Multicultural Counseling and Psychotherapy

A Lifespan Perspective

Fourth Edition

Leroy G. Baruth
Appalachian State University

M. Lee Manning
Old Dominion University

PEARSON

Merrill
Prentice Hall

Upper Saddle River, New Jersey
Columbus, Ohio

Library of Congress Cataloging in Publication Data

Baruth, Leroy G.
  Multicultural counseling and psychotherapy : a lifespan perspective / Leroy G. Baruth,
M. Lee Manning. — 4th ed.
      p. cm.
  Includes bibliographical references and indexes.
  ISBN 0-13-170681-0
    1. Cross-cultural counseling—United States. 2. Psychotherapy—United
States—Cross-cultural studies. 3. Developmental psychology—United
States—Cross-cultural studies. I. Manning, M. Lee. II. Title.

BF637.C6B283 2007
158'.3—dc22   2006044816

Vice President and Executive Publisher: Jeffery W. Johnston
Publisher: Kevin M. Davis
Editorial Assistant: Sarah N. Kenoyer
Production Editor: Mary Harlan
Production Coordinator: Rebecca K. Giusti, GGS Book Services
Design Coordinator: Diane C. Lorenzo
Text Design: GGS Book Services
Cover Design: Robert Davlin
Cover Image: SuperStock
Production Manager: Laura Messerly
Director of Marketing: David Gesell
Marketing Manager: Autumn Purdy
Marketing Coordinator: Brian Mounts

This book was set in Garamond by GGS Book Services. It was printed and bound by R. R Donnelley & Sons Company.
The cover was printed by R. R. Donnelley & Sons Company.

Pearson Education Ltd.
Pearson Education Singapore Pte. Ltd.
Pearson Education Canada, Ltd.
Pearson Education–Japan.

Pearson Education Australia Pty. Limited
Pearson Education North Asia Ltd.
Pearson Educación de Mexico, S.A. de C.V.
Pearson Education Malaysia Pte. Ltd.

10 9 8 7 6 5 4 3 2 1
ISBN: 0-13-170681-0

To all my students who have taught me so much during my forty years in the counseling field.

LGB

To Marianne, for her patience and respect for people.

MLM

Preface

The United States, which historically has been a haven for various cultural and ethnic groups, continues to benefit from the rich diversity of its people. The increasing cultural diversity of the U.S. population has given rise to a more intense need for effective multicultural counseling. Clients of various cultural backgrounds may bring to counseling sessions problems related to a particular lifespan stage or to the frustrations and challenges that often face cultural groups struggling to cope in U.S. society. Counselors who may not have been trained in multicultural intervention may underestimate or fail to recognize the powerful influence of a client's cultural background and developmental period; consequently, they may plan inappropriate counseling strategies.

Although few basic counseling strategies are designed for multicultural situations in particular, an understanding of client differences—cultural, ethnic, racial, gender, sexual orientation, disability, socioeconomic, and individual—is important in using existing strategies to their best advantage. Integrating multicultural and lifespan considerations is crucial to counseling effectiveness. Problems associated with multicultural intervention arise not only when majority-culture professionals counsel minority clients but also when minority counselors intervene with majority-culture clients.

Multicultural Counseling and Psychotherapy: A Lifespan Perspective was written to address these concerns. It provides majority-culture and minority-culture elementary and secondary school counselors, marriage and family therapists, rehabilitation agency counselors, mental health counselors, counselors in higher education, and social workers with a multicultural counseling text that explores the lives and potential counseling challenges of African American, American Indian, Asian American, European American, and Hispanic American clients at the various stages along the lifespan continuum.

The Lifespan Perspective and Selection of Cultures

The lifespan perspective that provides a framework for this text reflects the current emphasis on lifespan development and stresses that mental health issues and counseling problems differ for children, adolescents, adults, and elders. Effective multicultural counseling requires that counselors understand the problems unique to the client's culture, as well as the problems unique to the client's developmental period. It takes only a few examples to illustrate the need to consider both culture and development in counseling intervention: Mental health issues of the American

Indian child differ from those of the Asian American elder; similarly, African American children have unique problems that differ from those of Asian American children or even from those of African American adults.

Our emphasis on five cultural groups—African American, American Indian, Asian American, European American, and Hispanic American—was determined by two main factors. First, these five groups currently represent the most populous cultures in the United States. Second, these five cultural groups all have significant challenges that will increasingly require counseling intervention. Moreover, acculturation of younger generations threatens the continuance of the cherished values, traditions, and customs associated with each of these five cultures.

Organization of the Text

Multicultural Counseling and Psychotherapy: A Lifespan Perspective is organized into 3 parts and 17 chapters. Part I (Chapters 1–3) provides background knowledge for intervening with clients of differing backgrounds. Part II (Chapters 4–16) centers on understanding and counseling African American, American Indian, Asian American, European American, and Hispanic American clients as well as lesbian, gay, and bisexual clients in the various lifespan stages. Part III (Chapter 17 and the Epilogue) discusses professional issues in multicultural counseling and explores future directions in the field.

The organization of the text is consistent with our goal to enhance understanding of seven broad concepts:

1. The United States is a nation of many cultural groups and will continue to be enriched by increasing cultural diversity (Chapter 1).

2. A prerequisite to effective multicultural counseling is for both minority- and majority-culture counselors to understand their own cultural identities and how their identities affect counseling intervention (Chapter 2).

3. Majority-culture counselors can be trained to intervene effectively with minority clients, and minority counselors with majority-culture clients; minority counselors can be also trained to intervene effectively with minority clients of differing cultural backgrounds (Chapter 3).

4. Knowledge of a client's developmental period and of the problems and challenges of each lifespan period contributes to the counselor's expertise (Chapter 4).

5. Knowledge of a client's cultural background provides the counselor, regardless of cultural background, with a sound basis for multicultural counseling intervention (Chapters 5, 7, 9, 11, 13, and 15).

6. Counselors and their clients benefit from the selection and implementation of counseling strategies and techniques that are appropriate for specific cultural groups (Chapters 6, 8, 10, 12, 14, and 16).

7. In the coming years, counselors intervening in multicultural settings will be challenged by issues that deserve to be understood and addressed as multicultural counseling continues to gain recognition and respect (Chapter 17).

Special Features and Pedagogical Aids

To clarify and enliven the text and to provoke the reader's thought, several features are included:

- *Gender Perspectives* provide information and opinions related to gender and gender concerns as these areas relate to the topics being discussed.
- *A Focus on Research* features call the reader's attention to recent research on the topic under discussion. Empirical studies and scholarly writings on counseling, development, and multicultural populations are featured.
- *Up Close and Personal* vignettes describe individuals from each of the cultures and age groups. Various members of the fictional families are introduced, as well as lesbian, gay, and bisexual individuals in the four lifespan stages, providing a portrait of the child, the adolescent, the adult, and the elder within the family and/or the culture and within society at large.
- *Suggested Readings* lists journal articles that may be of special interest to readers who wish to improve their multicultural counseling effectiveness.
- *Appendix A* describes selected professional journals in which multicultural and developmental issues are sometimes considered.
- *Appendix B* lists experiential activities that can be used as a part of the multicultural counseling course.

At various points in the text, the reader is cautioned to keep in mind that each client is unique; that is, individual differences related to gender, sexual orientation, disability, generation, geographic location, and socioeconomic class must be accounted for in planning appropriate counseling intervention. Intracultural differences, as evidenced in the many Asian American, European American, and Hispanic American subgroups, also must be considered. To avoid stereotyping of cultures, we refer to specific populations whenever possible. It is crucial for counselors to recognize that the line between cultural descriptions and cultural stereotypes is very narrow and that the consequences of stereotypical thinking are potentially damaging to clients of all cultures and at all lifespan stages

Acknowledgments

We want to thank Dr. Katherine Bucher of Old Dominion University for her patience and willingness to locate reference sources. We also want to thank Kevin Davis for his assistance and for addressing our questions and concerns. Last, we want to thank the reviewers who offered insightful opinions and additional reference sources: Yvonne L. Callaway, Eastern Michigan University; Sharon Ferguson-Roberts, Virginia State University; Patricia J. Neufeld, Emporia State University; and Darren A. Wozny, Mississippi State University, Meridian Campus.

LGB

MLM

Discover the Companion Website Accompanying This Book

The Prentice Hall Companion Website: A Virtual Learning Environment

Technology is a constantly growing and changing aspect of our field that is creating a need for content and resources. To address this emerging need, Prentice Hall has developed an online learning environment for students and professors alike—Companion Websites—to support our textbooks.

In creating a Companion Website, our goal is to build on and enhance what the textbook already offers. For this reason, the content for each user-friendly website is organized by chapter and provides the professor and student with a variety of meaningful resources.

Common Companion Website features for students include:

- **Chapter Objectives**—Outline key concepts from the text.
- **Interactive Self-quizzes**—Complete with hints and automatic grading that provide immediate feedback for students. After students submit their answers for the interactive self-quizzes, the Companion Website **Results Reporter** computes a percentage grade, provides a graphic representation of how many questions were answered correctly and incorrectly, and gives a question-by-question analysis of the quiz. Students are given the option to send their quiz to up to four email addresses (professor, teaching assistant, study partner, etc.).
- **Web Destinations**—Links to www sites that relate to chapter content.

To take advantage of the many available resources, please visit the *Multicultural Counseling and Psychotherapy: A Lifespan Perspective,* Fourth Edition, Companion Website at

www.prenhall.com/baruth

Brief Contents

Contents

CHAPTER 5
Understanding African American Clients 109

CHAPTER 8
Counseling American Indian Clients 178

CHAPTER 9
Understanding Asian American Clients 199

CHAPTER 12
Counseling European American Clients 266

CHAPTER 16
Counseling Lesbian, Gay, and Bisexual Clients 355

PART III Professional Issues in Multicultural Counseling 385

Note: Every effort has been made to provide accurate and current Internet information in this book. However, the Internet and information posted on it are constantly changing, so it is inevitable that some of the Internet addresses listed in this textbook will change.

Overview

Chapters 1, 2, and 3 focus attention on the nature of multicultural counseling, the counselor's cultural identity, and the culturally effective counselor. These chapters lay a foundation for intervening with African American, American Indian, Asian American, European American, and Hispanic American clients along the lifespan continuum.

Introduction to Multicultural Counseling and Psychotherapy

Questions to Be Explored

1. What are the definitions of culture, race, and ethnicity relative to multicultural counseling?
2. What differences should counselors consider when planning counseling interventions?
3. Why is an understanding of lifespan development crucial for counselors?
4. What lifespan differences affect the outcome of the counseling intervention?
5. What is multicultural counseling and psychotherapy? What is multicultural group counseling?
6. What ethical issues should be considered when planning professional interventions?
7. Why should sexual orientation and disabilities be considered when planning professional intervention?
8. How should sexual orientation and disabilities be considered in multicultural counseling?
9. What cultural factors should be considered when planning individual, group, and family therapy?

Overview

America's doors have been open to people of diverse cultural, ethnic, and racial origins for many years. Some people entered the country with hopes of realizing the American dream. Others came to escape oppressive conditions in their home countries. Still others were brought against their will and were expected to conform culturally. Then, there were those who already inhabited the land that is now the United States. Through experiences commonly associated with daily living and working together, it was thought that this diverse range of people would acculturate or adopt "American" customs and values and, as in a "melting pot," assimilate into mainstream society. For any number of reasons, however, many people opted to hold on to their cultural heritages, traditions, and customs; they wanted their cultural characteristics and values recognized as different, rather than as inferior or wrong.

Considerable evidence suggests that the melting pot metaphor does not provide an accurate description of the many cultural groups living in the United States. For example, some groups have failed (or have elected not to try) to forsake cherished cultural characteristics in order to become "Americanized." Asians and Hispanics,* regardless of their generation, often reluctantly give up ethnic customs and traditions in favor of "middle-class American habits" that appear to them to be in direct contradiction to beliefs they acquired early in life. African Americans have fought to overcome cultural dominance and discrimination and, through efforts such as the civil rights movement, have sought to understand and maintain their cultural heritage. In essence, the United States is a nation of diverse peoples, and although cultural groups can be described with some accuracy, cultures are not monolithic in nature. This need to recognize and respect individual differences and similarities within cultures becomes clearer when one considers the generational differences and social class differences among the African American, American Indian, Asian American, European American, and Hispanic American cultures. The knowledgeable counselor can use these differences in working with a multicultural clientele.

Clients: Today and in the Future

The extent of the U.S. multicultural society and the role it plays in shaping people's lives will continue to become apparent to counseling professionals as increasing numbers of clients from diverse cultures seek mental health services. Undoubtedly, counselors and psychotherapists will increasingly counsel clients with differing customs, traditions, values, and perspectives toward life events and the counseling process. Will counselors, regardless of their cultural background, be able to provide effective counseling services for clients of differing backgrounds? The attitudes and skills that counselors bring to the multicultural counseling situation will depend significantly on their knowledge of cultures, their counseling effectiveness with clients, and their willingness to perceive cultural characteristics as differences rather than deficits.

For purposes of this text, we chose to concentrate on five cultures: African American, American Indian, Asian American, European American, and Hispanic American. The first determining factor was the population numbers, particularly the estimated growth increases associated with them. To date, these cultures have shown significant increases and are expected to continue to do so, either by increased birth rate or by immigration. The numbers are currently of a sufficient proportion that counselors—in schools, private practices, mental health institutions, or other settings of service delivery—will likely encounter clients from these cultures. Second, most available research data were drawn from these five groups. Third, these cultural groups have needs that warrant counseling, but individuals often are reluctant to seek counseling. Fourth, few counselors have sufficient knowledge of clients' cultural and other differences (especially the African, Asian, Hispanic, and American Indian cultures) and how these differences affect the process of providing effective, culturally responsive counseling intervention.

---

*Some scholars (e.g., Comas-Diaz, 2001) prefer other terms such as Latino (a) for this cultural group. Although we respect Comas-Diaz's opinion and the right of individuals to select a name for their culture, we have chosen to use the term Hispanic throughout this book, mainly because that is the term used by the U.S. Census Bureau. Still, whenever possible, we will refer specifically to persons from specific cultural backgrounds, such as Mexican Americans.

African Americans

Whether termed African Americans, Black Americans, or Afro-Americans, the majority of this group can trace their origin to western Africa. The term *African American* appears most popular as a replacement for *Black* or *Black American* because it recognizes cultural ties with Africa. African American also reflects cultural heritage (rather than only skin color), similar to terms designating Asian American, American Indian, and Hispanic American.

The term *African American* is being debated. The term is being questioned by some Blacks who have long lived in the United States, just as their ancestors. Also, it is being questioned by some people with roots in sub-Saharan Africa. Others simply prefer the term *Black* ('African-American' becomes a term for debate, 2004). It will take a number of years to determine which term will actually be selected to designate Black people and their culture.

American Indians

Ancestors of the people who are now known as Indians, Native Americans, or Native American Indians have continuously occupied North America for at least 30,000 years. Rather than emigrating from other lands and facing cultural assimilation into the majority culture, American Indians faced an influx of outsiders to their land who expected them to relinquish cherished cultural traditions. The American Indian people have been categorized into one group (see Chapter 7).

Asian Americans

Risking violation of sacred family traditions, many young Asians headed for the promised land of America around the turn of the twentieth century. Asian Americans were often forced to accept the lowest paid menial jobs and were denied the rights of citizenship and ownership of land. As discussed in Chapter 9, Asian Americans and Pacific Islanders in the United States include the following Asian cultures: Chinese, Filipino, Japanese, Korean, Asian Indian, and Vietnamese. Hawaiians, Samoans, and Guamanians are known as Pacific Islanders. The recent influx of another group of Asian Americans from Southeast Asia has further contributed to the diversity of the Asian cultures. Many Indochinese started their journey from rural and poor areas to refugee camps and finally to American towns and cities. Originating from such countries as Vietnam, Cambodia, Laos, and Thailand, these people differ from the most populous Asian groups (Japanese and Chinese). Southeast Asians are a diverse group. For example, refugees from Southeast Asia can include Blue, White, and Striped Hmong; Chinese, Krom, and Mi Khmer Cambodians; Chinese Mien, Thai Dam, and Khmer Laotians; and Lowlander and Highlander Vietnamese. Each group has its own distinct history and culture. However, a discussion of all the many Asian groups currently living in the United States is beyond the scope of this text.

European Americans

As discussed in Chapter 11, 53 categories of European Americans live in the United States. Although ambiguous, the term *White ethnic* originally referred to Southern and Eastern European immigrants, rather than to Americans of British or German ancestry. In later years, the term has referred to a broader range of people. European Americans have not received notable attention in the discussions of multiculturalism and diversity. It is also important to mention that European Americans are a diverse people in terms of thought, emotions, and group loyalty. European Americans emigrated from widely diverse places, such as western and southern Europe, as well as eastern Europe and the former Soviet Union. People of Greek, Italian, Polish, Irish, French, and German descent are well-known in the United States, whereas those from the Netherlands, Portugal, Spain, and Switzerland are less well-known.

Hispanic Americans

The Hispanic American culture includes Mexican Americans, Chicanos, Spanish Americans, Latinos, Mexicans, Puerto Ricans, Cubans, Guatemalans, and Salvadorans. All are recognized as Hispanics and share many values and goals. The soaring Hispanic population in the United States has been driven largely by waves of new immigrants—legal and illegal—as well as by more accurate counts by census takers. Hispanics are a large, young, rapidly increasing, highly diverse group of people. *Hispanic* is a catch-all term designed to cover a disparate array of people from various nationalities—from liberal Puerto Ricans in New York to conservative Cubans in Miami—who do not always have common interests (Schmitt, 2001). In fact, Hispanics should be considered an aggregate of distinct subcultures, rather than a homogeneous cultural group. For example, although Hispanics have cultural similarities, each Hispanic subgroup has its own distinct social and cultural practices. This increasing population is currently influencing mainstream American culture in such areas as communication, employment, education, and the arts. Chapter 13 describes the Hispanic population in more detail.

Understanding Diversity Among Clients in a Pluralistic Society

Currently, many counselors probably received their professional preparation at institutions that provided training for counseling majority-culture clients. Such training was unquestionably appropriate for counselors preparing to work with mainstream clients; however, the possible lack of training and clinical experiences with clients of diverse backgrounds indicates the need for improved understanding of appropriate intervention measures. A prerequisite to effective multicultural counseling is the professional's understanding of concepts related to the various cultural groups residing in the United States.

Culture, Subculture, and Intraculture

Even readers with limited awareness of cultures, intracultures, and subcultures and their many dimensions realize that these terms can be defined in various ways. Culture can be defined as institutions, communication, values, religions, genders, sexual orientations, disabilities, thinking, artistic expressions, and social and interpersonal relationships.

Culture should not be thought of as an abstract or relatively fixed set of attributions, shared traditions, country of origin, or even shared agreement about norms for living, common beliefs, etc. Culture is fluid and emergent as people constantly recreate themselves, their narratives, and their contexts and, in turn, are themselves changed. Culture is always a matter of intersections—of class, race, ethnicity, gender, age, and experiences—which themselves are diverse and changing (Laird, 2000).

Although counselors need to have an understanding of culture and its effects on counseling, the broad and inclusive perspective of culture recognizes that intragroup differences exist. Acquiring an objective picture of others' cultural backgrounds requires a determined attempt to understand clients' intragroup and intergroup cultural differences, as well as their subcultures and intracultures. One cannot group all Asian Americans into one cultural group or assume that all European or Hispanic American women are alike. One may assume that a Black client shares certain cultural characteristics with African Americans, but one should also recognize subcultural, intracultural, or individual differences in counseling intervention.

Subculture can be defined as a racial, ethnic, regional, economic, or social community (e.g., gang, drug, gay, elderly) that exhibits characteristic patterns of behavior sufficient to distinguish it from others in the dominant society or culture. A subculture provides its members with a history, social values, and expectations that may not be found elsewhere in the dominant culture. Therefore, meaningful communication between people who appear similar may be hampered because of differing subcultures.

Intraculture can be defined as a client's educational background, socioeconomic status, acculturation, and urban and rural background. A client may be a member of several subcultures and intracultures, each influencing the process and outcome of counseling intervention.

Race

Race refers to the way a group of people defines itself or is defined by others as being different from other groups because of assumed innate physical characteristics. It is based on characteristics such as skin and eye color and shape of the head, eyes, ears, lips, and nose.

Despite large numbers of people moving from one geographic region to another and increasing numbers of interracial marriages, the concept of race continues to play a role in distinguishing people. However, race contributes little to understanding clients' culture, ethnicity, sexual orientation, and lifespan differences. Considered as a single entity, racial identity does not reveal an individual's nationality, communication, or religion. Cultural groups that are defined by nationality, geography, communication, and religion seldom correspond with racial categories, at least not to the extent necessary to provide culturally relevant information. Therefore, although counselors should be cognizant of their clients' race, they will learn more about their clients' strengths, weaknesses, and challenges when other more individual aspects are identified.

Ethnicity

Ethnicity is the most distinguishing characteristic of Americans because we are categorized primarily based on our cultural identity or nationality. An *ethnic group* is a culturally distinct population whose members share a collective identity and a common heritage. Historically, the overwhelming majority of ethnic groups emerged in the United States as a result of one of the following processes: (1) migration, (2) consolidation of group forces in the face of impending threat from an aggressor, (3) annexation or changes in political boundary lines, or (4) religious schisms (Henderson, 2000).

Characteristics associated with ethnicity include (1) a shared group image and sense of identity derived from values, behaviors, beliefs, communication, and historical perspectives; (2) shared political, social, and economic interests; and (3) shared involuntary membership with a specific ethnic group.

Because of interracial marriage, many Americans have multiple ethnic and racial identities. Some persons of mixed lineage prefer to assume nondescript identities; for example, they label themselves as "White," "Black," "Indian," "Latino," "Asian," or merely "American" (Henderson, 2000, p. 12) in order to avoid any connection with their ancestors. The task of tracing their roots has become too taxing or unimportant. Even so, the effects of ethnicity and race are pervasive; disparate patterns of community relationships and economic opportunities haunt us. At some time in their history, all ethnic groups in the United States have been the underclass. Also, at different times, all ethnic groups have been the oppressed and the oppressors (Henderson, 2000).

Worldview

This section defines *worldview* and discusses overall aspects of the term. (Chapter 3 discusses assessment of and approaches to addressing worldviews.) Worldview may be defined as one's individual experiences and social, moral, religious, educational, economic, or political inputs shared with other members of one's reference group, such as culture group, racial or ethnic group, family, state, or country.

Recently, increasing attention has focused on the notion that different counseling and psychotherapy approaches reflect different worldviews. More specifically, the point has been made that counseling theories from different philosophical frames of reference ask differing questions about counseling.

It is important that counselors understand worldviews when planning professional intervention. Western counseling theories and research often depend heavily on abstractions, abstract words, cause-and-effect relationships, linear analytic thinking, and inductive and deductive reasoning—a thinking style that reflects Western worldviews. However, as international interactions increase in such areas as commerce, business, politics, science, and education, it is important to understand the effects of each culture's worldview on its people.

Understanding one's own worldview and those of other cultures, as well as perceiving their similarities and differences, facilitates interculturally sensitive relationships and communication. For example, if a school counselor wishes to facilitate the educational process of immigrant Chinese in the United States, he or she may be more successful if there is a clear understanding of the Chinese view of the structure, roles, functions, and purpose of hierarchical relationships compared with the American view of egalitarian relationships. In other words, understanding worldviews is important because a client's worldview is an overriding cognitive frame of reference that influences most of his or her perceptions and values. To understand an individual's response to a situation and to avoid a breakdown in communication, the counselor needs to understand the client's worldview.

Social Class

One of the most meaningful dimensions in people's lives is social class. Along with race and gender, social class is regarded as one of the three most important cultural cornerstones in multicultural theory and research. Yet unlike race and gender, social class remains one of the most elusive and least understood constructs in psychology. Although social class is potentially associated with many human experiences, the topic has not received much research attention. The available research and writings on the topic, however, do suggest social class is an important variable in the effectiveness of professional intervention (Liu, et al., 2004).

Social class differences play a significant role in determining how a person acts, lives, thinks, and relates to others and has the potential for limiting counseling effectiveness. Social class influences mental and physical health, family and peer relationships, occupational and career choice, and counseling process and outcome (Lee & Dean, 2004). Counselors and clients might see life events from different perspectives, and neither might be able to understand the other's perspectives on events. For example, the middle- to upper-class counselor may experience difficulty understanding the challenges (e.g., low wages, unemployment, feelings of helplessness) that a client from a lower socioeconomic level may experience on a daily basis. Another potential problem is that a person's social class is sometimes indicative of ambition or motivation to achieve. It is a serious mistake to believe that anyone can achieve a middle-class lifestyle by making the most of opportunities, for example, hard work, perseverance, and a little luck (Lee & Dean, 2004). Just because a person has succeeded or failed socioeconomically might have little to do with his or her motivation and determination to succeed.

The definition of mental health may change with social classes; therefore, declines in mental health may be regarded as a definitional problem rather than a reflection of mental health needs. In other words, as people move up the social class ladder, they might have less of a particular problem (e.g., lack of resources), but more of another problem usually not accessible to lower class individuals (e.g., negotiating privileges). Thus, counselors need to understand counseling needs and definitions of mental health from the perspective of the client's socioeconomic class (Liu, et al., 2004).

Client's socioeconomic status affects nearly all aspects of their lives. Factors such as household income, health insurance, and accumulated wealth can affect physical and psychological health as well as outlooks on life. The sad reality is that significant numbers of people in the United States live in poverty, with barely sustainable incomes, or without health insurance.

Figure 1.1 shows the poverty rates by age between 1959 and 2003.

Real median household money income between 2002 and 2003 was $43,318 and remained unchanged for non-Hispanic White, African American, and Asian households. Households with Hispanic householders (who can be of any race) experienced a real decline in median income of 2.6% between 2002 and 2003. African American households had the lowest median income. Their 2003 median income was about $30,000, which was 62% of the median for non-Hispanic White households (about $48,000). Median income for Hispanic households was about $33,000 in 2003, which was 69% of the median for non-Hispanic White households. Asian households had the highest median income among the racial groups. Their 2003 median income was about $55,500, 117% of the median for non-Hispanic White households.

Other socioeconomic data in 2003 on specific groups includes:

- American Indian and Alaska native peoples did not see a change ($32,866).

- Non-Hispanic Whites had a poverty rate of 8.2% unchanged from 2002.

- African American's poverty rate and the number in poverty changed between 2002 and 2003. People who reported Black as their only race, for example, had a poverty rate of 24.4%.

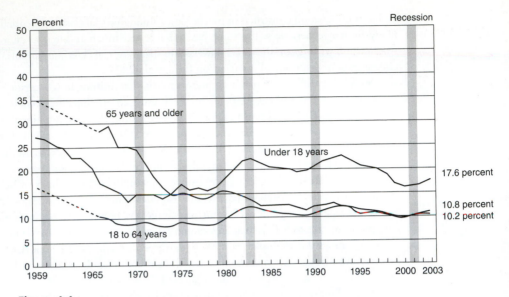

Figure 1.1
Poverty Rates by Age: 1959 to 2003
Note: The data points are placed at the midpoints of the respective years.
Data for people 18 to 64 and 65 and older are not available from 1960 to 1965.
Source: U.S. Census Bureau, Current Population Survey, 1960 to 2004 Annual Social and
Economic Supplements.

- Asians had an 11.8% poverty rate, up from 10.1% in 2002. The number in poverty rose, from 1.2 million to 1.4 million. Asians' poverty rate, regardless of whether they reported another race, increased to 11.8% and 1.5 million.

- Hispanics' poverty rate remained unchanged, at 22.5% in 2003, while the number in poverty increased from 8.6 million in 2002 to 9.1 million.

- American Indians' and Alaska natives' incomes did not change when comparing two-year averages from 2001–2002 and 2002–2003.

Table 1.1 and Table 1.2 provide examples of socioeconomic indicators.

People who do not reflect the middle-class values of traditional therapy (e.g., verbal ability, timeliness, psychological mindedness) may not receive the best counseling treatment. Other socioeconomic-related aspects of mental health and counseling include:

- Increases in monetary wealth do not always positively relate to a sense of well-being or happiness.

- Mental health providers may offer poorer quality health services to some minority groups.

- Low-income minority women are more likely to experience depression than White women.

Table 1.1

Socioeconomic Indicators: 2003

Developed from: U.S. Census Bureau. (2003). "Income, poverty, and health insurance coverage in the United States: 2003." Washington, DC: Author.

Income

- Real median household money income remained unchanged between 2002 and 2003 at $43,318.

- The ratio of female to male earnings in 2003 for full-time, year-round workers was 76%, a decline from 77% in 2002.

- The poverty rates for people 18 to 64 and for those 65 and older remained unchanged, but the poverty rate for children rose from 16.7% in 2002 to 17.6% in 2003, or 12.9 million.

- The poverty rate and number of families in poverty increased from 9.6% and 7.2 million in 2002 to 10.0% and 7.6 million in 2003.

- The official poverty rate in 2003 was 12.5%, up from 12.1% in 2002. Nearly 36 million people were in poverty, up 1.3 million from 2002.

- Poverty rates remained unchanged for Hispanics, non-Hispanic Whites, and Blacks, although it rose for Whites and Asians.

Health Insurance

- The number of people with health insurance rose by 1.0 million from 2002 to 2003; the number of people without health insurance rose by 1.4 million over that same period. The net result was that 15.6% of the population, or 45.0 million people, were without health coverage in 2003, up from 15.2% in 2002.

- The proportion of children not covered by health insurance did not change, remaining at 11.4% of all children.

- The uninsured rate did not change for African Americans (about 19.5%) or Asians (about 18.7%) between 2002 and 2003. Non-Hispanics who reported white as their only race saw their uninsured rate increase from 10.7% to 11.1%. The uninsured rate for Hispanics, who may be of any race, was 32.7% in 2003—unchanged from 2002.

- Lower-class individuals might be more prone to neurotic disorders.

- Lower social class individuals tend to have a lower sense of optimism and control over their lives.

- Members of lower social classes tend to have a higher prevalence of aggression and anxiety (Liu, et al., 2004).

Effective counseling intervention requires consideration of values, attitudes, behaviors, and beliefs among the various socioeconomic groups. These differences can have a significant impact on both the counselor's and the client's worldviews. Plus, socioeconomic differences can limit counseling effectiveness. Social class differences in some cases may be more pronounced than cultural differences. For example, because social class differences separate members of the European culture, a client from a particular socioeconomic class may share more cultural commonalities with someone of similar social class than with someone of another social class.

Table 1.2

Racial Groups and Poverty: 2003 (in thousands)

Developed from: U.S. Census Bureau. (2003). "Income, poverty, and health insurance coverage in the United States: 2003." Washington, DC: Author.

Racial Group [1,2]	Number	Percentage
White alone or in combination	24,950	10.6
White alone[3]	24,272	10.5
White alone, not Hispanic	15,902	8.2
Black alone or in combination	9,108	24.3
Black alone[4]	8,781	24.4
Asian alone or in combination	1,527	11.8
Asian alone[5]	1,401	11.8
Hispanic (of any race)	9,051	22.5

Note 1   American Indians and Alaska natives were not included in this census report.

Note 2   This census survey asked respondents to choose one or more races.

Note 3   White alone refers to people who reported White and did not report any other race category.

Note 4   Black alone refers to people who reported Black and did not report any other race category.

Note 5   Asian alone refers to people who reported Asian and did not report any other race category.

Generational Differences

Generational differences within a particular culture result in varying beliefs and values and represent another obstacle to achieving homogeneity within a culture. Older generations may be more prone to retain old-world values and traditions because of the tendency to live within close proximity of people of similar language, traditions, and customs. Because of public schooling and a tendency (or a requirement) to adopt the values of the majority culture in school, younger generations are more likely to accept values different from those of their elders.

One example illustrates generational differences among people. Older generations may have lived in cultural enclaves with others speaking their native languages, but younger generations who can communicate effectively in English cope better in a predominantly English-speaking society.

Although acculturation plays a role in generational differences, one's place on the lifespan continuum also plays a significant role. Whether because of wisdom, experience, or the way events are perceived during each lifespan stage, opinions and beliefs change as one matures. Generational differences often lead to interpersonal conflicts that have the potential to create psychological and emotional problems that warrant counseling intervention.

Gender

The influence of a client's gender in the counseling process and outcome has been vigorously debated. Counselors should recognize and understand gender-based differences, or those characteristics and traits that are unique to males and females and that affect their unique orientations toward problems and solutions. There are numerous possibilities for exploring gender-based differences in counseling. It is clear that gender plays a significant role during counseling, but

GENDER PERSPECTIVES 1.1
Immigrant Women and Counseling

Yakushko and Chronister (2005) believe that serving the mental health needs of immigrant women is a new frontier for American Counselors and research scholars. They used Urie Bronfenbrenner's ecological theory as a guide for counselors working with immigrant women because it highlights the significance of individual factors and larger social contexts on immigrant women's lives. Essentially, Yakushko and Chronister proposed the following contexts for consideration:

Individual—factors such as age, sex, physical and cognitive abilities, and language proficiency

Microsystem—factors such as family composition, urban or rural environment, occupational status, and racial and ethnic composition

Mesosystem—factors such as relations among immigrants' social support networks in the microsystem

Exosystem—factors such as political and economic climate of home and environment, relations between home and host countries, and legal immigration status

Macrosystem—factors such as cultural values of the home and host environment, gender and sexual identity, and political and economic values of the home and host countries.

These factors are only representative examples of the kind of information that might be helpful in working with immigrant women clients—readers wanting additional details and implications for counseling are referred to the article.

Source: "Immigrant women and counseling: The invisible others," by O. Yakushko, and K. M. Chronister, 2005, *Journal of Counseling and Development, 83,* pp. 292–298.

---

research focusing specifically on females of different cultural backgrounds does not consistently allow for generalizations across cultures.

Yakushko and Chronister (2005) maintain that global changes have resulted in an increase in the number of immigrant women in the United States. In Gender Perspectives 1.1, they focus on the experiences of Mexican immigrant women, mainly because Mexicans make up the majority of the Latino population.

Sexual Orientation

We believe that the multicultural counseling movement should include people of differing sexual orientations. Gays, lesbians, and bisexuals have a unique culture of their own, and they experience many of the same problems seen in other minorities. Counselors working with gay and lesbian clients must understand the special challenges (e.g., job discrimination, loneliness, isolation, ridicule) that gays and lesbians experience. Also, as discussed in Chapter 15, identity development models that show the different stages of identity development have been proposed for gays and lesbians.

Again, sexual orientation should be perceived as a unique characteristic, just as gender, culture, ethnicity, and social class are so considered. The counselor working with gay or lesbian

A FOCUS ON RESEARCH 1.1

Contributions of Multicultural Counseling to Lesbian, Gay, and Bisexual Clients

Israel and Selvidge outline the contributions of multi-cultural counseling to three areas of counselor competence with lesbian, gay male, and bisexual male and female clients. Actual counselor competence in working with LGB clients should be developed through supervision, consultation, and additional training. Ideally, this effort should provide guidance for professionals familiar with multicultural counseling to extend their work to counselor competence with LGB clients and will provide a framework for professionals in LGB psychology to build on the foundations established by multicultural counseling. The authors maintain that conceptualizing counselor competence includes knowledge, attitudes, and skills. Training in these three areas involves the content, the means of conveying the content, and the training environment (one that accepts and promotes an affirming environment).

Israel and Selvidge maintained that multicultural and LGB counseling can be strengthened by drawing on the foundations laid in each area. First, counselors should know the parallel literature in the other field. Second, researchers and scholars can identify similarities and differences in multicultural and LBG competence courses. Third, the incorporation of multicultural and gay issues in diversity courses can help students develop a fuller range of counselor competence and encourage counselor educators to bring together these two related fields.

Source: "Contributions of multicultural counseling to counselor competence with lesbian, gay, and bisexual clients," by T. Israel and M. M. D. Selvidge, 2003, *Journal of Multicultural Counseling and Development, 31,* pp. 84–98.

A FOCUS ON RESEARCH 1.2

Information and Attitude Exploration

Believing counselor education programs should train counselors who are competent to intervene with lesbian, gay, and bisexual clients, Israel and Hackett (2004) compared the effects of information-based and attitude-based interventions on counselor trainees' knowledge about and attitudes toward lesbian, gay, and bisexual clients.

Results showed that participants who received information on lesbian, gay, and bisexual clients were more knowledgeable than trainees who did not. Israel and Hackett maintain that counselor educators can have significant impact in providing knowledge to counselors in training. With the attitude exploration, the results were the opposite. Participants who underwent attitude training reported more negative atttitudes than did the participants who did not explore attitudes.

Although it is possible that exploring attitudes actually produced more negative attitudes, a more likely explanation is that the participants engaged in attitude exploration were challenged to reassess their actual feelings toward lesbian, gay, and bisexual clients.

Israel and Hackett concluded that the mental health field would benefit from a multidimensional model of counselor competence with lesbian, gay, and bisexual clients, much like the multicultural counseling literature has articulated for working with ethnically diverse clients.

Source: "Counselor education on lesbian, gay and bisexual issues: comparing information and attitude exploration," by T. Israel and G. Hackett, 2004, *Counselor Education and Supervision, 43,* pp. 179–191.

clients should base professional intervention on the clients' worldviews and overall perspectives of life. Understanding and counseling lesbians, gays, and bisexuals are the topics of Chapters 15 and 16. A Focus on Research 1.1 looks at the contributions of multicultural counseling to the gay, lesbian, and bisexual clients and the training needed for counselors to provide professional intervention with lesbians, gays, and bisexuals.

Ethical standards and accreditation standards as well as professional guidelines make clear the belief that counselors are charged with the task of providing sensitive and competent services for lesbian, gay, and bisexual clients and that training programs are responsible for helping counselors gain competence when intervening with this population (Israel & Hackett, 2004). A Focus on Research 1.2 looks at counseling programs providing information and exploring attitudes.

Disabilities

We think people with disabilities also have a culture of their own—the way they perceive themselves and think they are perceived by others; the mindsets and worldviews they share; and, unfortunately, the prejudice and discrimination they often experience. Also, just as some counselors may feel uncomfortable counseling a client from a different cultural background than their own (and some clients prefer a counselor from a similar cultural background), some counselors may feel uncomfortable counseling clients with disabilities. Similarly, some clients may have difficulty being counseled by a counselor with a disability. Reeve (2000) maintained that the oppression experienced by people who are disabled is sometimes replayed in counseling situations when counselors are unaware of their own disablist attitudes and prejudices. Reeve called for a new counseling approach, called disability counseling, that recognizes oppression during counseling intervention.

The most common psychological theories about personal responses to disability are based on the assumption that there will be psychological adjustment as an individual comes to terms with his or her disability. Similar to grief stage theories, people who are disabled are expected to grieve, mourn, and express feelings of anger and denial before they can become psychologically whole again. However, the loss theories often do not consider the social dimension of disability by assuming that the only loss will be of a personal nature. Other problems, such as losses in one's work or social life, also occur (Reeve, 2000).

Some counselors hold the assumption (albeit false) that all people with disabilities need counseling to help them deal with their losses. Such an opinion often comes from the belief that disabled people are bitter and self-pitying because of their inability to deal with their disability. Because people with disabilities are individuals and thus respond differently, some need counseling whereas others do not. Those who do seek counseling deserve counselors without biased attitudes and prejudices. These clients also deserve counseling intervention that is not based on false assumptions and conceptions about the disabled (Reeve, 2000).

Some people with disabilities experience problems similar to those without disabilities. Marital problems, stress, and childhood traumas affect many people, regardless of whether they are disabled. However, people with disabilities may experience additional difficulties that they may seek to resolve through counseling services. Special problems may include coping with pain and exhaustion, internalized oppression, and the experience of living in a society that discriminates against people with disabilities. Counselors should help clients with disabilities understand what counseling can and cannot do. Counseling cannot *fix* (italics Reeve's, 2000, p. 671) disability because disability is a problem created by society and not the individual; however, counseling can help people explore the ramifications of their disability and their feelings toward these issues (Reeve, 2000).

Just as the struggles for civil rights and equality have helped people from all cultural backgrounds, these struggles have also helped people who are disabled. For example, both affirmative action and the multicultural movements have contributed to the acceptance, available opportunities, and general welfare of people with disabilities. Still, considerable progress is needed for this group to have equal access to all opportunities available to people without disabilities.

Linking the civil rights movement and the disability rights movement, Middleton, Rollins, & Harley (1999) examined the disability rights movement as well as historical reforms, policies, and practices, especially their impact on racial and ethnic minorities. Their recommendations for counselors and counselor educators include:

1. Explore alternative ways to enable counselor education programs to develop training experiences that are responsive to clients with disabilities.
2. Develop interest in understanding of laws, regulations, and programs that affect persons with disabilities, specifically those of racial or ethnic minorities.
3. Support the emergence of disability policy as a significant field of study and research.
4. Use effective helping skills to better understand the nature and meaning of disability.

Lifespan Development

A major premise underlying this text is that clients differ with respect to their lifespan stages. Each lifespan stage (childhood, adolescence, adulthood, old age) has its own unique developmental characteristics and counseling problems. The dilemma is compounded, however, when counselors consider that their clients' lifespan differences and cultural characteristics are often closely intertwined. Examples include elderly Asian Americans who may exhibit considerable anxiety over the younger generation's acculturation, or the health concerns of elderly African Americans, or the machismo that is so important to Hispanic American adolescents. An adolescent client and an elderly client of the same culture, race, and ethnic group will probably perceive an issue from different perspectives. Problems, values, and beliefs vary so greatly with development that people functioning within the same lifespan stage may actually constitute a subgroup.

Human development is an ongoing process that starts at birth and continues to death, with cultural and individual variations existing within each lifespan period. The problems of children obviously differ from those of adults. Culturally perceptive counselors recognize that although African American and American Indian children may share similar developmental characteristics, they may be vastly different in many other respects. Likewise, although the elderly in all cultures often have common characteristics, elderly Asian Americans experience problems that differ from those of elderly American Indians or Hispanic Americans. It is important that counselors understand each client's cultural background and lifespan period as well as the intricate relationships between the two. Although studies in multicultural psychology and human development have become more sophisticated during the past decade or so, counselors are urged to draw conclusions and generalizations cautiously; the existing literature often does not allow for definitive conclusions. Sufficient evidence does indicate, however, that cultural differences undoubtedly exist across and within cultures, between generations, and throughout the lifespan. In this text, we examine cultural differences in terms of a lifespan approach and discuss their implications for counselors and psychotherapists in multicultural settings.

Research on human development relative to cultural diversity is limited. The paucity of literature in this area, however, does not excuse the counselor from making every effort to gain the maximum knowledge of the client's period on the lifespan. Increased recognition of cultural differences (and their implications for the counseling profession) has led to more and better research on multicultural populations and multicultural counseling processes. Nonetheless, much of the available literature must be considered as beginning points. Journals that publish research and scholarly opinion are too many to name here; however, a few representative journals that provide information for counselors include *Counseling Psychologist, Counseling and Human Development, Journal of Counseling and Development, American Psychologist, Journal of Cross–Cultural Psychology,* and *Journal of Multicultural Counseling and Development.* Readers interested in information pertaining to children and adolescents should consider *Child Development* and *Professional School Counseling;* those interested in adult development should consult *Human Development;* those counseling the elderly will benefit from reading selected issues of *Gerontologist* or *Journal of Gerontology.* (For a closer look at journals relating to human development and multicultural counseling, refer to Appendix A.) In summary, client differences such as culture, race, ethnicity, worldview, social class, lifespan, generation, gender, sexual orientation, and disability deserve counselors' attention and should be reflected in all aspects of multicultural counseling.

Counseling and Psychotherapy in a Multicultural Society

Multicultural counseling (sometimes called cross-cultural counseling) and psychotherapy have become major forces in counselor training and are recognized and endorsed by leading counselor education accrediting agencies. The National Council of Accreditation of Teacher Education (NCATE) and the council for Accreditation of Counseling and Related Educational Programs (CACREP) have adopted the position that multicultural education should be a part of the educational program for counselors. Considering our increasingly diverse society, it seems clear that culture will become an important construct for assessing, interpreting, and changing psychological processes in the future. However, the process of making culture central to the counseling process will require reconceptualizing our theories, tests, methods, strategies, and outcomes.

A Brief Historical Overview of Multicultural Counseling

Multicultural counseling as a specialization started with a small group of counselors and psychologists who were interested in cross-cultural differences. The civil rights movement of the 1960s provided tremendous impetus to the development of multicultural counseling. In addition, the growing recognition of racism and other forms of discrimination in American society resulted in ethnicity and minority status becoming a focus of interest within the field of counseling.

Until the mid-1960s, counseling and psychotherapy in America tended to overlook clients of differing cultural backgrounds who were at a disadvantage in a predominantly majority culture and a middle-class society. Likewise, psychotherapy limited its practice primarily to clients of the middle and upper classes and neglected people from lower classes and differing cultural backgrounds. However, by the mid-1970s, the number of studies focusing on the effects of race on counseling and psychotherapy had increased.

The movement gained momentum as people began to realize that certain minority-group clients were receiving unequal and poor mental health services. African American and American Indians were heavily overrepresented in community health centers in Seattle, whereas Hispanic American and Asian American clients were heavily underrepresented. The failure-to-return rate (after the first session) was over 50% for African Americans, American Indians, and Asian Americans, and 42% for both Hispanic Americans and European Americans (Pedersen, 1996). Obviously, more culturally relevant counseling services were needed. The number of publications on counseling minority groups in the United States began to increase. while initial efforts focused on Asian Americans, African Americans, and American Indians, the term *multiculturalism* was expanded to include other groups: various subcultures, racial groups, developmental periods, sexual orientation groups, gender groups, age groups, and social classes.

According to Pedersen (1996), counseling perspectives need to consider the rich traditions of counseling functions that predate the 19th and 20th centuries in both Western and non-Western cultures. Counselors need to acknowledge that the functions of counseling have been "alive and healthy" (Pedersen, 1996, p. 236) as long as civilizations have existed, even though the labels we use are relatively new. Incorporating a historical awareness into counseling will help counselors to identify culture-centered solutions to client problems in the client's own historical-cultural context.

Although the history of multicultural counseling and psychotherapy has been brief, current research and writing provide a basis for the prediction that the enthusiasm for counseling across cultures will continue.

Definitions

Several definitions offered by respected pioneers in the multicultural counseling field have withstood the test of time, including:

- counseling in which the counselor and client(s) are culturally different because of socialization acquired in distinct cultural, subcultural, racioethnic, or socioeconomic environments (Vontress, 1988); and
- a situation in which two or more people with different ways of perceiving their social environment are brought together in a helping relationship (Pedersen, 1988).

Although we respect the first two authors and their definitions, these definitions are more than a decade old and we prefer a newer definition of multicultural counseling:

Professional intervention and counseling relationships in which the counselor and the client belong to different cultural groups, subscribe to different worldviews, and have distinguishing differences such as gender, sexual orientation, disabilities, social class, and lifespan period.

Although counseling professionals often differ on their definition of multicultural counseling, most agree on several key aspects:

- Professional intervention techniques should reflect culturally different clients' cultural and ethnic backgrounds, lifespan period, gender perspectives, and sexual orientation.
- Counseling professionals plan accordingly for differences during counseling intervention as the dissonance between the cultural backgrounds of the counselor and the client increases.
- Counseling is perceived as culturally based, meaning both the counselor and the client bring their worldviews and cultural perspectives to the counseling process.
- Clients differ in the concerns they bring to counseling due to their cultural and ethnic backgrounds, lifespan period, gender perspectives, and sexual orientation.
- Counselors and their clients might vary in their perceptions of the counseling process as well as expected outcomes of the professional intervention.

Research Directions

Future research should include a focus on the various cultural groups, the relationship between culture and counseling, and developmental issues throughout the lifespan. For example, research directions may include: evaluating the impact of multicultural training, studying the effects of culture on counseling, examining the effectiveness of emic and etic approaches to counseling (discussed below), researching client–counselor matches to determine client preferences and counseling effectiveness, determining the role of gender on the process and outcome of counseling, examining how counselor and client worldviews affect professional intervention, and determining rationales for including gay and lesbian clients in multiculturalism (as well as meeting their counseling needs more effectively).

Draguns (1989) suggested that research investigations in multicultural counseling focus on either etic or emic approaches. An *etic* approach focuses on similarities and dissimilarities of the cultures being examined, whereas an *emic* approach examines a given culture itself, rather than making an external comparison of cultures. When choosing the former, an investigator might first assume that all human groups display aggressive behavior and then try to establish differences in aggression across cultures. In the latter approach, the investigator might consider an indigenous construct, such as the Japanese *amaeru* (translated as "presuming upon another person's benevolence"), and then relate it to a complex pattern of dependence on seeking gratification. The emic approach, then, proceeds from within the culture, whereas the etic approach is initiated from the outside, based on generic human dimensions (Draguns, 1989).

Counseling and Culture

To understand the close relationship between counseling and culture, counseling must be considered in its cultural context. For example, Draguns (1989) pointed out that counseling, as a product of 20-century Euro–American civilization, stresses individualism, self-determination, egalitarianism, social mobility, and social change attributes of the American culture. The counselor's traditional role was to be a "sympathetic but not meddlesome helper" (Draguns, 1989, p. 5).

Although American counselors considered the client's individuality, they did not give due recognition to the client's cultural background. Counselors often found that clients from culturally different backgrounds perceived counseling sessions as baffling, irrelevant, and unhelpful. The current emphasis on multicultural counseling further illustrates that counselors failed to recognize that their clients were products of differing cultural backgrounds (Draguns, 1989).

Counselors in multicultural settings carefully avoid three situations which can influence professional intervention and limit its effectiveness. First, they avoid overemphasizing similarities (e.g., culture, gender, sexual orientation, and lifespan period), which leads to a mindset that fails to recognize the differences that actually exist and affect counseling outcomes. The second situation is overgeneralizing differences, which leads to stereotyping. The third is assuming that one must emphasize either similarities or dissimilarities. These three situations can be avoided by focusing on the uniqueness of the client without dwelling on the client's similarities or differences.

Counseling and Counselor's Identity

Counselor's identity is influenced by several factors: culture, lifespan period, gender, developmental period, and prejudicial beliefs. Likewise, the counselor's perspectives toward individualism or collectivism affect counseling effectiveness. Why does all this matter, and does counselor identity have the potential for affecting the outcome of professional counseling intervention? Without doubt, the counselor's identity (and perspectives toward others) affects his or her ability to counsel effectively.

Effective counselors see the need to prepare and accept the responsibility to prepare for professional intervention in multicultural settings. Such responsibility and commitment require the close examination of one's identity. Counselors cannot understand others' cultural beliefs and worldviews until they understand others' cultural beliefs and worldviews until they understand their own; therefore, they should recognize their distinguishing cultural characteristics, beliefs, attitudes, and worldviews. In other words, they must learn "who they are" and "what they are becoming." This is especially true when counseling in multicultural situations, because clients will undoubtedly perceive events and situations through different lenses. Counselors need to understand the bases of their identities—their culture, ethnicity, social class, and gender—and how these orientations affect their response to clients.

A counselor's identity will influence how he or she intervenes. The European American counselor might emphasize rugged individualism; the Asian American and Hispanic American might feel obligated to show more concern for others. The African American counselor might expect European Americans to show more regard for family. Readers can likely name numerous other examples. The point is that counselors need to understand how their identities affect their feelings about clients' events and situations, and ultimately, counseling effectiveness. Perceptive counselors realize the necessity of working toward a neutral position regarding the value of these feelings and that client's entities affect how they perceive the forces affecting their lives.

Most counselor education programs provide training and first-hand experiences in individual and group counseling. Such training helps prospective counselors learn personal issues that might later interfere with their counseling effectiveness. This experience should also help prospective counselors become aware of their own ethnic and racial identities and how these views have shaped their personal identities, including their attitudes toward other ethnic and racial groups, the other gender, and people with differing sexual orientations. Counselors who completed counselor education programs prior to the emphasis on intervening with clients in multicultural settings and, more specifically, on understanding how counselor identity affects counseling intervention, have the professional responsibility to become aware of their own racial and ethnic identities, their perspectives toward differing cultural groups, and how their identities and perspectives affect the outcome of the counseling relationship.

Professional Status, Growth, and Progress

Scholarly research on culture and on counseling clients of differing cultural backgrounds appearing in counseling and psychology publications reflects the steadily rising professional status of multicultural counseling. Advances in multicultural human development research will further enhance the progress of the counseling movement by broadening the knowledge base through which clients in the various stages of the lifespan may be understood.

Patterson's (1996) belief that multicultural counseling is generic in nature and that all counseling is therefore multicultural drew responses from Pedersen (1996) and McFadden (1996). Pedersen (1996) stated that both similarities and dissimilarities need to be considered in multicultural counseling. Multiculturalism is more than an emphasis on techniques; the focus must always be on an effective therapeutic relationship, which will be assessed differently in each cultural context. Rather than using a universal approach that always works, counseling approaches must necessarily be "time-bound" and "culture-bound" (Patterson, 1996, p. 236) because each approach was itself developed in a cultural context. Multicultural skill is the ability to use time-bound and culture-bound theories, tests, or techniques in culturally appropriate ways.

In response to Patterson's (1996) theoretical positions, McFadden (1996) stated that, for multiculturalism to move forward toward a universal system of counseling, one should not presuppose abandonment of traditional counseling theories and techniques. Patterson's suggestion that multicultural counseling move from an emphasis on diversity in counseling techniques toward a more universal approach, however, raises certain concerns: (a) traditional systems of counseling do not meet the needs of clients of differing cultural and ethnic backgrounds, and (b) some ethnic minority clients have received unequal and poor mental health services. McFadden also suggested that some people think counselors who embrace multicultural counseling styles will "water down" or abandon traditional counseling theories and practices (1996, p. 232). Others think counselors who assent to a multicultural format will become chameleons, constantly changing their techniques to meet the special needs of minority clients. McFadden claimed that multicultural counseling does not presuppose the abandonment of traditional counseling or dilute the process. On the contrary, multicultural counseling attempts to blend cultural views and to create a broad social base for understanding problems in a pluralistic society, ultimately providing the most effective service for clients.

Resources and Guidelines

Counselors have several *resources* at their disposal when planning professional interventions in multicultural situations including:

- research-based findings on the cross-cultural counseling process;
- published accounts of personal experiences by other counselors;

- personally transmitted accounts;
- the counselor's own experiences with clients of differing backgrounds; and
- the counselor's professional, cultural, and personal sensitivity.

The following *guidelines* can potentially improve the overall effectiveness of multicultural counseling. Counselors should:

- be aware of their clients' and their own cultural group history and experiences;
- develop sensitivity toward their own personal beliefs and values;
- develop awareness and comprehension of their clients' histories and experiences within the cultural group;
- develop an awareness and comprehension of their clients' experiences in mainstream culture;
- develop perceptual sensitivity toward their clients' personal beliefs and values;
- demonstrate active listening and a broad repertoire of genuine verbal and nonverbal responses; and
- demonstrate genuine concern for their clients' individual situations.

Ethics

Ethics, without doubt, plays a significant role in multicultural counseling and influences its professional status, as well as its growth and progress. Because the topic of ethics is examined in Chapter 3 as a counselor responsibility, here we only briefly discuss the special ethical responsibilities of counselors who intervene with clients of culturally different backgrounds.

Counseling clients of various cultural backgrounds requires more than just knowledge of a particular client's cultural background. The client's perceptions, expectations, and expression of

---

A FOCUS ON RESEARCH 1.3

Multicultural Counseling and Ethical Practices

Addressing previous criticisms of the competencies, Arredondo and Toperek (2004) direct attention to seven criticisms: exclusiveness, research basis, racism, sociopolitical action, ethics and malpractice, mandating competence, and "diversity" and "multiculturalism." Maintaining that the competencies are a living document, Arredondo and Toperek offer future directions for counseling and ethical practices. Readers wanting a more detailed discussion are directed to Arredondo's and Toporek's excellent work.

Arredondo and Toperek maintained that when a mental health professional joins a professional

association and agrees to abide by the code of ethics, it is assumed the individual acts in accordance with its publicly acknowledged set of standards. Having a common document addressing multicultural competence helps the mental health professions achieve greater sophistication, preparation, and practice.

Source: "Multicultural counseling competence = Ethical practice," by P. Arredondo and R. Toporek, 2004, *Journal of Mental Health Counseling, 26,* pp. 44–55.

symptoms also warrant understanding from a cultural context. In fact, these should be understood from both the client's perspective and from that of the majority culture. Ethics comes into play when counselors try to understand (and subsequently plan interventions) that all people function from a culturally determined worldview which includes values, belief systems, lifestyles, and modes of problem-solving and decision-making. Ethical standards need to focus on professional training, assessment, and intervention practices especially as these aspects relate to counseling with clients of diverse cultural backgrounds. Arredondo and Toperek (2004) propose that multicultural competencies result in ethical counseling practices. They think the adoption of the competencies is indicative of ethical and culturally responsive practices. In A Focus on Research 1.3, Arredondo and Toperek (2004) write in support of the competencies developed by the Association of Counseling and Development (AMCD).

Challenges and Barriers

Several challenges have the potential for limiting the effectiveness of multicultural counseling. Although counselors can address challenges such as their own abilities to understand and counsel others who are different from themselves, they have less control over other challenges such as society's racism and discrimination.

Counselors' Mindsets and Efforts.   Challenges counselors may encounter when intervening with clients of differing cultural backgrounds include:

- lack of communication resulting from communication difficulties;
- counselor misunderstandings of the culture and its effects on the process and outcome of counseling (Atkinson, Morton & Sue, 1998);
- erroneous assumptions about cultural assimilation;
- differing social class values and orientations;
- stereotypical generalizations toward clients of other cultures;
- assumptions of racism or cultural bias on the part of either the counselor or the client; and
- lack of understanding of the client's worldview.

The existence of barriers does not imply that the counselor's challenge is too overwhelming to be tackled. Perceptive counselors can learn about clients' cultures, interact with people from different backgrounds, learn appropriate techniques for dealing with different clients, and, perhaps most importantly, examine their own beliefs and opinions concerning people of different cultures.

Lifespan Differences.   The increasingly pluralistic nature of the United States signifies a vast array of cultural, ethnic, gender, and racial differences deserving of counselors' respect and appreciation. It is also important for counselors to understand, however, that lifespan differences contribute to human diversity and, in many cases, are as important as a group's unique physical and cultural characteristics. A major premise of this text is that counselors should consider not only a client's cultural differences but also the client's lifespan period and the characteristics associated with each developmental stage, including potential psychological and emotional problems associated with each stage.

Stereotyping.   Stereotyping prohibits the effectiveness of multicultural counseling. Stereotypes produce a generalized mental picture of a person or an entire culture. Although a stereotype may hold some validity in a particular case, effective counselors have a professional responsibility to consider all stereotypes with skepticism and to acknowledge that prejudice and approval or disapproval accompany these images. Because stereotypes all too often contribute to racism and ageism, effective counselors should seek to understand and respond appropriately to their own and others' cultural and age-level beliefs.

Stereotypes about lifespan stage also affect one's perceptions of clients. Do children lack the power to change their lives? Are adolescents rebellious troublemakers obsessed with sex? Are adults always preoccupied with progress and material gains? Are the elderly "over the hill," without power or purpose? A counselor who holds such beliefs could place clients in a difficult situation. Likewise if a client subscribes to these beliefs, then the therapeutic relationship may be undermined.

Racism.   Racism is a complex ideology and occurs at individual, cultural, and institutional levels. The disturbing reality is that racism remains deeply embedded in individual value systems and in economical, political, and social institutions (Hays & Chang, 2003).

Racism and its effects continue to affect society with great force. The impact can be seen within various societal institutions, including education, government, business, housing, and criminal justice. Some people believe that advancements made during the civil rights movement have stalled or been reversed, whereas other people encourage us to believe that the wrongs of the past have been rectified because we now live in a "colorblind society" (p. 119) where individual effort and determination will enable anyone to succeed (Manglitz, 2003).

Efforts to combat racism have almost always addressed the issue from the perspective of the groups affected by discriminatory policies and practices. During most of the 20th century, racial relations and the problem of racism have focused almost exclusively on various aspects of the experiences of the victims of racism, oppression, and other forms of oppression. Such an approach revealed almost nothing about the motivations of Whites or other perpetrators of racism. These practices derive from the belief that racial prejudice and bias grow from personal ignorance and can be addressed primarily by education and information, thus ignoring the institutional and cultural components of racism and their conflation with power and priviledge (Manglitz, 2003).

Some cultural groups in the United States have clearly suffered the consequences of racism. African Americans continue to face discrimination in housing, employment, schooling, and various other areas despite civil rights legislation. Hispanic Americans are still exploited as migrant farmworkers. Asian Americans were denied entry into the United States during the early 1900s. American Indians had their land taken from them and were placed on reservations where today approximately half the population lives.

Unfortunately, racism or general dislike of those who are "different" often results in crimes committed against people based on their culture, sexual orientation, or other differences. Racism sometimes results in new forms of extremism to hurt others, both physically and psychologically. *Hate crime*, like domestic violence, sexual harassment, stalking, and date rape, is a relatively new term in the American lexicon of criminal law and public policy, although intergroup conflict and violence have been enduring characteristics of human societies. Since 1985, the definition of hate crime has come to include acts of violence based on sexual orientation, gender, and disability. Counselors should understand that all people, regardless of cultural background or other diversity, are at risk for being victims of a hate crime.

Racism appears in various forms and dimensions. For example, people (a) harbor negative feelings about another group because they consider that group to be a threat to their cultural beliefs; (b) harbor negative feelings about another cultural group, yet will not openly admit their racial feelings; (c) demonstrate friendly attitudes to other cultural groups only in some situations; and (d) fail to understand others' cultural beliefs and traditions and therefore harbor negative feelings because of ignorance and misunderstanding. Jones (2000) developed a framework for understanding what she calls the three levels of racism: institutional, personally mediated, and internalized.

Institutional racism is defined as different access to the goods, services, and opportunities of society because of race. This insidious form of racism plagues American society and impedes social acceptance and economic progress. Whereas the more obvious forms of racism can be identified and addressed, institutional racism may be more covert, including policies and practices of decision-making. Because this type of racism can be legal and often has been codified in institutions of law and custom, there may be no identifiable perpetrator. Nevertheless, it still manifests an inherent disadvantage. Institutionalized racism manifests itself both in material conditions and in access to power. For example, material conditions may include limited access to quality education, housing, employment, medical facilities, and a safe environment. With regard to access to power, examples include limited access to information directly pertaining to oneself (such as medical, financial, family), resources (such as wealth and organization infrastructure), and voice (such as voting rights, representation in government, and control of the media).

Personally mediated racism is defined as prejudice and discrimination, where prejudice means different assumptions about the abilities, motives, and intentions of others based on their race, and discrimination means different actions toward others based on their race. This type of racism can be intentional or unintentional and includes acts of commission as well as those of omission. It can take many forms, including: lack of respect, such as poor or no service; suspicion, such as shopkeeper's vigilance, avoidance of others, street crossing, purse clutching, and standing when empty seats are available; and devaluation, such as surprise at competence and the discouraging of aspirations.

Internalized racism is defined as acceptance of negative messages by members of stigmatized races about their own abilities and intrinsic worth. It is characterized by their not believing in others who look like them and not believing in themselves. It involves accepting limitations to one's full humanity, including one's spectrum of dreams, one's right to self-determination, and one's range of allowable self-expression. It can be seen in an embracing of "whiteness" (Jones, 2000, p. 1213), such as the use of hair straighteners and bleaching creams; self-devaluation, such as nicknames and rejection of ancestral culture; and feelings of resignation, helplessness, and hopelessness, such as dropping out of school and engaging in risky health practices (Jones, 2000).

The effects of racism are often denied and considered a taboo subject in racially mixed settings. Also, many people, regardless of their racial-group membership, have been socialized to think of the United States as a just society and fail to recognize the impact of racism on their own and others' lives (Henze, Lucas, & Scott, 1998).

White Privilege.   White privilege has been described as the resulting benefits that accrue to those who have been constructed as possessing "Whiteness" (p. 122) or who are seen as White (Manglitz, 2003). White privilege can also be defined as the belief that only one's own standards and opinions are accurate (to the exclusion of all other standards and opinions) and that these standards and opinions are defined and supported by Whites in a way to continually reinforce social distance between oppressed groups (Hays & Chang, 2003). Jackson (1999) refers to White privilege as a club that enrolls only certain people at birth, without their consent, and brings them up according to rules and expectations. Such privilege is an often overlooked condition that is lived but not recognized by Whites and greatly influences and limits racial interactions, guides appropriate ways of living for society, and gives Whites entitlement to take the initiative in discussing or refusing to discuss racism and being White. Whites' acceptance of their dominant culture role obscures their perceptions of themselves and others and has the potential for resulting in unequal power relations.

Within the social science literature, there are two general perspectives about what we should do with White being a racial category and associated with unequal access to resources and opportunities. One perspective equates Whiteness with privilege and oppression and calls for renunciation and abolition of the concept of Whiteness. The second perspective calls for serious efforts to rearticulate Whiteness into a progressive, antiracist White identity. Both perspectives share similarities and assumptions about Whiteness—an awareness that all racial categories are racially constructed, fluid, and affected by changing historical, societal, and political conditions; the recognition of the impact of interlocking oppression and privilege; the assertion that Whiteness and White privilege are used to position others as inferior, with compelling effects on people's lives; the importance of examining Whiteness within the contexts of power and societal systems; and the need to address systemic and institutionalized racism by creating spaces for Whites to examine their identity and how it is implicated in racism (Manglitz, 2003).

White privilege brings several advantages to its "members." Whites can feel confident when they look at the newspaper or television that they will see other Whites. Having white skin usually allows people to assimilate into the dominant culture in a way that most people of color cannot. Whites are fairly sure they will not be followed or harassed in a store. Having white skin may protect people from certain degrading, distasteful, and discriminatory experiences. Generally speaking, Whites do not have to spend the psychological effort or economic resources recovering from others' prejudices (Lucal, 1996).

Privilege can also be considered in terms of power, access, advantage, and a majority status. *Power* is having control, choice, autonomy, and authority or influence over others. *Access* is having money, opportunities, and/or material possessions. *Advantage* is having connections, favorable treatment, entitlement, social support, or lack of concern for others. *Majority* is simply being part of the majority in number, social standing, and/or social norms. The opposite of privilege, *oppression* is the lack of privilege, power, access, and majority status (Hays, Chang, & Dean, 2004).

For many Whites, race is invisible, just as gender is for men, sexuality for heterosexuals, and socioeconomic class for the middle class. Because they personify the privileged cultural categories in Western society, White male heterosexuals can think of themselves as individuals. Some people argue that viewing oneself as not belonging to a particular race is also an example of privilege. Members of the dominant group use race to distinguish others from themselves, and thus ascribe race only to others (Lucal, 1996).

White people are often unaware or unwilling to acknowledge that they are privileged (Willis & Lewis, 1999). Still, White privilege exists regardless of a particular White person's attitudes. In the United States, being White opens many doors for people, regardless of whether they approve of the way dominance has been placed upon them (Lucal, 1996). In order for an individual to deny something, he or she must be aware of its existence (Jackson, 1999).

White people also need to acknowledge that institutionalized inequality exists and that it favors them. In fact, some Whites see inequality as only a Black or Hispanic issue. Others think that because they are White, they do not have anything to add to discussions on racial issues. Many race- and ethnicity-based privileges are invisible to and taken for granted by most Whites, and even by some people of color (Pence & Fields, 1999). Racial inequality is explained in ways that do not implicate White society; the responsibility of Whites for the persistence of racism is obscured. As a result, Whites often look at racial discrimination with detachment (Lucal, 1996).

A premise of cultural pluralism approaches is that people will learn about others who are different and will come to appreciate others as individuals through deepened understanding and respect for their worldview. Unfortunately, this approach fails to take into consideration historical inequities among different groups, institutional and individual biases, and differential power relations. There needs to be a greater understanding of those with less power and privilege who have legitimate reasons to be angry, hurt, and frustrated (Henze, Lucas, & Scott, 1998).

This unearned White privilege along with the awareness of racism can create feelings of "White guilt." In fact, this guilt can result in Whites looking more favorably on affirmative action programs that might ameliorate the impact of White privilege (Swim & Miller, 1999). Whites often experience anxiety because of guilt stemming from the awareness of "ill-gotten" (Swim & Miller, 1999, p. 501) advantage. To be aware of White privilege and discrimination or to believe this discrimination is wrong, one must presumably have little prejudice against people from other cultures (Swim & Miller, 1999).

White guilt describes the dysphoria felt by European Americans who see their group as responsible for illegitimate advantages held over other racial groups. White guilt can include white people feeling good about their favored social position. Some evidence suggests that the advantaged can experience something akin to pride when they see themselves as superior to members of other groups. Still, even feeling a sense of pride, these people might also fell bad when systemic inequality illegitimately favors their group and disadvantages others. For example, European Americans can fell guilty about the ways in which racial inequality advantages them and disadvantages other groups. Although White guilt is based on the perception of illegitimate racial inequality, it does not always lead to support of general efforts to achieve racial equality (Iyer, Leach, & Crosby, 2003).

What does all this have to do with counselors? White counselors respond to White privilege and oppression with varying levels of awareness. Depending on their level of awareness, White counselors report anger, guilt, confusion, defensiveness, sadness, and a sense of responsibility and need for advocacy when discussing these topics. Other counselors might not have such a sense of awareness. Because Whiteness remains invisible to Whites, they might look at racial discrimination with detachment and feel little responsibility for changing the status quo. Although discussing these realities may create strong emotions, they are helpful in increasing counselors' awareness of advocacy, oppression, and cultural identity (Hays, Chang, & Dean, 2004).

Value of Understanding a Client's Developmental Stage

The number of research studies on lifespan development has resulted in a broad spectrum of publications, textbooks, and conference proceedings. Counselors who understand the developmental characteristics and unique cultural characteristics of their clients and the complex relationship between these two dimensions bring an enhanced perspective to counseling and psychotherapy.

As we have already mentioned, a major premise of this text is the importance of recognizing and understanding a client's developmental stage when planning and implementing counseling intervention. Rather than assuming a developmental homogeneity that may not actually exist, counselors benefit from knowing the problems, tasks, and challenges of each developmental period. The decision to use a specific technique should always be based on a sound rationale, rather than simply on a counselor's style, training, or preference. The relevance of human development theories becomes clear as counselors select techniques and counseling strategies based on the client's developmental level and the goals being worked toward. Counselors need to know counseling strategies that reflect cultural (and other) differences and developmental levels, as well as short-term and long-term counseling goals.

Counseling Intervention: Cultural Considerations

Regardless of culture and social class, professionals must often reach difficult decisions concerning whether to use individual, group, or family therapy for their clients. In multicultural situations, such decisions can be particularly difficult as cultural, intracultural, and generational differences are brought into play.

Individual and Group Therapy

Selecting individual or group counseling techniques becomes intricately complex, considering that some cultures may not react favorably to traditional counseling situations. For example, because of the commitment of Asian Americans to protecting the family name and honor at all costs, an Asian American client may be reluctant to reveal significant personal or family information; a Hispanic male client may be reluctant to disclose events or situations that may reflect negatively on his family or his manhood; the Western society's tendency to encourage the sharing of one's personal feelings runs counter to American Indians' reluctance to allow "outsiders" to intervene in their personal affairs. Whereas a client may be reluctant to disclose significant information during individual therapy, this reluctance might grow more acute during group therapy. Clients, both minority and majority culture, may distrust the counselor, again both minority and majority culture, because they believe that the counselor does not understand a cultural perspective other than his or her own.

The terms "multicultural group counseling" and "multicultural counseling groups" are used interchangeably to refer to group counseling situations in which counselors and clients differ in their cultural, ethnic, or racial characteristics. Many counselors agree that group counseling services can be used in both a preventive and a remedial manner with people from diverse ethnoracial backgrounds. Although intervening with group counseling may foster positive psychological outcomes, the effective and ethical practice of multicultural group counseling depends largely on the practitioner's understanding and competence in this area. Because multicultural group counseling represents a new service modality in the counseling profession, few mental health practitioners have knowledge and professional preparation in this realm (D'Andrea & Daniels, 1996).

Multicultural counseling groups may be reflected in a wide range of configurations, as shown in the following examples:

- White counselors work with a group of clients in which only one or two participants come from non-White, non-European backgrounds.
- White counselors work with a group of clients who all come from non-White, non-European backgrounds.
- A White counselor and a non-White counselor cofacilitate a group of clients who all come from non-White, non-European backgrounds.
- Non-White (African American) counselors facilitate a group whose members all come from other cultural/racial backgrounds (Asian Americans, Hispanic Americans, American Indians);
- Non-White counselors work in a group counseling setting in which all the clients share a common White–European background (D'Andrea & Daniels, 1996).

In A Focus on Research 1.4 (See p. 29), Conyne (2003), a former editor of the *Journal for Specialists in Group Work*, discusses group work issues and offers several predictions for the future.

A FOCUS ON RESEARCH 1.4
Group Work Issues

Conyne (2003) provides examples of special issues during his tenure as editor. Examples include: groups and structures, life coping skills, organizational development, ethical issues, substance abuse, and women's issues. He draws the conclusion that group work has become a major force in education and mental health. Recognizing "the lunacy of prediction" (p. 293), Conyne offered several predictions for the future of group work.

- Group work will be matched with an interdependent, ecological framework.
- Group work will continue to be used therapeutically and preventively.
- Group work will provide a framework for education.

- Group work will be a prime connector.
- Group work will be used increasingly for social betterment.
- Group work will be used to heal and to prevent and/or reduce international conflict.

Overall, Conyne's article did an excellent job of showing previous issues that have challenged group work and of showing future directions for group work and for the *Journal for Specialists in Group Work*.

Source: "Group work with issues: Past, present, and future." by R. K. Conyne, 2003, *Journal for Specialists in Group Work, 28* (4), pp. 291–298.

Marriage and Family

The Western world's tradition of encouraging males and females to share feelings and to communicate openly, freely, and on an equal footing may not be accepted by many Asian Americans, who have long accepted the superiority of the male and his valued role as the family spokesperson. In fact, it is unlikely that certain minority women will assume a significant speaking role during marriage and family counseling sessions. Although younger generations may have acculturated somewhat, the dominance of the male and his control over the family in some cultures should be understood by mental health professionals who may have intervened predominantly with clients of other cultural backgrounds.

Turner, Wieling, and Allen (2004) in A Focus on Research 1.5 point out that some family scholars have developed a greater sensitivity to the relative neglect of families of color in clinical and empirical research.

When planning intervention strategies, the counselor should consider the extent to which the client's cultural traditions affect therapy sessions and their outcome. Specifically, how will

---

A FOCUS ON RESEARCH 1.5
Culturally Effective Family-Based Research Programs

Turner, Wieling, and Allen (2004) discuss some of the etiological and methodical issues associated with planning, conducting, and disseminating family-based prevention and intervention research with ethnic minority families. Their overall purpose was to address some of the thought processes that they believe are instrumental to conducting ethical and responsible research with ethnic minority families.

Major topics explored by Turner, Wieling, and Allen include "The Complexity of Conducting Research in Diverse Contexts," "Toward Developing Conceptual Clarity of Race, Culture, and Ethnicity," and "Establishing Culturally Based Research Priorities for the Field of Marriage and Family Therapy."

Turner, Wieling, and Allen offered seven guiding questions for researchers and seven guiding questions for marriage and family therapists (MFTs). Selected guiding questions include:

Guiding Questions for Researchers:

1. What are your motivations for conducting research that involves families/communities of color?

2. What is your role/responsibility as a researcher vis-a-vis communities of color?

3. How does your ethnic and racial background inform the type of research you conduct with communities of color?

Guiding Questions for MFT practitioners:

1. What are your motivations for conducting clinical work with families/communities of color?

2. What is your role/responsibility as a MFT practitioner/trainer/supervisor vis-a-vis communities of color?

3. How does your ethnic and racial background inform your clinical work with communities of color?

We strongly recommend this article by Turner, Wieling, and Allen for both researchers and practitioners of marriage and family therapy.

Source: "Developing culturally-based effective family-based research programs: Implications for family therapists," by W. L. Turner, E. Wieling, & W. D. Allen, 2004, *Journal of Marital and Family Therapy, 30* (3), pp. 257–270.

the client in a multicultural setting respond to the presence of a spouse or children during a session? Will the wife respond during family therapy, or will she let the husband speak for the family? Such questions can be answered only by considering individual clients; their cultural characteristics, generation, and degree of acculturation; and the nature and severity of the problem.

What does the future of multicultural counseling look like? This question is taken up in the next section.

A Point of Departure

The development of multicultural counseling from its beginnings to its current status in both counselor education and mental health centers indicates that its growth will continue. Clients will benefit even more with the increasing recognition of lifespan differences. Counselors of the future might very well receive advanced degrees in multicultural counseling, which will contribute even further to the growth of this subspecialty and to the effectiveness of intervention strategies.

Challenges Confronting Counselors in Multicultural Settings

Professionals' expertise in counseling clients who are culturally different and their knowledge of lifespan differences will undoubtedly increase as multicultural counseling competencies are included in counselor education programs. Counselors are challenged to understand diversity of all types, understand clients and their differences, develop competency in multicultural counseling, and understand cultural and lifespan issues that affect counseling across cultures and developmental stages. In meeting these challenges, professionals are also responsible for being aware of the ethics involved in counseling across cultures.

Summary

Predicted population trends indicate that cultural diversity in the United States will continue to grow. Counselors will increasingly be called on to counsel clients of different backgrounds and ages in the lifespan continuum. Understanding concepts of culture, race, and ethnicity, as well as lifespan differences, is prerequisite to effective multicultural counseling. A significant challenge faces current and future counselors: to provide the most effective counseling intervention with clients of various cultures, racial and ethnic backgrounds, and stages on the lifespan.

Appendix B provides counselors with "Suggested Multicultural Experiential Exercises" as they learn more about multicultural counseling.

Suggested Readings

Chubbuck, S. (2004). Whiteness enacted, whiteness disrupted. The complexity of personal congruence. *American Educational Research Journal, 41*(2), 301–333.

Chubbuck concluded that neither an abolition of Whiteness nor a rearticulation of Whiteness includes a sufficiently complex understanding of how disruption of Whiteness is influenced by the interplay of personal identity, the need to maintain personal congruence, and the cultural constraints of Whiteness.

Chung, R. C. (2005). Women, human rights, and counseling: Crossing international boundaries. *Journal of Counseling and Development, 83,* 262–268. Maintaining that psychological and counseling issues are becoming more pronounced as the world become more globalized, Chung brings attention to women identified as victims of social injustices and human rights violence.

Goh, M. (2005). Cultural competence and master therapists: An inextricable relationship., *Journal of Mental Health Counseling, 27,* 71–82. Goh calls for counselors to learn two concepts simultaneously—cultural competence and counseling expertise.

Kim, C. J. (2004). Imagining race and nation in multiculturalist America. *Ethnic and Racial Studies, 27*(6), 987–1005. Kim looks at demographic changes since 1965 and maintains that national political leaders have promoted a discourse that discourages Americans from addressing intergroup tensions.

Reynolds, A. L., & Constantine, M. G. (2004). Feminism and multiculturalism: Parallels and intersections. *Journal of Multicultural Counseling and Development, 32,* 346–357. These authors call for exploring the connections of feminist concerns and multicultural concerns.

Sanchez, D. T., & Crocker, J. (2005). How investment in gender ideals affects well-being: The role of external contingencies of self-worth. *Psychology of Women Quarterly, 29,* 63–77. Sanchez and Crocker examined the relationship between investment in gender ideals and well-being and the role of external contingencies of self-worth.

Skovholt, T. M. (2005). The cycle of caring: A model of expertise in the helping profession. *Journal of Mental Health Counseling, 27*(1), 82–93. Skovholt describes the Cycle of Caring—Empathetic Attachment, Active Involvment, and Felt Separation and also describes the work of the counselor.

Identity Development and Models

Questions to Be Explored

1. How do factors such as culture, gender, sexual orientation, and development affect counselor identity?

2. How does prejudice affect counselor identity, and how should the counselor respond to it?

3. How does the American belief in individualism and self-sufficiency affect counselor identity as well as counselor perception of clients who may feel more regard and concern for the welfare of others?

4. What is meant by Helms's (1984, 1990, 1994) White racial identity attitude theory (WRIAT) model and Rowe, Bennett, and Atkinson's (1994) White racial consciousness (WRC) model, and what are their similarities?

5. Why should counselors develop an awareness of the perspective of their own culture, gender, sexual orientation, and development stage as well as those of their clients?

6. What difficulties and hurdles are associated with counselors understanding their own identity in an effort to achieve more effective intervention with clients in multicultural settings?

Overview

Counselor identity plays a major role in shaping how counselors perceive themselves and how they perceive others and their cultural backgrounds. Counselors in multicultural settings often face seemingly confusing situations, customs, and worldviews that differ from their own and have the potential for affecting the efficacy of counseling intervention. Their clients, regardless of the lifespan stage, can have attitudes and beliefs that contradict counselors' long-held and valued beliefs. For example, the African American counselor may fail to understand the American Indian perspective toward sharing and love of the earth, or males may not understand females' perspectives and vice versa. Misunderstandings that result from differences between the counselor and the client, such as differing cultural backgrounds, social class, or gender perspectives, can cloud judgments and inhibit decision-making processes. This chapter focuses on counselor identity, how identity can affect the counseling relationship, and the need for counselors, regardless of cultural background, to understand their own and others' cultural identities.

Understanding Identity

Scholars of social psychology, personality theory, feminist thought, and psychoanalytic theory have developed elaborate and thoughtful theories of the self and identity that have the potential for enhancing our understanding of counseling practice (Blustein & Noumair, 1996).

Cultural identity can be defined as one's cultural identification—the distinguishing character or personality of an individual and her or his self-perception as a cultural being, as well as beliefs, attitudes, and worldviews. The definition can also be viewed in terms of personal identity or who one is. Identity is the partly conscious, largely unconscious sense of who one is, both as a person and as a contributor to society. Undoubtedly, counselors can offer other definitions; however, regardless of the selected definition, a well-grounded, mature psychosocial identity is necessary. Identity, a complex and multifaceted entity, can be perceived in terms of culture, development, and gender, and directly influences how counselors perceive situations as well as their counseling effectiveness.

Racial identity development is important for at least two reasons. First, it helps shape individuals' attitudes about themselves, their attitudes about other individuals in their racial/ethnic minority group, and their attitudes about individuals from the majority. Second, it emphasizes that individuals from a particular cultural group differ, with widely varying attitudes and preferences.

Culture and Identity

Identity is inseparable from the specific culture that shapes it. One's culture—communication, social structures, rituals, and taboos—shapes one's identity in terms of what to think about situations and events. In other words, identity is influenced by how people perceive their communication, both as their native communication and in comparison with the majority communication. For example, an Asian American may look favorably on her native language in her enclaves yet perceive her native language as inferior when forced to participate in the broader English-speaking society. Similar conclusions can hold true for mannerisms, beliefs, and values. For example, a Hispanic American counselor might have difficulty understanding a European American's motivation to achieve and to excel at the expense of others. Before counselors can understand the cultural orientation of others, it will be necessary for them to understand their own culture and its effects on their counseling intervention.

Identity is firmly based in culture, cultural backgrounds, and opinions of how others perceive their culture. Although all people need to be aware of the relationship between culture and identity, counselors have an even greater responsibility to examine perceptions of their own and others' cultures and identities. The counselor needs an identity that contributes to the acceptance of culturally different people. Counseling effectiveness will be diminished when the counselor places value judgments on clients' cultures and judges events and situations through his or her identity expectations.

Development and Identity

Identity is well-grounded in the developmental changes that occur from childhood to old age. Identity formation begins early in life, but it continues to develop throughout the lifespan. Other factors that affect identity include the passage of time, social change, role requirements, and one's perceptions of others' opinions.

Pope (2002) examined the relationship between psychosocial development and racial identity of Black American (Pope used the term Black American because some participants were Caribbean American), Asian American, and Hispanic American traditionally aged undergraduate college students to learn the developmental needs and issues of college students of color and the impact of race and racial identity on their development. Implications of Pope's study included (1) ensuring that programs targeted at assisting students in the development of these areas (psychosocial development and racial identity) reflect consideration for differences in Asian American students; (2) focusing on individual interactions, such as advisement and career counseling sessions, to pass on important information and skills for psychosocial development and racial identity; (3) avoiding making assumptions about the students' levels of psychosocial development without first considering their racial identity and how they perceive themselves as racial beings; (4) addressing students' unique histories, cultural values, and perspectives of the various racial groups by targeting different types of workshops, personal approaches, mentoring, and advising and counseling efforts; and (5) considering both race and racial identity as important factors in understanding the development of students of color.

As we have said, identity formation actually begins in young children (as they learn the identifying characteristics of their culture), and significant development occurs during adolescence, when maturational ability allows self-determination, abstract future-oriented thought, expanding social roles, and more astute recognitions of one's culture and those of others. Thus, counselors working in multicultural settings need to understand both culture and development. Understanding one entity and not the other limits the counselor's ability to intervene, especially with clients of differing cultural backgrounds.

It is often difficult for people to understand the perspectives of others in differing lifespan stages. Although many people remember certain events of their childhood, they may forget what it is like to be a child. Likewise, it is difficult for an adolescent to imagine life as a middle-aged or elderly person. The lifespan period of the client has serious implications for counselors. First, counselors need to understand the various tasks and challenges of each developmental stage. Second, counselors need to understand the value placed on the elderly in some cultures. Third, and probably most important, counselors need to understand their own developmental period in itself and in relation to other developmental stages.

Gender and Identity

Gender can be defined as the differences in masculinity and femininity—the thoughts, feelings, and behaviors that suggest masculine or feminine orientations. Effective counselors accept and understand that individual and societal expectations of acceptable behavior for men and women vary across cultures. As with culture, gender has a direct influence on identity and vice versa. All people's identities, regardless of cultural background, are influenced by gender and gender expectations.

GENDER PERSPECTIVES 2.1
The Lives of Women with Severe Work Disabilities

Moore (2005) explored how women with severe disabilities attributed meaning to their lives, experiences, and decisions. Unquestionably, women with severe work disabilities face substantial barriers to participation in social, educational, and work roles.

Moore provided several implications for working with and counseling women with severe disabilities:

1. Connection with others—counselors should assess the loss of relationships and relational opportunities in clients' lives.

2. Unpaid and paid work—counselors can explore the meaning of work in clients' lives because they need to feel their abilities are being utilized, their needs are being met, and their lives are being valued.

3. Religion/spirituality—counselors should realize that church involvement and spirituality can be significant avenues that help to clarify meaning in life. Moore also thinks that the traditional medical model of counseling and rehabilitation disregards the inherent tendency in human beings toward wellness, self-actualization, and growth.

Source: "Expanding the view: The lives of women with severe work disabilities in context," by D. L. Moore, 2005, *Journal of Counseling and Development, 83*, pp. 343–348.

Several issues surface when counselors consider gender and its effects. Counselors need to understand their own gender—their maleness or femaleness—and how these orientations affect their counseling orientations and effectiveness. Likewise, counselors need to understand others' cultural orientations toward gender, such as cultures that place females in "less valued" positions. Also, changing gender orientations deserve consideration; that is, some people in Western cultures have been more accepting of males adopting traditionally female expectations and vice versa. Counselors should use considerable caution, however, not to transfer Western perspectives to people of other cultural backgrounds. Similarly, counselors from cultures that traditionally have adhered to strict gender roles, such as some Asian cultures, should be conscious of their own gender perspectives when intervening with Western-culture clients.

Counselors are often called upon to provide professional intervention with people who are disabled. Gender Perspectives 2.1 looks at women with severe work disabilities. It is important for counselors to understand their identity as well as clients who are disabled in some manner.

Prejudice and Identity

Identity can lead to prejudice when people consider their culture or values to be better than those of another person. Prejudice results when people believe their identities to be superior to others' and others' beliefs, attitudes, and worldviews to be wrong or inferior. Rather than perceive differences as enriching and worthy, people harboring prejudicial thoughts attempt to convince, subtly or blatantly, that others' cultural characteristics are wrong. Prejudice has harmful effects on both the harborer and the recipient. The identity of the prejudiced person is based on a belief of superiority that clouds her or his perspective of others and limits her or his ability to provide psychological intervention. The person to whom prejudice is directed does not have a fair chance of being understood and accepted.

It is imperative that counselors of all cultures determine whether they harbor traces of prejudice before they intervene with clients of differing cultural backgrounds. Counselors need to erase all personal prejudices before intervening with clients who are different in some way. For example, Hispanic American counselors should eliminate (or reduce as much as possible) all prejudices when intervening with European Americans and vice versa. Addressing one's prejudices requires understanding one's cultural identity and the perceptions of others.

Some counselors adhere to Western identity norms of individualism that can lead to a lack of acceptance of others or even outright prejudice. This constitutes a serious but not insurmountable challenge; counselors, regardless of cultural background, need to perceive situational events from their clients' cultural perspectives. Rather than use their own cultural perspectives when intervening with Eastern clients, Western counselors should intervene from the clients' perspectives. The reverse also holds true; counselors with Eastern cultural backgrounds should consider Westerners' cultural perspectives.

A Focus on Research 2.1 looks at White racial identity and racism.

A FOCUS ON RESEARCH 2.1
White Racial Identity and Racism

Although Denevi focuses on schools and educators, many of her thoughts on White racial identity, privilege, and racism apply to counselors. She maintains that professionals committed to the development of a multicultural community need to confront the question of White racial identity and privilege.

Rather than using guilt, Denevi's work has focused on the research on identity development and social justice initiatives. Many White people have been taught that their way of living is the American way and often feel a need to defend their culture, thus creating animosity and fear of interaction with others and equating Whiteness as rightness. One way of looking at White identity development is through the establishment of White affinity groups. These groups refer to a gathering of people who all share a similar experience—in this case, being White. This does not mean that everyone shares the same experiences, but rather that participants recognize that racial identity has an effect on the way they move through the world.

Denevi suggests that White professionals:

- explore their whiteness and recognize their ethnic identity—in other words, think about what it means to be White;
- consider themselves as diverse and recognize that multicultural does not mean "other than White;"
- distinguish between group and individual identity;
- understand the social, political, and historical roles of teaching (or in this case, providing counseling intervention); and
- learn the distinction between speaking for someone and speaking with someone.

While Denevi limits her discussion to White racial identity, she offers some excellent recommendations for Whites as they consider their racial identity and privilege.

Source: "White on White: Exploring White racial identity, privilege, and racism," by E. Denevi, 2004, *Independent School, 63* (4), pp. 84–87.

Individualism and Identity

C. H. Hoare (1991) maintained that an emphasis on individualism has resulted in an increase in preoccupation with fulfilling the needs of self and a decrease in value placed on equality for all. A current theory of person, perhaps best called insular individualism, has resulted in counselors, as well as other people, placing priority on personal needs and valuing personal identity at the expense of others. In the United States, the trend toward individualism and self-centrality reflects the American idea of the person, yet these concepts do not contribute to an understanding and acceptance of identity in other cultures. Autonomy, a traditional American value, places priority on self and personal achievement, yet a higher developmental identity reflects acceptance and inclusion of others in a more connected and relational world. Such an identity contributes to acceptance of self and others and to rejection of prejudice. Although "self" and "identity" have various connotations for different cultures, it is theoretically possible for people to share common ground with others in a manner that extends beyond individualism. What are the implications of this trend toward individualism for counselors who work with clients of other cultures? Counselors need to realize that some clients may not understand the concept of individualism. The counselor must intervene with caution, because some clients—for example, American Indians or Hispanic Americans, who often feel responsible for others' welfare—may perceive individualism as antithetical to cultural expectations. Counselors in multicultural settings need to understand how clients of some cultures feel a sense of collectivism toward others. Counseling intervention often falters when clients think that the counselor does not understand that their cultural identities place value on helping others.

Cultural identity development theory identifies levels of cultural awareness and stresses that counselors and therapists must recognize their clients' cultural identities or awareness levels. Counselors who understand their own and others' identities can match the interviewing style to the level of client awareness. For example, many non-African American therapists may be ineffective when intervening with African Americans because of an inability to relate to the client's cultural identity. Likewise, African American therapists can be expected to experience some difficulties with African American clients who have differing worldviews from their own (Ivey, Ivey, & Simela-Morgan, 1997).

Several models of identity development have appeared (sexual orientation, female, and biracial) in recent years. Although an examination of all identity models is beyond the scope of this text, selected models are examined briefly in terms of how counseling intervention will be effected. Following a discussion of how identities develop, a more detailed examination focuses on racial identity models in White counselors.

The Counselor's Identity: Developing Self-Awareness

Self-Awareness

Self-awareness is a person's consciousness of specific events that influence his or her psychological, social, emotional, and cultural attributes. It includes identity (what one thinks of oneself) and one's sense of identity as influenced by the perception of self and others. Identity includes many factors, such as race, ethnicity, and gender (Brown, Parham, & Yonker, 1996).

Ideally, counselors should develop an awareness of their cultural heritage and how it has shaped their beliefs, attitudes, and values, especially those involving other people. To provide effective counseling intervention, counselors who work with clients of a particular racial or ethnic minority must acquire specific knowledge about that particular group. Counselors also need a general understanding (and an awareness of their perspective of this understanding) of the sociopolitical systems operative in the United States with respect to minorities and the institutional barriers that prevent minorities from using mental health services (Das, 1995).

Counselors can develop or promote self-awareness by examining personal attitudes and beliefs. This process of increasing understanding of oneself and one's identity should begin with exploration of one's culture and how it affects personal psychosocial development. Of particular importance is a careful examination of factors that have contributed to the formation of the counselor's ethnic identity during childhood and adolescence. Such self-exploration leads to self-awareness, which is crucial in developing a set of personal attitudes and beliefs to guide multicultural counseling practices (C. C. Lee, 1995b).

For cross-cultural awareness and subsequent effective counseling to occur, counselors need to develop several "awarenesses" in addition to just self-awareness (however, these additional awarenesses do not negate the importance of self-awareness). In addition to self-awareness and awareness of one's own culture, other awarenesses include:

- awareness of racism, sexism, and poverty;
- awareness of individual differences;
- awareness of others' culture(s); and
- awareness of diversity (Locke & Parker, 1994).

Awareness of One's Culture and Sensitivity to One's Cultural Heritage

Arredondo and colleagues (1996) published an extensive article focusing on multicultural counseling competencies. In the section "Counselor Awareness of Own Cultural Values and Biases," they stated that counselors should be able to:

- identify culture(s) to which they belong;
- identify specific cultural groups from which they derived fundamental cultural heritage and significant beliefs and attitudes;
- recognize the impact of their beliefs on their ability to respect others;
- identify specific attitudes, beliefs, and values from their own cultural heritage that support behaviors demonstrating respect and valuing;
- engage in an ongoing process of challenging their own beliefs and attitudes that do not support respecting and valuing of differences;
- appreciate and articulate positive aspects of their own heritage that provide them with strengths in understanding differences; and
- recognize the influence of other personal dimensions of identity and their role in self-awareness.

Awareness and Attitudes, Values, and Biases About Psychological Processes

To gain understanding of personal identity and development of self-awareness, counselors must develop an awareness of how their own cultural backgrounds and experiences influence their attitudes, values, and biases about psychological processes. For example, counselors need to be able to:

- identify the history of their culture in relation to educational opportunities and current worldview;
- identify relevant personal cultural traits and explain their influences on cultural values;
- identify social and cultural influences on cognitive development;
- identify social and cultural influences in their history that have influenced their views, which may affect counseling; and
- articulate the beliefs of their own cultural and religious groups as these relate to sexual orientation, able-bodiedness, and the impact of these beliefs on counseling relationships (Arredondo, et al., 1996).

A significant and growing amount of attention has focused on White identity (Behrens, 1997, p. 3) as scholars increasingly realize the profound implications that the racial outlook of Whites may have for research, training, and counseling outcomes. For example, in regard to research, White identity holds promise of serving as a within-group variable that may bring to light important differences that might otherwise be obscured. In terms of practice, an understanding of White racial outlook has the potential to significantly improve multicultural counseling services through analysis of dyadic interactions (Behrens, 1997).

Several factors suggest a need for a section in this text concerning the White counselor. First, realistically speaking, the United States has more White counselors than non-White counselors. As members of the majority culture, White counselors might have a greater need to understand minority cultures and the racism, prejudice, and discrimination that minority cultures often face. Second, substantial research has not focused on the identity development of counselors of other cultural backgrounds. As will be seen in the next section, Ponterotto's (1988) research focused on White counselor trainees. Likewise, Helms (1984, 1990, 1994) and Rowe, Bennett, Atkinson (1994) focused their work on White counselors. Perhaps researchers do not see a need for studying minority counselors' identities, or perhaps multicultural counseling has not yet progressed to this point, but the fact remains that research has focused primarily on White counselor trainees and practicing counselors.

The Ponterotto Model—The White Counselor's Identity

Ponterotto (1988) proposed a model of identity development for white counselor trainees; that is, the White counselor often works through the following stages when confronted with multicultural concerns:

Stage 1: *Pre-exposure:* The White counselor trainee has not thought about counseling and therapy as multicultural phenomena. The trainee may believe that people are just people, and in counseling practice may engage in unconscious racism or sexism or try to treat all clients the same.

Stage 2: *Exposure:* The counselor trainee recognizes multicultural issues, learns about cultural differences and discrimination and oppression, and realizes that previous educational experiences have been incomplete. In this stage, the trainee may become perturbed and confused by the many apparent incongruities.

Stage 3: *Zealotry and Defensiveness:* Counselor trainees are faced with the challenge of multicultural issues and may move in one of two directions: Some may become angry and active proponents of multiculturalism, whereas others may retreat into quiet defensiveness and adopt criticisms of Eurocentric culture in general (Ivey et al., 1997) and of therapeutic theory specifically. These individuals become passive recipients of information and return to the safer perspectives of the White culture.

Stage 4: *Integration:* The counselor trainee acquires respect for and awareness of cultural differences, understanding how personal and family history can affect the counseling intervention plan. An acceptance evolves that one cannot know all the dimensions of multicultural counseling and therapy all at once and that developing multicultural counseling expertise takes time and the development of a plan (Ivey et al., 1997).

Although Ponterotto (1988) developed his model for White counselors, the model also has implications for counselor trainees of other cultural backgrounds. For example, a Lakota Sioux counselor may have developed an awareness of her or his own culture and be aware of Midwestern European Americans but may not have had contact with Hispanic Americans or African Americans. Therefore, it is likely that all counselors will have to face issues in multicultural counseling that are reflected in Ponterotto's model. Perceptive readers can easily see the importance of counselors understanding their own identities as well as the identities of their clients (Ivey et al., 1997).

Identity Development Models

Minority Racial/Cultural Identity Model

The Racial/Cultural Identity (R/CID) development model (Sue & Sue, 2003) is a conceptual framework to aid therapists in understanding their culturally different clients' attitudes and behaviors. The model describes five stages of development that people experience as they struggle to understand themselves in terms of their own culture, the dominant culture, and the relationships between cultures: conformity, dissonance, resistance and immersion introspection, and integrative awareness.

In the *conformity stage*, minority individuals prefer dominant cultural values over their own. Physical and cultural characteristics toward the self (or one's own racial/cultural group) are perceived negatively, as something to be avoided or denied. Basically, in this stage, minority individuals identify with and appreciate White Americans and their lifestyles value systems, and cultural/physical characteristics. The attitudes and beliefs toward members of the same minority group might be similar to those they perceive as held by the majority culture, yet they see themselves as different or an exception to the rule. Little thought or validity is given to other cultural viewpoints. To be more like the majority culture, some minority individuals in this stage might attempt to mimic what is perceived as White mannerisms, speech patterns, dress, and goals (Sue & Sue, 2003).

In the *dissonance stage*, no matter how much one attempts to deny his or her own racial/cultural heritage, an individual will encounter information or experiences that are inconsistent with culturally held beliefs, attitudes, and values. For example, an Asian American who believes that Asians are inhibited, passive, inarticulate, and poor in people relationships may encounter an Asian leader who seems to break all these stereotypes. In all probability, movement into the dissonance stage is a gradual process. The individual is in conflict between different information or experiences that challenge his or her current self-concept. People generally move into this stage slowly, but a traumatic event may propel some individuals to move into dissonance at a much more rapid pace. Attitudes and beliefs about the self include a growing sense of personal awareness that racism does exist, that not all aspects of the minority or majority culture are good or bad, and that one cannot escape one's cultural heritage. The person begins to accept the possibility of positive attributes in the minority cultures and an accompanying sense of pride in self. Attitudes toward members of the same minority change (Sue & Sue, 2003).

During the third stage, the *resistance and immersion stage*, the person tends to endorse minority-held views completely and to reject the dominant value of society and culture. The person seems dedicated to reacting against White society and rejects White social, cultural, and institutional standards. Desire to eliminate oppression of the individual's minority group becomes an important motivation of the individual's behavior. Three feelings—guilt, shame, and anger—surface. Feelings of guilt and shame result from thinking that, in the past, minority individuals have rejected or downplayed their own cultural and racial groups. These feelings are associated with a sense of anger at the oppression and feelings of being brainwashed by forces in the White society.

This stage includes a sense of rediscovery of one's own history and culture. People seek information that enhances a person's sense of identity and worth. Cultural and racial characteristics that once elicited feelings of shame and disgust become symbols of pride and honor. Negative self-esteem resulting from prejudice and racism is now actively challenged in order to raise self-esteem. A growing sense of comradeship develops with persons from his or her own minority group, and a strong sense of cultural pride develops. There are fewer attempts to reach out and understand other racial/cultural minority groups and their values and customs. Characterized by both withdrawal from the dominant culture and immersion in one's cultural heritage, there is also considerable anger and hostility directed at White society (Sue & Sue, 2003).

The *introspection stage* is the fourth level and includes the individual beginning to discover that this level of anger directed at White people is psychologically draining and does not permit one to devote more critical energies to understanding themselves or to their own racial/cultural group. The person now feels that he or she has too rigidly held onto minority group views and notions in order to submerge personal autonomy. This conflict now becomes significant in terms of responsibility and allegiance to one's own minority group versus notions of personal independence and autonomy. Thus, the individual begins to spend more and more time and energy trying to sort out these aspects of self-identity and begins to demand individual autonomy. The person might also see his or her own group taking positions that might be considered extreme. There is a greater uneasiness with cultureocentrism and an attempt is made to reach out to other groups in learning what types of oppression they experienced and how they handled oppressive experiences. Last, the person experiences distrust for the dominant society and culture. Conflict occurs because the person begins to recognize that there are many elements in U.S. culture that are highly functional and desirable, yet there is a confusion as to how to incorporate these elements into the minority culture (Sue & Sue, 2003).

In fifth and last stage, *integrative awareness stage,* minority persons have developed a sense of security and now can own and appreciate unique aspects of their culture as well as others' cultures. Minority culture is not necessarily in conflict with White dominant cultural ways. Many conflicts and discomforts are resolved, allowing greater individual control and flexibility. There is now the belief that there are acceptable and unacceptable aspects in all cultures and that it is very important for the person to be able to examine and accept or reject those aspects of a culture that are not seen as desirable.

The person develops a positive self-image and experiences a strong sense of self-worth and confidence. Racial pride in identity and culture develop as well as a sense of autonomy. In essence, the individual becomes bicultural or multicultural. There is no longer a conflict over disagreeing with group goals and values. He or she reaches out to other minority groups to understand their cultural values and ways of life. Last, the individual experiences a sense of trust and liking from members of the dominant group who seek to eliminate oppressive activities. The individual becomes open to constructive elements of the dominant culture (Sue & Sue, 2003).

The R/CID development model has several implications for counseling intervention. First, an understanding of cultural identity development should sensitize counselors to the role that oppression plays in a minority individual's development. Second, the model will aid counselors in recognizing differences between members of the same minority group with respect to their cultural identity. Third, the model allows counselors to realize the potentially changing and developing nature of cultural identity among clients (Sue & Sue, 2003).

Biracial Identity Development Model

Poston (1990) proposed a five-stage, progressive, developmental model for biracial identity development, as follows:

Stage 1: *Personal Identity:* People in this stage are commonly very young, and membership in any particular ethnic group is just becoming salient. Children will tend to have a sense of self that is somewhat independent of their ethnic background. However, they develop an awareness of their race and ethnicity. Opinions vary as to how much racial awareness actually occurs. Phinney and Rotherham (1987) found no substantial research data on how and when children understand themselves as racial or ethnic beings. Young children often demonstrate idiosyncratic and inconsistent feelings about such matters, sometimes showing no awareness of race and identity. Ponterotto (1988) noted, however, that older children have a greater sense of ethnic identity than was previously thought.

Stage 2: *Choice of Group Categorization:* Individuals in this stage feel a need to choose an identity, usually of one ethnic group. Although individuals differ, this stage can be a time of crisis and alienation. Many biracial people feel forced to make a specific racial choice in order to participate in or belong to peer, family, and social groups. Biracial people think they have two choices: (1) They can choose a multicultural existence that emphasizes the racial

A FOCUS ON RESEARCH 2.2

African Americans' Racial Identity and Socially Desirable Responding

Abrams and Trusty developed a model of the relationship between racial identity development (RID) and socially desirable responding. The authors maintained that RID is often assessed through self-report instruments. This process can result in response bias when clients try to present themselves in an overly positive manner. In other words, clients present a biased presentation that may reflect an unconscious attempt to appear positive (e.g., positive, perceived control, and adjustment) to others. This type of responding may threaten the validity of self-report measures.

The researchers underscored the need for incorporating sophisticated measures of social desirability in racial identity research and clinical practice because clients made a deliberate attempt to endorse certain scale items and not to endorse others. In particular, future RID instrument developers should use thorough and theoretically consistent methods or quantifying social desirability. Abrams and Trusty recommended that RID instrument developers broaden their perspectives. Counselors and other professionals should be aware that literature pertinent to RID exists in various disciplines such as social psychology, sociology, and anthropology.

Source: "African Americans' racial identity and socially desirable responding: An empirical model." by L. Abrams and J. Trusty, 2004, *Journal of Counseling and Development, 82* (3), pp. 365–374.

heritage of both parents, or (2) they can choose one parent's culture or racial heritage as dominant over the other. Factors influencing this decision include status of parents' ethnic backgrounds; neighborhood demographics; ethnicity of peers; acceptance and participation in cultures of various groups; and parental and familial acceptance, physical appearance, knowledge of languages other than English, cultural knowledge, age, political involvement, and individual personality differences. It would be unusual for an individual to choose a multiethnic identity, because this requires some level of knowledge of multiple cultures and a level of cognitive development beyond that which is characteristic of this age group.

Stage 3: *Enmeshment/Denial:* This stage is characterized by confusion and guilt at having to choose one identity that is not fully expressive of one's background. Individuals in this stage often experience feelings of guilt, self-hatred, and lack of acceptance of one or more groups. A multiethnic child, unable to identify with both parents, may experience feelings of being disloyal and of guilt over rejection of one parent. During this stage, the biracial adolescent might be ashamed of and might fear having friends meet the parent whose racial background differs from the norm in the neighborhood. Eventually, these feelings must be resolved and the individual must learn to appreciate both parental cultures.

Stage 4: *Appreciation:* Individuals begin to appreciate their multiple identities and to broaden their reference group orientation. They may begin to learn about their racial/ethnic heritages and cultures, but also may continue to identify with only one group. The choice of which group to identify with continues to be influenced by the factors described in Stage 2.

Stage 5: *Integration:* Individuals in this stage experience a wholeness and tend to recognize and value all of their ethnic identities. At this stage, they have developed secure, integrated identities (Poston, 1990).

Poston's (1990) model of biracial identity introduces several important issues and assumptions. First, biracial individuals may tend to have identity problems when they internalize outside prejudice and values. Second, numerous factors, such as family and peer influences, affect individuals' identity choices. Third, biracial individuals may experience alienation at the choice phase and make a choice even though they are uncomfortable with it. Fourth, the choice of one identity over another at the choice phase and the resultant denial can be associated with feelings of guilt and disloyalty. Fifth, integration is important and is associated with positive indicators of mental health. Finally, the most difficult adjustment and identity confusion occurs during the enmeshment/denial stage.

A focus on Research 2.2 looks at how African Americans' racial identity might be affected by clients offering what they consider to be socially desirable responses.

White Racial Identity Attitude Theory (WRIAT) Model

In the past few years (Block & Carter, 1996; Helms, 1984, 1990, 1994; Rowe, Bennett, & Atkinson, 1994), research has focused on the White counselor's racial identity and how it affects counseling intervention. Racial identity development can be defined as the process or series of stages through which a person passes as the person's attitudes toward his or her own racial/ethnic group and the White population develop, ultimately achieving a healthy identity. Although the number of stages and the specifics of each stage varies among models, the first stage typically involves acceptance of the stereotypes that the dominant society has attributed to the group. The second stage is typically one of conflict or dissonance, in which the individual begins to question previously held stereotypes. The third stage involves an immersion in the culture of the racial/ethnic group and a militant rejection of individuals and values outside the group. In the final stage, the individual retains a positive racial/ethnic identity while coming to accept the positive attributes of individuals and cultures outside the reference group (Rowe et al., 1994).

Several White racial identity development models [e.g., Helms' White Racial Identity Attitude Theory (WRIAT) model and Rowe's et al. White Racial Consciousness Model (WRC)] have been proposed in the last decade or so. The model selected for discussion is Helm's WRIAT model (Helms, 1984, 1990, 1994).

Helms (1984, 1990, 1994) proposed that White racial identity develops through six stages: contact, disintegration, reintegration, pseudoindependence, immersion/emersion, and autonomy. Each stage involves conceptions of self as a racial being, as well as conceptions of others and of oneself relative to other racial groups. Helms's model includes two phases: the abandonment of racism and the development of a positive White identity.

The six stages of WRIAT are as follows:

Stage 1: *Contact:* This stage involves a lack of consciousness of one's own race and a naïve curiosity or timidity with respect to other groups. People usually pretend that racial differences do not matter, perhaps because they lacked meaningful contact with members of other cultural groups or were raised in a familial atmosphere that did not discuss racial differences.

Stage 2: *Disintegration:* This stage involves guilt and confusion. This stage represents Whites first acknowledgement of social implications that often force them to face moral dilemmas that arise from being considered superior to other groups. These feelings can lead to guilt and anxiety when discussions and life experiences focus on racial issues. During this stage, people may embrace immoral racial values and beliefs because these are the norms for the White group to which they have been exposed. The identity may become exclusively White as people attempt escape from the painful feelings by denying that racism exists.

Stage 3: *Reintegration:* Because of the intrapersonal conflict experienced in the previous stage, the reintegration stage involves people adopting an orientation in which all aspects of being White are considered superior. People have a tendency to stereotype other groups negatively and to exaggerate the differences between one's own group and others. Common reactions include rigidity in beliefs, reclusiveness, and out-group aggression and hostility in mixed racial environments. Those in this stage generally believe that Whites are better than other cultural groups and that Whites should control society. Feelings include views of cultural superiority and denigration and hostility toward other groups.

Stage 4: *Pseudoindependence:* This stage represents the initial step toward a positive, nonracist identity. People in this stage attempt to control tumultuous feelings aroused during earlier stages by thoughtfully considering other people's racial problems and by trying to acculturate them to the White culture. These people continue to believe in the superiority of the White race; that is, they believe that other racial issues can be resolved by learning the White culture and by associating with Whites.

Stage 5: *Immersion/emersion:* This stage involves White people beginning to seek a personally meaningful definition of Whiteness and to reeducate other White people about race and racism. People are consciously aware of being White and may have feelings of anger and confusion and an insensitivity to other Whites. They sometimes believe that they should relate to, and identify with, other Whites in their environment but that the other Whites perhaps have not resolved their own racial issues.

Stage 6: *Autonomy:* This stage might be best thought of as an ongoing process of refinement of one's racial identity. Primary themes include internalizing, nurturing, and applying the new personal definition of Whiteness that has evolved in earlier stages. Individuals in this stage are nonracist Whites and are able to conceive of being White without being racist; they recognize that core values and beliefs are absorbed from the White culture. Because these people can actively question the tenets of the White culture, they now have the capacity to choose those aspects of White culture that feel right to them. People in this stage are actually multiracial; that is, they increasingly become aware of the commonalities inherent in various forms of oppression and try to eliminate all forms of oppression from society.

Biracial Identity Model

Biracial identity development is a complicated and important process in the life of any individual of ethnically different parents. Although most individuals seem to move through identity development successfully and eventually become well-adjusted individuals, some people experience difficulty negotiating the numerous hurdles. Biracial persons often struggle with converging their various identities.

Aldarondo (2001) maintains that although individuals of mixed ethnic and racial heritage are increasing in numbers among the general population, many gaps remain in the literature in terms of guidelines for counselors working with these individuals. Aldarondo suggest's that counselors should determine the extent to which the client adheres to a particular culture. Such a determination should be made not on the basis of racial or ethnic membership but on cultural/racial identity. Other suggested methods include degree of social support from family and community members, the number of and degree of racial incidents, and the actual counseling relationship itself. For example, the counselor will need to examine his or her own attitudes and beliefs about interracial marriage and biracial children with other individuals. As with other forms of counseling, the relationship between client and counselor should be genuine and built on trust.

Asian Identity Model

Sue and Sue (2003) maintain that Asian American identity models have not been advanced as far as some other identity models. They explain that while some models have been proposed, the early models had several shortcomings. First, the early models failed to provide a clear rationale as to why an individual develops one ethnic type over another. Second, the early proposals seemed too simplistic to account for the complexity of racial identity development. Third, these models were too population specific in that they described only one Asian American cultural group. In response to these criticisms, theorists have begun moving toward the development of stage/process models of Asian American identity development. Sue and Sue (2003) describe John Kim's model with third generation Japanese American women to posit a progressive and sequential stage model of Asian American identity development. His model integrates the influence of acculturation, exposure to cultural differences, environmental negativism to racial differences, personal methods of handling race-related conflicts, and the effects of group or social movements on the Asian American individual.

The *ethnic awareness stage* begins around the age of 3 or 4, when the child's family members serve as the significant ethnic group model. Positive or neutral attitudes toward one's own ethnic origin are formed depending on the amount of ethnic exposure conveyed by caretakers.

The *White identification stage* begins when children enter school, where peers and the surroundings become powerful forces in conveying racial prejudice that negatively impacts their self-esteem and identity. The realization of "differentness" (quotes Sue's and Sue's) from such interactions leads to self-blame and desire to escape racial heritage by identifying with White society.

The awakening to *social political consciousness stage* means the adoption of a new perspective, often correlated with political awareness. The civil rights movement and the women's movement, as well as other significant political events, often precipitate this new awakening. The primary result is an abandoning of identification with White society and a consequent understanding of oppression and oppressed groups.

The *redirection stage* means recommendation or renewed connection with one's Asian American heritage and culture. This is often followed by the realization that White oppression is the culprit for the negative experiences of youth. Anger against White racism may become a defining theme with concomitant increases of Asian American self-pride and group pride.

The *incorporation stage* represents the highest form of identity evolution. It encompasses the development of a positive and comfortable identity as Asian American and consequent respect for other cultural/racial heritages. Identification for or against White culture is no longer an important issue (Sue & Sue, 2003).

A FOCUS ON RESEARCH 2.3

Pilipino American Identity Development Model

Nadal examines identity development in F/Pilipino Americans. In his article, he proposes a six-stage identity development model. The model describes the process of ethnic identity formation for native-born/second-generation F/Pilipino Americans in the United States. This nonlinear model will not be completed by all F/Pilipino Americans. Plus, the stages should not be viewed as positive or negative but should be used to understand the acculturation levels of F/Pilipino Americans for more accurate and appropriate therapeutic or psychological practice. While Nadal provides a detailed description and discussion of the six stages, space only allows us to list the stages:

Stage 1	Ethnic Awareness
Stage 2	Assimilation to Dominant Culture
Stage 3	Social Political Awakening
Stage 4	Panethnic Asian American Consciousness
Stage 5	Ethnocentric Realization
Stage 6	Incorporation

Readers wanting a more detailed discussion of Nadal's model are referred to the original reference.

Nadal also provides several excellent implications for counseling F/Pilipino Americans. First, the model is nonlinear, meaning that participants may advance through the stages in a progressive manner but may occasionally move back and forth between stages. Second, it is important to understand that some people may not progress through all the stages. Depending on their environments, surroundings, and influences, clients may remain in certain stages for their entire lives. Third, it is important to realize that it is not the duty of the counselor to help a client progress through these stages. The counselor may challenge the client to think in different perspectives yet should not and could not force the client to advance to any other stage.

Source: "Pilipino American identity development model," by K. L. Nadal, 2004, *Journal of Multicultural Counseling and Development, 32*(1), pp. 45–62.

Alvarez and Kimura (2001) believe that racism has been a persistent and significant theme in the life experiences of Asians in the United States. Asian Americans continue to be the targets of racially motivated verbal harassment, property vandalism theft, physical assaults, and in some cases, homicides. Such racial incidents undoubtedly affect Asian Americans' identity development. Their struggle with racial issues have mental health implications for the counseling community, yet most of the psychological literature has focused on the prevalence of rates of mental health, utilization rates for mental health services, and counselor preferences. In fact, surprisingly little attention is paid to race and racism. Alvarez and Kimura (2001) maintain that racism should be considered a valid psychological stressor for Asian Americans and call for increased cultural competency of counselors working within the Asian American community.

Nadal (2004) explains *F/Pilipino*, the term he uses to describe Americans of Philippine backgrounds from different geographic regions and different stages of identity development who use both Filipino and Pilipino as ethnic identities. Some F/Pilipinos will use Pilipino as a political statement because there is no "F" in the Tagalog/Pilipino language. However, some F/Pilipinos will identify with Filipino because it is the term that has been used most commonly for centuries.

Nadal (2004) maintains that the sociocultural experience of F/Pilipino Americans is distinct from that of their Asian American counterparts due to a variety of factors, including a lower socioeconomic status, F/Pilipino American–specific health concerns, educational barriers, and marginalization within the Asian American community. All these factors have the potential for influencing cultural identity development. In A Focus on Research 2.3. Nadal examines the Pilipino American identity development model.

Collins (2000) investigated the complexity of biracial identity development in Japanese Americans and found that these individuals have many problems: identity development, self-hatred, alienation, denial of self, feelings of guilt and disloyalty, substance abuse, gender identity confusion, and suicide. His findings relate to participants' initiating explorations of identity and perseverance in pursuing a biracial identity, which depend on the degree of support or negative experience within their own social networks. Service providers need to be familiar with the developmental phases of biracial individuals to better plan intervention strategies. Collins suggests that clinicians use the model to gain a better understanding of biracial identity development; perceive biracial identity development as being dynamic rather than static; acknowledge clients' multiethnic heritage as different and positive; encourage clients to seek relationships with peers from many different backgrounds and suggest they search for multiethnic role models; and teach parents and significant others skills that promote healthy self-concepts by providing children with a multiethnic label, teaching them about their multiethnic backgrounds, and emphasizing the positive aspects of each ethnic group.

Hispanic Identity Model

Robinson (2005) cites the work of Ferdman and Gallegos (2001) in her discussion of Hispanic identity development. It is worth noting that Robinson chooses to use the term *Latino* rather than *Hispanic*. Still, her synopsis of Ferdman and Gallegos's (2001) work is valid and helpful to counselors intervening with Hispanic clients. According to Robinson (2005) and Ferdman and Gallegos (2001), there are key dimensions involved in defining a nonlinear Hispanic orientation. The first dimension is the *lens* (italics Robinson's) toward identity, how a person chooses to identify herself or himself, how Latinos as a group are seen, how Whites are seen, and how race fits into the equation. The various orientations include:

Hispanic (or Latino) Integrated.   Persons who have reached this orientation are able to embrace the fullness of the Latino identity and integrate this into other identities, such as class, profession, and gender. These persons feel comfortable with all types of Latinos because they use a broad lens to see themselves, White people, and others.

Hispanic Identified.   This group has more of a pan-Hispanic identity, with a view of race as uniquely Hispanic or Latin. A deep and abiding understanding exists of the political struggle and a desire to be united with other Hispanics in racial unity. Despite the awareness of and vigilant stand against institutional racism, Hispanic-identified persons may see Whites, Blacks, and others in a rigid way.

Subgroup Identified.   Persons of this group see themselves as distinct from White people, but do not necessarily identify with other Hispanics or with people of color. These people do not reflect broad pan-Hispanics orientations. Other Latino subgroups may be viewed in an inferior way. People's allegiance to a particular subgroup is nearly exclusive. Race is not a central or clear organizing concept, but nationality, ethnicity, and culture are primary.

Hispanic as "Other."   Persons with this orientation see themselves as people of color. This may be a function of biracial or multiracial status, ambiguous phenotype, or dominant construction of race. In certain contexts, the person sees herself or himself as a minority person and not as White. There is no identification with Latino cultural norms or with White culture, and an understanding of Latino history and culture is missing.

Undifferentiated.   Persons with this orientation regard themselves as simply "people" (quote Robinson's) with a color-blind eye. The emphasis on racial classification is not a part of their framework. The desire to associate with other Latinos is not prominent because contact with others is distinct from a person's race or ethnic identity.

White Identified.   White-identified persons perceive themselves as White and thus superior to people of color. Assimilation into White culture is a possibility as is connection to other subgroups. There is an acceptance of the status quo and a valuing of Whiteness to the extent that marrying White is preferred over marrying dark.

Although not a linear model, the strength of this model is that it helps counselors and clients ascertain identity development for Hispanics who differ greatly across acculturation level, skin color, national origin, and political ideology (Robinson, 2005).

Feminist Identity Model

Downing and Roush (1985) offer a model based on an earlier theory (Cross, 1971) of Black identity development: feminist identity development. They base their theory on the premise that women who live in contemporary society must first acknowledge, then struggle with, and repeatedly work through their feelings about the prejudice and discrimination they experience to achieve an authentic and positive feminist identity. The authors assert that feminist and nonsexist counseling and psychotherapies are needed to reflect a developmental model of feminist identity.

The Downing and Roush (1985) model of feminist identity development has five stages:

Stage 1: *Passive Acceptance:* The woman is unaware of or denies the individual, institutional, and cultural prejudice and discrimination against her. She considers traditional sex roles to be advantageous; that is, when asked to use such terms as woman or man, she prefers to use girl or boy because she thinks the terms have some type of advantage. Likewise, she accepts the White male social system and the perspective of the dominant, majority culture.

Stage 2: *Revelation:* This stage evolves from a series of crises that result in open questioning of self and roles and feelings of anger and guilt. Although events leading to such revelations vary with individuals, typical events include attending consciousness-raising groups, realizing discrimination against female children, ending a relationship, getting a divorce, being denied credit or employment, or becoming involved in a women's empowerment movement.

Traditional female socialization includes a distrust of one's perceptions, a mechanism that helps perpetuate women's subordinate status. An increased sense of trust in one's perceptions is necessary in order to begin the process of questioning oneself and one's role and to eventually make the transition to the revelation stage. During revelation, women primarily experience feelings of anger and secondary feelings of guilt because they believe that they have participated in their own past oppression. They see men as negative and women as positive. They perceive other women in this stage as having mature, positive identities, when in reality they have developed "pseudo-identities" (Downing & Roush, 1985, p. 700) based on negation of traditional femininity and the dominant culture.

Stage 3: *Embeddedness–Emanation*: Women attaining this stage encounter several barriers. These barriers are subtle in nature, are chronic in duration, and may be posed by significant others as well as by society. Most women are so integrally involved in the dominant culture through marriage, work, and children that it is difficult for them to embed themselves in a female subculture. Because they often are considered as only wives, mothers, lovers, sisters, and daughters of men, women in this stage commonly feel the need to end their marriages or significant relationships as they immerse themselves in female subcultures. Women's centers, women's studies classes, and women's support groups serve as havens for women experiencing embeddedness.

During the latter part of this stage, women experience emanation—the beginnings of an openness to alternative viewpoints and to a more relativistic rather than dualistic perspective. Although the need to reduce dissonance between the newly emerging identity and the repeated experience of being treated as subordinate may cause some women to revert to earlier stages, others tolerate these discrepancies and emerge from this uncomfortable state with a healthier, multidimensional, and adaptive perspective. Interaction with men during the latter part of embeddedness–emanation is usually cautious.

Stage 4: *Synthesis*: In this stage, women increasingly value the positive aspects of being female and they are able to integrate these qualities with their unique personal attributes into a positive and realistic self-concept. They are able to transcend traditional gender roles, make choices for themselves based on well-defined personal values, and evaluate men on an individual, rather than stereotypical, basis. They have reached a balance with others and are able to channel their energies productively but also to respond appropriately to experiences of oppression and discrimination.

Stage 5: *Active Commitment*: This stage involves the transition of the newly developed, consolidated identity into meaningful and effective action. Women carefully select an issue based on their unique talents and the possibility of both personal gratification and effecting social change. A consolidation of the feminist identity occurs, and actions are personalized and rational. Women consider men as equal yet not the same as women. Few women truly evolve to the active commitment stage. Most women dedicated to working for women's equal rights may actually be functioning out of needs from earlier stages, such as revelation and embeddedness–emanation.

Lesbian/Gay Identity Development Model

Several models of lesbian/gay identity development have been proposed. Proposing various numbers of stages and times of acceptance of lesbian and gay identity development, each model can help counseling psychologists better understand their own sexual orientations and identities as well as identity development in gay and lesbian clients. It is not feasible to explore in detail all the models of gay and lesbian identity development in Chapter 1; however, several models are examined in Chapter 15.

Multicultural Identity Model

People who are exposed to diversity and challenges for multicultural adaptation continuously modify their opinions of both self and others, as well as their philosophy of life. These modifications and a commitment to growth by examining self and others lead people to develop multicultural identities wherein they no longer see themselves as products of one culture or group. Instead, they express a strong, lifelong commitment to the well-being of all peoples, cultures, and groups (Ramirez, 1994).

It is hoped that counselors intervening in multicultural settings will work to develop multicultural identities. Through examining their identities and developing an understanding of their own identities, counselors can emerge from their ethnocentrism or cultural encapsulation and recognize how their identity perspectives influence the effectiveness of the counseling process. Counselors, regardless of their cultural heritage, need to work toward this goal because they can provide effective professional intervention with others only when they understand their own identities.

Multiple Dimensions of Identity

Jones and McEwen (2000) recognize previous efforts to explain identity models such as racial identities, ethnic identities, sexual identities, and gender identities, yet they maintain that many models address only a single dimension of identity (e.g., race, sexual orientation) rather than considering intersecting social identities.

Jones and McEwen (2000) propose a broader conceptual model of multiple dimensions of identity, one that considers significant identity dimensions and contextual influences on identity development. Their conceptual model (see Figure 2.1) is intended to capture the essence of the core dimension (e.g., personal attributes, personal characteristics, personal identity), as well as other dimensions of identity development, for a diverse group of women college students.

Rather than being a fixed or stable model, the model of multiple dimensions of identity represents the ongoing construction of identity and the changing contexts on the experience of the identity. In essence, the model illustrates one person's identity construction at a particular time. The model also depicts the possibility of living comfortably with multiple dimensions, rather than simply describing multiple dimensions of identity. As Figure 2.1 shows, the core categories include sexual orientation, race, culture, gender, religion, and social class. These six influences and overall identity development are affected by family background, sociocultural conditions, current experiences, career decisions, and life planning. The intersecting circles of identity and the related contextual influences represent development of the multiple dimensions of identity. The circles intersect with one another to demonstrate that one dimension cannot be understood in isolation; it can be understood only in relation to other dimensions.

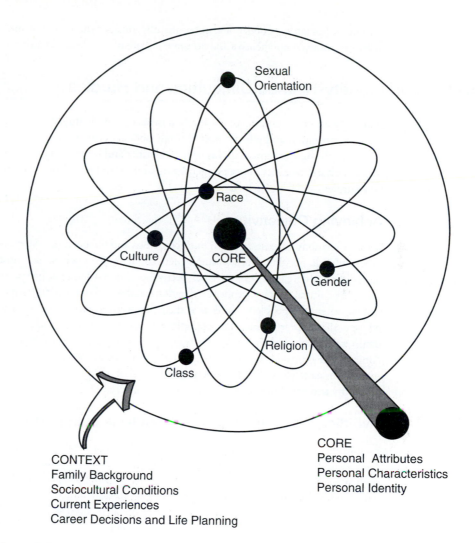

Figure 2.1
Model of Multiple Dimensions of Identity
Source: "A conceptual model of multiple dimensions of identity," by S. R. Jones and
M. K. McEwen, 2000, *Journal of College Student Development, 41* (4), p. 409. Reprinted
by permission.

The work of Jones and McEwen (2000) is relevant because many factors affect identity development. A Jewish lesbian who is disabled will have multiple dimensions to her identity. Proposing that she has only a gender, religious, or sexual orientation identity misses the multi-faceted aspects of her life. The relevance of Jones and McEwen's work does not negate the importance of other models. The most effective counselors probably consider both singular models and the multiple dimension model. If a counselor knows that a client is gay, then the counselor can consider a lesbian/gay model, and subsequently consider the model of multiple dimensions to develop a more comprehensive and accurate picture of the client's identity development.

Addressing Identity-Related Difficulties and Hurdles

Achieving an understanding of the many dimensions of identity and how identity affects counseling intervention and effectiveness will not be an overnight task; it might take years for the counselor to come to terms with his or her identities and how they have been shaped by such factors as culture, race, development, gender, disability, and sexual orientation. Several difficulties and hurdles can be highlighted.

Achieving Objectivity

A direct relationship exists between one's conscious and unconscious biases and the ability to help others who do not share one's culturally derived views. Counselors, like most people, sometimes have difficulty developing objective perspectives of others. Opinions, perspectives, and worldviews forged by cultural heritage, gender expectations, and sexual orientation (to name a few influencing factors) often lead people to think that their perspectives, views, and ways of thinking are right, whereas all others are wrong. For example, a European American male counselor must not condemn a American Indian woman for wanting to share material wealth nor condemn an African American or Hispanic American for placing family welfare over individual desires. Such objectivity requires counselors of both genders and all cultural backgrounds to perceive clients' differences as worthy and enriching rather than as wrong or in need of change or remediation.

Avoiding Western Identity Perspectives of Individualism

As previously mentioned, counselors should avoid using perspectives based on Western perspectives of individualism during intervention. European American counselors, perhaps men more so than women, might have a tendency to intervene by using perspectives that suggest individualism. Counseling from Western perspectives can create conflict between counselor and client worldviews; that is, the counselor's perspectives on such issues as individualism, family welfare, and concern for others do not coincide with the clients'.

A Point of Departure

Challenges Confronting Counselors in Multicultural Settings

Several challenges confront counselors intervening in multicultural settings. Addressing these challenges can result in successful outcomes and holds the potential for improving the counseling relationship. Counseling can take several directions, all with potential for developing respect for the identities of both counselor and clients. Counselors should:

- develop an understanding and respect for clients' different worldviews, the effects of those differences, and the implications for counseling intervention;
- consider and accept perspectives that vary from their own identity perspectives;

- accept and respect their cultural identity, values, and perspectives, yet be open to those of others; and

- listen carefully, ask sensitive questions, and read and study about clients' cultural, racial, and ethnic backgrounds as well as sexual orientation.

Summary

Counselors need to understand their own identities and the factors that contribute to their development. Counselor identity shapes how counselors perceive themselves and how they perceive others and their cultural backgrounds. Counselors in multicultural settings may face different situations, customs, and worldviews that could affect counseling effectiveness. Clients in multicultural situations may have attitudes and beliefs that threaten or disturb the counselor of another cultural background. It is important for counselors to understand their identities and how these are affected by culture, gender, parental expectations and teachings, and sexual preference. Undoubtedly, counselor identity affects counseling intervention and therefore should be understood in relation to both self and others.

Appendix B provides counselors with "Suggested Multicultural Experiential Exercises" as they learn more about counselor identity.

Suggested Readings

Abram, L., & Trusty, J. (2004). African Americans' racial identity and socially desirable responding: An empirical model. *Journal of Counseling and Development, 82*(3), 365–374. Abrams and Trusty developed a model of the relationships between racial identity development and socially desirable responding.

Carter, T. T., Helms, J. E., & Juby, H. L. (2004). The relationship between racism and racial identity for White Americans: A profile analysis. *Journal of Multicultural Counseling and Development, 32*(1), 2–17. These authors investigate how racial identity profiles are related to racist attitudes and provide implications for counseling practice.

Denevi, E. (2004). White on White: Exploring White racial identity, privilege, and racism. *Independent School, 63*(4), 84–87. Denevi maintains that professionals committed to the development of a multicultural community need to confront the question of White racial identity and privilege.

Hoffman, R. M. (2004). Conceptualizing heterosexual identity development: Issues and challenges. *Journal of Counseling and Development, 82*(3), 375–380. Hoffman provides an overview of two independently developed models of heterosexual identity development and discusses implications for counseling practice.

Moradi, B. (2005). Advancing womanist identity development: Where we are and where we must go. *The Counseling Psychologist, 33*(2), 225–253. Moradi focuses on a womanist identity development model as a model of gender-related identity development that has been argued to be applicable to women across racial/ethnic, class, and other groups.

Munley, P. H., Lidderdale, M. A,. Thiagarajan, M., & Null, U. (2004). Identity development and multicultural competency. *Journal of Multicultural Counseling and Development, 32*, 283–295. These authors investigate the relationship of identity development and multicultural counseling competencies.

3

The Culturally Effective Counselor

Questions to Be Explored

1. How does cultural diversity affect counseling intervention? Why should counselors seek special preparation for counseling clients of differing cultures?

2. What barriers, myths, assumptions, and stereotypes interfere with effective multicultural counseling?

3. What characteristics describe effective counselors?

4. What specific beliefs/attitudes, understandings, skills, and ethical concerns should be addressed during professional preparation for multicultural counseling?

5. What is a worldview, and how can a counselor assess a client's worldview?

6. What ethical standards pertain to multicultural counseling?

7. What is a social constructivism model for ethical decision-making?

8. How do competent counselors provide a positive and supportive counseling environment for homosexual and bisexual clients?

Overview

American society undoubtedly benefits from the richness of cultural diversity. Counselors who are trained in traditional counseling approaches, however, often experience difficulty when working with clients of differing cultural backgrounds. Formal preparation and firsthand experiences with people of differing cultural backgrounds are essential for multicultural counseling to be effective. In this chapter, we look at why counselors need multicultural counseling competence, with emphasis on the beliefs/attitudes, knowledge, and skills needed for effective intervention.

Cultural Diversity and the Counseling Profession

As the population of the United States grows more pluralistic and all forms of diversity are increasingly recognized, counselors will be called on to provide professional intervention with clients of differing cultural backgrounds. White counselors will be challenged to provide culturally appropriate counseling intervention. Such contact can initially lead to questioning, confusion, guilt, and anxiety about racial topics. Regardless of their racial and cultural background, counselors will be expected to intervene with clients of differing cultural backgrounds.

Mental health professionals need multicultural counseling training programs because mental health services should differ, depending on the culture and lifespan period of the individual client. Counseling competence across cultural boundaries requires special training as a part of mental health training.

The already complex nature of the counseling process is further complicated when client and counselor come from different cultures. Problems and issues may arise during counseling sessions when, for example, the counselor is a middle-class European American and the client is lower-class African American and vice versa. Generational, intracultural, lifespan, and other individual differences complicate the counseling process to an even greater degree.

Counselors who are most different from their clients, especially with respect to race and social class, have the greatest difficulty effecting constructive changes; those who are most similar to their clients in these respects have a greater facility for helping appropriately (Pedersen, 1988).

Increased attention is also being given to multiculturalism and marriage and family counseling or, more specifically, to how cultural and other forms of diversity affect families and marriage and family counseling. The traditional family unit (a married man and woman parenting two children) of the 1950s and 1960s is no longer the norm. Counselors cannot assume that the practices that are effective with traditional family structures are effective with diverse family systems. Counselors will increasingly work with diverse family systems such as single-parent families, stepfamilies, families of mixed cultural heritages, and gay families. Effective marriage and family counselors consider the various family arrangements, the need for different approaches and ways of thinking about families, how cultural differences need to be reflected in counseling.

Minority Counseling Professionals

Although middle-class European American counselors are the most numerous providers of mental health services, many clients receiving such services are from other cultural backgrounds. If only majority-culture counselors are available, problems may arise because of differing value orientations, differing expectations and attitudes toward immediate and extended families, ineffective verbal and nonverbal communication, and the counselors' lack of understanding of the racism and discrimination that clients of diverse cultural backgrounds so often encounter.

The question may be raised as to whether problems resulting from differing cultural backgrounds can be reduced by carefully matching clients with counselors of similar cultural and socioeconomic backgrounds. Realistically, however, the relatively small number of minority counselors reduces the possibility of counselor–client match-ups. As a result, counseling often fails to meet the needs of minority clients and, in some cases, is even counterproductive to their well-being (Atkinson, Morten, & Sue, 1998).

There may be several reasons for the relatively small number of minorities entering the counseling profession. First, minority students considering the profession may be dissuaded by the small number of minorities already in the profession. Where would these students find mentors? Who could guide them appropriately or offer needed support? Second, institutional racism may discourage students wanting to become counselors.

It is essential that counselor education programs employ faculty members of diverse backgrounds because they can serve as role models for minority students. Similarly, having diverse faculty members in tenure-track positions serves as a highly visible statement that cultural diversity is respected and valued in the counseling program.

Barriers to Effective Multicultural Counseling

Barriers have impeded counselors' efforts with clients in multicultural settings. Counselors intervening in multicultural settings should recognize and then formulate a plan for addressing the barriers.

Differing Class and Cultural Values.   Counselors' class values, which are partly determined by their own socioeconomic class, influence the effectiveness of multicultural counseling. Pedersen, Fukuyama, and Heath (1996) presented evidence that indicates that professional mental health services are class bound and that a dangerous situation develops when the counselor (especially the counselor with a middle- or upper-class background) attributes mental health "disorders" to a client's culture or social structure. The importance of being aware of class- and culture-bound values should be recognized, especially when counselors consider the consequences that could result from misunderstanding those values.

Cultural differences that affect counseling relationships include the varying amounts of time needed to establish deep personal relationships, some clients' tendencies not to disclose personal information to an unfamiliar person, and differing definitions of psychological well-being. In fact, some cultures (e.g., American Indians) may consider traditional counseling to be in violation of their basic philosophy of life.

Differing Languages Between Counselor and Client.   Language, dialect, or overall communication differences between counselor and client may present formidable barriers to effective counseling relationships. The monolingual nature of Western society may unfairly discriminate against clients from bilingual and lower-class backgrounds. Regardless of the client's native communication and cultural background, building rapport during counseling sessions depends significantly on communication between counselor and client. For example, a middle- or upper-class African American professional may experience difficulty and frustration in trying to understand the street talk of a lower-class African American client. A Spanish-speaking person of Puerto Rican descent may not understand the dialect of a Mexican American migrant worker from California. These examples illustrate the importance of counselors exercising caution in communication to avoid assumptions that may affect diagnosis and counseling intervention.

A FOCUS ON RESEARCH 3.1

Supervision in Bilingual Counseling

Fuertas reviews selected literature on the topics of bilingual and multicultural counseling and supervision and provides a framework for understanding issues in the delivery of bilingual services. With respect to linguistically diverse clients, the guidelines are clear that the client be offered services in the language that she or he prefers and, if this is not possible, that the counselor refer the client to a professional who speaks the client's language. The guidelines also instruct counselors, as an option, to offer services to the client with the use of a properly trained translator who shares the client's cultural background.

Supervisors have definite roles as they work with their supervisees: (1) Supervisors should educate their supervisees about the APA guidelines and model them as part of the supervision process; (2) supervisors should assess any disparities in language ability or cultural knowledge between themselves and their supevisees; (3) supervisors may communicate his or her comfort with either language and allow, or even encourage variations in English use in supervision; and (4) supervisors should monitor when and why language mixing and switching occur.

In addition to language, Fuertas also looks at acculturation; theory, technique, and skill; clients' sociopolitical realities; and future research directions. Readers who are interested in language issues are referred to this excellent article.

Source: "Supervision in bilingual counseling: Service delivery, training, and research considerations," by J. N. Fuertas, 2004, *Journal of Multicultural Counseling and Development, 32* (2), pp. 84–94.

Fuertas (2004) A Focus on Research 3.1 looks at supervision in bilingual counseling.

Stereotyping Clients.   Counseling professionals, regardless of whether they are from a minority or majority culture, need to consider their stereotypical beliefs toward clients of differing cultures. It is often easier to rely on stereotypical beliefs about others than to learn about cultures and to get to know people on a firsthand basis. Stereotyping can result both from a counselor's personal prejudices and biases as well as from a lack of factual information about cultures and individuals.

Stereotyping crosses cultural lines and deserves the attention of counseling professionals of all cultural backgrounds. Just as European American counselors might hold stereotypical perceptions about African American, Asian American, Hispanic American, and American Indian clients, counselors from these cultural groups might also hold stereotypical perceptions about European American clients. Significant problems can accrue from counselors using stereotypical generalizations to describe their clients: It is ethically wrong, counseling is based in erroneous information, and the counselor is guilty either of not having sufficient knowledge of cultural backgrounds or of failing to take the initiative to learn factual and accurate information.

Counselor Encapsulation.   Counselor encapsulation can be described as substituting stereotypes for the real world, disregarding cultural variations among clients, and dogmatizing a technique-oriented definition of the counseling process (Pedersen et al., 1996). The culturally encapsulated counselor may evade reality through ethnocentrism. The individual is "cocooned" by internalized value assumptions he or she believes are best for society. Counselors need to become culturally sensitive individuals with new knowledge and skills and to reorganize old knowledge that no longer applies to current situations. Casas and Vasquez (1989) summarize in this way:

> At this time, given the availability of research, the question is no longer whether counselors are personally and professionally encapsulated and biased but to what degree and in what ways. Each and every human … is encapsulated by the values and beliefs of the society and ethnicity that nurtured that individual. (p. 162)

Counselors Understanding Their Own Cultures.   Counselors need to understand their own cultures in order to successfully understand the cultures of others. Ivey, Ivey, & Simek-Morgan (1997) devised an exercise in cultural awareness for professionals preparing for counseling in multicultural situations. Ivey and colleagues (p. 43) suggested that counselors answer the following questions to start them thinking about how their cultural heritage may affect their counseling:

1.   *Ethnic heritage.* With what ethnic background do you primarily identify? First identify your nationality—U.S. citizen, Canadian, Mexican, etc. Beyond this first answer, you may find that the words White, Black, Indian, Polish, Mormon, Jewish, or others come to mind. Record these words.

   Where did your grandparents come from? Great-grandparents? Can you trace a family history, perhaps with different ethnic, religious, and racial backgrounds? Trace your heritage in list form or in a family tree. Do not forget your heritage from the country within which you live.

2.   *Are you monocultural, bicultural, or more?* Review the list you developed and pick out the central cultural, ethnic, religious, or other types of groups that have been involved in your development.

3.   *What messages do you receive from each cultural group you have listed?* List the values, behaviors, and expectations that people in your group have emphasized over time. How have you personally internalized these messages? If you are aware of the message, you have probably made some deviation from the family, ethnic, or religious value. If you are unaware, you may have so internalized the values that you are a "culture-bearer" without knowing it. Becoming aware of obvious but unconscious culture-bearer messages may become the most difficult task of all.

4.   *How might your cultural messages affect your counseling and therapeutic work?* This final question is the most important. If you believe in the supremacy of individuality, given your family history, then you may tend to miss the relational family orientation of many Asian Americans and African Americans. If you come from a relational orientation, you may have difficulty understanding individualistic WASPs (White Anglo-Saxon Protestants) and label them as "cold" and "calculating." Because we all have cultural histories, it is easy to believe that our way of being in the world is "the way things are and should be."*

Client Reluctance and Resistance.   Evidence (Atkinson et al., 1998) supports the belief that people in some cultural groups prefer to discuss personal, emotional, and other problems with parents, friends, and relatives, rather than with professional counselors. The lack of minority counselors in many counseling agencies may contribute to the underuse of professional services by minorities. American Indians may believe that counseling services are not responsive

---

*From *Counseling and Psychotherapy: Integrating Skills, Theory and Practice* (4th ed.), (p. 43), by A. E. Ivey, M. B. Ivey, and L. Simek-Downing, 1993, Upper Saddle River, NJ: Prentice Hall, Inc. Adapted with permission of Prentice Hall, Inc.

to their cultural and individual needs. Other clients, such as Chinese Americans (and many other Asian American people), traditionally seek family assistance with personal problems, rather than disclose problems to outsiders. In the Asian American culture, it is a social taboo to ask detailed questions about physical and mental illnesses. By recognizing these cultural beliefs, the culturally effective counselor will want to avoid explicit questions that clients might consider an invasion of their privacy.

Differing Worldviews and Lack of Cultural Relativity.   An understanding of counselor and client worldviews is key in multicultural counseling situations. *Worldview* can be defined as a person's value-laden beliefs and assumptions about life aspects, such as relationships with others and with the broader world, as well as perspectives of past and present events and outlook about the future. Although definitions of worldview vary, effective counselors in multicultural settings understand their and clients' worldviews, how these worldviews affect the outcomes of counseling intervention, and how to provide culturally sensitive intervention that reflects clients' worldviews.

Why should counselors consider worldviews, especially in multicultural settings? One's worldview is a culturally based variable that influences the essence of the counseling relationship. Additionally, the counselor's and the client's lack of cultural relativity can result in disparate perceptions of problems. An effective counselor in a multicultural situation must perceive the client's problems from a cultural perspective. What a client perceives as a problem may not be so perceived by the counselor and vice versa; it is the counselor's responsibility to attempt to perceive situations from the client's worldview.

Labeling Women, Multicultural Populations, and the Poor.   Cultural groups, as well as women and the poor, often have been labeled as mentally ill when they have varied from so-called normal patterns of behaving. Likewise, counselors sometimes label women's physiological illnesses as psychogenic and label mental health disorders in African American clients as psychoses.

Expecting All Clients to Conform to Counselors' Standards and Expectations.
Another common barrier in multicultural counseling is presented when counselors expect (perhaps unconsciously) clients to conform to the counselors' cultural standards and expectations. For example, expecting African American women to emulate European American standards of beauty (or vice versa) has a demoralizing effect. Putting pressure on adolescent African American mothers to undergo sterilization denies them an important source of self-worth and fails to consider the extended kinship network that figures so prominently in child-rearing and mothering among African American women.

Clients of various cultural backgrounds may also be treated differently from European clients. Certain approaches may reflect paternalistic behavior or the counselor's belief that he or she is doing what is best for the client. In some cases, the counselor may even distort information if she or he thinks such a practice benefits the client.

Another equally serious issue that may threaten the counselor–client relationship involves the cultural dictates surrounding gender roles. Traditional and stereotypical gender roles prohibit strong disagreement between authority figures and clients. Thus, communication and individual decision-making by women may be discouraged.

Counselors who strive to be culturally effective will respond to a variety of issues: the different ways cultural backgrounds influence counseling relationships; the need to evaluate their own cultural biases; the ways problems and solutions vary among cultures; and the question whether counseling itself is culturally encapsulated (Pedersen, 1988). Will counselors understand, for example, the strong sense of family and community shared by many African Americans? Will they understand American Indians' love of nature or commitment to sharing, or the loyalty of Hispanic American men to machismo? Such understanding, together with knowledge of development factors during each stage of the lifespan, significantly determines the effectiveness of counseling efforts. Likewise, African American, Asian American, Hispanic American, and American Indian counselors need to understand the European American perspectives of individualism, family, and other cultural characteristics.

Worldviews: Assessment Approaches

As previously mentioned, differing worldviews of counselor and client are potential barriers to effective multicultural counseling. Here, we discuss how counselors can assess worldviews.

The first step in any counseling or psychotherapy encounter is to understand the client and the issues, problems, symptoms, and pain that led the client to seek help and relief. Assessment of a client's worldview, beliefs, values, and perspectives may be accomplished by two specific approaches. Sue (1978b) proposed an approach based on internal/external locus of responsibility; Ibrahim and Kahn (1984, 1987) proposed the Scale to Assess World Views (SAWV).

Sue (1978b) defined worldview as the way an individual perceives his or her relationship to the world. Worldview is based on the client's locus of responsibility or the perceived control over life events. Sue based one part of his theory on Rotter's (1975) distinction between internal control (IC), in which reinforcement is contingent on a person's own actions, and external control (EC), in which consequences are perceived to result from luck, chance, or fate. Next, Sue added the dimension of internal locus of responsibility (IR), in which success is attributed to a person's skills, resulting in a "person blame," and an external locus of responsibility (ER), in which the sociocultural environment is more powerful than the individual, resulting in "system blame." For example, an IC-IR worldview exemplifies European middle-class cultural perceptions, whereas an EC-IR view reflects the worldview of minorities who believe that they have little control over the way others define them. The EC–ER view is often prevalent among minorities who blame their problems on an oppressive social system, and the IC–ER view assumes the ability of an individual to achieve personal goals if given a chance (Pedersen, Fukuyama, & Heath, 1996).

Another means of assessing worldview is the Scale to Assess World Views (SAWV). Ibrahim and Kahn (1984, 1987) designed this paper-and-pencil instrument which can be used as a structured interview informally administered to the client through discussion of the client's values, beliefs, and perspectives on five dimensions: (1) human nature, (2) social relationships, (3) nature, (4) time, and (5) human activity. Within these dimensions, it is important to differentiate and understand the client's worldview, the worldview held by the client's family, and the worldview of the client's primary and secondary groups (Lonner & Ibrahim, 1996).

Counselors can use the SAWV to better understand clients' values and assumptions and how they relate to their cognitive, emotional, and social perceptions and interactions with the world. The SAWV also clarifies the issues and problems the client brings to counseling. Thus, counselors can formulate approaches and techniques to be used in identifying goals that would be meaningful to a particular cultural group (Lonner & Ibrahim, 1996).

Culturally Effective Counselors

This section examines characteristics of culturally effective counselors, such as being aware of self, developing multicultural counseling competencies (in terms of attitudes and beliefs, understandings, and skills), and recognizing and addressing their values and biases, as well as understanding clients' worldviews, learning culturally appropriate intervention strategies, and understanding and adhering to ethics associated with multicultural counseling.

Awareness of Self

Ideally, counselors should develop an awareness of their own cultural heritage and how it has shaped their cultural beliefs, attitudes, and values, especially those involving other people. To provide effective counseling intervention, the counselor working with clients of a particular racial or ethnic minority has to acquire specific knowledge about the particular groups.

Developing self-awareness also includes developing an awareness of how one's own cultural background and experiences influence one's attitudes, values, and biases about psychological processes. For example, counselors should be able to do the following:

- Identify the history of their culture in relation to educational opportunities and current worldview.
- Identify relevant personal cultural traits and explain their influences on cultural values.
- Identify social and cultural influences on cognitive development.
- Identify social and cultural influences in their history that have influenced their views (which would affect counseling).
- Articulate the beliefs of their own cultural and religious groups as these relate to sexual orientation, able-bodiedness, etc., and the impact of these beliefs on the counseling relationship.

Counselors should also be able to do the following:

- Identify the culture(s) to which they belong.
- Identify specific cultural groups from which they derived fundamental cultural heritage and significant beliefs and attitudes.
- Recognize the impact of their beliefs on their ability to respect others.
- Identify specific attitudes, beliefs, and values from their own cultural heritage that support behaviors demonstrating respect and valuing.
- Engage in an ongoing process of challenging their own beliefs and attitudes that do not support respecting and valuing of differences.

- Appreciate and articulate positive aspects of their own heritage that provide them with strengths in understanding differences.
- Recognize the influence of other personal dimensions of identity and their role in self-awareness (Arredondo et al., 1996).

Multicultural Counseling Competencies

Whereas all counselors need an array of professional competencies, those who provide multi-cultural counseling need specific competencies related to culture and its effects on counseling. Culturally competent counselors need an understanding of their own cultural characteristics and of how their cultural values and biases may affect clients, an ability to resolve differences of race and beliefs between counselor and client, and an ability to know when a client should be referred to a counselor of the client's own race or culture. They also need a wide range of verbal and non-verbal response skills, a knowledge of the client's developmental stage, and the skill to send and receive accurate and appropriate verbal and nonverbal messages.

Arredondo and coworkers (1996) published an extensive article focusing on multicultural counseling competencies. One key reference tool in the process of developing these competencies was the dimensions of personal identity model. Premises of this model are as follows:

- We are all multicultural individuals.
- We all possess a personal, political, and historical culture.
- We are all affected by sociocultural, political, environmental, and historical events.
- Multiculturalism also intersects with multiple factors of individual diversity.

Dimensions of the personal identity model are as follows:

- *A Dimensions:* Age, culture, ethnicity, gender, language, physical disability, race, sexual orientation, social class.
- *B Dimensions:* Educational background, geographic location, income, marital status, religion, work experience, citizenship status, military experience, hobbies/recreational interests.
- *C Dimensions:* Historical moments/eras.

Arredondo and colleagues' (1996) list of multicultural counseling competencies is based on the dimensions of the personal identity model (Arredondo & Glauner, 1992):

I. Counselor Awareness of Own Cultural Values and Biases
   A. Attitudes and Beliefs
      1. Culturally skilled counselors believe that cultural self-awareness and sensitivity to one's own cultural heritage is essential.
      2. Culturally skilled counselors are aware of how their own cultural background and experiences have influenced attitudes, values, and biases about psychological processes.

3.   Culturally skilled counselors are able to recognize the limits of their multicultural competency and expertise.

4.   Culturally skilled counselors recognize their sources of discomfort with differences that exist between themselves and clients in terms of race, ethnicity, and culture.

B.   Knowledge

1.   Culturally skilled counselors have specific knowledge about their own racial and cultural heritage and how it personally and professionally affects their definitions of and biases about normality/abnormality and the process of counseling.

2.   Culturally skilled counselors possess knowledge and understanding about how oppression, racism, discrimination, and stereotyping affect them personally and in their work. This allows individuals to acknowledge their own racist attitudes, beliefs, and feelings. Although this standard applies to all groups, for White counselors it may mean that they understand how they may have directly or indirectly benefited from individual, institutional, and cultural racism as outlined in White identity development models.

3.   Culturally skilled counselors possess knowledge about their social impact on others. They are knowledgeable about communication style differences, how their style may clash with or foster the counseling process with persons of color or others different from themselves based on the A, B, and C Dimensions, and how to anticipate the impact it may have on others.

C.   Skills

1.   Culturally skilled counselors seek out educational, consultative, and training experiences to improve their understandings and effectiveness in working with culturally different populations. Being able to recognize the limits of their competencies, they (a) seek consultation, (b) seek further training or education, (c) refer to more qualified individuals or resources, or (d) engage in a combination of these.

2.   Culturally skilled counselors are constantly seeking to understand themselves as racial and cultural beings and are actively seeking a nonracist identity.

II.   Counselor Awareness of Clients' Worldview

A.   Attitudes and Beliefs

1.   Culturally skilled counselors are aware of their negative and positive emotional reactions toward other racial and ethnic groups that may prove detrimental to the counseling relationship. They are willing to contrast their own beliefs and attitudes with those of their culturally different clients in a nonjudgmental fashion.

2.   Culturally skilled counselors are aware of their stereotypes and preconceived notions that they may hold toward other racial and ethnic minority groups.

B.   Knowledge

1.   Culturally skilled counselors possess specific knowledge and information about the particular group with which they are aware of the life experiences, cultural heritage, and historical background of their culturally different clients. This

particular competency is strongly linked to the minority identity development models available in the literature.

2. Culturally skilled counselors understand how race, culture, ethnicity, and so forth may affect personality formation, vocational choices, manifestation of psychological disorders, help-seeking behavior, and the appropriateness or inappropriateness of counseling approaches.

3. Culturally skilled counselors understand and have knowledge about sociopolitical influences that impinge on the life of racial and ethnic minorities. Immigration issues, poverty, racism, stereotyping, and powerlessness may affect self-esteem and self-concept in the counseling process.

C. Skills

1. Culturally skilled counselors should familiarize themselves with relevant research and the latest findings regarding mental health and mental disorders that affect various ethnic and racial groups. They should actively seek out educational experiences that enrich their knowledge, understanding, and cross-cultural counseling behavior.

2. Culturally skilled counselors become actively involved with minority individuals outside the counseling setting (e.g., community events, social and political functions, celebrations, friendships, neighborhood groups) so that their perspective of minorities is more than an academic or helping exercise.

III. Culturally Appropriate Intervention Strategies

A. Beliefs and Attitudes

1. Culturally skilled counselors respect clients' religious and spiritual beliefs and values, including attributions and taboos, because these affect worldview, psychosocial healing, and expressions of distress.

2. Culturally skilled counselors respect indigenous helping practices and respect help-giving networks among communities of color.

3. Culturally skilled counselors value bilingualism and do not view another language as an impediment to counseling ("monolingualism" may be the culprit).

B. Knowledge

1. Culturally skilled counselors have a clear and explicit knowledge and understanding of the generic characteristics of counseling and therapy (culture bound, class bound, and monolingual) and how they may clash with the cultural values of various cultural groups.

2. Culturally skilled counselors are aware of institutional barriers that prevent minorities from using mental health services.

3. Culturally skilled counselors have knowledge of the potential bias in assessment instruments and use procedures and interpret findings in a way that recognizes the cultural and linguistic characteristics of the clients.

4. Culturally skilled counselors have knowledge of family structures, hierarchies, values, and beliefs from various cultural perspectives. They are knowledgeable

about the community where a particular cultural group may reside and the resources in the community.

5. Culturally skilled counselors should be aware of relevant discriminatory practices at the social and the community level that may be affecting the psychological welfare of the population being served.

C. Skills

1. Culturally skilled counselors are able to engage in a variety of verbal and nonverbal helping responses. They are able to send and receive both verbal and nonverbal messages accurately and appropriately. They are not tied down to only one method or approach to helping, but recognize that helping styles and approaches may be culture bound. When they sense that their helping style is limited and potentially inappropriate, they can anticipate and modify it.

2. Culturally skilled counselors are able to exercise institutional intervention on behalf of their clients. They can help clients determine whether a "problem" stems from racism or bias in others (the concept of healthy paranoia) so that clients do not inappropriately personalize problems.

3. Culturally skilled counselors are not averse to seeking consultation with traditional healers or religious and spiritual leaders and practitioners in the treatment of culturally different clients when appropriate.

4. Culturally skilled counselors take responsibility for interacting in the language requested by the client and, if not feasible, make appropriate referrals. A serious problem arises when the linguistic skills of the counselor do not match the language of the client. This being the case, counselors should (a) seek a translator with cultural knowledge and appropriate professional background or (b) refer to a knowledgeable and competent bilingual counselor.

5. Culturally skilled counselors have training and expertise in the use of traditional assessment and testing instruments. They not only understand the technical aspects of the instruments but are also aware of the cultural limitations. This allows them to use test instruments for the welfare of culturally different clients.

6. Culturally skilled counselors should attend to, as well as work to eliminate, biases, prejudices, and discriminatory contexts in conducting evaluations and providing interventions, and should develop sensitivity to issues of oppression, sexism, heterosexism, elitism, and racism.

7. Culturally skilled counselors take responsibility for educating their clients to the processes of psychological intervention, such as their goals, expectations, legal rights, and the counselor's orientation.

Providing a Supportive Environment for Lesbian, Gay, and Bisexual Clients.

Effective and competent counselors in multicultural settings provide supportive environments for lesbian, gay, and bisexual (LGB) clients and also provide appropriate professional intervention (see Chapter 16). This section looks at some variables that contribute to counselors providing supportive environments for LGB clients. As with all aspects of this text, readers should remember LGB clients pass through all four lifespan stages; therefore, it is important to clarify misconceptions (for example, children and the elderly do not face LGB issues). First, we will look at some recent research, and then seek ways to provide positive and supportive environments. The study of counselor attitudes provides evidence that negative attitudes toward LGB clients continue to persist, which definitely is devastating to a humane and supportive counseling environment. According to a study by Bieschke, McClanahan, Tozer, Grzegorek, and Park (2000), some counselors consider LGB clients to be weaker, more powerless, and less active than heterosexual clients; continue to hold stereotypical beliefs about LGB clients, as well as harbor homophobic attitudes (resulting in counselors discouraging, inhibiting, avoiding discussion of, and ignoring LGB clients' and their sexuality); and consider LGB clients as pathological, disordered, and deviant.

Other obstacles limit humane and supportive counseling environments for these clients. Because LGB clients fall outside the heterosexual norm, they must create their own identities, relationships, and communities. Therapists who work with LGB clients must understand the daunting nature of these tasks. Because some therapists lack exposure to information and to LGB clients, they do not have the resources or first-hand contact to counter the prejudices faced by these clients. Competent counselors who work toward supportive environments for LGB clients seek accurate and objective information as well as first-hand contact with them. Therapists must also confront problems resulting from religious biases, societal norms, gender restrictions, and fears surrounding sexuality resulting in homophobia, heterosexism, prejudice, and discrimination against LGB clients. Counselors should also be sensitive toward subgroups of nonheterosexuals. For example, bisexuals often are not included in research studies; therefore, the knowledge base of lesbians and gays continues to increase, but at the expense of bisexuals (Bieschke et al., 2000).

Therapists who demonstrate competence with LGB clients take responsibility for professional development and for confronting biases. They want to project positive feelings toward LGB clients and, in doing so, contribute to client growth and healing. Likewise, they avoid attributing all the LGB clients' problems to sexual orientation. Similarly, competent therapists encourage the development of a positive LGB identity (Morrow, 2000). Last, therapists whose gender role orientations are particularly rigid must avoid making incorrect assessments of LGB clients who do not fit the societal gender roles. For example, a counselor should not diagnose depression in a lesbian client simply because she does not use make-up and keeps a "wash-n-go haircut" (Morrow, 2000, p. 141).

To promote a positive and supportive environment for LGB clients, the therapist should:

- avoid overemphasizing similarities and differences, regardless of therapists' sexual orientation;
- be sufficiently comfortable with his or her sexuality, so that disclosure is not fraught with ambivalence;
- provide therapy to LGB clients only when the counselor is comfortable with his or her own sexual orientation;
- avoid assuming that lesbian, gay, and bisexual couples are similar to or very different from their own sexual orientation;

- understand that being a good therapist for LGB clients requires more than just being an LGB therapist; and

- refuse to believe that simply changing a sexual orientation will solve many of one's problems (Morrow, 2000).

Other strategies that contribute to a positive and supportive counseling environment include the counselor respecting client confidentiality, being supportive and accepting, allowing clients to consider their sexual orientation, making a genuine offer of help, providing accurate and objective information, and being informed when making referrals to community and social organizations.

Bernstein (2000) uses a cultural literacy model to sensitize marital and family therapists (MFTs) to work with lesbians, gays, and their families. Although most MFTs have lesbian and gay clients, differences in sexual orientation between therapist and clients are often insufficiently addressed, thus closing off therapeutic possibilities. Bernstein thinks MFTs should assess homophobic and heterosexist assumptions in both personal attitudes and professional practice. She also thinks effective straight MFTs must be willing to examine themselves, their own privilege as heterosexuals, and their attitudes, feelings, and beliefs about lesbian, gay, bisexual, and transgendered people.

Straight MFTs need to create a working alliance that cultivates client trust and the continued self-monitoring for homophobia and heterosexualism in one's therapeutic model and one's personal assumptions and values. Aspects of this working alliance include:

- disclosure, trust, and talking about sexual orientation;

- trust and becoming trustworthy;

- establishing a rapport that fosters open communication; and

- the gay–straight therapeutic relationship.

As emphasized in Chapters 15 and 16, clients' sexual orientation should be considered a part of their culture. Therefore, culturally effective counselors will understand and respect a client's sexual orientation in addition to practicing appropriate counseling techniques.

Providing Counseling for People With Disabilities.   Chapter 1 and Chapter 17, advance the idea that people with disabilities have a culture of their own. Based on that idea, counselors should provide a supportive environment and effective professional intervention with clients with disabilities. In fact, Reeve (2000) called for an actual counseling approach called *disability counseling*. Part of her rationale is that oppression lies at the root of multicultural counseling and feminist counseling. Because people with disabilities experience similar oppression, it is time for a new approach, disability counseling, which will openly challenge disablist attitudes and prejudices in a manner similar to the way in which multicultural counseling challenges racism and other forms of oppression.

According to Ryan and Harvey (1999), for years the career development field and college career placement centers served a fairly homogeneous student population: affluent, able-bodied White males. Although one should avoid using today's standards to judge career development leaders of the past, it is important to note that women, minorities, people with disabilities, and people of lower- or middle-socioeconomic class did not seek higher education in large numbers at that time. Only with the passage of the Rehabilitation Act of 1973 and the Americans With Disabilities Act (ADA) of 1990 did colleges make serious efforts to address and resolve accessibility issues.

Considerations in counseling students with disabilities include the following:

- Encourage professionals involved in campus disability services to provide inservices for all interested people on the effects of certain disabilities on students' abilities to perform various job functions.

- Learn disability etiquette, or know what to do and what not to do (e.g., do not pet guide dogs or lean on a students' wheelchair).

- Ensure that all offices, programs, and services are accessible to students.

- Understand that all professionals' feelings about disabilities should be put in perspective—people with disabilities can be an uncomfortable reminder of how easily one can acquire a disability.

- Avoid overcompensating when talking to a student with labored speech (ask students with labored speech to repeat themselves—they will rather be asked to repeat themselves than be misunderstood).

- Embrace an ideology that emphasizes serving an increasingly diverse student body—ideology should extend beyond legal obligations.

- Incorporate disability-related issues into job search and career planning workshops for students with disabilities.

- Understand that some students with disabilities may engage in an act of self-sabotage wherein they ruin their chances of getting a job—they may present themselves in a less positive light as a means of denial, fear of the unknown, or anger.

- Provide role models with successful careers for students with disabilities (Ryan & Harvey, 1999).

Ethics in Multicultural Counseling

Ethics are rules of conduct or moral principles that guide the practices of professional counselors. Multicultural principles have been included in the American Psychological Association's (APA's) *Ethical Principles* and the American Association for Counseling and Development's (AACD's) *Ethical Standards* (W. M. L. Lee, 1996). Ethically conscientious counselors want to provide the best possible services to their clients and practice in a manner that reflects the profession's highest standards (Herlihy, 1996). The nature of the counseling process—that is, the close involvement between counselor and client—makes ethical standards a crucial aspect of the counseling process.

1995 ACA Code of Ethics

Herlihy (1996) reports on the 1995 American Counseling Association (ACA) Code of Ethics. The new organization included eight major sections in its guidelines:

1. Section A: *The Counseling Relationship* addresses important issues that arise in forming, maintaining, and ending the counseling relationship.

2. Section B: *Confidentiality* emphasizes the client's right to privacy of records and information shared during sessions.

3. Section C: *Professional Responsibility* contains standards related to maintaining competence.

4. Section D: *Relationships With Other Professionals* highlights the importance of respecting professionals in related mental health professions.

5. Section E: *Evaluation, Assessment, and Interpretation* contains standards that govern the use of tests in counseling.

6. Section F: *Teaching, Training, and Supervision* includes ethical guidelines for counselor educators and trainers, for counselor preparation programs, and for students and supervisees.

7. Section G: *Research and Publication* addresses a range of issues, including protection of human subjects, informed consent for research participants, honesty and accuracy in reporting research results, and ethical problems in seeking publication.

8. Section H: *Resolving Ethical Issues* emphasizes the responsibility of counselors to know their ethical standards and explains procedures for resolving and reporting suspected ethical violations. (Herlihy, 1996)

In their discussion of ethical issues in training, LaFromboise, Foster, and James (1996) maintain that efforts to achieve parity for ethnic minorities in psychology have been characterized as showing both progress and stagnation. Although diversity does exist in the profession, additional progress is needed. LaFromboise et al. conclude that there is a wide gap between idealistic policy statements laden with multicultural platitudes and the reality of current training.

In her article on multicultural counseling, Herlihy (1996) calls for counselors to be aware of cultural differences so that they can modify their approaches and increase their effectiveness when working with clients of differing cultural backgrounds. Recognizing diversity in our society and developing intercultural competence are fundamental to ethical counseling practice. The preamble to the ACA Code of Ethics states that counselors should embrace a cross-cultural approach; similarly, specific standards related to nondiscrimination and multicultural competence are found throughout the code. Although the code provides guidelines for sound multicultural practice in such areas as testing (Standard E.8) and counselor training (Standards F.1.a and F.2.i), these standards need to be considered seriously and thoughtfully and with intentionality toward culturally sensitive practice.

Lonborg and Bowen (2004) discuss the ethical implications of spiritual diversity for school counseling in rural communities, an area they think should be in the multicultural counseling realm. Their opinions and suggestions, however, apply to nearly all counselors who at least sometimes deal with spiritual issues. By design, members of the counseling profession assist students and clients in the important process of identity development, of which spiritual identity is one important aspect. School counselors should work with their colleagues to create a school environment in which people of differing spiritual traditions feel welcome. Counselors as individuals may be on their own spiritual journeys; however, as school professionals, their challenge is to find ways to live out their own spiritual traditions and beliefs while carrying out their important responsibilities to a school community that likely enjoys tremendous spiritual and religious diversity.

Lonborg and Bowen (2004) provide practical suggestions for school counselors working with spiritual issues. First, school counselors should anticipate the ethical challenges associated with their highly visible lives. Second, counselors should identify and be prepared to use an ethical decision-making model when confronted with questions about multiple relationships, confidentiality, and boundaries of competence. Third, counselors must become familiar with community norms and values so that they may thoughtfully consider the impact of their personal and professional behavior on the school community as well as on the lives of their current and future clients. Fourth, ethical school counseling requires an understanding of one's own worldview, including spirituality as well as an awareness of diverse worldviews that exist in the community. Fifth, in light of their important role in promoting school climate, school counselors should advocate for multicultural competence in all members of the school community.

In A Focus on Research 3.2, Sadeghi, Fischer, and House (2003) look at ethical dilemmas in multicultural counseling. Several standards relate to being nondiscriminatory toward and respectful of differences in counseling relationships. Counselors should actively attempt to understand the diverse cultural backgrounds of clients and work to learn how their own cultural/ethnic/racial identities affect their personal values and beliefs about the counseling process (Standard A.2.b). Not only do conscientious counselors practice within their boundaries of competence, but they also are committed to stretching their boundaries by gaining knowledge, personal awareness, sensitivity, and skills for working with diverse client populations (Standard C.2.a). Counselors are expected to keep current with the diverse and special populations with whom they work (Herlihy, 1996).

A FOCUS ON RESEARCH 3.2

Ethical Dilemmas in Multicultural Counseling

Sadeghi, Fischer, and House (2003) maintain that, included in ethical issues, are the counseling programs that lack culturally sensitive material, that provide inadequate training, that fail to adequately recognize the ramifications of culture or to address issues that pertain to ethnic minorities, and that fail to prepare counselors to interpret the ethical guidelines with sensitivity to racial and ethnic minority groups.

Sadeghi, Fischer, and House (2003) identify eight dilemmas. Selected dilemmas include dealing with discrimination, leaving one's family to promote individual growth, ending an abusive marriage, seeking treatment based on Western medical practices, and treating clients while not having culturally specific competencies.

The results of their study have important implications for the practice of counseling, the continued improvement of counseling programs, and research application. Providing inservice training, workshops, and continuing education opportunities for practicing counselors with these multicultural ethical dilemmas as the basis for open discussions, analysis, and clarification would enhance the delivery of counseling services to the expanding population of the United States. As counseling programs increasingly focus on competency-based skills, the ability to successfully negotiate multicultural ethical dilemmas should be considered a task requiring proficiency. Counseling programs that are committed to including diversity issues in their curriculum must recognize the importance of preparing students for the ethical situations that arise during multicultural counseling.

Source: "Ethical dilemmas in multicultural counseling," by M. Sadeghi, J. M. Fischer, and S. G. House, 2003, *Journal of Multicultural Counseling and Development 31* (3), pp. 179–191.

To maintain a diversity-sensitive counseling practice, Herlihy makes the following recommendations:

- Be open to examining your own values, biases, and assumptions.
- Expand your repertoire of intervention strategies to include nontraditional roles and system-oriented approaches that might be appropriate for diverse clients.
- Read some of the excellent articles and new books available on multicultural counseling.
- Attend workshops and seminars to broaden your knowledge and understandings of different cultures in the United States.
- Seek consultation or work under supervision while stretching boundaries of competence in working with diverse client populations.

Cottone (2001) proposes a social constructivism model for ethical decision-making in counseling. He defines constructivism as an intellectual movement in the mental health field that directs a social consensual interpretation of reality. A social constructivism approach redefines the ethical decision-making process as an interactive, rather than an individual, process, which involves negotiation, consensualization and, when necessary, arbitration. The social constructivism model involves several steps: (a) Obtain information from those involved, (b) assess the nature of the relationships operating at that moment, (c) consult valued colleagues and professional expert opinion, (including ethics codes and literature), (d) negotiate when disagreement occurs, and (e) respond in a way that allows for reasonable consensus as to a solution or what really occurred (Cottone, 2001). Detailed discussion of Cottone's constructivism model is beyond the scope of this text; however, the reference is listed in Suggested Readings for readers wanting additional information.

Professional Training and Preparation

The vast cultural and ethnic differences that characterize the U.S. population provide a sound rationale for including culturally appropriate professional experiences in training for counselors. Rather than counselors merely using slightly modified techniques that were originally designed for European middle-class clients, current thought calls for culturally effective counselors having special professional preparation in counseling clients of various cultural backgrounds.

Kim and Lyons (2003) describe the use of experiential learning activities as a method of instilling multicultural competence in counselor trainees. Experiential learning can be a powerful means to stimulate multicultural awareness and can be used to help individuals confront and overcome racial–ethnic biases. When used with didactic methods, experiential learning can provide trainees with opportunities to observe and practice skills that they have read and have been taught.

Arthur and Achenbach (2002) maintain students can experience cultural similarities and differences through experiential learning. Students can be encouraged to process their experience in both cognitive and affective domains. First, cognitive learning challenges students to examine their worldview and beliefs about self and others. Cognitive behavior can be examined by including topics such as social and cultural bases of behavior, attitudes, and beliefs to be reflective about the impact of professional role. Second, curriculum designed to increase counselors' self-awareness needs to go beyond cognitive learning and to encourage students to engage in affective learning. To challenge ethnocentrism, students require experiences that help them to bring feelings, attitudes, and values to the surface. Experiential learning can promote self-awareness through demonstrating the important influences of thoughts and feelings in the counseling role. Third, experiential learning facilitates students' experience of cultural similarities and differences in a structured environment with relatively low risks. Thus, students may be able both to process and to resolve new information prior to working directly with culturally diverse clients.

Playing the role of counselor or client may not necessarily challenge students to process cultural information in new ways. Assuming a specific role during experiential learning may lead to externalizing the behavior, thoughts, and feelings that emerge without personalizing learning. Therefore, special efforts must be made to explore hidden messages of clients and counselors (Arthur & Achenbach, 2002).

Counseling faculty have a responsibility to address several ethical considerations. First, to protect students, educators should make clear that participation in the experiential learning is voluntary and not a condition of the course or evaluation. Second, educators should seek informed consent from participants prior to engaging in experiential learning. Third, a safe context must be fostered during experiential learning to prevent levels of stress that could be counterproductive for learning goals or harmful to students. Fourth, counselor educators should limit the amount of student self-disclosure in reaction to experiential learning. Fifth, faculty must be knowledgeable of the content in multicultural counseling, skillful facilitators at orchestrating learning environments, skillful supporters of individual learners' reactions, and able to help students link their personal experiences to the development of multicultural competencies.

Several suggestions for using experiential learning foster multicultural counseling experiences include the following:

- Select experiential learning exercises to match specific learning goals in the domains of self-awareness, knowledge and skills.
- Review experiential learning exercises to consider which values are reinforced and which values may be excluded or devalued.
- Review ethical considerations, including the competence of faculty, safety in the learning environment, student consent for voluntary participation, and sufficient time for debriefing.
- Be aware of experiential learning based on the simulation of oppression may lead to defensiveness and pose a barrier to student learning.
- Personalize experiential learning and encourage students to pay attention to feelings, thoughts, and behaviors in exploring their world views.
- Encourage discussion in which contrasting points of view, values, and beliefs can help students experience cultural diversity with their peers.
- Structure learning so that students can be reflective about self-awareness, knowledge, and skills.

GENDER PERSPECTIVES 3.1
Feminism and Feminist Therapy

Evans, Kincade, Marbley, and Seem (2005) explain that feminist therapy incorporates the psychology of women, developmental research, cognitive–behavioral techniques, multicultural awareness, and social activism in a coherent "theoretical and therapeutic package" (p. 269). The authors, first, provide a history of feminist therapy, beginning with the 1960s and also provide an interesting explanation of feminist foremothers.

They emphasize that one cannot speak of one feminist therapy—counselors need to realize there are many feminist therapies, but they all share a valuing of gender as a central organizing aspect in an individual's life and the tenet that people cannot be separated from their culture.

Feminism and feminist therapy has impacted family therapy, which has existed since the 1940s, but only in the past decade has it become a driving force in counseling and psychotherapy. The authors also explore career counseling and state that one of the most

significant advantages of the feminist movement is to emphasize that women should have the same opportunities as men.

Another excellent section focused on counselor education and training where the authors examined feminist content in counseling sessions and trainee reactions to feminist pedagogy and content. After looking at multitracial feminist theories and female consciousness of African American women, the authors offered their opinions on feminist counseling and the twenty-first century.

Undoubtedly, counselors need to be effectively prepared to understand feminism and provide appropriate feminist therapies.

Source: "Feminism and feminist therapy: Lessons from the past and for the future," by K. M. Evans, E. A. Kincade, A. F. Marbley, and S. R. Seem, 2005, _Journal of Counseling and Development, 83,_ pp. 269–277.

- Help students identify strategies beyond the experiential learning exercise to review and incorporate their learning into professional practice.

- Encourage students to continue the process of reflective practice beyond course work and in their professional work as multicultural counselors.

- Incorporate both process and outcome measures to evaluate the ways that students' multicultural competencies are affected through experiential learning (Arthur & Achenbach, 2002).

In Gender Perspectives 3.1, Evans, Kincade, Marbley, and Seem (2005) explore feminism and feminist therapy and call for counselors to be trained in these aspects of professional intervention.

Cross-Cultural Counseling Supervision

Counselor education and counseling psychology programs are increasingly devoting attention to how to train counselors to work with people of differing backgrounds most effectively. Counselor supervision is an important topic in counselor education literature. Recommendations included that supervisors (a) acquaint themselves with recent counselor education models designed to promote the effectiveness of multicultural counseling; (b) recognize the complex nature of cultural factors and mental health variables; and (c) learn about prospective counselors' cultural backgrounds as will as their other diversities.

As with other areas of professional training, counselors-in-training need culturally appropriate supervisory experiences. Leong, Wagner, and Kim (1994) offered several recommendations regarding counselor supervision:

- Questions such as the following need to be answered: Is cross-cultural counseling supervision a developmental process? Do the stages of these models apply to all supervisor–supervisee–client interracial triads, or are specific stage models needed for different racial–ethnic combinations?

- Directions need to be determined concerning techniques that can help supervisors promote awareness, increase knowledge, and develop cross-cultural counseling skills in their trainees.

- Theoretical models of cross-cultural counseling supervision need to include formulations about the role and impact of personality dynamics.

A primary goal of multicultural counseling courses is to help students reflect on their thinking and its influence on both their feelings and behaviors toward clients (Faubert, Locke, & Lanier, 1996).

Training and Preparation Issues

Counselor educators often face the realities that counseling professionals are not adequately trained to meet the mental health needs of clients of various cultures. They also question counseling methods and techniques that are most effective with clients of differing cultural backgrounds.

Should counselor educators provide training in multicultural counseling for undergraduate students or should such training be reserved only for the graduate level? Estrada, Durlak, and Juarez (2002) believe it is possible to promote multicultural counseling competencies in undergraduate students. Their goal was to train students who have little knowledge of multicultural counseling and to provide a highly structured and supportive academic environment for undergraduate students to explore diversity. Although multicultural counseling competency cannot be achieved completely in a single course, exposing undergraduate students to multicultural concepts can enhance some competencies and motivate students to develop additional expertise.

Training occurred in a one-semester counseling course that was designed to introduce undergraduate students to current multicultural concepts and principles in counseling and psychotherapy; to increase students' awareness of multicultural concepts and knowledge about the clinical needs of clients from culturally diverse backgrounds; and to increase students' ability to conceptualize counseling cases from multicultural perspectives. Instead of teaching actual counseling skills, the counseling course adopted a broad definition of multiculturalism to include racial and ethnic issues, sex, socioeconomic status, sexual orientataion, and national origin. The beginning of the course focused on providing a rationale for and a definition of multicultural counseling, including a review of sociopolitical, historical, and developmental factors that may account for the existence of clinically underserved populations. Assigned readings focused on racism, sexism, and other forms of oppression, ethical issues in multicultural counseling, the notion of with-in group differences or variance; and the etic or universal approaches as contrasted to emic or culture-specific approaches to understanding human behavior. The second part of the course was a review and critique of traditional theories of psychotherapy from multicultural perspectives. The last part of the course was a review of the psychotherapy literature on sex, gays, and lesbians as well as the most visible racial and cultural minority groups in the United States, including African Americans, Asian Americans, Hispanic Americans, and Native Americans.

The *genogram* is a commonly used technique in counseling and counselor training. The genogram has its roots in family counseling and facilitates an examination of historical influences on current issues in a person's life. Genograms usually expand three generations and are used as visual aids to uncover patterns and the multigenerational transmission of family influences. Genograms also can be used to trace family influences, understand career influences, delineate family influence on academic success, and examine the impact of the family on sexual functioning. Within the counseling profession, the genogram is considered an important tool for helping therapists develop self-understanding and is a common assignment in family counseling courses (Granello, Hothersall, & Osborne, 2000).

A Focus on Research 3.3 focuses on *developmental advocacy* whereby school counselor education faculty can use contemporary developmental research to train counseling students to serve as developmental advocates.

A FOCUS ON RESEARCH 3.3
School Counselors as Developmental Advocates

Akos and Galassi (2004) maintain that counselor educators continue to debate the persistent questions of the role and function of the school counselor. School counselor education faculty can use contemporary developmental research to train counseling students. The primary role of a developmental advocate is to promote positive student developmental outcomes and to identify environments that nurture these outcomes.

Akos and Galassi (2004) explain that the developmental advocacy framework extends earlier forms of developmental counseling and provides a foundational role in development for school counselors. Training school counselors to be developmental advocates requires programs to integrate a philosophy of *developmental promotion* (italics Akos' and Galassi's) as part of a professional identity, to infuse developmental content in all courses, and to revise curriculum and training to enable school counselors to function in the role of developmental promotion.

The authors focus on topics such as helping relationships, social and cultural diversity, group work, school counseling curriculum, and clinical experience and supervision. According to the authors, some may view developmental advocacy as a mere restatement of older developmental counseling models, but what is distinctive about the developmental advocacy is that contemporary research moves beyond traditional notions of developmental needs and tasks. This research identifies the characteristics of skills of resilient youth and environments and actually promotes positive youth development.

Source: "Training school counselors as developmental advocates," by P. Akos, and J. P. Galassi, 2004, *Counselor Education & Supervision, 43,* pp. 192–206.

Counselor Self-Development

Current counselor education programs use a variety of models to provide training in multicultural counseling. However, the question remains: How can counselors who were trained prior to the emphasis on cultural diversity most effectively plan a program of self-development? Although any efforts of these counselors to improve their multicultural competence are commendable, minority clients deserve (and the ethics of the counseling profession require) counselors who are qualified and competent to intervene in multicultural situations. Counselors who are planning a program of self-development may take several approaches:

- Make a commitment to recognize the value of a client's cultural, ethnic, racial, socioeconomic, lifespan, and all other differences.

- Strive to participate in firsthand social interactions with people from various cultures, individually and in groups.

- Become familiar with the literature on multicultural counseling, including professional publications that focus on cultural diversity and lifespan issues (e.g., those listed in Appendix A); attend seminars offered by counseling organizations; and participate in additional formal coursework.

- Use available tools, such as the cultural attitudes repertory technique (CART). Exercises of this type provide opportunities to gain a better understanding of one's own personal values and attitudes and those of others from different backgrounds.

- Engage in critical reflection to identify possible racist attitudes and to examine personal behaviors, perceptions, and feelings that might compromise effective and competent multicultural counseling.

As with other professional tasks to be mastered, the success a counselor achieves toward improving multicultural counseling effectiveness depends significantly on the level of enthusiasm and commitment brought to the effort.

Granello, Hothersall, and Osborne (2000) suggest the use of academic genograms for students during doctoral orientation in a counselor education course. The genogram encourages students to trace their academic roots. They might select their academic mentor (perhaps their master's or doctoral level advisor) as a beginning point. They interview the selected faculty member and then perhaps interview the faculty member's mentor. Students can contact mentors by phone, e-mail, or letter, but they should be encouraged to seek information from secondary sources. Important collateral information can be obtained from spouses, former colleagues, and former advisees. The selection of people to interview is intentionally vague. Also, there is no specified number of people from whom to seek information. Selected professional themes include faculty as agents of socialization of change, research agendas, and intellectual and personal development.

The authors remind readers that some mentors are busy with their own agendas and may not wish to participate or may participate with differing levels of enthusiasm. In such cases, students can seek other sources or entirely skip a generation. Some faculty mentors have composed a short biography for students to use; others feel that social and verbal interaction is preferable to written statements. A major advantage of the academic genogram is that there is no one prescribed method. Students need to determine individually how best to complete their own academic genogram.

A Point of Departure

Challenges Confronting Effective Counselors

Counselors whose professional training focused mainly on European American middle-class adult clients will experience frustration and feelings of inadequacy as the number of clients from various cultures and age groups continues to increase. No longer can counselors expect to intervene with only European American clients of a similar social class. Similarly, counselors of various cultural backgrounds will be challenged to intervene with European American clients and with clients of cultures different from their own.

Contemporary counselors will increasingly interact with clients who have differing values, backgrounds, and outlooks toward family, friends, and life in general. A counselor might be threatened by an inability to understand the client's motives and reasoning, to communicate the objectives and processes of counseling, and to establish an effective counseling relationship. Becoming a culturally effective counselor requires professional education and training, knowledge of cultural diversity, an understanding of and respect for others, and an ability to plan and implement intervention that is appropriate to culture and lifespan level.

Summary

There are three essential aspects of becoming an effective counselor. First, the counselor needs to have an appreciation for cultural diversity, an understanding of the individual culture, and a sense of empathy for clients. Second, the counselor needs appropriate beliefs/attitudes, understandings, and skills to intervene effectively in multicultural situations. Third, professional preparation, firsthand experiences with people of various cultures, and an adherence to ethical standards established by the counseling profession can reduce the barriers to effective multicultural counseling.

Appendix B provides counselors with "Suggested Multicultural Experiential Exercises" as they learn more about the qualifications and characteristics of effective counselors.

Suggested Readings

DeRicco, J. N., & Sciarra, D. T. (2005). The immersion experience in multicultural counselor training: Confronting covert racism. *Journal of Multicultural Counseling and Development, 33,* 2–8. These authors report on the use of immersion experiences in a multicultural counseling course as a means of confronting unacknowledged racism on the part of White students.

Fier, E. B., & Ramsey, M. (2005). Ethical challenges in the teaching of multicultural course work. *Journal of Multicultural Counseling and Development, 33,* 94–107. Fier and Ramsey explore the ethical issues and challenges frequently encountered by counselor educators of multicultural counseling course work.

Fraga, E. D., Atkinson, D. R., & Wampold, B. E. (2004). Ethnic group preferences for multicultural counseling competencies. *Cultural Diversity & Ethnic Minority Psychology, 10*(1), 53–65. As the title implies, this article looked at group preferences for multicultural counseling competencies and found that participants regarded some multicultural counseling competencies as more important than others.

Kitaoka, S. K. (2005). Multicultural counseling competencies: Lessons from assessment. *Journal of Multicultural*

Counseling and Development, 33, 37–43. Kitakoka discusses multicultural counseling from the perspective quantitative assessment.

Liu, W. M., Soleck, G., Hopps, J., Dunston, K., & Pickett, T. (2004). A new framework to understand social class in counseling: The social class worldview model and modern classism theory. *Journal of Multicultural Counseling, 32* (2), 95–122. These authors maintain that social class and classism remain elusive constructs in psychology and suggest a foundation for the Social Class Worldview and Modern Classism Theory.

Lonborg, S. D., & Bowen, N. (2004). Counselors, communities, and spirituality: Ethical and multicultural considerations. *Professional School Counseling, 7*(5), 318–325. Lonborg and Bowen look at ethical and multicultural concerns as they maintain that spiritual counseling should be a part of multicultural counseling.

Smith-Adcock, S., Rogers-Huilman, B., Choate, L. H. (2004). Feminist teaching in counselor education: Promoting multicultural understanding. *Journal of Multicultural and Development, 32,* 402–413. These authors maintain that feminist teaching is a promising pedagogy for counselors' multicultural understanding.

Toperak, R. L., Ortaga-Villalobos, L., & Pope-Davis, D. B. (2004). Critical incidents in multicultural supervision: Exploring supervisees' and supervisors' experience. *Journal of Multicultural Counseling and Development, 32* (2), 66–83. These authors report supervisees' and supervisors' experiences in multicultural supervision and identify recommendations for improving supervision.

PART

II

Understanding and Counseling Clients in Multicultural Settings and Throughout the Lifespan

Chapter 4 looks at multicultural growth and development; Chapters 5 through 16 focus attention on understanding and counseling African American, American Indian, Asian American, European American, and Hispanic American clients along the lifespan continuum. Specifically, Chapters 5, 7, 9, 11, and 13 look at understanding clients and their respective cultures. Chapters 6, 8, 10, 12, and 14 look at counseling children, adolescents, adults, and the elderly in these cultural groups. Chapters 15 and 16 focus on understanding lesbian, gay, and bisexual clients.

Multicultural Human Growth and Development

Questions to Be Explored

1. Why are the prenatal and infancy stages important in a lifespan approach?

2. How do historical and contemporary perspectives of infancy, childhood, adolescence, adulthood, and old age differ?

3. Does each lifespan stage have a "culture"? What makes each stage unique? What role do cultural differences play during each lifespan stage?

4. What are some issues and questions that pertain to multicultural lifespan development?

5. What are the physical, psychosocial, and intellectual characteristics of clients at each lifespan stage?

6. What special problems and concerns face African American, American Indian, Asian American, European American, and Hispanic American clients at each lifespan stage?

7. What are some research findings in the multicultural development area? What implications do they have for mental health professionals?

8. What challenges confront counselors working with clients at the various lifespan stages, and what resources can be suggested?

Overview

Although most counseling professionals have recognized for some time that understanding cultural differences enhances intervention, the need to take the client's lifespan stage into account has been emphasized only recently. Understanding developmental characteristics and the unique crises, tasks, and problems associated with a particular lifespan period provides counselors with insights into the counseling needs of children, adolescents, adults, and the elderly. To underscore the importance of recognizing and understanding lifespan differences, this chapter begins with a discussion of cross-cultural research and an overview of lifespan development, followed by a description of developmental characteristics of the four lifespan stages and relevant issues occurring during each.

Cross-cultural research on developmental issues and the relationship of development to culture has made considerable progress (Rice, 2001). By looking at people from different cultural groups, researchers can learn in what ways development is culturally universal and in what ways it differs. One important reason to conduct research among different cultural groups is to recognize biases in traditional Western research and theories that often have gone unquestioned. Such biases have led many people to define typical development in Western nations as the norm. Measuring development against Western norms leads to narrow and often incorrect ideas (Papalia, Olds, & Feldman, 2001).

Maintaining the field of developmental psychology has been dominted by European American perspectives, Wainryb (2004), in A Focus On Research 4.1, looks at diversity and human development and calls for study of human diversity.

Table 4.1 presents several questions that need to be addressed for more enhanced understanding of the effects of culture on development.

In Table 4.2, Papalia, Olds, and Feldman (2001) divided the lifespan into eight periods rather than the four stages chosen for this volume; for example, they have three childhood stages and three adulthood stages. Although Papalia and colleagues' (2004) more detailed look at development is worthwhile, these counseling chapters will discuss only the four main lifespan stages. Also, readers are encouraged to remember that all clients differ according to socioeconomic class, sexual orientation, disability, and cultural factors.

A FOCUS ON RESEARCH 4.1
Diversity and Human Development

Wainryb maintains that the emphasis on the study of diversity, a growing area of research in developmental psychology, reflects an increasing awareness of the need to recognize the value of the differences among people. Wainryb reviews scholarly writing that maintains that the field of developmental psychology is an ethnocentric one dominated by European American perspectives. When one group, the majority, has the exclusive power to define the nature of itself and all other groups in a society, all minority groups are disenfranchised. Such an ethnocentric approach does not yield an accurate account of human development.

The call to address these biases has been taken seriously. Minority groups are now routinely included in developmental research. In this context, psychologists have championed culture as the main source of development—the origin and organizer of the self, emotion, cognition, and values.

Over the years, psychologists have begun to realize that most cultures are not homogeneous. Such an approach is better at capturing aspects of the multifaceted experiences that make up life within cultures; most importantly, it allows for the possibility that conflicts arise, within a society, between the features and goals characteristic of different orientations. Still, this approach has flaws. For example, although becoming a member of a culture might involve acquiring more than one cultural orientation, this approach leaves little room for the varied and often critical interpretations and judgements that individuals (adults and children, males and females, have and have-nots) make about their societies' values, traditions, and practices.

Source: "The study of diversity in human development: Culture, urgencies, and perils," by C. Wainryb, 2004, *Human Development, 47,* pp. 131–137.

Table 4.1
Cross-Cultural Child
Development: Crucial
Questions

- How do culture and ethnicity affect children's development?
- What developmental similarities do children share across cultures?
- How do children differ developmentally across cultures?
- How do cultural beliefs about maternal and paternal parenting affect child development?
- How should professional intervention reflect both culture and the childhood stage of development?
- Do the research findings of Piaget, Vygotsky, and Erikson have relevance for development in minority children?
- How can mental health professionals most effectively intervene with children of differing cultures?

Table 4.2
Developmental Characteristics Throughout the Lifespan Continuum

Age Period	Physical Developments	Cognitive Developments	Psychosocial Developments
Prenatal (conception to birth)	Conception occurs. The genetic endowment interacts with environmental influences from the start. Basic body structures and organs form. Brain growth spurt begins. Physical growth is the most rapid in the lifespan. Fetus hears and responds to sensory stimuli. Vulnerability to environmental influences is great.	Abilities to learn and remember are present during fetal stage.	Fetus responds to mother's voice and develops a preference for it.
Infancy and Toddlerhood (birth to age 3)	All senses operate at birth to varying degrees. The brain grows in complexity and is highly sensitive to environmental influence.	Abilities to learn and remember are present, even in early weeks. Use of symbols and ability to solve problems develop by end of second year.	Attachments to parents and others form. Self-awareness develops. Shift from dependence to autonomy occurs.

Table 4.2 *continued*
Developmental Characteristics Throughout the Lifespan Continuum

Age Period	Physical Developments	Cognitive Developments	Psychosocial Developments
	Physical growth and development of motor skills are rapid.	Comprehension and use of language develop rapidly.	Interest in other children increases.
Early Childhood (3 to 6 years)	Growth is steady; appearance becomes more slender and proportions more adultlike.	Thinking is somewhat egocentric but understanding of other people's perspective grows.	Self-concept and understanding of emotions become more complex; self-esteem is global.
	Appetite diminishes, and sleep problems are common.	Cognitive immaturity leads to some illogical ideas about the world.	Independence, initiative, self-control, and self-care increase.
	Handedness appears; fine and gross motor skills and strength improve.	Memory and language improve.	Gender identity develops.
		Intelligence becomes more predictable.	
			Play becomes more imaginative, more elaborate, and more social.
			Altruism, aggression, and fearfulness are common.
			Family is still focus of social life, but other children become more important.
			Attending preschool is common.
Middle Childhood (6 to 11 years)	Growth slows.	Egocentrism diminishes.	Self-concept becomes more complex, affecting self-esteem.
	Strength and athletic skills improve.	Children begin to think logically but concretely.	Coregulation reflects gradual shift in control from parents to child.
	Respiratory illnesses are common, but health is generally better than at any other time in lifespan.	Memory and language skills increase.	Peers assume central importance.
		Cognitive gains permit children to benefit from formal schooling.	
		Some children show special educational needs and strengths.	

Table 4.2 *continued*
Developmental Characteristics Throughout the Lifespan Continuum

Age Period	Physical Developments	Cognitive Developments	Psychosocial Developments
Adolescence (11 to about 20 years)	Physical growth and other changes are rapid and profound. Reproductive maturity occurs. Major health risks arise from behavioral issues, such as eating disorders and drug abuse.	Ability to think abstractly and use scientific reasoning develops. Immature thinking persists in some attitudes and behaviors. Education focuses on preparation for college or vocation.	Search for identity, including sexual identity, becomes central. Relationships with parents are generally good. Peer groups help develop and test self-concept, but also may exert an antisocial influence.
Young Adulthood (20 to 40 Years)	Physical condition peaks, then declines slightly. Lifestyle choices influence health.	Cognitive abilities and moral judgments assure more complexity. Educational and career choices are made.	Personality traits and styles become relatively stable, but changes in personality may be influenced by life stages and events. Decisions are made about intimate relationships and personal lifestyles. Most people marry, and most become parents.
Middle Adulthood (40 to 65 years)	Some deterioration of sensory abilities, health, stamina, and prowess may take place. Women experience menopause.	Most basic mental abilities peak; expertise and practical problem-solving skills are high. Creative output may decline but improve in quality. For some, career success and earning powers peak; for others, burnout or career change may occur.	Sense of identity continues to develop; stressful midlife transition may occur. Double responsibilities of caring for children and elderly parents may cause stress. Launching of children leaves empty nest.

Table 4.2 *continued*
Developmental Characteristics Throughout the Lifespan Continuum

Age Period	Physical Developments	Cognitive Developments	Psychosocial Developments
Late Adulthood (65 years and over)	Most people are healthy and active, although health and physical abilities decline somewhat. Slowing of reaction time affects some aspects of functioning.	Most people are mentally alert. Although intelligence and memory may deteriorate in some areas, most people find ways to compensate.	Retirement from workforce may offer new options for use of time. People need to cope with personal losses and impending death. Relationships with family and close friends can provide important support. Search for meaning in life assumes central importance.

Source: Human Development (8th ed. p. 14–15), by D. E. Papalia, S. W. Olds, and R. D. Feldman, 2001, Boston: McGraw-Hill.

Prenatal and Infancy Stages

Crucial Periods

The nine months preceding birth are so obviously significant in lifelong development that their inclusion here requires no explanation. An infant's overall size, health, and weight are all affected by the mother's nutritional intake during pregnancy. Smoking and drug and alcohol use can harm the fetus. Improper nutrition may be a result of lack of financial resources, lack of knowledge, the tendency to rely on relatives rather than to consult physicians, and or communication barriers that cause misunderstanding. Also, the ingestion of certain medications and toxins during early pregnancy can harm the fetus (Vander Zanden, Crandell, & Crandell, 2003). For these and other reasons, minority children or those from lower socioeconomic backgrounds may begin life at a disadvantage.

Although smoking and use of alcohol or drugs is a conscious choice made by the pregnant woman, maternal malnutrition is more difficult to control and particularly affects minority groups. Malnutrition-related problems, such as low birth weight, rickets, physical and neural defects, and failure to thrive, occur most frequently in African American, American Indian, and Hispanic American children, whose mothers are more likely to be undernourished than are mothers of European American children (Vander Zanden, Crandell, & Crandell, 2003).

Single mothers can face increased stress due to housing and financial problems as well as the challenges of raising children alone. Some unmarried women may also lack adequate health care during pregnancy. They may be unable to afford proper health care, be too embarrassed

Figure 4.1
Percentages of Births
to Unmarried Women

Source: "American families," by
S. M. Branchi and L. M. Caspar,
2000, *Population Bulletin,*
55(4), p. 22.

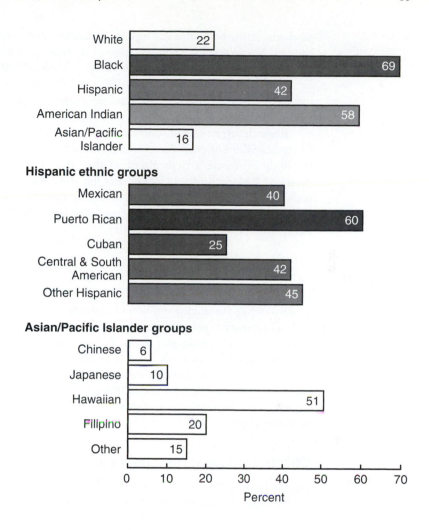

to seek help, or be unaware or uninformed of available health services due to inadequate English-speaking skills. The stress, frustration, and anxiety that sometimes accompany single motherhood can result in problems which require counseling intervention. Still, it must be acknowledged that not all unmarried women experience such problems—some women have the financial means, English-language skills to seek assistance, and the emotional support of extended family members.

Multicultural Differences

Is infant behavior universal, or does even infant behavior vary according to culture? Surprising to some observers, research suggests that infants demonstrate culture-specific behaviors. A typical behavior of Western newborns is the Moro reflex. To test this reflex, the baby's body is lifted, with the head supported. The head is then released and allowed to drop. Typical European American newborns extend both arms and legs, cry persistently, and move about in an agitated manner. In contrast, Navajo newborns typically respond in a more reduced reflex extension of the limbs; crying is rare, and agitated motion ceases almost immediately. African American infants appear to be more precocious in gross motor skills, and Asian American infants to a lesser degree, than infants of European origin. Asian American infants are typically more docile and may tend to stay closer to their parents (Papalia et al., 2004).

Research suggests Asian American infants have a lower level of arousal than White infants. Compared with European American infants, newborn Asian American infants are calmer and less likely to remove a cloth placed on their face, and they are more easily consoled when distressed. Chinese American infants were less active, less vocal, and smiled less often at the presentation of visual and auditory events during their first year than did European American infants. Also, Japanese American infants were less easily aroused and are less reactive than European American infants (Rice, 2001).

Children

Understanding the unique position of children in the lifespan continuum and the historical and contemporary perspectives surrounding the concept of the childhood years presents professionals with challenging tasks. Because their physical, psychological, and intellectual characteristics differ from those of their older counterparts on the lifespan, children have unique developmental characteristics that professionals should understand and consider when planning counseling intervention. Although all children progress in the same developmental sequence, it is imperative to recognize the effects of diverse cultural and ethnic backgrounds on young clients.

Childhood Years: Historical and Contemporary Perspectives

Interest in the unique growth and developmental aspects of children and recognition of the need for special counseling for children have been demonstrated only fairly recently. Because they lacked social standing and legal rights, children were considered by many to be possessions and were treated as the adults pleased. There was no concept of childhood—children were seen as miniature adults. The prevailing opinion of the adult culture was that "children should be seen and not heard." For society to accept that children also differed culturally proved difficult.

Contemporary perceptions of the childhood years hold that childhood has its own unique culture that differs significantly from other lifespan cultures. Although children differ across cultures, they have their own characteristics that differ substantially from those of adults. Children, by virtue of their developmental characteristics, have their own communication patterns, senses of humor, likes and dislikes, and types of social activity and play. Their unique ways of speaking, acting, and perceiving events in their lives indicate that professionals should duly consider the distinct culture of the childhood years.

Counseling professionals who consider children unique and developing individuals rather than "miniature adults" tend to counsel children more effectively. In essence, counselors and psychotherapists who intervene with children from varying cultures should understand

(a) the culture of childhood; (b) the physical, psychosocial, and intellectual characteristics of developing children; and (c) the cultural differences among children.

Multicultural Differences

A discussion of cultural differences in children should consider differences from a cultural perspective. For example, Hawaiians and Navajos offer an interesting comparison. Both groups have been incorporated into the United States by conquest and are highly similar in survival perspectives. Still, they differ sharply in dimensions of individualism versus collectivism. For Hawaiians, the island ecological system produced a collective productive economy and a socialization system that contributed to a collective style. The nomadic system of the Athabascan peoples (of which the Navajo are the most salient group) produced a much more individualistic orientation. Although the patterns of individualism are still collectivistic in nature in comparison with European American perspectives, Navajo children differ distinctly from Hawaiian children in their thinking about individualism and collectivism (Tharp, 1994).

Actual physical differences also exist between cultures. In the United States, African American children tend to have longer legs and be taller than European American children who, in turn, are taller than Asian American children. In Canada, English-speaking children tend to be taller than French-speaking children (Rice, 2001). Similarly, African American boys and girls tend to grow faster than European American children, and thus be a bit taller and heavier at the same age. By about six years of age, African American girls have more muscle and bone mass than European American or Hispanic American girls. Hispanic American girls have a higher percentage of body fat than European American girls of the same age (Papalia et al., 2001).

Child Development

The present-day emphasis on child growth and development illustrates the recognition and value currently being placed on the childhood years. Developmentally, an array of physical, psychosocial, and intellectual changes occur simultaneously: Muscles and body proportions grow, social interests increasingly move outside the immediate family to a broader community and society, and intellectual problem-solving and reasoning skills increase.

Three physical changes are (1) the rapid growth of legs and arms, resulting in a slimmer appearance; (2) a lengthening of the jaw and an increase in face size as permanent teeth replace baby teeth; and (3) an increase in muscle tissue in boys and adipose tissue (fat) in girls.

Children emerge from the socially secure confines of a parent-centered home into a socially expanding world of extended family, with closer and more meaningful friendships and a recognition of peers. As children build their complex social networks of friends and significant peers, they also change their self-concept, their opinions of others, and their perceptions of the world in relation to themselves. Closely related to physical and psychosocial–emotional development is intellectual development, which opens vast new worlds of increased thinking ability. No longer confined to the physical or concrete worlds, a child now experiences increased flexibility of thought, ability to reverse operations, enhanced memory, and ability to share another's point of view. As always, culturally perceptive counselors need to remember that physical, psychosocial, and intellectual development differ across cultures and that each client should be considered unique (Papalia et al., 2001).

Development, family relationships, and culture are complexly intertwined. In her cross-cultural research with Asian and Australian children, Keats (2000) reported that far-reaching changes challenge traditional cultural values in family relationships and child-rearing practices. The author examines aspects such as the role of communication, development of values, and culturally related differences. Western ideas of desirable practices in the development of children often conflict with an Asian culture's traditional views and more recent ideologies. Examples of conflicts include Islamic views of child development and the attitudes of many Westerners toward China's one-child policy. Also, Asian countries have all been undergoing massive lifestyle changes, including economic, social, and psychological, which threaten many traditional child-rearing practices and values.

Gender Differences

Although physical gender differences are fairly easy to recognize, other differences between girls and boys are more subtle. Counselors and other professionals should carefully avoid stereotyping girls and boys. For too many years, people have considered girls and boys in gender-specific terms to the detriment of both genders. Table 4.3 looks at selected gender differences among girls and boys.

Self-Concept

Two closely related aspects surface as the social status of children changes: self-concept and locus of control. Children around six or seven years of age begin to think of themselves in external terms—what they look like, where they live, and what they are doing. This developing self-concept takes

Table 4.3
Selected Gender Differences in Children
Source: Developed from *Development through the lifespan* (2nd ed.), by L. E. Berk, 2004, Boston: Allyn and Bacon; *Human development* (8th ed.), by D. E. Papalia, S. W. Olds, and R. D. Feldman, 2004, Boston: McGraw-Hill; *Human development: A life-span approach*, by F. P. Rice, 2001, Upper Saddle River, NJ: Prentice-Hall.

- In infancy, girls are slightly shorter and lighter and have a higher ratio of fat to muscle than boys; girls in some Asian cultures are below growth norms for North American children of the same age; and African American girls are slightly ahead of European American children of all ages.

- Attention-deficit hyperactivity disorder (ADHD) is diagnosed five to ten times more often in boys than in girls; however, many girls with ADHD may be overlooked because their symptoms usually are not as obvious.

- Boys are more likely to have asthma, although heredity contributes to this condition in both boys and girls.

- Temperamental differences may result from gender-differentiated maternal child-raising attitudes as well as inherited genetic differences.

- Boys sometimes exhibit a tendency to be active and daring, whereas girls may be more anxious and timid, perhaps because parents often teach boys to be physically active and teach girls to seek help and physical closeness.

- During the early childhood years boys are slightly ahead of girls in skills that emphasize force and power, perhaps because boys and girls are encouraged to engage in different activities.

two forms: the real self and the ideal self. The former refers to the child's concept of what she or he is actually like; the latter refers to what the child would like to be like (Papalia et al., 2001). Thus, children continually evaluate themselves to determine their degree of self-worth and their sense of adequacy. Positive self-concept comes from development of the sense of industry, when children feel successful in learning the knowledge, tasks, and technology of their society. The negative side of this sense of industry—feelings of inferiority and inadequacy—results in anxiety and poor self-concept (Erikson, 1963).

Locus of control refers to the degree to which a person perceives control over his or her life. Briefly put, children who have an internal locus of control believe that they can determine what happens to them; on the other hand, children who have an external locus of control believe that outside forces control their lives. Locus of control has implications for counselors intervening in multicultural settings; children (as well as adults and the elderly) may think that racism and discrimination prohibit them from taking control of their lives.

Self-concept varies among children of differing cultural backgrounds. Children have to learn skills that are valued in their society. Arapesh boys in Guinea learn to make bows and arrows and to lay traps for rats; others learn to plant, weed, and harvest. Inuit children of Alaska learn to hunt. Children in industrialized nations learn to read, write, and count. Regardless of the skills they learn, children compare their abilities with those of their peers, thus determining their sense of self-worth (Papalia et al., 2004).

Learning about cross-cultural developmental studies helps mental health professionals avoid inappropriate generalizations about aspects of children and their social world. A knowledge of cultural differences and an understanding of child growth and development are essential for counselors working with children of differing cultural backgrounds. In one sense, counselors should be able to think from a child's perspective and to "see" situations from a child's point of view. This will often include recognizing and understanding how a child of a particular age thinks—the child's self-perception of physical growth and changes, the child's psychosocial self-concept, and the child's level of intellectual development.

Stress

Gil, Vega, and Dimas (1994) maintain that acculturation and personal adjustment can result in stress for Hispanic boys. Counselors who understand acculturative stress and its effects on psychological well-being can look for indicators of stress and can plan appropriate professional intervention. Gil et al. (1994) reported several findings: (a) Foreign-born Hispanics report considerably more acculturative stress than U.S.-born Hispanics; (b) U.S.-born Hispanics experience low self-esteem stemming from acculturative stress and low family pride; (c) high acculturation appears to have a powerful degenerative effect on family pride among foreign-born Hispanics; and (d) U.S.-born Hispanics are more prone to low family pride regardless of acculturative level.

What should counselors remember when intervening with children of various cultures? First, children are developmentally unique and should not be considered "little adults." Second, contrary to some adult thinking, children do have problems and may feel helpless to change life situations, may be victims of discrimination (because of both their cultural diversity and their developmental period), and may lack the intellectual capacity to perceive problems and solutions. Third, understanding the relationship between children's development and their cultural diversity improves counseling intervention.

Adolescents

The adolescent years have traditionally gone unrecognized as a genuine developmental period on the lifespan. As a result, adolescence has been plagued with misconceptions, general misunderstandings, and damaging stereotypes. No longer children but not yet adults, adolescents very often experience feelings that tend to lower their self-esteem. Psychosocial and intellectual changes that parallel the more visible physical changes cause adolescents to adopt childlike behaviors at times and to conform with adult standards at other times. Adolescents often experience identity confusion. Professionals working with adolescent clients need a sound understanding of this lifespan period; they also need to recognize cultural differences that influence adolescent behavior.

Adolescent Years: Historical and Contemporary Perspectives

Some observers define adolescence in terms of a specific age range, whereas others equate the beginning of adolescence with the onset of puberty and its ending with certain cultural factors.

Contrary to popular belief, the term *adolescence* has not been in use very long; in fact, it was hardly accepted before the nineteenth century. Moreover, proposing the term to suggest a continuation of childhood beyond puberty was considered even more ludicrous than not recognizing it at all.

Multicultural Differences

Adolescents vary from culture to culture, just as children do. What is considered normal behavior in one culture may be considered inappropriate in another. For example, many European American adolescents feel a strong need to act in accordance with peer pressure, whereas Asian American adolescents may believe that loyalty to parents takes precedence over any peer pressure that may be experienced. Similarly, the sense of "machismo" that so strongly influences the behavior of many Hispanic Americans is less important to their European American and Asian American counterparts.

Adolescent Identity

Adolescents ask themselves: Who am I? What am I to become? One main task of adolescence is to build a reasonably stable identity. Identity refers to a person's sense of placement within the world; in other words, it is the meaning that one attaches to oneself in the broader context of life (Vander Zanden, Crandell, & Crandell, 2003).

Adolescents often develop individual and cultural identities under difficult circumstances involving racism, discrimination, and injustice. The "culture of poverty" image may influence American Indian identities; similarly, African Americans who hear repeatedly that their culture is "inferior" may develop negative identities. In fact, African American youths have historically been confronted with many challenges to their cultural identity that have negatively affected their physical and psychological development. They have encountered problems with education, unemployment, delinquency, substance abuse, adolescent pregnancy, and suicide. Evidence in schools includes declines in grade point averages and attendance and in rates of participation in extracurricular activities, as well as increases in psychosocial stress and problem behaviors. One must carefully avoid blaming the victim in this case—African Americans, just as adolescents in other cultures, have faced serious racism and discrimination.

Gender Differences

Perceptive counselors understand the importance of gender differences and their effect on adolescent girls and boys. Considerable caution is needed when considering gender. People often make statements such as "Boys like to compete; girls like to collaborate" or "Boys like a large social network; girls like a few close friends." Although such statements can be true, counselors should avoid basing professional intervention on these and similar assumptions. With that said, Table 4.4 looks at several selected gender differences among adolescent girls and boys.

Yager and Rotheram-Borus (2000) investigated ethnic, gender, and developmental differences in the social expectations of African American, Hispanic American, and European American high school students. The four domains included group orientation, expressiveness, assertiveness, and aggressiveness. Yager and Rotheram-Borus reached several conclusions, but only their findings on gender will be briefly mentioned here. Males' social expectations were less group oriented and assertive and more expressive and aggressive. Females' expectations for assertiveness increased with grade level. Ethnic and gender differences were similar across youth of different ages.

Self-Concept

The significance of self-concept during all periods of the lifespan cannot be overstated. An adolescent's degree of self-worth can have long-lasting effects on identity formation, social development, and academic achievement. Self-perception is vital in determining

---

Table 4.4
Selected Gender Differences in Adolescents
Source: Developed from *Development through the lifespan* (2nd ed.), by L. E. Berk, 2004, Boston: Allyn and Bacon; *Human development* (8th ed.), by D. E. Papalia, S. W. Olds, and R. D. Feldman, 2004, Boston: McGraw-Hill; *Human development: A life-span approach*, by F. P. Rice, 2001, Upper Saddle River, NJ: Prentice-Hall.

- Typically girls satisfy communal needs through friendships, whereas boys satisfy status and mastery needs.
- Girls normally seek more emotional closeness in friendships, whereas boys look for more physical activity—for example, sports and competitive games.
- Girls experience greater decreases in self-esteem, perhaps because they are concerned about physical abilities and feel more insecure about these abilities.
- Girls often develop a sense of infant-caregiver which carries over for future intimate ties; boys often form a masculine gender identity, stressing individuation and independence.
- Girls are more prone to depression (but this is limited to industrialized nations); however, suicide rates are higher for boys (probably four- or five-fold greater).

whether the adolescent will become alienated from parents, peers, and society or whether he or she will become a sociable person who is capable of sustaining satisfactory relationships.

Although self-concept begins to develop at birth and continues to develop until death, the real crisis in identity occurs during adolescence. Emerging from this crisis with a strong, healthy, and independent self-concept allows the adolescent to progress further and to face the challenges of the adult world. Adolescents who are unable to develop positive self-concepts may withdraw from others or develop negative identities. Successful mastery of the developmental tasks that lead to a healthy self-concept is even more difficult for minority group members. Failure can result in academic problems, loneliness, and isolation.

Self-concept among African Americans has improved over the years due to the civil rights movement and the Black consciousness movement. Still, understandably, some African American adolescents have high self-esteem and others have lower self-esteem. Those who have established close friendships and have achieved some degree of intimacy have positive self-concepts and feel good about themselves. This finding suggests that counselors should focus intervention on social adjustments (Rice, 2001).

The self-concept of adolescents of all cultures may be enhanced by (a) learning about their respective cultural histories, (b) identifying the effects of past and contemporary relationships (both intracultural and intercultural), (c) learning historical and contemporary accomplishments and contributions of respective cultural groups, and (d) working to reduce acculturative stress, especially for immigrants and first-generation adolescents.

Adolescents Who Are at Risk

Although suicide, accidents, and homicides account for most adolescent deaths, many adolescents are at risk due to eating disorders, drug abuse, and sexually transmitted diseases (STDs). Common eating disorders include anorexia nervosa and bulimia, which are characterized by a distorted body perception and a preoccupation with food. Substance abuse may involve alcohol, tobacco, and marijuana or other illicit drugs, which may lead to use of still more powerful drugs. AIDS and STDs are becoming increasingly serious problems, with particular implications for adolescents. Three out of four cases of STDs involve young people from 15 to 24 years of age. Chlamydia, gonorrhea, syphilis, and herpes simplex are a few STDs that take a considerable toll on adolescents (Papalia et al., 2004).

It takes special commitment and expertise to intervene with adolescents of various cultures. Adolescents may experience frustrations not only from being at an age between childhood and adulthood but also from being a minority in a predominantly European American society. At a time when development of positive self-concept and identity is crucial, adolescents often find themselves caught between their parents' admonitions and their peers' pressure to experiment with risky behavior. In fact, being culturally different has the potential for making the already difficult adolescent years even more so. The American Indian adolescent who values noninterference with others and the Asian American adolescent who believes that errant behavior brings shame and disgrace on the family can encounter problems with identity formation. Understanding the complex relationship between development and cultural diversity provides counselors with clearer insights into counseling adolescents from differing cultures.

Adults

Although adults are often thought to be "grown and not developing," they do, in fact, continue to experience physical, psychosocial, and intellectual developmental changes. Tasks that face counselors of adult clients include a commitment (a) to consider adulthood a unique developmental period between adolescence and the elderly years and (b) to take into account multicultural differences among adults.

Adulthood Years: Historical and Contemporary Perspectives

The term *adulthood* has only recently begun to receive attention and respect as a valid period on the lifespan. Because it lacks the specific developmental characteristics of childhood or adolescence, adulthood was used as an all-encompassing term to describe all developmental changes in adults, beginning at age 18, 21, or some other age. Researchers consider the adult stage a largely unexplored phase of the lifespan. Once thought to be homogeneous, fully developed "products," adults are currently recognized by researchers and scholars as diverse and continually changing and developing.

Adult Development

As previously mentioned, to assume that adults do not continue to experience both visible and invisible developmental changes demonstrates a lack of knowledge of human development. From the time of conception, humans experience many developmental changes, both desirable and undesirable, that continue until death. Considerable individuality is associated with these developmental changes: Some adults experience them without psychological turmoil, whereas others require counseling interventions.

Erikson (1963, 1968, 1982) offers a theory of psychosocial development for all stages of the lifespan. Wastell (1996) suggests that Erikson's theories have potential in counseling intervention with clients of varying cultural backgrounds. However, Erikson's theories have received considerable criticism from feminist groups who believe that females need their own developmental theory and feminist-based counseling models. Criticisms of Erikson's theories include an intrinsic weakness of the theory (e.g., mechanisms for resolving crises are not delineated; conditions of transition from one stage to another are not clearly explained; the specific stages, particularly in adulthood, have not been empirically demonstrated; the specific way society influences development has not been elaborated). Specific feminist criticisms have focused on the nature of the model. The theory is dominated by a male, Eurocentric perspective, with emphasis on the emergence of the individual and the task of achieving "autonomy." Feminists claim that, in Erikson's theory, the male is seen as the model of normal development; that is, his theory emphasizes separation and autonomy, whereas females need to be connected and to be able to develop and maintain relationships (Wastell, 1996).

In Gender Perspectives 4.1, Saucier (2004) discussed the issues related to aging that are becoming more evident in Western culture as the baby boomers reach middle age and beyond.

Adult developmental stages basically can be divided into three arbitrary age ranges: early, middle, and late. The early adult age range is 20 to 40 years. During these years, early adults

GENDER PERSPECTIVES 4.1

Midlife and Beyond: Issues for Aging Women

Saucier looks at issues confronted by aging women, particularly those related to ageism and body image, emphasizing society's role in influencing women's perceptions of their bodies. Issues include unattainable beauty (e.g., the ideal female body represents the thinnest 5% of women), the influence of the media, and declining self-concept about one's body.

Saucier offered several implications for counseling professionals. First, the impact of ageism should be explored, and issues that could be affected by this cultural bias should be discussed: Saucier suggests assertiveness training and creating a more positive attitude toward aging. Second, women need help in acknowledging changes in their physical appearance and in dealing with emotions associated with these changes: Saucier suggests congnitive-behavioral approaches and also help for women to understand that there is nothing inherently pathological and irrational about wanting to

achieve a culturally valued appearance. Third, the influence of the media takes a toll on women: Saucier suggests encouraging women to view the media with a more critical eye and to view the marketing schemes emphasizing youth and beauty as hype. Also, she suggests feminist therapy can be beneficial in dealing with the media because it encourages the expression of anger toward injustices and teaches assertiveness.

In summary, Saucier maintains that the issues confronting aging women are influenced by many factors, most of which are societal. The implication seems to be that because women are held to higher standards of physical attractiveness throughtout their lives, they are more negatively influenced by ageism and the aging process.

Source: "Midlife and beyond: Issues for aging women." by M. G. Saucier, 2004, *Journal of Counseling and Development, 82,* pp. 420–425.

make decisions regarding marriage and careers that will affect the rest of their lives. The middle age range is approximately 40 to 65 years. (The late age range arbitrarily begins at age 65; it is discussed in the next section.) Middle age brings with it an aging physical appearance, development of a distinct adult intelligence, and changes in personality. Although the transition from early adult to middle age may go virtually unnoticed, counselors can still benefit from determining the stage at which clients think they are. Transitions are culture based, which means that middle age in one culture may not coincide with the previously suggested age range of 40 to 65 that is often considered appropriate for the Western world (Papalia et al., 2001).

It is essential that readers realize that developmental tasks may differ among cultures, genders, disabilities, and sexual orientations. A developmental task in one culture might appear earlier or later, or possibly not at all, in another culture.

Gender Differences

Table 4.5 looks at several selected gender differences among adult women and men. As mentioned in other sections in this chapter, readers should avoid gender stereotyping. The only accurate and reliable way to determine specific gender characteristics is to gain firsthand knowledge about individual clients.

Table 4.5

Selected Gender Differences in Adults

Source: Developed from *Development through the lifespan* (2nd ed.), by L. E. Berk, 2004, Boston: Allyn and Bacon; *Human development* (8th ed.), by D. E. Papalia, S. W. Olds, and R. D. Feldman, 2004, Boston: McGraw-Hill; *Human development: A life-span approach*, by F. P. Rice, 2001, Upper Saddle River, NJ: Prentice-Hall.

- About 13% of men and 3% of women are heavy drinkers. About one-third of heavy drinkers are alcoholics.

- The number of single adults (individuals not living with an intimate partner) has risen six-fold since 1970—to 29% in never-married males and 21% in similar females.

- Disability due to arthritis affects 45% of men over age 65; in women, the number is higher—50% of those ages 65 to 75 and 60% of those over age 75.

- Men and women experience reproductive health problems; in other health areas, men experience more lung cancer (although this cancer is increasing in women), and women experience more eating disorders, rheumatoid arthritis, and osteoporosis.

- Women tend to have higher life expectancies than men and lower death rates throughout life.

Concerns and Tasks of Adulthood

Adults, perhaps unknowingly, experience several concerns and tasks during the adult years. Challenges may include growing older, developing adult identities, forming positive self-esteem, and progressing through the stages of moral development. These are all affected by adults' cultural backgrounds, their opinions of their cultural heritages, and their acculturative stress. People of all cultures may experience problems associated with poverty, alcoholism, drug use, and violence. Concerns and tasks undoubtedly reflect the stage of adulthood (between early adult and middle-aged adult). Other differences in developmental concerns and tasks occur among clients of differing sexual orientations. The counselor's challenge is to understand problems from the adult's perspective and to plan intervention that reflects both the client's lifespan stage and culture.

Havighurst (1972) compiled a list of developmental tasks that he maintained were age-level appropriate for both early and middle adulthood. Success or failure in these tasks determined future happiness or unhappiness. Tasks during early adulthood include selecting a mate, learning to live with a partner, starting a family, rearing children, managing a home, and getting started in an occupation. Tasks during middle adulthood include assisting teenage children to become responsible adults, assuming social and civic responsibility, performing satisfactorily in one's chosen occupation, developing leisure activities, relating to one's spouse as an individual, accepting the physiological changes of middle age, and adjusting to aging parents.

In recognizing the role of cultural and socioeconomic factors in mastering these developmental tasks, Havighurst (1972) acknowledges that they are extremely important. A person in one culture might be encouraged to seek financial independence; in another culture, financial dependence might be the norm. Whereas a successful middle-aged European American might be established and performing satisfactorily in an occupation, the unemployed middle-aged African American, American Indian, or Hispanic American with few marketable skills might still be seeking gainful employment. Similarly, socioeconomic differences affect one's leisure activities, degree of social and civic responsibility, and ability to manage a home. Although Havighurst's developmental theories undoubtedly contribute to our knowledge of adults, many questions still remain as to the complex interaction of development, culture, and socio-economic class in a nation of increasing diversity.

Developmental changes during the substages of the adult period are as distinctive as the previously discussed child and adolescent developmental changes; hence, the need for specific counseling strategies planned for early, middle, and late adulthood. Intervening with adults of various cultures requires an understanding of the physical and psychosocial effects of aging, the different tasks and crises among cultures, and the complex relationship between an individual's development and culture.

Stress and Stress-Related Illnesses

The more stressful the changes that occur in a person's life, the greater the likelihood of illness within the next year or two. Change, even positive change, can be stressful, and some people react to stress by becoming ill. In addition, there are different types of stressors or stressful experiences. Hassles of everyday living are associated with minor physical ills such as colds and may have a stronger effect on mental health than major life events or transitions. Stress is currently being examined as a factor in such diseases as hypertension, heart disease, stroke, peptic ulcers, and cancer. The most frequently reported symptoms of stress include headache, stomachache, muscle pain or tension, and fatigue. The most common psychological symptoms include nervousness, anxiety, tension, anger, irritability, and depression (Papalia et al., 2001).

Lovejoy (2001) compares body image disturbance and eating disorders among African American and White women to determine major ethnic differences in these areas. In her feminist sociological analysis, Lovejoy offers three arguments for the differences among African American and White women: (1) African American women may develop a strong positive self-valuation and an alternative beauty aesthetic to resist societal stigmatization; (2) African American women may be less likely to acquire eating disorders due to differences in the cultural construction of femininity in Black communities; and (3) positive body image among African American women may sometimes reflect a defensive need to deny health problems such as compulsive eating and obesity.

Several societal factors have the potential for contributing to stress and stress-related illnesses. Racism, prejudice, discrimination, and the threat of hate crimes can all act as stressors. Minorities, regardless of their cultural and ethnic backgrounds, can experience stress in housing or work situations where the majority culture (whatever it might be) fails to treat them fairly and equitably. Also, the lack of English-language proficiency and the accompanying problems can result in stress.

Counselors who identify a client's problem as stress or stress-related should look for the actual stressor and, whenever possible, assist the client in reducing the stressful experiences. Still, counselors should not automatically assume that a client's stress is a result of racism, prejudice, and discrimination.

Early Adulthood and Middle Adulthood

Adult concerns differ with each substage (early, middle, late) and with culture and socioeconomic status. Concerns associated with specific cultures might include (being careful to avoid basing counseling on stereotypes) high unemployment rates among African Americans, Hispanic

Americans, and American Indians; alcoholism among American Indians; acculturation (and attendant rejection of old-world values) of Asian Americans; the portrayal of African American males as violent and prone to drug use; and the emerging role of African American women as family heads.

Racial Identity and Self-Esteem

How adults develop and perceive their racial identity will affect their mental health and overall outlook on life. Developing a positive racial identity can be difficult in U.S. society because of racism, sexism, classism, and heterosexism. The identity development process, initiated during the childhood years, requires each individual to build a sense of self: personal and cultural beliefs, feelings about the self and culture, and perceptions about his or her "place" in the overall U.S. society. A close relationship exists between racial identity and self-esteem: Both are intertwined and affect each other. How one feels about one's culture undoubtedly affects feelings about one-self and vice versa.

The Elderly

America's population is undeniably growing older. People are increasingly living longer. Since 1900, the percentage of people over age 65 has grown from 4% to 13%; by the year 2030, 20% of the U.S. population will likely be in that group. The elderly population itself is also aging. Its fastest growing segment consists of people 85 and older, and by 2030 their number could more than double. Census estimates reveal that the number of people living past their 100th birthday nearly doubled during the 1990s to more than 70,000. Figure 4.2 shows how the 50+ population will increase during the next 20 years.

Ethnic diversity is also increasing among the elderly, as in other age groups. By 2030, 25% of older Americans will be members of a minority group. The proportion of older Hispanic Americans is likely to more than triple from 5.1% to 17.4% by 2030, exceeding the older African American population (Papalia et al., 2001).

The "graying" of the population can be attributed to several factors, primarily high birthrates, high immigration rates during the early to mid-twentieth century, better medical care, and healthier lifestyles. At the same time, the trend toward smaller families has reduced the relative size of younger age groups (Papalia et al., 2004).

Elderly Years: Historical and Contemporary Perspectives

What does it mean to be elderly in a culture that emphasizes youth? What does it mean to be an elderly minority person in such a culture? Chronological age alone is a poor measure of physical condition or aging (Rice, 2001), especially because elderly people are so diverse in terms of physical, psychosocial, and cognitive abilities.

Although views of aging differ within cultures and with individual people, indications are that the European culture favors youthfulness. The elderly are often perceived as incapable of

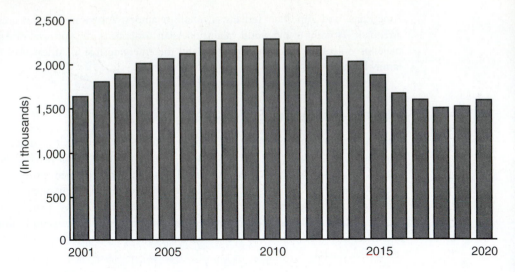

Figure 4.2
Annual increase in the 50+ population by 2001–2020. This population will increase
by 40 million in the next 20 years
Source: © 2001 AARP, Beyond 50, A Report to the Nation on Economic Security

thinking clearly, of learning new things, of enjoying sex, of contributing to the community, and of holding responsible jobs. The elderly in many other cultures, however, do not suffer such negative attitudes. For example, in the Chinese and Japanese cultures, the elderly are accorded a higher status than their American counterparts. Papalia and colleagues (2001) reported that although it is considered rude in most Western countries to ask a person's age, people are often asked their age in other countries (e.g., Japan), so that they can be accorded greater respect and proper deference.

In the United States, aging is generally seen as undesirable. Even today, older people often are categorized in derogatory terms such as "fading fast," "over the hill," "out to pasture," "geezer," and "biddy." Other terms are kinder (e.g., "older Americans," "golden-agers," "senior citizens"), but we seem to be somewhat baffled as to how to describe the elderly, especially those from various cultures.

Stereotypes about elderly people reflect widespread misconceptions: that older people are usually tired, poorly coordinated, and prone to infections and accidents; that most of them live in institutions; that they can neither remember nor learn; that they have no interest in sexual activity; that they are isolated from others; that they do not use their time productively; and that they are grouchy and self-pitying (Papalia et al., 2001).

Myths and stereotypes surrounding the elderly have long cast them in an undesirable light. They are often misunderstood, neglected, and abused. Undoubtedly, the elderly client may present difficult problems for the counselor: Planning appropriate intervention requires an understanding of the declining capacity of the body to function properly and the health problems and concerns that often plague the elderly of differing cultural backgrounds.

A FOCUS ON RESEARCH 4.2

Gay, Lesbian, and Bisexual Elders: Needs and Concerns

Orel (2004) maintains that the gay, lesbian, and bisexual senior population is growing, yet there has been little attention given to identifying and understanding the needs of this population. She reports on the results of a series of focus groups and in-depth interviews with GLB elders. The beliefs, attitudes, and opinions from participants revealed seven major areas of concern: physical health, legal rights, housing, spirituality, family, mental health, and social networks. While the numbers of gay, lesbian, and bisexual elders will likely increase during the next few decades, obtaining accurate population numbers is difficult, since sexual orientation as a research variable has been absent in almost all gerontological research. Also, the pervasive homophobic attitudes of society have discouraged the GLB elder population from coming out. Implicaions of the research include

1. The research suggests that a needs assessment information instrument is necessary to identify the prevalence of issues in the general community. This instrument can also evaluate the effectiveness of current programs and services.

2. The research suggests that GLB elders will benefit from programs and services that address their unique needs and concerns.

3. The research suggests that the aging network is more homophobic and heterosexist than the general health system because its attitudes and beliefs have gone unchallenged.

4. Professionals should become more politically involved in the complex arena of public policy and support legislation that benefits GLB elders.

Source: "Gay, lesbian, and bisexual elders: Expressed needs and concerns across focus groups," by N. A. Orel, 2004, *Journal of Gerontological Social Work, 43*(2/3), pp. 57–77.

The last several decades have witnessed a new interest in the elderly years, with more attention focused on minority elderly. Gerontology (the study of aging) has come into its own, and there is increasing awareness that the reality of being elderly differs across cultures. These enhanced perspectives will help to shed light on the particular needs of people in this lifespan period and to clear up some of the misconceptions surrounding it.

In A Focus on Research 4.2, Orel looks at the concerns and needs of gay, lesbian, and bisexual elders.

Elderly Development

Changes in physical appearance, such as graying hair, balding, and wrinkling skin, usually indicate advancing age; however, many other less visible changes occur as people age. Understanding the elderly requires conscientious effort, because various cultures perceive and treat the elderly differently. See Table 4.2 for physical, psychosocial, and cognitive development changes that occur as people grow older.

Desselle and Proctor (2000) reported that one in nine people in the United States is affected by hearing loss. One in four adults aged 65 through 74 years is hearing impaired, and almost two in five adults aged 75 and older experience disabling hearing loss.

Although Desselle and Proctor (2000) wrote their article primarily for social workers, their conclusions and recommendations are also relevant for counselors. Hearing impairment is an "invisible disability" (p. 277), and these authors want social workers to be aware that sounds amplified by hearing aids may be fuzzy, unclear, and confusing. In addition, hearing aids amplify background noises and jumble sounds the user is trying to hear.

Desselle and Proctor (2000) offer several practice interventions for improving communication with hearing-impaired clients:

- Face the person, maintain eye contact, speak slowly, pause between words, and enunciate each word clearly.
- Speak in a louder tone, but do not shout or yell (which can embarrass these clients).
- Never speak directly into the person's ear; to do so will eliminate visual cues.
- After finishing a thought, check with the person to determine whether he or she understands what was said.
- If the client is having trouble understanding a phrase, try rephrasing it.
- Be an advocate. If someone is ignoring the hearing-impaired person, explain that the hearing-impaired person is interested in what is being said.
- Be patient and treat the client with respect.
- Help these clients accept the natural consequences of hearing impairment by teaching them to be assertive and to cultivate a sense of humor about inevitable conversation errors.
- Get the client's attention before beginning to speak.

Gender Differences

Gender differences exist among the elderly, just as they do among individuals in the other three lifespan stages (Table 4.6). Some characteristics are gender-specific (such as reproductive system problems), whereas others such as sleeping difficulties, sexual relations, and suicide vary among individuals. Therefore, when counseling elderly women and men, awareness of selected gender characteristics can be worthwhile, but it does not eliminate the need to assess women and men as individuals.

Health Problems and Concerns of the Elderly

There are common misperceptions about the health status of the elderly. Most people over age 65 do not have to limit any significant activities for health reasons, and not until age 85 do more than half of the elderly population report such limitations. Even those aged 85 and older are usually able to take care of their own basic needs. Thus, the stereotype of the elderly as helpless is not based on reality (Papalia et al., 2001). This is not meant to imply, however, that the health problems of the elderly do not warrant special attention.

A Focus On Research 4.3 looks at traumatic experiences, emotional support, and life satisfaction among older adults.

Table 4.6

Selected Gender Differences in the Elderly

Source: Developed from *Development through the lifespan* (2nd ed.), by L. E. Berk, 2004, Boston: Allyn and Bacon; *Human development* (8th ed.), by D. E. Papalia, S. W. Olds, and R. D. Feldman, 2004, Boston: McGraw-Hill; *Human development: A life-span approach*, by F. P. Rice, 2001, Upper Saddle River, NJ: Prentice-Hall.

- Men and women have varying sleeping difficulties, a trend that starts earlier for men than women; until age 70 or 80, men experience more sleep disturbances than women, probably due to enlargement of the prostate gland (causing more frequent urination) and sleep apnea, a condition where breathing stops for 10 seconds or longer.

- Nearly 50% of women aged 65 and older are widowed, compared with only 15% of men.

- Among unmarried people over 65, about 70% of men and 50% of women have sex occasionally.

- Women experience a greater dissatisfaction when marital dissatisfaction exists—they usually try to confront marital problems in an attempt to solve them, which can be taxing to physical and mental health.

- Suicide rates peak during late life, climbing to their highest levels in people aged 75 years and older.

A FOCUS ON RESEARCH 4.3

Trauma, Support, and Satisfaction Among Older Adults

Krause examines the relationships among lifetime exposure to traumatic events, emotional support, and life satisfaction in older adults. He divided his subjects into three groups: the old-old (65–74 years old), the older-old (75–84 years old), and the oldest-old (85 years and older). Examples of traumatic events include a spouse or child dying, a child given up shortly after birth, life-threatening illness or accident, or a near-fatal accident. Life satisfaction includes statements of one's opinion of her or his life. Emotional support includes the support one has been given within the past year.

The findings underscore the needs to develop interventions that help older people deal more effectively with lifetime trauma. Specifically, results include

1. Greater exposure to trauma is associated with lower levels of life satisfaction.

2. Deleterious effects of lifetime trauma appear to be reduced for older adults who receive strong

emotional support from their family members and close friends.

3. Trauma and emotional support do not affect all older people in the same way.

There are three ways in which the findings from the present study may be useful in specifying intervention strategies. First, the data suggests that older adults who have been exposed to lifetime trauma are at risk. Second, the findings reveal that those who do not have sufficient emotional support should be included in the intervention group, especially the oldest-old group. Third, when working with members of the oldest-old group, the results indicate that elders who encountered traumatic events between the ages of 18 and 64 appear to be the most vulnerable.

Source: "Lifetime trauma, emotional support, and life satisfaction among older adults," by N. Krause, 2004, *The Gerontologist, 44*(5), pp. 615–623.

The need to consider the cultural aspects of health is becoming increasingly clear. Keeping in mind individual differences, as well as differing environmental conditions, we can now summarize the health problems facing the elderly in several cultures.

African Americans.   African Americans have a number of risk factors:

- Almost one-third of the excessive mortality of middle-aged African Americans can be traced to six risk factors: high blood pressure, high cholesterol levels, obesity, diabetes, smoking, and alcohol intake.
- The death rate for middle-aged African Americans is nearly twice that for European Americans.
- Almost twice as many African Americans as European Americans ages 45 to 64 die of heart disease, close to one and a half times as many die of cancer, and more than three times as many die from stroke.
- About one in three African American adults has hypertension, compared with one in four European Americans; hypertension accounts for one in five deaths of African Americans, twice the number occurring in European Americans.
- African American women are at higher risk of hypertension and are more than likely to be overweight than European American Women. (Papalia et al., 2001).

Elder abuse also occurs among elderly African Americans, just as in all cultures. Elder abuse is a difficult term to define and depends on how physicians, social workers, lawyers, or other professionals choose to define it. It is often a catch-all term used to describe physical maltreatment, financial exploitation, neglect (by self or others), misuse of medication, violation of rights, and psychological abuse. Regardless of the definition and type, elderly African Americans are increasingly susceptible to abuse and deserve the attention of mental health professionals.

American Indians.   The average life expectancy for American Indians is only 65 years, eight years less than that of European Americans. The major health problems of elderly American Indians are tuberculosis, diabetes, liver and kidney disease, high blood pressure, pneumonia, and malnutrition. The majority of elderly American Indians rarely visit a physician, primarily because they often live in isolated areas and lack transportation. Other reasons relate to a long-standing reliance on ritual folk healing and a different cultural understanding of disease.

Asian Americans.   Hypertension, tuberculosis, and certain types of cancers are major health concerns of elderly Asians and Pacific Islanders. This population is less likely to use formal health care services, such as those reimbursed under Medicare, primarily because of cultural and language differences, a reliance on folk medicine, and a distrust of Western medicine.

European Americans.   The concerns of elderly European Americans include health problems and long-term illnesses and hospital care; fear of living alone; lack of financial means; inability to deal with medical professionals and social service workers; and increased medical bills. They also experience lack of physical mobility, terminal diseases, and often worry a great deal about health concerns and about paying for needed medical care.

Hispanic Americans.   Twenty-four percent of Hispanic Americans aged 65 and over live in poverty, which contributes to their health problems and overall poor living conditions. Also, Hispanics between the ages of 65 and 84 experience health problems greater than the general population. Primary health problems in this population include cardiovascular disease and diabetes (Berk, 2004).

Educational, occupational, and income advantages of Cuban Americans in early adulthood may translate into better overall health for them, compared with other Hispanics. The greater impoverishment of Puerto Ricans points to higher morbidity rates among this population compared with Cuban Americans and Mexican Americans. A larger proportion of older Cuban Americans and Puerto Ricans reported more illnesses than Mexican Americans. A significantly smaller proportion of Mexican Americans than Cubans and Puerto Ricans reported being hospitalized during the past 12 months (Berk, 2004).

Some other statistics include

- Central/South American men and Puerto Rican women are most likely to live alone.
- Central/South American women and Cuban men are most likely to live with family.
- Cuban women prefer living alone relative to living with family members.
- Older Central/South American men may have migrated as individual workers rather than as household heads and consequently have few kin available for coresidence.

A Point of Departure: Challenges Confronting Counselors

Counselors need to understand the insights that can be gained from understanding multicultural differences from a lifespan perspective. Counselors who work with clients at the four lifespan stages face several challenges that have potential for improving the counseling intervention and enhancing the client–counselor relationship, including

- understanding the historical and contemporary perspectives of each lifespan stage;
- understanding the importance of human growth and development in the counseling process;
- understanding that clients differ both within and across cultures; and
- understanding the complex relationship among counseling, culture, and human growth and development.

Summary

Counseling developmentally different clients from differing cultures requires knowledge of their cultural backgrounds as well as their physical, psychosocial, and intellectual characteristics. Although some human needs cross developmental levels and cultural boundaries, other concerns, problems, and tasks differ according to lifespan stage and cultural background. Understanding each client's individual needs and the complex relationship between culture, development, and counseling provides a solid framework for counseling intervention.

Suggested Readings

Barnes, P. W., & Lightsey, O. R. (2005). Perceived racist discrimination, coping, stress, and life satisfaction. *Journal of Mutilcultural Couseling and Development, 33*, 48–61. Barnes and Lightsey studied life satisfaction in African Americans and maintain that fostering problem solving and reducing avoidance may help to alleviate racism-related stress.

Lachman, M. E. (2004). Development in midlife. *Annual Review of Psychology, 55*, 305–332. Lachman maintains that the midlife period in the lifespan is characterized by a complex interplay of multiple roles.

Sanders, J. L., & Bradley, C. (2005). Multiple lens paradigm: Evaluating African American girls and their development. *Journal of Counseling and Development, 83*, 299–304. Sanders and Bradley look at African American girls' identities using gender, race, ethnicity, and social class.

Saucier, M. G. (2004). Midlife and Beyond: Issues for aging women. *Journal of Counseling and Development, 82*, 420–425. Saucier explains issues confronted by aging women, particularly those related to ageism and body image.

Scollon, C. N., Deiner, E., Oishi, S., Biswas-Diener, R. (2004). Emotions across cultures and methods. *Journal of Cross-Cultural Psychology, 35* (3), 304–326. These authors examined cultural differences among participants during a specific week—they found cultural differences for almost every measure investigated.

Watkins, K. J., & Baldo, T. D. (2004). The infertility experience: Biopsychosocial effects and suggestions for counselors. *Journal of Counseling and Development, 82* (4), 394–402. Using a case study, these authors provide an overview of infertility and its psychosocial and sociological effects.

Winter, A., & Daniluk, J. C. (2004). A gift from the heart: The experiences of women whose egg donations helped their sisters become mothers. *Journal of Counseling and Development, 82*, 483–495. Three women whose egg donations resulted in the birth of a child for their sisters discuss their donation motivations and decisions.

Understanding African American Clients

Questions to Be Explored

1. What are the childhood, adolescent, adult, and elderly years like in the African American culture?

2. What social and cultural, familial, and communication characteristics describe African Americans along the lifespan continuum?

3. What unique challenges face African Americans during the various lifespan stages?

4. How do selected African American women view marriage, motherhood, and mothering?

5. What unique challenges face counselors providing mental health services to African Americans in the four lifespan stages?

6. What sources of information are available for counselors intervening with African American children, adolescents, adults, and elders?

Overview

Counselors who work effectively with African American children, adolescents, adults, and elderly recognize the challenges associated with each lifespan stage as well as the rich diversity of African American culture. Providing appropriate counseling intervention for African American clients requires an understanding of each individual's culture, family, and communication, all of which interact in a complex fashion to create clients with unique needs. Effective counselors also recognize and gain an understanding of the decades of racism and discrimination that the African American people have experienced. This chapter examines African Americans in all stages of the lifespan continuum and explores counseling issues germane to these clients.

African Americans: Demographics

African Americans comprise one of the nation's largest ethnic minority groups. In fact, projected population numbers suggest that African Americans will total 40,454,00 by 2010 and (U.S. Census Bureau, 2004–2005). Figure 5.1 provides a population breakdown by age, sex, and race. one can readily see the African American population is young, and one can project significant birth rates in the next several decades.

Although significant number of African American live in metropolitan areas susch as New York, Detroit, Washington, D.C., New Orleans, Baltimore, Chicago, and Memphis, the majority of African Americans live in the South (55%), a similar proportion (18%) live in the Northeast and Midwest, and 9% live in the West. Selected states with significant numbers of African Americans include New York (3,425,000), Florida (2,703,000), Texas (2,555,000) Georgia (2,497,000), California (2,442,000), Illinois (1,920,000), and North Carolina (1,838,000) (U.S. Census Bureau, 2004). Figure 5.2 shows a more detailed look at the geographic regions in which African Americans reside. Figure 5.3 shows the percentages of African Americans and non-Hispanic Whites in metropolitan and nonmetropolitan.

While this section looks only at population numbers and regions of residences, other figures in this chapter focus on age of children, educational attainment, socioecomic factors (e.g., poverty rates), marital status, and family characteristics.

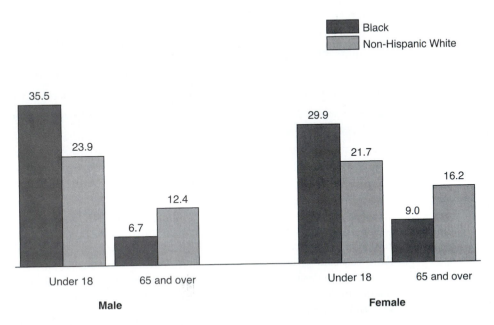

Figure 5.1
Population by Age, Sex, and Race: 2002 (Percent of population)
Source: From *Annual Demographic Supplement to the March 2002 Current Population Survey* by U.S. Census Bureau, 2002, Washington, D.C.: Author.

Figure 5.2
Region of Residence by Race:
2002 (Percent of population)

Source: From *Annual Demographic Supplement to the March 2002 Current Population Survey,* by U.S. Census Bureau, 2002, Washington, D.C.: Author.

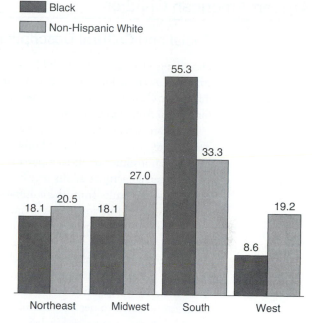

Figure 5.3
Metropolitan and Nonmetropolitan Residence by Race: 2002 (Percent of population)

Source: From *Annual Demographic Supplement to the March 2002 Current Population Survey,* by U.S. Census Bureau, 2002, Washington, D.C.: Author.

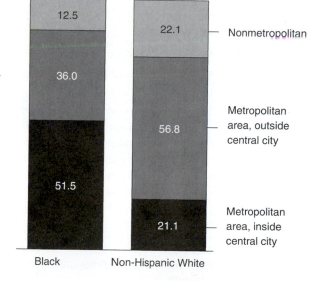

Mental health professionals practicing in metropolitan areas will increasingly work with significant numbers of African Americans; however, many African Americans continue to live in rural areas in the South and will need professional intervention for problems throughout their lifespan continuum.

African American Children

Social and Cultural Description

Describing African American children requires an understanding of the differences within their culture. Lower, middle, and higher socioeconomic groups live differently; likewise, significant differences characterize urban and rural African Americans. Table 5.1 shows population numbers for African American children.

African American children interact with two cultures on a daily basis: the African American culture of their home/neighborhood and the European American culture of schools and other social institutions. It is important for counselors to remember that the actions of other children and sometimes adults may cause feelings of inferiority in African American children. Such thinking results from the culturally deficient model in which people consider cultural differences to be inferior. African American children should be afforded the opportunity to grow up in a society in which unique characteristics are considered different rather than deficient.

Governmental social programs such as Head Start and Follow-Through have undoubtedly improved the lives of many African American children. Still, many African American children continue to live in poverty, just as do children of other cultures. In fact, 3,467,000 of African American children under 18 years of age live below the poverty level. Percentage of children living below the poverty level include

- under 5 years—36.7%;
- 5 years old—35.2%;
- 6–11 years—33.5%; and
- 12–17 years—29.4% (U.S. Census Bureau, 2004).

These numbers provide a bleak picture of the future of many children.

Self-concept may be the most influential factor in a child's development. African American children's self-concepts (i.e., what children think of themselves, their abilities, and their culture) influence not only academic achievement but also many other social and psychological aspects of their development. For example, African American children may tend to accept others' views, either negative or positive, of themselves and their culture. Racism and discrimination

Table 5.1
Population: African American Children

Source: From *Statistical Abstracts of the United States* (124th ed.), by U.S. Census Bureau, 2004–2005, Washington, D.C.: Author.

Age	Number
Under 5 years	2,998,000
5 to 14 years	6,463,000

undoubtedly have affected the African American community; however, increased pride in African American experience has resulted in considerable gains relative to African American self-concept. Other gains may be attributed to African American parents fostering positive self-concept development in their children.

Counselors and educators should also objectively consider the African American child's achievement (which is closely related to self-concept), rather than rely on traditional stereotypes of achievement expectations. Although some African American students lag behind European American students on standardized tests, there is considerable controversy about where the responsibility for lower academic performance lies. School officials often blame the child's "disadvantaged" or "culturally deprived" home. Some educators now call for effective schools where teachers have an objective understanding of African American children and similar expectations for these children as well as for children from other cultural backgrounds.

Communication

The degree to which African American children experience communication problems varies considerably with socioeconomic class, geographic location, and language of the parents. Children of educated and socially mobile urban African American parents may speak a different dialect than children of rural parents of a lower socioeconomic status.

African American children are likely to face several problems in a society that places emphasis on standard English, for the following reasons:

- Their dialect, albeit an excellent means of communication in the African American culture, might result in communication difficulties and other problems generally associated with not being understood by the majority culture.

- Their self-esteem might be lowered as they hear negative statements about their dialect and are urged to change to a more "standard" form of English.

- Children might not experience communication difficulties at home or in the neighborhood; however, problems may result when speech patterns vary considerably between home/neighborhood and school settings. Children's communication skills often determine their scores on intelligence and achievement tests or, perhaps more accurately, linguistic intelligence.

What directions should counselors take when working with African American children? Rather than imply that Black dialect is "wrong," "inferior," or "substandard," they should attempt to understand the role that dialect plays for people who have experienced a history of injustices and of struggle for survival. Counselors should not expect African American children to change their dialect during counseling sessions or to abandon it in all situations in favor of standard English; however, African American children and their educators should understand the frustrations and problems that might result from speaking differently among people who speak predominantly standard English.

Families

African American children grow up in homes that may be very different from European American homes. Two examples follow.

1.   African Americans rely extensively on family kinship networks, which include blood relatives and close friends called *kin*. Young African American children are often taken into the households of their grandparents. These arrangements reflect a sense of family responsibility; that is, children belong to an extended family, not merely to the parents. Consequently, uncles, aunts, cousins, and grandparents all exert considerable authority in the family and are responsible for the care and rearing of children and for teaching them appropriate skills and values. These strong kinship bonds probably originated from the African ethos of survival of the tribe and the oneness of being. Kinship care can be an important factor in an examination of African American families. A Focus on Research 5.1 looks at resilience among African American children.

A FOCUS ON RESEARCH 5.1
Resilience and African American Children

Kinship care is the full-time nurturing and protection of children by relatives subsequent to a legal parent–child separation. In most cases, these children have been removed from parents' homes because of neglect or abuse. African Americans represent the largest percentage of children in kinship care. These children encounter numerous challenges—they frequently contend with economic hardship and the stress associated with the estrangement from their birth parents. Johnson-Garner and Meyers studied 30 African American resilient and nonresilient children to examine why some succeed in their placements while others do not.

Their findings include the following.

- The most critical dynamic was family adaptability, or the ability to adjust to family roles in response to change—kinship givers with resilient children demonstrated a clear awareness of new family issues. The families acknowledged their newfound responsibilities.
- Virtually all kinship caregivers believed that the immediate family was close—they emphasized

themes such as loyalty and interdependence and also felt open communication promoted their sense of family cohesion.

- Caregivers of resilient children emphasized that they frequently relied on numerous extended family members for emotional comfort, financial assistance, advice, and help in meeting their care-taking responsibilities.

Directions for future research and clinical implications include using larger samples for the investigations of African American children; using more subjects (e.g., birth parents, teachers, and therapists); examining the impact of factors such as children's ages, developmental period, and developmental histories; and using qualitative approaches such as case studies.

Source: "What factors contribute to the resilience of African-American children under kinship care," by M. Y. Johnson-Garner, and S. A. Meyers, 2003, *Child & Youth Care Forum, 32*(5), pp. 255–269.

2.   Religion is another important aspect of African American life; however, there has been little research focused on the role of religion in the development of the African American child. More attention has been focused on religion with respect to the civil rights movement, economic leadership, and the quest for equal opportunities. It is clear, though, that children perceive the church as a hub of social life, the provider of a peer group, and a source of leadership in the community.

Islam and African American Families.   Raising children in an Islamic family in a non-Islamic society is a difficult task. Some African American Muslims enroll their children in public or private secular schools; others may home-school or educate their children in private Islamic schools. In the latter case, classes are separated by gender, and, along with their regular curriculum, Arabic and Qur'anic studies are taught. Muslim families place great emphasis on education, and studious, well-behaved children are prized (Mahmoud, 1996).

Muslim families who are too strict, punitive, or shaming in their parenting raise rebellious children, who will sometimes do the very things their parents forbid. These children also are subject to all the pressures that maturation brings and struggle to define their identity and the place that Islam has in their lives. Because of the restriction on dress, girls will often struggle with wearing a *hijab* in their adolescence unless they are in a supportive community. Some Muslim girls who go to secular high schools wear a *hijab*, but others choose not to because of the negative stereotypes about covering their hair. Dating is not allowed in Islam unless there is an intent to marry, so pressure from non-Muslim society to do so may cause difficulties for both sexes. Parents must work very hard to ensure that their children have a large enough peer group with whom to relate. Muslim women are not supposed to marry non-Muslim men, but Muslim men may marry outside their religion as long as their intended wife believes in the oneness of God (e.g., Christian, Jewish). Because the man is expected to be the spiritual leader in the home, a woman is thought to be vulnerable to oppression for her beliefs if she marries a non-Muslim (Mahmoud, 1996).

Unique Challenges Confronting African American Children

African American children growing up in a predominantly European American society, with an increasing Hispanic American population, face difficult problems that can impede their overall development into adulthood. These problems result from their culture being different from mainstream American culture and from years of discrimination and misunderstanding with respect to their culture and their developmental period. Communication barriers, lower academic achievement, and poor self-esteem are a few problems that confront these children. Thus, it is imperative that counselors and other professionals consider individual differences, rather than perpetuate stereotypical images of the African American child—not all African American children are struggling and problem-laden. Counselors need to take into account individuality among African American children and recognize that motivation and determination are powerful determinants of success, even in the face of hardship.

Up Close and Personal 5.1 describes Carl, an African American child.

UP CLOSE AND PERSONAL 5.1

Carl, an African American Child

Five-year-old Carl lives with his mother, father, grandmother, one older brother, and two older sisters in a lower middle-class neighborhood in a large city. Several aunts and uncles and six cousins live in the immediate neighborhood. William, his father, has completed 11 years of schooling and works in a local manufacturing plant. His mother, Cynthia, has had a similar formal education. She works as a hospital aide.

Carl spends a considerable amount of time with his grandmother. He considers his aunts and uncles to be "parents away from home." He visits them often and plays with his cousins and other children in the neighborhood. The closeness of the family has its advantages. When Carl is ill and unable to attend kindergarten, he stays home with his grandmother or at the homes of other relatives; hence, his parents do not have to miss work.

Carl's neighborhood is predominantly African American, although several Puerto Rican and Cuban families have recently rented houses in the area. Carl already realizes that people of different ethnic groups have different customs and lifestyles. He attends the neighborhood integrated school with a racial composition that is approximately 50% African American, 30% European American, and 20% Hispanic American. The teachers are predominantly middle-class African Americans. Although Carl tries in school, his readiness scores and performance on kindergarten objectives place him below average. His teacher assumes that his problems stem from a poor home environment and blames Carl and his parents for the difficulties. Carl's self-esteem is low; sometimes he blames himself for not doing as well as the other children. Although his dialect works well with his parents and in the neighborhood, it is not viewed favorably at school. Sometimes he does not understand his teacher or class materials. The teacher frequently corrects Carl's speech because, she says, students will need to use "correct English" when they enter the real world.

Carl is in a cross-cultural bind. Is one culture wrong and one right? Is his culture somehow inferior?

African American Adolescents

Social and Cultural Description

Census reports indicate that 6,229,000 African Americans aged 10 to 19 currently reside in the United States, and these numbers are expected to increase to 6,421,000 by the year 2010 (U.S. Census Bureau, 2000).

Identity development is a major task for all adolescents, but more so for racial and ethnic minorities given their often oppressive environments. Unfortunately, many African American youth have numerous obstacles to overcome, such as poverty, substandard housing, and inferior schools. In addition, their socialization and identity development occur in the context of racial discrimination and oppression, an environment that is not conducive to mental health. African American adolescents face overcoming the stigma of negative social stereotypes; too often they are portrayed as school dropouts, drug abusers, and lawbreakers. Negative stereotypes used to describe the African American culture and the adolescent lifespan period lower the self-esteem of these adolescents. It is imperative that counselors recognize the considerable individual

A FOCUS ON RESEARCH 5.2
Risk in Early Adolescent African American Youth

These authors examined the degree to which single- and multiple-risk profiles were evident in samples of African American early adolescents in low-income, inner-city, rural, and suburban schools. One study explored early adolescent risk status and later adjustment—youth who experienced a single risk in early adolescence had moderately increased levels of school dropout, criminal arrests, and teen parenthood. Another study examined the extent to which single- and multiple-risk profiles were evident in African American youth from low-income, inner-city and rural areas. Overall, more than 60% of African American youth in these two samples did not evidence risk for later adjustment problems.

Although the study yielded a wealth of interesting findings, several stood out as being important. First, the relationship between early adolescent profiles and later outcomes of risk status may be different for European American and African American youth. Second, African American youth tended to have higher rates of teenage parenthood and police arrests than their European American counterparts with the same risk status.

Source: "Exploring risk in early adolescent African American youth," by T. W. Farmer, L. N. Price, K. K. O'Neal, M. C. Leung, J. B. Goforth, B. D. Cairns, and L. E. Reese, *American Journal of Community Psychology, 33*(1), pp. 51—60.

differences among African American adolescents, rather than automatically stereotyping them. In A Focus on Research 5.2, the investigators sought to determine risk in early adolescent African American youth and reached some interesting comparisons with European American students of the same developmental period.

Many African American adolescents harbor an inclination to mistrust Whites, especially in the areas of education, training, business and work, interpersonal and social relations, and politics and law. This distrust, sometimes called cultural paranoia, has increased over the years. Cultural mistrust research has focused on the effects of counseling process, counseling outcomes, and educational and occupational expectations (Phelps, Taylor, & Gerard, 2001).

If counselors understand the African American culture, they will appreciate the predicament of many African American adolescents. These adolescents want to retain the cultural heritage with which they feel comfortable; however, they may also believe that some acculturation must take place for their economic and psychological survival. A balance must be struck whereby African American adolescents can retain their cultural heritage and at the same time achieve success in a pluralistic society.

Belgrave, Chase-Vaughn, and colleagues (2000) investigated the role of cultural factors in explaining the sexual attitudes among African American urban girls aged 10 to 13. They reported disturbing findings: African American teenagers comprise only 14% of the adolescent population yet they account for 29% of all teen births. Early sexual activity also increases the risk of sexually transmitted diseases, including HIV, as reflected in the continued increase of AIDS cases among young African American women. Early sexual activity also contributes to lowered academic success and limits vocational and career plans. Other problems include conflicts with the family, peer difficulties, lowered self-esteem, depression, and other emotional problems. The researchers maintained that antecedents of early sexual activity include contextual factors such as family and community, self-esteem and locus of control, peer and interpersonal relationships, and school interest and achievement.

Communication

Appreciation of one's own language and communication styles, along with the development of communication skills sufficient for understanding others and for being understood, significantly influences an adolescent's ability to adjust to societal expectations. Emphasis should be placed on understanding and accepting adolescents' valuing of their language and communication styles rather than on subscribing to a language-deficit belief in which some languages are judged to be "unworthy" and destined for extinction.

The dialect of African Americans, sometimes called Black English (or African American Language [AAL] or Ebonics), is used in varying degrees, depending on the individual person and the situation. Its widespread use among African Americans continues to arouse concern among people who do not understand the language, its background, and the African American culture. Although some of these concerns result from a lack of knowledge and appreciation of the language, some educators question whether the contrast between AAL and Standard English may result in severe consequences for African American students ("Ebonics Controversy," 1997).

The Ebonics controversy brought the African American language to the nation's attention when the Oakland, California, school board proposed applying for federal bilingual education funds to support its Ebonics program. The board's intention was to establish a climate where students who did not speak standard English would be nurtured and empowered to learn without being subject to debilitating, negative judgments based on their actual speech patterns. A month later, the board backed off from references to Ebonics being the primary language of African American students; however, its proposal still received national attention ("Ebonics Controversy," 1997).

Some people have sought to "change" the African American dialect. Some, no doubt with good intentions, have sought to teach standard English to African Americans. The African American dialect, however, persists as an integral aspect of the culture for several reasons. First, it provides a vehicle for expressing the uniqueness of the African American culture. Second, it binds African Americans together and traverses the barriers of education and social position.

Rather than perceive the Black dialect as wrong or substandard, the counselor should help these adolescents understand that Black English is a unique and valuable aspect of their culture. As they develop into adulthood and into an ever-widening social world, they must also be made to realize the implications of using a language that is not wholeheartedly accepted by the majority culture. During the crucial time of moving away from the safe confines of family and home, adolescents will benefit from speaking a language that is accepted and understood outside the predominantly African American community. Feeling and being understood in their own community but being rejected by the prevailing culture has the potential for damaging self-concept and retarding development.

Families

Counselors intervening with African American adolescents need to understand the African American family from a historical perspective rather than allow misconceptions and stereotypes to cloud their perceptions. Throughout centuries of cultural oppression and repression, the African American family has developed an appreciation for extended family networks. The family plays a crucial role in determining an adolescent's capacity and readiness to develop a sense of self and an identity.

Understanding African American family customs contributes to effective counseling intervention. Also, European American counselors and counselors from other cultures will benefit from an objective understanding of the adolescent developmental period. It should be recognized that not all African American adolescents experience role confusion. They are not all impoverished or uneducated. Nor do they all come from single-parent households. African American adolescents must be perceived in a more objective light.

Considerable concern has been expressed for adolescent identity formation, especially in African American households and in single-parent homes from which the father is absent. A disturbing number of African American families lives in poverty, and there is a growing trend of female-headed families and households.

Unique Challenges Confronting African American Adolescents

African American adolescents face several challenges that will significantly influence their identity development and transition into adulthood. First, they must accept the challenge of combating the racism and discrimination that have plagued their culture for decades. Second, they must reject stereotypes of their culture and developmental period. Acceptance of misperceptions and stereotypes precludes an objective examination of one's personal abilities and, without doubt, may retard the development of a cultural identity and a strong self-concept. Third, they must develop identities that embody the African American culture, adolescence, and their own individual abilities, skills, and characteristics. To do otherwise results in role confusion and a loss of potential.

African American adolescents are also challenged to understand the importance and necessity of education in their lives. Adolescents living in poor neighborhoods often perceive little reward from working for academic achievement and may underestimate their opportunities. Counselors can make significant contributions when they help these adolescents understand the benefits of education.

Even with these challenges, many African American preadolescent females demonstrate strength and resiliency. For example, Belgrave, Chase-Vaughn, Gray, Addison, and Cherry (2000) report that significant numbers of young African American females assume adult responsibilities early, have high self-esteem, have levels of independence, have lower levels of substance abuse, and have more positive body image than their White counterparts. Belgrave et al. (2000) concluded that positive feelings about oneself, one's culture, and one's ethnic group are linked to positive behaviors and decreases in risky behaviors.

Up Close and Personal 5.2 focuses on Tyrone, an African American adolescent.

UP CLOSE AND PERSONAL 5.2

Tyrone, an African American Adolescent

Tyrone, a 16-year-old African American, is in the ninth grade and lives with his parents, grandmother, younger brother, and two younger sisters. Because most of Tyrone's relatives also live in his lower middle-class neighborhood, he enjoys the extended family network. Tyrone feels free to visit his relatives in their homes, and they often spend time at his home. When Tyrone cannot attend school because of illness, he usually goes to the home of his adolescent cousins.

Tyrone has experienced several "identity crises." He has questioned his success in developing from childhood to adulthood, and he has also questioned the significance of being African American in a predominantly European American society. Although he has learned much about his cultural heritage and is proud to be African American, he also realizes that racism and discrimination will very likely limit his opportunities. Also, being an adolescent has not been easy. Even though his parents and siblings view him as "not yet grown," his peers think he is ready for adult activities. Should he listen to his family, or should he go along with his friends?

Another problem confronting Tyrone is his education. Quite frankly, he is not sure he will graduate from high school. His grades in elementary school were below average, but his grades are even lower now, and this is his second year in the ninth grade. He thinks he could do the work, but his recent academic record discourages him, and he admits to a changing world of many interests. He does not have many behavior problems in school (except perhaps talking with his friends too much at times), but he thinks his teachers are not too interested in him. Also, although he has both African American and European American teachers, he doubts whether any of them really understand what it is like being an African American adolescent in a large school. His parents talk with him often about the importance of education and encourage him to do his best work, but neither parent is able to help him much with homework.

Tyrone continues to speak his dialect. He communicates well with his parents, extended family, and friends. In fact, he is proud of his Black English even though his teachers do not like it. Language puzzles Tyrone. The European American teachers "don't sound right," he says. It appears, however, that he will have to be the one to change.

Although Tyrone has not confided in his friends, he has several concerns: What will he do if he cannot improve his grades? Because the teachers insist that he speak a more standard form of English, can he still maintain his cultural heritage? Will he be able to accommodate his parents' insistence on academic achievement, his own motivation, and the expectations of his peers? Sometimes Tyrone actually wishes that the adolescent years would end so that he could begin his adult life.

African American Adults

Social and Cultural Description

Describing the African American population is difficult because of its tremendous diversity. Differences resulting from social class, intracultural aspects, geographic location, educational attainment, and individuality contribute to the tremendous diversity of the African American people.

Although some economic improvements had been made during the prior several decades, African Americans continued to experience significant levels of poverty in 2002: 8,602,000

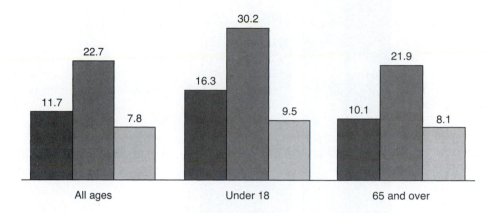

Figure 5.4
Poverty Rate by Age and Race: 2001 (Percent of population)
Source: From *Annual Demographic Supplement to the March 2002 Current Population Survey* by U.S. Census Bureau, 2002, Washington, D.C.: Author.

(24.1%) African American families lived below the poverty level (U.S. Census Bureau, 2004–2005). The roots of most African Americans can be traced to the rural South, where they were poorly prepared for urban living. Specifically, the education they received, the skills they learned, and the society in which they lived left them unable to cope well in an urban setting. Figure 5.4 shows poverty rates by age, race, and sex of African Americans. Figure 5.5 shows the civilian labor force participation rate and unemployment rate by sex and race. Last, Figure 5.6 shows family income by family type and race of householder.

These figures show the economic hardships being experienced by many African Americans—hardships that can lead to the need for counseling intervention.

The high incidence of health problems in African American males is so serious that their life expectancy is declining. Many African American males are at risk because of homicide, drug addiction, and AIDS. In 2002, an estimated 162,412 African Americans were infected with AIDS (U.S. Census Bureau, 2004–2005). Estimated life expectancy for African American males in 2005 was 69.9 years and was 76.8 years for females. For 2010, the life expectancy 70.9 for African American males and 77.8 years for females (U.S. Census Bureau, 2004–2005). Homicide is the leading cause of death in African American males. The prevalence of drug use and violence in the African American community has reduced the quantity and quality of African American life.

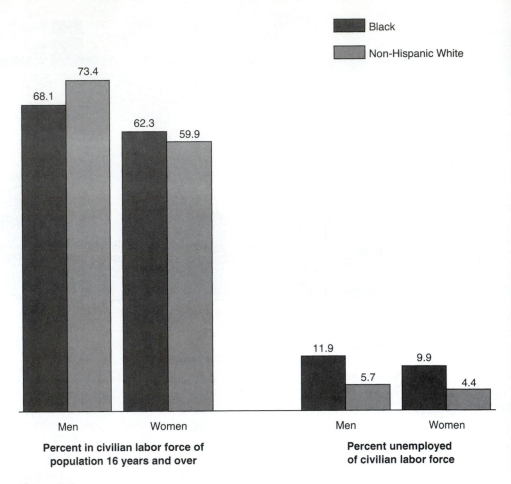

Figure 5.5
Civilian Labor Force Participation Rate and Unemployment Rate by Sex
and Race: 2002
Source: From *Annual Demographic Supplement to the March 2002 Current Population Survey*
by U.S. Census Bureau, 2002, Washington, D.C.: Author.

A related problem facing African Americans is health insurance coverage. In 2002, 6,683,000 (16.8%) of African Americans were not covered by health insurance (U.S. Census Bureau, 2004–2005). The cumulative effects of health disadvantages and the tendency to avoid medical visits until conditions are serious predispose African American adults to higher incidences of chronic disability and illness.

Mattis, Fontenot, Hatcher-Kay, Grayman, and Beale (2004) believe the research on African American religious life demonstrates that religion shapes the ways that members of this community view, understand, and respond to the world in which they live. Religion, both formal and individuals' private religious beliefs, as well as religious institutions and religious leaders have been shown to play key roles in shapint the way that people cope with adversity.

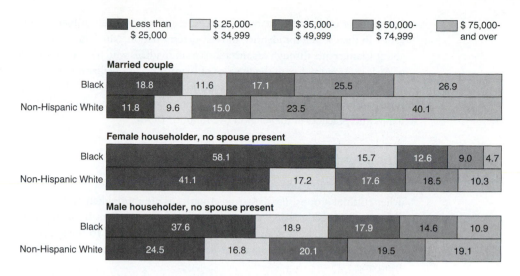

Figure 5.6

Family Income by Family Type and Race of Householder: 2001 (Percent distribution of families)

Source: From *Annual Demographic Supplement to the March 2002 Current Population Survey,* by U.S. Census Bureau, 2002, Washington, D.C.: Author.

McRae, Thompson, and Cooper (1999) maintain that the Black church, as an institution, has been a vital social, economic, and political resource for the African American community. Churches have had a longstanding tradition of actively addressing social needs, organizing educational initiatives, mobilizing economic support for Black businesses, promoting civil rights awareness, and providing a safe haven for the expression of the Black experience. As a social institution, the Black church serves as a significant support network for its congregation. Members experience fellowship, develop friendships, and assist each other in times of need. Churches are also an important support system for families, providing a sense of tradition, moral guidance, and services for parents, children, and the elderly. As a religious institution, the Black church provides spiritual and moral guidance. The church has also been shown to have a positive effect on the health and well-being of its members. Counselors need to understand that the Black church provides a source of strength. Counselors need to be trained to understand the role and function of Black churches in the lives of its members. Counselors also need to understand the importance of religion and spirituality to many African Americans; in fact, the communalism of the Black church environment provides a sense of shared identity, values, and mutual support.

Some African Americans, either by choice or by necessity, have somewhat adopted the social and cultural patterns of the larger society in which they live. Significant cultural adaptation among middle- and upper-class African Americans often makes these groups barely distinguishable culturally from European Americans of comparable socioeconomic levels. Some evidence points to an overconforming to middle-class standards in religious observances, dress, sexual behavior, and child-rearing practices.

On the other hand, many African Americans have been influenced by Islam and Islamic values in their search for identity and self-determination. Much of what African Americans learn about Islam comes through organizations or individuals who have attempted to blend the culture of African Americans with the practice of Islam. This reconciliation of culture and religion is not an unusual occurrence in the Islamic world. Although the tenets of the religion do not change from culture to culture, usually each culture puts its distinct cultural stamp on the everyday habits and practices of the religion (Mahmoud, 1996).

Communication

Considerable differences are found in the speech patterns of African Americans and those of other cultural groups. First, African Americans are more likely to interject such comments as "all right," "make it plain," and "that all right" into conversations, whereas European Americans are more likely to sit quietly or perhaps smile or nod. To the speaker, the oral comments are perceived as signs of encouragement; African Americans do not consider them rude or annoying.

Although the subject is controversial, Black English has been considered a full-fledged linguistic system with the range of inherent variation of all languages. As a language, Black English is systematic and rule-governed in its syntax, phonology, and semantics. The major pronunciation differences between Black English and standard English include word variability, sound variability, contrast variability, and final consonants. Although some studies have shown that African Americans hold Black English in high regard, other studies indicate that African Americans prefer standard English. Black English has traditionally been viewed by the dominant culture as an inferior system of communication and its speakers as ignorant or lazy. However, some African Americans engage in code switching (using two or more linguistic varieties)—they speak one dialect or the other, depending on the communicational situation. Although code switching has been espoused as a goal for African Americans, it has not been universally accepted and has been subject to objections; some people consider it racist for African Americans to have to shoulder the entire burden for language and communication.

Still, people's communication styles and their culture often are inseparable. Although not all African Americans speak Black English, the linguistic elements of the language are believed to represent important markers of group identity and group solidarity. This idea holds that African Americans should feel positively about themselves because it is an important way to distinguish themselves from other groups. Still, negative stereotypes of Black English are often inconsistent with upwardly mobile individuals. To maintain cultural ties and at the same time advance in mainstream society, code switching or switching communication styles becomes the necessary and preferred mode of interaction. According to Koch, Gross, and Kolts (2001), African Americans should balance the need to identify with their own culture with the need to function effectively within the context of the larger dominant culture.

African Americans' nonverbal communication may play an important role in the counseling relationship. Effective counselors understand such communication and work toward correct interpretations. The directness of some African Americans during counseling may be considered offensive or hostile. For example, African Americans, especially males, may act overly confident and unconcerned, which may be a means of defense that limits disclosure, involvement, and revealing embarrassing or difficult issues.

Families

Several economic factors affect the African American family. First, Conger, Wallace, Sun, Simons, McLoyd, and Brody (2002) believe economic hardships positively relate to economic pressure in families. Economic pressure relates to emotional distress of caregivers, which in turn affects the caregiver relationship. Plus, families' economic difficulties have adverse affects on the cognitive, behavioral, emotional, and physical development of children and adolescents. Second, the effects of unemployment and underemployment on African American men and their families present a clear problem for the culture. One result of unemployment is family disruption, which increases homicide and robbery rates (Koch, Gross, & Kolts, 2001). Third, the high crime rates in urban African American communities appear to stem from the combination of unemployment, economic deprivation, and family disruption. Changes in the family include higher divorce rates, decreased marriage rates, increasing numbers of female-headed households, and increasing percentages of children living in single-parent households. In 2001, 58.1% of African American households were headed by a female householder (with no spouse present) earning less than $25,000 per year (U.S. Census Bureau, 2003). Also, women who had never married represented the largest number of females heading households. Another challenge to economic security: In 2002, 68.2 percent of African American births were to unmarried mothers (U.S. Census Bureau, 2003). Consequences of these situations become clear when one considers that most African American children in single-parent households also live in lower socioeconomic circumstances.

In A Focus on Research 5.3, Ross D. Parke, looks at development in the family. His article has implications for mental health professionls.

A FOCUS ON RESEARCH 5.3
Development in the Family

Parke, a noted authority on the family and family matters looks at development of the family and reviews some recent advances in our understanding African American families. Since his article is much too long to summarize here, interested readers are referred to the entire work.

Parke begins by looking at the theoretical perspective on the family and then focuses on family subsystems, such as parent–child, martial, and sibling subsystems. Next, he looks at the determinants of family socialization, such as child characteristics, personal resources, familial and social capital, and ethnicity and development in the family. Also interesting is his discussion of new directions in family research: employment and its impact of family socialization, gay and lesbian couples, the effects of new reproductive technologies on parenting, and parental incarceration and children. Without doubt, his comprehensive article is excellent and provides a wealth of information for counselors working with families or seeking to know the impact of families.

Source: "Development in the family," by R. D. Parke, 2004, *Annual Review of Psychology*, 55, pp. 365–400.

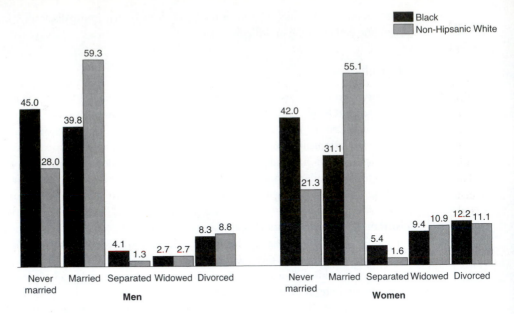

Figure 5.7
Marital Status by Sex and Race: 2002 (Percent of population 5 and over)
Source: From *Annual Demographic Supplement to the March 2002 Current Population Survey* by U.S. Census Bureau, 2002, Washington, D.C.: Author.

Figure 5.7 shows the marital status by sex and race of the African American population.

The increasing number of interracial marriages is another factor affecting African American families. Only 40 years ago, states still had the power to prohibit such marriages. Even after the U.S. Supreme Court declared such laws unconstitutional in 1967, social taboos against Blacks marrying Whites persisted. During the last decade or so, however, interracial marriages have risen dramatically.

Child-rearing techniques and practices in African American families differ from those of European American families. Parents in African American families are generally stricter and more authoritarian in the use of discipline than European American parents.

Counselors providing professional intervention for African American women should also understand that some take care of relatives with HIV/AIDS. Tolliver (2001) reported that approximately two-thirds of the total assistance given to people living with AIDS is provided by relatives. This situation is particularly salient for the African American community, which has been disproportionately affected by the AIDS epidemic. AIDS has a tremendous impact on the entire family system, particularly on the individual who is the primary caregiver.

Thomas (2004) maintains that the life experience of Black women have never fit neatly within the traditional boundaries created by the field of psychology since its emergence as an independent intellectual and academic discipline. In Gender Perspectives 5.1, she advances the psychology of Black women by offering some insightful points.

The Psychology of Black Woman

Thomas (2004) provides a critical analysis of the psychology of Black woman, discusses the relevant epistemologies and conceptual framework's that can inform such a perspective, and suggests a set of guiding principles for advancing theory and research on Black women within a historically and contextually relevant framework.

Thomas maintains that Black women bring uniqueness to psychology stemming from a historical legacy that continues to relegate them to membership in multiple oppressed groups. No other group has been victimized and dominated as Black women have been in American society.

Believing psychology has found itself in the paradoxical position of talking more about diversity and knowing less what to do about it, Thomas contends this has been made more difficult by a long-standing tradition of psychological theorizing and research that are products of deeply racialized and gender-stratified roots. In studying the lives of Black women in context, there remains an urgent need for psychologists to learn how to understand another's experience and to judge it by its own standards. Also, during the last few years, there has been a movement towards multicultural foundations of understanding people and their life perspectives.

Unique Challenges Confronting African American Adults

African Americans face several problems. As previously mentioned, dialect differences will present a continuous challenge. Although their distinctive dialect is a unique cultural characteristic, some African Americans are beginning to view it as a handicap to success in a society that demands the use of standard English. Second, African Americans must address the problem of their negative image. The stereotype of being violent may affect their economic opportunities and social progress. Third, their low socioeconomic status must also be addressed. Complicating these problems is the fact that many African Americans live in an environment in which social conditions are often detrimental to self-improvement.

McNair and Prather (2004) maintain African American women represent the fastest growing group of individuals infected with HIV in the United States. When the epidemic began, White gay men were most likely to be infected; however, by the early 1990s, women become the fastest growing group infected with HIV, having rates that continue to increase faster than those for the highest risk group, such as men who have sex with men and injection drug users. Developing and implementing strategies to provide support and hope may be the greatest challenge facing mental health professionals working with African American women with AIDS. With increased knowledge, sensitivity, and awareness of social risks confronting the lives of African American women, mental health providers can develop more effective programs.

Historically, suicide rates for European Americans have exceeded those of African American by a ratio of 2:1. These low rates for African American are attributable to misclassification of suicides for African Americans, underreporting due to the heightened stigma associated with suicidal behavior in this population, and the presence of a number of protective factors. Actually, the number of suicides among African Americans may be higher if the number of deaths misclassified as homicides or accidents were included. The rates of suicide in the African American

A FOCUS ON RESEARCH 5.4
Person Factors and Suicidal Behaviors

In their article, Kaslow, et al. (2004) maintain that only recently have investigators examined psychological factors associated with suicidal behavior in African Americans. Their discussion contends that strong group difference were found between attempters and nonattempters on all variable studied:

Psychological Distress: Compared with nonattempters, African American suicide attempters reported higher levels of psychological distress, depressive symptoms, and hopelessness and lower levels of hopefulness.

Aggression and Impulsivity: Compared with nonattempters, African American suicide attempters reported higher levels of physical aggression, anger, hostility, and impulsivity.

Substance Abuse: Compared with nonattempters, African American suicide attempters (especially men), reported higher levels of substance abuse.

Cognitive Processes: Compared with nonattempters, African American suicide attempters were more likely to use maladaptive coping strategies such as escape, avoidance, and depressive attributional styles and less likely to use adaptive strategies such as seeking social support, problem-solving, or positive reappraisal.

Spirituality and Religiosity: Compared with nonattempters, African American suicide attempters endorsed lower levels of religious involvement and spiritual well-being.

Ethnic Diversity: Compared with nonattempters, African American suicide attempters felt less connected and affirmed by their own ethnic group as well as more distant from other ethnic groups.

The findings have several implications for clinical practice. First, when assessing African Americans, one should query those with elevated levels of psychological distress, aggression, and substance use; maladaptive cognitive processes; and low levels of religiosity, spirituality, and ethnic identity regarding suicidal tendencies and history of suicidal behavior. Second, preventative interventions for suicidal African Americans and those at risk for suicidal behavior should target reducing psychological symptoms, increasing feelings of helpfulness, and reducing substance use via the teaching of effective strategies for the management of aggression.

Source: "Person factors associated with suicidal behavior among African American women and men," by N. J. Kaslow, A. W. Price, S. Wyckoff, M. B. Grall, A. Sherry, S. Young, L. Scholl, V. M. Upshaw, A. Rashid, E. B. Jackson, & K. Bethea, *Cultural Diversity and Ethnic Minority Psychology,* 10(1), pp. 5–22.

---

community, particularly among younger men, are on the rise. Also, across racial and ethnic lines, men are four times more likely than women to commit suicide (Kaslow, et al., 2004). A Focus on Research 5.4 looks at suicidal behavior among African American women and men.

Neal-Barnett and Crowther (2000) propose that the double minority status of gender and ethnicity places African American women at higher risk for anxiety. African American women often experience panic, phobias, obsessive–compulsive disorders, help-seeking, and victimization. They maintain that middle-class African American women are unlikely to seek help for anxiety-related problems but are likely to seek help when relationship problems or bereavement reach crisis proportions. Although middle-class African American women perceive panic and anxiety disorders as problematic, they do not perceive them as serious enough to warrant

UP CLOSE AND PERSONAL 5.3

Cynthia, an African American Woman

Cynthia, age 33, considers herself fairly fortunate. Her family consists of her husband, William; two sons, Tyrone and Carl; two daughters, Karen and Jennifer; and children's grandmother. William has not been laid off recently at the manufacturing plant, and she works as a hospital aide. Although Cynthia knows that William is worried about being laid off, she feels fairly secure about her job. Having William's mother in the home is another plus; she looks after the family when Cynthia is at work.

Cythia's life is not problem-free, however. Providing for four children is often difficult, especially when William is without work. Furthermore, her own lack of formal education and marketable skills is holding her down. She is also concerned about her lower middle-class neighborhood, which appears to be deteriorating in several areas. Drugs are becoming increasingly visible, the police are being called more frequently, delinquency and vandalism are more rampant, and it is rumored that there are three cases of AIDS. Just the

other day, she thought she overheard Carl ask Tyrone whether he had smoked pot. Cynthia questions whether her children should be growing up in such an environment. She understands the temptations that 5-year-old Carl and 16-year-old Tyrone may experience. Also, she wonders about the safety of her family. She tends to be nonaggressive and has always been opposed to guns in the home. Recent neighborhood events, however, are making her more receptive to William's suggestion of buying a gun for protection. Also, although her two young daughters are not currently on the streets much, they are developing rapidly and will soon be leaving the safe confines of their home.

Cythia sometimes thinks of herself, too—her frustrations and accomplishments. Shouldn't life be more than just work and survival? Is this the way it will always be? Will Carl and Tyrone be around when she grows old? Will she still be healthy? Although Cynthia does not dwell on her concerns, she is somewhat apprehensive about the future.

professional help. It is also possible that a cultural mistrust of mental health providers prevents African American women from seeking counseling intervention.

Up Close and Personal 5.3 focuses on Cynthia, an African American adult.

African American Elderly

Social and Cultural Description

African Americans aged 65 and older number about 2.8 million people; about 390,000 people in this age demographic are aged 85 or older (U.S. Census Bureau, 2004–2005). The elderly are the fastest growing segment of the African American population. Approximately 20% of African American elderly live in nonmetropolitan areas and most are concentrated in the Southeast; only about 25% of their European American counterparts live there.

Three closely related factors influence the quality of life of the African American elderly: education, employment, and income. Many African American elderly who seek counseling were educated in U.S. school systems when access to equal education was severely limited; many African American elderly have no formal education. The employment rate is about equal for African American and European American elderly; however, income levels tend to be lower for elderly African Americans than for elderly European Americans. Lack of income is probably the most serious problem faced by aging African Americans in the United States. In fact, 718,000 African Americans aged 65 and over live in poverty (U.S. Census Bureau, 2004–2005). Elderly African American women are usually worse off financially than African American men and people of other cultural backgrounds.

Although housing costs consume a substantial portion of African Americans' incomes, the money spent does not contribute to their general life satisfaction. In addition, increasing rents and maintenance costs cause additional financial hardships for those with fixed incomes. Urban-dwelling elderly African Americans tend to be clustered in low-income areas in the central districts of cities, often in crowded apartments.

Elderly African Americans, especially those living in rural areas, experience serious health and social problems. Common health problems include high blood pressure, musculoskeletal disorders, and cancer. (In fact, cancer is a leading cause of mortality among elderly African Americans.) Yet, elderly African Americans, especially rural residents, often have limited access to health care.

Many elderly African Americans view themselves as sick and disabled and as being in poor health. There is a higher incidence of chronic disease, functional impairments, and risk factors, such as high blood pressure, in this group. African American men have the highest incidence of prostate cancer, and they tend to be hospitalized more frequently and for longer periods of time than European Americans.

Religion plays a major role in the lives of many elderly African Americans. Their pragmatic and family-oriented belief system enables them to cope with the stress of their daily lives.

A FOCUS ON RESEARCH 5.5

Life Experiences of African American Elders

In her excellent article, Shellman focuses attention on the themes (1) "Nobody Ever Asked Me Before," (2) "Stories of Discrimination," (3) "Coping with Discrimination," (4) "Hurt of Discrimination," and (5) "Self-Discoveries." The cumulative effect of poverty, racial segregation, neglect, and disregard experienced by African American elders throughout their lifetime have left their mark.

Interestingly, the theme called "Nobody Ever Asked Me Before," reveals that the elders had never been asked about their life experiences. The general feeling was that no one actually cared about what they had been through during their life. The theme, "Stories of Discrimination," reveals some painful times of discrimination at school, health care, Army life, and work. "Coping with Discrimination," the third theme, includes how the mother had been a source of comfort,

family caring for family, home remedies (for medical conditions), strength of faith, and coming North. The fourth theme, "The Hurt of Discrimination," includes topics such as life regrets, being abused, and feeling different. The last theme, "Self-Discoveries," notes that the interviews created opportunities for the elders to discover something positive about themselves and that some felt good that they could overcome adversity.

Shellman's article provides valuable insight into the struggles faced by African American elders. Although many of the stories are disturbing and sad, they also give mental health professionals a clearer perspective on African American elders' life experiences.

Source: "'Nobody ever asked me before': Understanding life experiences of African American elders," by J. Shellman, 2004, *Journal of Transcultural Nursing, 15*(4), pp. 308–316.

Participation in church-related activities is valued early in life and continues to be important later in life. Historically, the church served as a frame of reference for African Americans coping with racial discrimination, and it continues to play a key role in their survival and advancement. The church has been one of the few institutions to remain under African American control and relatively free from the influence of the majority culture. The church often embraces many religions, including the traditional African American Protestant denominations, such as Baptist and Methodist, as well as other more fundamentalist groups. African American religious services tend to be celebrations; worshipers are inclined to be more demonstrative than worshipers in other cultures.

African American elders represents a quickly growing segment of the geriatric population. Population numbers of African American elders are expected to continue to increase, and, in fact, by the year 2030, they will be the highest number of minority elders in the United States (Shellman, 2004). A Focus on Research 5.5 looks at life experiences of African American elders.

Communication

The aging process takes its toll on the vocal mechanisms, just as it does on the rest of the body. Elderly African Americans' health problems extend to their language mechanisms. Age-related losses can be seen in at least two aspects of language production. The first is retrieving words from long-term memory. When conversing with others, elderly clients may have difficulty thinking of the correct words to convey their thoughts. Consequently, their speech contains a greater number of pronouns and other unclear references than it did at younger ages. They may also speak more slowly and pause more often, in part because they need time to search their memory for certain words. Second, the elderly need time to plan what to say and how to convey their thoughts. Consequently, their speech may contain more hesitations, false starts, word repetitions, and sentence fragments as they age (Berk, 2004).

The language used in church has relevance for elderly African Americans and for the congregation as a whole. The congregation responds to the minister with frequent "amens" or "right-ons" to offer encouragement and to indicate agreement. Dialectal differences in language on the part of minister and congregation have genuine meaning for African American elderly.

Families

Accurate perceptions of the role of elderly African Americans and their contributions to immediate and extended kinship networks contribute to counseling effectiveness. The African American family has long existed within a well-defined, close-knit system of relationships. Several underlying themes, such as respect for the elderly, strong kinship bonds, and pulling together in efforts to achieve common family goals, characterize African American family relationships. For example, family responsibility involves combining resources so all family members will feel economically and emotionally secure.

African American elderly occupy a unique position in the family that differs considerably from the position of European American elderly. In the African American family structure, the elderly are often regarded as immediate family members; hence, they are expected to care for the young. Elderly African American women in particular play an important role in this extended family network. African Americans often value elderly family members because they are important role models. For example, they are valued for their accumulation of wisdom, knowledge, and common sense about life; their ability to accomplish much with little; their ability to accept the reality of aging; and their sense of hope and optimism for a better future.

Living arrangements of elderly African Americans are important for counselors, especially marriage and family counselors, to comprehend. The majority of African American and European American men aged 65 and older are married, whereas the majority of women are widowed.

Unique Challenges Confronting the African American Elderly

Problems that pose challenges for elderly African Americans include the following:

- They are reluctant to participate in health-related activities because few health care providers and researchers are African Americans.

- Low annual income affects housing, nutrition, health care, and nearly all other aspects of their living standards.

- Widowed, separated, or divorced elderly African Americans who are not accepted into the extended kinship network must live alone and face potentially serious problems; not being a part of a traditional family unit is likely to be especially difficult for African Americans because they place such a high value on the kinship network.

UP CLOSE AND PERSONAL 5.4

Eloise, an Elderly African American

Eloise, better known as Miss Eloise to her younger friends and as Aunt Ellie to her grandchildren, is 74 years old. She moved in with her son William and his family after her husband died. Eloise has worked hard all her life, usually at low-paying jobs with no retirement plans. She lives primarily off her Social Security payments, which allow for necessities. Although she cannot contribute financially to William's household, Eloise does take care of the children and helps his wife, Cynthia, with light housecleaning. She also makes a few extra dollars caring for several children for a neighbor who works. She often cares for nieces and nephews, too, but free of charge because they are family. Eloise enjoys living with her son and his family. It has proved to be a mutually satisfying relationship, and it means a lot to her.

Eloise's problems are common to many elderly African Americans. If she did not have a home with William and Cynthia, she would barely be able to afford a place of her own. Although her health is still fairly good, she worries about falling ill, especially because so many of her friends are in poor health or have died. Another worry, the increasing incidence of crime in the neighborhood, is one she shares with William. When she grew up, times were difficult for African Americans, but the problems that her grandchildren must face—drugs and AIDS—were not a concern back then.

Eloise has always gone to church and she continues to attend. Her religion has seen her through some difficult times and is still a source of strength for her. William and the family also give her strength. Because of them, she has avoided serious financial woes, loneliness, and the fear of growing old alone. In fact, Eloise may be luckier than most other elderly people; she enjoys good health, she has her family by her, and she feels needed.

- They experience more frequent and longer hospitalization stays than the elderly of other cultures; health problems, or the fear of health problems, may require counseling intervention.

- They may experience discrimination and unequal treatment on two counts: age and minority status.

Up Close and Personal 5.4 features Eloise, an elderly African American.

In summary, elderly African Americans are better off now that their culture and age-group are receiving increased attention. However, there are still hurdles to overcome in the areas of equal housing, equal access to medical care, and equal opportunities in education and employment.

A Point of Departure: Challenges Confronting Counselors of African Americans

Counselors who intervene with African American children, adolescents, adults, and elderly will have several difficult, but not insurmountable, challenges; for example:

- understanding both historical and contemporary perspectives of the African American culture and its people;

- understanding the challenges that African Americans commonly experience during each lifespan stage;

- understanding changing African American family structures and how these changes can affect marriage, child-rearing, and gender perceptions;

- recognizing and responding appropriately to the dilemma surrounding use of Black English and standard English; and

- understanding intracultural, geographic, socioeconomic, and other differences that contribute to "individuality."

Summary

Understanding African American people and the challenges commonly associated with respective lifespan periods is prerequisite to acquiring the knowledge, attitudes, and skills necessary for counseling African American children, adolescents, adults, and elderly. In addition, counselors of African Americans will need to understand issues of particular interest to women.

Providing effective mental health intervention to such a diverse group (especially considering both cultural and lifespan differences) is not an easy task; it requires counselors who have developed appropriate counseling skills and who have the motivation and determination to provide effective, sensitive professional counseling intervention.

Suggested Readings

Brook, J. S., Adams, R. E., Balka, E. B., Whiteman, M., Zhang, C., & Sugerman, R. (2004). Illicit drug use and risky behavior among African American and Puerto Rican urban adolescents: The longitudinal links. *Journal of Genetic Psychology, 165*(2), 203–221. In this useful article by mental health counselors, the authors look at the relationship between illicit drug use and later risky sexual activity.

Farmer, T. W., Estell, D. B., Bishop, J. L., O'Neal, K. K., & Cairns, B. (2003). Rejected bullies or popular leaders? The social relations of aggressive subtypes of rural African American early adolescents. *Developmental Psychology, 39*(6), 993–1004. These authors use teacher assessments of interpersonal characteristics that were used to identify rural African American early adolescents who had lower levels of social prominence and social skills.

Li, H., Edwards, D., & Morrow-Howell, N. (2004). Informal caregiving networks and use of formal services by inner-city African American elderly with dementia. *Families in Society: The Journal of Contemporary Human Services, 85*(1), 55–63. These authors maintain that caregiving networks are the primary source of support for elderly African American persons with Alzheimer's disease.

Patterson, K. L (2004). A longitudinal study of African American women and the maintenance of a healthy self-esteem. *Journal of Black Psychology, 30*(3), 307–328. Patterson examines that self-esteem of African American women over a 14-year period. Although historical analysis of self-esteem predicted low self-esteem, the women had maintained a high self-esteem because of social networks and achievement outcomes.

Powers, K. (2005). Promoting school achivement among American Indian students throughout the school years. *Chidhood Education, 81*(6), 338–342. Powers describes a research project that focused on urban American Indian youth—her project directed attention to student achievement motivation, teacher expectations, family involvement, and safe and drug-free schools.

Steinman, K. J., & Zimmerman, M. A. (2004). Religious activity and risk behavior among African American adolescents: Concurrent and developmental effects. *American Journal of Community Psychology, 33*(3–4), 151–162. Examining the relationship of religious activity and risk behaviors among African American adolescents, Steinman and Zimmerman found higher levels of religious activity predicted smaller increase in marijuana use; and larger decreases in religious activity predicted increased alcohol use among males and sexual intercourse among females.

Counseling African American Clients

Questions to Be Explored

1. What unique challenges and differences can counselors expect when intervening with African American children, adolescents, adults, and elderly?

2. How can counselors, especially those from differing cultural backgrounds, effectively plan counseling intervention for African American clients, considering African Americans' many geographic, socioeconomic, and individual differences?

3. How can counselors assist in lessening the effects of racism and discrimination that have long affected African Americans?

4. How can counselors accommodate for African Americans' differences when selecting individual, group, or family therapy?

5. What concerns and problems related to development might African American clients at different lifespan stages present to counselors?

6. How can counselors of differing cultural backgrounds and lifespan stages intervene with African Americans of other lifespan stages?

7. What additional resources are available for professionals intervening with African American clients?

Overview

As a cultural group, African Americans have been victims of discrimination and racism for many years. In general, African Americans have higher unemployment rates; lower economic status and, in some cases, poverty; more drug abuse problems; overall poorer health; lower life expectancy, and higher infant mortality rates than other U.S. groups. Also, as with other cultural groups, African American clients will have problems that are unique to specific developmental stages. For example, this chapter looks at biracial children; counselor–parent collaboration, empowerment groups, and challenges facing the elderly. At the outset, it is important to note that considerable geographic, socioeconomic, and individual differences exist among African Americans, and therefore all clients should be considered individually.

African American Children

Potential Problems Warranting Counseling Intervention

Problems that African American children may experience include

- failure to develop a strong African American identity and self-esteem;
- adverse effects of stereotypes, prejudices, and injustices against African American children and the childhood years in general;
- adverse effects of inappropriate value judgments based on differences;
- academic problems because of either the children's lack of educational experiences or the school's inability to build on such experiences;
- inability to overcome society's perception of African American children as "behavior problems";
- language problems and different nonverbal communication styles;
- different home life and cultural concept of "family";
- physical, psychosocial, and intellectual differences;
- health and nutritional problems associated with low-income families;
- increasing desire to move from a parent-centered world to a peer-centered world; and
- failure to attain competence in developmental tasks such as getting along with peers (from the same culture and other cultures) and in learning appropriate masculine or feminine social roles.

Counseling Considerations

Counselors intervening with African American children are often at a loss in choosing appropriate strategies. Before making counseling decisions involving these children, professionals should assess their abilities and personal biases objectively. Often, African American children are assessed by instruments that were designed primarily for European Americans, which could result in a culturally biased picture. If the counseling professional views a child in an unfavorable light, the child's self-perception may be affected.

Examples of tests that are designed specifically for African American children or are appropriate for them include

- *The Black Intelligence Test of Cultural Homogeneity*—a test to identify early indicators of intelligence in Black children. Included are items on Black American folklore, history, life experiences, and dialect.
- *Themes of Black Awareness (TOBA)*—a 40-item sentence-completion instrument that elicits thematic material relative to an individual's level of Black awareness.
- *Themes Concerning Black (TCB)*—an instrument to measure various aspects of a Black person's personality.
- *Multicultural Pluralistic Assessment (MPA)*—a test to be used with culturally diverse children ages 5 to 11 years. Based on the assumption that American society is pluralistic, both

A FOCUS ON RESEARCH 6.1

Counselors Collaborating with African American Parents

The changing demographics of public schools have been a catalyst for examining the role of school counselors, especially their multicultural competence to deal with students of color and to work with parents for the benefit of students' academic and developmental success. Some African American parents may be inhibited by the fact that many school personnel are White, middle-class women without sufficient pre-service training with African American parents. Although "moments of inclusion" (p. 424) occur when African American parents are encouraged to participate in school activities such as parent–teacher conferences and athletic events, interactions with African American parents often does not occur outside these traditional events.

Bradley, Johnson, Rawls, and Dodson-Sims offer nine strategies for collaborating with African American parents:

1. Explore your own attitudes about African American families and their children.

2. Obtain an accurate and well-balanced perspective of African American family life.

3. Establish respectful and positive rapport.

4. Make flexible meeting times.

5. Establish community relationships.

6. Perceive African American students as "at promise" (p. 426)

7. Establish parent groups.

8. Advocate on behalf of African American parents and children.

9. Appreciate the strengths of African American families.

Source: "School counselors collaborating with African American counselors," by C. Bradley, P. Johnson, G. Rawls, and A. Dodson-Sims, 2005, *Professional School Counseling,* 8(5), 424–427.

culturally and structurally, this assessment tool includes an interview with parents, a medical examination, and a Wechsler Intelligence Scale for Children (WISC).

Elementary school counselors working with African American children should respect and appreciate cultural differences, actively participate in the African American community, ask questions about the African American culture, and hold high academic and social expectations for African American children.

Milan and Keiley (2000) believe that biracial youth are a particularly vulnerable group in terms of self-reported delinquency, difficulty in school, internalizing problems, and self-regard. As a group, they are more likely to receive some form of psychological intervention than their counterparts of other cultures. Biracial children do not differ significantly from White children or monoracial minority children in their perceptions of family relationships. However, they report more maladjustment than other youth in such aspects as behavioral conduct, school problems, and general self-worth. When counseling biracial clients, counselors should be careful to avoid assuming that clients' problems result from their biracial cultural backgrounds.

Counseling strategies suggested by Milan and Keiley (2000) include the following:

• Have both parents construct a cultural genogram that focuses on their ancestors' identities, coping strategies, childbearing practices, strengths, and adversities.

- Use reflecting teams that consist of a group of therapists and therapists-in-training who watch a therapy session, and then discuss their reactions with each other and with family members.
- Use externalizing language whereby the therapist attempts to separate the problem from the client by talking about the problem as a adversarial entity (e.g., "bulimia") that is trying to gain control of the family.

Parent participation has been strongly linked to student success, yet in urban schools, African American parents are often uninvolved. In A Focus on Research 6.1, Bradley, Johnson, Rawls, and Dodson-Sims (2005) present nine strategies that school counselors can use to better collaborate with African American parents.

Individual and Group Therapy.   Larrabee (1986) advocates an affirmation approach to counseling African American males. He presents the following dialogue of a therapist counseling a 14-year-old boy by using individual therapy:

COUNSELOR: Hi, you must be Joe ; I'm Mr. _____ (Ms.) _____. Come on in and have a seat. We don't know each other, but the assistant principal told me that he wanted you to come to see me. Now that you're here, I'd like to get acquainted and find out the reason he thought you should come in.

JOE: [He is quiet as he looks over the office with a somewhat sullen expression.] Look, I don't know what all this is about.

COUNSELOR: If there is no real reason why you're here, what would you like to talk about?

JOE: [pause] I don't want to talk about nothin'.... You know, he just said I had to come. I figure, it's better than sittin' in math.

COUNSELOR: Because the assistant principal insisted, you decided it would be better than math class?

JOE: Sure, I hate Ms. _____ anyway.

COUNSELOR: One of the advantages of being here is not having to deal with Ms. _____ . What are some other good reasons for talking a bit with me today?

JOE: [laughing] I can get that S.O.B., Mr. _____, off my back.

COUNSELOR: So you can dump Mr. _____'s pressure and avoid Ms. _____ then by coming in and getting to know me a little bit.

JOE: Yeah, I guess.... He's always on me about somethin'.

COUNSELOR: What seems to bug him the most?

JOE: Oh, he thinks I bust ass too much.

COUNSELOR: Then, it bothers you that he thinks you fight too much.

JOE: Nope, he's buttin' in where he don't belong sendin' me to see you when he already settles it.

COUNSELOR:	It just bugs you that he dealt with you on the fighting and then sent you to me, too.
JOE:	Yeah.
COUNSELOR:	It seems like one of the advantages of us getting together is to get Mr. _____ off your back. You know it might just help me out, too. Because I don't usually get involved in stuff like fighting. I think talking with you would help me understand kids who get in fights better. If you decided to come in to talk a few times about your experiences with fighting, it might keep the assistant principal off your case and kind of educate me about some of the things that go on with kids who fight. What do you think about that?
JOE:	Well, I don't know... but maybe it'd be okay if I get out of math.
COUNSELOR:	Okay, let's see what we can work out. I have time during this period on Wednesdays. How many times would you want to miss math on Wednesdays?
JOE:	Hey, I'll cut every day if you want.
COUNSELOR:	[chuckling] I can't handle that. What would you think about this time on Wednesdays for about the next month? Is it a deal?
JOE:	Ya got a deal! Shake? (pp. 31–33)

Groups often provide a more natural setting than individual counseling for working with children. Children function as members of groups in their daily activities (e.g., in the family, in the classroom, in the peer group). Group counseling has been advocated as an effective method of counseling several children simultaneously. An even more important advantage is that children can learn appropriate behaviors and new ways of relating more easily through interaction and feedback in a safe situation with their peers.

Family Therapy.   Counseling African American children in family therapy settings can be particularly useful. First, all family members are part of a counseling process, in which each member works to achieve unity and working order. Second, family relationships can be redefined during the session as each family member adds input. The close-knit nature of the African American family (both immediate and extended) may also contribute to the effectiveness of family therapy.

What status and what role will the African American child be accorded during family therapy? In essence, how will the child be perceived by the family and the counselor? Three factors are particularly relevant in answering these questions. First, African American families generally accord equal status to sons and daughters. Second, clear responsibilities are assigned to siblings on the basis of age. Third, the firstborn, regardless of gender, receives special preparation for the leadership role in the child group. Also, because of the reality of racism and discrimination, some African American parents feel determined to create a more favorable environment for their children.

Several strategies will contribute to counselors' success with African American children and their families in group sessions. First, as a matter of procedure, the counselor should meet with the child, the family, and school officials to clarify issues and to facilitate change. Second, successful counselors communicate respect and openly acknowledge the family's strengths. Third, the counselor should avoid using jargon and relate to the family in a direct but supportive

---

UP CLOSE AND PERSONAL 6.1

Counseling Carl, an African American child

What concerns and needs will 5-year-old Carl bring to the counseling session? Carl's kindergarten teacher referred him to the counselor because she thought Carl was not achieving at the appropriate level for 5-year-olds. After talking with Carl, the Hispanic American counselor thought that, although his readiness scores and kindergarten objectives were below average, he indeed had been putting forth considerable effort. The counselor concluded that Carl's poor self-concept was adversely affecting his schoolwork: Carl believed that he could not do the work the teacher expected. The counselor also thought that Carl's dialect was another factor contributing to his problems. The dialect worked well at home but did not seem to be acceptable at school. Although his teacher was a middle-class African American, she encouraged Carl to give up the neighborhood language for a "school language." Although Carl did not want to change, he did recognize that his dialect was quite different from the language he heard at school.

Also apparent to the counselor was Carl's confusion regarding his cultural identity. Carl wondered why so many people encouraged him to change his "ways," especially because his family spoke and acted the same way at home and in the community. The counselor summed up the assessment: If Carl could improve his self-concept and establish a strong cultural identity, his overall school achievement might improve and he might show an increased interest in school. The counselor decided to try to help Carl understand that his dialect was a natural aspect of his culture and to talk with Carl's teacher to obtain information that might help in the intervention with Carl.

---

manner. Fourth, counselors should avoid assuming familiarity with adult family members; for example, the counselor who uses first names prematurely and without permission may offend adult family members, who may view this as showing disrespect in front of their children.

Up Close and Personal 6.1 looks at a counselor's efforts with Carl, a 5-year-old African American child.

African American Adolescents

Potential Problems Warranting Counseling Intervention

Problems that African American adolescents may experience include

- failure to develop a positive self-esteem and a strong African American identity;
- poor academic achievement;
- communication problems, both verbal and nonverbal, in part because Black English is accepted in the home and community but is deemed inappropriate at school;
- absence of the father from the home;
- adverse effects of the culture being perceived as inferior or in need of change;
- cultural and social class differences;
- developmental differences (e.g., height, weight, coordination);
- problems associated with increasing socialization of the adolescent outside the African American community;

- adverse effects of racism, prejudice, and discrimination;
- role confusion because of stereotypes and prejudices involving both the adolescent developmental period and the African American culture; and
- achievement of developmental tasks, such as getting along with peers and progressing toward personal independence. This may be difficult for adolescents who differ racially and culturally from the mainstream and for those with disabilities or different sexual orientation.

Compared to other cultural groups, urban, African American male adolescents experience disproportionately higher rates of discipline referrals, suspension, and expulsion which have been related to ecological factors, including misunderstandings between the student's culture of origin and school. A Focus on Research 6.2, Day-Vines and Day-Hairston (2005) explained the logic that guides certain behaviors of urban, African American adolescents, so counselors can develop culturally congruent intervention strategies.

A FOCUS ON RESEARCH 6.2

Intervention Strategies for African American Male Adolescents

Day-Vines and Day-Hairston (2005) summarize the various problems (e.g., their high suspension rate) faced by many African American male adolescents. They maintain that these problems arise at least in part from racial and gender discrepancies in the dispensation of disciplinary measures that result in more severe measures for urban, African American male adolescents.

Some of urban, African American male adolescents' problems result from cultural perspectives, male subcultures, and communication styles. First, cultural perspectives include a mainstream American cultural orientation that endorses competition, individualism, a nuclear family, and religion as separate from other aspects of life. The African American cultural orientation endorses collective orientation, extended family networks, and religion as integral to family life. The authors maintain that these characteristics apply to many people, but certainly not all. Second, the urban African American male often endorses values that reflect the direct antithesis of healthy psychosocial functioning, for example, academic underachievement, aggression, substance abuse, sexual promiscuity, and illegal activity. Third, communicational styles (e.g., loud, intense, and confrontational without having feelings of anger) exhibit an affiliation

that does not conform to norms and expectations in mainstream educational settings.

To address the problems faced by urban males, Day-Vines and Day-Hairston (2005) recommend culturally congruent strategies.

1. Use individual and small-group counseling and mentoring programs.
2. Overcome the counselor's own inhibitions.
3. Use bibliotherapy.
4. Provide instruction in social skills.
5. Teach students that behavior in some situation (e.g., home) may not be acceptable at school—Day-Vines and Day-Hairston (2005) called this "code switching" (p. 241)
6. Promote democratic values, such as civic responsibility, service learning, and collaboration

Source: Day-Vines, D. L., & Day-Hairston, B. O. (2005). Culturally congruent strategies for addressing the behavioral needs of urban, African American male adolescents. *Professional School Counseling, 8*(3), 236–243.

Counseling Considerations

Bailey and Paisley (2004) describe the challenging situations facing African American males as follows. They often give up on schools and education because they do not see schools and social systems as places for them to succeed. The poor academic and social performance of African American males has been linked to the lack of role models, low self-esteem, hopelessness, and low expectations of schools and communities. Realistically speaking, African American males face problems in both educational institutions and in U.S. society. The best chance of changing negative social and educational trends for African American males lies within the school environment and will require innovative strategies. In A Focus on Research 6.3, Bailey and Paisley (2004) look at "Project: Gentleman on the Move," a developmental and comprehensive approach to helping African American males achieve their potential.

Two European American counselors implemented a counseling group for African American females in a suburban high school outside of Baltimore, Maryland. The counselors were concerned about African American females in a predominantly European American high school and about the underrepresentation of African American students in counseling groups. Also, the counselors thought African American females faced multiple levels of discrimination; for example, being African American females in a predominantly European American school, being teenagers in an adult-run society, and facing sexism.

The goals of the counseling group included the following:

1. Identify and discuss feelings related to being African American women (e.g., joy, pride, worry, frustration, hope).

A FOCUS ON RESEARCH 6.3

Nurturing Excellence in African American Males

After reviewing characteristics of successful intervention programs, Bailey and Paisley (2004) describe the "Project: Gentleman on the Move," (or PGOTM). Intervention programs need to be developmental and comprehensive in their approach. Developmentally, they should consider where each member is compared to where he should be psychosocially and academically. Development gaps should be addressed, and the foundation should be laid for preventing future gaps. Comprehensively, the programs should include contact with parents, community service projects that provide a quality service to the community, opportunities for participants to interact and share experiences with other adolescents, instruction on what it means to be African American, and personal and business etiquette training and leadership opportunities.

Bailey and Paisley (2004) describe the PGOTM and its assumptions, program background, expectations of members, and requirements and outcomes of the program. Recommendations for counselors include developing an awareness of the African culture, acknowledging personal biases, developing meaningful rapport with male African Americans, identifying positive African American males in the community, identifying existing programs for helping African American males, creating a system that matches students to existing programs, and serving as true advocates for African American male adolescents in the school and community.

Source: "Developing and nurturing excellence in African American males," by D. F. Bailey, and P. O. Paisley, 2004, *Journal of Counseling and Development, 82,* pp. 10–17.

2. Discuss expectations for themselves, expectations of others, and their feelings about those expectations.

3. Discuss relationships with other females, males, teachers, parents, siblings, friends, and neighbors.

4. Discuss feelings about and experiences with racism and prejudice.

5. Identify goals and dreams for the future.

The group also offered suggestions for European American counselors working with African American women's groups: Counselors should be honest, open, relaxed, respectful, and good listeners. They should not be afraid to make mistakes, refrain from taking things personally, ask for help or for clarification from the group when needed, communicate honestly even when discussing sensitive topics, and avoid being overly sensitive to issues related to racism, prejudice, and stereotyping. As with all cross-cultural counseling, professional counselors must be aware of the limitations of their own beliefs and assumptions about others. European American professionals need to consider their own prejudices (as should counselors of all cultures) and be open to and genuinely respectful of culturally different attitudes and behaviors (Muller, 2000).

As previously mentioned, language differences and communication barriers can be factors in determining the success of counseling intervention. In fact, the ability to communicate effectively is considered more important than similarity to the client's racial membership group. What, then, must counselors of African American adolescents recognize to ensure effective communication? First, some African Americans resent counselors' attempts to use slang to show understanding. Second, counselors who are unfamiliar with the directness of some African Americans may find their style of communication offensive and may interpret directness as hostility. Some clients may be hesitant to speak altogether for fear that their speech will be evaluated negatively; thus therapists sometimes label African Americans as nonverbal and incapable of dealing with feelings. In fact, African Americans often deal with anxiety by becoming either passive or aggressive: Either they say nothing or they become loud, threatening, and abusive. Passive or aggressive behavior during therapy may be a manifestation of frustration and displaced anger toward the therapist, particularly the European American therapist. Consider the following dialogue between Jessie and her counselor:

JESSIE:	Well, you're the one who wanted to talk, so talk.
COUNSELOR:	Yes, the absence list showed you weren't in school for 3 days. Didn't we have an agreement that when things weren't going right for you, we'd talk, rather than you cutting out?
JESSIE:	All this same White counselor talk. You Whites always coming down on us and jiving us.
COUNSELOR:	Jessie, I thought we were going to talk about what happened during the 3 days of absence.
JESSIE:	This whole damn system of yours—it's hooked us all into money.
COUNSELOR:	Would you cut out all that crap about the system and talk about what's been going on with you the last 3 days? You know we can talk about what you can do for you, but that other thing is out there and not in here.
JESSIE:	Uh? Tell me more, ha!

COUNSELOR: Jessie, I know you believe unfair things happen to you, but I want you to talk about what's been happening to you the last few days and try to forget that other for now.

JESSIE: Uh? Well, uh, see. Our check didn't come in, and we had the bills, and I had to get us some quick bread and.*

Competent skills and techniques needed for counseling African Americans include the consideration of family and community life from an African American perspective. African American counselors should be available in areas that have large African populations. When an African American high school student goes to a counselor, particularly a European American counselor, and is reluctant to reveal information, the student may be experiencing inner conflicts with racial identity and may choose not to participate in the counseling relationship. Because having access to only European American counselors may have a detrimental impact on African American adolescents, it is important for these adolescents to experience feelings of acceptance in counselor–client relationships.

Advocacy, proactive services, and outreach should figure prominently in school guidance programs designed to effectively address the career development needs of African American adolescents. Advocacy activities include in-school action to address policies and procedures that may affect educational opportunities negatively.

Concerns that African American adolescents bring to counseling sessions include establishing a meaningful personal identity, academic performance, interpersonal relations, autonomy, sexual and aggressive feelings, and long-term career plans.

Individual and Group Therapy.   A primary task for counselors during initial counseling intervention is to determine the appropriateness of individual and group therapy. Deciding which technique to use requires a basic understanding of intervention strategies and a careful consideration of the client(s)' culture and developmental period.

Johnson and Johnson (2005) think the Empowerment Groups for Academic Success (EGAS) provides a means of group counseling in urban schools to increase students' academic achievement and personal/social competencies. In A Focus on Research 6.4, they describe how EGAS can be a viable means of providing group counseling.

Choosing the appropriate intervention mode requires consideration of several questions: Is the African American adolescent more likely to disclose personal information during individual or group sessions? In individual and group therapy, how effective is counseling if the family is not involved? Although adolescents tend to prefer group therapy sessions because their age-level peers may have similar problems, will African American adolescents speak of personal matters in the presence of adolescents from other cultures? Answering these questions requires getting to know the individual adolescent and the nature of the problem.

The following are recommendations for effective counseling of African American youths:

- Encourage African American students to talk about themselves, their families, and their experiences to determine strengths.

---

*Dialogue from *Counseling and Development in a Multicultural Society* (p. 432), by J. A. Axelson, 1999, Monterey, CA: Brooks/Cole.

- Ask students to describe their social class status, rather than make assumptions based on their behaviors.
- Ask students to describe their social kin networks.

A FOCUS ON RESEARCH 6.4
Group Counseling

Johnson and Johnson (2005) maintain that the Empowerment Groups for Academic Success (EGAS) model utilizes some of the traditional strategies for group counseling. These strategies include using a group leader, establishing a set number of meetings, setting individual objectives, and building group cohesion and support. However, the model goes beyond the traditional approach by including a multicultural approach that is sensitive to students living in urban settings. The approach also uses the strengths of an unstructured process group, with clearly defined goals to develop individual student success. The belief that group members can develop ownership and have choices about discussing their personal and social problems is fundamental to the success of the EGAS model.

One strength of the EGAS model is that it utilize knowledge and skills that counselors have learned in their counselor preparation program. Since it is not a new delivery system, it takes little additional training to implement the model. Still, it is a new perspective on how group counseling can effectively address directions, goals, and missions of the counseling program and the larger educational efforts within a school. Plus, conducting meetings, facilitating group sessions, providing training for parents and staff, as well as using group processes, are critical to developing comprehensive programs.

Source: "Group counseling: Beyond the traditional," by S. K. Johnson, and C. D. Johnson, 2005, *Professional School Counseling, 8*(5), pp. 399–400.

GENDER PERSPECTIVES 6.1
Empowerment Groups for At-Risk Urban African American Girls

In their article, Bemak, Chung, and Siroskey-Sabdo (2005) describe an innovative counseling approach called Empowerment Groups for Academic Success (EGAS), which was implemented in a Midwest inner-city school that was experiencing high rates of expulsions and suspensions, teenage pregnancies, absenteeism, poverty, and poor academic records.

The EGAS approach to group counseling is unique and different in its emphasis on empowerment through group processes, moving away from psycho-educational and traditionally structured groups filled with exercises and activities planned by the facilitator. Topics of discussion chosen by the participants included family and peer relationships, the

death of friends and loved ones, pregnancy and single parenting, experiences with first sexual encounters, smoking, confrontations and poor relationships with teachers, and general school and academic concerns.

For an excellent description of EGAS, we highly recommend counselors read the Bemak, Chung, and Siroskey-Sabdo article.

Source: "Empowerment groups for academic success: An innovative approach to prevent high school failure for at-risk, urban African American girls," by F. Bemak, R. C. Chung, and L. A. Siroskey-Sabdo, 2005, *Professional School Counseling, 8*(5), pp. 377–386.

- Ask students to describe concerns about whether the counselor will be able to help them.
- When possible, visit the homes of African American youths.

Factors affecting the outcome of individual/group counseling include developmental levels and gender roles. Possible interventions include group assertiveness training, which has been found to reduce classroom displays of aggression; expressive group therapy, which has positive effects on male youths; and self-instructional techniques, which modify African American adolescent males' behavioral risks.

Bemak, Chung, and Siroskey-Sabdo (2005) (see Gender Perspectives 6.1) maintain that urban schools face unique challenges as they provide culturally responsive experiences for diverse populations. The many problems facing at-risk urban African American girls include academic

UP CLOSE AND PERSONAL 6.2

Counseling Tyrone, an African American Adolescent

Tyrone, age 16, was recommended by his teacher for a districtwide school drop-out prevention program. A requirement for enrolling in the "at risk" program was at least one session (one part of an overall assessment) with a community agency counselor. After the initial visit, the counselor used established guidelines in deciding whether additional sessions were warranted. Tyrone was brought from his school to the 35-year-old European American counselor, who met with students individually at the agency. Tyrone's greatest in-class behavior problem was talking too much with his friends; he was adamantly opposed to being placed in the at-risk drop-out program and being sent to the counselor.

The counselor introduced herself and explained to Tyrone the reason for the referral. Tyrone stated, "Nothin's wrong with me. The problem's the teacher, who don't like me 'cause I'm Black. I'll be glad to get out of that honky school. I'd quit now if my parents wouldn't find out about it." Tyrone mostly looked down at the floor or at the picture on the office wall. His failure to look her in the eye concerned the counselor, but she realized it was a common habit among her African American clients.

The counselor assessed Tyrone's case. His academic problems qualified him for the drop-out program, and he appeared to harbor strong feelings that he was a victim of racism in his school. Still, she had to note that not all of Tyrone's teachers were European American. Could it be that his African American teachers, who had been academically successful, had lost perspective of what it meant to be poor and African American? Although the counselor did not want to imply that racism was not a factor, she hoped to help Tyrone get the situation in perspective.

During Tyrone's first session, the counselor tried to make him feel comfortable talking to her. She was of European cultural background and might not understand what it was like to be poor and African American, but she sought to learn more about him, his friends, and his culture. She realized that establishing rapport was all-important. She informed Tyrone that she wanted him to return for additional counseling. She carefully explained that this was not punishment. She wanted to help him and would not "put him and his race down," as he thought his teachers did. Another decision was to continue individual therapy until she could determine whether there were enough students in Tyrone's situation to form a small group. Also, she considered future family counseling because the referral slip mentioned that Tyrone's parents were interested in his academic work. Yes, she thought, maybe Tyrone's parents could help with this situation.

achievement, high dropout rates, negative stereotyping, and fewer educational resources—many of which result from social problems, poverty, violence, and discrimination.

School counselors serve in a unique position to assume leadership roles in reducing academic disparties. Gender Perspectives 6.1 looks at the problems facing urban, African American girls and suggests using the EGAs model.

Family Therapy.   As with individual and group therapy, a fundamental step is to consider whether the adolescent will disclose personal information during family counseling sessions. Another point to consider is the extent to which the family can assist during and after the counseling session. The likelihood of family members helping to facilitate change may be better when they are involved in therapy sessions.

The family therapist sees a client's problems as a result of family interactions, as affecting other family members, or as being amenable to family members providing assistance and insights. Although African American families differ in many aspects and deserve individual consideration, two cultural characteristics that might contribute to family counseling include their concern for group welfare and their extended family networks. Grandparents, aunts and uncles, and cousins might also play active roles in family counseling. They might be able to offer insights that the parents do not realize.

Unless there is a court-ordered mandate for family counseling, an individual interview is probably the most effective means of deciding whether the client will benefit from family members being included.

Up Close and Personal 6.2 looks at a counselor's efforts with Tyrone, a 16-year-old African American adolescent.

African American Adults

Potential Problems Warranting Counseling Intervention

Problems African American adults may experience include

- communication problems caused by misunderstood communication patterns and dialects;
- African American women often being more religiously active than their mates;
- adverse effects of myths and stereotypes regarding the African American culture;
- historical and contemporary ill treatments from other cultures;
- low self-esteem, confused cultural identity, and feelings of rejection;
- lack of education;
- differing cultural characteristics and customs;
- unequal employment and housing opportunities;
- underemployment, unemployment, and low socioeconomic status;
- increasing number of single-parent and/or female-headed households;
- inability to cope with problems associated with adulthood (e.g., appearance and personality changes, psychosocial crises, marital discord);

- depression and depressive symptoms resulting from living in high-stress environments (e.g., low income, high crime rate, high unemployment);

- coping with signs of aging (e.g., strength and stamina decrease, gray hair and wrinkles increase, the body frame begins to stoop) (Papalia, Olds, & Feldman, 2001);

- taking stock of one's life during the adult period, including past accomplishments and the possibilities of attaining future goals (financial, personal, and societal); and

- perception of how age has affected sexuality.

Counseling Considerations

Counseling services for adults are based on the premise that all individuals have the capacity for controlled growth and development in psychosocial, vocational, emotional, and other areas. Furthermore, life transitions in adulthood often give rise to conflict; such conflict may cause individuals to be less effective in coping with aspects of daily living. Counselors of adults seek to provide services that maximize the growth and coping abilities of clients and that help them explore these areas of their lives.

Effective intervention with African American clients includes a mutual understanding on the part of client and counselor about their racial identities and how racial identity influences counseling dynamics. Counselors who are knowledgeable of the African American identity development process and assess the interactive nature of racial identities have a better understanding of these clients and can provide more effective intervention.

It is important to mention that some African American Muslims have a great distrust and suspicion of European American counseling professionals. This suspicion has resulted from the acute awareness of oppression brought on by intense study of African American history by many members, the historical reality of how Islam in America has been closely associated with cultural nationalism, and the individual experiences of members with racism, which may have contributed to their conversion (Mahmoud, 1996). Distrust of the therapist, skepticism about the therapist's attitudes toward Muslims, and African Americans' sensitivity to misperception and distortion are common concerns that one may encounter in the therapeutic relationship with African American Muslims (Mahmoud, 1996).

African Americans often underuse counseling services because they perceive counselors as insensitive to their needs and as not accepting, understanding, and respecting their cultural differences. Other reasons for underuse include attitudes of mental health professionals as well as clients, the limited number of African American counselors, and the limitations of multicultural counseling training. African Americans also often rely heavily on their church rather than on counseling intervention. Mental health professionals increasingly recognize the mental health benefits of religious involvement and the extent to which a strong spiritual base is central to the client's improved mental health.

Mental health help-seeking among African American women is a complex issue and is influenced by factors such as age, socioeconomic status, education, cultural beliefs, religion, and unique life experience. A large number of middle-class, working-class, and low-income African American women seek help from sources other than traditional mental health institutions. These sources include Black churches, beauty/barber shops, respected elders in the community, and sister circles. If and when African American women seek help from traditional mental health service providers,

A FOCUS ON RESEARCH 6.5

Menopause Symptoms and Attitudes of African American Women

Huffman, Myers, Tingle, and Bond (2005) report that available literature on women's attitudes toward menopause have primarily involved Caucasian, middle- and upper-class, well-educated women. If counselors and health care professionals are going to help African American women understand their challenges, it will be necessary to understand menopause in their cultural perspectives.

If there had been a taboo related to speaking about menopause in the African American culture, it did not appear to affect this population of women. Relatively few had any problem discussing the topic. It appears that this taboo has not only weakened in the larger U.S. culture but also in the African American community.

Implications for counselors include the following items:

1. Realize that both commonalities and differences regarding menopause exist within ethnic/cultural groups.

2. Remember that although most women reported an overall positive attitude toward menopause and similar symptoms, individual experiences may vary greatly from the norms.

3. Understand that women considering menopause for the first time might also be considering for the first time what it means to grow older in a society that supports ageism.

4. Understand that African American women might have to deal with ageism, sexism, and racism—all hurdles that threatens their well-being.

5. Network with other health care professionals through initiatives such as community coalitions whose agendas support both psychological and medical care needs.

Readers wanting additional information are referred to this highly recommended research article.

Source: "Menopause symptoms and attitudes of African American women: Closing the knowledge gap and expanding opportunities for counseling" by S. B. Huffman, J. E. Myers, L. R. Tingle, and L. A. Bond, 2005, *Journal of Counseling & Development, 83,* pp. 48–56.

it is not until a problem has reached a crisis state. Even then, African American women are less likely to seek help from community mental health centers (Neal-Barnett & Crowther, 2000).

The question remains whether a non-African American therapist can intervene effectively with African American clients. Perhaps it would be preferable to match counselors and clients whenever possible with respect to race. Some African Americans may not want to see an Asian American therapist, just as some women may not want to see a male therapist. A client's choice of therapist usually is indicative of self-perceptions and certain expectations for the counseling relationship.

Some problems may result from African Americans' racial, historical, cultural, and structural position in American society. A major task for the counselor continues to be engaging reluctant African American men to participate in counseling. Men often feel they should work out their own difficulties; consequently, they do not want to disclose personal feelings, which further complicates the counseling process.

Killian (2001) explored how interracial spouses construct narratives about their racial histories, identities, and experiences in their relationships. Compared with White spouses, Black spouses demonstrate a greater awareness of and sensitivity to social resistance to interracial couples. Marrying a partner of another race can have serious social and psychological implications for the partners' relationships with family and friends. Close friends and relatives typically reinforce established social norms with respect to homogamy and often actively discourage couples from marrying interracially. Even best friends who themselves have chosen to marry across race and ethnicity may strongly oppose a couple's interracial union.

Killian suggests a narrative-informed approach to provide interracial couples with opportunities to share individual and couple experiences of racism and prejudice, stories about their families of origin, and personal and family histories. This approach offers potential for empowerment and a hopeful outlook. Counselors can also create an atmosphere of support and sensitive interest as partners disclose painful memories and histories.

Huffman, Myers, Tingle, and Bond (2005) maintain that menopause, a normal midlife transition for women, remains poorly understood for minority women. A Focus on Research 6.5 looks at menopause symptoms and attitudes of African American women.

Individual and Group Therapy.   When planning intervention for African American clients, the counselor must decide whether to use individual or group counseling. While some counselors might prefer individual counseling, group counseling often has advantages and deserves consideration. Some advantages are that group counseling can be more cost-effective in terms of the counselor's time, and clients often feel support from other participants who have similar problems and challenges. Still, the welfare of the client is always the final determinant. The decision about whether to use individual or group approaches should depend on several factors.

First, is the group developmentally compatible with a particular client? For example, an African American adolescent will likely face different problems than an African American elderly person. Although they both might experience discrimination, the younger client may be experiencing job discrimination or identity concerns, whereas the older one may be facing health problems and financial concerns. As always, individual differences and challenges deserve consideration. While the counselor might be able to plan counseling intervention that addresses some diversity in age and level of development, participants might benefit from having all group members in a similar developmental period.

Second, how will the African American adult respond in group counseling? Some clients who are quite vocal in individual counseling are reluctant to speak in front of groups, especially when they feel their situations reflect negatively on their ability to provide for the family, maintain a job and the household, and serve as suitable role models for children and adolescents. Do they have the social skills, communicational skills, and emotional stability to benefit from group interaction? Are they receptive to sharing feelings as well as accepting others' feelings? These decisions can be made only through consideration of individual clients.

Gender differences also deserve consideration when deciding between individual or group therapy. Although African American women are more likely than their spouse/significant other to be receptive to discussing problems in groups, women in mixed gender groups may not be as willing to discuss their push for equality and the problems associated with female-headed households. Counselors providing group therapy with African American women should assume the role of an active facilitator; understand nonverbal communication, such as the meanings of gestures, postures, and movements; enlist group members' feedback; and experiment with exercises that help group members gain greater awareness.

Family Therapy.   To work effectively with African American families, therapists must be willing to explore the impact of the social, political, socioeconomic, and broader environmental conditions of families. Therapists must also be willing to expand the definition of family to a more extended kinship system. Relatives often live in proximity to and expect to rely on one another in times of need. They may interchange functions, and they frequently share responsibilities for child-rearing. This is an important point to understand, because counseling sessions may be attended by family members who counselors usually would not expect to do so.

Counseling interventions that emphasize social functioning over inner feelings are most appropriate for African Americans. Counselors need to attend to the specifics of African Americans' historical and cultural experiences, as well as their socioeconomic conditions. Family therapists should also be aware of the important roles that extended family members, social institutions, and churches play in the lives of African American families.

A therapist working with an African American Muslim family needs to know to which community the family belongs and how its members feel about their particular religious community. Mahmoud (1996) categorizes African American Muslims as follows:

1.   *Cultural nationalists*: those who belong to a community that stresses Black nationalism and Islam and stresses separation and independence from the dominant community.

2.   *Sunni or Orthodox African American–centered leadership*: those who belong to communities that practice and adhere to the traditional practice of Islam and, while stressing self-determination and pride, see themselves as believers whose faith defines them as well as their place in secular culture. Their communities are usually led by an African American.

3.   *Sunni or Orthodox African- or Arab-centered leadership*: those who belong to communities that practice and adhere to the traditional practices of Islam but stress the universality of the religion and are most comfortable in an international, multicultural Islamic community.

Essentials for successfully counseling African American families include discussing their goals for the intervention; understanding and respecting the African American culture, especially family traditions; assisting the family to adopt the counseling plan; and assisting the family to evaluate the plan and its effectiveness.

Counselors should avoid assuming too many generalizations about African Americans. They differ in many ways, such as socioeconomic status and place of origin, to name a few. For example, African Americans do not always experience similar problems: Lower-class families may experience economic problems, high crime and mortality rates, and employment and social discrimination. Although counseling intervention always has potential, some social problems facing African Americans are beyond their control. A helpful approach is for the therapist to point out areas of life where they do have control, and empower them to make changes where they can.

Suggestions for providing family therapy for African Americans include understanding the worldview of these families as being different from that of the larger society; considering family strengths, such as religious/spiritual orientations, adaptability of family roles, acknowledging differences between counselor and client and exploring how these differences can influence the counseling process; and learning to acknowledge and to feel comfortable with the family's cultural differences.

Recommendations or principles for counselors working with African American families experiencing divorce, separation, or other problems include encouraging couples to (a) maintain

Counseling Cynthia, an African American Adult

Cynthia, age 33, referred herself for counseling through a counseling program operated for the hospital staff. In this program, counselors, who are in private practice or are employed by community mental health organizations, conduct counseling sessions at the hospital on a regular basis.

During Cynthia's first session, the 38-year-old Asian American female counselor discussed Cynthia's reasons for the self-referral. Speaking in Black dialect interspersed with standard English, Cynthia explained that she felt trapped. Her husband tried hard to make a living: His work record was good, he never did time in jail, and he did not have a drinking problem. Still, Cynthia wanted more; she was already over 30, and nothing

much was changing in her life. Although she had not spoken with her husband about her plans, Cynthia was thinking about attending school at night. She had a desire to improve her life. The counselor listened intently, took notes, and encouraged Cynthia to examine her goals carefully and to consider the impact of her decision on her family. The counselor accepted Cynthia as a client. First, she would meet with her several times individually, then move to a group session (other women working in the hospital likely had similar concerns), and finally, depending on Cynthia's progress and her husband's reaction, she might schedule family sessions by which other family members could see the reasons for Cynthia's concerns and understand her goals.

an open, honest, and direct communication with children about divorce or separation; (b) maintain a strong coalition despite marital discord; (c) provide understanding, availability, and support to the children; (d) build a new life, establish a new identity, and redefine the relationship with the ex-spouse or estranged spouse; and (e) maintain an image of competence and self-confidence.

Up Close and Personal 6.3 looks at a counselor's efforts with Cynthia, a 33-year-old African American woman.

Respect is key to successfully engaging the family during a family counseling session. The therapist should openly acknowledge the family's strengths, avoid professional jargon, and relate to the family in a direct but supportive manner.

The literature has focused primarily on urban African American families whose lives differ from those of non-African American, middle-class therapists. Family therapy may not always be the treatment of choice in such situations. Again, individual consideration of African American clients is essential. In essence, until definitive research suggests appropriate treatment strategies, the wisest policy continues to be consideration of individual clients and their particular circumstances.

African American Elderly

Potential Problems Warranting Counseling Intervention

Problems that elderly African Americans may experience include

- adverse effects of stereotypes about the culture and elderly status;
- the possibility of multiple jeopardy (i.e., combination of being culturally different, aged, and/or disabled);

A FOCUS ON RESEARCH 6.6

Ethnic Differences in Family Caregiving

Pinguart and Sorensen (2005) investigated ethnic differences in caregiving backgrounds, stressors, beliefs about filial obligations, psychological and social resources, coping processes, and psychological and physical health.

Ethnic minority caregivers had a lower socioeconomic status, were younger, were less likely to be a spouse, and were more likely to receive informal support. They also provided more care than White caregivers and had stronger beliefs about filial obligations than White caregivers. Asian caregivers, but not African and Hispanic caregivers, used less formal support than non-Hispanic White caregivers. Whereas African American caregivers had lower levels of caregiver burden and depression than White caregivers, Hispanic and Asian caregivers were more depressed than White non-Hispanic peers. All non-White groups of caregivers reported worse physical health than Whites.

Since differences exist, interventions need to vary among ethnic groups and caregivers.

Source: "Ethnic differences in stressors, resources, and psychological outcomes of family caregiving: A meta-analysis," by M. Pinguart, and S. Sorensen, 2005, *The Gerontologist,* 45(1), 90–106.

- lack of education, lack of employment, and low socioeconomic status;
- cultural differences, traditions, and customs;
- high divorce/separation rates;
- problems with generational differences because of the acculturation of younger African Americans; and
- health problems; longer and more frequent hospital stays; chronic diseases, functional impairments, prostate cancer, and risk indicators such as high blood pressure. (U.S. Census Bureau, 2004–2005)

Pierce (2001) reports that approximately 4 million Americans live with the effects of stroke. Annually, 500,000 persons have an initial stroke, and the average life expectancy post-stroke is 5 to 10 years. This is particularly relevant to African Americans and other minorities because of the high prevalence of stroke in these groups.

Stroke can result in cognitive, emotional, social, behavioral, and functional impairments, thus creating problems for family members who must become caregivers. For low-income, urban families, caregiving problems may be magnified because of meager or depleted resources and the social problems that are compounded by the erosion and decay of many urban communities.

In A Focus on Research 6.6, Pinguart and Sorensen (2005) looked at ethnic differences and caregiving and drew some interesting conclusions.

Counseling Considerations

Counselors should first try to gain an understanding of what it means to be elderly and African American, and to be aging in a society that glorifies youth. As with other stages of human development, counselors working with elderly African Americans should be aware of the body of knowledge pertaining to the elderly developmental period in this culture. Specific research and scholarly opinion on counseling African American elderly, however, is scarce. Counselors must synthesize their understanding of the culture with their knowledge of the lifespan period to form a basis for counseling decisions.

Most techniques used in counseling adults also apply to the elderly. What steps, then, can counselors take to improve the likelihood of a positive counselor–client relationship? First, rapport should be established by convincing the client that the counselor empathizes with the concerns of the elderly, such as health problems, financial problems, loneliness, and expectations of family and church. The elderly client may think, "You're too young and too White to know my problems and to know how I feel," but the counselor can still try to gain the client's confidence by demonstrating a "feel" for the various aspects of aging. Several characteristics of African American family life may result in the need for counseling intervention for the elderly. One example is the orientation toward kinship bonds, wherein a wide array of uncles, aunts, "big mamas," boyfriends, older brothers and sisters, deacons, preachers, and others frequent the African American home. The increasing number of three-generation families may result in "boundary" or responsibility problems involving the elderly. Another example is African Americans' strong religious orientation. Consider the following family dialogue that illustrates the powerful influence of the church:

THERAPIST:	(to Ms. K.) Do you understand why your children worry about you?
MS. K:	No.
THERAPIST:	Find out from them now.
MS. K:	Why? Do you think I'm gonna die?
CYNTHIA:	The way daddy be hitting on you.
MS. K:	Ray don't hit on me.
KAREN:	What he fought you that time.
MS. K:	John, you think I'm gonna die?
JOHN:	The way you two get in serious arguments sometimes (pause)—someone might get injured.
MS. K:	Nobody gets serious injuries. You know the Bible says everybody is gonna die but they come back, John.
JOHN:	I know.
MS. K:	Then you all don't have anything to worry about. Jehovah tells you that you're not supposed to worry about anything like that 'cause he'll take care of his people, and we'll live right back here on this earth. If you be good. Dying is something to get out of all this agony now. (Hines & Boyd-Franklin, 2005, p. 97)

Clearly, the children's valid concerns for Ms. K's safety are being blocked by her religious beliefs. Counselors who are confronted with such situations are in a better position to intervene successfully if they understand the traditional role of the church and the influence that it exerts.

Individual/Group Therapy.   The first several sessions should focus mainly on individual therapy directed toward building rapport and letting the elderly client know what to expect from a counseling relationship; however, if other clients with similar problems participate (and, in all likelihood, there will be such clients), group therapy may be feasible. Group therapy for elderly African Americans is most beneficial when several clients have problems in common with their culture, their age, or racism and discrimination.

Up Close and Personal 6.4 looks at a counselor's efforts with Eloise, a 74-year-old African American woman.

Family Therapy.   Family therapy may be particularly appropriate for elderly African American clients in certain situations. Consider the following example of a "boundary" problem in which the therapist worked with three generations:

> A 10-year-old boy was brought in for treatment because of stealing. The first session was attended by the parents and their two children. Both parents appeared bewildered and unsure of their parenting skills. Upon learning the grandmother had the primary child care responsibility, the counselor asked her to join the family sessions. It became apparent that the grandmother ran the household. She had her way of handling the children, and the parents had theirs.

The therapist's goal was to form a working alliance between the parents and the grandmother so that the children were no longer given conflicting messages. This was accomplished by having a number of joint meetings with the parents and the grandmother to discuss family rules, division of labor, and child care policies. Disputes and differences of opinions were discussed. Later, the children were included in sessions in order to clarify the boundaries of the family (Hines & Boyd-Franklin, 2005, p. 92).

What other problems might African American elderly bring to counseling sessions? Possibilities include problems with adult children, interracial marriages, and divorces or remarriages. Of course, some problems are specific to aging—for example, grief and growing old in a society that

---

UP CLOSE AND PERSONAL 6.4
Counseling Eloise, an Elderly African American

Eloise, aged 74, visited her community medical doctor for stomach pains and was referred to a community mental health counselor. She decided to keep her appointment mainly because the agency was near her son's home. The 34-year-old European American female counselor recognized that Eloise had a few problems, but generally she was in much better shape than most other elderly African American clients. Although Eloise was poor, she was better off financially than many African American women, her health was relatively good, and she felt needed by her grandchildren, nieces, and nephews. The counselor decided that the best strategy for this first session was to gain Eloise's confidence and to learn more about her. Conversation

focused on Eloise's life, her age, and her family and church. At the end of the session, Eloise concluded that the counselor was, indeed, interested and that she knew a little about what being an elderly African American woman was like.

The counselor reached several conclusions during this first session. Although Eloise did not have any serious problems, she did feel that she lacked control over her life. Financial problems were a possibility, and her neighborhood was becoming more dangerous. The counselor decided to meet with Eloise again one-on-one, and then maybe a group session could be arranged. Also, the supportiveness of Eloise's family suggested to the counselor that a family session might be beneficial.

favors youth. In summary, counselors need to understand the elderly period in the lifespan, the problems experienced by elderly African Americans, and the strategies employed in family therapy.

A Point of Departure: Challenges Confronting Counselors of African Americans

Counselors working with African American children, adolescents, adults, and elders need a comprehensive understanding of African American culture and the four lifespan stages. They will also need to understand African Americans' geographic, socioeconomic, generational, and individual differences. Childhood years on the lifespan should be perceived as a critical developmental period for forming individual and cultural identities. The adolescent developmental period presents important challenges, such as identity formation and self-concept development. Counselors intervening with African American adults need to understand the challenges associated with the adult lifespan stage. Relatively few counselors have adequate training and counseling skills to deal with the problems of the elderly in a cultural context. In general, counselors with African American clients face several challenges: understanding the African American culture, understanding the four lifespan periods, understanding the relationship between culture and development, and understanding the effects of racism and discrimination on African Americans. These challenges are monumental but not insurmountable.

Summary

Counseling African American clients can be a rewarding experience when counselors understand these clients' cultural backgrounds and developmental periods. Knowing when to use individual, group, and family therapy and where to seek additional knowledge about cultural differences are prerequisites to planning and implementing effective counseling for these clients. Simply having knowledge, however, is insufficient; it is necessary to appreciate the life circumstances of African American clients.

To determine appropriate counseling interventions, such factors as racial and ethnic differences, language and communication barriers, and concerns associated with lifespan differences must be understood. Particularly challenging to counselors are class and generational differences and other cultural group differences that sometimes may not be so obvious. Because few professionals have been trained to work with African American clients from all four lifespan stages, it is imperative that counselors seek such training, either through accredited training programs or through other professional development avenues, or refer clients to colleagues with the appropriate expertise.

Suggested Readings

Bailey, D. F., & Paisley, P. O. (2004). Developing and nurturing excellence in African American males. *Journal of Counseling and Development, 82,* 10–17. In this excellent article, Bailey and Paisley describe the "Project: Gentlemen on the Move," a project designed to assist African American adolescent males.

Barnes, P. W., & Lightsey, O. R. (2005). Perceived racist discrimination, coping, stress, and life satisfaction. *Journal of Multicultural Counseling and Development, 33,* 48–61. These authors investigated 114 African Americans to determine the effects of perceived racism.

Fall, K. A., Levitov, J. E., Anderson, L. & Clay, H. (2005). African Americans' perceptions of mental health professions. *International Journal of the Advancement of Counseling, 27*(1), 47–56. This study found that African Americans were confident in counselors' abilities to treat less severe cases, and less confident in their abilities to treat more severe cases.

Huffman, S. B., Myers, J. E., Tingle, L. R., Bond, L. A. (2005). Menopause symptoms and attitudes of African American women: Closing the knowledge gap and expanding opportunities for counseling. *Journal of Counseling and Development, 83,* 48–56. Maintaining that menopause remains poorly understood, especially for minority women, these authors investigated the health status, stressful life events, social support, and demographics of African American midlife women.

Rosenthal, D. A. (2004). Effects of client race on clinical judgment of practicing European American vocational rehabilitation counselors. *Rehabilitation Counseling Bulletin, 47*(3), 131–141. Rosenthal investigated vocational rehabilitation counselors and found that African American clients were judged more negatively than European American clients.

Want, V., Parham, T. A., & Baker, R. C. (2004). African Americans students' ratings of Caucasian and African American counselors varying in racial consciousness. *Cultural Diversity and Ethnic Minority Psychology, 10*(2), 123–136. These authors found that African American counselors were rated more favorably than White counselors and that highly racially conscious counselors were rated more favorably than low racially conscious counselors.

Understanding American Indian Clients

Questions to Be Explored

1. What are the childhood, adolescent, adult, and elderly years like in the American Indian culture?

2. What social and cultural, familial, and communication characteristics describe American Indians along the lifespan continuum?

3. What unique challenges (e.g., low educational attainment, poverty) face American Indians during the various lifespan stages?

4. What cultural discontinuities do American Indian children and adolescents experience as they deal with issues in their homes and communities and in majority-culture or reservation schools?

5. What do psychologists and researchers mean by two-spirit people, especially concerning American Indians?

6. What unique challenges face counselors providing mental health services to American Indians in the four lifespan stages?

7. What sources of information are available for counselors intervening with American Indian children, adolescents, adults, and elders?

Overview

Professional intervention with American Indian children, adolescents, adults, and elders requires an understanding of the challenges associated with each lifespan stage, the tremendous diversity within the American Indian culture, and the many challenges this culture faces. Providing appropriate counseling intervention for the American Indian client requires an understanding of the individual's culture, family, communication, and many problems, all of which interact in a complex fashion. To be effective, counselors need to recognize and gain an understanding of racism and injustices forced, and still being forced, on American Indians. This chapter examines American Indian children, adolescents, adults, and elders, their characteristics, and their daily challenges.

American Indians: Demographics

Early American colonists treated American Indians with contempt and hostility and engaged in wars against them that bordered on genocide. Later, the native peoples were driven from the coastal plains to make way for a massive movement by White settlers pushing West (Henderson, 2000). History is filled with examples of racism and discrimination against American Indians, and they continue to face such realities and the accompanying effects of poverty, unemployment, and low educational attainments. Research suggests a dismal picture for many American Indians. They often rank at the bottom of every social indicator: highest unemployment rates, lowest levels of educational attainment, and poorest housing and transportation (Ramasamy, 1996).

Across the United States, there are more than 558 federally recognized and several hundred state recognized American Indian nations; together, they consist of a diverse population of 2.3 million people (Russell, 1998; Garrett & Wilbur, 1999), speaking 252 languages and comprising 505 federally recognized tribes and 365 state recognized tribes (Garrett, M.W. 1995). The larger tribes (those with more than 100,000 members) include the Cherokee, Navajo, Chippewa, and Sioux. Tribes with about 50,000 members include the Choctaw, Pueblo, and Apache. Fourteen tribes have populations between 10,000 and 21,000, but most tribes have fewer than 10,000 members. Currently, nearly half of all American Indians live west of the Mississippi River. In 1998, more than half of the American Indian population lived in just six states: California, Oklahoma, Arizona, New Mexico, Washington, and Alaska (with large numbers of Aleuts). Table 7.1 shows the states in which significant numbers of American Indians live.

Table 7.1
American Indian Population for Selected States

Source: From *Statistical Abstracts of the United States: 2004–2005* (124th ed.), U.S. Census Bureau. Washington, D.C.: Author.

State	American Indian Population
California	413,000
Oklahoma	280,000
Arizona	294,000
New Mexico	187,000
Washington	100,000
Alaska	103,000
North Carolina	108,000
Texas	147,000
New York	105,000
Michigan	60,000

The U.S. Census Bureau offers other facts about American Indians and their demographics; however, caution is urged as counselors and social workers intervene with American Indians. This culture is very diverse: American Indians constitute a significant cultural group with very different values, problems, and resources, compared with the general population. Therefore, to avoid basing professional intervention on stereotypical generalizations, counselors need to consider tribal, geographic, socioeconomic, educational, and other differences.

First, American Indians are a young and growing population. The median age of the American Indian population is considerably younger than the U.S. median. Also, the relatively young age of the population results in higher fertility rates overall.

Second, educational attainments of American Indians, Eskimos, and Aleuts are dismal: Of the population that is 25 years and older, 29.2% of American Indian students have completed high school, and 7.6% have a bachelor's degree.

Third, significant numbers (i.e., 608,000) of American Indians live below the poverty line. The proportion of American Indian, Eskimo, and Aleut persons and families living below the poverty level is considerably higher than for the total population. In 2002, about 303,000 Native Americans qualified for food stamps (U.S. Census Bureau, 2004–2005).

Fourth, about 54% of American Indians (including Eskimos and Aleuts) live on reservations and trust lands. Also of interest, American Indians living on reservations are considerably younger than the general population. In addition, educational attainments differ substantially among reservations (U.S. Census Bureau, 2004–2005).

American Indian Children

Social and Cultural Description

It is crucial that professionals intervening with American Indian children understand the history of the United States from the American Indian point of view and from the child's perspective. The assumption that American Indians belong to one homogeneous tribe is far from the truth. They are a culture of many peoples, with diverse educational attainments, economic levels, and tribal differences. Table 7.2 shows an age breakdown of American Indian, Eskimo, and Aleut children.

Although physical and cultural diversity has long characterized American Indians, certain similarities with respect to values and beliefs allow for a broad-based description of the American Indian child. As mentioned previously, caution must be exercised when developing such a portrait, because considerable intracultural variation is to be expected. Particularly relevant is the

Table 7.2
Population of American Indian, Eskimo, and Aleut Children

Source: Statistical Abstracts of the United States: 2004–2005 (124th ed.), by U.S. Census Bureau. Washington, D.C.: Author.

Age	Total
Under 5 years	208,000
5 to 14 years	509,000

location of a child's residence (on or off the reservation), the child's school (predominantly American Indian or European American), and the parents' socioeconomic class.

The values and beliefs of American Indians often differ from those of European Americans. Whereas European American children are taught that they have considerable freedom as long as their actions remain within the law, American Indian children are taught that their actions must be in harmony with nature. American Indians also prize self-sufficiency and learning gained from the natural world. Children are taught to respect and protect the aged, who provide wisdom and acquaint the younger generations with traditions, customs, and legends (Axelson, 1999). Elderly American Indians teach younger family members traditional crafts and handiwork as well as cultural morals. Other distinct cultural values are reflected in interpersonal relationships. For example, children receive the same degree of respect as adults, group cooperation and harmony are encouraged, and individuals are judged by their contribution to the group. American Indians have an unhurried lifestyle that is present-time oriented. A deep respect for tradition is evident.

For more than a century, tens of thousands of American Indians surrendered their childhoods at Indian boarding schools. The federal Bureau of Indian Affairs began opening boarding schools in the late 1870s, conjoining a parallel system of religious boarding schools operated by Christian missionaries. The number of students at these boarding schools swelled from 6,200 in 60 schools in 1885 to more than 17,000 in 153 schools by 1900. By 1931, nearly one-third (about 24,000) of Indian children attended boarding schools. Currently, enrollments at 52 federal boarding schools have declined to less than half that number.

The stories of misery and abuse told by native children in these schools are disturbing, especially since the goal was to obliterate all that was Indian, or "Kill the Indian, save the man" Children were beaten, were forced to eat lye soap for speaking their tribal languages, had their hair cropped, were paddled for carrying medicine bundles, and were forced to walk a gauntlet of classmates wielding sticks and belts. Some schools banned parents from visiting because they might "infect" their children with tribal culture. Because they were separated from their parents for years, the children never learned about good parenting skills (Former students recall beatings, April 30, 1999).

In the 1970s, a survey of the Association of American Indian Affairs found that 25% to 35% of all native children had been separated from their families (Cross, Earle, & Simmons, 2000). In 16 states in 1969, 8.5% of the Indian children were placed with non-Indian families. From 1971 to 1972, approximately 35,000 children lived in institutional settings, more than 68% of those in Bureau of Indian Affairs schools. The tragic, long-range effects of the placement of thousands of native people away from their homes were only then beginning to be realized (Cross, Earle, & Simmons, 2000).

Cross, Earle, and Simmons (200) also looked at American Indians' heritage of cultural child protection and the impact of humanitarian efforts, relocation programs, and learned abuse patterns. The Indian Child Welfare Act (ICWA), which reaffirmed tribal authority to protect children, was passed in 1978. Cross and colleagues maintained that the ICWA was a step in the right direction, however, other factors (e.g., funding, desire, training) posed problems. For Indian tribes, program development has been hampered by lack of funding, jurisdictional barriers, lack of trained personnel, lack of information about the extent of abuse and neglect, lack of culturally appropriate service models, and community denial of these problems. Despite these obstacles, tribes have been able to develop services to a degree beyond what could reasonably be expected.

A FOCUS ON RESEARCH 7.1

Identity and Pride in American Indian Children

Horne, an American Indian, attended a Bureau of Indian Affairs boarding school. Then she completed her teacher education training and taught one year at a boarding school and 35 years at an Indian school.

Horne explains how well-meaning school employees sought to take the "Indianness" out of Indians. In her paper, she explains that she wants to share her thoughts on educating American Indians as well as on promoting the development of their pride and identity:

1. Become a creative educator.

2. Rediscover and reaffirm the cultural heritage of American Indian students.

3. Create successful learning experiences,

4. Develop language and communication skills.

5. Work to reduce discrimination and intolerance of differences.

6. Encourage family and community involvement in teaching and learning.

7. Teach old Indian values.

Horne includes a special section on what she terms old Indian values—bravery, individual freedom, generosity and sharing, adjustment to nature, and Indian wisdom.

Many of Horne's suggestions for teachers are also relevant for counselors who want to promote identity development in American Indian children.

Source: "The development of identity and pride in the Indian child," by E.B. Horne, 2003, (edited by C.B. Leung), *Multicultural Education, 10(4)*, pp. 32–38."

Programs designed to serve tribal communities should have

- direct access to funds for tribes;

- funding formulas for the distribution of tribal funds that emphasize need, equity, and the administrative capacities of tribes;

- regulations that provide tribes with the ability to design and operate a program that meets the unique circumstances and values of their communities; and

- streamlined application procedures and more realistic reporting requirements. (Cross et al., 2000)

In A Focus on Research 7.1, Horne (2003), an educator of American Indian children for 36 years, explains the need for educators and counselors to promote the development of identity and pride in American Indian Children.

Communication

American Indian languages can be divided into about a dozen stocks, with each stock divided into distinct languages. Most classifications of American Indians into nations, tribes, or peoples have been linguistic rather than political. This broad and diversified communication background, albeit personal and sacred to the American Indian, has not contributed to the European American definition of school success. Moreover, widespread differences exist in American Indians' ability to speak English.

Nonverbal communication of American Indian children adds another dimension to counseling intervention. It is essential for professionals to understand American Indian gestures, body movements, and general social behavior. Although considerable diversity exists, American Indian children speak more softly than European children and at a slower rate. They also tend to avoid direct interaction between speaker and listener as expressed by signs such as head nods and similar gestures.

Families

American Indian immediate and extended families contribute to their children's cultural identities and play a significant role in overall child development. Extended family members retain official and symbolic leadership in family communities. They monitor children's behavior and have a voice in child-rearing practices (Wilson, Kohn, & Lee, 2000).

American Indian children are respected, and they are also taught to respect others. It has been said that Indian child-rearing methods are marked by extraordinary patience and tolerance; that is, Indian children usually are brought up without restraint or severe physical punishment. Obedience is achieved through moral or psychological persuasion, building on tribal beliefs in supernatural beings. Many tribes have stories of supernatural beings who watch children and punish them when they are disobedient. Through the telling of myths and legends, children are given a clear picture of expectations for desired behavior and the consequences of deviant behavior (Cross, Earle, & Simmons, 2000).

In the American Indian culture, family extends well beyond the immediate relatives to extended family relatives through second cousins, members of one's clan, members of the community, all other living creatures in this world, nature as a whole, and the universe itself. The entire universe is thought of as a family, with every one of its members serving a useful and necessary function. American Indian children develop a heightened sensitivity for everything of which they are a part, for the cyclical motion of life, and for the customs and traditions of their people (Garrett, M. W., 1995).

The American Indian family thinks of children as gifts worthy of sharing with others, whereas the European family holds that children constitute private property to be disciplined as deemed necessary. In essence, children have fewer rules to obey in the American Indian culture, whereas European children have more rules, with strict consequences for disobedience. Also, contrary to the individualism prized in European American society, the American Indian family places more emphasis on group welfare (Axelson, 1999).

American Indian child-rearing practices and differing cultural family expectations for behavior sometimes result in confusion and frustration for American Indian children growing up in European American society. They may demonstrate feelings of isolation, rejection, and anxiety that can result in alienation, poor self-image, and withdrawal. Such feelings undoubtedly affect achievement aspirations of American Indian children and can cause them to question the worth of their family life.

Up Close and Personal 7.1 describes Bill Lonetree, an American Indian child.

Bill Lonetree, an American Indian Child

Eight-year-old Bill Lonetree lives with his parents, 10-year-old sister, 15-year-old brother, and elderly grandmother. The Lonetree family home is in a small community several miles from a reservation. Although the family's financial status is above the poverty level, money often poses a problem. For many years, Bill's ancestors lived on the reservation, but his grandparents moved to a European American Community in an attempt to better their deteriorating financial status. After Bill's grandfather died, his grandmother moved in with Bill's parents.

Bill, a quiet and often reflective child, is a third grader at the local European American school. Although he generally likes his school and has several American Indian friends, he experiences difficulty making European American friends. The European American children have much in common with Bill, but their differences make "an understanding of one another" difficult.

Bill's schoolwork is below average. In home and neighborhood situations, he appears to be relatively bright and thoughtful. His European American teacher, who recently began teaching at the school, encourages Bill to try harder, to listen attentively, and to be more proactive in his learning. In her attempts to motivate Bill, she sometimes tells him of her learning experiences in high school and college and encourages him to prepare for similar experiences that he can someday enjoy. She hopes that Bill will "speak up" and give her some indications that he is at least listening to her. Bill's

parents think he is trying hard in school, although he is not performing at the level they would like. They hope that his grades will not decline further at about sixth grade, as was the case with Bill's older brother.

When Bill is asked about his academic problems, he responds that he is trying, but admits that he does not always understand what the teacher is saying. He admits that reading the textbooks and other materials is difficult for him. Understanding (and speaking) two languages is often confusing for him.

In Bill's family, there is a sense of mutual respect and appreciation for one another. His grandmother, although elderly and unable to contribute financially, is close to Bill. He has tremendous respect for her and listens attentively when she tells him of the rich heritage of the American Indian culture. Also, he feels a sense of loyalty to her. On the days when she is ill, Bill stays home from school to watch over her and to assist her with her needs.

In many ways, Bill is a typical third grader. He is looking for a sense of self-worth (although perhaps not the same "self-worth" his teacher considers important), and he desires friendships. His poor self-concept, however, makes it difficult for him to find new friends and to develop self-worth. He sometimes feels "caught in the middle" between his American Indian home and his European American school. Conforming to American Indian cultural expectations at home and European American expectations at school often seems to be too much for Bill to handle.

Unique Challenges Confronting American Indian Children

Several obstacles may hinder counseling interventions for American Indian children. First, previous injustices by Whites have resulted in significant feelings of suspicion and distrust of White professionals and institutions. Second, communication problems, such as nonverbal or body language, may result in misunderstanding, mistrust, and inability to develop rapport, which may hinder counseling efforts. The American Indian child who may appear to be unemotional or detached may only be painfully shy and overly sensitive to strangers because of communication problems and mistrust of European Americans.

Attention deficit hyperactivity disorder (ADHD) affects children of all races, not only American Indian children, but counselors should recognize the characteristics of the disorder and possible accommodations for Indian children. According to Reid (2001), an estimated 3% to 5% of American children have ADHD (a neuropsychological disorder) and thus are at higher risk for learning, behavioral, and emotional problems, including (a) short attention span or being easily distracted, which sometimes results in minor discipline problems; (b) difficulty starting work and following class routines; (c) fidgeting and inability to stay seated; (d) sloppiness, disorganization, failure to complete or return assignments; (e) difficulty completing work or maintaining effort; and (f) having a "bad day" (p. 3). Implications for teachers and counselors include (a) having a few good rules; (b) keeping rules short and simple; (c) keeping rules positive; (d) posting rules prominently; (e) teaching the rules; and (f) reinforcing compliance.

American Indian Adolescents

Social and Cultural Description

Although the words Indian and adolescent combined tend to evoke stereotypical images, this developmental period in the American Indian culture varies greatly. Significant physical and cultural variance is found within the American Indian population, but individual differences during the adolescent years are even more marked. Some common characteristics emerge when studying American Indian adolescents, but one must be careful not to oversimplify or ignore intracultural and individual differences.

Each day, American Indian youths face the dilemma of constant change in our dynamic multicultural society. Conflicts include being expected to adapt to new and changing values and traditions. American Indian youths are an extremely high-risk population, with dramatically higher rates (compared with national averages) of dropping out of high school, alcohol and drug abuse, teenage pregnancy, learning disabilities, out-of-home placement, and suicide (Safran, Safran, & Pirozak, 1994). Many American Indian youths also experience racism from European Americans, and probably from other cultural groups as well. Deyhle (1995) tells about the racism that young Navajo men and women face daily in a border reservation community. She describes racist acts and racial conflicts that occurred, such as Navajos receiving the worst jobs or being turned down for jobs, and other forms of discrimination in the school and workplace.

Cultural beliefs and traditions of the American Indian people particularly influence developing adolescents and their evolving identity. Adolescents who live in American Indian families and attend European American schools may experience cultural confusion and often question allegiance to their cultural identity. This can be particularly serious for adolescents who want to retain their rich cultural heritage and at the same time be accepted in European American mainstream society.

Cooperation, Competition, and Sharing.   Many Americans place value and emphasis on competition. American society values individuality and achievement; for many people, being successful means having the most cars, wealth, and material possessions. Many American Indians, however, view success communally, by contributing toward the maintenance of the group identity and by promoting a harmonious whole. They value sharing and seeking to acquire only what is necessary to satisfy current needs. In games requiring talent and skills, players may choose to play in such a way that places group cooperation over individual winning. A similar situation may occur in the classroom, where competitive academic achievement may be shunned to avoid causing some students to be perceived as losers (Safran et al., 1994).

Patience and Passivity.   American Indian adolescents learn to be patient, to control emotions, and to avoid passionate outbursts over small matters. Such attributes as poise under duress, self-containment, and aloofness often conflict with European American tendencies toward impatience and competitiveness. Therefore, people of other cultures sometimes perceive American Indians as lazy, uncaring, and inactive (Lewis & Ho, 1989). American Indians show patience and poise as they lower their voices when angry, unlike European American adolescents, who tend to be strident in expressing their anger. Other differences exist; for example, some American Indian groups indicate respect by looking downward to avoid eye contact. Also, whereas a firm handshake is regarded positively in the majority culture, such a gesture is perceived by American Indians as an aggressive and disrespectful act (Safran et al., 1994).

Noninterference.   Generally speaking, American Indians strive to attain a harmonius relationship with nature and all living things. Noninterference with others and a deep respect for the rights and dignity of individuals constitute a basic premise of the American Indian culture. Adolescents are taught early on to respect the rights and privileges of others and to work together toward common goals in harmony with nature. American Indians place high regard on building relationships and on an all-encompassing sense of belonging with one's people and the practice of noninterference. The highest form of respect for another person is respecting his or her natural right to self-determination. This means not interfering with another person's ability to choose, even if it means not preventing a person from doing something foolish or dangerous. Noninterference means caring in a respectful way (Garrett, M.W., 1995). American Indian life is an unhurried, never-ending process, with a basic philosophy of "live and let live" (Garrett, M.W., 1995, p. 51).

The school drop-out rate of American Indian adolescents is high. Factors that undoubtedly contribute to the high drop-out rate include growing feelings of isolation, cultural conflicts between American Indian adolescents and European American teachers, cultural and individual rejection, and anxiety resulting from differences in cultural values. Many Navajo and other American Indian adolescents often experience school curricula and program development that result in formidable challenges.

Communication

American Indian adolescents, like adolescents of other cultures, need the security and psychological safety provided by a common language. However, this may be complicated by the fact that some American Indian adolescents speak only their American Indian language, some speak only English, and others are bilingual. Self-concept and individual and cultural identities are being formed during the adolescent's transition from the family-centered world to a wider social world. No longer is communication limited to that with elders, parents, and siblings. An American

Indian adolescent's ability to reach out to a wider world depends greatly on his/her ability to speak and understand the language of the majority and other cultures.

Attending a school staffed by European American teachers and facing problems associated with not being understood may affect the adolescent's perceived ability to cope successfully in a predominantly European American world. Communication problems also may contribute to the adolescent's tendency to decline in academic achievement and self-esteem. Also, adolescents often have to decide which language to speak. American Indians respect their language as a part of their culture. This regard for their native language, however, conflicts with the European American opinion that English is the means to success (or at least the European definition of success) and should be the predominant form of communication.

Families

Although an adolescent's developing social consciousness results in a gradual transition from a family-centered to a more peer-centered environment, the traditional American Indian respect for and commitment to the family continue. Adolescents seek social acceptance and approval

---

UP CLOSE AND PERSONAL 7.2

Ed Lonetree, an American Indian Adolescent

Ed, aged 15, lives with his parents, sister, elderly grandmother, and his 8-year-old brother, Bill. The family still lives several miles from the reservation and continues to have some financial difficulty.

Ed, who is midway through his adolescent years, has problems that Bill has yet to experience. Although Ed was a relatively small child, his growth spurt began at about age 12, accompanied by considerable physical and psychosocial changes. He thinks about these changes and does not always understand what is happening. He wonders whether all the changes are normal. Sometimes he admits to feelings of confusion. "How can I be a child, an adolescent, and an adult?" Ed asks himself.

Ed is in the eighth grade for the second time. Although he thought he was trying last year, the schoolwork was difficult and he experienced language problems. In fact, language may be his greatest problem. He thinks his "choice of language" will depend on where he lives when he grows up. He will speak the American Indian language if he returns to the reservation; he will speak English if he lives in the local community. Meanwhile, he speaks the American Indian language with his grandmother (and sometimes with his father) and English at school.

Ed is thinking of joining the Indian League when he turns 16. The organization is concerned with the civil rights of American Indians and generally promotes their interests. Ed's dad thinks he will be too young and that finishing school and speaking English would be best for Ed. Secretly, Ed knows that he will not join if his grandmother opposes the idea. Disappointing his grandmother would not be worth joining the group. And, after all, she has always given him good advice in the past.

Ed has experienced a few problems at school. His teachers continue to write notes on his report cards, referring to his lack of interest. Ed thinks he is interested and motivated, but the issue is not worth confronting the teachers. Also, he has tried to make friends with some European American adolescents but has not had a great deal of success.

Ed wonders about the future. Will he return to the reservation? Will he choose to speak the American Indian language, English, or both? Will he ever pass the eighth grade? Will he have White friends? These questions continue to plague Ed.

from older members of the family as well as from younger ones. Unlike European American culture, which emphasizes youth and the self, American Indian culture places family before self and fosters a great respect for elders and their wisdom. Wisdom is gained through interaction with older people, whose task is to acquaint the young with the traditions, customs, legends, and myths of their culture. All family members care for the aged and accept death as a natural fact of life (Axelson, 1999).

Early training received by American Indian adolescents continues to have an impact during the adolescent years. Although loyalty to and dependence on the immediate and surrounding family continue to be valued, adolescents grow increasingly independent and confident of their abilities to deal with the world outside the family. Their early training, however, might contribute to their confusion. For example, some outside cultures may have difficulty understanding the American Indian belief that great wealth and materialistic possessions should not be accumulated at the expense of sharing with one's fellow human beings. Likewise, self-gain cannot be achieved at the expense of family or tribal members or at the expense of harming any aspect of the natural world.

Up Close and Personal 7.2 introduces Ed Lonetree.

Unique Challenges Confronting American Indian Adolescents

Three specific issues have particular relevance for American Indian adolescents: (1) Should American Indian or European American values (or some "cultural combination") provide the basis for the adolescent's developing identity? (2) Should proficiency in both the American Indian language and English be encouraged? and (3) Can harmony with family and nature be maintained while the adolescent is surviving in the European American world? Survival in the majority culture often requires American Indians to question the priorities of their own culture.

American Indian adolescents are in a unique and often difficult situation. Not only must they reconcile the values of American Indian and European American cultures, they must also deal with the usual problems of adolescence as a developmental period on the lifespan continuum. Educational and societal dilemmas, as well as cultural conflicts, during these crucial developmental years often cause feelings of frustration, hopelessness, alienation, and loss of confidence. The steady decline often seen in adolescents' academic achievement may further contribute to feelings of hopelessness.

Jeffries and Singer (2003) maintain that several mechanisms have focused on forcing American Indians to assimilate. Although some efforts sounded good on paper, in theory and practice, acculturation relegated the various cultural practices to a status below the dominant culture. For example, the Bureau of Indian Affairs proposed educational initiatives such as off- and on-reservation boarding schools and day schools. Many of these efforts actually weakened the pride and solidarity found among American Indians and Alaska Native children. In A Focus on Research 7.2, Jeffries and Singer describe a successful program to educate urban American Indian students.

A FOCUS ON RESEARCH 7.2

Alternative School Formats for American Indians

In their article, Jeffries and Singer (2003) explore the use of culturally relevant practices and a responsive alternative school. Specifically, they provide a framework for examining the use of culturally relevant experiences for American Indians. They also examine the impact of school size, the implementation of a format and governance, and the use of culturally responsive educational experiences.

Alternative schools provide an educational environment that lends itself to students who have difficulty in traditional educational settings. Also, Jeffries and Singer (2003) maintain that alternative schools have a positive effect on student achievement, allow students greater access to activities, and provide opportunities for increased interaction and communication.

In their study, they report some very interesting student comments regarding topics such as teachers, classes, and other students.

For alternative schools to meet the cultural needs of American Indians, the authors suggest an exemplary leader, culturally responsive teachers, and culturally relevant pedagogy. These have the potential for promoting academic achievement and reducing the power of extrinsic rewards that often distract marginalized students from educational success.

Source: "Successfully educating urban American Indian students," by R. B. Jeffries, and L. C. Singer, 2003, *Journal of American Indian Education, 42*(3), pp. 40–57.

American Indian Adults

Social and Cultural Description

The lack of acceptance of American Indian culture has contributed to the difficulties faced by American Indians. Currently, American Indians continue to struggle to overcome others' negative images of them; even worse, they may have to overcome their own negative self-images. When the American Indian culture is mentioned, the image too often brought to mind is of a lazy, deceptive individual who is prone to excessive drinking and violent and erratic behavior. This stereotypical image has led many American Indians to view themselves in a negative light. Undoubtedly, self-denigration has contributed to American Indians' lack of success in a predominantly European American society.

Historically, in American Indian communities, adults were universally responsible for child-rearing. Every adult played a role in teaching and caring for younger members of the tribe. First-born children were often raised by grandparents, who were responsible for teaching the children about social mores and values, including sexuality and appropriate behaviors that ensured the tribe's survival. Children learned creation stories, naming ceremonies, spiritual teachings, puberty ceremonies, spiritual and social songs, and dances. They learned gender roles, some of which were of a practical nature and others which fell within the spiritual realm (Day, 1995).

Spirituality plays a major role in the lives of many American Indians and thus should be recognized by counselors during intervention. Garrett and Wilbur (1999) describe a number of basic American Indian spiritual and traditional beliefs:

1. There is a single higher power known as Creator, Great Creator, Great Spirit, or Great One, among other names. Lesser beings are known as spirit beings or spirit helpers.

2. Plants and animals, like humans, are part of the spirit world. The spirit world exists conjointly with and intermingles with the physical world. Moreover, the spirit existed in the spirit world before it manifested as a physical body, and it will continue to exist after the body dies.

3. Human beings are made up of a spirit, mind, and body, all of which are interconnected; therefore, illness affects the mind and spirit as well as the body.

4. Wellness is harmony in body, mind, and spirit; unwellness is disharmony in mind, body, and spirit.

5. Natural unwellness is caused by a violation of a sacred social and natural law of creation (e.g., participating in a sacred ceremony while under the influence of alcohol, drugs, or having had sex within 4 days of a ceremony).

6. Unnatural wellness is caused by conjuring (witchcraft) from those with destructive intentions.

7. Each individual is responsible for his or her own wellness by being attuned to self, relations, environment, and universe (Garrett & Wilbur, 1999).

Garrett and Wilbur offer several implications for counseling:

1. Counselors should recognize culturally specific meanings and practices that may play a critical role in understanding the client's issues (and appropriate ways of dealing with the issues) and also understanding the world in which the client lives.

2. Counselors should seek to understand the client's level of acculturation.

3. Counselors should pose questions in a respectful and unobtrusive manner.

4. Counselors should not assume that a client who "looks Indian" (p. 202) is traditional; similarly, it should not be assumed that a client who "does not look Indian" (p. 202) is not traditional.

5. Counselors working with a client who has very traditional values and beliefs should consider inviting a medicine man or medicine woman to participate in the counseling process as the client moves through important personal transitions.

Most professionals agree that the American Indian population has a proportionately greater percentage of problems than other minority populations. Compared with African and Asian Americans, American Indians have significant income, education, and medical needs. In addition, arrest, alcoholism, and unemployment rates are higher among American Indians than among other ethnic groups.

Researchers have long been interested in alcohol use and alcoholism among American Indians. Taylor, M.J. (2000) explored several myths about alcohol use and abuse. First, the "firewater myth" (p. 153) holds that American Indians experience rapid intoxication from small amounts of alcohol and then demonstrate boisterous, raucous behavior. A second myth is that alcoholism rates are inordinately high among all Native American people. Interestingly, however, an estimated 60% of Navajos abstain from alcohol, wheras surveys show that greater than 80% of Utes and Ojibwas have used alcohol (Taylor, M.J., 2000). A third myth is that alcohol use and abuse are the root causes of many problems (e.g., poverty) that Indian people currently face. Taylor maintains that there are two types of alcohol users in Indian communities. The anxiety drinkers account for about one-fourth of Indians who are chronic alcohol users; they are often older, unemployed, and live a marginal existence. The recreational drinkers are episodic binge drinkers and often are younger than anxiety drinkers.

Taylor also found that when the goal of substance abuse programs is to enhance individuals' self-esteem, professionals should also consider addressing client self-efficacy. Individuals who feel more confident about their skills and abilities may be less prone to use alcohol or participate in other risky behaviors.

Although American Indians' diversity should always be considered, several cultural practices and lifestyles characterize American Indians. Common traits include (a) relative passivity and shyness in dealing with professionals, (b) sensitivity to strangers (resulting in soft-spokenness), (c) a tendency to focus on the present, (d) a fatalistic view of life, (e) strong family obligations, (f) noninterference with others, and (g) avoidance of assertive or aggressive situations.

Communication

At one time or another American Indians have spoken over 2,000 different languages. The difficulty of categorizing these languages into major families attests to the fact that understanding the communication patterns of this culture requires considerable effort.

Littlebear (2003) maintains that the loss of American Indian languages has recently accelerated, and he calls for the preservation of spiritual identities and endangered languages.

Although verbal communication is the usual means by which adults interact, nonverbal communication is also extremely important. Professionals are increasingly realizing the urgent

---

A FOCUS ON RESEARCH 7.3

Strengthening the Northern Cheyenne in Language and Culture

Littlebear claims that the United States is a graveyard for hundreds of native languages. Some are only a generation away from extinction. The loss of American Indian languages has been well-chronicled by ethnologists, linguists, anthropologists, missionaries, and even some government-run schools. Although there is nothing wrong with American Indian languages, systematic attempts have sought to eradicate these languages and have the potential for damaging American Indian identities.

Littlebear (2003) describes a program at Chief Dull Knife College that is designed to save the Cheyenne language. The goal of the program is to strengthen the Cheyenne language through the application of oral-based methodologies.

In his description of the program, Littlebear addresses several points (the uppercase letters are Littlebear's): (1) What is the language strengthening program actually going to do? (2) Is it going TO TEACH the language? (3) Is it going TO TEACH ABOUT the language? (4) Is it going TO TEACH WITH the language? (5) Is it going TO TEACH FOR ACADEMIC CREDIT?

In conclusion, Littlebear points out that languages can help people preserve their individual and cultural identities.

Source: "Chief Dull Knife community is strengthening the Northern Cheyenne in language and culture," by R. E. Littlebear, 2003, *Journal of American Indian Education, 42*(1), pp. 75–84.

need to understand how messages are communicated. Because it is deeply rooted in Indian cultural heritage, nonverbal communication must be recognized and appreciated as a cherished cultural tradition. Common nonverbal behaviors of American Indian adults include avoiding eye contact, listening with an indirect gaze, and looking away after initial acknowledgment. European Americans who tend to look each other in the eye may be disturbed by clients who are indeed listening but are looking in another direction.

Families

American Indian families, just as individuals of the culture, have widely differing personality traits, cultural practices, and lifestyles. Several common characteristics of families, however, appear to pertain to large segments of the culture.

UP CLOSE AND PERSONAL 7.3

John Lonetree, an American Indian Adult

John, age 38, shares traits common to fathers of all cultural backgrounds. His main goals are to provide financial support and a home for his 8-year-old and 15-year-old sons, his 10-year-old daughter, his wife of 17 years, and his elderly mother. John works at a manufacturing plant and wonders where he could find another job if he were laid off. He realizes the difficulty that job hunting would entail, especially with his limited education, lack of marketable skills, and poor English.

Through hard work at the same job for 9 years, John's condition belies that of the stereotypical American Indian. John has a job, does not have a drinking problem, has never been in jail, and is not overly self-critical, as many American Indians are thought to be. The fact that he does not have extensive material possessions is of little concern to him; he thinks people should appreciate him as a person rather than for what he owns. He is aware that he has experienced fewer problems than many of his friends.

John has several family concerns that adults of other cultures often share. He sometimes worries about his children's education. They will need a better education than he has had in order to compete in the predominantly European American society. He is

concerned about his mother, who is showing signs of advancing age. Although she doesn't make a direct financial contribution to the family, she is an important source of advice and counsel. Also, she takes care of the children when they are too ill to attend school. Because of her age, she deserves to be protected and respected. John often seeks her advice on how to raise the children.

Although John is fairly content and happy compared with many of his friends, he does have problems. As previously mentioned, he wants his children to finish high school. Then he wants to do something to help those friends who have not been as fortunate as he. He would also like to rid himself, his family, and his people of the stereotypical image of the drunken, lazy, uneducated American Indian that continues to be so demoralizing. Finally, because he is accustomed to speaking a combination of two languages with his friends, he sometimes experiences communication difficulties when he travels outside his American Indian community.

John has doubts about his future: With his current skills, will he always have a job? Will his children finish high school?

How will his family change when his mother passes away?

In the American Indian culture, because survival of the individual is synonymous with that of the community, the family holds a prominent place in the lives of American Indians, who view the concept of family much more broadly than does mainstream America. Structural characteristics of the extended family network and the tribal network function as facilitators of social responsibility, reciprocity, and values transmission. Family relationships extend far beyond the biological connections of the nuclear family (Garrett, M.W., 1995).

Several characteristics of American Indian families are worth mentioning. Each has implications for counselors planning professional intervention.

First, the culture expects adults to demonstrate strong allegiance to, respect for, and protection of the elderly.

Second, American Indian child-rearing practices include an emphasis on self-sufficiency, with physical development and psychological learning being in harmony with knowledge gained from the natural world.

Third, with respect to women, American Indian society differs from other ethnic minority groups. Historically, African, Latin, and Asian cultures have exhibited a patriarchal structure. Some American Indian subcultures, however, have perceived the roles of women differently. In the past, American Indian women held great political and economic power. In fact, they had considerable power and status in their tribes at the time Europeans arrived in North America (Porter, 2000).

Up Close and Personal 7.3 looks at John Lonetree, an American Indian adult.

Unique Challenges Confronting American Indian Adults

Several challenges facing American Indian adults deserve counselors' attention. First, despite the considerable progress made over the past 20 years in addressing the health care needs of American Indians and Alaskan Natives, their overall health care lags well behind that of other racial groups in the United States (Portman, 2001). Second, education has always been a controversial issue that basically revolves around the pressures of domination, value conflict, and self-determination. Regardless of these factors, however, the poor academic attainment of American Indians has been a major drawback to their progress. Third, alcoholism is another challenge that significant numbers of American Indians experience, just as do people of all cultural backgrounds. Fourth, perhaps one of the most significant problems for American Indians, is the collection of destructive stereotypical images that are often perpetuated in literature and in the media. These stereotypes can potentially influence the decisions of counselors and the career and employment aspirations of their clients.

Solutions to the challenges confronting American Indian adults must be sought by both clients and their counselors in a cooperative spirit. Many of their problems stem from a history of discrimination and prejudice. Although the reasons for American Indians' personal and social conditions should be recognized and understood, counseling interventions should focus on solutions to the obstacles hampering personal and social progress.

American Indian Elderly

Social and Cultural Description

Counselors need to have an objective understanding of the population, education, employment, income, and health of elderly American Indians. Table 7.3 shows the population numbers of Native Americans age 65 and older.

Knowledge of several interesting facts will help mental health professionals understand elderly American Indian clients:

- About one-fourth of Native American elderly live on American Indian reservations or in Alaskan Native villages. Almost half are concentrated in the southwestern states of Oklahoma, Arizona, New Mexico, and Texas. Most of the remainder live in states along the Canadian border.

- Educationally, elderly American Indians lag significantly. In fact, nearly 10% of all American Indian elderly do not have any formal education, and only about one-third have a high school diploma. Those who did receive an education almost exclusively attended school systems that—either on or off the reservation—often have been considered poor quality.

- Many American Indians live in poverty. Twenty-five percent of American Indians live in poverty; 26% of American Indian elderly live in poverty (U.S. Census Bureau, 2000).

- The health status of elderly American Indians also poses problems. American Indians' life expectancy is about 8 years shorter than that of European Americans. American Indians and Alaskan Natives are 10 times more likely than European Americans to develop diabetes. In addition, alcohol abuse is a leading cause of health problems in American Indians. Other health problems include injuries from accidents, suicide, homicide, tuberculosis, liver and kidney diseases, high blood pressure, pneumonia, and malnutrition (U.S. Census Bureau, 2000)

Counseling professionals should focus their efforts on the prevention and management of chronic illnesses and conditions in this population. Disease patterns in American Indians have followed several trends, including a shift from acute, infectious diseases to those of a more degenerative type. Chronic illnesses and conditions seen in significant numbers of American Indians include diabetes, heart disease, substance use, and fetal alcohol syndrome.

Table 7.3
Population of Elderly American Indian, Eskimo, and Aleut
Source: Statistical Abstracts of the United States: 2004–2005 (124th ed.), by U.S. Census Bureau. Washington, D.C.: Author.

Age	Total
65 to 74 years	172,000
75 to 84 years	68,000
85 years and older	17,000

Many American Indian elderly rarely see a physician, primarily because those who need medical attention often live in isolated areas and lack transportation. American Indian traditions of ritual folk healing and the spiritual aspect of disease also have deterred reliance on a strictly scientific medical community.

Although the American Indian population continues to be young relative to the total population, the number of elderly American Indians continues to grow. Based on their unique cultural and lifespan characteristics, many of these elderly are likely to require counseling.

It is imperative that counselors be aware of the often disturbing living conditions of American Indian elderly. Social programs cannot immunize American Indian elderly from a lifetime of deprivation, such as inadequate nutrition, housing, and health services. Significant changes will be needed for future generations of elderly American Indians to witness improvement in their standard of living.

Communication

American Indian elderly seem to experience communication problems similar to those of American Indian adults; however, there is no evidence that they encounter special problems as a result of their age. American Indian elderly experience frustration in seeking attention to their health and retirement benefits. Also, as with other minority adults, differing cultures may misunderstand or misinterpret the elderly American Indian's nonverbal communication style.

Families

As previously mentioned, the elderly receive considerable respect in the American Indian culture. This may be because of their advanced age or cultural tradition. Regardless of the reason, younger generations seek the opinions of elders and consider their advice with reverence (Axelson, 1999).

Understanding the actual role the elderly play in American Indian families provides counselors with insights about their problems and the questions that might be raised during counseling sessions. The extended family continues to play a significant role in family life. Elderly family members provide significant services, such as assisting with the traditional child-rearing practices. In turn, younger family members respect the symbolic leadership of the elderly and expect them to have an official voice in child-rearing. Parents defer to the authority of their elders and rarely overrule the latter's decisions regarding the children. Relationships with all family members are an important source of strength for the elderly (Garrett, M.W., 1995).

It is important for counselors to understand the living arrangements of American Indian elderly. Among Native American and European Americans age 65 and older, the majority of men are married and the majority of women are widowed. However, more American Indian women than European American women tend to marry in their later years.

Up Close and Personal 7.4 focuses on Wenonah Lonetree, an elderly American Indian woman.

UP CLOSE AND PERSONAL 7.4

Wenonah Lonetree, an American Indian Elder

At age 72, Wenonah Lonetree does not doubt that she is growing old. She senses it in the way she feels and in the way she is treated by her family and others. Growing old has both rewards and drawbacks. She realizes that attaining the age of 72 is unusual for a person in her American Indian culture; she has already outlived many of her friends. Although Wenonah is financially poor, not having money is nothing new to her. She lives with her son John, his wife, and their family and contributes to the family by helping with the children. In fact, she has assumed virtually all responsibility for child-rearing. The children have learned that Wenonah's word represents authority; their parents never question her decisions. The family equates Wenonah's years with great wisdom.

Wenonah has the typical problems of elderly members of the American Indian culture. Her only schooling was a few years in a reservation school, and she suffers the usual ailments of the aged. Although her community does not lack medical facilities, Wenonah seldom visits the physician. She has no means of transportation when John and his wife are at work; besides,

she places her trust in healing rituals. Finances are also a problem, because living with John and his family off the reservation has lowered her government benefits.

Living with John's family can be both rewarding and frustrating. She likes being close to the children, and her son conscientiously works to provide a good home. Also, telling the children stories and teaching them about customs and traditions allows her to relive old memories. However, she is troubled by the growing problems of her grandchildren. The school apparently has little regard for American Indian youths, and her grandson Ed is talking about joining the Indian League. "That's just not the way to make progress," Wenonah says quietly, yet adamantly.

When Wenonah looks back on her life, she celebrates her accomplishments—her family, her wisdom, and her knowledge that gains her the respect of her family. But the future is uncertain. What will the next few years bring? How much longer will she be able to help John and his family? Will she become sick and need someone to take care of her?

Unique Challenges Confronting the American Indian Elderly

First, American Indians' poverty translates into alarming statistics: Indian Health Service figures show that the average life expectancy for American Indians is 8 years less than that for European Americans (Garrett, M.W., 1995). Second, the relatively small size of the elderly American Indian population has not been sufficient to attract attention to their problems. Dealing successfully with government agencies, such as the Bureau of Indian Affairs and the Public Health Service, continues to be frustrating, especially for American Indians who lack English proficiency and knowledge of their legal rights.

A Point of Departure: Challenges Confronting Counselors of American Indians

American Indians in all four lifespan stages have problems that might be brought to counseling sessions. Counselors who intervene from the perspective of any other cultural background will fail to understand American Indians' worldviews and cultural perspectives, such as their main concern being in the "here and now," their reluctance to compete at the expense of others, and their tendency to practice noninterference. In addition, counselors, regardless of cultural background and world-view, need to have an accurate perspective of such American Indian problems as unemployment, illiteracy, poverty, and substandard housing. Undoubtedly, counselors will need an understanding of such factors as injustice, prejudice, and discrimination that contribute to these problems.

Counselors working with American Indian clients, regardless of lifespan stage, should understand their cultural characteristics and worldviews and then plan counseling interventions that will be effective with, and make sense to, these clients.

Summary

Professionals who counsel American Indian children, adolescents, adults, and elders have a responsibility to understand the American Indian culture as well as the specific challenges commonly associated with each life-span period. American Indian women are perceived differently from women in most other cultures, and they have traditionally played significant family and tribal roles. Providing effective mental health intervention to such a diverse and challenged cultural group requires training and experience. Counselors will need to develop appropriate counseling skills and to make the commitment to provide culturally effective counseling intervention.

Suggested Readings

Lews, G. (2004). Were American Indians the victims of genocide? *Commentary, 118*(2), 55–64. Lews looks at the population numbers of American Indians and builds a case for genocide.

Paltoo, D. N., Chu, K. C. (2004). Patterns in cancer incidence among American Indians/Alaska Natives, United States, 1992–1999. *Public Health Reports, 119*(4), 443–449. As the title suggests, these authors look at population numbers and the incidence of cancer, and concluded the 5-year survival rate for American Indians was the poorest of any major ethnic group.

Powers, K. (2005). Promoting school achievement among American Indian students throughout the school years. *Childhood Education, 81*(6), 338–342. Powers describes a research project that focused on urban American Indian Youth. Her project directed attention to student achievement, motivation, teacher expectations, family involvement, and safe and drug-free schools.

Wahoo, E., & Olson, L. (2004). Intimate partner violence and sexual assault in Native American communities. *Trauma, Violence, and Abuse: A Review Journal, 5*(4), 353–366. Maintaining that Native American women experience the highest rate of violence of any ethnic or racial group, Wahoo and Olson address the issue of partner violence and sexual assault among Native Americans.

8

Counseling American Indian Clients

Questions to Be Explored

1. What unique challenges and differences can counselors expect when intervening with American Indian children, adolescents, adults, and elders?

2. How can non–American Indian counselors effectively plan counseling intervention for American Indian clients, considering the latter's diverse cultural, tribal, and individual differences?

3. How has a history of ill treatment affected American Indians and their worldviews?

4. How can counselors address American Indians' tendency toward early withdrawal from counseling services?

5. How can counselors conduct individual, group, and family therapy for American Indians?

6. What developmental concerns and problems might American Indian child, adolescent, adult, and elderly clients present to counselors?

7. How can counselors address American Indians' many problems, such as low educational attainment, high unemployment levels, and low socioeconomic conditions?

8. What additional sources provide information for professionals intervening with American Indian children, adolescents, adults, and elders?

Overview

Counselors intervening with American Indian children, adolescents, adults, and elders need both an understanding of and appreciation for the American Indian culture and worldview. Such a task will not be easy, considering the differing languages, lifestyles, religions, kinship systems, tribes, and reservations. Counseling therapy that may be appropriate for an American Indian adult living on the East Coast may be inappropriate for such an adult living in the western plains region. Each tribe's customs and values affect both individual identity and family dynamics. Counselors will find that American Indians withdraw from counseling at alarmingly high rates. The initial consultation should be substantive in nature, and the nature and process of counseling intervention should be explained to the client. Also, counselors need to understand that mainstream individual and group counseling processes often conflict with American Indians' values and perspectives—for example, cooperation, harmony, generosity, sharing, living in the present, ancient legends and cultural traditions, peace, and politeness. Last, lifespan differences will also determine American Indians' worldviews, as well as their perceived problems.

American Indian Children

Potential Problems Warranting Counseling Intervention

Problems American Indian children may experience include

- failure to develop a strong cultural identity and a positive self-concept;
- adverse effects of misperceptions about American Indians and the childhood years;
- adverse effects of discrimination;
- distrust of European American professionals;
- poor English proficiency and confusion in communication;
- nonverbal communication style, which may result in misunderstandings;
- inability to reconcile American Indian cultural values with other cultural values;
- lower academic achievement after the fourth grade;
- increasing socialization from a parent-centered to a peer-centered world;
- physical, psychosocial, and intellectual differences;
- differences in size and growth rate resulting from cultural factors, genetics, environment, and socioeconomic status;
- hair texture, facial features, and skin colors of American Indian children, which may be considered by other cultures as "inferior" or "wrong," rather than "different"; and
- academic difficulties, which may cause American Indian children to conclude that they simply are not smart enough to achieve success in school.

American Indian youth often face social and cultural challenges during identity development. In A Focus on Research 8.1, Newman reports on her study of ego development and ethnic identity formation in a rural Southeastern American Indian community. Although A Focus on Research 8.1 deals primarily with younger adolescents, it also shows the problems of younger children and the conclusions that counselors should recognize.

A FOCUS ON RESEARCH 8.1

Ego Development and Ethnic Identity Formation

Newman (2005) maintains that the identity development process for ethnic minority adolescents provides an added dimension highlighting the importance of ethnicity in developing a sense of self. She studied Lumbee Indian adolescents living in a rural county in North Carolina, an area she describes as poor and economically limited by low-quality public education and employment opportunities. Specifically, she investigated ego development, ethnic identity, and interpersonal relationships.

Her conclusions include (1) impulsive adolescents had the least developed ethnic identities and highest levels of interpersonal vulnerability; (2) conformist adolescents expressed positive feelings about ethnic group affiliation and described relationships as harmonious, but demonstrated social anxiety; and (3) post-conformist

adolescents had the highest levels of social competence and identity achievement but also had high levels of psychological distress and family conflict.

American Indians also face a number of challenges to their ego development and ethnic identity formation. For example, they are influenced by the mainstream media: the imagery of American Indians, omission of their history in social and political history, references to American Indians as being savages, and the various cultural stereotypes. Newman provides a wealth of information on American Indians in this valuable article.

Source: "Ego development and ethnic identity formation in rural American Indian adolescents." by D. L. Newman, 2005, *Child Development, 76* (3), pp. 734–747.

Counseling Considerations

Counselors who work with American Indian children should first learn as much as possible about the American Indian culture. Well-informed, objective, and appropriate counseling requires an unbiased perception of American Indian children and their many cultural and individual variations.

Behavior that may appear bizarre to the counselor might be the cultural norm for American Indian children. For example, American Indian children may pilfer objects from teachers, peers, or the counselor. When confronted, they will usually admit taking the objects; however, they are likely to be both surprised and hurt if the act is referred to as "stealing." These children have been taught that people of rank and importance share. The counselor could tell the children that sharing with one's family is acceptable, but that one should ask before "borrowing" objects outside the home. In addition, freedom in the American Indian culture extends to the childhood years: Children are allowed considerable involvement in decision-making and are usually given choices. Counselors working with American Indian children may want to provide them with opportunities to make decisions during counseling sessions.

Although mental health clinics have programs that address the needs of children, elementary school counselors probably represent the largest group of counselors working with American Indian children. These counselors should consider the stereotypical perceptions of the American Indian people and culture, the contributions of the culture, the special needs of young American Indians, and the barriers that hamper communication between American Indians and their counselors. To promote counseling effectiveness, these counselors may want to improve their understanding of the American Indian child's perceptions, language (both verbal and nonverbal), values, and cultural heritage.

Individual and Group Therapy.   Current counseling orientations require American Indian children to adopt unfamiliar ways of acting and thinking and to reject their traditional ways of storytelling and participation in healing rituals and ceremonies. School counselors need a deeper understanding of the effects of environment (the present and historical) and culture on counseling. Most counseling models evolved from European American middle-class perspectives and thus reflect the concerns, problems, and values of that group (Herring, 1996).

Counselors working with American Indian children should remember several key points. First, eye contact, which is valued in European American society, may be considered rude or discourteous by some American Indian children (depending on the tribe), who may be taught to listen without looking directly at the speaker. Second, counselors should exercise caution in placing children in situations requiring self-praise, because speaking of one's accomplishments may be considered in poor taste. Particularly in group sessions, considerable strain is placed on children who are asked to talk about their strengths. They may resort to telling unbelievable stories or may refuse to speak altogether; praise must always come from someone else. Third, it is important that clients receive positive reinforcement during group therapy; however, it may be more appropriate to provide reinforcement in individual situations. Receiving praise in front of one's peers in the initial stages of group therapy may be embarrassing and culturally inappropriate when working with American Indians. Once group cohesion is developed, group members may provide positive support to one another.

Group therapy appears to be a worthwhile intervention for American Indian children because their culture places more value on group contributions than on individual successes and accomplishments. As with other cultures, many topics are appropriate for group counseling with children: discussing developmental concerns, dealing with death and divorce, developing friendships, or improving study skills.

Counselors working with American Indian children should

- provide individualized counseling intervention that addresses the specific needs of the American Indian child;

- provide assessment that has minimal socioeconomic or cultural bias;

- recognize that "life purposes" of American Indians differ from most other cultures; and

- intervene with strategies that value the child's culture as well as place high value on self-worth.

American Indian children learn early that nonverbal communication plays an important role in their lives. A significant factor in counseling effectiveness will be the counselor's own nonverbal communication style and personality. For example, communication will break down and the client may wish to leave if the counselor gives the impression of being busy or preoccupied.

Family Therapy.   Because the extended family is a major source of support for the American Indian people, counselors should plan intervention strategies that involve the entire family. Although individual situations exist, generally speaking, the American Indian people prefer counseling intervention that involves the entire family.

Prior to counseling American Indian children in family situations, the counselor needs to understand American Indian children and families. Counselors should understand the reason for participants seeking counseling, establish relationships that American Indians will deem positive,

UP CLOSE AND PERSONAL 8.1

Counseling Bill Lonetree, an American Indian Child

Eight-year-old Bill was referred for counseling by his African American teacher, who reported that Bill does not listen, shows little emotion, and appears anxious or stressed at times. The counselor, a European American, has met with Bill weekly for about 4 weeks, and Bill is just beginning to open up to him. Bill was suspicious at first, but slowly and reluctantly he has begun to confide that the teacher urges him to try harder, to listen attentively, and to take a more active role in the learning process. Bill does not understand the teacher's suggestions: He is listening and he does try; however, he admits to a lack of interest in the future. The counselor has noticed that Bill tends to look away as he speaks, although he appears to listen attentively. The counselor

has also observed that Bill seems nervous when he talks about his schoolwork. Bill has admitted that he wants to do well in school, but school is not like home. Things are different in school—the communication, for example. Besides, he has no European American friends. The counselor has reached several conclusions: (a) Bill's comments indicate that some of his problems might stem from the teacher, who neither understands the American Indian culture nor recognizes the differences between Bill's home life and school life; (b) Bill is experiencing stress because of his lack of school progress; and (c) Bill should be counseled in individual sessions several times and then participate in a group session with other American Indian children.

respond appropriately to children's and family's distrust, and explain how counseling procedures work. The counselor should also explain clearly to the family who he or she is, his or her role in counseling intervention, and the reason for the session. Up Close and Personal 8.1 looks at a counselor's efforts with Bill, an American Indian child.

Group sessions with American Indian families may involve participation of extended family members, members of the clan or tribe, or significant others. These sessions may need to be informal and may require long periods of time to develop relationships and to achieve desired goals.

American Indian Adolescents

Potential Problems Warranting Counseling Intervention

Problems American Indian adolescents may experience include

- suicide, alcohol abuse and other substance abuse (e.g., tobacco and inhalants), and high school and college dropout rates;

- failure to develop positive individual and American Indian identities;

- misperceptions and stereotypical images of American Indian adolescents that may result in poor self-image;

- communication problems (e.g., English as a second language; nonverbal communication being misunderstood; and differences between "reservation" or "tribal" languages and "school" languages);

- conflict between loyalty to family and elders and a desire to conform to peer standards;

- adverse effects of being misunderstood by other-culture teachers;

A FOCUS ON RESEARCH 8.2

Minority Adolescents and Substance Abuse

These researchers maintain that inhalant use is a growing problem, particularly among American Indian youth. In their article, they review the limited literature on risk factors associated with inhalant abuse, outline their theoretical analysis, and offer a summary of their findings.

In their study in Washington state, they found cigarettes and inhalants showed the lowest age of initiation. In general, predictors of lifetime use of marijuana, alcohol, and inhalants included attachment to parents, parents' drug use, and school attachment. Although peer drug use was a strong predictor of marijuana and

alcohol use, it was not a significant predictor of adolescents' use of inhalants.

These authors conclude that inhalant use is more common among American Indian youth than among other American cultural groups. They also conclude that inhalant abuse should be addressed specifically rather than in more general categories of drugs.

Source: "Minority adolescents and substance use risk/protective factors: A focus on inhalant use." by C. Mosher, T. Rotola, D. Phillips, A. Krupski, and K. D Stark, 2004, *Adolescence, 39*, pp. 489–502.

- poor academic achievement;

- poor self-concept;

- drug or alcohol addiction;

- adverse effects of racism and discrimination;

- generational conflict caused by parents' allegiance to American Indian values and the adolescent's acculturation into mainstream culture; and

- disagreements between adolescents and families about appropriate ages for certain activities—for example, one culture allowing or encouraging activities that another culture frowns upon.

Despite the fact that inhalant abuse is a growing problem among adolescents, little attention has been given to demographic and social factors. Mosher, Rotola, Phillips, Krupski and Stark (2004) in A Focus on Research 8.2 look at inhalant abuse in Native American adolescents.

Counseling Considerations

As previously stated, because there are relatively few American Indian counselors, most American Indian adolescents will probably be counseled by European American counselors, or perhaps by other minority counselors. The non–American Indian counselor planning intervention with American Indian adolescents should consider the following questions: What unique American Indian cultural and developmental characteristics are important to know? In what stage is the American Indian adolescent's identity? How can the counselor develop trust, rapport, and genuine respect for American Indian adolescents? Will individual, family, or group therapy be most effective?

Although diversity among the various tribes does not allow for the establishment of clear rules for counseling American Indians, the counselor's understanding of the culture's unique characteristics is prerequisite to effective counseling. Following are several aspects of the culture that are important for counselors to remember:

- Adolescents are respected to the same degree as adults.
- Cooperation and harmony are valued.
- Generosity and sharing are important, and individuals are judged on their contributions.
- Competition may be encouraged as long as it does not hurt anyone.
- Life is lived in the present, with little concern for planning for the future.
- Some behaviors may be considered strange or rude (e.g., loud talking, reprimands).
- Ancient legends and cultural traditions are important.
- Peace and politeness are essential; confrontation is considered rude.

The American Indian adolescent's attitude toward silence differs significantly from that of adolescents in other cultures. The American Indian does not feel a need to fill time with meaningless speech just to avoid silence. Also, it is culturally appropriate to avoid eye contact with the speaker during conversation. The non-American Indian counselor might treat silence, embellished metaphors, and indirectness as signs of resistance, when they actually represent forms of communication. Professionals working with these adolescents need to monitor their feelings about these communication differences. They must resist the urge to interrupt and be willing to admit to confusion and misunderstanding. Therapists should be especially aware of nonverbal communication, particularly when "nothing is taking place." How one enters the room, what is in it, and how one responds to silence are all forms of communication (Sutton & Broken Nose, 2005).

Perceived trust is the most important variable in how an American Indian adolescent decides whether a counselor should be viewed as a helper. The American Indian may harbor a general distrust of counselors of another cultural background. Once trust in the counselor and the counseling process is established, rapport and mutual respect likely will follow.

The first meeting with the American Indian adolescent should be designed to build trust. Effective listening and empathic responding are helpful in this regard. Counselors who are able to show genuine appreciation for the American Indian culture and its values and traditions likely will reduce their clients' distrust. During the first session, it is important that counselors work diligently to accommodate the American Indian time orientation and fatalistic view of life.

A study by Subia, Dauphinais, LaFromboise, Bennett, and Rowe (1992) revealed several interesting findings about American Indian secondary school students' preferences for counselors. These researchers concluded that (a) American Indian secondary students who expressed a strong commitment to the American Indian culture preferred talking with an American Indian counselor, (b) female American Indian students expressed a strong preference for talking with a female American Indian counselor, and (c) students expressed a strong preference for an American Indian counselor regardless of whether the problem was academic or personal. If a student had a personal concern, having a same-gender counselor seemed to be preferable.

Individual and Group Therapy.   In counseling American Indian adolescents, as in counseling other adolescents, the cultural perceptions (the counselor's as well as the client) play a large part in shaping counseling goals and intervention techniques. Once an adolescent has been referred or has initiated a self-referral, the counselor can decide whether individual or group therapy will be the most effective approach. Counselors often prefer group sessions because most adolescents find it easier to speak freely in a group setting. They believe that their peers will understand and accept their deficiencies more readily than will adults.

As previously mentioned, group therapy may be the most valuable counseling approach for working with American Indian students. Group therapy relieves individual students of some of the pressures to talk and self-disclose and allows them to learn from the experiences of other adolescents. Groups should be kept small and should include some students who have successfully handled problems. Leaders must be respected and trusted by group members. Group counseling should take a general approach in which the students are asked to suggest topics to consider.

Counseling adolescents in individual or group situations has drawbacks. Clients may change their behavior, but on returning to the family, they might return to old behaviors. It is also important to remember that in some cases group therapy may cause American Indian adolescents to be somewhat reserved because of their lack of trust or their tendency toward noninterference with others. Their soft-spokenness and suspicion of strangers might also impede the counseling process in a group situation.

Family Therapy.   Practical and immediate solutions to problems during family therapy may be more relevant than future-oriented philosophical goals. As a reflection of American Indian values, group decisions will take precedence over individual decisions during family counseling sessions. Whenever possible, the therapist should involve all family members, even extended family members, in selecting therapy goals. This process of involving all family members is often so therapeutic in itself that further counseling intervention may be unnecessary.

Ho (1987) related the cases of Phillip and Debbie. In Phillip's case, the misunderstanding regarded the extended family:

> Phillip, a 15-year-old probationer, was brought to the attention of a court-related worker when she received a complaint that Phillip was running around from house to house visiting female friends without parental supervision. When the worker inquired about Phillip's family background, she discovered that he had several aunts and cousins. When the worker called all Phillip's aunts and cousins together for a family conference, she discovered that all his cousins were young girls. The worker later learned that Phillip's behavior was very natural in the extended family system. (p. 97)

In the case of adolescent Debbie, it was necessary to mobilize a social support network to assist her:

> Although she had been a "good" student in the past, Debbie, the teenage daughter of the Tiger family, has recently been missing school. When her parents were informed of this, they displayed no surprise, but expressed willingness to cooperate with the school official in getting Debbie back to school regularly. The school social worker, who served as a family therapist, happened to live in the same neighborhood as the Tigers, and she volunteered to transport Debbie back and forth to school. Through this consistent relationship, the therapist became a trusted friend of the Tiger family. To express the family's gratitude and friendship, Mrs. Tiger provided the therapist with a regular supply of home-grown vegetables. Through this informal exchange, the therapist learned that the Tigers were totally shut off from the community, with Mr. Tiger labeled as "crazy" and "not to be trusted." Mr. Tiger did not have a regular job. On his days off, "he managed to get drunk," according to Mrs. Tiger. Although Mrs. Tiger was willing to get some therapy for their family problems, Mr. Tiger

UP CLOSE AND PERSONAL 8.2

Counseling Ed Lonetree, an American Indian Adolescent

Ed, aged 15, was referred to the school guidance counselor by his teacher for poor academic achievement. On the referral slip, the teacher's notation read "poor grades, lack of interest, and unmotivated." During Ed's first session, he demonstrated some apprehensiveness and distrust of the European American counselor. The counselor and Ed discussed Ed's development and his American Indian culture. Ed was somewhat hesitant to share information ("You can't trust people in this school"), and he made vague references to the counselor "doing something to him."

During the first session, the counselor sought to lessen Ed's anxiety and to develop rapport. Ed's poor communication skills made conversation a bit difficult, but the counselor worked to overcome this barrier. The counselor noticed that Ed paused a lot in his speech—it seemed as if he could not find anything to say. Yet, silent periods didn't seem to bother him.

After talking at length with Ed, the counselor came to two conclusions. First, Ed's academic problems resulted from poor language skills; second, Ed's teacher did not understand American Indian mannerisms. The teacher failed to recognize that Ed was indeed interested in school and motivated to learn.

The counselor decided to do three things: First, he would offer to assist Ed's teacher in understanding Ed's behavior. Then, because many of Ed's academic problems stemmed from his communication problem, the counselor would recommend Ed for special language classes. Finally, he would follow up on Ed's progress in individual sessions. The prospect of Ed speaking up in group therapy sessions seemed unlikely unless all other members of the group had similar academic and communication problems. After Ed's communication problem improved, however, the counselor thought that he could be considered for group therapy.

insisted that he would not have any of "that stuff" (therapy). After learning that the Tigers were religious individuals who attended church regularly, the therapist referred the Tigers to a minister for consultation. The minister, although a non-Indian, was highly respected by the Indians who also attended the same church but belonged to different tribes. Through such extended interaction with other Indians, Mrs. Tiger became more relaxed and paid attention to Debbie, who managed to attend school regularly without the family therapist's assistance. (pp. 100–101)

Up Close and Personal 8.2 looks at a counselor's efforts with Ed, an American Indian adolescent.

American Indian Adults

Potential Problems Warranting Counseling Intervention

Problems American Indian adults may experience include

- difficulties in overcoming myths that their culture is lazy, savage, and inferior;
- adverse effects of injustice, discrimination, hardship, and degradation;
- adverse effects of a "culture of poverty," such as high unemployment and low socioeconomic status;
- differing cultural characteristics;

- high suicide rate and low life expectancy;

- communication problems, including "on reservation" and "off reservation" languages and the majority culture's misunderstanding of nonverbal mannerisms;

- midlife difficulties such as coping with the effects of aging, marriage crises, psychosocial crises, and developmental tasks;

- problems with alcohol or other drugs;

- poor self-concept and feelings of rejection; and

- low educational level.

Garrett and Carroll (2000) report that the images of the "lazy drunken Indian" (p. 379) and "Indians just can't hold their liquor" (p. 379) are age-old beliefs that have been seared into American society's consciousness through media images and social attitudes toward American Indians. They also report that the shortcomings of some individuals have been generalized to an entire group of people.

Garrett and Carroll (2000) report that clear answers do not exist. According to these authors, American Indians may actually have an abstinence rate higher than that of the general U.S. population; 70% of Americans say they drink compared to 63% of those in American Indian tribes/nations. This may suggest that those American Indians who do drink experience more adverse consequences than others, contrary to the perception that alcoholism among American Indians is innate. Still, Garrett and Carroll think alcoholism in this culture is a problem that counselors need to address. For example, alcohol-related deaths among American Indians are 4.8 times greater than in the general U.S. population, and the mortality rate from chronic liver disease and cirrhosis is 4.5 times greater than in other racial or ethnic groups. Garrett and Carroll also report that 75% to 80% of American Indian suicides involve the use of alcohol or other mind-altering drugs.

Counseling Considerations

From an American Indian perspective, the entire ordeal of substance dependence is a matter of mental, physical, spiritual, and environmental dimensions. Factors that seem to be related to alcohol abuse in American Indians include cultural disassociation (not feeling a part of the traditional American Indian culture or the general U.S. culture), the lack of clear sanctions or punishments for alcohol abuse, and strong peer pressure and support for alcohol abuse. Other factors related to alcohol abuse include poverty, school failure, unemployment, poor health, feelings of hopelessness, and the breakdown of American Indian family life. Compared with the majority population, the alcohol-related mortality rate in American Indians is four-fold greater and the rates of alcohol-related accidental death, suicide, and homicide are three-fold greater (Thomason, 2000).

American Indians may be more successful in stopping or controlling their alcohol use if the treatment approach includes a family, group, or community component. However, this may be true only for traditionally oriented American Indians who are not highly acculturated into the general U.S. culture. Although acculturative stress, poverty, and racism may influence drinking behavior, there is no evidence to suggest that these are causative factors.

Thomason (2000) offers several conclusions:

- There is no evidence that a single treatment modality works especially well with American Indians.

- Counseling interventions should include assessment of the client's identity and acculturation level and modalities such as brief interventions, social skills training, motivational enhancement, and community reinforcement.

- Clients who have a strong American Indian identity and are involved in their traditional culture may respond better to a treatment program that considers their culture; for example, it has been reported that treatment programs which incorporate the use of sweat lodges, talking circles or medicine wheels, and other American Indian rituals and traditional ceremonies are helpful.

- Group therapy with an American Indian counselor and all American Indian clients may be difficult to initiate because of the shortage of American Indian treatment providers and the lack of standardized American Indian treatments. The shortage of American Indian counselors also presents difficulties because traditional American Indian healing strategies are meant to be practiced only by trained American Indian healers.

Working with American Indian clients presents counselors with numerous challenges: tribal and individual diversity, lifestyle preferences that can vary considerably from one client to another, verbal and nonverbal language differences, and the reluctance of clients to disclose personal or embarrassing thoughts. Still, counselors should learn about and plan sessions for American Indian clients as individuals and be cautious about making assumptions. The goals of counseling will largely depend on the tribal values and traditions of the American Indian client.

Lokken and Twohey (2004) maintain that the history of oppression of American Indians by Euro-Americans has resulted in American Indians being distrustful and reluctant to become involved with mental health professionals. A Focus on Research 8.3 looks at Lokken and Twohey's (2004) investigation of American Indian perspectives of Euro-American counseling behaviors.

Garrett and Carroll (2000) explain the American Indian concept of the circle as a symbol of power, relation, peace, and unity. The circle reminds people of the sacred relationship humans share with all living things and humanity's responsibility as a helper and contributor to the flow of the Circle of Life by living in harmony and balance with all living things. They explain the importance of the following concepts in a Native context: life energy, harmony and balance, spiritual practices, and substance dependence.

Six practical recommendations for counseling American Indians with substance abuse problems include the following:

- *Greeting.* Offer a gentle handshake if any handshake at all. A firm handshake is considered an aggressive show of power and can be construed as an insult.

- *Hospitality.* Offer a beverage or snack because American Indians have a traditional emphasis on generosity and kindness.

- *Silence.* Maintain a time of quietness at the beginning of the session to give both the counselor and the client a chance to orient themselves to the situation, get in touch with themselves, and experience the presence of the other person.

A FOCUS ON RESEARCH 8.3

American Indian Perspectives of Euro-American Counseling Behavior

Although American Indians often distrust Euro-American mental health professionals, ethnically similar counselors are not always available, and when they are, their communication styles sometimes remain a salient factor in American Indians' perceptions of helpfulness.

Some American Indian clients perceive negative consequences for participating in counseling: having children taken away, being treated in a condescending manner, and having medications prescribed without getting to the cause of the problem. In one example, when parents sought help to stop abusing, they were reported for abusing their children, a process that is very shameful for parents.

Reported barriers to counseling include inaccessible locations, lack of availability of counselors, lack of knowledge about counseling, and lack of money for mental health counseling.

Factors associated with perceptions of counselor trustworthiness include authenticity, respectfulness, concern, signs of listening behavior, self-disclosure, and slow pace. Participants indicated that they were more able to trust a counselor who self-disclosed, because it gave them an additional context in which to learn about the counselor.

Source: "American Indian perspectives of Euro-American counseling behavior," by J. M. Lokken, and D. Twohey, 2004, *Journal of Multicultural Counseling and Development, 32,* 320–331.

- *Acculturation.* Get a sense of the client's acculturation by formally assessing his or her values, geographic origin/residence, and tribal affiliation.

- *Eye contact.* Respect American Indian's practice of avoiding eye contact—the eyes are considered a pathway to the spirit. It may be acceptable to glance occasionally at the client, but generally it should be remembered that listening is "something that happens with the ears and heart" (Garrett & Carroll, 2000, p. 386).

- *Direction.* Offer suggestions rather than directions due to clients' respect for personal choice (Garrett & Carroll, 2000).

American Indian clients who seek counseling are usually hoping for concrete, practical advice about problems that is sensitive to their cultural beliefs and differences. Historically, American Indians have had negative experiences with professionals who were supposedly there to "help" them. Missionaries, teachers, and social workers have tried to address American Indians' needs by changing American Indians' value systems, thereby alienating them from the strength and support of their own people and traditions (Sutton & Broken Nose, 2005).

It is the counselor's task to help these clients accept and value their culture and to help them resolve difficult conflicts that can impede personal and social growth. Consider the following example (Axelson, 1999) in which a European American counselor helps an American Indian client consider his cultural beliefs about religion:

CLIENT: Where can I start? Take religion, for instance. Okay? I have a strong traditional Indian background... and I try to cope with whatever is good in the non-Indian society. But, coming from the Indian way of life, I feel that how I can relate myself to the way of praying to nature is not the same as saying I got to be good and go to church on Sunday and pray to a certain god. How can I relate myself to that way?

COUNSELOR: You're saying that you are religious, that you don't find that the White religion is in harmony with what you are; you find conflict in some practices of the White religion.

CLIENT: I'm not sure that you understood.

COUNSELOR: Would you try to explain to me again?

CLIENT: I know that I feel there is something around me that is good. I can take a piece of rock and say that it was formed from something that I believe in. I can take a tree branch and say that I pray to this tree and feel good. I feel the obligation that is imposing on me to make me go to church; and I don't want to do that.

COUNSELOR: You feel an obligation to go to church and somehow you want to resist the obligation. You're caught in the middle in giving in to it and fighting against it. You'd rather fight against it than do it; somehow you're not quite free to do that.

(Pause)

CLIENT: Do you think I should?...go to church?

(Pause)

COUNSELOR: I'm wondering if going to church would help you, like anybody else, since you feel so reluctant. It just doesn't seem to be you.

CLIENT: Eh...they tell me I should go to church.

COUNSELOR: Who are "they"?

CLIENT: The people who taught me about their religion. The Catholic Church.

COUNSELOR: You don't want to do this. Somehow I'm puzzled because you don't want to do it; in other words, you feel an obligation to go to church because they told you to. And yet you don't feel a real need inside yourself to go.

(Pause)

CLIENT: I think...(Pause)...I think the need is there.

COUNSELOR: The need to go to church on Sunday?

CLIENT: Eh...I think the need is there because...I don't know...I don't know what to say. It's kind of confusing now.

COUNSELOR: You sound like you don't understand yourself. It's almost like someone sneaked up and put this need in you.

CLIENT: I think I know what is good, and I know that there is something there that is good. You know, why should I go to church on Sunday when I know that there is the same thing outside the church?

COUNSELOR: One thing. You see yourself as a good man. Is that right? And, as a good man, you recognize good within this Catholic religion and that gives a…

CLIENT: I don't know what's good within the Catholic religion.

COUNSELOR: You feel some kind of obligation or attraction to the good that you see there, but not enough obligation to make you feel that you want to go to church, or go to that church. That you can be good by praying before the stone or tree branch. Or by doing whatever you do on Sunday besides going to church.

CLIENT: What do you think I should do?

COUNSELOR: (sighs)…What do you want to do?

(Pause) What do you think a good man would do in your situation?

(Pause)

CLIENT: I'm confused. I don't want to talk about it.[*]

American Indians often judge people by who they are, rather than by what they are. On entering a therapist's office, they will probably look for indications of who the therapist is, rather than for a particular diploma on the wall. Thus, personal authenticity, genuine respect, and concern for the client are essential for initiating a relationship between counselor and client (Sutton & Broken Nose, 2005).

Traditionally, many counselors have not received training in counseling the American Indian population; therefore, they often do not feel the need to discuss the family's American Indian background and culture, to ask questions in a manner that does not cause discomfort, and to use cultural information in assessment decisions.

Also, traditionally, the contributions and roles of American Indian women have not been considered. Historical and counseling literature have generally failed to provide explanations of their contributions to the American Indian culture. Awe, Portman, and Garrett (2005) maintain that historically, women have wielded a remarkable amount of sociopolitical power with tribal nations, yet as a rule, counseling professionals rely heavily on theories and interventions that reflect a Western, masculinized worldview. In Gender Perspectives 8.1, Awe, Portman, and Garrett (2005) provide a look at historical leadership of American Indian women and the cultural teachings they modeled and valued.

Examples of questions and statements that can open lines of communication and reveal culturally relevant information include the following:

- Where do you come from?
- Tell me about your family.

---

[*]*Source: Dialogue from Counseling and Development in a Multicultural Society* (pp. 428–430), by J. A. Axelson, 1999, Monterey, CA: Brooks/Cole. Reprinted with permission.

GENDER PERSPECTIVES 8.1

Beloved Women and the Sacred Fire of Leadership

Awe, Portman, and Garrett (2005) provide an alternative view of American Indian leadership and attempt to build a bridge between American Indian perspectives of nurturing leadership. Rather than Indian governance being filled with the notion of wise, supreme, and all-knowing chiefs, decisions were made by tribal councils or communities made up of multiple male and female leaders holding leadership positions.

The authors provide an excellent summary of historical leadership of American Indian women. They provide succinct summaries of Nancy Nanyehi Ward (an 18th century Cherokee women), Susan LaFlesche Picotte (the first American Indian female doctor in the U.S.), Wilma Mankiller (former Principal Chief of the Cherokee Nation of Oklahoma and the first female leader of the Cherokee Nation in modern history), and Carolyn Attneave (a Delaware and Cherokee women who made significant contributions to the advancement of American Indian mental health). Leadership perspectives from American Indian females included collectivism, collaboration, compassion, and courage.

While implications are offered throughout this excellent article, selected implications for the counseling profession include that institutions of higher education, as well as other organizations, should move to a more collectivistic organization mentoring style; that mentoring of women should occur in a collectivistic relationship that fosters interdependence among colleagues and group success as relational norms; and that women require relationships to develop their own sense of identity and purpose—nurturing and mentoring women require an examination of a women's sense of place and being in the world.

This article is highly recommended because it addresses American Indian women, explains their historical leadership roles, and provides clear implications for mental health professionals.

Source: "Beloved women: Nurturing the sacred fire of leadership from an American Indian perspective," by T. Awe, A. Portman and M. T. Garrett, 2005, *Journal of Counseling and Development, 83* (3), 284–292.

- What tribe or nation are you? Tell me a little about that.
- Tell me about yourself as a person, culturally and spiritually.
- Tell me how you identify yourself culturally.
- Tell me how your culture and spirituality plays into how you live your life.
- Tell me about your life as you see it—past, present, and future (Garrett & Wilbur, 1999).

Counseling American Indian adults requires techniques that are carefully planned to accommodate these clients' cultural characteristics. Using counseling techniques developed for clients of other cultural backgrounds with only slight modifications is not sufficient. Counseling and psychotherapy often are based on Western values that may be antagonistic to American Indian value systems. Not only should culturally appropriate counseling be planned, but counselors should also be aware of personal characteristics that may offend or confuse the client.

It is essential that counselors working with American Indian clients be adaptive and flexible in their professional intervention and understand that a counselor's personal identification with the culture of the client does not guarantee sufficient understanding of the client. Counselors should recognize their own personal biases and stereotypes, and should use counseling approaches that involve empathy, caring, and a sense of importance of the human potential.

Although some counseling strategies are effective for all cultures, the following strategies have the potential to enhance the effectiveness of counseling sessions with American Indians:

- Counselors may admit to not fully understanding the American Indian culture and request to be corrected if a cultural error is made.

- Counselors who empathize with others appreciate the greatness of the American Indian culture and its many accomplishments.

- Counselors should take the attitude that they can help best by listening.

- Counselors should have a small, homey, lived-in office. Pictures in the office of American Indians may help put clients at ease. Rather than sit side by side, some clients may prefer that the counselor sit behind a desk (to provide a form of separation).

- Counselors should not lean toward clients to study them. They also should not be upset with long pauses in the conversation. Counselors may want to take short notes and summarize at the end to let clients know they have been listening.

Counselors should give special attention to their manner of speaking. It is wise to summarize or confirm the client's thoughts after he or she has been talking for a while. In particular, counselors should not talk for too long and should not "talk down" to the client. Instead, the counselor's sentences should be short and lucid and should make clear that the counselor's views are only general opinions, rather than absolute truths or facts.

The counselor might also explore such practical resources as a communication class, participation in ceremonies at a local powwow, or involvement with American Indian organizations or centers (Sutton & Broken Nose, 2005).

Individual and Group Therapy.   Counselors working with American Indians need to remember several points. First, they should understand that counseling interventions do not always effectively address the problems of American Indians. Second, counselors need to understand American Indians' emphasis on nonverbal communication. American Indians express many thoughts in natural-world metaphors. Third, counselors need to understand the special needs of American Indians—that is, understand their familial structures and their values. Fourth, counselors need to show sincere interest in American Indians—carefully consider family theories, individual counseling styles, and assessment instruments.

The decision whether to use individual or group therapy should be based on the individual client's needs and culture. One advantage of group therapy is that clients may share similar problems and frustrations. Disadvantages of group therapy include American Indian clients' possible reluctance to share personal concerns and their cultural tendency toward noninterference with others.

It is worth reiterating the following important points with regard to counseling American Indians. First, the client is apt to be silent for what may seem like a long time. Second, restating or summarizing the client's comments at the end of the session may enhance understanding.

Family Therapy.   Family therapy often has more successful outcomes for American Indians than individual counseling sessions. The American Indian family structure allows for the growth of bonding between generations. Counselors should incorporate as many family members as possible in family sessions, particularly during the first two or three sessions.

The American Indian culture emphasizes harmony with nature, noninterference with others, and a strong belief that people are inherently good and deserving of respect. Such traits, however, make it difficult for families experiencing problems to seek counseling or other professional help. Their fear and mistrust of European Americans make it difficult for them to allow a European American family therapist entry into their family system. Also, American Indians' lack of knowledge as to what a family therapist actually does often contributes to their reluctance to initiate or participate in counseling.

In American Indian culture, families work together to solve problems. Fortunately, family therapy, with its systemic approach and emphasis on relationships, is particularly effective in working with American Indians, whose life cycle orientation blends well with this therapy approach (Sutton & Broken Nose, 2005).

As previously mentioned, the American Indian attitude toward silence can be extremely frustrating to counselors providing family therapy. This silence may sometimes be used as a safe response to defend against outsiders who are perceived as intruders; still, counselors sometimes experience frustration when several sessions are needed to get effective counseling underway.

Up Close and Personal 8.3 looks at a counselor's efforts with John, an American Indian adult.

The close-knit family structure of American Indians and their cultural tradition of keeping family matters private may result in few opportunities for family therapy. After engaging

UP CLOSE AND PERSONAL 8.3

Counseling John Lonetree, an American Indian Adult

John Lonetree, age 38, was referred by his physician to a community mental health clinic that provides free counseling to qualified American Indians. John had complained of headaches for several months, and the physician had been unable to pinpoint the cause.

The 45-year-old European American counselor greeted John at the office door and tried to make him feel as comfortable as possible. The counselor sat behind a small desk and requested that John sit across from him. The counselor took special care to let John know that he was fairly unaccustomed to counseling American Indians. He also encouraged John to make him aware of any misconceptions he might have about the culture. The counselor avoided looking John in the eye for long intervals while speaking. Being off the reservation, John experienced problems with English, which made communication somewhat difficult.

The counselor concluded that John had several problems related to his age and to the financial and emotional demands placed on him. First, John was nearly 40; relative to his life expectancy, 40 was "older" for him than for his age peers in other cultures. Second, with John's advancing age, his responsibilities seemed to be growing heavier and harder to bear. He was concerned about his children and their schoolwork. In addition, he was concerned about what he would do if he lost his job. So many people depended on him for financial support. The counselor suggested additional sessions, to which John agreed, somewhat to the surprise of the counselor, who was aware that American Indians often place a high premium on noninterference. Also, because John considered his problems to be family-oriented, the counselor decided that group counseling was inappropriate at this stage. The decision whether to include John's family would have to wait until the counselor knew more about the family situation.

the family, the counselor should proceed cautiously to allow family members to deal with problems at their own pace. An overbearing or manipulative counselor will almost certainly alienate American Indian clients.

American Indian Elderly

Potential Problems Warranting Counseling Intervention

Problems that elderly American Indians may experience include

- difficulties overcoming culture- and age-related stereotypical images;
- double or multiple jeopardy as a result of being elderly, minority, and perhaps disabled;
- low socioeconomic status;
- inadequate nutrition and housing;
- low life expectancy;
- health problems, such as tuberculosis, diabetes, pneumonia, liver and kidney disease, and high blood pressure;
- inadequate health services, either because of lack of communication skills or overdependence on folk rituals;
- low self-esteem and poor self-concept;
- lack of education;
- generational differences because of the acculturation of younger American Indians;
- physical changes, such as visible signs of aging or a deteriorating skeletomuscular system, or psychosocial–emotional changes, such as adjusting to poor health, the death of a spouse, or relocation to a reservation for economic reasons;
- lack of health care opportunities that contribute to physical and mental well-being; and
- lack of transportation to acquire mental health counseling and other health services.

Counseling Considerations

Counselors working with older American Indians have a special task of understanding the trials and joys of the elderly period from the standpoint of American Indians. Many problems require an understanding of the complex relationship between age and cultural background.

Although the literature on counseling American Indian elderly as a specific population is sketchy at best, counselors can use their existing knowledge of the elderly and their knowledge of the American Indian culture as a basis for formulating appropriate counseling strategies. It is also important for counselors to acknowledge the centuries of deprivation and discrimination that American Indians have endured, the current status of uneducated American Indian elderly trying to live and cope with the stress common in contemporary society, and the elderly client's hesitation to seek professional counseling from a non–American Indian professional.

In addition to understanding the culture and the lifespan period, there are other prerequisites for effective counseling of the American Indian elderly. For example, counselors must build rapport with their elderly clients. American Indian history is full of broken treaties and promises. American Indian clients often must be convinced that professionals can be trusted to think in terms of American Indian welfare and well-being. Also, counselors must use their knowledge about the aging process in the counseling relationship. Finally, they should make sure that clients understand the counselor's role and know what to expect in the counseling relationship.

What specifically can counselors do to promote an effective counseling relationship? The following strategies may be considered:

- Allow adequate time to get acquainted. The atmosphere should be relaxed. Counseling professionals will not want to give the impression that they are uninterested or in a hurry.

- Allow for pauses and be patient when the client avoids eye contact or appears to just sit and think.

- Let elderly clients know that their age is accepted. Although counselors may not be aware of the realities of being elderly, it is imperative that they communicate a willingness to listen to and learn from their elderly clients.

- Allow a paraprofessional from the client's ethnic background to assist with communication barriers.

- Understand the client's cultural background and elderly status and the complex relationship between the two.

Individual and Group Therapy.   The decision regarding what type of therapy to use should be based on the individual American Indian client. One intervention approach is to use individual therapy at first and then to move to a group therapy session. Of course, the individual client's willingness to speak in group sessions should be considered. How willing are elderly American Indians to disclose feelings of grief in group settings? What about concerns over decreasing strength or sexual abilities? Counselors should first explore the elderly American Indian's problems in individual sessions and then decide on the feasibility of group therapy.

Family Therapy.   Counselors intervening with American Indian families first need to be relaxed. Elderly American Indians, who are accustomed to noninterference with others and unaccustomed to counseling procedures, tend to be silent for prolonged periods. Conversational exchanges may be relatively short. This pattern might last throughout the session or perhaps stretch into two sessions.

During the initial session with an elderly American Indian client, it may be useful to ask open-ended questions designed to elicit a family history. Showing genuine interest without being judgmental helps to establish rapport. It allows the client and the family members to get to know the therapist and vice versa.

Effective counseling sessions might emphasize the elder's "place" in the family structure and the counselor's awareness of the respect traditionally given to American Indian elderly. The counselor should keep in mind that elderly clients may not want to disclose personal information with their families present and that family members may look to the elderly client to act as spokesperson for the family,

UP CLOSE AND PERSONAL 8.4

Counseling Wenonah Lonetree, an Elderly American Indian

Wenonah, age 72, was referred to a free counseling clinic when she went to a government office to try to increase her monthly benefit check. Wenonah's poverty, lack of education, and communication problems indicated that she could qualify for counseling assistance. Although Wenonah at first refused to go, her son John convinced her to visit the clinic, especially because he was off work that day and could take her there. However, she was not at all sure that she was doing the right thing.

The 38-year-old, female, European American counselor immediately recognized Wenonah's many problems. It was clear that she rarely visited a physician and saw her only role in life as taking care of her grandchildren. The counselor spoke to Wenonah alone while John waited outside. She began very slowly with Wenonah—she did not urge her on nor confront her when she paused or looked the other way during conversations. The counselor made Wenonah feel that her age was respected and that her problems were important and deserving of attention.

The counselor decided that Wenonah's problems were related primarily to communication difficulties and poverty. She suggested that Wenonah meet with the agency's language specialist, but Wenonah immediately responded that she did not have regular transportation to the clinic. In the meantime, the counselor told Wenonah that she would speak to the government agency to see whether Wenonah's benefits could be raised sooner. What about another session? What could be addressed? The counselor pointed to several issues, including Wenonah's feelings about growing old and about how society was changing. The counselor asked Wenonah to return, and she managed to schedule an appointment when John was off work and could bring her. In future sessions, the counselor would try to convince Wenonah to see a physician for a medical check-up.

Up Close and Personal 8.4 looks at a counselor's efforts with Wenonah, an elderly American Indian.

A Point of Departure: Challenges Confronting Counselors of American Indians

Counselors, psychotherapists, and social workers working with American Indian children, adolescents, adults, and elders need a comprehensive understanding of the American Indian culture, the four lifespan stages, and American Indians' specific problems. Counselors will also need to understand American Indians' diversity: individual, tribal, communication, geographic, and so forth. Any of the following problems may be brought to counseling sessions: children's challenges in school, adolescents forming self-esteem and cultural identities while torn between two worlds, adults' financial and educational problems, and the elders' health problems. Counselors need to be prepared to provide counseling intervention that reflects American Indian values and perspectives rather than using professional intervention techniques that reflect European American middle-class perspectives. Counselors will also be challenged to understand American Indians' proud heritage, appreciation of land and nature, and love of peace and harmony.

Counselors and psychotherapists, regardless of cultural background, have professional responsibilities in three broad areas: (a) to learn about the individual American Indian client, (b) to learn about the client with respect to developmental stage, and (c) to plan effective counseling intervention that reflects American Indian worldviews.

Summary

This chapter examined American Indians, their cultural characteristics and perspectives, the richness of their culture, and problems that clients might bring to counseling sessions. The American Indian people have endured a long history of adversity since White settlers came to this country, and they continue to experience racism and discrimination. The counselor's role will include understanding American Indians' problems (and their historical and contemporary contexts) and knowing when to use individual, group, and family therapy.

Professional counselors need to recognize their counseling strengths, professional areas needing improvement, and resources regarding American Indian cultural differences and effective counseling for these clients.

Suggested Readings

Aragon, S. R. (2004). Learning and study practices of post-secondary American Indian/Alaskan native students. *Journal of American Indian Education, 43* (2) 1–18. Using a survey design, Aragon looks at study practices such as motivation, ability to select main ideas, use of test strategies, and concentration.

Awe, T., Portman, A., & Garrett, M, T. (2005). Beloved women: Nurturing the sacred fire of leadership from an American Indian perspective. *Journal of Counseling and Development, 83* (3), 284–292. These authors address American Indian women, explain their historical leadership roles, and provide clear implications for mental health professionals.

Garrett, M. T., & Barrett, B. (2003). Two spirit: Counseling Native American gay, lesbian, and bisexual people. *Journal of Multicultural Counseling and Development, 31*, 131–142. These authors maintain that the *Two Spirit* is the traditional role of Native individuals believed to be both male and female spirit.

Newman, D. L. (2005). Ego development and ethnic identity formation in rural American Indian adolescents. *Child Development, 76* (3), 734–747. Newman examines the identity development process for ethnic minority adolescents among Lumbee Indian adolescents living in a rural county in North Carolina.

Running Wolf, P., & Rickard, J. A. (2003). Talking Circles: A Native American approach to experimental learning. *Journal of Multicultural Counseling and Development, 31*, 39–43. These authors explain Talking Circles, an unique instructional approach used to stimulate multicultural awareness while fostering respect for individual differences and facilitating group cohesion.

Understanding Asian American Clients

Questions to Be Explored

1. What are the childhood, adolescent, adult, and elderly years like in the Asian American culture?

2. What social and cultural, familial, and communication characteristics describe Asian Americans along the lifespan continuum?

3. What unique challenges face Asian Americans during the various lifespan stages?

4. What communication problems affect Asian Americans, and how do these problems affect educational attainment, employment, and the seeking of health care services?

5. What unique challenges face counselors providing mental health services to Asian Americans in the four lifespan stages?

6. What sources of information are available for counselors intervening with Asian American children, adolescents, adults, and elders?

Overview

Planning counseling intervention for Asian American clients requires an understanding of their cultural characteristics, communication style and languages, families, and individual challenges. The diversity among Asian American clients also requires a consideration of their geographic, generational, and socioeconomic differences, as well as their intracultural and individual characteristics. Although clients from all cultures have been labeled with stereotypical beliefs, the notable successes of Asian American people have resulted in "model minority" stereotype that sometimes leads mental health professionals to expect exemplary achievement and behavior, as well as few mental health problems. This chapter examines the social and cultural, communication, and familial characteristics of Asian Americans so that counselors working with children, adolescents, adults, and elders in the Asian American culture will have a valid and objective basis for counseling decisions and strategies.

Asian Americans: Demographics

"Asian" refers to people with origins in any of the original peoples of the Far East, Southeast Asian, or the Indian subcontinent, including, for example, people from Cambodia, China, India, Japan, Korea, Malaysia, Pakistan, the Philippine Islands, Thailand, and Vietnam. "Pacific Islander" refers to people with origins in any of the original peoples of Hawaii, Guam, Samoa, or other Pacific Islands. The Asian and Pacific Islander population is not a homogeneous group; rather, it comprises many groups who differ in language, culture, and length of residence in the United States. Some of the Asian groups, such as the Chinese and Japanese, have been in the United States for several generations. Others, such as the Hmong, Vietnamese, Laotians, and Cambodians, are comparatively recent immigrants. Relatively few Pacific Islanders are foreign born (Reeves & Bennett, 2003).

The amount of available information on Asian groups varies. Although considerable demographic information can be found on Asian groups from China, Korea, and Japan, less information is available about groups from India, Pakistan, and Bangladesh. Still, counselors should realize that the latter are Asian groups and that the diversity of all Asian groups calls for individual consideration during counseling.

Although the Asian American population is small compared to other minority groups (such as African Americans and Hispanic Americans), they represent a rapidly growing, diverse culture in America. Table 9.1 shows states with significant numbers of Asian Americans. Figure 9.1 shows the distribution of population by region of the United States.

Immigrants to the United States sometimes experience psychological problems. In addition, some immigrants enter the United States without adequate English-speaking skills, which can contribute to or create psychological problems. Shin, Berkson, and Crittenden (2000) examined Korean immigrants' mental health problems and help-seeking behaviors. They examined perceptions of professional and informal support as related to their traditionalism and, in particular, perceptions of problems unique to Korean-speaking immigrants and perceptions of helpfulness of professional and informal social support. Participants spoke

Table 9.1
States with Significant Numbers of Asian Americans

Source: Statistical abstracts of the United States 2004–2005 (124th ed.), by U.S. Census Bureau, 2005, Washington, D.C.: Author.

States	Total
California	4,148,000
New York	1,242,000
New Jersey	565,000
Hawaii	529,000
Illinois	501,000
Washington	369,000
Virginia	310,000
Massachusetts	285,000
Pennsylvania	263,000
Maryland	248,000

Figure 9.1
Residence by Region of the
United States (Percent
distribution of population)

Source: "The Asian and Pacific
Islander population in the
United States: March 2002,"
by T. Reevas and C. Bennett,
2003, *Current Population Reports*,
pp. 20–540, U.S. Census Bureau,
Washington, D.C.

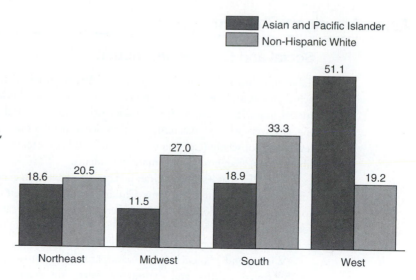

Korean as a primary language and attended churches in the metropolitan Chicago area.
Selected findings include:

1. People who were more adapted to U.S. society tended to think of family members or friends
   as less helpful in solving psychological problems—parents were considered least helpful,
   which was surprising considering the traditional roles that parents play in the Korean culture.

2. Although marital problems existed, couples considered the spouse as the best helper to
   solve psychological problems.

3. Ministers rated comparably with counselors on helpfulness in solving psychological
   problems.

4. Younger individuals tended to have less traditional values and to make more positive
   comments about the helpfulness of psychological support.

Poverty and its accompanying circumstances also affect Asian Americans, just as it does
people of all cultures. Table 9.2 shows the percentages of Asian Americans living in poverty for
the various age groups.

Table 9.2
Poverty Status for Selected Age
Groups (percentages)

Source: "The Asian and Pacific
Islander Population in the United
States: March 2002," by T. Reevas
and C. Bennett, 2003, *Current
Population Reports*, pp. 20–540, U.S.
Census Bureau, Washington, D.C.

Selected Age Group	Total	Male	Female
Total	10.2	10.1	10.4
Under 18 years	11.5	11.5	11.4
18 to 64 years	9.7	9.1	10.4
65 years and over	10.2	13.8	7.4

Asian American Children

Social and Cultural Description

Table 9.3 shows the population of Asian American children by age group. Because of their achievement and behavior in schools, Asian American children are often considered to be a model minority. Teachers often consider Asian children ideal students—studious, high achieving, and well-behaved, Asian American students spend more time doing homework, attend more lessons out of school (e.g., tutoring sessions), and participate in more educational activities (e.g., library trips) than non-Asian American students.

It may be that Asian American parents who have high expectations of their children are also unwilling to negotiate these terms. Children understand their parents' message and are obligated to their parents to do well in school. Perhaps Asian American students think their parents will feel displeasure with low school performance. Just perceiving how their parents might feel about their achievement may be a motivating factor.

Whang and Hancock (1994) compared the motivation and mathematics achievement of 353 fourth-, fifth-, and sixth-grade Asian American and non-Asian American students and found that the former had lower self-concepts of their mathematics ability and believed that their parents shared this belief. The researchers also found that Asian American students were more likely to learn mathematics "because they do not want to look dumb"(p. 314). As for other differences, children in Asian cultures thought they had no choice except to master mathematics skills, whereas European American children thought that low proficiency in or dislike of mathematics meant they could excel at something else. In essence, the Asian American students thought mathematics achievement was required, whereas the European American students did not think such achievement was necessary (Whang & Hancock, 1994).

The diverse nationalities comprising the Asian American culture make a general description difficult. Wide variation is found in physical characteristics, as well as in attitudes, values, and ethnic institutions. For example, Japanese Americans have been described as quiet, reticent, or aloof. Compared with European American children, Asian American children may be more dependent, conforming, obedient to authority, and willing to place family welfare above individual wishes (Sue & Sue, 2003). Also, some Asian American students, just as students of all cultures, experience academic problems. Some have learning problems, some lack motivation or proficiency in English, and some have parents who do not understand the American school system because of cultural differences and language barriers.

Table 9.3
Population: Asian American Children (By Age)

Source: Statistical abstracts of the United States 2004–2005 (124th ed.), by U.S. Census Bureau, 2005, Washington, D.C.: Author.

Age	Total
Under 5 years	777,000
5 to 14 years	1,536,000

Communication

The considerable emphasis that Asian cultures place on education has contributed to the academic success of many Asian American children. However, communication difficulties do exist and must be overcome. Communication difficulties may be traced to the fact that Asian Americans often come from bilingual backgrounds. Furthermore, cultural traditions and customs often restrict or impede verbal communication. For example, some Asian American children learn to value one-way communication in which parents are the primary speakers in the family.

Counselors should remember several factors relative to Asian American children's languages to avoid stereotypical thinking, First, it should be remembered that many Asian American students communicate in the equivalent of a second language. Although English may be their predominant language, these children may still continue to speak and hear their parents' native language at home. Second, the Asian American child should not be viewed as a clumsy, inarticulate child who is good with numbers but poor with words (Atkinson, Morten, & Sue, 1998). Third, although many Asian American children have proved to be quite successful academically, all children deserve individual consideration of their unique strengths and weaknesses. Fourth, generational differences and socioeconomic factors warrant consideration; second- and third-generation children with educated and successful parents will probably have fewer communication problems than first-generation children of lower socioconomic status.

Parette and Huer (2002) maintain that the increase in students with disabilities from Asian backgrounds who receive special education and related services places greater responsibility on professionals providing augmentative and alternative communication (AAC). Plus, they think that numerous values that are deeply embedded in Asian American families may influence the success of family involvement in team decision-making processes as well as subsequent AAC interventions. With projected population changes, there will probably be an impact on the practices in AAC in which teams of professionals interacting with Asian American family members in making decisions about specific interventions provided children and families. In Focus on Research 9.1, Parrete and Huer (2002) call attention to Asian American children with augmentative and alternative certification needs.

Families.   Family allegiance and respect for parents and family significantly affect the achievement and behavior of Asian American children. In traditional Asian American families, children

- *View elders with great reverence and respect.* Children are taught that the father is the head of the family, with absolute authority.
- *Learn specific family roles.* The primary duty of the boys and men is to be a good son; the obligation to be a good husband or father is second to duty as a son. Females are primarily the child bearers and nurturing caretakers and are responsible for domestic chores. Children obey their parents and elders, and parents and elders are responsible for the support, upbringing, and education of the children. Both parents and children demonstrate respect for elders of the household; in return, ancestral spirits are believed to protect the family. The interdependency of family members works as a mechanism to keep the family together (Sue & Sue, 2003).

A FOCUS ON RESEARCH 9.1

Asian American Children with Augmentative and Alternative Certification Needs

In their excellent article, Parrete and Huer (2002) focus on a wealth of useful information (and six specific and useful tables), but due to space considerations, only Asian values that have the potential to affect professional decision-making will be reviewed here. Readers wanting additional information are referred to the original article.

One example shows how cultures view disabilities differently. Asian American families may believe disability results from fate or by sins committed by parents and ancestors, may think only children with physical disabilities should receive services, and may perceive disabilities as sources of shame. In contrast, European American families view disability as resulting from multiple causes, think disability may be prevented with proper health and living conditions, differ in reactions to disabilities, and assume full responsibility for children with disabilities. Readers need to consider the individuality of both Asian American

and European American cultures, just as of all cultures. Plus, acculturation and social class also affect views on disability.

Parrete and Huer maintain that professional collaboration with families of Asian American children needs to be reality-based; that is, it must consider changing demographics and views on disability and professional consultation. Also, children and their parents need to feel the professional is culturally competent. Through an increased awareness of the perceived role of the family, the impact of cultural differences, of Asian American family values, and of preferred communication styles and preferences, the optimal family-centered approach may be maximized.

Source: "Working with Asian American families whose children have augmentative and alternative certification needs," by P. Parette and M. B. Huer, 2002, *Journal of Special Education Technology, 17*(4), pp. 5–13.

- *Feel their families have high expectations for their achievement and behavior.* Children are expected to excel in American society yet retain the values and traditions of their Asian American culture.

- *Sense a powerful message not to bring embarrassment and shame to the family.* The inculcation of guilt and shame is the principal technique used to control the behavior of family members. Parents emphasize the children's obligation to the family and their responsibility to meet family expectations. If a child acts contrary to the family's wishes, the child is considered selfish, inconsiderate, and ungrateful. Aberrant behavior is usually hidden from outsiders and is handled within the family. Outstanding achievement, in contrast, is a source of great pride; it, too, reflects not only on the child but also on the entire family.

The Asian and Pacific Islander family structure has the potential for creating conflicts and the need for counseling intervention. American-born children sometimes defy and reject their ancestors' ways of living. They may feel torn between the demands of becoming Americanized and the desires of parents to adhere to traditional values. If they believe that their parents have unreasonable expectations and are at odds with American expectations of life, children may openly voice their opposing opinions—for example, disdain for their cultural background. They may even make rude remarks about their parents' national origin.

Second-generation children often differ dramatically from their parents who immigrated to the United States. Many values, such as bringing honor and praise to the family by practicing filial piety, expressing deference to elders, and making personal sacrifices for family members, may become less meaningful to Asian American children.

Up Close and Personal 9.1 introduces Mina, an Asian American child.

Unique Challenges Confronting Asian American Children

Asian American children face several challenges. One challenge is their ability to speak English. Speaking English and being understood can be a source of difficulty for Asian American children. A second challenge for Asian American children is reconciling loyalties to two different cultural traditions. In a pluralistic society, children are faced with the challenge of maintaining their ethnic identities while meeting differing cultural expectations of home and school (Sue & Sue,

UP CLOSE AND PERSONAL 9.1
Mina, an Asian American Child

Mina, a 10-year-old Japanese American, lives with her parents, older sister, younger brother, and elderly grandfather. Although her community is predominantly Asian American, the immediate area in which she lives is as diverse as her culture; she has many opportunities to meet both Asian American and European American children.

Mina lives in a close-knit family. Her father works two jobs, and her mother works one; together, they provide a comfortable standard of living. Mina's grandfather does not work outside the home, but he does take an active part in child-rearing and has other household responsibilities. The whole family looks to him for advice in making everyday decisions. In essence, the family is an interdependent unit working toward common goals and toward solving its own problems. Each member accepts his or her own specific role and is committed to not disappointing other family members. Mina does not question the dominance of her father's authority nor does she question that her younger brother seems to have more important roles and privileges than she has.

Mina has demonstrated above-average academic achievement. She plays the piano, works part-time at the school library, and is a member of the school's

Honor Society. Her family views education as an avenue to success and has always insisted that Mina excel in whatever she does. Although her teacher is concerned that Mina is a bit quiet and aloof, she also appreciates Mina's obedience and fine academic work. Mina does not think she is too quiet, but she does realize that her commitment to fulfill family expectations influences her interpersonal conduct and social standing. She feels pressured to excel in both personal conduct and academics. To do otherwise would bring shame and disappointment to her family.

Although Mina wants very much to please the members of her family, their high expectations have given rise to several problems. English does not come easily for her; it requires a considerable amount of work. Also, her European American peers and some of her Asian American friends think she is somewhat aloof—a bit of a goody-goody, in fact. Mina thinks her academic success has caused some of her fellow students to reject her. Of course, she wants to have friends and to be accepted by her peers, but family expectations must come first. Meanwhile, Mina continues to work diligently to fulfill her family obligations and to maintain her excellent academic standing. At the same time, she is trying to develop her own identity.

2003). Third, Asian American children may face peer pressure that conflicts with basic family values and traditions. Fourth, the model minority stereotype presents a significant dilemma for these children. Not all of them fit the mold, and even those who do may have trouble meeting unrealistic expectations. Fifth, some Asian Americans experience low socioeconomic status, with its inherent problems and risk factors.

Asian American Adolescents

Social and Cultural Description

According to the U.S. Census Bureau (2004–2005), the Asian American and Pacific Islander population aged 15 to 19 years was 821,000 in 2003 and is expected to grow to 1,178,000 in 2010. Asian American adolescents, much like African American adolescents, must overcome a stereotype that has the potential for affecting their identity formation, self-concept, and others' perception of them. The academic success of many Asian Americans has led to a perception that all Asian Americans are bound to succeed in all their pursuits. However, to make this assumption based on culture alone has no greater validity than assuming that all African Americans are incapable of high academic achievement or that all American Indians live on reservations.

The importance of identity formation and personality development during the adolescent years must be considered from a cultural perspective. Family beliefs and values play an important role in shaping the emerging adult. Asian Americans often adopt a more practical approach to life and problems than do European Americans. Although some acculturation has occurred, cultural emphasis continues to be placed on diligence, harmony, taking responsibility, respect for authority, emphasis on education, and, respect for elders, and family loyalty.

Many Asian American adolescents spend more time on homework, take more advanced high school courses, and graduate with more credits. In addition, a higher percentage of these young people complete high school and college than do their European American peers. However, the high expectations for Asian American adolescents often work to their disadvantage. For example, expectations based on stereotypes mask individuality. Not all Asian American adolescents excel; indeed, many have academic problems that are serious enough to warrant their dropping out of school.

Duan and Vu (2000) studied the acculturation levels of Vietnamese college students born either in Vietnam or in the United States who had received pre-college education and entered college in the United States. The main purpose of the study was to determine whether these students' acculturation levels were related to the community settings at college. The authors compared the acculturation level of students who lived in or near the Vietnamese community while attending college with that of those who lived away from the Vietnamese community during their college years. Whereas one finding was expected, a second finding was somewhat surprising. First, the community setting of residency at college did relate to the Vietnamese college students' acculturation into U.S. culture. However, Duan and Vu found it "intriguing that participants who lived in a Vietnamese community were more acculturated than those who lived in a non-Vietnamese community at college, rather than the opposite" (p. 236). Also, the differences between the two groups seemed to be in their functional integration with mainstream society but not in cultural values and attitudes.

Communication

For effective multicultural counseling, it is crucial that the counselor recognize the problems some Asian Americans have with English and understand their unique forms of nonverbal communication. Without doubt, communication barriers and problems confronting Asian American adolescents make educational attainment even more significant. Although many Asian American parents encourage the use of English, large numbers of adolescents live in homes where the primary language spoken continues to be the native language.

In many cases, additional coursework is recommended to remedy the language and communication deficiencies of Asian American students. Some of these students have such difficulty understanding English and making themselves understood that considerably more study is required to achieve even minimal competency. Moreover, the direct teaching of English. Communication skills to correct language and communication deficiencies indicates a failure to understand Asian Americans' difficulty with English and has caused remedial programs to become generally ineffective (Sue & Sue, 2003).

Some nonverbal behavior patterns demonstrated by Asian Americans differ distinctly from those of other cultures. For example, the forward and backward leaning of the body indicates feelings: A backward lean indicates a degree of discomfort with the conversation and a withdrawal from it, whereas a forward lean lets the speaker know the listener is interested, concerned, and flexible. Also, counselors should be aware that Japanese American females express anxiety through increased vocalization, whereas Japanese American males express anxiety through silence. Also, Japanese Americans often communicate nonverbally through gestures. Rubbing or scratching the back of the head or neck, for example indicates shame or discomfort.

Families

Children learn early on that the father is the head of the household in the traditional Asian American family. Each family member recognizes and respects rigidly defined roles. The father–son relationship is held in the highest esteem. A son is a prized and valued family member who receives greater privileges and responsibilities than does a daughter. A son is obligated to respect and obey his father; in turn, the father assists his son with his education and marriage and provides him with an inheritance. Also, sons have a greater voice in family decisions and enjoy freedoms that daughters do not. Understandably, in this culture, adolescent boys are given more freedom than adolescent girls (Axelson, 1999).

Respect for family values and expectations influence the behavior of adolescents. If adolescents demonstrate disrespect or any form of undesirable behavior, it reflects poorly on the entire family. The Chinese American family serves as a source of emotional security and personal identity and as a reference point for individual members. In turn, the family exerts control over interpersonal conduct and social relations, even over the choice of a career or marriage partner. Although acculturation has contributed to increasing individualism, such cultural characteristics as avoidance of shame, indirect communication, self-effacement, and modesty appear to be maintained in recent generations. Adolescent behavior will continue to be strongly influenced by old-world family expectations.

Unique Challenges Confronting Asian American Adolescents

Because they live in a predominantly European American culture and yet must continue to meet the expectations of their respective cultures, Asian American adolescents will probably experience problems that may warrant counseling intervention. Loyalty to Asian American family expectations may result in conflicts, especially during this period of pressure to conform to European American standards and to make the transition into a wider social world.

One of the authors taught a Japanese American student whose achievement record outpaced all others in the class. Her language problems often exacted a burdensome toll: She studied far longer and more conscientiously, sought more assistance, relied heavily on her Japanese–American dictionary, and usually requested additional time for in-class assignments. With all her language difficulties, however, her persistence and determination overcame her deficiencies in English.

Vietnamese Americans constitute a growing ethnic group as the result of the influx of refugees. Many of these refugees were young when they entered the United States and are now experiencing problems resulting from tasks associated with adjusting to a new culture (Duan & Vu, 2000).

A Focus on Research 9.2 looks at mental health symptoms of Chinese, Korean, and Japanese immigrant youth. Yeh (2003) maintains that her research has particularly helpful

---

A FOCUS ON RESEARCH 9.2

Mental Health Symptoms of Chinese, Korean, and Japanese Immigrant Youth

Yeh's (2003) investigation looked at Chinese, Korean, and Japanese immigrant youth in terms of age, acculturation, cultural adjustment difficulties, and general mental health concerns. Previous theories have found mental health concerns of Asian immigrants to be unique; for example., immigrant adolescents often have high expectations for what their life will be like when they move to the United States, and they experience disappointment, resentment, depression, and shock when their expectations are inaccurate. Another problem results when their family values do not match those of mainstream society. These factors can have a detrimental effect on one's mental health. Dealing with language difficulties, forming a sense of identity, assimilating to a new culture, relating to peers, and learning new role relations can take a significant toll. Yeh maintains that considering Asian Americans' adjustment processes was important because Asian American youths are often characterized as model minorities in education, work, and social settings.

Yeh concludes that Korean immigrant students

1. experience higher levels of mental health symptoms in comparison to Chinese and Japanese students;

2. experience shame and humiliation in seeking help for their cultural conflicts;

3. face particular challenges as they approach adulthood, such as child care, working for money, and increased housework; and

4. experience increasing parent–adolescent conflict due to contrasting ideas about youth authority and autonomy.

Source: "Age, acculturation, cultural adjustment, and mental health symptoms of Chinese, Korean, and Japanese immigrant youth," by C. Yeh, 2003, *Cultural Diversity and Ethnic Minority Psychology, 9*(1), pp. 34–48.

implications for research, training, and counseling Asian immigrant youth. Understanding the factors contributing to mental health symptoms in Chinese, Korean, and Japanese immigrant youth will help educators, administrators, and counselors better serve these groups through direct services, program development, and counselor training.

The European American emphasis on individualism presents challenges for Asian American adolescents seeking to satisfy the demands of contemporary society and still remain loyal to family traditions. Asian American girls, in particular, may experience the cultural conflict between traditional values and the more contemporary European American values and thus question their role in life: Will females continue to be relegated to second-class status in the Asian American family? Should they seek more equitable standing, such as exists in European American families? Female Asian Americans are often forced to make additional cultural compromises to achieve success in the majority culture.

Up Close and Personal 9.2 introduces Rieko, an Asian American adolescent.

UP CLOSE AND PERSONAL 9.2

Rieko, an Asian American Adolescent

Rieko, a 16-year-old Japanese American, lives with her parents, younger sister Mina, her younger brother, and her elderly grandfather. Rieko enjoys the closeness of her family and in particular seeks the advice of her grandfather, who is always available to listen to her concerns.

Rieko is in the 10th grade and does above-average work, but her studies take up most of her time. She is not sure why her studies take so much more time than for European American students, but she suspects that her language problem is the reason. She has not discussed this with her family, however, because they continually emphasize the value of education. Also, she does not want them to know that her English is not as good as that of other students. Rieko does pride herself, however, on being able to speak Japanese. In fact, she and her grandfather sometimes speak his native tongue. She enjoys the fact that speaking Japanese makes her grandfather proud of her.

Besides excelling in schoolwork, Rieko has also learned the responsibilities of running a household. She can cook, clean, sew, and shop for groceries. Because her mother is responsible for these tasks, Rieko was encouraged to learn them, too. She is aware, though, that her younger brother is not being taught how to care for the household. She accepts the fact that girls must assume more responsibility despite having fewer privileges, but she sometimes envies her European American girlfriends, who have considerably more freedom. What will it be like after she finishes high school and college (if her family can afford to send her) and enters a predominately European American world? Secretly, she wonders whether she will be drawn away from her Asian American culture.

Sometimes, but not often, Rieko worries about her situation. Will she be more accepted by her fellow European American students next semester? Are they a bit standoffish because of her culture, because of her good grades, or because she tries to satisfy her teachers? If it is her grades and behavior, there isn't much she can do. She would never disappoint her family. Will her English improve? She has been working very hard on it lately, but there is only so much time between schoolwork and household chores. She also wants to spend some time with her grandfather. Right now, these problems do not seem overwhelming to Rieko. She has always persisted, and besides, she knows her family is there to support her.

Asian American Adults

Social and Cultural Description

Historically, Asians and Pacific Islanders were often forced to accept the lowest paid, menial jobs and were denied the rights of citizenship and of land ownership. Without the opportunity to live and work in European American communities, Asian Americans often formed their own cultural enclaves, such as Chinatowns. In these isolated enclaves, they continued to speak their native language and maintain their old-world traditions (Sue & Sue, 2003).

Phan, Rivera, and Roberts-Wilbur (2005) believe that there is a lack of knowledge about the identity development of Vietnamese women. Gender Perspectives 9.1 examines identity development in Vietnamese women.

Although statistics indicate that many Asian Americans have experienced considerable economic and academic success, a comprehensive picture deserves consideration before reaching conclusions.

GENDER PERSPECTIVES 9.1

Understanding Vietnamese Women Refugees

Phan, Rivera, and Roberta-Wilbur (2005) first provide a brief history of Vietnamese populations and their problems (e.g., culture shock, depression, homesickness, and stresses). Next, they maintain that traditional models of identity development do not assist counselors in understanding ethnic minorities in the United States. One cannot assume all women have the same issues—there is not a universal women's experience. Likewise, similarities between racial and ethnic identity exist, but gender is not always included.

Phan, Rivera, and Roberts-Wilbur (2005) describe an Asian American ethnic identity development model, but maintain that some of these studies overlook the effect of womanhood development on ethnic identity development for Asian American women, specifically on particular ethnic groups such as Vietnamese women. In an interesting section, the authors provide an historical overview of colonization, mainly early Vietnamese culture, Chinese influence, French influence, and U.S. influence.

They feel the available ethnic identity models do not adequately describe the unique and multifaceted reality of Vietnamese women. In addition, Vietnamese women face complications such as discrimination, oppression, prejudice, and sexism.

Implications for practice include that counselors should

- understand issues of identity such as gender stereotypes, racial stereotypes, family, marriage, gender role conflict, and interracial marriage;

- recognize the multiple dimensions of Vietnamese refugee women, such as the influence of sociopolitical, sociohistorical, and inherited traditional aspects of the Vietnamese culture;

- understand that Vietnamese women have become better educated over the years, which as led them to freedom and progressive thinking; and

- realize that traditional ways of thinking about the Vietnamese culture may no longer be valid.

Source: "Understanding Vietnamese refugees women's identity development from a sociopolitical and historical perspective," by L. T. Phan, E. T. Rivera, and J. Roberts-Wilbur, 2005, *Journal of Counseling and Development, 83*, pp. 305–312.

First, the stereotype of economic success does not take into account that the culture has a high percentage of more than one wage earner per household. It is true that some Asian Americans work in high-paying occupations, in part, because of high educational attainments. Still, some Asian Americans experience poverty conditions, for example, 10.1% of Asian Americans lived in poverty in 2002 and 11.8% lived in poverty in 2003. Plus, in 2003, 18.7% of Asian Americans did not have health insurance (DeNavas, Proctor, & Mills, 2004).

Second, taking care to avoid stereotyping, Asian Americans as a whole have had impressive academic achievements. For example, the U.S. Census Bureau (2004–2005) reports significant numbers of Asian Americans receiving academic degrees at all levels. In 2002, 20.5% had completed 4 years of high school, and 50.9% had completed 4 years of college (Reeves & Bennett, 2003). Also, 22% of Asian American households earn $100,000 or more annually (compared to 14% of all U.S. households) (Ahmed, 2003). Even with these educational and financial success rates, communication problems pose problems for significant numbers of Asian Americans and constitute a major barrier to success.

Some Asian Americans believe that discussing unpleasant events will actually cause them to happen. In fact, discussing sickness, mental illness, or death with members of the Chinese culture often constitutes a social taboo. In some situations, an entire family might be ostracized if it is learned that one family member has a mental illness; however, that is also true in some other cultures.

Religious rites and ceremonies play a significant role in the lives of many Asian Americans. Formal religions include Buddhism, Protestantism, and Catholicism. Protestant and Buddhist churches serve specific Asian groups, such as the Japanese, Chinese, Filipino, Korean, and Vietnamese, whereas members of the Catholic church are generally integrated with other ethnic groups in a geographic parish. Religious values of Asian Americans tend to be closely intertwined with family obligations and expectations.

Communication

Asian Americans speak at least 32 different primary languages. Within each cultural subgroup, various dialects are spoken. Proficiency in English varies greatly among the different groups. English is generally the first and often the only language of American-born Asians. In contrast, most foreign-born Asian Americans speak a language other than English. Many are fluently bilingual and even multilingual or speak more than one dialect of their native Asian language. Those with limited English proficiency generally live in households where a language other than English predominates (Hume, 2002).

Many Asian Americans feel uncomfortable with direct forms of communication, especially those involving challenges, confrontation, interruption, and assertiveness. Asians often use subtle, indirect means of communication to allow all those involved to save face. Many Asian American people convey information nonverbally, such as through silence and eye contact. Maintaining silence during a conversation often indicates an expression of respect. Direct eye contact is usually avoided, especially with an elder, because it might indicate disrespect.

Understanding that an Asian American's communication structure changes with differing situations provides counselors with additional cultural insights. Communication forms change with regard to syntax, word endings, and terminology, depending on the individuals involved and the nature of relationships.

Effective communication, regardless of the counselor's cultural background, is essential when working with Asian and Pacific Islander clients. Infusing cultural sensitivity into professional intervention requires counselors to be aware of communication that is reflective of cultural styles and mannerisms.

Families

The Asian American family is characterized by unique familial roles and expectations that warrant the counselor's attention. Of great importance is the fact that this culture consists of many different populations shaped by environmental, historical, and social pressures. These groups differ not only among themselves but also in important aspects from the broader European American culture.

Most Asian American families are headed by married couples. Table 9.4 shows the family types among Asian Americans.

The family-first concept of Asian and Pacific Islander families plays a significant role in promoting and maintaining cohesiveness and stability in the family. The cultural obligation to place the family's needs above one's personal needs can result in problems that need counseling intervention.

Despite some changes in values and the shifting trend toward increasing individualism, such concepts as family loyalty, respect and obligation, and harmony and group cooperation all continue to play significant roles in determining family and individual behavior. Many Asians continue to hold on to a cultural value of humility and an orientation of collectivism. These beliefs, which emphasize the connections among self, family, and community, stand in stark contrast with Western individualistic values. Counselors with cultural backgrounds that value individualism and independence may want to examine how these values affect their personal attitudes toward Asian American families who value harmony and interdependence.

Family honor is often maintained through highly developed feelings of obligation. The family provides a reference point, a source of personal identity and emotional security. The concept of loss of face involves not only the exposure of an individual's actions for all to see but also the possible withdrawal of the confidence and support of the family, community, or society.

Chung, Bemak, and Wong (2000) outline how the first wave of Vietnamese refugees came to America shortly after the fall of Saigon in 1975; the second and subsequent waves came in the postwar era. As the authors show, second and subsequent waves of Vietnamese refugees have experienced more psychosocial adjustment problems than did first-wave refugees.

Table 9.4

Family Types Among Asian Americans (percentages)

Source: "The Asian and Pacific Islander population in the United States: March 2002," by T. Reeves and C. Bennett, 2003, *Current Population Reports*, pp. 20–540, U.S. Census Bureau, Washington, D.C.

Family Types	Total
Total	100
Married, spouse present	53.3
Married, spouse absent	3.2
Widowed	4.2
Divorced	5.0
Separated	1.4
Never Married	32.9

In an effort to understand psychosocial postmigration adjustment, Chung, Bemak, and Wong (2000) studied variables such as acculturation, social support, and psychological distress in Vietnamese refugees. In their discussion, the researchers maintained that their study provided important implications for mental health counselors who work with Vietnamese and other refugees. They found that the second-wave Vietnamese refugees reported more psychological distress than did first-wave refugees. Also, first-wave refugees (who came to America when they were approximately 3 years of age) reported greater acculturation and satisfaction with their social support than did second-wave refugees (who arrived when they were about 11 years old). The second-wave refugees arrived in America during a later developmental period, when their social and cultural identity were particularly important, thereby requiring rapid cultural adaptation and language acquisition. Chung, Bemak, and Wong offer several recommendations for counselors:

1. Provide therapeutic interventions for existing dysfunctional families and social networks.
2. Support and reinforce already established health social networks that go beyond the counseling interventions for troubled families and groups.
3. Re-create social networks where there is an absence of family or friends in order to facilitate interpersonal awareness and experiences.

Unique Challenges Confronting Asian American Adults

Communication problems, dismal employment opportunities for unskilled minorities, the model minority stereotype, and conflicting familial roles and expectations all create unique challenges for Asian American adults. First, communication problems will continue to challenge selected Asian groups. Second, the commonly held stereotype of Asian Americans achieving academic and financial success poses a problem. Third, problems may arise when family roles and expectations conflict with those of the European American culture. With acculturation, Asian Americans place increasing emphasis on the European ideals of individuality and personal achievement. Fourth, Hwang, Chun, Takeuchi, Myers, and Siddarth (2005) investigated depression in Chinese Americans and concluded that although most people experience depression during the late teens and early adulthood, Chinese Americans differ in the onset of depression. In fact, Chinese Americans in their study evidenced low risk during late teens and early adulthood. They also concluded that depression onset with Chinese Americans varies as a function of age at immigration and length of residence in the United States.

Sharma (2004) maintained that approximately one-fourth of Americans over the age of 15 have a physiological dependence on at least one substance. Still, while there is not any particular predilection for or prevalence of substance abuse, there is a glaring omission of data from groups with culturally diverse backgrounds. In A Focus on Research 9.3, Sharma looks at substance abuse and Asian Americans and the need for more research.

Another challenge is life satisfaction after immigration to the United States. Chinese American immigrants who experience problems with communication and social isolation expressed less satisfaction. Counselors intervening with Chinese Americans, especially immigrants, need to realize the factors (e.g., language, discrimination, social isolation) that affect life satisfaction and thus plan counseling strategies to address these life stressors.

Up Close and Personal 9.3 introduces Han, an Asian American adult.

A FOCUS ON RESEARCH 9.3

Substance Abuse and Asian Americans

Despite serious gaps in the research and conclusions, Sharma (2004) concludes that Asian Americans bear a disproportionate burden of substance abuse. One-third of Asian American youth are smokers, which is much greater than other ethnic groups. Recent reviews of the tobacco industry have revealed aggressive marketing directed toward Asian Americans. Several reasons exist for these marketing efforts: Asian Americans' rapidly increasing population growth, higher purchasing power of some Asian Americans, higher rates of tobacco use in countries of origin, higher proportions of retail businesses under Asian American ownerships, and Asian Americans' difficulties adapting to mainstream American society. In Asian societies, youth are taught to be more dependent on others (e.g., parents, elders, and peers) in making decisions. As a result, Asians often get confused while making decisions that focus on everyday living and problems.

Educational interventions aimed at preventing the initiation of substance abuse, such as developing refusal skills, developing media interpretation skills, restoring peoples' sense of purpose and meaning, training in relaxation, and mediation methods, are available.

Source: "Substance abuse and Asian Americans: Need for more research," by M. Sharma, 2004, *Journal of Alcohol Drug Education, 47*(3), pp. 1–3.

UP CLOSE AND PERSONAL 9.3

Han, an Asian American Adult

Han, a 36-year-old Japanese American, lives in a predominantly Asian American neighborhood with his elderly father, his wife, 10-year-old daughter Mina, 16-year-old daughter Reiko, and his son. Han really appreciates the grandfather's presence in his household, especially when his two jobs leave him weary and in need of encouragement. Han's full-time job is with a European American company; his part-time job is with an Asian American friend who owns a small, struggling construction company. Although he likes his friend, Han would prefer to have only one job. The extra money is handy, but he has little time to spend with his family.

Han views his role as crucial to the welfare of the family. He makes most financial and household decisions. Some of his European American friends question his strong, authoritarian hand, but he feels that's the way it was with his father and that's the way it should be. Han is not sure he could change even if he wanted to. What would his wife and children think? What would the grandfather think? Everyone in his family expects him to make all the important decisions.

Han is proud of his daughter Mina. Her part-time library job, her musical gifts, and her recent initiation into the school's Honor Society please him. In fact, all his family members are worthy. Only once did Mina's younger brother appear to be a bit lax in his behavior at school. Before taking action, Han went to the grandfather to seek his advice. The solution was to approach the problem indirectly and with great tact. The boy did not suffer great shame or embarrassment, but he knew what his father expected him to do.

Han acknowledges that he has problems: working two jobs, uncertainty about whether he should allow his wife to work to supplement his salaries, and his aging father. He is fairly content and is proud of his close-knit family, but today's changing society is likely to change the family, too. Han is uncertain about what the future will bring.

Asian American Elderly

Social and Cultural Description

Table 9.5 provides a breakdown of Asian Americans 60 years and older.

The number of older Americans is growing considerably. The percentage of adults age 65 and older is 12.4%, with a projected increase to 13.5% by 2010. Nationally, the number of ethnically diverse adults is rising. It is projected that by 2020, approximately 22% of the older adult population will be composed of ethnic minority elders. The numbers suggest major changes and challenges for mental health providers in the immediate future (Watari & Gatz, 2004). According to the U.S. Census Bureau (2004–2005), approximately 7% of Asian American elderly live in nonmetropolitan areas. More than 60% live in California and Hawaii; most of the remaining 40% live in New York, New Jersey, Illinois, Texas, and Washington.

Counselors should remember that many elderly Asian Americans who seek counseling experienced considerable hardships decades ago (and, in many cases, still do). After arriving in the United States, Asians (especially the Japanese) experienced racism, injustices, and discrimination, such as legal acts forbidding them to own land. They also had limited educational and political opportunities. During World War II, many Japanese Americans were moved to internment camps in the western United States, where they remained until the end of the war. Counselors working with elderly Asian Americans who have suffered the effects of racism and discrimination need to understand how injustices affect these clients' current outlooks and worldviews.

It is a popular misconception that Asian American elderly have no need for assistance because they do not have significant problems and their adjustments to mainstream society have been relatively simple. Although many Asian Americans have demonstrated an amazing ability to achieve success in the predominantly European American society, Asian Americans, especially the elderly, should not be saddled with such an "all is well" image.

Compared with other minorities, the Asian American culture ranks closest to the European American in education and income, but professionals must still remember that moat

Table 9.5
Asian Populations: 60 and over

Source: Statistical abstracts of the United States 2004–2005 (124th ed.), by U.S. Census Bureau, 2005, Washington, D.C.: Author.

Ages	Total
60–64 yrs.	418,000
65–69 yrs.	330,000
70–74 yrs.	260,000
75–79 yrs.	193,000
80–84 yrs.	121,000
85–90 yrs.	59,000
90–94 yrs.	23,000
95–99 yrs.	6,000

A FOCUS ON RESEARCH 9.4

Caring for Filipino, Southeastern Asian, and Indian Patients

Pennachio (2004) offers information on the special needs of Chinese, Japanese, and Korean patients. Her article outlines some cultural clues to help professionals working with these cultures. Examples of Pennachio's suggestions include:

Filipinos

Filipinos sometimes think

- rapid shifts from hot to cold lead to illness, and a warm environment is essential to maintaining optimal health.

- illnesses result from ancestors for unfulfilled obligations which can be countered by healers or priests with massage, herbal treatments, incantations, and offerings.

- they should resist screening programs such as mammograms, Pap smears, and blood tests for cholesterol and glucose.

Southeast Asians

Southeast Asians sometimes think

- elders should be involved in medical decision-making.

- actions of the past affect the circumstances in which one is born and lives his life, as well as reincarnation of ancestral spirits.

- the head is sacred—if the head must be touched, touch both sides of the head, so the person will think balance is being respected and maintained.

Indians

People from India sometimes think

- ayurvedic medicine, an ancient, intricate system of healing, is effective and worthy of respect.

- professionals should take charge and have answers to their problems.

- maintaining spiritual peace is an essential part of health.

While Pennachio's beneficial article focuses primary emphasis on medical practice, counseling professions will gain significant information about working with these cultural groups.

Source: "Caring for your Filipino, Southeastern Asian, and Indian patients: More than half of Asian Americans say their doctors don't understand their cultures: Sensitivity to diversity is essential for good patient care," by D. L. Pennachio, 2004, *Medical Economics, 81*(2), pp. 36–42.

studies have focused on Asian Americans in general rather than on the elderly in particular. An appropriate perception of the elderly requires knowledge of the culture, the elderly years, and the elderly as individuals. Compared with elderly European Americans, elderly Asian Americans fall short in several areas crucial to individual well-being. For example, although the more recent Asian American immigrants include well-educated professionals, the percentage of Asian American elderly who lack formal education continues to be disturbingly high.

Although acculturation undoubtedly continues to occur, most elderly in the Asian American culture continue to receive considerable respect. For example, many Japanese Americans equate old age with prestige and honor. Respect for elders is evident in the language used when addressing the elderly and in behavior such as bowing to them and observing strict rules of etiquette.

Each Japanese American generation has a unique title which emphasizes the importance of the role that generations play:

Generation	Name
1st	Issei
2nd	Nisei
3rd	Sansei
4th	Yonsei

The values brought to America by first-generation Chinese Americans are often quite different from the prevailing views of American society. For example, Chinese society discourages financial independence from parents and instead encourages interdependence. The American values of achievement, upward mobility, and competition are contrary to Chinese beliefs. In the Chinese culture, the elderly maintain control over income, property, and jobs, whereas European American culture does not recognize such control or power of the elderly.

First-generation Asian American elders have come to expect a reverence and respect that second and third generations (who have adopted many European American customs) may no longer support. Thus, these Chinese Americans have difficulty maintaining the old-world traditions, lifestyle, and status they were taught to cherish in their homeland.

In A Focus on Research 9.5, Watari and Gatz (2004) examined help-seeking behaviors for dementia and Alzheimer's disease among older Korean Americans.

A FOCUS ON RESEARCH 9.5

Pathways to Caring for Alzheimer's Disease Among Korean Americans

Watari and Gatz (2004) investigated Alzheimer's disease among Korean Americans. Barriers to seeking help for mental health symptoms include both structural and cultural barriers. Structural barriers include lack of health insurance, low income, and limited knowledge of the English language. Cultural barriers include how patients and families view illness and whether the illness was conceptualized in religious terms. For example, if the person considered the illness to be related to religious aspects, he or she was less likely to seek mental health counseling. Another related barrier is the lack of knowledge of Alzheimer's disease and dementia.

Watari and Gatz conclude that a higher proportion of Korean American patients are married or living with other family members. Also, their knowledge of Alzheimer's disease and dementia is quite limited. The authors also conclude that Korean Americans underutilize community health services for dementia-related problems; delay visits to seek mental health services; and depend on family to buffer symptoms (which sometimes result in more cognitive declines). Memory problems alone were unlikely to be a cause of seeking assistance. Reasons for the delay may be found in the main barriers to seeking help, including the belief that more rest or religion could help with the memory problems and also the belief that knowledge of the problem should be confined to family members.

Source: "Pathways to caring for Alzheimer's disease among Korean Americans," by K. Watari, and M. Gatz, 2004, *Cultural Diversity and Ethnic Minority Psychology, 10*(1), pp. 23–28.

As do all older Americans, elderly Asian Americans experience various changes related to advancing age: declining physical strength, increased leisure time, and the imminence of death. In addition, elderly Asian Americans must adjust to challenges to their established traditions. In short, the difficulties faced by Asian Americans are also faced by other cultural groups.

Communication

Communication barriers cause considerable problems and frustrations for Asian American elderly. Communication problems have undoubtedly played a major role in preventing Asian Americans from seeking community services as well as public social and health services. Communication difficulties have also hampered their adjustment to a predominantly European American culture. Because elderly Chinese Americans have lived most of their lives in predominantly Chinese-speaking communities, communication poses a major barrier for them. They may not have the option to improve their living conditions by moving outside their ethnic neighborhoods. They may also not seek medical attention unless their illnesses are extremely severe, and then they visit only Chinese-speaking doctors in their neighborhood.

For Asian American elderly, communication problems are compounded by attitudes and limitations associated with advanced years. Because of the lack of motivation, the difficulty of learning a second language, or the lack of proper professional assistance, it is unlikely that the elderly will undertake any serious effort to improve their communication skills. The feeling that "it's too late in life to begin such an enormous task" or the lack of motivation to improve language skills continues to be a contributing factor to such hardships as substandard housing and inadequate medical attention and nutrition experienced by many elderly Asian Americans.

Families

Families, both immediate and extended, have traditionally played a significant role in the Asian American culture and are characterized by specific roles, relationships, and respect for elders. Although historically the responsibility for the elderly rested with the oldest son, more contemporary expectations do not include the oldest son accepting such responsibility. Elderly family members do, however, expect their children to assist them. In the traditional Japanese and Chinese cultures, the extended family unit functions as a supportive institution, and all family members share individual incomes. Although these values carried over to some degree in the United States and continue to be appreciated by first-generation Asian Americans, cultural changes in younger generations indicate that practices toward the elderly might be changing. It is ironic that, at the very time the elderly need stability and adherence to cultural traditions, many younger generation Asian Americans are beginning to emphasize the values of the traditional European American society, such as financial independence from parents and extended family. Without doubt, the "Americanization" of Asian American youths is forcing many older Asian Americans to compromise their old-world values.

Unique Challenges Confronting Asian American Elderly

Asian American elderly have been erroneously portrayed as a cultural group without need of assistance and as an age group that has all of its financial and emotional needs met by younger generations. Professionals with a knowledge and understanding of Asian American elderly clearly recognize the fallacy of such thinking. Elderly Asian Americans experience challenges unique to their age on the lifespan and to their culture:

- Certain types of cancers, high blood pressure and tuberculosis are major health concerns of elderly Asian/Pacific Islander Americans (U.S. Census Bureau, 2004–2005).

- Elderly Asian Americans are less likely to use formal health care services, such as those reimbursed under Medicare. Reasons include communication differences and a distrust of Western medicine.

- Language continues to be a serious problem for elderly Asian Americans. Because of lack of proficiency in English, they may be forced to live in low-income neighborhoods, where they often receive inappropriate medical care and cannot take advantage of social services.

- Because of low wages, lack of education, and limited skills, significant numbers of elderly Asian Americans live in poverty.

- An alarmingly high rate of drug use and suicide among older Asian Americans exists, especially in older men without family or ideological ties to the larger community.

- Increasing generational differences put additional stress on the elderly at a time when they especially need stability.

The elderly often face expensive and sometimes preventable consequences as a result of chronic illness. For example, Cataldo (2001) investigated the relationship of hardiness and depression to disability in aged persons in a nursing home. Her sample included elderly people who were relatively diverse both racially and ethnically. She directed attention toward aspects such as physiological factors and disability; psychological factors and disability; and depression and disability. Selected aspects of her discussion include the following:

- Physiological factors alone do not totally explain degree of disability.

- Psychological factors may increase a person's degree of disability beyond what might be expected from physical illness or injury alone.

- People who have experienced high degrees of stress with low levels of disability have a personality characteristic called "hardiness" (p. 33). The hardy person with a sense of control and a continued commitment to health and life who views his or her illness and nursing home stay as a challenge rather than a threat may be less likely to experience a magnification of disability.

- Hardiness and depression contribute more to explaining disability than health status and length of nursing home stay.

- Depressed individuals are less active, both physically and cognitively, and inactivity can lead to an increase in the disability level.

It is ironic that an age group and a culture with so many problems and challenges can be stereotyped as a cultural group without significant problems. Elderly Asian Americans are not likely to seek assistance for a variety of reasons: pride, communication barriers, fear of discrimination outside Asian American communities, and a mistrust of Western medicine. Furthermore, Asian American elderly may be forced to accept rejection of their traditional values as their children and grandchildren assimilate into the majority culture.

Up Close and Personal 9.4 introduces Grandfather Sukuzi, an elderly Asian American.

UP CLOSE AND PERSONAL 9.4

Grandfather Sukuzi: An Asian American Elder

Eighty-five-year-old Grandfather Sukuzi lives with Han and his wife, their daughters, Mina and Rieko, and their youngest child, a son. He feels very fortunate to live in the same house with his family; some of his elderly friends are not as fortunate and must live either alone or with other elderly people in small apartments. He no longer works outside the home and does very little housework. "Keeping the house is women's work," Grandfather says. Besides Han's wife and daughters do a very good job taking care of the house. Grandfather does feel needed, however; he helps the family by giving advice and instructing the children in traditional Japanese customs.

Grandfather's health is generally good, but he does have the usual problems associated with growing old, such as dizziness, aches and pains, and a slight lose of hearing. He is somewhat frail and moves slowly. His forgetfulness worries him. Could it be Alzheimer's disease? He has heard of it, but he does not know much about it. Grandfather seldom sees a physician; in fact, he has not been to one in several years. Because Han has two jobs, Grandfather must go alone, which means he will not have help translating what the physician says. He also wonders whether the physician understands him. Although Grandfather probably could receive government benefits of some kind, he always puts off seeking assistance. "They ask too many questions," he tells Han. Grandfather's pride and lack of language facility are more likely the reasons for his reluctance to apply for benefits.

Although Grandfather has lived in the United States since he was in his early 20s, his English is still poor. He never attended an American school, and the only English he knows is what he has picked up from talking with others and occasionally watching television. Moreover, living in the Japanese community has relieved him of undue pressure; everyone there speaks his language.

Although Grandfather is quite content, he does sense some erosion of traditional Japanese values. Of course, the family treats him with great respect, but the younger generations are somehow different now. It is difficult to pinpoint specific examples, but sometimes Han seems to want too much financial independence, and he does not seek out Grandfather's advice as much as he once did. Evidence of change is clearer in the neighborhood. Some of his elderly friends seem to be forgotten by their children, who seldom visit their elders.

Grandfather is closest to his grandchildren. He and Rieko speak Japanese at times, and although she is not fluent, she is making progress and Grandfather enjoys teaching her. Strangely enough, it seems that Rieko is more interested in the traditional Japanese culture than her parents are.

What does the future hold for Grandfather? Right now, he is respected and needed by his family. It pleases him that the cultural assimilation of some Asian Americans is not affecting them to any significant degree. He is growing old, but his place in the family is secure.

A Point of Departure: Challenges Confronting Counselors of Asian Americans

Racial and ethnic minorities in the United States demonstrate a remarkable ability to sustain well-being, adapt to situations, and succeed in life, despite the persistent discrimination in society (Lee, R. M., 2005). Still, some Asian Americans, as well as people of other cultures, encounter difficulties that require mental health counseling. Counselors of Asian American children, adolescents, adults, and elders face several challenges that require culturally appropriate knowledge, attitudes, and skills. Slight modifications in counseling intervention will not suffice. Counselors intervening with Asian Americans will need to recognize

- the rich diversity among the Asian cultures and that knowledge gained from working with Chinese American clients, for instance, may not be applicable to Samoan or Tongan clients;

- the communication problems facing many Asian Americans, such as limited English language skills (comprehension and speaking);

- the incidence of poverty, which occurs in some Asian cultures more so than in others;

- society's expectations that all Asians fit a stereotypical mold; and

- cultural differences that relate to the respective lifespan stage, such as possible differences between partially acculturated children and their grandparents.

Counselors, regardless of their cultural background, will be challenged to understand the complexity of Asian cultures. For example, Hispanic American counselors will need to learn both the Asian client's lifespan stage and cultural characteristics (and vice versa). Asian American counselors face acute challenges; for example, a young Japanese American counselor can make few assumptions when working with a Chinese American elderly person. Similar challenges hold true when working with clients in the four lifespan stages and from all Asian American subcultures.

Summary

The rapidly increasing populations of Asian American children, adolescents, adults, and elders indicate that counselors will be called on to provide mental health intervention for this vastly diverse culture of people. Trying to fit an Asian American client into a mold or a model will only cause frustration for both client and counselor. Counselors who work effectively with Asian American clients will understand the need to learn about each client's specific culture and developmental stage. Such an undertaking will not be an easy task, especially considering Asian Americans' differing cultural characteristics, language proficiency levels, educational attainments, and income levels, as well as the challenges associated with each developmental stage. The task can be achieved, however, when counselors learn about Asian cultures and commit to a genuine effort to learn about their individual clients.

Suggested Readings

Hwang, W., Chun, C., Takeuchi, D. T., Myers, H. F., & Siddarth, P. (2005). Age of first onset of major depression in Chinese Americans. *Cultural Diversity and Ethnic Minority Psychology, 11*(1), 16–27. Focusing on depression in Chinese American, Hwang et al examines issues such as gender differences, age of depression onset, immigration and acculturation, and length of residence in the United States.

Prey, L. L., & Roysircar, G. (2005). Effects of acculturation and worldview for White American, South American, South Asian, and Southeast Asian students. *International Journal for the Advancement of Counseling, 26*(3), 229–248. These authors emphasize the importance of counseling approaches that respond to cultural variations, thus avoiding misattribution of behavior and ensuring culturally competent counseling assessment and intervention.

Lee, R. M. (2005). Resilience against discrimination: Ethnic identity and other-group orientation as protective factors for Korean Americans. *Journal of Counseling Psychology, 52*(1), 36–44. Lee investigates the resilience of Korean Americans and concludes ethnic identity pride and perceived discrimination affect self-esteem.

Rahman, O., & Rollock, D. (2004). Acculturation, competence, and mental health among South Asian students in the United States, *Journal of Multicultural Counseling and Development 32*, 130–142. Rahman and Rollock studied South Asian international students in the United States to determine levels of depressive symptoms due to higher perceived prejudice—interestingly, depressive symptoms differ by gender.

Yoon, S. M, (2005). The characteristics and needs of Asian American grandparent caregivers: A study of Chinese American and Korean American grandparents in New York City. *Journal of Gerontological Social Work, 44* (3/4), 75–94. Yoon finds that most Asian Americans who provide a significant proportion of their grandchildren's day care do not have legal guardianship yet continue to provide essential child care.

Counseling Asian American Clients

Questions to Be Explored

1. What unique challenges can counselors expect when intervening with Asian American children, adolescents, adults, and elders?

2. How can counselors, especially counselors from other cultural backgrounds, effectively plan counseling intervention for Asian American clients, considering Asian Americans' unique cultural and individual differences?

3. How have years of discrimination and injustice affected Asian Americans and their worldviews?

4. How can counselors address Asian Americans' tendency to seek mental health advice from sources other than counselors and psychotherapists?

5. How can counselors conduct individual, group, and family therapy for Asian Americans?

6. What concerns and problems related to development might Asian American child, adolescent, adult, and elder clients present to counselors?

7. How can counselors of differing cultural backgrounds and lifespan stages intervene with Asian Americans of other backgrounds and lifespan stages?

Overview

Counselors need to understand the Asian American people from historical, cultural, and lifespan perspectives. Many Asian Americans have experienced considerable hardships in the United States. Efforts to prohibit home ownership and to restrict educational, occupational, and political opportunities have taken a considerable toll on Asian Americans. Counselors also need to avoid making generalizations about this vastly diverse group of people. Given Asian Americans' diversity, it is essential that counselors consider languages, religions, and individual differences. As with all cultures, it is imperative that counselors learn about differences between younger generation and older generation Asian Americans. This chapter looks at how counselors can provide culturally appropriate individual, group, and family therapy to Asian American clients.

Since many Asian Americans have been successful in U.S. society, some people erroneously believe that discrimination is minimal or less severe and Asian Americans do not need counseling intervention (Lee, 2003). Such an opinion often hides potential counseling problems resulting from acculturation, economic stress, family conflicts, or substance abuse. Lee (2003) also thought Asians might avoid situations and circumstances in which discrimination has already occurred.

Asian American Children

Potential Problems Warranting Counseling Intervention

Problems Asian American children may experience include:

- failure to develop a strong Asian American cultural identity and a positive self-concept;
- the perception that they constitute a model minority; that is, they are all intellectually superior, hardworking, and academically successful, with superior mathematical skills;
- differing cultural characteristics;
- the inability to reconcile loyalties with conflicting Asian and majority cultures;
- pressures to excel in the majority-culture society yet maintain old-world Asian values;
- communication difficulties, which may hamper academic achievement and socialization;
- adverse effects of overt or covert racism, injustice, discrimination, and cultural history of oppression;
- an increasing tendency to move from a parent-centered world to a peer-centered world;
- family conflicts arising from children moving toward a peer-centered world and away from the parent-centered world;
- parents who are unwilling to accept contemporary Western viewpoints on child–family allegiances; and
- smaller physical size that may create problems for children when small stature causes them to feel inadequate in other ways.

Counseling Considerations

Issues relative to Asian American children include (a) conflicts related to children's cultural background and the Western values advocated in school, (b) the significant influence of the patriarchal role of the father in nearly all aspects of children's lives, and (c) the European American cultural challenge to children's traditional place in the Asian family (valuing boys over girls, determining authority by sibling age, maintaining unquestioned obedience, or upholding the family's honor at all costs).

Recommendations for working effectively with Asian American children include the following:

- Determine individual strengths, experiences and challenges.
- Determine the children's degree of acculturation to Western society.

- Understand Asian Americans' difficulty in being self-disclosing and open, especially with strangers, when discussing family matters.

- Understand that confrontational, emotionally intense approaches may cause additional problems and turmoil for Asian American clients.

- Learn about childern as individuals and their respective cultural beliefs.

Asian American children experience many social, economic, and educational inequities that may warrant the intervention of elementary school counselors. These children may feel uncomfortable with or unable to deal with school situations. They may experience social and health problems or problems resulting from conflicting values and language differences. Asian American children often learn early in life to keep personal and family problems within the confines of the family so as to avoid shame and embarrassment. Therefore, children might feel unfamiliar with counseling procedures and be reluctant to reveal inner feelings with a counselor with whom trust has not been established. Counselors who are aware of these cultural factors are in a better position to develop rapport that is conductive to the counseling process.

Individual and Group Therapy.   What strategies are most appropriate for working with Asian American and Pacific Islander children? Counselors who understand the reserved demeanor of Asian Amercian children and develop an enthusiasm for their Asian cultural heritage can enhance the client–counselor relationship. To promote cultural understanding, each child should be encouraged to share his or her background, values, needs, and problems.

Counselors should not misinterpret silence as apathy. During the session, Asian Americans may remain silent for quite some time, briefly verbalize a problem, and then wait for the counselor to offer directions.

Counselors should understand issues relating to four major areas: group orientation, concepts of time, communication and learning skills, and appropriate behavior. Counselors can understand the following issues:

- Individual competition should be minimized; children should not be recognized or punished in front of the group.

- Counseling activities should focus on the present time.

- Participation of parents and elders from the community should be sought whenever possible.

- The counselor should take the role of a mentor because Asian American children and their parents might be reluctant to seek professional assistance.

In examining counseling techniques used with Asian Americans, counselors should be more formal and less confrontational than when working with European Americans. Also, although counseling decisions deserve individual consideration, group therapy sessions should be used less often with Asian American children; these children may be reluctant to disclose personal problems that could reflect negatively on the family. The child who might disclose problems and

A FOCUS ON RESEARCH 10.1

Asian Shades of Spirituality

Hanna and Green think school counselors should consider the spiritual backgrounds and traditions of Asian students. Such an understanding will improve counseling effectiveness and will also prove beneficial in establishing trust with Asian parents. When a counselor can demonstrate some depth of knowledge of an Asian parent's religious tradition, the degree of trust generated can be deeper and even more inspired than what results from a counselor's understanding of culture. In their article, Hanna and Green succinctly explain Hinduism, Buddhism, and Islam. They also provide a case example for each.

The key to establishing spiritual connections with Asian clients is through communicating empathic understanding. The concept of cultural empathy best explains the integration of cultural knowledge, counselor wisdom, and the awareness necessary for connecting with a student from a different spiritual background. It is not enough to simply understand a religion, it is also important to understand the religion in a cultural context of how it is practiced and who is practicing. It is also important to understand that a spiritual practice varies within the culture; that is, just as not all Christians are alike, not all Buddhists are alike.

An ethical dilemma sometimes occurs. It is important that a counselor does not impose her or his beliefs on the student. No matter how much a highly religious counselor may experience incongruence with a student, she or he must avoid letting her or his own religious beliefs dictate that Asian perspectives are unacceptable.

Source: "Asian shades of spirituality: Implications for school counseling," by F. J. Hanna, and A. Green, 2004, *Professional School Counseling, 7*(5), pp. 326–333.

concerns in individual sessions may not wish to risk peers in a group session knowing personal or family problems.

In school counseling, little consideration is given to the spiritual background of students of Asian culture. In A Focus on Research 10.1, Hanna and Green (2004) maintain that Asian students can often be better served when counselors understand the spiritual aspects of their religious traditions.

Family Therapy.   The Asian American family's sense of cohesiveness and their loyalty to the family welfare should not rule out family therapy altogether. Realistically, however, Asian American children may have to be encouraged to disclose significant information. Also, a child in a family therapy situation will probably be reluctant to speak, because the father is generally expected to speak for the family. Furthermore, the child's disclosure of a significant problem might reflect poorly on the father's ability to manage his home and family.

Elementary school counselors may want to involve parents and families in certain situations. Essential factors to consider include (a) reviewing the parents' backgrounds, (b) being aware of cultural differences, (c) developing a sense of trust, (d) respecting the "pride and shame" aspect, (e) recognizing the family's need to save face, and (f) learning how the parents feel about school.

Up Close and Personal 10.1 looks at a counselor's efforts with Mina, a 10-year-old Japanese American girl.

UP CLOSE AND PERSONAL 10.1

Counseling Mina, an Asian American Child

Mina's teacher had asked her on several occasions whether she wanted to see the counselor, and although the teacher thought that Mina had several concerns, Mina was always hesitant. Finally, the teacher took the initiative to arrange an appointment.

During the first and second sessions, the counselor found that Mina was reluctant to reveal her problems. Mina trusted her teachers; they had shown a great deal of interest in her and her schoolwork. But as for the counselor— well, Mina couldn't imagine what to talk about.

Mina lived in a close-knit family in which her father reigned supreme. He made all the decisions, and Mina was afraid to ask him whether she could participate in the extracurricular activities her peers enjoyed. After completing her schoolwork and her piano practice, little time was left over; however, she did regard her peers with a sense of envy. Why couldn't she do some of the things they did? When would her father change? Couldn't he see that living in America required some change of ways? She worked very hard to live up to his high expectations

for her, but her few friends did not have to meet such expectations. They enjoyed play a lot more than work. Mina thought that the exceptional demands of her family might be costing her friends.

Mina's other concern, which she was slow to admit, was her developing body. Was she developing too slowly, perhaps? Were all the changes normal? Luckily, her counselor was a woman; but even so, Mina did not admit her concerns until the eighth session. Now Mina feels fortunate that she has the counselor to answer her questions because no one at home is willing to discuss such matters.

The counselor tried diligently to establish a trusting counseling relationship and proceeded slowly so as not to confront Mina "head-on." Finally, the counselor determined that Mina's problems could be attributed primarily to the pressure placed on her to excel in all endeavors, her perceived rejection by her peers, and her developing body. Because Mina probably would not disclose information in a group setting, the counselor scheduled several more individual sessions with her.

Asian American Adolescents

Potential Problems Warranting Counseling Intervention

Problems Asian American adolescents may experience include

- failure to develop positive adolescent and Asian American identities;
- adverse effects of the model minority stereotype;
- failure to meet cultural expectations for behavior (e.g., restraint of strong feelings, avoidance of outspokenness);
- conflicts involving family cultural characteristics (e.g., rigidly defined roles);
- problems with English language proficiency and non–Asian Americans' inability to understand nonverbal communication;
- conflicts between "individualism" and the Asian American commitment to family and the welfare of others;
- conflicts arising from generational differences between adolescents and elders;
- developmental differences (e.g., in height and weight);

- problems associated with social interests expanding from family to the wider community and peers; and

- adverse effects of racism, prejudice, and discrimination.

Counseling Considerations

Several challenges confront counselors working with Asian American adolescents. First, these adolescents often believe that they should seek out family members for advice and assistance rather than share concerns with an outsider. This situation may lead to the counselor having to explain the objectives, procedures, and confidentiality of the counseling process. Second, parent–adolescent conflicts stem from the traditional Asian commitment to the family, thus resulting in problems from acculturation, generational differences, and differing peer and family expectations (Lee, Su, & Yoshida, 2005). Third, nonverbal behaviors may be misinterpreted; Asian Americans' forward and backward leaning indicates specific feelings (a forward lean indicates politeness and concern; a backward lean indicates that the listener wants to withdraw from the conversation). Fourth, Asian Americans may choose to remain silent, perhaps due to their uncomfortableness with the counselor. Last, Asian American college students may experience somatic discomforts, such as headaches, insomnia, palpitations, dizziness, and fatigue for which they may seek counseling services (Lee, Su, & Yoshida, 2005).

Another barrier that interferes with the counseling of Asian Americans is a tendency to avoid disclosing personal problems. For example, Asian American students frequently have difficulty admitting emotional problems because of the shame it might bring to their families. These students may request help indirectly by referring to academic problems or somatic complaints. Asian Americans' difficulties with disclosure often require the counselor to emphasize the confidentiality of counseling relationships. Asian American clients often open up and express feelings quite directly once they develop trust in the counselor (Lippincott & Mierzwa, 1995; Yeh & Haung, 1996). Asian students tend to view counseling as a directive, paternalistic, and authoritarian process. Hence, they are likely to expect the counselor to provide advice and a recommended course of action.

Individual and Group Therapy.   Several characteristics of group-oriented cultures—collectivism and primacy of group survival over individual survival—make them especially compatible with group career counseling techniques (Pope, 1999).

Although Asian Americans generally tend to underutilize formal mental health services, they tend to use or overuse career counseling. In Asian cultures, seeking assistance for career issues does not have the same stigma associated with seeking help for mental health issues (e.g., depression). Group career counselors must build self-credibility as well as credibility for the process of group career counseling. Specific group career counseling interventions include exploration groups, job interview skills, and culturally appropriate career decision-making skills (Pope, 1999).

Asian American adolescents may be reluctant to seek counseling, either with individual or group therapy. Ringel (2005), in A Focus on Research 10.2, maintains that Asian Americans, specifically Chinese, Japanese, and Koreans, underutilize mental health services due to a variety of reasons, such as lack of access to counseling services, lack of familiarity with Western counseling models, and differences in values and worldviews. A Focus on Research 10.2 looks at how

A FOCUS ON RESEARCH 10.2
Therapeutic Dilemmas in Cross-Cultural Practice

Ringel looks at therapeutic dilemmas in cross-cultural practice that often occur when counselors with Western cultural perspectives intervene with Asian American adolescents. The author examined the process of cross-cultural intervention with Asian American adolescents from the perspective of their non–Asian American therapists. The study included the therapists' thoughts, reflections, and their use of self in relation to specific cultural-based dilemmas. In her study, Ringel examined differences in family structure and view of self, views of psychopathology, and underutilization of mental health services.

Ringel concludes that typical Western adolescent developmental themes such as individuation, identity consolidation, and peer relationships may be viewed very differently from an Asian immigrant family's point of view. This cultural difference has to be understood and appreciated by their non–Asian American clinicians.

Also, Ringel found that some therapists advocated a Western point of view, encouraging their clients to become more independent of their family and more expressive with their feelings. Other therapists viewed their clients from the perspective of their Asian traditions, but perhaps missed some important aspects of their unique individuality. The culturally experienced therapists presented the most skillful ways of balancing their clients' individual struggles with their unique cultural traditions.

Source: "Therapeutic dilemmas in cross-cultural practice with Asian American adolescents," by S. Ringel, 2005, *Child and Adolescent Social Work, 22* (1), pp. 57–69.

differences in client and counselor cultural perspectives and worldviews can affect counseling effectiveness.

When deciding whether to use individual or group therapy with adolescents, counselors should recognize that Asian American adults might consider group counseling a threat because they want to protect and honor the family's name. For those who hold such an expectation, group therapy may be threatening. Adolescents may fear that friends and parents will learn of their counseling sessions; therefore, information that could jeopardize the adolescents' or families' status is not likely to be disclosed. Asian American adolescents frequently refuse to participate in group counseling; in a group setting, they may be quiet and withdrawn.

Asian Americans may be reluctant to disclose information during group sessions. Family sessions may be characterized by only the father speaking or by holding back information that casts doubt on his ability. Ethical dilemmas may arise when family members, who feel a sense of collectivism for the family and do not understand the confidentiality associated with the counseling profession, ask the counselor what another family member revealed during sessions.

Group therapy has the potential to be effective with Southeast Asian refugee adolescents: They have an opportunity to share troublesome experiences with others and to participate in the healing process. This sharing experience provided by group therapy decreases alienation and the belief that one's own experiences are unique. This is particularly relevant for counseling with adolescents in Vietnamese and Cambodian cultures, given the traditional nature of privacy and personal boundaries outside the family system. Groups could be structured to provide psychotherapy that addresses depression, isolation, loss, and post-traumatic stress (Bemak & Greenberg, 1994).

Generational differences between parents and adolescents in the United States reflect the ongoing acculturation process of Asian Americans. Some adolescent clients experience a dislike for their own culture, especially in their social life. Such a situation is illustrated in the following counseling interchange, wherein the Asian American adolescent girl discusses her parents' reluctance toward her dating European Americans:

COUNSELOR: You seem to prefer dating Caucasians . . . .

CLIENT: Well . . . . It's so stupid for my parents to think that they can keep all their customs and values. I really resent being Chinese and having to date all those Chinese guys. They're so passive, and I can make them do almost anything I want. Others [Chinese] are on a big ego trip and expect me to be passive and do whatever they say. Yes . . . I do prefer Caucasians.

COUNSELOR: Is that an alternative open to you?

CLIENT: Yes . . . but my parents would feel hurt . . . they'd probably disown me. They keep on telling me to go out with Chinese guys. A few months ago they got me to go out with this guy—I must have been the first girl he ever dated—I wasn't even polite to him.

COUNSELOR: I guess things were doubly bad. You didn't like the guy, and you didn't like your parents pushing him on you.

CLIENT: Well . . . actually I felt a little sorry for him. I don't like to hurt my parents or those [Chinese] guys, but things always work out that way. (p. 100)

The client's last statement reflects feelings of guilt over her rudeness toward her date. Although she was open and honest, she confused her desire to be independent with her need to reject her parents' attempts to influence her life. During a later session, she was able to express her conflict:

CLIENT: I used to think that I was being independent if I went out with guys that my parents disapproved of. But that isn't really being independent. I just did that to spite them. I guess I should feel guilty if I purposely hurt them, but not if I really want to do something for myself.*

Family Therapy.   Asian American clients often do not understand family therapy; therefore, the first session should be planned so that the client and the family will want to return for future sessions. Often misunderstanding the role of a family therapist, clients sometimes perceive the therapist as a knowledgeable expert who will guide them through their problem. They expect the counselor to be more directive than passive. Being directive does not mean the counselor must tell family members how to live their lives, but it does involve guiding the family therapy process. In such cases, the family therapist must convey confidence and should not hesitate to disclose educational background and work experience. Asian Americans need to feel that the counselor has received proper training and has the ability to help them with their problems.

---

*From *Counseling American Minorities* (pp. 100–101), by Donald R. Atkinson, George Morten, and Derald Wing Sue, 1983. Dubuque, IA: Brown. Reprinted with permission of McGraw-Hill Companies.

Counseling Rieko, an Asian American Adolescent

Rieko, age 16, was referred by her teacher for counseling. The teacher had advised Rieko to refer herself, but Rieko secretly thought that counseling was out of the question because she valued her family's wishes to keep problems within the family. Therefore, the teacher had referred her, promising Rieko that her peers would not know and that her family's name and honor would not be shamed.

The 32-year-old European American counselor knew she would have to move cautiously with Rieko by ensuring confidentiality, building trust, explaining the counseling process and the client–counselor relationship, and allaying Rieko's fears about shaming the family. During the first session, Rieko was quiet and unwilling to disclose significant information. After the third session, the counselor decided that Rieko's two major problems were her lack of non–Asian American friends and her difficulties with English. Specifically,

Rieko's loyalty to her family's wishes and her commitment to excel in all endeavors "turned off" some potential friends, and her problems with English resulted in an inability to communicate with ease. The counselor's goal was to help Rieko believe in herself as a worthwhile person, regardless of whether or not she had non–Asian American friends. Also, remedial assistance with the communication problems was long overdue, especially because Rieko's communication problems required her to study much harder than most of her peers.

The counselor decided that Rieko should enroll in a special English class and that she would continue in counseling on a regular basis to discuss making friends in multicultural situations and to explore ways for her to deal with students who seemed to turn their backs on her. The counselor quickly ruled out both group and family therapy because Rieko would be very unlikely to disclose information in either situation.

A basic consideration in implementing family therapy with Asian Americans is to plan counseling therapy in such a manner that all family members will feel free to speak. In family counseling situations, the father, acting as the head of the household, might assume the spokesperson role, with other family members for the most part remaining silent. Up Close and Personal 10.2 looks at a counselor's efforts with Rieko, a 16-year-old Asian American girl.

Asian American Adults

Potential Problems Warranting Counseling Intervention

Problems Asian American adults may experience include

- acceptance of the model minority stereotype and the belief that Asian Americans do not need counseling;
- adverse effects of historical and contemporary discrimination;
- low socioeconomic status of many Asian Americans;
- the belief that discussing physical and mental problems actually causes these problems;
- language and communication difficulties;
- adverse effects of rigid and authoritarian family structures;

- conflicts arising from acculturation, such as perceived discrimination, homesickness, stress due to culture shock, and refugees' guilt about leaving loved ones behind;

- the belief that seeking counseling reflects negatively on the family;

- problems associated with midlife (e.g., aging, successfully meeting adult tasks and crises); and

- problems resulting from marriage and family situations (e.g., expecting to maintain traditional Asian American family roles in a majority culture that emphasizes equality).

Counseling Considerations

Traditional Western psychotherapeutic approaches based on individualism, independence, self-disclosure, verbal expression of feelings, and long-term insight therapy may be counterproductive for Asian Americans, who often value interdependence, self-control, repression of emotions, and short-term, results-oriented solutions (F. Y. Lee, 1995).

Kim, Ng, and Ahn (2005) maintain that Asian American adults underutilize and prematurely terminate from counseling services, although their need is no less than that of other cultural groups. In A Focus on Research 10.3, Kim, Ng, and Ahn (2005) look at Asian Americans and client expectations.

Yeh and Wang (2000) propose that Asian Americans talk with familial and social relations rather than with health care professionals. Korean Americans are significantly more likely to cope

---

A FOCUS ON RESEARCH 10.3

Asian Americans and Client Expectations

Kim, Ng, and Ahn (2005) suggest that Asian Americans favor a logical, rational, and directive counseling style over a reflective, affective, and nondirective one, especially if the counselor is Asian American. Also, Asian Americans perceive culturally sensitive counselors as being more credible and culturally component than less sensitive counselors.

Kim, Ng, and Ahn (2005) studied Asian American volunteer clients who either matched or mismatched the counselor's worldview. They concluded that

- clients in the worldview match condition perceived stronger client–counselor alliance and counselor empathy than those in the mismatch condition;

- client adherence to Asian cultural values was positively related to client–counselor working alliance;

- client adherence to European American values was positively associated with client–counselor working alliance and session depth; and

- clients with high expectation for counseling success and strong adherence to European American cultural values had increased perceptions of counselor empathy.

Source: "Effects of client expectation for counseling success, client–counselor worldview match, and client adherence to Asian and European American cultural values on counseling process with Asian Americans," by B. S. K. Kim, G. F. Ng, and A. J. Ahn, 2005, *Journal of Counseling Psychology, 52* (1), pp. 67–76.

with problems by engaging in religious activities, such as speaking with a religious leader. Asian American females are significantly more likely to have positive attitudes toward seeking professional counseling.

Other Asian cultures (e.g., Filipino) associate a stigma with mental health illness. Many Filipino people vehemently deny mental illnesses or try to hide the presence of any disorder among family members. They believe that only people who are dangerously insane and socially disruptive require psychiatric treatment; therefore, those who are believed to be mentally ill are treated with apprehension and disdain. The notion that mental illness is indicative of "bad blood" or a familial flaw is also very strong (Rita, 1996, p. 327).

Counselors should understand the reasons why Asian Americans tend to underuse mental health services and should also attempt to convince these individuals that use of such services may be in their best interest. Although Asian Americans have emotional disturbances just like the rest of the population, their problems usually pertain to academics and careers. For Asian Americans, talking about problems of this nature is not as threatening as disclosing personal and emotional concerns. Counselors who understand the values and motivations of Asian Americans will use techniques that encourage these clients to be open about personal and family matters.

Traditionally, some Koreans have resolved conflicts with the help of mediators chosen for their fairness and wisdom, whereas others have sought the help of shamans and fortune tellers, who are superb listeners and astute observers of people. In the Korean culture, shamans exorcise evil spirits with elaborate and often costly ceremonies, whereas fortune tellers console and prescribe a course of action or inaction. Deprived of these sources of help in the United States, Korean immigrants turn to relatives, close friends, clergy, and lawyers for help with emotional, psychological, and relational problems. They seldom seek help from a professional counselor because they define both the problems and the remedies differently than do European Americans (Kim, 1996).

Once the counselor understands the Asian American culture and its tendency to underuse counseling services, what counseling strategies are appropriate? Specifically, what should the counselor do or not do? Counselors working with Chinese American clients should

- Exhibit considerable involvement by modulating voice tone and by asking questions at appropriate times concerning the clients' problems or feelings. Caution should be used, however, because clients may think they are being interrogated. It is important that questions be posed with tact and that they not be excessive.

- Demonstrate self-confidence, through voice control and sureness of presentation. Moderate pitch and volume suggest self-confidence; paraphrasing a client's comments often seems unnatural and suggests hesitancy or weakness on the part of the counselor.

- Present himself or herself as an expert, by projecting a solid, secure, and trustworthy image. Because too much movement may be perceived as nervousness or insecurity, the counselor should remain relatively still and not gesticulate excessively.

- Offer self-disclosing remarks to convey a sense of trustworthiness as well as a sense of caring.

Much of the literature on multicultural counseling suggests that traditional, nondirective counseling approaches may be in conflict with the values and life experiences of Asian American clients. Because of Asian American cultural orientations, nondirective approaches may even be counterproductive. Asian American clients also assign more credibility to counselors who employ a directive approach than to counselors who use a nondirective approach. It follows then that Chinese American clients expect to assume a passive role and expect the counselor to be more assertive. Exum and Lau (1988) suggest that counselors should use a directive counseling approach with Cantonese-speaking Chinese students, as in the following dialogue:

COUNSELOR: What would you like to share with me today?

CLIENT: (sigh) Well, I'm not sure if it's going to help to talk about it.

COUNSELOR: Since you're here, there must be something bothering you. I do believe that talking about it would help.

CLIENT: Maybe the more I talk about it, the worse I'll feel. Maybe I shouldn't talk as much and let time take care of itself.

COUNSELOR: Seems like you're feeling a great pain inside you. Can you tell me more about it? We'll see if we can find some ways to solve the problem.

CLIENT: Yeah, maybe I should do that; since you've seen so many difficult problems before, you might be able to give me some suggestions.

COUNSELOR: Well, since this is something bothering you so much, you might feel even worse if you keep it all inside. I think it's very courageous of you to come to seek counseling. (p. 92)

Axelson (1999) used the following exchange between a career training counselor and a Vietnamese American client to illustrate how the communication barrier poses a problem:

COUNSELOR: How are things going now that you and your family have settled into your new apartment?

CLIENT: Yes. (Smiles and glances down)

COUNSELOR: Sometimes moving into a strange neighborhood and new home brings problems.

CLIENT: Many things for Kien fix up, work hard . . . need stove, one [burner] only work, but cos' so much. Friends [sponsors] help get good price, and get TV.

COUNSELOR: A TV?

CLIENT: Yes, they get good education, get better life. Can no teach English Kim and Van, school help . . . (pauses) . . . worry abou' Lan. Change so much, go far from Vietnamese way. She have American boyfriend. Want be like American. (Smiles, and becomes very quiet, looks at floor, seems embarrassed by what she has said)

COUNSELOR: You seem sad.

CLIENT: (Grins and laughs) My father tell me take care of Lan. My brothers all made dead by soldiers . . . only me left to watch Lan . . . (pauses) . . . our boat ge' Thai pirates. Lan and me make face black, hide in boat . . . no see us! (Laughs and begins to sob quietly) Oh, excuse me.

COUNSELOR: That's okay. I know it's difficult to talk about those past days and the things that hurt you. And it's a big responsibility to look out for Lan. It's all right to show how you feel to me. I won't take it as being impolite to me and I'll try to help you in any way I can—including listening and caring for how you feel about something that hurts or makes you sad or angry. It's my job to help you with things that are difficult for you.

CLIENT: Oh (faint smile) so many problems wan' to please father; help Kien . . .

COUNSELOR: Yes, that's all important to you. How is Kien's job training going for him?

CLIENT: Kien in Vietnam, big navy officer . . . now nothing feel bad, but training good . . . become computer-electronic man. That good for him, get job, more money, feel better.

COUNSELOR: Yes, that's a good thing for your family.

CLIENT: Thank you.

COUNSELOR: Let's talk now about the work that you want. You said before that you like to sew. That's a skill that you have that you can use right now to add to the family income.

CLIENT: Yes, make clothes for children, mend Kien's shirt.

COUNSELOR: I know. You showed me some of the good work you have done. There's a job that I'd like to see you try at the store. It will be to alter clothes that customers buy.

CLIENT: Oh…speak little English, so har' for me, makes others feel bad . . . no way go store . . . can't find . . . where bus?*

In working with some Asian American clients, counselors should realize that modesty, discretion, and self-deprecation should not be considered a negative opinion of oneself. Discussing family matters calls for considerable discretion; likewise, obtaining sexual information may prove difficult, due to modesty and feelings of privacy.

When intervening with Vietnamese Americans, counselors may wish to remember several suggestions:

- Build trust and concern for the client and the client's family.
- Understand and address communication barriers (both verbal and nonverbal) and their effects.
- Understand Vietnamese concepts of rigidly defined gender roles.

Writing specifically of South Asian people (e.g., Indian Americans and Pakistani Americans), Ibrahim, Ohnishi, and Sandhu (1997) offer several implications for counseling. For

---

*From *Counseling and Development in a Multicultural Society* (pp. 447–448), by J. A. Axelson, 1999. Monterey, CA: Used with permission.

example, for effective intervention with South Asian clients, the mental health counselor should do the following:

- Respect the client's cultural identity and worldview (South Asian clients want to feel that interventions are self-generated and that a mutually respectful relationship exists between them and the mental health professional).
- Understand the client's level of acculturation and identity status before planning counseling intervention.
- Clarify the client's spiritual identity before deciding on counseling goals and outcomes.
- Provide multidimensional interventions by using cognitive, behavioral, ecological, spiritual, and other relevant domains for these clients.
- Recognize the importance of the client's life stage and age.
- Be aware that the client may not understand the counselor's nonverbal attitudes.
- Recognize the role of humility in the client's cultural identity.
- Respect the client's integrity and individualism.
- Allow clients to educate the counselor regarding their identification level with their subcultures, religions, values and worldviews, and the mainstream society.
- Use a relational style that allows both counselor and client to explore value systems in conjunction with each other.

Individual and Group Therapy.   Counselors need to realize several myths that often surround group therapy: (a) Discussion of racial or cultural differences will offend group members, (b) groups can be truly homogeneous, (c) group member differences do not affect the process and outcome of groups, and (d) group work theory is appropriate for all clients.

According to Yu and Gregg (1993), Asian Americans underuse counseling sessions in general, and group counseling services in particular. These clients might be reluctant to share information and might be offended by, or react negatively to, other group members sharing their values and feelings and attempting to assimilate the minority member. They perceive requests for self-disclosure, comments on the group process, and requests for feedback as rude demands and attempts at domination. In fact, Asian American clients may be confused by traditional group counseling approaches that emphasize verbalization, confrontation, conflict resolution, individualism, and autonomy. The counselor who is unaware of or elects to ignore this confusion faces the possibility of a negative outcome, including premature termination of counseling.

Yu and Gregg (1993) also suggest for counselors the following:

- *Counselor self-exploration:* Counselors should recognize their biases and prejudices toward members of specific cultural groups.
- *Client orientation:* During the pregroup interview, counselors should take special care to explain to the Asian client the expectations of group membership, the purpose of the group, and the roles of the members and the leader.

- *Group composition:* Counselors should group Asian clients accordingly, such as in groups that are culturally homogeneous, that allow members to better understand others' communication styles, and that allow Asian clients of a particular nationality or geographic locale to be together.

- *Rapport building:* Throughout the orientation session, counselors should develop rapport between all members and the leader.

- *Group orientation:* Counselors should begin professional intervention so that group members will be aware of cultural differences and eventually unite all group members.

- *Group facilitation:* Counselors need to recognize the special circumstances and values that Asian clients bring to the group.

Even when Asian Americans do engage in group therapy and psychotherapy, the likelihood of negative outcomes between the demands of the group therapy process and the cultural values of Asian Americans is high. This conflict includes verbal unassertiveness, reluctance to display strong emotion, and unwillingness to disclose problems to strangers. Conflicts may be exacerbated if the counselor is unaware of Asian American culture-based behavior. Such pressure may cause the client to withdraw from group counseling.

Professional intervention with the most potential for positive outcomes are those in which the groups are homogeneous in terms of gender, background, profession, and social class. Goal-oriented sessions are probably more productive than free-floating, process-oriented sessions.

Johnson, Torres, Coleman, and Smith (1995) offered the following suggestions for group leaders:

- Conduct an assessment of potential members' values, interests, abilities, personalities, and decision-making patterns.

- Challenge members to examine the basis for their assumptions, attitudes, and beliefs.

- Help members generate alternatives to their existing beliefs.

- Assist members in testing their assumptions by requesting that members verify information outside the group and bring that information back to share with the group.

- Help members receive feedback from other group members about the logic of their attitudes and beliefs.

Han and Vasquez (2000) reported that South Asian refugees showed greater approval of group therapy that had a bicultural focus, provided practical information, met concrete needs, and demonstrated flexibility.

Family Therapy.   Family therapy usually focuses on one individual, protects the dignity of the individual, and preserves the honor of the family. Counselors often find the technique valuable with Asian Americans because it allows them to define and clarify family relationships by speaking directly to the therapist rather than, for example, by a husband or wife speaking with one another.

Discussions of feelings or psychological motives for a behavior are uncommon in most Asian American homes. Disturbed behavior is often attributed to lack of will, supernatural causes, or physical illness. Hard work, effort, and developing character are thought to be the most effective means to address the majority of problems.

Kung (2001) maintains that mental health professionals will continue to face challenges when working with Chinese American families, especially due to the cultural belief that families should be involved in clients' lives. Kung suggests educating the population, especially recent immigrants, about the prevention and treatment of mental disorders; ensuring the availability of accessible services provided by mental health professionals who speak their language or dialect; enhancing the sensitivity of clinicians to the needs and expectations of these clients in order to reduce the drop-out rate; and developing culturally sensitive information models to fit specific cultural needs.

Counselors may want to talk with the husband prior to the wife to show respect for Asian custom and tradition. They may also choose to place the husband and wife in different groups to prevent the wife's speaking being considered an affront to the husband.

When working with Chinese families, clinicians should follow these guidelines: (a) Convey expertise and caution in establishing egalitarian therapeutic relationships (Chinese families view the family in terms of a vertical hierarchy), (b) convey an air of confidence, (c) establish rapport and a sense of genuine caring and empathy, (d) engage in nonjudgmental listening, (e) demonstrate flexibility and willingness to assume various helping roles, and (f) identify the decision makers in the family and gain their support. Special caution is advised when counselors and psychotherapists share similar cultural backgrounds with their clients. Shared backgrounds may create particular difficulties and blind spots. For example, a young Chinese clinician who is struggling with cultural identity and dependency toward his or her parents may overidentify with the teenagers in the family being counseled (E. Lee, 1996).

In family therapy, it is important for the therapist to take an active role in the therapeutic process, rather than the traditional passive and facilitory process favored by many Western-trained therapists. In particular, Vietnamese clients likely see the therapist in the role of teacher, adviser,

UP CLOSE AND PERSONAL 10.3

Counseling Han, an Asian American Adult

Han, age 36, was referred by his company's physician to a mental health counseling organization. The physician wrote to the counselor that Han was experiencing stress. "If it hadn't been for the physical examination, I wouldn't have to see that counselor, who will probably ask a lot of nosey questions," Han thought.

The 44-year-old African American male counselor immediately picked up several cues that did not bode well for the counseling relationship: (a) Han was reluctant to come to counseling, (b) he was quiet and withdrawn, and (c) he did not want to discuss personal problems with a stranger. The counselor explained the counseling process, its confidentiality, and its intent. Then the counselor cautiously encouraged Han to talk (taking care not to give the impression of interrogating or snooping). Although it was difficult at first for Han

to reveal his problems, the counselor was able to reach several conclusions after several sessions: (a) Han was working two jobs and felt uncomfortable about being away from his family; (b) he was worried about his wife seeking a part-time job (not only would this reflect badly on him, but who would take care of Grandfather?); and (c) he was also worried about his preadolescent daughter Mina (so far, she had been an excellent daughter and student and had brought much honor to the family, but would she be swayed by her friends?).

The counselor decided to meet with Han individually for several more sessions. A group session would allow Han to see that other men shared similar problems, but Han would be unwilling to share personal information in such a setting. Also, Han's traditional ways of thinking would undermine the effectiveness of family sessions.

and someone who is able to give guidance in time of trouble (Leung & Boehnlein, 1996). Up Close and Personal 10.3 looks at a counselor's efforts with Han, a Japanese American adult.

Asian American Elderly

Potential Problems Warranting Counseling Intervention

Problems elderly Asian Americans may experience include

- adverse effects of stereotypes;
- being both Asian and elderly—the possibility of double or multiple jeopardy;
- discrimination and injustices because of age and culture;
- cultural differences and characteristics;
- poor English language skills;
- distrust of social and governmental agencies;
- lack of education, low income, unemployment, and poor housing;
- reluctance to disclose personal information;
- problems with developmental tasks and psychosocial crises;
- lack of systematically kept records with specific ethnic classifications;
- major health-related concerns, such as certain types of cancers, high blood pressure, and tuberculosis; and
- communication or cultural barriers that prevent them from receiving health benefits and services to which they are entitled.

Ageism has been well-documented (Ryan, Jin, Anas, & Luh, 2004) in both the United States and Europe. Older adults are marginalized, given low status, and either ignored in the mass media or portrayed in roles reinforcing negative stereotypes. Unfavorable stereotypes characterize older people as forgetful, sick, unattractive, and useless. While strong traditional Confucian norms in the East have resulted in more positive images of old age, there are still images of declining vitality and negativity in the East (Ryan, et al).

Gender Perspectives 10.1 looks at gender differences in the financial status and overall well-being of older Asians.

In the past 25 years, mental health professionals have given increased attention to the role of families in mental health treatment and rehabilitation processes. Part of this trend is due to an effort to move discharged patients into the community, thereby necessitating caregiving and assistance from their families.

Counseling Considerations

Problems that elderly Asian American clients bring to counseling sessions often center around differing intergenerational expectations and the elderly's expectation that their kin and younger generations will care for them. When younger generations of the family attain middle-class or higher status, the elderly often experience conflict and strain: Will they continue to be cared

GENDER PERSPECTIVES 10.1

Gender Differences in Economic Support

Concern over the vulnerability of the older population in general, and old women in particular, has been a major impetus for much of the research on, and the considerable attention given to, population aging. These authors did a comprehensive study of older Asians to determine overall economic support and well-being. Multiple economic factors were examined: sources of income, receipt of financial and material support, income levels, ownership of assets, and subjective well-being.

The study shows substantial variations in gender differences and provides information on the disadvantaged position of older women. Other findings include:

- Whereas men tend to report higher levels of income than women, there is generally little

gender difference in housing characteristics, in asset ownership, or in subjective reports of economic well-being;

- Unmarried women are economically advantaged as compared to unmarried men in some respects, in part because they are more likely to be embedded in multigenerational households and receive both direct and indirect forms of support from family members.

Source: "Gender differences in economic support and well-being of older Asians," by M. B. Ofstedal, E. Reidy, and J. Knodel, 2004, *Journal of Cross-Cultural Gerontology, 19,* pp. 165–201.

for? Will they receive the same respect? It is imperative to understand the history of Asian family loyalty and allegiances and the concerns of the elderly as younger generations rapidly acculturate. Counselors may have to encourage elderly Asian Americans to utilize available services. They may need to provide a convincing argument that counseling professionals can be trusted, and they may need to overcome the reluctance of Asian Americans to reveal the family's personal problems and secrets.

Counselors are often at a loss to explain why Chinese Americans do not participate more actively in counseling sessions. Barriers might include external barriers such as language, culturally generated distrust of service providers, and lack of bilingual and bicultural staff or internal barriers such as individual negative attitudes, cultural beliefs toward services, and preferred helping courses (Liu, 2003) as well as a simple "never thought of it" (Li, 2004, p. 253).

Counselors might interpret the undemonstrative demeanor of Asian Americans as the result of repressed emotional conflicts. Professionals should remember that behaving openly with strangers can be quite difficult for Asian Americans. To overcome this potential impediment to counseling progress, counselors should (a) show respect for elderly clients and their culture, (b) establish a trusting atmosphere and develop rapport, (c) understand that elderly Asian Americans may be hesitant to disclose personal problems, and (d) explain the counseling process to clients, including the concept of confidentiality. These strategies may encourage participation and self-disclosure in Asian American clients (Liu, 2003).

Individual and Group Therapy.   The decision whether to use individual or group therapy should take into consideration the individual Asian American client. Individual therapy might be the most effective technique, unless the client chooses to disclose personal information in a group session. Reluctance to reveal personal information may stem from the Asian American client's fear of shaming or degrading the family. Even in an individual counseling situation, Asian American men will be hesitant to reveal information that could reflect negatively on the family or on their performance in meeting responsibilities to the family.

Writing specifically about elderly Japanese American clients, Itai and McRae (1994) maintain that such individuals may be reluctant to engage in any counseling therapy. For example, the Japanese traditionally have not looked for causes of illnesses in the psychological realm. For this culture, "paying to talk" (Itai & McRae, p. 374) is a difficult concept to understand, and asking someone for help with one's emotional problems has been regarded with shame. Thus, emotional difficulties have been converted to physical problems because physical symptoms have been more acceptable. The Japanese also have considerable respect for self-sufficiency and independence. All of these factors can contribute to Asian Americans, and especially Japanese Americans, being reluctant to participate in counseling therapy.

Up Close and Personal 10.4 looks at a counselor's efforts with Grandfather Sukuzi, an Asian American elder.

Family Therapy.   It is important for counselors and elderly Asian American clients to understand their expectations of each other. For example, elderly Asian Americans may be reluctant to admit their need for counseling; also, they might have unrealistic or erroneous expectations of the counselor and counseling. The Asian American elder might view the

---

UP CLOSE AND PERSONAL 10.4
Counseling Grandfather Sukuzi, an Asian American Elder

Grandfather Sukuzi, age 85, finally decided to visit a physician because of his worsening dizziness, fading hearing, and forgetfulness. His son Han took a half day off from work and drove Grandfather to the physician's office. The physician diagnosed the dizziness as the result of an ear infection, for which he prescribed an antibiotic. The mild hearing loss was nothing to worry about; it was common for people of Grandfather's age. The physician did refer Grandfather to a counselor, however, to discuss his fears that the family was becoming too Americanized.

The 43-year-old Hispanic counselor experienced considerable difficulty with Grandfather Sukuzi. The client could hardly speak English, he was reluctant to talk about himself or his family, and he seemed to be waiting for the counselor to do something so that he could finally leave. Obviously, Grandfather was

extremely uncomfortable. Little could be done, the counselor thought, during this first session except try to build trust. He would show Grandfather that he was interested in him and assure him that the counseling relationship would remain confidential.

The counselor decided to schedule at least two or three more sessions with Grandfather to try to build rapport and to give Grandfather a chance to disclose significant personal information. Group therapy was out of the question because Grandfather would not want to share his concerns in a group setting. Family therapy was impossible, too, because Grandfather would do all the talking for the family. In this case, the counselor thought, progress will be slow. Not only was there a communication barrier, but his client would not always have transportation, and the chance of Grandfather revealing personal information was remote.

counselor as a knowledgeable expert who will guide family behavior in the proper course. During the first session, the effective counselor will take an active role rather than wait for the elderly client or a family member to initiate interaction. The counselor who adopts a passive approach to professional intervention might be considered lacking in knowledge or skill.

Counselors readily recognize the importance of communication in any counseling effort. Thus, they may find communication with Asian Americans to be difficult and frustrating. The elderly Asian American's reluctance to speak could result from limited English proficiency or an unwillingness to disclose personal information. To address these barriers, counselors may choose to develop a trusting and comfortable alliance with the family, especially the elderly, to whom other family members will look for direction.

Another factor that must be considered during family therapy is the powerful Asian belief that the father is head of the household and the spokesperson for the family. This belief may cause other family members to remain silent. Certainly, family members would be unlikely to disagree with the father under any circumstances. It is important for counselors to recognize this family dynamic in evaluating their clients' behavior.

A Point of Departure: Challenges Confronting Counselors of Asian Americans

Several challenges await counselors of Asian American children, adolescents, adults, and elders: (a) understanding the Asian American culture and its tradition of individuals and families caring for those with mental health problems; (b) understanding Asian American cultural mannerisms (e.g., silence) and cherished cultural beliefs (e.g., filial duty); (c) understanding the adverse effects of racism, injustice, and discrimination among Asian Americans; and (d) understanding Asian Americans' unique problems, such as communication barriers, portrayal as a model minority, and the stress caused by younger generations acculturating toward individualistic perspectives and the older generations expecting to be cared for.

Summary

Counseling Asian Americans requires knowledge of their developmental periods and cultural backgrounds, as well as being able to predict how clients will respond to individual, group, and family therapy. To determine appropriate counseling intervention, counselors need to know how Asian Americans will react to various counseling situations, such as disclosing significant personal and familial information. The vast cultural and lifespan diversity of the Asian American people requires that counselors, regardless of their cultural background, be prepared to intervene with clients who differ from Africans, Europeans, Hispanics, and American Indians. Counselors who feel the need for additional knowledge, skills, and competencies can pursue several resources and professional avenues, all of which can benefit both clients and counselors.

Suggested Readings

Anetzberger, G. J. (2005). The reality of elder abuse. *Clinical Gerontologist, 28*, 1–2, 1–25. As the title implies, Anetzberger looks at elder abuse and provides an overview of elder abuse as a social and health problem for older people.

Fraga, D. D., Atkinson, D. R., & Wampold, B. E. (2004). Ethnic group preferences for multicultural counseling competencies. *Cultural Diversity and Ethnic Minority Psychology, 10* (1), 53–65. These authors conclude that some college students view some multicultural counseling competencies as more important than others, and their preferences for multicultural counseling competencies vary by race/ethnicity.

Kim, B. S. K., Ng, G. F., & Ahn, A. J. (2005). Effects of client expectation for counseling success, client–counselor worldview match, and client adherence to Asian and European American cultural values on counseling process with Asian Americans. *Journal of Counseling Psychology, 52* (1), 67–76. These authors suggest that Asian Americans favor a logical, rational, and directive counseling style over a reflective, affective, and nondirective style.

Kim, B. S., & Omizo, M. M. (2005). Asian and European American cultural values, collective self-esteem, acculturative stress, cognitive flexibility, and general self-efficacy among Asian American college students. *Journal of Counseling Psychology, 52*(3), 412–419. Kim and Omizo examine Asian American college students' adherence to Asian and European cultural values and their collective self-esteem, acculturative stress, and several other factors that might lead to the need for professional help.

Lee, R. M., Su, J., & Yoshida, E. (2005). Coping with intergenerational family conflict among Asian American college students. *Journal of Counseling Psychology, 52* (3), 389–399. Two coping factors—problem solving and social support seeking—were found to be significant with intergenerational family conflicts.

Young-Kyong, E., Bean, R. A., & Harper, J. M. (2004). Do general treatment guidelines for Asian American families have applications to specific ethnic groups? The case of culturally-competent therapy with Korean Americans. *The Journal of Martial and Family Theraphy, 30*(3), 359–374. Maintaining the importance of cultural competence, these authors propose eleven guidelines for effective intervention with Korean American families.

Understanding European American Clients

Questions to Be Explored

1. How many European Americans live in the United States today and what are their origins?
2. What societal, cultural, communication, familial, and socioeconomic characteristics most accurately describe contemporary European Americans?
3. What stereotypes should counselors of European Americans be aware of and work to avoid?
4. What lifespan differences exist among European American children, adolescents, adults, and elders, and what are the counseling implications?
5. What are the unique challenges faced by European American children, adolescents, adults, and elders, and how can counselors most effectively address these challenges?
6. What challenges confront counselors intervening with European Americans?
7. What suggested readings can be offered to counselors preparing to work with or currently working with European Americans along the lifespan continuum?

Overview

As with all other cultures in America, European Americans enrich and contribute to the nation's diversity with their varied traditions, customs, languages, and dialects. Counselors, regardless of their cultural background, need to understand this plethora of differences and how they affect counseling intervention. As with African, Asian, and Hispanic Americans whose origins are quite diverse, European Americans originated from many locations, including England, France, Germany, Greece, Hungary, Ireland, Italy, Poland, and Portugal. This chapter focuses on European Americans in the four lifespan stages and their cultural, socioeconomic, family, and language diversity. To avoid overgeneralizing, specific cultural groups are discussed whenever possible.

European Americans: Demographics

Although they are generically referred to as Whites, there are 53 categories of European Americans living in the United States. The term *White ethnic* refers to all non-Hispanic White families of European American heritage. The term is quite ambiguous, because it originally referred to southern and eastern European immigrants rather than to Americans of British or German ancestry. More recently, it has been used to refer to a broader range of people. According to the U.S. Census Bureau (2000), the White population in 2000 numbered 226,266,000, and this number is projected to increase to 265,306,000 in 2025 and 302,453,000 in 2050. European ancestry groups with largest population numbers include German, Irish, English, Italian, French, Polish, Dutch, Scotch-Irish, Scottish, and Swedish. Europeans with smaller numbers include Czechs, Danes, Greeks, Hungarians, Norwegians, Russians, Slovaks, and Welsh (U.S. Census Bureau, 2004).

At the time of the American Revolution, the American population was composed largely of English Protestants who had absorbed a substantial number of German and Scotch-Irish settlers and a smaller number of French, Dutch, Swedish, Polish, Swiss, Irish, and other immigrants. The colonies had a modest number of Catholics and a smaller number of Jews (Henderson, 2000).

Over time, the White population crossed ethnic lines to create a conglomerate, but culturally homogeneous, society. People of different ethnic groups—English, Irish, German, Huguenot, Dutch, and Swedish—intermarried. Some writers incorrectly described the nation as having "melted" into one ethnic group: American. However, in reality, non-White Americans or people from non-English-speaking western and northern Europe were not included in the Eurocentric cultural pot and, in fact, experienced considerable discrimination. The slowness of some of those immigrants (particularly Germans) to learn English, their tendency to live in enclaves, and their establishment of ethnic-language newspapers caused friction among various ethnic groups (Henderson, 2000).

The period from 1830 to 1930 was a time of mass immigration to the United States. In colonial days, most immigrants came from Great Britain and Ireland, with a few from Germany, France, The Netherlands, Belgium, and Luxembourg; later, they were followed by Norwegians and Swedes. Italians began arriving in 1890, and from 1900 until the start of World War I, about one-fourth of all immigrants to America were Italians. Many Germans arrived in the United States following World War II. Greek immigration began in the 1880s, when the Greek economy failed to show signs of improvement. Most Poles immigrated to the United States as a result of mass migration and World War II.

Significant numbers of Jews of the former Soviet Union migrated to Israel and to the United States. Jews in the Soviet Union, who were once thought to be locked away forever from mainstream Jewish life, began migrating as the result of several events: *perestroika* (the restructuring of the Soviet economy and bureaucracy that was begun in the mid-1980s), *glasnost* (the policy of the Soviet government emphasizing candor in discussion of social problems), the crumbling of the economic system, and the resurgence of anti-Semitism. Although the majority of these Jewish immigrants chose Israel as their new home, 40,000 immigrated to the United States. However, this wave of Jewish immigrants was not the first to arrive in the United States; some immigrated from the Soviet Union following the Six Day War and the Leningrad Trial in the 1970s. At first, nearly all of those immigrating from the Soviet Union chose to live in Israel;

however, following 1972, a growing number chose other countries. The majority of the 90,000 Soviet Jews who chose the United States came from Russia, Byelorussia, and the Ukraine (Abrams, 1993).

European American Children

Social and Cultural Description

As with the many Asian and Hispanic cultures, the diversity of the many European American cultures makes accurate description difficult. A prerequisite to any discussion of such a diverse population is to recognize the tremendous societal, cultural and intracultural, socioeconomic, and individual diversity of these groups. Because children in all European cultures have not been studied, conclusions must be drawn from the most reliable available evidence. Acculturation also affects what children believe. Although first-generation children often hold onto native cultural beliefs, significant acculturation has occurred in subsequent generations. Table 11.1 shows the population numbers of the various age groups of European American children.

Members of some European American cultures (e.g., Greeks) want their children to hold on to cherished traditional values and beliefs. Rapid acculturation often occurs as a result of U.S. schooling, which creates a strong pressure to adopt the predominant culture of the school.

Depending on their individual culture and degree of acculturation, it is likely that European American children feel a sense of bicultural allegiance. For example, European American children, especially first- or second-generation, may feel pulled between two cultures when they strive to accommodate majority-culture beliefs, values, and customs, as well as family expectations to maintain allegiance to old-world and time-honored traditions. Considerable stress and guilt can occur when other children of differing cultural backgrounds question a child's attire, foods, religious beliefs, or mannerisms.

One of the challenges facing European American children is actually due to another person's condition or lifestyle. In A Focus on Research 11.1, Elden, Edwards, and Leonard (2004) look at children of alcoholic and nonalcoholic fathers.

Communication

Some European American groups speak English sufficiently well so that English has become the primary medium of communication and the language spoken at home. In all likelihood, many of these people encourage their children to speak English in order to assimilate into mainstream

Table 11.1
European American Children: Population Numbers

Source: Statistical abstracts of the United States 2004–2005 (124th ed.), by U.S. Census Bureau, 2004, Washington, D.C.: Author.

Age Group	Total
Under 5 years	15,119,000
5 to 9 years	15,098,000
10 to 14 years	16,192,000

A FOCUS ON RESEARCH 11.1

Children of Alcoholic and Nonalcoholic Fathers

Elden, Edwards, and Leonard (2004) examined the association between fathers' alcoholism and children's effortful control. *Effortful control* is the capacity to plan and to suppress inappropriate approach responses and is an important dimension of developing self-control, curtailing impulsive behaviors, and the externalizing of behavior problems in general.

Counselors of children (and, in fact, adults) should find several conclusions interesting: 1) Boys of alcoholic fathers exhibit lower overall levels of effortful control than boys of nonalcoholic fathers; 2) maternal warmth was a unique predictor of effortful control in boys; and 3) for girls, fathers' alcoholism was associated with lower

paternal warmth, which was in turn, a significant predictor of effortful control. Overall, the researchers found that sons of alcoholic fathers are at an increased risk of problems in self-regulation (or self-control) at young ages. Paternal warmth mediates the association between fathers' alcoholism and self-regulation for both boys and girls, although the nature of the mediation may vary with gender.

Source: "Predictors of effortful control among alcoholic and nonalcoholic fathers," by R. N. Elden, E. P. Edwards, and K. E. Leonard, 2004, *Journal of Studies on Alcohol, 65*(3), pp. 309–320.

America. People who are less fluent in English may feel incapable of helping their children learn English and thus avoid situations requiring proficiency in English.

One significant problem usually associated with language-minority children is that they face two different sets of cultural perspectives and are forced to orient themselves to two different worlds, both socioculturally and psychologically. Such a communication dilemma often results in children thinking they have to choose between the cultural heritage of their parents and the culture of the school. The result is that some children try to develop both a school language and a home language, thereby taking on additional learning challenges. Others who adopt English as their primary language risk disappointing their elders, who may consider adherence to the native language to be an essential element of their cultural heritage.

Families

European American families differ, just as African American, Asian American, Hispanic American, and American Indian families differ. Differences may result from socioeconomic, cultural, intracultural, and other factors. Some European American families hold on to traditional beliefs, such as preference being shown to boys, expectations for girls to perform household duties, and expectations of both genders to show strong support and concern for the family. Likewise, the success or welfare of the family is more important than the welfare of the individual.

Children in some European American groups are taught traditional family values, such as maintenance of positive family relationships, nurturance of children, and obligations of the children toward the family. Depending on the cultural group, parents also instruct their children to respect and assist extended family members.

Up Close and Personal 11.1 tells about 9-year-old Christina, who is growing up in a predominantly Greek American world.

UP CLOSE AND PERSONAL 11.1

Christina, a European American Child

Nine-year-old Christina Anastasopoulos is the middle child in a Greek American family. She and her family live in the inner city of a relatively large urban area on the East Coast. She is a fourth grader at a Greek American elementary school sponsored by her church; it has a culturally rich student body of Greek, African, Italian, and few other European Americans.

Christina is a better-than-average student and takes part in school activities. Even though she has positive self-esteem and a positive perception of her Greek heritage, she does have concerns. She questions her world: Her neighborhood is predominantly Greek, her teachers are all Greek, most of her friends are Greek, and her family continues to follow Greek traditions. All this is fine with Christina, but she is beginning to perceive a wider social world outside her immediate Greek American family and school. Increasingly, she understands that she must interact in a predominantly non-Greek world. Not far away in her neighborhood are African Americans and Italian Americans, and when she visits other parts of the city, she comes in contact with many other European Americans. She has no problem with the two cultures—Greek and non-Greek—but she does wonder what living in a totally Greek culture would be like.

Christina's family relationships are generally positive. She thinks her older brother, Nikos, gets to do more than she does, but he is 16 years old. Still, she wonders whether he gets to do more because he is older or because he is a boy. She often asks herself, Will I be allowed to do everything he does when I am 16?

Christina enjoys spending time with her grandfather, Costas, who tells her about Greece and what his life was like when he was young. She is a perceptive 9-year-old, who realizes that she must deal with a predominantly non-Greek world, that her mother and father have financial problems (although not severe) and want the best for her and her brother and sister, and that as her aging grandfather gets older, he seems to have more health problems. These problems do not actively worry Christina, but she is aware of the problems faced by her family.

Living in a predominantly Greek American neighborhood and attending a Greek school, she has not encountered racism and discrimination, but she does hear stories of how other Greek Americans are treated when they leave their own community. Will she be liked and accepted by other people, such as African American, Italian American, and other cultural groups living outside her Greek American community? Because she is only 9 years old, she does not consider these to be major concerns, but she does think about her future: What will it be like? Will she have friends other than Greeks? Will she attend a Greek high school, or will she attend a public high school? These and other questions and concerns occasionally arise and challenge Christina for answers and solutions.

Unique Challenges Confronting European American Children

Several challenges unique to European American children deserve the attention of counselors in multicultural settings (it is important to note, however, that counselors should avoid stereotypical conclusions about European American children; a problem faced by a specific child might be an entirely individual situation and have little or no cultural basis):

- Children, by the nature of their developmental period, may feel ignored or powerless to gain needed attention. Their mental health needs may go unrecognized until problems grow acute.

- Children may feel the need to become more bicultural to maintain social relationships in a majority-culture society. This need for biculturalism could result in guilt feelings as the children choose between majority-culture values and their parents' long-held cultural beliefs and traditions.

- Children learning English as a second language may have both social and academic problems in school and may feel overwhelmed and unable to deal with the demands of English language schools.

- Children of some European American cultures may have difficulty with the usually greater freedom allowed girls in the United States. They may be accustomed to seeing boys in more authoritarian roles and may be shocked at the gender equality in American schools.

- Children may experience academic problems because they lack understanding of the U.S. school system and of the roles of educators and counselors.

- Children may experience a decline in self-esteem because of being in a majority-culture school and because of their different cultural values, beliefs, and traditions.

Although these examples are representative of European American children's problems, other problems undoubtedly exist and will require the individual attention of the counselor to pinpoint them and to devise culturally appropriate intervention strategies.

European American Adolescents

Social and Cultural Description

According to the U.S. Census Bureau (2000), the number of European American adolescents ages 15 to 19 years was 15,755,000 in 2000 and is projected to be 16,804,000 in 2010. Although adolescents vary among cultures, they experience certain common developmental characteristics or tasks regardless of culture: making friendships, dealing with peer pressures, moving away from the immediate family to an expanding social world (this undoubtedly varies among cultures), and beginning the transition toward economic independence. These tasks may be more difficult for European American adolescents because they might be dealing with different cultural expectations for making and keeping friends, speaking a language other than English, and experiencing difficulty equating family and peer expectations.

Adolescents living in cultural enclaves (e.g., predominantly Italian, German, Hungarian, or Polish) might experience only minor difficulties. However, when forced to extend life activities outside the boundaries of the cultural enclave, adolescents might encounter problems with different world customs and expectations. For example, school activities may require adolescents to leave their cultural enclaves to participate in athletic events, academic competitions, school plays, and other activities requiring intraschool participation.

Although self-esteem (as well as a positive cultural identity) is important during all life-span developmental periods, counselors need to recognize the importance of self-esteem during the adolescent years. Adolescents form self-esteem that might last a lifetime and that influences their attitudes toward self, significant others, and life's challenges. Yet, self-esteem often declines, especially for females, during this developmental period. Living, socializing, and functioning in a majority-culture society may intensify problems with self-esteem. Adolescents' self-esteem can be damaged when they believe that significant others consider "cultural differences" wrong or in need of change, or when adolescents believe it is necessary to change long-held traditions and beliefs in order to gain acceptance in the majority-culture society. Although it is common for self-esteem to decline for both adolescent girls and boys, girls usually experience a more active decline. Cultural and societal expectations as well as students' self-esteem can either promote or limit career aspirations and decisions of whether to seek employment in the United States or to return to one's native land.

Hazler and Mellin (2004) in Gender Perspectives 11.1 maintains that one of every four girls is likely to experience moderate to severe symptoms of depression during adolescence.

Communication

Communication plays a significant role in the socialization of adolescents, who increasingly widen their social worlds away from their immediate families to a widening circle of friends and peers. Although some European American cultures continue to have a high regard for and close allegiance to family members (immediate and extended), the demands of adolescence require increased socialization and communication. The ability to socialize with peers and others, as well

---

GENDER PERSPECTIVES 11.1

Female Adolescents and Depression

In this excellent article, Hazler and Mellin (2004) maintain that rates of female to male depression rapidly soar during adolescence to a 2:1 ratio despite fairly equal rates throughout childhood. The fact is that female adolescents face emotional, academic, and social problems more often and more extensively than male adolescents at this critical age. With this clear problem, there has been a lack of research on the unique difficulties female adolescents face and the identification of techniques designed to meet their specific needs. Existing research suggests that throughout childhood and preadolescence, depression rates between the sexes tend to be fairly equal, but at about the age of 14, female adolescents begin experiencing depressive disorders at twice the rate of male adolescents.

Factors associated with developmental aspects include social development, social role expectations, and biological changes. Specific problems needing attention

include belonging, social isolation, neediness, and biological and medication issues.

Hazler and Mellin suggest that the next steps in research and practice on adolescent female depression include (1) understanding the variables that contribute to the onset of significant gender differences in depression during adolescence—this will be a first step toward better prevention, detection, and treatment of this disorder; (2) investigating the social challenges experienced at this age to delineate what role they may be playing in the onset of depression for female adolescents; and (3) focusing on developing treatment techniques that best meet the unique needs of young girls struggling with depression.

Source: "The developmental origins and treatment needs of female adolescents with depression," by R. J. Hazler, and E. A. Mellin, 2004, *Journal of Counseling and Development, 82,* pp. 18–24.

as the ability to speak English to teachers and counselors, illustrates the importance of being able to communicate effectively.

The tremendous communication diversity among European Americans makes it difficult to draw conclusions. Just as with adolescents from Asian and Hispanic cultures, some European American parents speak English very well, whereas others do not. Counselors intervening with European American clients will find that an adolescent's ability to speak the language will influence greatly academic success and the ability to build satisfactory interpersonal relationships. Therefore, although an adolescent's native language should be a respected aspect of the cultural background, an increasing proficiency in English should be encouraged, especially if the adolescent's reasons for seeking or being referred for counseling stem from an inability to communicate in English.

European American adolescents who are confident in their English language proficiency will be more likely to engage in the verbal interaction necessary for desirable socialization and social development. Conversely, adolescents who do not feel confident with their English-speaking abilities will probably avoid situations requiring English language proficiency. Counselors working with students who have communication difficulties will readily recognize potential problems, such as academic, socialization, and employment difficulties. Taking care to avoid casting the adolescent's native language in a negative light, the counselor needs to help the adolescent client understand that at least a minimal degree of communication competency will be needed to cope in an English-speaking society.

Families

It is a commonly held belief that a primary source of problems for immigrant families is the differing values held by parents and adolescents. Even though adolescents and their families might disagree on issues and expectations, conflicts may not be as acute as some might expect. Such a lack of serious problems may result from adolescents being taught from an early age the importance of adhering to family expectations.

However, adolescent children of immigrants, unlike their parents, are often attracted to majority-culture values and behavior models in school and society. At the same time, their socialization is heavily influenced by their parents' ancestral cultures at home and in the community. Perceptive counselors recognize potential adolescent–family conflicts and that these problems will warrant serious consideration and attention.

Depending on the European culture, adolescents may perceive a conflict between the expectations and traditions of the majority culture and those of their own culture. Such a conflict may or may not cause a problem, depending on the adolescent's commitment to adhere to traditional family beliefs. For example, some aspects of adolescents' cultural backgrounds include (a) the father as the authority figure, (b) the mother as the nurturer, (c) more freedom and a more responsible place in the family for sons than daughters, (d) the expectation that daughters stay closer to home, both during adolescence and adulthood, than sons, and (e) the high regard for the welfare of elderly family members. Acculturation often has dramatic effects on these expectations; second- or third-generation European American families might differ significantly from first-generation families.

Up Close and Personal 11.2 tells about Nikos, an adolescent European American.

UP CLOSE AND PERSONAL 11.2

Nikos, a European American Adolescent

Nikos, age 16, is Christina's older brother. Nikos is in the ninth grade in the Greek high school sponsored by his family's church. He makes passing grades and has no behavior problems, but he shows little signs of excelling. He is a member of at least one club in the school.

Nikos has strong friendships with several other Greek American boys, but because he attends the Greek school and lives in a predominantly Greek neighborhood, he has few opportunities to make friends in other cultural groups. The lack of non-Greek friends does not seem to be a major problem for Nikos, but he knows he must eventually interact with people in other cultural groups. At this time, however, he feels a degree of security and acceptance in having only Greek friends.

Nikos senses that being male carries distinct advantages. Although he is the oldest of three siblings in the family, he thinks being male is more influential than being the oldest. He accepts responsibility for few household chores, but he is more confident in how the family works and functions—its problems, challenges, joys, and relationships. He has a close relationship with his father. They often discuss familial aspects that

Christina (because she if only 9) knows nothing about. Again, he thinks this is because he is male, but he realizes it could be because he is the eldest.

Nikos realizes that he faces several challenges: How can he improve his grades (he feels guilty that his parents pay for his education, yet he does not always do his best)? How will he be able to make friends in a predominantly non-Greek world? How will he equate peer and family expectations, especially when he starts making non-Greek friends? How will his parents respond if he dates non-Greek girls? How will he relate in either higher education or a job when he finishes high school? And how will he accept greater responsibility for the family as his grandfather grows older? These and other questions concern Nikos, but they do not appear to affect his mental health.

Nikos has briefly discussed these problems with his guidance counselor, but she deals with so many students that she cannot give him the extensive time he needs, especially because she does not consider his problems acute. She also thinks many other boys in the school have similar problems.

Unique Challenges Confronting European American Adolescents

Tasks usually associated with adolescence, coupled with approaching adulthood in a majority-culture society, can have profound and intertwining effects on adolescents. Unique challenges that European American adolescents may face include

- problems resulting from trying to hold on to their family's traditional cultural beliefs while adopting the majority-culture beliefs necessary for social and economic survival;

- problems resulting from peer pressure to engage in popular social and school activities that their parents find objectionable;

- communication problems stemming from poor English-language proficiency or forced bilinguality;

- problems moving toward marriage or economic independence;

- inability to accept the responsibility that their parents expect children to accept (e.g., responsibility for helping the parents and elderly family members); and

A FOCUS ON RESEARCH 11.2

Adolescent Violence

Although this study comprehensively investigated adolescent violence, space only allows a look at the risk factors and conclusions. Readers interested in this topic are encouraged to thoughtfully consider the entire article.

Individual risk factors include perpetrators having been bullied, teased, isolated, or ostracized. *Juvenile delinquency risk factors* suggest that violent offenders were more likely to come from a single-parent house headed by a mother; have siblings or parents who have been involved with the criminal justice system; report use of cigarettes, alcohol, and marijuana at an early age; earn money selling crack cocaine; have a friend who sells drugs; have excellent achievement in mathematics but not in reading; have high rates of school suspension or expulsion; report early sexual activity and numerous partners; and exhibit no aspiration for higher education. *Economic risk factors* include that wealthier families are less likely to engage in weapon carrying. Also, racial/ethnic differences in family structure and poverty play a role in violent behavior. In homes headed only by a woman, 27% of White families compared with 44% of Black families were classified as poor. Lack of resources means that children

in these families may not receive good health care, may have lower reading skills, may live in high crime areas, may have more responsibility for self-care, and may have limited adult contact.

Conclusions include that youth who have parents who try to understand their point of view, who tell youth they are loved and want good things for them, and who talk with them about their problems are less likely to be involved in physical fighting. Also, youth who can say no to activities that they think are wrong, who can identify the positive and negative consequences of their behavior, who make decisions to achieve their goals, and who organize their time to get their work done are significantly less likely to be involved in physical fighting. Last, gender differences include male youth being more at risk for both fighting and weapon carrying when compared with female youth, and some racial/ethnic groups were more likely to carry weapons than others.

Source: "Adolescent violence: The protective effects of youth assets," by C. B. Aspy, R. F. Oman, S. K. Vesely, K. McLeroy, S. Rodine, and L. Marshall, *Journal of counseling and Development, 82,* pp. 268–276.

- pregnancies in unwed adolescent mothers. (In 1998, 11.1% of births were to teenagers of European ancestry [U.S. Census Bureau, 2000]).

Adolescent violence is a problem facing many counselors—violent adolescents and the harm they inflict upon others are not limited to any specific culture. Unfortunately, adolescents in all cultures are perpetrators and victims.

A Focus on Research 11.2 looks at the problem of adolescent violence. Some interesting conclusions have relevance for counselors working with this specific developmental period.

European American Adults

Social and Cultural Description

Social and cultural characteristics vary among cultures, generational status, social class, gender, and age. Just as it is difficult to describe a typical Hispanic American because of the culture's many different origins and cultural backgrounds, it is equally difficult to describe a typical European

Table 11.2
Educational Attainments:
European Americans (25 Years
and Older)

*Source: Statistical abstracts of the
United States 2004–2005* (124th ed.),
by U.S. Census Bureau, 2004,
Washington, D. C.: Author.

Educational Attainment	Number	Percentage of Population
Not a high school graduate	10,084,000	6.6%
High school graduate	49,332,000	32.2%
Some college or Associate degree	38,774,000	25.3%
Bachelor's degree or advanced degree	42,308,000	27.6%

American adult. Likewise, a southern European man will probably differ significantly from an eastern European woman. Therefore, the most valid cultural descriptions come from considering individual cultures (even then, one should use considerable caution because of intracultural and individual differences). Educational attainment varies with cultural group. Some of this variation results from lack of opportunity or motivation to seek education. Nevertheless, one's education is indicative of one's potential to achieve economically and socially in U.S. society. Table 11.2 shows U.S. Census Bureau (2004) data on educational attainment of European Americans age 25 and older.

Greek Americans may have difficulty cooperating with others, especially in business deals; they prefer a competitive atmosphere and usually are not willing to put aside their individual interests for the sake of the group. Greek Americans also (a) have clearly defined status and roles in work situations, (b) have patriarchal control and deeply binding extended kinship networks, (c) have a strong need to defend family honor, and (d) generally love *philotimo*, or honor (Scourby, 1984).

Italian Americans (a) have a strong allegiance to the family, (b) have a strong affection for living where they grew up, (c) believe that young people should be taught by their elders, (d) have an allegiance to a church, (e) are suspicious of strangers, and (e) expect filial obedience. Some of these tendencies (e.g., suspicion of strangers) decrease with education and advancing occupational position (Alba, 1985).

The religions of European Americans deserve careful consideration because a culture's religion often depends on its geographic origin and its members' degree of acculturation. Italian Americans remain heavily Catholic; in fact, in one survey, 90% of respondents had been raised as Catholics and 80% considered themselves Catholic at the time of the interview (Scourby, 1984). Because the Catholic Church has stood for tradition, family, and community, Italians continue to offer their support (Alba, 1985). Polish Americans also have a powerful allegiance to the Catholic Church. By 1923, about 140 Greek churches existed in the United States. Each community of Greeks formed a board of directors whose function was to build a Greek Orthodox Church. Attempts were made to consolidate the Greek Church with other Eastern churches into an American Orthodoxy, but this did not materialize; the church seemed inextricably intertwined with its role as transmitter of the Greek heritage (Scourby, 1984).

Most newly arrived Soviet Jews view their primary motivation in leaving the Soviet Union as fear of anti-Semitism, rather than as the desire for religious freedom. Most Soviet Jews view themselves as culturally Jewish and are interested in the Jewish culture as expressed through history and literature (Abrams, 1993).

A FOCUS ON RESEARCH 11.3

Marital Quality in Black and White Marriages

Broman (2005) sought to extend prior research on race and marital quality through an investigation of the role of spouse behavior. Broman reviewed the research suggesting race differences between Blacks and Whites in marital quality. Studies (Broman, 2005) maintain that Blacks have lower levels of marital stability than do Whites. For example, collaborative styles have been found to be more important for Blacks than Whites; Blacks are more likely to participate in household chores; and conflictual styles do not seem to be as detrimental to Black marriages as they are for Whites.

In his study of Black and White marriages, he concluded: Black spouses characterize their spouse's behavior as more negative than do Whites, thus resulting in lower levels of marital quality. Specifically, Broman concludes that Blacks feel less loved and feel their spouse

wastes money, hits or pushes (or exhibits more physical violence in general), and has affairs. He also raises the possibility of whether Blacks are just more honest and open to discussing their marriage and spouse behavior than Whites; however, his research did not address this question.

Although critical differences evidently exist between Black and White marriages, factors such as socioeconomic status and length of the marriage should be considered. Still, counselors intervening with both Black couples and White couples should understand that differences exist and deserve consideration during counseling.

Source: "Marital quality in Black and White marriages," by C. L. Broman, 2005, *Journal of Family Issues, 26*(4), pp. 431–441.

Describing the socioeconomic status of the many European cultures is nearly impossible, because many variations exist among cultures. For example, there are both wealthy and poor Italians. Many criteria affect family and individual socioeconomic status: Is the husband or father present? Does the wife work outside the home? How many children are in the family? Is the cost of living in the neighborhood high or low? How well do family members manage their money?

Heller and Wood (2000) investigated whether religious and ethnic similarities and differences function in the development of intimacy in the early stages of marriage. They concluded that clinicians and religious leaders should not assume intermarriage is doomed to low levels of intimacy, nor should it be assumed that intramarriage assures high intimacy. Professionals should assist spouses, regardless of ethnic differences and similarities, to enhance their shared similarities, negotiate their differences, and foster better understanding of each other.

Broman (2005) maintains that high quality in marriage is important in its own right for a sense of well-being as well as being important for marital stability, yet the limited focus on the role of race on marital quality poses a barrier to our understanding of marriage. In A Focus on Research 11.3, Broman looks at marital quality in both Black and White marriages.

Communication

Most European Americans feel confident in their ability to speak English and probably place priority on speaking English in the home. In contrast with some Hispanic American cultures that continue to place high priority on speaking Spanish, some European American cultures, such as people from Germany, the United Kingdom, and Italy, value speaking English. European Americans with English-language proficiency probably cope better economically and socially than their counterparts with less proficient English-speaking skills. People who speak English fluently and who perceive English as their major medium of communication most likely live in mainstream society. Others feel forced to live and work in a native-language enclave with people speaking the same language or speaking English with a similar proficiency. Counselors may have clients with communication-related problems—problems resulting from the frustration of having limited English-speaking skills in a majority-English society. Potential problems include inability to interact socially, difficulty finding suitable employment, or difficulty conducting business transactions in a non-native language. It will be important for counselors to understand the dilemmas caused by communication problems. For example, English-speaking or Spanish-speaking counselors need to realize the frustrations of their Greek- or Russian-speaking clients and vice versa.

As for people in all cultures, considerable variation exists in the English-language proficiency of European Americans. Cultural groups such as Italian Americans and German Americans may experience difficulty with the language. Due to tremendous individual differences, it is impossible to determine which cultures will and will not have language problems. Several factors influence an individual's ability to learn and speak English: (a) Parents and families live in language enclaves where native people speak native languages, (b) parents speak the native language in the home, (c) parents try to learn to speak the language, and (d) schools provide English as a second language (ESL) programs and show appreciation for native languages.

Families

Any discussion of family characteristics should be approached with considerable caution. Generally, adult European Americans grew up in families that taught men and women to be independent, strong, and self-sufficient. Exploration of the world was encouraged, self-control was highly valued, suffering was borne in silence, and conflicts were concealed, especially in public (McGoldrick, Giordano & Garcia-Preto, 2005). Like all cultures, however, European Americans form a heterogeneous group. Family patterns differ according to time of immigration, region of origin, economic class, and religious background. Many factors influence how a family lives, the roles of the husband and wife, how parents view their children, and the emphasis placed on extended family members. Although counselors need information about European families, providing a full description of these families risks stereotyping. To avoid stereotyping, an attempt is made here to use only the most objective information and the most widely accepted resources.

Table 11.3 shows the percentages of European American families with children under age 18.

Table 11.3
Number and Percentages of European American Families with Children Under Age 18

Source: Statistical abstracts of the United States 2004–2005 (124th ed.), by U.S. Census Bureau, 2004, Washington, D.C.: Author.

No. of Children Under Age 18	Number of Families	Percentage of Families
0	33,656,000	54%
1	11,913,000	19%
2	10,993,000	18%
3+	5,735,000	9%

In the German American family, the husband/father is the head of the household and leader of the family. Traditionally, the father, although he is sometimes sentimental, has a stern side. He is usually self-controlled, reserved, unduly strict, and stubborn. The German American father is often somewhat distant and less emotionally available to the children than their mother. The German American woman is regarded as hardworking, dutiful, and subservient. She adopts her husband's family and friends and gains his social status. Her contributions center primarily around household and family duties. In contemporary times, the wife's main tasks continue to be focused on the house and family; in fact, the appearance of her husband and children can be a source of pride (Winawer & Wetzel, 2005).

The Greek American family continues to maintain strict gender roles, with little overlap between these roles. Men provide economic necessities; women cater to men's desires and wish to be considered good wives. Men are authoritarian fathers and husbands, who often seem emotionally distant, and they are parsimonious with praise and generous with criticism. They often tease their children (some say to toughen them), and the children learn that teasing is part of being loved. Typically, Greek men revere their mothers, value the family honor, and believe that a woman's place is in the home. Women expect to comply with tradition and view motherhood as fulfillment. Male children are still preferred over females, even in the urban areas of the United States; having a son is a wife's main source of prestige. Parents believe that some emotions, such as uncertainty, anxiety, and fear, are weaknesses and should be hidden from their children. Gay and lesbian couples or families are sometimes reluctant to seek counseling services because alternative lifestyles are usually stigmatized in the Greek community. In fact, gay and lesbian Greeks usually tend to seek services outside the culture (Killian & Agathangelou, 2005).

Irish American women have traditionally dominated family life, have primarily found their social life through the church, and have enjoyed more independence compared with women in other cultures. Unlike other cultures, the immigration rate of Irish women ranked higher than that of Irish men. Irish families often paid as much attention to the education of their daughters as to that of their sons. Traditionally, fathers have been shadowy or absent figures, and husbands dealt with wives primarily by avoidance. Discipline is still maintained by ridicule, belittling, and shaming. Children are generally raised to be polite, respectable, obedient, and well-behaved. Children are rarely praised by their parents or made the center of attention (McGoldrick, 2005).

A major characteristic of Polish American families is respect for family members. The father/husband is the acknowledged leader of the household, whose wishes are to be respected and obeyed. Children are raised in a strict tradition of discipline and are expected to give their fathers unquestioning obedience. Discipline is physical and sometimes harsh. Second-generation children have become acculturated, but physical discipline continues to be practiced (Mondykowski, 1982).

In the Portuguese American family, the husband/father maintains great physical and emotional strength to combat life's difficulties. He tends to conceal his feelings to avoid the loss of respect or power. As a father, he expects his children to respect and obey him. Virtue and purity are desirable feminine qualities for the Portuguese woman. Her role includes loving, honoring, and obeying her husband and caring for her family's many needs. Children are expected to be seen and not heard. They receive the most physical and emotional attention from their parents from infancy to about school age. Girls tend to receive overt displays of affection from both parents, whereas boys are often ignored in this area, particularly by the father (Moitoza, 1982).

Italian Americans learn that the family is all-important and that sharing meals is a symbol of nurturing and family connectedness and a wonderful source of enjoyment. In Italian American homes, gender roles are distinct and defined; men always dominate, and women nurture (Giordano, McGoldrick, & Klages, 2005).

The Dutch American family shares a strong sense of responsibility. The nuclear family maintains close ties with the family at large. Clear boundaries are maintained in the family consistent with the values of individualism and respect for privacy and personal freedom. Role definition and responsibilities are clear. Families expect the man to provide overall direction to the family, provide economic support, and set an example of uprightness in the community. The woman provides a rich home life for her husband, nurtures the children, and attends to and promotes social and cultural input for the family (De Master & Giordano, 2005).

Emotionality, romanticism, pessimism, isolation, and duality of identification between Eastern and Western values are common Hungarian characteristics. An old proverb says that Hungarians are happiest when they are in tears. They want music at weddings and at funerals; the Hungarian culture has always appealed more to emotions than to logic. Although Hungarians are generally an emotional people, certain negative emotions are not always expressed openly. For example, conflicts, anger, and pain are not openly expressed, perhaps to preserve family loyalty (Laszloffy, 2005).

Up Close and Personal 11.3 describes Olympia, a European American adult.

UP CLOSE AND PERSONAL 11.3

Olympia, a European American Adult

Olympia is in her mid-40s. She is the mother of Nikos, Christina, and a younger child. Although she does not work outside the home, Olympia has little free time, especially because she takes care of three children, her husband, and a grandfather, Costas. In addition, she volunteers at her church and occasionally at the Greek school that Christina attends. She does relatively simple (yet important) tasks at the school because she is not an educated or specially trained person. She volunteers because she enjoys being a part of the Greek school and because she thinks the school expects parental assistance. She also thinks it is an opportunity to help her children in their education, which is a priority for her.

Olympia feels a great deal of allegiance to her husband. Even though she realizes that some Greek women are becoming more assertive and independent, Olympia continues to feel strongly that the husband/father has the final word on family decisions. She looks to her husband for advice on household and family matters, and although she has a significant voice in child-rearing decisions, she listens attentively to his opinions. Olympia is aware that her husband does not exert his authority like his father and grandfather did, but he still continues to place Greek traditions in high regard. Olympia respects his feelings and opinions as well as traditional Greek beliefs.

Although she feels fairly psychologically safe with her family and her home, Olympia has several frustrations: (a) The family needs more money; (b) the grandfather's health has declined in the past several months; (c) Nikos's grades reflect his lack of motivation; (d) Christina will be changing schools in a few years (will she go to the Greek high school or the public high school?); and (e) she thinks her children are forsaking age-old Greek traditions for more "accepted" and "popular" beliefs. Olympia does not know what to do about these concerns; she sometimes feels overwhelmed, but she sees little she can do to remedy her concerns. She has somewhat accepted them as facts of life.

Unique Challenges Confronting European American Adults

European American adults face several challenges, including the five now described. First, European groups, like all cultural groups, have been negatively stereotyped by other groups. Italians and Jews, in particular, have stood out because of the frightful stereotypes associated with them. Italians have been characterized as being "swarthy," bearing signs of physical degradation (e.g., low foreheads), having criminal tendencies, and being prone to passion and violence. Jews have been stereotyped as being "stingy," "shrewd," and "intellectual" (Atkinson, 2004). Poles have been subject to offensive and distasteful jokes and other ethnic slurs. The list continues, but this brief discussion serves to show the dangers of stereotyping.

Second, European Americans, especially first- and second-generation families, may have financial problems because of discrimination, unemployment or underemployment, poor English-language skills, and lack of education. According to the U.S. Census Bureau (2004), 4,829,000 (8%) White families and 23,454,000 (10.5%) White persons live below the poverty level. Substantial numbers of these people participate in the food stamp program (U.S. Census Bureau, 2004).

Third, European Americans, probably primarily first- and second-generation, may experience communication problems. People who choose to live (or are forced to live) in cultural enclaves where the majority of residents speak the same language will likely enhance their social interaction and economic survival; however, problems may arise when these people must venture out among predominantly English-speaking populations. Regardless of a counselor's native language, it may be advisable to encourage clients to improve their English-language skills as an excellent beginning point to solving communication problems caused by poor English proficiency.

Fourth, European Americans may experience confusion and frustration as family members increasingly move toward majority-culture family expectations. Traditional expectations of the father/husband being the breadwinner and decision-maker and the mother/wife being the homemaker and nurturer may be affected by acculturation. For example, both men and women may experience psychological difficulties as women perceive the advantages associated with more egalitarian and liberated views. Older generations and men (and also women) who are accustomed to strict family traditions and customs sometimes experience problems with others' tendencies to forsake cherished cultural traditions in favor of a more acculturated lifestyle.

Last, some European Americans, like people of other cultures, are coping with HIV/AIDS. In 1999, there were 14,813 reported AIDS cases in European Americans, down from 15,984 in 1998.

European American Elderly

Social and Cultural Description

European American elderly, like clients in all cultures and developmental stages, must be considered as individuals because, for example, Romanian Americans differ from German Americans just as Mexican Americans differ from Cuban Americans. A number of factors—intracultural, socioeconomic, gender, and geographic—can affect the way European Americans think and live. Counselors in multicultural settings need to learn about individual European American elderly in an attempt to provide the most effective counseling intervention.

Table 11.4
Total Number of European
Americans: 65 and Older

*Source: Statistical abstracts of
the United States 2004–2005*
(124th ed.), by U.S. Census Bureau,
2004, Washington, D.C.: Author.

Age Group	Total
65 to 69 years	8,335,000
70 to 74 years	7,480,000
75 to 79 years	6,601,000
80 to 84 years	4,856,000
85 to 89 years	2,715,000
90 to 94 years	1,164,000
95 to 99 years	315,000

Table 11.4 shows the total population numbers of elderly European Americans.

Demographic data indicate that the population of adults ages 65 and older is growing steadily. By 2030, the elderly population will be about 70 million. As the elderly population continues to grow, counselors will increasingly be faced with meeting the needs of older adults and their families.

Some acculturation has undoubtedly occurred among second- and third-generation (and, to some extent, first-generation) European Americans. The degree of acculturation depends on educational level, initiative and ability to be a part of majority-culture activities, and residence in a cultural enclave.

European American elderly may be more likely than younger generations to retain valued cultural traditions and customs, such as the authority role of husbands/fathers. Elderly family members might look on with disbelief as younger women take assertive roles, men allow (and, in some cases, encourage) women to take crucial family roles, both men and women allow their children and adolescents greater freedom and independence, and younger family members place greater emphasis on proficiency in English. Another potentially threatening cultural belief is the nontraditional egalitarian value placed on both daughters and sons, rather than giving sons privileged positions within the family.

Although cultures and generations vary, some European American cultures place the elderly in high regard and believe that they deserve respect and care. Elderly European Americans may feel neglected because of changing familial status and changing cultural attitudes toward the elderly. They may think their children are accepting more majority-culture values that favor personal concerns over traditional cultural beliefs toward the elderly.

Communication

As with the elderly in other cultures, considerable diversity exists among European Americans in their ability to speak English. The elderly in some European American cultures speak fluent English, whereas others continue to hold on to their native languages, live in language enclaves to avoid the realities of a predominantly English-speaking society, or experience difficulty because they are confronted with a new language. Regrettably, there is no reliable information on the numbers of elderly who speak native languages to avoid English. First-generation elderly European Americans who may not have mastered English and elderly persons who have elected, or been forced, to live in language enclaves may experience the most serious communication problems.

Communication problems among some elderly persons indicate the need for intervention. Counselors working with elderly European Americans must understand the common problems of the elderly, as well as the special problems resulting from limited English-speaking skills. Language-minority persons, whether French, German, Romanian, Hungarian, or any other language, may have several problems—speaking with physicians and nurses, especially on the telephone; dealing with social services agencies designed to assist the elderly; getting groceries and medicines delivered to the home (even in places where businesses still provide such services); and other problems. Aging can potentially aggravate the existing problems seen in European Americans in other stages along the lifespan continuum. Perceptive counselors will recognize a possible double jeopardy—being elderly and a language minority—and plan counseling intervention that addresses the problems that are associated with aging.

Families

In most cases, the elderly hold on to cherished familial beliefs about family roles and treatment of the elderly. For example, elderly Italian Americans continue to see the family's role as providing family members with the training necessary to cope in a difficult world. The father

---

UP CLOSE AND PERSONAL 11.4

Costas, an Elderly European American

Grandfather Costas, who is in his late 70s, lives with his son, his daughter-in-law Olympia, and their three children. He feels fairly lucky because he is spending his later years with the family he has known and loved for so long.

Costas would like to make a more valuable contribution to the family, but he has the satisfaction of knowing that he did what he could in his earlier years. He does not feel like a burden to the family and does not think that they consider him one.

He thinks his health has declined within the past several years. He has less energy, more aches and pains, failing eyesight, and perhaps a hearing problem. He does not see a physician as he should because he finds such visits to be frustrating. He is concerned about the costs involved, transportation to and from the physician's office, and the fact that he and the physician do not always communicate well. Rather than see the physician at regular intervals, Costas tends to procrastinate and makes an appointment only when something is clearly wrong. He has never considered any of his problems and concerns serious enough to see a mental health counselor. He always believed that

people (especially men) should take care of their own problems—people should either deal with them or ignore them, he always thought.

Costas has a few friends near his age in the neighborhood. They also experience problems—physical and mental—similar to his. They usually get together once or twice a week to talk about their families and the world in general.

Although health matters do bother Costas a great deal, he has other concerns, too. He thinks about Christina and Nikos and whether they will forsake Greek traditions for more popular majority-culture values and traditions. He sees other families, especially the adolescents, adopt more majority-culture customs. He thinks they should hold on to the Greek beliefs that have helped him, and family members before him, deal with life. Change for the worse, as Costas views it, should not occur.

Costas does not plan to begin visiting a physician on a regular basis and has never considered seeing a mental health counselor for any problem or concern. He feels fortunate; his health problems are not life-threatening, and he has his family.

has traditionally been the family's undisputed head—often authoritarian in his rule—who sets behavioral guidelines. He still usually takes seriously his responsibilities to provide for his family. As the ultimate authority on living, he offers advice on major issues. The mother provides the emotional sustenance. She yields authority to the father and traditionally assumes responsibility for the emotional aspects of the family. Her life centers around domestic duties, and she is expected to receive her primary pleasure from nurturing and serving her family. For children, there is marked differentiation between sons and daughters. Sons are given much more latitude. Daughters are expected to assume primary caregiving responsibility for an aging or sick parent. The extended family plays a central role in all aspects of Italian family life, including decision-making (Giordano, McGoldrick, & Klages, 2005). Because many elderly European Americans continue to cling to such beliefs, seeing younger generations apparently adopt majority-culture values can pose difficult dilemmas for some elderly family members.

Up Close and Personal 11.4 looks at Costas, an elderly European American.

Unique Challenges Confronting Elderly European Americans

European American elders may face several challenges that are unique to their culture and developmental period. Challenges will, of course, depend on the client's generational status, overall health, economic status, and living arrangements (living alone or with relatives).

First, communication difficulties can pose a problem, especially for elderly European Americans who either have been unable to learn English or have lived in cultural enclaves where learning English seemed unnecessary. Coping with life's everyday demands and expectations can be hampered by lack of English-speaking ability. Communication problems between counselor and client can also limit the effectiveness of counseling intervention. In fact, some acute communication difficulties may result in the need for an interpreter.

Second, changing cultural expectations (e.g., perspectives toward family traditions, children living near and caring for the elderly, husband/father primarily assuming authoritarian roles) can result in frustration and confusion that counselors may need to address. Older European Americans may not have lived as long in the majority culture as their children and grandchildren and thus may be more reluctant to forsake cherished cultural customs and beliefs. The older generation's observations of younger generations acculturating toward majority-culture ways may create conflicts that require counseling intervention.

Third, elderly European Americans may experience financial problems. Difficulties arising from individuals being unable to work and possibly unable to benefit from some social

Table 11.5

Number and Percentage of European Americans (65 to 75+ years) Living in Poverty

Source: Statistical abstracts of the United States 2004–2005 (124th ed.), by U.S. Census Bureau, 2004, Washington, D.C.: Author.

Age Group	Total	Percentages
65 to 74 years	1,224,000	7.9%
75+ years	1,515,000	10.5%

services and monetary programs can necessitate a need for counseling. Investigating poverty risks in the elderly, McLaughlin and Jensen (2000) looked at employment history, demographic characteristics, marital status, and residential context. McLaughlin and Jensen maintain that despite improved economic well-being of elders, poverty remains prevalent among minorities, women, and rural residents. Clear links exist between poverty, minority culture, lower educational attainment, residence in rural or nonmetropolitan areas, female gender, and living alone. People who did better financially during their working life do better after they retire; that is, the advantages experienced during younger years will accumulate to enhance relative well-being during older ages. Other findings included that (1) metropolitan residents were less likely to make a transition into poverty after age 55 than were their nonmetropolitan counterparts; and (2) many women who were widowed, divorced, or single when they reached age 55 were already poor as a result of their prior martial and labor force histories. Table 11.5 looks at the numbers of European American (65 years to 75+) living below the poverty level.

A FOCUS ON RESEARCH 11.4

Alcohol Problems Among Aging Adults

Finfgeld-Connett (2005) describes the alcohol problems among aging adults and discusses self-directed treatment models and their importance in helping aging adults resolve early- and late-onset alcohol abuse problems. In general, early-onset alcohol abusers began abusing alcohol in their thirties and forties and may be well-known to the health care and social service providers. Late-onset alcohol abusers develop problems in their fifties and sixties. These drinkers are often perceived as reactive drinkers because their problems stem from retirement or death of a spouse. Although distinct differences exist among the two types, they also share similarities. Both groups are likely to drink at home, alone, and in response to negative emotional states. Most consume alcohol on a daily basis, are widowed or divorced, are retired, and have minimal social support.

Finfgeld-Connett (2005) describes the Gerontology Alcohol Project (GAP): The major premise of this model is that alcohol misuse is a result of inadequate problem-focused coping skills and low self-efficacy. As such, when alcohol abuse occurs, individuals experience diminished confidence in their ability to change their situations, and they become reliant on the short-term relief that alcohol may provide. Thus, the focus of the GAP self-management treatment model is to increase the individual's repertoire of problem-focused behavioral coping skills

and to enhance self-efficacy in high-risk situations. Stages of GAP include: *Stage 1*—Assessing the Consequences of Drinking; *Stage 2*—Teaching the ABCs (e.g., reasons for alcohol abuse, dangers, etc.); and *Stage 3*—Teaching Self-Management Strategies.

Suggestions for counselors and social workers (as well as others in the helping profession) include the following:

1. Employ age-specific, group treatment using a supportive versus a confrontational approach.
2. Concentrate on managing negative emotional states such as depression and loneliness.
3. Foster the expansion of social support networks.
4. Present treatment content at a pace that is appropriate for older workers.
5. Avoid using terms such as group *leader, therapist,* or *treatment program* (to preserve self-esteem)—instead, use terms such as *teacher, student,* and *class.*

Source: "Self management of alcohol problems among aging adults," by D. L. Finfgeld-Connett, 2005, *Journal of Gerontological Nursing, 31*(5), pp. 51–58.

Fourth, European American elderly, like their counterparts in other cultures, often experience declining health and increased medical expenses. The elderly often worry about health concerns ranging from impaired physical mobility to terminal diseases, living alone while ill, and paying for needed medical care. Thus, the elderly may need counseling to help them cope with these problems.

Fifth, although not isolated to one cultural group, alcohol abuse is considered to be one of the fastest growing health problems among aging adults in the United States. It is estimated that 2% of the 10% of community-based older adults have alcohol problems and 21% of aging hospitalized patients have a diagnosis of alcoholism. In A Focus on Research 11.4, Finfgeld-Connett (2005) discusses alcohol problems in aging adults and self-directed treatment models and their importance in helping aging adults resolve early and late onset of alcohol abuse problems.

A Point of Departure: Challenges Confronting Counselors of European Americans

Counselors of European American children, adolescents, adults, and elders face several challenges that call for resolution prior to effective counseling intervention.

First, counselors, regardless of their cultural background, need to understand their own culture as well as their clients' cultures. Attention should focus on understanding differences and similarities in worldviews and how these worldviews affect counseling intervention. Counselors also need to recognize that their clients' developmental stages will affect worldviews and their perception of counseling strategies.

Second, counselors and clients may experience communication problems (including nonverbal mannerisms), which can potentially limit counseling effectiveness. For example, a counselor whose native language is Spanish may have difficulty communicating with a client whose native language is German. Any number of communication difficulties can arise, depending on the extent of language differences between counselor and client.

Third, counselors, regardless of cultural background, will need to choose counseling strategies that are appropriate for clients and their respective cultures. For example, an African American or Hispanic American counselor will be challenged to select a counseling intervention that is appropriate for a client with a European American cultural perspective and worldview.

Summary

European Americans bring diverse cultural traditions and characteristics to counseling sessions with social workers and mental health professionals. A counselor from a non–European American background may have difficulty understanding European American worldviews. Similarly, a young or middle-aged counselor may have difficulty understanding the developmental perspectives of children, adolescents, and elders. Counselors, regardless of their cultural background, need an understanding of European American perspectives on development, family, and languages, to name a few aspects. Likewise, because of the tremendous diversity within the greater European American culture, counselors may experience difficulty understanding some European American subcultures; for example, a French American counselor might experience difficulty intervening with a Romanian American client. As our nation's cultural diversity increases, counselors will be increasingly challenged to provide counseling intervention with clients of differing cultural backgrounds. Perceptive counselors in multicultural settings readily recognize that clients of European American cultural backgrounds differ as do those of other diverse cultures, such as Asian or Hispanic. Professional responsibility demands, first, an understanding of the client in the individual European American culture and, second, the selection of culturally appropriate counseling strategies.

Suggested Readings

Cortina, L. M., & Wasti, A. (2005). Profiles in coping: Response to sexual harassment across persons, organizations, and cultures. *Journal of Applied Psychology, 90* (1), 182–192. These authors investigate sexual harassment among working-class Ango Americans, professional Turks, and Professional Anglo Americans.

Hawkins, N. A., Ditto, P. H., Danks, J. H., Smucker, W. D. (2005). Micromanaging death: Process Preferences, values, and goals in end-of-life medical decision making. *The Gerontologist, 45* (1), 107–117. The authors examine patients' and surrogates' attitudes about using advance directives to manage end-of-life medical care and also examine how patients want decisions to be made.

12

Counseling European American Clients

Questions to Be Explored

1. What unique challenges can counselors expect when intervening with European American children, adolescents, adults, and elders?

2. How can counselors, especially those from other cultural backgrounds, effectively plan counseling intervention for such a diverse group as European American clients? How can counselors avoid cultural stereotypes?

3. How can counselors accommodate cultural differences in selecting individual, group, and family therapy?

4. What concerns and problems related to development might child, adolescent, adult, and elderly clients present to counselors?

5. How can counselors of differing cultural backgrounds and lifespan stages intervene with European Americans of other lifespan stages?

6. How can counselors most effectively plan and implement counseling intervention for gay, lesbian, and bisexual European American clients?

7. What sources provide information for professionals intervening with European American children, adolescents, adults, and elders?

Overview

European Americans and their diverse traditions, customs, languages, dialects, and communication styles will challenge counselors to plan counseling interventions that reflect both cultural backgrounds and lifespan stages. European Americans originate from diverse locations, including France, Germany, Greece, Hungary, Ireland, Italy, Poland, and Portugal. Perceptive counselors realize the need to consider European Americans' cultural differences, languages, family issues, and developmental concerns. This chapter examines European Americans in the four lifespan stages and how counselors can plan effective professional intervention. Also, gender differences and gay and lesbian perspectives have the potential for affecting the outcome of counselor interventions and are examined whenever possible. Last, this chapter includes a discussion of individual, group, and family therapies that may be appropriate for European American clients.

European American Children

Potential Problems Warranting Counseling Intervention

Problems that European American children may experience include the following:

- Parents and families discourage children from seeking counseling at school; for example, children in some European cultures learn early that they alone understand their problems, the causes, and the possible solutions.

- Conflicts are caused by being raised in a culture that teaches children that the father is the primary decision-maker and authority figure, while attending more egalitarian-oriented schools.

- Old-world values taught at home may conflict with values of other cultures in the neighborhood and school (e.g., allegiance to the family, affection for the homeland, respect for elders, allegiance to a church).

- There may be peer pressure to engage in behaviors that would be considered "culturally inappropriate" by parents and families.

- Strangers are suspect.

- Communication difficulties may occur, especially when English is spoken at school and a different language is spoken in the home.

- Developmental and health concerns can include eating disorders and common childhood diseases and ailments.

Ingersoll, Bauer, and Burns (2004) report that estimates of from 7.5 million to 14 million children in the United States experience significant mental health problems, many of which will be treated with psychotropic medications. The range is vague due to the ambiguity of psychiatric diagnoses and general problems with epidemiological research on diagnostic categories. In A Focus on Research 12.1, Ingersoll, Bauer, and Burns look at children's medication and recommend advocacy counseling.

Counseling Considerations

Counseling European American children requires consideration of individual children and their respective cultures. Some children disclose freely, whereas others believe that talking about problems reflects negatively on their families as well as on their ability to deal with life tasks. Children, especially younger children, may not understand the purposes of counseling and may lack the

A FOCUS ON RESEARCH 12.1

Children and Psychotropic Medicine

During the last 5 years, there has been a growing emphasis on advocacy counseling. During the last 10 years, there has been an enormous increase of psychotropic medicines for children. The medical world in Western society, with its focus on alleviating symptoms using psychotropic medicines, continues to dominate in the treatment of emotional disorders. The convergence of increasing psychotropic medicines for children, the dominance of the medical model, and the economic power wielded by pharmaceutical companies are all issues that could be addressed through advocacy counseling.

Topics addressed in this excellent article include trends in describing medicines, power issues (e.g., relationships among the Federal Drug Administration, the *Diagnostic and Statistical Manual of Mental Disorders,*

and pharmaceutical companies), the ethics of counselors discussing psychotropic medicines, and advocacy issues (e.g., treatment versus medication).

In closing, Ingersoll, Bauer, and Burns (2004) raise the primary issue of how counselors can best advocate for clients and their families regarding children and psychotropic medications. Even though treatment might involve some form of medication, advocacy counseling can help families explore treatment options, evaluate relevant literature, and become empowered to stand up against pharmaceutical companies.

Source: "Children and psychotropic medication: What role should advocacy counseling play?" by R. E. Ingersoll, A. Bauer, and L. Burns, 2004, *Journal of Counseling and Development, 82,* pp. 337–343.

cognitive structures and social skills to respond to counselors' efforts. Some children experience communication problems and others may view counseling as the family's role. Counseling European American children will differ from counseling clients in other lifespan stages and other cultural groups. A client's willingness to talk, to discuss family matters, and to trust counseling professionals varies significantly from culture to culture.

Counseling children is full of challenges. Children's limited concept of time may make it difficult for them to receive maximum benefit from the standard once-a-week session. Thus, the counselor may wish to schedule shorter, twice-weekly (or more) sessions so that children can experience carryover between the sessions. Counseling effectiveness may also be hampered by communication difficulties resulting from differences in both communication and nonverbal behavior styles. Third, children are still in the process of developing a sense of self-esteem and a cultural identity. Thus, both counselor and child may benefit greatly from activities that enable the child to explore the culture and immediate environment in a concrete fashion.

Counselors who work with children benefit from the realization that children, because of their developmental period, often feel that they are powerless and without a voice. In some situations, the counselor working with family issues might be perceived as a helpful force; in other ways, the counselor might be seen as further complicating the problem. For example, children may question whether to place allegiance with the counselor or with the family. Also, counselors will have to make individual decisions whether to select individual, group, or family counseling. One child might benefit from listening to other children talk about psychological discomfort resulting from family and peer allegiances, but for another child, hearing other children discuss problems might only solidify or intensify family concerns.

Individual/Group Therapy.   Children can be confused in their thinking and may need the counselor to help them structure their ideas and feelings. In fact, many elementary-grade children simply do not understand counseling terms and the actual meaning of words. In such situations, the counselor's intuitive style and questioning skills become especially important. Other problems associated with thinking, language, and understanding counseling terminology might be even more acute with children from the vast number of European American subcultures. Ivey, Ivey, and Simek-Morgan (1997) suggested the development of a 5-stage interview structure that may require as many as 10 sessions. Several sessions may be necessary to establish rapport, an essential prerequisite when working with children, especially if the cultural backgrounds of the child and the counselor differ.

The model proposed by Ivey and colleagues (1997) is as follows:

1. *Establishing rapport:* The counselor needs to tap personal and cultural strengths to establish rapport. Giving a smile, playing a game, or allowing children to do artwork or something with their hands as they talk might open communication and build a sense of rapport or trust. Traditional therapy that begins with talk will probably be less effective with children.

2. *Gathering data that emphasizes strengths:* Children often talk in short, random, and concrete segments. The counselor who works effectively with children often allows them to talk freely and in their own fashion while the counselor paraphrases, reflects feelings, and summarizes frequently. Children may need help organizing their thoughts as well as expressing themselves. With the less talkative child, it will be important to ask questions to encourage the child to talk, without leading the child in a specific direction. The counselor's questions and concepts should be concrete, rather than abstract. Data gathering also includes identifying children's strengths and assets. Children may sense if the counselor feels boredom, impatience, or frustration, which will negatively affect the intervention.

3. *Determining goals:* During this stage, the counselor can ask children what they want to happen. Such questioning gives children an opportunity to explore an ideal world and to discover fantasies and desires. Some goals might be impossible (e.g., stopping their parents' divorce), but the counselor should try to get children to work toward concrete and realistic goals.

4. *Generating alternative solutions and actions:* Children respond well to brainstorming, which helps the counselor to break down the problem into small, workable steps. Often, listing solution alternatives can be useful. This 5-stage model is also useful in group work. For example, when three to five children who share similar problems are brought together in group therapy, they can often help one another or at least see that other children share similar problems. Simultaneously, imagining the future and the emotional consequences of alternatives can be especially helpful.

5. *Generalizing:* The counselor should try to give children a concrete goal for the next counseling session. Assignments work well when children know they need to work on specific things. Children should know that the counseling session had a specific purpose and that, afterward, they have a specific "assignment" to do prior to the next session.

Only the counselor can consider cultural and individual differences to determine the feasibility of individual and group therapy. As with other cultures and other lifespan stages, wide differences exist among European Americans. Also, both individual and group therapies have their advantages. Individual sessions allow children to tell and enact their own stories; such counseling interviews are conducted with an awareness of self in relation to others, family, and culture. In group therapy, friendship, social skills, and sharing groups can be useful for children, for example, groups of children who all experience alcoholism in the home or self-esteem groups focused on the values of varying cultural groups (Ivey et al., 1997).

Family Therapy.   Family therapy can be beneficial, especially if the counselor plans sessions to reflect the child's developmental stage and concerns. Several considerations are prerequisite to effective family therapy. The counselor needs to recognize the child's capabilities and potentialities and to plan the length of counseling sessions to reflect the child's shorter attention span and interest level (Thompson & Rudolph, 1988).

The counselor should first set the mood of the session by: (a) asking questions in a warm, specific, matter-of-fact way; (b) creating settings in which people can risk looking clearly and objectively at themselves and at their actions; and (c) asking questions the child will be able to handle. The counselor needs to be sure that the child understands the counseling process and the family's goals. The importance of communication should be emphasized—the child should feel free to agree or disagree with family members, say what they really think, and bring disagreements out in the open. The child needs to feel that she or he will be treated with respect (Thompson & Rudolph, 1988).

Each child in the family should be spoken with individually. The counselor needs to convey sincerity in honoring all the child's questions, thus demonstrating that asking questions does not constitute troublemaking. Also, the counselor should convey expectations of the child to increase the likelihood of the child rising to meet them. The child should be asked about expectations of and reasons for seeking or referral to counseling. The counselor should repeat what the child says to make sure the child's meaning is understood. In essence, the counselor (a) learns about communication within the family, (b) encourages the children to talk about themselves and their feelings in relation to the family, (c) helps the children to express frustration and anger, (d) encourages the children to question family members about troublesome issues, (e) uses confronting questions to provoke the children's thoughts, and (f) discusses the roles of family. After establishing rapport and a comfortable atmosphere, the counselor begins to bring out underlying feelings and confronts family members concerning the factors that are causing the family dysfunction (Thompson & Rudolph, 1988).

Although Thompson and Rudolph (1988) provide excellent suggestions for counseling children, it is important to look at family therapy from a cultural perspective. Counselors may experience more difficulty when intervening by using family therapy with some European American cultural groups. For example, some children are more reluctant to speak and voice concerns in family therapy because they have been taught to consider parents with great respect. In patriarchal families, children might think problems or disagreements reflect negatively on the father's ability to manage his household and family. Also, some families might perceive children in a subordinate role—children should be silent and avoid commenting on family matters. Next, on the one hand, communication problems might interfere with the effectiveness of a counseling session; some family members can communicate effectively, whereas others (perhaps older

UP CLOSE AND PERSONAL 12.1

Counseling Christina, a European American Child

A teacher in Christina's school recommended her for counseling. Because Christina attended a school sponsored by the Greek Orthodox Church, no full-time school counselor was available. However, a guidance counselor who had been contracted to work among several Greek schools was available. Although Christina did not exhibit serious emotional problems, the teacher did think Christina had concerns of sufficient merit to warrant the counselor's attention. For example, Christina had demonstrated several stress-related ailments and had voiced a concern about venturing out from her Greek enclave and taking an active role in the broader majority-culture society.

After several meetings with Christina, the counselor found that Christina's basic problem centered around her lack of confidence in her ability to interact with potential friends in the majority-culture society. Her self-esteem allowed her to relate positively in her Greek American surroundings, yet she had considerable concerns, particularly when she visited other schools with her school teams.

Christina's counselor reached two conclusions: (a) Although Christina had the ability and motivation to deal interpersonally outside her immediate community, her perceived inadequacies deserved to be addressed; and (b) the counselor planned to initially provide individual counseling and the move to several small-group sessions. Specific plans included helping Christina realize that her ability to make friends and form interpersonal relationships within the Greek culture could transfer to the majority culture. Also, although Christina's self-esteem was not currently a problem, the counselor wanted to help Christina preserve her self-esteem and continue to respect the Greek culture. She had to convince Christina that it was not necessary to give up her Greek heritage to gain acceptance in a broader society.

generations) may experience more difficulty with English. On the other hand, having family members present may be beneficial; those with greater facility in English can assist other members who have difficulty. Last, some cultures might be reluctant to discuss family issues (particularly those of a personal nature) with a counselor of a different culture; for example, a Greek American family may feel uncomfortable with a female counselor or a non-Greek American counselor. Such a reluctance could, of course, occur in any counseling situation regardless of individual, group, or family.

Up Close and Personal 12.1 looks at a counselor's efforts with Christina, a European American child.

European American Adolescents

Potential Problems Warranting Counseling Intervention

Problems that European American adolescents may experience include

- conflicts between the quest for freedom and independence typically associated with adolescent conflict and the adolescent's traditional cultural expectations;

- frustration and stress caused by increased communication demands and limited English proficiency skills;

A FOCUS ON RESEARCH 12.2
Person-Centered Counseling and Sexual Minority Adolescents

Adolescents who are stigmatized as sexual minorities possess unique and complex needs that must be considered in the dynamics of counseling. This particular population includes lesbian, gay, bisexual, and transgender/sexual (LGBT) adolescents who are questioning and struggling to accept their sexual identity.

In this article, Lemoire and Chen described the sexual identity development of LGBT adolescents and advocate Carl Roger's person-centered approach for counseling intervention. They argue that this counseling approach seems to have potential to create the necessary conditions that counteract stigmatization, allowing adolescents who are associated with a stigmatized sexual group to cope with their sexual identity in a manner that is constructive for them.

Lemoire and Chen maintain the person-centered approach has particular strengths such as unconditional positive regard, congruence, and empathy; adoption of the client's perspective; the notion of self-concept; and growth process being client-directed.

Source: "Applying person-centered counseling to sexual minority adolescents," by S. J. Lemoire, and C. P. Chen, 2005, Journal of Counseling and Development, 83, pp. 148–154.

- a decreasing respect for oneself and one's cultural background as adolescents' social worlds broaden;
- increased stressors, such as arguments about getting chores done at home, pressure to get good grades or excel in school sports, and increased adolescent resistance to participating in family activities;
- acculturative stress resulting from being a first- or second-generation culture in a school and neighborhood where another culture is the majority;
- peer pressure to experiment with illicit substances and to engage in other illegal activities;
- stereotypes often associated with certain European cultures; and
- typical concerns and stresses of the adolescent lifespan period, such as developing an identity, conflicts between independence and dependence, being an adult in certain aspects and only an older child in others.

Although the general society, as a whole, in North America is becoming more "tolerant" (Lemoire & Chen, 2005, p. 153) of the existence of diversity of sexual orientations, substantial homophobic feelings toward and perceptions about lesbian, gay, bisexual, and transgender/sexual (LGBT) still exist. As a result, sexual minority groups are still being stigmatized and discriminated against, either intentionally or unintentionally. In A Focus on Research 12.2, Lemoire and Chen suggest Carl Rogers's person-centered therapy for counselors intervening with LGBT adolescents.

Counseling Considerations

Adolescents referred to the counselor by a teacher, parent, principal, or other authority figure often project onto the counselor the authority of those who "force" them to be in counseling. Whenever possible, adolescents should self-refer to avoid the feeling that another adult "made" them see a counselor. Even youths who have elected to seek counseling may find it difficult to share problems and concerns.

The counselor can take several directions to help the adolescent experiencing stress and frustration caused by inadequate communication skills. First, during intervention, the counselor may determine a need for a translator. There are drawbacks to having a translator present (e.g., the translator's choice of words and tone of voice), but if unaided, the client's problems with English (or the counselor's inability to speak the client's native language) may intensify the client's problems. Second, depending on the severity of the communication problem, the counselor may seek help from another professional (e.g., an English as a second language [ESL] specialist) who can evaluate specific problems and provide an appropriate English-language program. Third, the counselor may decide to identify and arrange for intervention with a counselor whose native language is the same as the client's. This approach should be considered a short-term solution, however, because eventually the client will need to develop proficiency in English. Fourth, rather than take a comprehensive approach to intervention, the counselor may decide to focus intervention only on those areas related to the adolescent's development (e.g., communication for socialization or for dealing with a widening social world outside the immediate home and language enclave).

Maintaining prevention factors has become a major programmatic and investigative force in child and adolescent mental health specialty. Counselors seeking to enhance the counselor–client relationship should work to be perceived as different from the adolescent's parents and teachers. Counselors should be perceived as being able to keep adolescents' disclosures confidential. They should be sensitive and sympathetic, yet honest, and work cooperatively with the client in providing feedback and openly seeking feedback from the client. Also, counselors should remember that developmental characteristics and cultural differences play a significant role in the counseling process and in the determination of counseling strategies.

Counselors intervening with adolescents will want to use as many resources as possible. These resources may include health departments, urban leagues, hospitals with comprehensive health programs, and other organizations geared toward helping adolescents. Counselors should maintain a current file of such organizations, especially service groups.

Individual and Group Therapy.   Bruce (1995) reported that busy school days and counselors' heavy workloads suggest a brief counseling model, in which the counselor limits the number of sessions or conceptually plans short-term interventions. The brief counseling process adapts effective counseling practices and is time-limited by design, rather than by failing to provide effective intervention.

The brief counseling model relies on four components necessary for successful therapeutic change:

1. *A strong working alliance:* The counselor listens attentively, enters the worldview of the student, and joins in the process of mutual understanding. The counselor is nonjudgmental, understands and accepts patterns of behavior, and offers collaborative support for the student's exploration of the problem in a respectful climate.

2. *Recognition and use of the student's strengths and resources:* Counselor roles include helping students exercise their power by affirming them as the source for change and by believing

in their capabilities, by fostering self-confidence, and by encouraging students to take charge of directing change in their lives.

3. *Involvement:* A high level of counselor and student affective and behavioral involvement is predictive of successful outcomes. During counseling intervention, the counselor uses role-playing and experiential work to get the student to reframe problematic situations.

4. *Establishing clear, concrete goals:* The counselor and the student need to know that success is achieved. Rather than focus on the past, the counselor and student focus on current patterns of behavior, future plans, and expectations for change. The counselor also expresses hopes for change, as well as for the maintenance and generalization of the initial change.

Counselors working with adolescents might need to consider several points. First, solution-focused counseling provides adolescent clients with an opportunity to see that other adolescents have problems and, in many cases, share similar problems. Second, some adolescent clients in multicultural situations are reluctant to disclose personal information in group sessions; thus, perceptive counselors will determine whether group counseling would be appropriate. If adolescents demonstrate a reluctance to disclose significant information with the group, the counselor can still employ solution-focused counseling on an individual basis (LaFountain, Garner, & Eliason, 1996).

Family Therapy.   The extent to which families teach their adolescents to suspect professional counselors and other cultures and to rely on family support networks, such as the extended family and the church, will determine or significantly influence adolescents' tendencies toward, or rejection of, family intervention.

Family interventions with ethnically different families often require that counselors deal with suspicion among groups, myths of sameness, treatment expectations, processes of acculturation, and communication barriers. Traditionally, family members have relied on informal support networks such as the extended family and the church. Some have suggested that reliance on natural support systems results in fewer feelings of guilt, humiliation, and powerlessness when compared with reliance on outside institutions. Although more ethnic minorities are beginning to take advantage of family therapy, these issues and problems should be addressed before trust can be developed (Wilson, Kohn, & Lee, 2000).

Family therapy with adolescents who function in neither the child nor the adult developmental stage requires an understanding of developmental factors that have the potential for affecting counseling intervention. Adolescents may be reluctant to participate in any type of therapy if their parents have taught them that mental health problems should be addressed only in the family. Some beliefs (e.g., families should take care of their problems, problems can reflect negatively on the father and his ability to manage the family) will contribute to adolescents' reluctance to disclose information.

Counselors working with adolescents from European American cultures might choose to meet with these clients several times prior to actual family counseling sessions to inform them of expectations and techniques. Counselors may also need to encourage adolescents to disclose information without making them feel guilty about disobeying their parents' wishes.

UP CLOSE AND PERSONAL 12.2
Counseling Nikos, a European American Adolescent

The school counselor, the same one who travels to various schools and works with Nikos' sister Christina, was asked to meet with Nikos because of his low academic achievement. Although Nikos was passing and did not exhibit significant behavior problems, he was not excelling, he felt guilty about his lack of academic achievement, he wanted to make friends outside the Greek community, and he questioned how he would equate family and peer expectations, especially when he started making friends of another cultural background. What would his parents think if he dated non-Greek girls? With his academic achievement, how would he locate a job or continue his education if he decided to do so? What would his parents think if they knew he was not working up to his potential? He confided these concerns to the counselor in an individual counseling session.

The counselor made several decisions regarding Nikos's problems. First, he had legitimate concerns, especially his feelings of guilt about letting his family down and concerns about equating family and peer expectations. As with Nikos's sister, the counselor decided on several individual counseling sessions with Nikos to be followed by several group sessions with other adolescents who had similar problems. Also, she decided to include two or three adolescents of other cultures with Nikos's group counseling sessions so that he could learn to appreciate his Greek culture yet simultaneously realize that he could relate to non-Greek peers. Next, she wanted to work on Nikos's feelings of guilt over schoolwork (his failure to meet his family's expectations). Last, if Nikos did not disclose significant or confidential information during group counseling sessions, she would try to schedule more individual counseling sessions.

Up Close and Personal 12.2 looks at a counselor's efforts with Nikos, a European American adolescent.

European American Adults

Potential Problems Warranting Counseling Intervention

Problems that European American adults may experience include

- reluctance to seek mental health counseling because of confidence in their ability to determine and handle personal problems;
- the belief that if they seek counseling services, the counselor's role will be to tell them what to do rather than to help them resolve their own situation;
- suspicion of authority and actual distrust of strangers;
- stereotypical generalizations;
- conflicts caused by women seeking increased freedom, more equality in their marriages and families, more decision-making powers, more freedom to seek careers, and an overall egalitarian family life;
- problems associated with employment such as discrimination, underemployment, unemployment, or decisions about career moves;

- challenges with children and adolescents who disobey parental expectations for behavior and family roles;

- age-related concerns such as midlife crises, the trials of caring for an elderly family member, and the difficulty of seeing one's children growing older and more independent;

- fear of illnesses and diseases;

- disruptions such as divorce, alcoholism, death of a loved one, relocation, loss of a job, and dual-career marriages; and

- racism (both individual and institutional), discrimination, prejudice, and stereotypes associated with differing European cultures.

Basically, social phobia can be defined as a persistent fear of social performance, one that has the potential for causing the person to experience embarrassment (see A Focus on Research 12.3). Approximately 60% of the people who experience social phobia experience other troubling disorders such as depression and obsessive–compulsive disorder and are at greater risk of experiencing suicide ideation and suicide attempts. Curtis, Kimball, and Stroup (2004) look at this problem and offer implications for counseling intervention.

A FOCUS ON RESEARCH 12.3
Understanding and Treating Social Phobia

Although people with social phobias report that the condition interfere with their lives, less than 20% seek professional help and only 6% say they have medications to treat the condition. Low treatment use results from the lack of information made available to people with social phobia about treatment options coupled with their fear of social interactions, including making contact with helping professionals.

For people with social phobia, exposure to social situations can cause extreme anxiety and even panic. Symptoms include trembling, twitching, dizziness, rapid heart rate, feeling faint, difficulty speaking or swallowing, and sweating. Commonly feared situations include eating in public places, giving and receiving compliments, unexpectedly bumping into someone previously known, making eye contact, taking with unfamiliar people, and speaking to an audience.

Curtis, Kimball, and Stroup (2004) offer several implications for counseling intervention. Counselors should

- make the general public more aware of social phobia, since most people with the condition never seek treatment;

- understand that anxiety can be a symptom of many medical conditions, such as diabetes, heart arrhythmia, thyroid conditions, and anemia;

- help clients change their irrational beliefs through cognitive restructuring and exposure to feared situations through role-play and then in-vivo exposure;

- encourage clients to invite close family members and significant others to participate in therapy.

Source: "Understanding and treating social phobia," by R. C. Curtis, A. Kimball, and E. L. Stroup, 2004, *Journal of Counseling and Development, 82,* pp. 3–8.

Counseling Considerations

Counselors who work with clients of differing cultures often contend with the negative consequences of racism and discrimination, as well as with the problems associated with clients' differing worldviews and structures of reasoning. To prepare for counseling European American adults, counselors should obtain a list of service and community organizations and agencies that assist with specific situations. Such organizations include crisis hotlines, family shelters, rape crisis networks, Sistercare for Abused Women, the Salvation Army, and the Urban League. Counselors will also have to determine whether individual or family therapy will be most beneficial for European American adults.

Gender-related issues and needs should be addressed in counseling sessions. As counselors become increasingly sensitive to multicultural concerns, the culture of genders should be included for the male segment of the population to be better served. With traditional men being socialized to be independent, it is not surprising that they have sought the services of mental health professionals less often than women do. In treating men, specific factors need to be considered: counselors' flexibility and gender sensitivity as well as learning from male clients in the counseling process. Also, recognizing strengths that men bring to the counseling process can be integral. Gender Perspectives 12.1 looks at counseling within a traditional male gender role.

The counselor should be cautious when intervening in family issues such as the following: (a) problems dealing with the defining of family roles; (b) frustrations of living in a patriarchal family in an egalitarian society; (c) frustrations of wanting to follow one's desires while feeling obligations to extended kinship networks; and (d) valuing and equating independence, rather than individualism, among people. These issues may be more or less acute, depending on the generational status of the family. For example, first-generation adults might experience more acculturation problems as their children adopt mainstream values, whereas second- or third-generation adults may have grown accustomed to these changes in values.

Although the feminist critiques and proposals have spurred some progress, as evidenced by the 1988 mandate that gender topics be part of the curriculum of American Association for

---

GENDER PERSPECTIVES 12.1

Counseling and Traditional Male Gender Role

McCarthy and Holliday (2004) maintain that a traditional male gender role reflects an affirmation of masculine identity with such qualities as success and reliance. They suggest that this gender role may affect many men's help-seeking attitudes and behaviors. In their excellent article, McCarthy and Holliday briefly review the research on men's approaches to help-seeking; draw connections with the Multicultural Counseling Competencies; and offer suggestions for working with men.

McCarthy's and Holliday's (2004) suggestions include preparing clients to enter and undertake counseling, understanding stereotypes and how they may enter into counseling, considering positive and negative perceptions of cultural groups, and offering possible gender-specific strategies (understanding that no intervention works for every client).

Source: "Help-seeking and counseling within a traditional male gender role: An examination from a multicultural perspective," by J. McCarthy, and E. L. Holiday, 2004, *Journal of Counseling and Development, 82,* pp. 25–30.

Marriage and Family Therapy (AAMFT) accredited programs, Haddock, Zimmerman, and MacPhee (2000) reported that most family therapists remain reluctant to address gender-related issues in their practice.

Individual and Group Therapy.   The array of problems and issues that European American adults bring to counseling sessions will be as diverse as their individual cultures. Thus, counselors cannot begin a session with a predetermined mindset of a Hungarian American family's problems, for example. Once a problem has been determined, the counselor has the professional responsibility to decide whether individual or group therapy will be most effective. Only after an individual assessment will the counselor be able to determine whether to use individual or group therapy. To make this determination, the counselor may ask questions such as the following: Will the client disclose personal information in front of group members? How uncommon (e.g., individual or personal) are the individual's problems? Will the degree of cultural diversity of the counseling group contribute to or decrease the effectiveness of the counseling intervention?

Once the decision is made to use individual or group therapy, there are several guidelines that contribute to the effectiveness of counseling with European Americans.

Guidelines for individual therapy include (a) considering individual European American cultures, rather than relying on stereotypical generalizations; (b) considering communication problems and making accommodations whenever possible; (c) considering individual problems, rather than problems commonly associated with the cultural group; (d) considering problems and issues related to the adult lifespan period, rather than overgeneralizing problems of other lifespan periods; and (e) basing decisions about whether to use individual therapy on specific and factual information.

Guidelines for group therapy include (a) knowing when group therapy is most effective— that is, if clients are willing to disclose personal information; (b) knowing "cultural backgrounds" sufficiently well to recognize how culture affects adult clients; (c) understanding issues such as sexual orientation, disabilities, and other differences; and (d) periodically reassessing group therapy to determine its continued effectiveness.

Family Therapy.   Ethnicity is a filter through which families and individuals understand and interpret their symptoms, their beliefs about the causes of their illnesses, their attitudes toward helpers, and their preferred intervention methods. For example, Italian and Jewish family members may tend toward emotional expressiveness in sharing suffering, whereas Irish and British family members may tend to withdraw into themselves and not discuss their feelings with others. Attitudes toward mental health also vary. For example, Italians generally rely primarily on the family and seek professional help only as a last resort (Ivey et al., 1997).

Plus, the needs of lesbian and gay clients also deserve to be understood and addressed. (These topics are addressed in considerable detail in Chapters 15 and 16.) Laird (2000) explored lesbian relationships and offered several implications for marital and family therapists:

1. Lesbian couples seek therapy for many of the issues that trouble other couples—the loss of partner or job, help in negotiating conflicts in parenting or work sharing, or relationships with their families of origin.

2. Models of marital and family therapy that have proved useful with heterosexual couples will likely prove helpful with lesbian couples (however, therapists should be knowledgeable about lesbian life, recognize the sexist, heterosexist, and homophobic biases in theories and models, and work to overcome their own sexism, heterosexism, racism, and classism).

3. "Matching" (p. 463) the gender and/or sexual orientation of therapist and client is not necessary—what is important is the therapeutic approach that follows.

Counselors employing family therapy with European American adults can maximize effectiveness by (a) preparing individual family members for family therapy (e.g., explaining the purposes of family therapy, the counselor's and family members' roles and responsibilities), (b) learning as much as possible about each family member's cultural background and developmental period, (c) understanding power structures and expectations within the family, and (d) formulating an intervention plan with clearly defined goals that reflect adults' cultural and developmental perspectives.

Rather than consider the European American family through the lens of the counselor (regardless of the counselor's cultural background), the counselor should use caution to develop an accurate cultural perspective of the family. Counseling based on middle-class, majority-culture perspectives (again, regardless of the counselor's cultural background) will not suffice, especially with European American adults who have a powerful allegiance to old-world customs and beliefs. In other words, family intervention needs to be based on and reflect the individual European American culture.

Franco Americans have a history of self-help and of accepting advice from kinship networks or the local priest, rather than from outsiders, who are viewed with suspicion and mistrust. Frequently clannish, most Franco Americans are reluctant to acknowledge the need to seek help from mental health workers and resent any implication that they should. Personal problems, especially family issues, are considered too personal to share with a therapist. When therapy is sought as a last resort, Franco Americans prefer a male who is the same age or older, Catholic, and also Franco American. Because French is the primary language of most first-generation Franco Americans, they will probably seek a parish priest or a sympathetic layperson who speaks French. The counselor needs to avoid misunderstandings that result from cross-cultural and intrafamilial confusion (Langelier & Langelier, 2005).

Counseling German American families often violates a tacit rule: "Do it yourself" (Winawer & Wetzel, 2005, p. 565). German Americans who seek therapy think they have no other choice; for example, a marriage is on the verge of collapse or some symptom impedes the family's functioning. During the initial interview, the therapist should move slowly and not be discouraged by a labored beginning. The German style of forming relationships is generally very structured and takes time. Once the therapist has been accepted in the family, German Americans usually take therapy seriously. Family therapists should understand that the German family is characterized by gender role complementarity (e.g., fathers provide for the family, and mothers take care of the household and the children) (Winawer & Wetzel, 2005).

With Greek American families, the first step is to ensure that each family member feels understood. During the first session, the therapist should display culturally sensitive behaviors to reassure family members that they are not involved with a complete outsider. The therapist should be respectful of relationship values and the traditional hierarchical family organization. If the therapist is unsure about the Greek culture, the session can begin by conducting an enthographic interview in which the family members are treated as experts. Inquiries can begin with cultural customs and lead to questions about the family's patterns. Because gender roles are rigidly defined in the Greek culture, the gender of the therapist will be a powerful determinant in the interactions among family members. Male and female counselors are perceived as having different kinds of power. It is likely that Greek parents will generally be more impressed with a formal, conservative manner (Killian & Agathangelou, 2005).

When Irish Americans attend family therapy, they probably view therapy sessions as being like a confession, during which they admit their sins and ask forgiveness. They may not understand their feelings and may experience considerable embarrassment during the process. As a general rule, structured therapy that is focused on a specific problem will be the most helpful to these clients. Brief, goal-oriented, and clearly stated therapy will likely have the greatest appeal. Value centered, introspective, open-ended therapy may be considered very threatening. Therapy that is oriented toward uncovering hidden psychological problems probably increases clients' anxiety and their conviction that they are "bad" and deserve to suffer. Irish American clients may be helped more effectively by somewhat mysterious, paradoxical, and humorous techniques. For example, the counselor might use techniques that encourage clients to change without dwelling on their negative feelings, and organize therapy around building on a positive connotation and a more hopeful vision of their lives (McGoldrick, 2005).

Italian Americans traditionally have turned to the family, rather than to mental health professionals, for help in solving problems. When they do seek outside help, the problem has probably reached a serious level, and they may feel ashamed that they are unable to solve it. The therapist needs to reassure these clients that they are not to blame and ensure that the family will be involved in counseling intervention. Gaining the family's trust is important because Italian Americans mistrust nearly everyone outside the family. Italian fathers, in particular, may feel threatened because seeking outside help implies their inability to remain in control of their families. In the beginning stages of therapy, the counselor can build trust by sharing common values, which makes the counselor seem warm and approachable (Giordano & McGoldrick, & Klages, 2005).

Therapists intervening with Scandinavian Americans should understand and respect several points. First, Scandinavians emphasize egalitarianism and, because of their suspicion of authority, will probably mistrust the therapist. Second, although most Scandinavians realize that depression negatively affects their lives, they do not admit depressive symptoms or seek professional help. Because Scandinavians are a pragmatic people, they prefer solution-focused approaches during which therapists need to be indirect. Therapy that emphasizes a total-reality approach may be considered shaming, thereby exposing them to humiliation for having called special attention to themselves. Perhaps the most effective way of intervening with Scandinavian Americans is to allow them to figure out as much for themselves as they can, with guidance. Such an approach allows them to maintain their dignity, independence, and sense of control of their lives (Erickson, 2005).

Up Close and Personal 12.3 looks at the counselor's efforts with Olympia, a European American adult.

UP CLOSE AND PERSONAL 12.3
Counseling Olympia, a European American Adult

Olympia's Greek church provides a counselor 1 day per week to discuss problems experienced by members of the church, A friend suggested that Olympia visit the counselor, especially because the church provided the counseling services. Although Olympia did not think she had any serious problems, she agreed to see the counselor, mainly to satisfy her friend's request. Olympia revealed several potential problems, such as her belief that some Greek women were becoming more independent and assertive, whereas she was not; her placing Greek traditions in high regard even though she realized that both Christina and Nikos were experiencing considerable acculturation; the family's need of more money; and the grandfather's declining health. Again, she felt fortunate; her problems were not as serious as those of some of her friends, but she did have a better understanding of the problems that she and her family faced.

The counselor considered Olympia's problems to be somewhat typical of many women in the Greek culture who were torn between tradition—their own and their husbands' Greek traditions—and the acculturation of their children. They wanted a better life for their children and viewed the school (sponsored by the Greek Orthodox Church) as the means to achieve a better life. Also, like many other women, she felt obligated (although not resentful) to take care of older family members—in this case, Grandfather Costas. The counselor decided to include Olympia in a small-group counseling session at first. Then, if she could convince Olympia's husband to attend and participate, she might plan one or more family counseling sessions. The counselor realized that convincing Olympia's husband to attend might be difficult, especially because he probably did not understand Olympia's feelings. The counselor considered how many other Greek women might share similar feelings and concerns and wondered what special programs she might initiate at the church specifically to meet the needs of Greek women.

European American Elderly

Potential Problems Warranting Counseling Intervention

Problems that European American elders may experience include

- varying degrees of acculturation, which affects their motivation and ability to deal with life;

- communication proficiency, which will depend on their generational status and whether they live in a native language enclave where learning English seems unnecessary;

- the belief that younger generations should give emotional and financial support, offer respect and loyalty, and in some cases live in proximity to them;

- health problems, physical and psychological, that limit mobility and their ability to deal with personal problems;

- lower standards of living and, in some cases, poverty and substandard housing;

- illness or death of a spouse or other loved ones;

- health problems and chronic illnesses and medical care;

A FOCUS ON RESEARCH 12.4

Obesity and Older American Men and Women

Reynolds, Saito, and Crimmins (2005) estimated the effect of obesity on life expectancy. In their review of the literature, they found that obesity leads to higher mortality rates. Conflicting research holds that the relationship between obesity and life expectancy may differ by age; that is, some evidence suggests lower death rates among the obese at older ages. The effects of obesity may be more significant for younger rather than older adults.

Reynolds, Saito, and Crimmins conclude that obesity has little effect on life expectancy in adults age 70 and older; however, the obese are more likely to become disabled. That means obese older adults live more years and a higher proportion of their remaining lives disabled. One significant implication is that health professionals and health care providers should realize obesity-related death is less of a concern than obesity-related disability in this age range. Given the steady increases in obesity among older Americans, more research is needed on the effects of obesity on life expectancy and disability.

Source: "The impact of obesity on active life expectancy in older American men and women," by S. L. Reynolds, Y. Saito, and E. M. Crimmins, 2005, *The Gerontologist, 45*(4), pp. 438–444.

- fear of living alone and lack of financial means to do so;
- communication problems that hamper the ability to deal with medical professionals and social service workers;
- changes resulting from acculturation and the younger generations' seeming lack of allegiance; and
- fear of counseling intervention that might appear intrusive or threatening.

One problem facing significant numbers of older adults (and many other age groups) is obesity, caused by heredity, poor eating habits, and lack of proper exercise. In A Focus on Research 12.4, Reynolds, Saito, and Crimmins (2005) look at the impact of obesity on active life expectancy in older American men and women and conclude that obesity has more effect on disability than it does on life expectancy.

Counseling Considerations

Counselors will increasingly be called on to work with the elderly from various cultural backgrounds. However, without special training, counselors might feel unprepared to provide counseling intervention with elderly clients. Also, counselors must understand the need to redefine terminology that defines elderly people and perhaps be instrumental in the redefining process.

Decisions regarding counseling therapies with elderly European Americans should be grounded both in cultural and developmental perspectives. Problems of elderly European Americans might result from their individual cultural diversity, limited communication skills, family problems, and concerns about growing older. No single intervention method can be suggested for a particular culture; such a decision must be reached on an individual counseling basis and must reflect the most effective approach for individual elderly persons. As with other cultures and developmental periods, the literature does not conclusively suggest a specific counseling approach.

Counselors may use several approaches with elderly European American clients who have communication problems, keeping in mind the value that these clients place on their languages. Counselors working with these clients may (a) arrange for a translator to assist with communication problems during counseling intervention, (b) arrange for English-language instruction from a person trained to work with the elderly, and (c) seek the help of bilingual social services specialists.

Individual and Group Therapy.   Counselors employing individual therapy should (a) understand the perspectives of elderly European Americans and the challenges associated with the lifespan period; (b) build an effective counseling relationship (i.e., obtain the trust and confidence of the elderly client); (c) understand and address, whenever possible, problems resulting from limited English-language skills; and (d) determine the effectiveness of individual therapy.

Similarly, counselors intervening with group therapy can benefit from several guidelines, including the following: (a) An increased number of clients can be counseled simultaneously (although clients' individuality should never be forgotten); (b) comments and disclosures of other clients can contribute to the overall goals of counseling; (c) recognition of individual cultures and their members' propensity and reluctance to disclose personal information should guide intervention; and (d) disclosure should be encouraged, yet cultural perceptions of confidentiality should be respected.

UP CLOSE AND PERSONAL 12.4

Counseling Costas, a European American Elder

Grandfather Costas was recommended for counseling when he visited his physician for arthritic-type pains. Costas visited a physician only rarely, and he thought it was even less likely that he would attend a counseling session. After being encouraged by the physician and his own family, however, he decided to attend "one or two" sessions. After extending considerable effort to get Costas to disclose personal information, the counselor listened attentively to Costas's concerns about his declining health, failing eyesight, and a slight loss of hearing. Other concerns included his dislike of Nikos and Christina increasingly adopting mainstream American values. "It is not like the old days," Costas once said with mixed emotions of concern and dismay.

The male counselor realized that Costas was experiencing concerns (aging, failing health, fear of losing traditions) similar to those of many elderly clients.

In his determination of appropriate counseling interventions, he thought Costa might disclose more in individual sessions than in group or family sessions; however, family sessions might be most effective because other family members could learn how to help him. However, because Costas was the eldest male in the family and thought he had to be a "tower of strength," he probably would not disclose significant information or feelings in front of family members. Although one objective of counseling would be to address acculturation issues, the counselor might also be able to convince Costas to get visual and hearing tests to determine how he might be helped in those areas. The counselor decided that individual counseling would be most appropriate and he would try to accomplish as much as possible in the first session because he was doubtful that Costas would attend many sessions before deciding to withdraw from counseling.

Family Therapy.   Family therapy with elderly European Americans requires that counselors (a) consider whether family members will respond to or disclose information, especially in cultures placing the elderly in high regard (family problems and issues might reflect negatively on the elderly or vice versa); (b) take advantage of family dynamics by establishing goals for all family members, not just the elderly client; (c) learn how elderly family members fit into the overall family structure; (d) understand language problems, especially if the family speaks a native language at home; and (e) recognize that generational differences might interfere with counseling effectiveness.

Up Close and Personal 12.4 tells of the efforts of Grandfather Costas and his counselor during an intervention session.

A Point of Departure: Challenges Confronting Counselors of European Americans

Counselors of European American clients along the lifespan continuum may face several unique challenges. Counselors should avoid assuming that European Americans are a homogeneous group of people with similar problems and challenges; learn cultural and developmental characteristics and the complex relationship between the two; make valid decisions concerning when to use individual, group, and family therapies; provide for communication differences, both verbal and nonverbal, and recognize when to request the services of a translator; and realize the impossibility of learning about all European American groups and commit to learning about individual European cultural groups.

Summary

European Americans originate from diverse geographic locations and bring to counseling a wide array of cultures, traditions, customs, religions, and languages. Contributing to this diversity are lifespan periods and individual differences. Counselors have a professional responsibility to learn about individual European American clients and to plan professional intervention to meet their needs. Such a task requires individual initiative to acquire additional knowledge of cultural groups, to develop attitudes that contribute to counseling, and to acquire skills for effective counseling. Rewards will be worth the effort as counselors provide effective counseling and clients benefit from counseling intervention.

Suggested Readings

Coy, D. R., & Kovacs-Long, J. (2005). Maslow and Miller: An exploration of gender and affiliation in the journey of competence. *Journal of Counseling and Developing, 83*, 138–145. Coy and Kovacs-Long examine Maslow and Miller and maintain that they took different paths to the same conclusion: gender and affiliation affect competence.

Curtis, R. C., Kimball, A., & Stroup, E. L. (2004). Understanding and treating social phobia. *Journal of Counseling and Development, 82,* 3–8. In this excellent article, these authors describe social phobia and offer implications for counselors.

Lawson, D. M., & Brossart, D. F. (2004). The association between current intergenerational family relationships and sibling structures. *Journal of Counseling and Development, 82,* 472–482. This article focuses on the relationship between sibling structure, sibling spacing, number of siblings, and birth order, as well as all men and all women siblings.

Steinke, E. E (2005). Intimacy needs and chronic illness: Strategies for sexual counseling and self-management. *Journal of Gerontological Nursing, 31*(5), 40–50. The authors of this article identifies intimacy needs and strategies for sexual counseling for individuals with cardiovascular illnesses and chronic lung problems.

Townsend, K. C., & McWhirter, B. T. (2005). Connectedness: A review of the literature with implications for counseling, assessment, and research. *Journal of Counseling and Development, 83,* 191–201. The authors review the current conceptual and empirical literature from a variety of disciplines dealing with the construct of connectedness.

Watkins, K. J., & Baldo, T. D. (2004). The infertility experience: Biophysical effects and suggestions for counselors. *Journal of Counseling & Development, 82,* 394–402. This article begins with a couple who have experienced infertility but do not identify infertility as their presenting problem. Valuable resources are also mentioned.

13

Understanding Hispanic American Clients

Questions to Be Explored

1. What are the childhood, adolescent, adult, and elderly years like in the Hispanic American culture?

2. What social and cultural characteristics (e.g., *afecto*, *dignidad*, *machismo*, *respeto*) and familial traditions describe Hispanic Americans along the lifespan continuum?

3. What unique challenges face Hispanic Americans during the various lifespan stages?

4. What communication problems (and Hispanics' tendencies to hold on to the Spanish language) affect Hispanic Americans, and how do these problems and tendencies affect educational attainment, employment, and economic success?

5. What unique challenges face counselors providing mental health services to Hispanic Americans in the four lifespan stages?

6. What sources of information are available for counselors intervening with Hispanic American children, adolescents, adults, and elders?

Overview

Counselors undoubtedly will be called on to provide professional intervention for Hispanic Americans, the nation's fastest growing cultural group. Hispanic Americans will challenge counselors and psychotherapists, regardless of gender and cultural background, to understand Hispanic heritages, allegiances to the Spanish language, and cultural customs and practices. Also, Hispanic Americans experience problems on a daily basis that potentially can result in the need for professional counseling. Problems such as lack of English-language skills, low educational attainment, unemployment, poverty, discrimination, and acculturative stress can exact serious tolls on Hispanic Americans. This chapter looks at Hispanic Americans in the four lifespan stages and presents a portrait of Hispanic Americans and the lives they live.

Hispanic Americans: Demographics

Hispanic Americans may be identified as Mexican Americans, Central and South Americans, Chicanos, Spanish Americans, Latin Americans, Mexicans, Puerto Ricans, Cubans, Guatemalans, and Salvadorans. Mexican-origin people live predominantly in the Southwest and Midwest, Puerto Ricans tend to live in the Northeast, and Cubans are mostly concentrated in the Southeast. The Hispanic American population has steadily increased, from 22,379,000 in 1990, to 35,306,000 in 2000, and 39,899,000 in 2003 (U.S. Census Bureau, 2004). Table 13.1 shows the states with the greatest numbers of Hispanic Americans.

Hispanics share many values and goals, yet they also differ in many aspects. In some ways, Hispanics constitute members of a single cultural group with a fairly common history and the sharing of language, values, and customs; in other ways, aspects point to a significantly heterogeneous population that should be conceptualized as an aggregate of distinct subcultures. Tremendous cultural diversity exists among Hispanic Americans, such as the differences between Mexican Americans and Cuban Americans, among generations, and among Hispanics living in different geographic locations in the United States. Thus, mental health professionals and social workers are encouraged to learn about individual clients and their respective cultural characteristics.

Like the arrival of European immigrants at the turn of the century, the tide of Hispanic immigrants and the fast growth of Hispanic American families have injected a new energy into the nation's cities. Hispanic Americans are changing the way the country looks, feels, thinks, and votes. From teeming immigrant meccas to small towns, they are filling churches (Hispanics are overwhelmingly Catholic; 42% attend church once per week), building businesses, and celebrating their Hispanic heritage (Latino American, 1999).

The Hispanic American vote will become an increasingly important factor among politicians running for office. Nagourney (1999) maintained that at one time, politicians visited Spanish-speaking neighborhoods as a last stop on their election campaign tours; they would eat a few Hispanic dishes, speak a few words of Spanish, and then leave. Now, the growing Hispanic vote cannot be taken for granted. Not only are there increasing numbers of voters, but the growing number of Spanish-language newspapers, radio stations, and television stations are better educating Hispanic voters about political issues.

Readers should not assume Hispanic Americans' economic problems stem from lack of motivation or ambition. In A Focus on Research 13.1, Mason (2004) found evidence to suggest

Table 13.1
States With Largest Hispanic American Populations

Source: Statistical abstracts of the United States 2004–2005 (124th ed.), by U.S. Census Bureau, 2004, Washington, D.C.: Author.

State	Population
California	12,176,000
Texas	7,557,000
New York	3,132,000
Florida	3,160,000
Illinois	1,727,000
New Jersey	1,254,000
Colorado	847,000
New Mexico	810,000

A FOCUS ON RESEARCH 13.1

Annual Income, Hourly Wages Among Mexican Americans and Other Latinos

In his study of acculturation and income equality, Mason (2004) focuses on Hispanics because of their heterogeneity that includes phenotype, color, nativity, and language usage, and also because of their recent large-scale integration into mainstream U.S. society. Mason's main focus is to examine Hispanics' acculturation and labor market discrimination because of skin color.

After a literature review of identity formation among Hispanics, Mason examined identity and income. He found evidence to support acculturation among Mexican Americans and Cuban Americans but less evidence suggesting that Puerto Ricans are

acculturating (and increasing annual income and hourly wages) into a non-Hispanic white racial identity. Neither the abandonment of Spanish nor the abandonment of a specifically Hispanic racial self-identity is sufficient to overcome the penalties associated with having a dark complexion and non-European phenotype.

Mason also concluded that labor market discrimination and acculturation remain important issues for Hispanic Americans.

Source: "Annual income, hourly wages, and identity among Mexican Americans and other Latinos," by P. L. Mason, 2004, *Industrial Relations, 43* (4), pp. 817–834.

Hispanics' socioeconomic conditions might be attributed to their overall lack of acculturation into non-Hispanic labor markets due to labor market discrimination.

Hispanic American Children

Social and Cultural Description

A general cultural description of Hispanic Americans is difficult because of the marked diversity of the various subcultures. Diversity also exists in individual differences, generational differences, and socioeconomic levels within each Hispanic cultural group. In considering the social and cultural characteristics of Hispanic American children, counselors and psychotherapists must keep this intracultural diversity in mind to avoid the pitfalls of stereotyping. Table 13.2 shows population numbers of Hispanic American children, ages 5–14.

Several cultural characteristics and values are instilled in children at an early age.

- *Children are taught about machismo.* This term may be translated as a strong sense of masculine pride and is used flatteringly among Hispanic Americans. Both Hispanic American boys and girls learn that machismo refers to manhood, the courage to fight, the masculine traits of honor and dignity, keeping one's word, and protecting one's name. More subtly, machismo also

Table 13.2
Population Numbers of Hispanic American Children

Source: Statistical abstracts of the United States 2004–2005 (124th ed.), by U.S. Census Bureau, 2004, Washington, D.C.: Author.

Age	Total
Under 5 years	4,158,000
5 to 9 years	3,830,000
10 to 14 years	3,661,000

refers to dignity in personal conduct, respect for others, love for family, and affection for children. The term also implies a clear-cut distinction between the sexes, whereby males enjoy rights and privileges that are denied to females, a fact that Hispanic children often learn early in life.

• *Children are taught to avoid competition and behaviors that would set them apart from their group.* To stand out among one's peers is to place oneself in great jeopardy and is to be avoided at all costs.

• *Children in some Hispanic groups*, such as Mexican Americans, are *often taught to regard European Americans with fear and hostility.* Children who are taught such attitudes have difficulty believing that a European American counselor has their best interests at heart.

Before discussing communication and families, it must be repeated that the tremendous cultural diversity among Hispanic Americans warrants consideration. For example, Mexican Americans and Cuban Americans may be very different with respect to culture-based values. In fact, each of the numerous Hispanic subgroups adheres to unique and distinguishing cultural and social practices. Acculturation rates, socioeconomic factors, educational levels, and region of residency deserve consideration.

As the number of single-parent families in the United States has continued to increase, so have concerns about the health and well-being of young children. Although exceptions certainly exist, as a whole, the majority of single parents are women, less educated, poorer, and more likely to experience racial discrimination than is the case for women in two-parent families. In A Focus on Research 13.2, Ricciuti (2004) investigates the effects of single parenthood on 12–13-year-old white, black, and Hispanic children.

A FOCUS ON RESEARCH 13.2

Single Parenthood and White, Black, and Hispanic Children

Ricciuti (2004) reports that several unfavorable outcomes are often associated with single parenting, particularly for children in late childhood, adolescence, and young adulthood. Although he emphasizes these findings are not always consistent, some reports suggest problems might include dropping out of high school, poor school achievement, problem behavior, increased health risk, and severe behavioral difficulties. In addition to the inconsistent findings, considerable variation occurs among single-parent families due to their social and economic resources.

With a sample of White, Black, and Hispanic children ages 12–13, Ricciuti did a follow-up to determine whether being in a single-parent family had adverse effects. He found little or no evidence of adverse effects of single parenthood when the children reached 12–13.

Ricciuti concludes that the results suggest that, even in the presence of reduced income, the potential negative consequences for children of single parents may be significantly attenuated or offset by the presence of maternal or family characteristics that support and enhance positive parenting and childcare. These characteristics include mothers' competence and education, as well as positive maternal expectations and attitudes toward children's schooling and developmental potential, all of which tend to be associated positively with their children's achievement.

Source: "Single parenthood, achievement, and problem behavior in white, black, and Hispanic children," by H. N. Ricciuti, 2004, *Journal of Educational Research, 97*(4), pp. 196–206.

Communication

Spanish-speaking people represent the largest language-minority population in the nation. Often, Hispanic American children feel encouraged to speak Spanish at home yet feel compelled to speak English at school. Which language should be considered the language of choice? Although children want their parents' approval for choice of language, they often hear in school that English contributes to academic success. Also, nonverbal language, as in other cultures, is important in the Hispanic American culture and should be understood by professionals of all cultures; for example, many Hispanic Americans tend to stand close while communicating and to touch one another; eye contact may be avoided.

Also, many Hispanic American children are taught distinct communication customs, some of which professionals fail to understand. For example, children of Hispanic immigrants are taught to respect adult authority rather than express their own knowledge and opinions, yet teachers and counselors in the United States often value assertive speaking and typically equate Hispanic American children's silence as a negative attitude toward learning and professionals. Using a culturally valid communication style, the child listens politely and attentively but does not answer; then the counselor who misunderstands this communication custom thinks the child is being difficult or obstinate.

Families

Family lifestyles and activities in the Hispanic American culture play a large part in determining what the developing child will be like as an adult. Ethnic awareness in children is perpetuated by family gatherings for cultural holidays. Puerto Rican Americans have a deep sense of commitment to the immediate and extended family—kinship networks of Hispanic Americans are widely recognized.

The father in the Hispanic American family is clearly head of the household. Children learn early that their father's authority goes unchallenged, that he often makes decisions without consulting their mother, and that he expects to be obeyed when he gives commands. Male dominance extends to sons, who have more and earlier independence than daughters.

Professionals working with Hispanic American children and their families need to understand the traditionally defined gender roles. They should also be aware that changes are occurring: Hispanic American women are increasingly exerting their influence; indeed, in many cases, they are seeking equality with men. As women continue to redefine their roles in the Hispanic and White societies, children will also experience changes.

Up Close and Personal 13.1 provides a portrait of Ramon, a Hispanic American child.

Unique Challenges Confronting Hispanic American Children

Hispanic American children face several challenges with regard to poverty, communication, and education. First, many Hispanic American children live in poverty. The U.S. Census Bureau (2004) reports that 28.2% of all Hispanic American children under age 18 live below the poverty level. Second, communication problems continue to plague Hispanic American children; their tendency to speak their native language at home and in the community but to speak English at school may prolong communication problems. In fact, 23.4% of Hispanic children (5–17 years)

UP CLOSE AND PERSONAL 13.1
Ramon, a Hispanic American Child

Ramon, an 8-year-old Puerto Rican boy, lives with his parents, a younger brother, an older sister, and an older brother in a dilapidated apartment building. Ramon's grandfather, Rafael, lives on the same floor of the building. Another brother, the eldest of the five children, is married and lives with his wife across the street. The community is predominantly Hispanic American and quite diverse. Ramon's Puerto Rican cultural traditions are very different, for example, from those of the Mexican Americans in the neighborhood.

Ramon's father is, without doubt, the head of the family. Although Ramon's mother has begun to receive more respect as an individual and as a valued family member, his father continues to make nearly all the decisions concerning the household. The immediate family and extended relatives function as a unit, and Ramon's grandfather has considerable influence in family matters. Ramon likes the arrangement. His married brother continues to visit nearly every day, and his grandfather, who lives in Ramon's building, spends lots of time with him, telling stories of his life in Puerto Rico.

Despite a relatively tranquil home life, Ramon is troubled at school, and his European American teachers are at a loss for appropriate solutions. Ramon's parents acknowledge his academic problems; however, their limited knowledge of the American school system and their lack of proficiency in English make it difficult for them to assist the school professionals. Ramon's teachers consider him unmotivated and uninterested in schoolwork. The school counselor, however, thinks

Ramon's troubles can be traced to specific causes. For example, one of Ramon's fights involved two other Hispanic American boys; the three of them were trying to "impress" their friends. Ramon admitted that he wanted his peers to think he could defend himself like his father and older brothers. Ramon's communication problem stems from his home, where Spanish continues to be the primary language. In fact, Ramon speaks Spanish at home and in his neighborhood and English only at school. He has problems understanding the teacher and reading the textbooks. Although his counselor has spoken to Ramon on several occasions, a persistent problem continues to handicap the counseling situation: Ramon does not trust the counselor. He has learned from his family and friends that European American professionals cannot always be trusted and must be viewed with suspicion.

Still another problem is that Ramon never wants to stand out among his peers. He once confided to the counselor that "making good" might be costly in terms of peer approval. Reconciling himself to mediocre schoolwork while demonstrating machismo was Ramon's chosen path.

Ramon will continue to have problems as long as English is spoken only at school and Spanish at home. His European American teachers tell him that machismo is unimportant, but his friends disagree. Meanwhile, Ramon's self-concept and academic achievement suffer as he struggles to reconcile the differences of two cultures.

speak a language other than English at home and have difficulty with everyday English usage (U.S. Census Bureau, 2004).

Hispanic American children face several educational challenges: (a) Compared with European Americans, Hispanic American children and adolescents begin school with less preschool experience; (b) gaps in Hispanic Americans' academic achievement appear at age 9 and persist through age 17; (c) the school drop-out rate for Hispanic American adolescents is declining but still remains high; (d) Hispanic American high school seniors experience more learning disruptions (e.g., fights, gang behaviors) than their European American counterparts; (e) Hispanic

Americans take fewer advanced mathematics and science courses; and (f) Hispanic Americans have lower educational aspirations and are about half as likely to complete 4 years of college ("Educating Hispanic students," 1996).

Hispanic American Adolescents

Social and Cultural Description

Hispanic American adolescents represent a sizable percentage of the Hispanic population. According to the U.S. Census Bureau (2004), 3,247,000 Hispanic American adolescents (15–19 years) were living in the United States in 2004. They represent a diverse group with varying levels of acculturation, socioeconomic class, proficiency in English, and region of residency within the United States.

Forces that influence the lives of Hispanic American adolescents include the social and psychological changes that accompany adolescence as well as the cultural customs and traditions considered sacred to the culture. These two forces, along with Hispanics' tendencies to speak only Spanish in the home or to live in predominantly bilingual areas, challenge both adolescents and their counselors.

Several Hispanic American cultural characteristics illustrate that European American standards are inappropriate when intervening with Hispanic Americans. First, European Americans often believe that equality within the family and self-advancement are consistent with the ideals of freedom, democracy, and progress. In contrast, Mexican Americans value placing one's family above self. Second, the adolescent male must adhere to cultural expectations or risk the loss of respect for himself and his manhood.

Too often, Hispanic American adolescents are negatively stereotyped. Emphasis has been placed on such issues as delinquency, gangs, drug and alcohol abuse, poor academic achievement, and dropping out of school, rather than on the more average adolescent behavior in the culture. This is not to suggest that the negative aspects should be ignored, only that they should receive an objective and cautious interpretation.

A Focus on Research 13.3 looks at anger in adolescents, especially in Hispanic American adolescents.

A cultural description of Spanish-speaking people must include an understanding of certain attributes that play a significant role (in varying degrees, depending on the individual group) in the Hispanic American culture. These attributes include the following:

Spanish Term	Meaning
afecto	literally "affect"; refers to warmth and demonstrativeness
dignidad	dignity; one may oppose another person but should never take away his or her dignity
machismo	a strong sense of masculine pride; sometimes taken by non-Hispanics to imply an innate inferiority of women
respeto	respect for authority, family, and tradition

A FOCUS ON RESEARCH 13.3

Anger in Adolescents

Reyes, Meininger, Liehr, Chan and Mueller (2003) explain that experience, and expression, of anger are common occurrences throughout the adolescent years. Feelings of unjust treatment or of frustration often precipitate anger arousal. Although the experience of anger and the expression of anger are normal for everyone, emerging data suggest a relationship between how anger is experienced and expressed and risk factors for cardiovascular disease. Significant relationships have been found between anger control and a number of health conditions, for example, blood pressure and overall current health.

The State-Trait Anger Expression Inventory (STAXI), a questionnaire, is designed to measure the experience and expression of anger. It is well established with African and European Americans, but Reyes, Meininger, Liehr, Chan and Mueller (2003)

maintain that little is known about its use with Hispanic American adolescents. The objectives of this study was to test ethnic, sex, and age differences in STAXI scores in a sample of 11-year-old to 16-year-old African, Hispanic, and European Americans, with an emphasis on Hispanic youth for whom no data are available.

Reyes, Meininger, Liehr, Chan and Mueller (2003) reported that all scales of the STAXI, excluding one scale, have adequate reliability and validity for African, Hispanic, and European adolescents (11–16 years of age).

Source: "Anger, and in adolescents: Sex, ethnicity, age difference, and psychometric properties," by L. R. Reyes, J. C. Meininger, P. Liehr, W. Chan, W. H. Mueller, 2003, _Nursing Research, 52_ (1), pp. 2–11.

Poverty continues to plague the Hispanic American population and affects developing adolescents. Although some Puerto Ricans have experienced substantial improvement in socioeconomic status, poverty continues to be widespread in this population. For example, 26.2% of adolescents aged 12 to 17 years live below the poverty level (U.S. Census Bureau, 2004). Furthermore, the unemployment rate of Puerto Rican males is twice as high as for European American males. Another factor contributing to the poor socioeconomic status of Hispanic Americans is the increase in the number of female-headed households (Latino Americans: The face of the future, 1999).

Determining appropriate programs and efforts has proved difficult because of the paucity of research on the mental health needs of some Hispanic adolescents (e.g., Mexican Americans). Despite the many risk factors for Hispanic American adolescents, research and scholarly literature on this population are almost nonexistent. Available research usually focuses on one of four categories: dropping out of school, substance abuse, delinquency, and teenage pregnancy. Although these topics are important, other areas of concern need attention so that counselors, social workers, and other mental health professionals will be able to plan appropriate intervention.

Communication

Spanish-speaking adolescents have much in common with other cultural groups. For example, communication poses a problem outside the immediate neighborhood. Many Hispanic Americans prefer to retain their native tongue rather than make the transition to English.

Because they do not perceive a need to develop proficiency, some Spanish-speaking people continue to risk survival in a bilingual world. In the southwestern United States, many Hispanic Americans live in Spanish-speaking communities that are isolated from the English-speaking community.

A major concern in the education of Hispanic American adolescents is their language proficiency and literacy. Approximately one out of every six Mexican American high school students has not acquired academic English-language skills adequate for the levels of performance required to succeed in the various subject areas. Anyone trying to survive in a society speaking a language that is different from the dominant language can attest to the problems encountered. Communication problems during the adolescent years, however, have the potential for negatively affecting both individual self-concept and developing cultural identity.

Counselors working with significant numbers of Hispanic American adolescents need to address their problems with English. Counselors, especially school counselors, might be called on to work with regular classroom teachers, bilingual specialists, and special educators. Addressing Hispanic Americans' communication challenges is a difficult task because of the tremendous cultural and language diversity. No one model or program meets all of the needs of Hispanic American students.

Families

A counselor's understanding of the family's role in the Hispanic American culture is a prerequisite to understanding and counseling an adolescent client. A deep feeling for family, both immediate and extended, permeates the culture and often becomes the basis for individual and group decisions.

The Hispanic American family is like families of other cultures in some respects and different in others. First, as in Asian American and African American families, the extended kinship network plays a vital role; also, in the Hispanic American family the natural superiority of the male is a basic tenet. Grandparents and other family members may live in the same household or nearby in separate households and visit frequently. Second, with respect to the dominance of the male, in the Puerto Rican family the husband exercises the authority in the family and makes decisions without consulting his wife. It follows that he expects to be obeyed when he gives commands. Third, like American Indian and Asian American families, there is an emphasis on cooperation and placing the family's needs ahead of individual concerns. This does not imply that the family impedes individual achievement and advancement. One must be careful to distinguish between being cooperative and respectful and being docile and dependent. Any discussion of Hispanic American families must consider the effects of acculturation and recognize that second- and third-generation Hispanics have experienced change. Women are demanding more active and equal roles and increasingly are heading households.

Hispanic American adolescents living in single-parent, female-headed households have higher rates of alcohol and drug use, overall risk-taking behaviors, and earlier onset of sexual activity than adolescents living with both parents. These observations suggest that adolescents engage in these risky behaviors in the absence of nuclear family structures. It has also been argued that the quality of the parenting relationship is more significant than the family's composition in predicting social deviance, substance use, and dropping out (Ricciuti, 2004).

Up Close and Personal 13.2 introduces Carlos, a Hispanic American adolescent.

UP CLOSE AND PERSONAL 13.2

Carlos, a Hispanic American Adolescent

Carlos, a 16-year-old Puerto Rican American, lives with his family in a predominantly Hispanic American neighborhood. Although Carlos is experiencing the changes of adolescence, he still enjoys spending time with his brother, 8-year-old Ramon. His Hispanic American friends and peers in the community and school are becoming increasingly important to him, though. He continues to have a close relationship with his immediate family, his grandfather Rafael, who lives in his apartment building, and his married brother, who lives across the street. The Suarez family has financial problems because the father, a laborer, has been unemployed for several weeks. Carlos does not feel too bad about the situation, though, because many of his friends also have fathers who are without jobs.

Carlos is faced with several difficult situations. Although he has never been arrested, several of his friends have been involved in delinquent behavior either in school or in the neighborhood. Because he lacks European American friends at school, he spends much time with several Hispanic American youths in the neighborhood. Although his parents and grandfather do not like these boys, Carlos needs friends, and he is not sure what other friends he can make.

Although he does not always agree with these friends, he does enjoy spending time with them. They all speak Spanish and share Hispanic American values. Besides, they accept him for who he is and do not question his cultural habits.

Carlos wonders which language he will eventually speak. He now speaks English in his classroom because his teachers say he should, but he speaks Spanish at home and in the neighborhood. In fact, he nearly always speaks Spanish with his grandfather. He would not, however, qualify as bilingual. His teachers insist that English is important, yet Carlos feels a commitment to the native language of his parents and friends.

Carlos is experiencing academic problems, which are hurting his self-esteem and making him dislike school. He admits that his communication difficulties might be contributing to his poor academic achievement. Of course, he wants to do better, but if he improves significantly, he might "stand out" among his Hispanic American peers, which could hurt his friendships. Trying to deal with schoolwork, maintain his friendships, and continue to satisfy his parents and family are becoming harder and harder for Carlos to cope with.

Unique Challenges Confronting Hispanic American Adolescents

Counselors working with Hispanic American adolescents need to be aware of several challenges confronting this group. First, they are often stereotyped as being gang members and involved with drugs. Second, these adolescents must try to reconcile the different family structures of the Hispanic American and European American cultures. Third, many adolescent Hispanic American mothers have little chance of escaping the cycle of poverty. Fourth, Spanish-speaking adolescents are faced with recognizing the need to speak the language of the majority culture; although the desire to maintain an allegiance to their native tongue is natural, learning English increases their chances of success in a predominantly English-speaking nation. Problems worsen when adolescents have some type of disabling condition (e.g., a learning disability).

Hispanic American Adults

Social and Cultural Description

Counselors should avoid labeling Hispanic Americans as a single cultural group based on their common language. Race and ethnicity figure largely in the diversity among Hispanic Americans, which is influenced by geographic origin (e.g., Mexico, Cuba, Puerto Rico, El Salvador, the Dominican Republic, Colombia, Venezuela).

Some interesting facts about Hispanic Americans include the following: (a) Large numbers of Hispanic families are concentrated in just a few states, such as California, Texas, and New York; (b) Hispanic families are more highly urbanized than non-Hispanics; (c) the Hispanic population has a younger age distribution; (d) the Hispanic youth population is expected to increase substantially; (e) compared with non-Hispanics, Hispanics have the largest family size (U.S. Census Bureau, 2004).

Hispanic Americans have experienced considerable difficulty achieving academic and economic successes in the United States. Whether a result of cultural discrimination, poor English-language skills, lack of employment skills, or problems coping in a predominantly European American society, the Hispanic American population generally has not made gains comparable to those of other cultural groups. Table 13.3 shows the numbers of Hispanic American adults who live in poverty.

Although the educational level of Hispanic Americans continues to rise, considerable diversity continues to exist among Hispanic groups. Table 13.4 shows Hispanics' educational attainment.

As previously mentioned, Hispanic Americans are reluctant to forsake their native language. They continue to emphasize *respeto, machismo,* and *dignidad* and to persevere in defining rigid family roles.

Recently immigrated Hispanics who have a low sense of intercultural and intracultural proficiency may experience increased stress (Torres & Rollock, 2004). People who have not experienced the trials of acculturation cannot fully understand the loss and enormity of the challenges of the process. Acculturation stress may occur in various stages, just as one experiences stress during the acceptance of any loss, such as the death of a loved one, divorce, or disability. For Hispanic Americans, perhaps the most significant aspect of acculturative stress results from loss of social support in the form of family ties and close interpersonal relationships. Other forms of acculturative stress may result from discrimination on the basis of skin color, the unique Hispanic emphasis on social and family ties, and illegal immigration.

Table 13.3
Hispanic American Adults Living in Poverty (by Age)
Source: Statistical abstracts of the United States 2004–2005 (124th ed.), by U.S. Census Bureau, 2004, Washington, D.C.: Author.

Age	Number	Percentage
25 to 34 years	1,410,000	19%
35 to 44 years	1,016,000	17.2%
45 to 54 years	559,000	15.2%
55 to 59 years	169,000	14.2%

Table 13.4
Educational Attainment Among
Hispanic Americans
Source: Statistical abstracts of the
United States 2004–2005
(124th ed.), by U.S. Census Bureau,
2004, Washington, D.C.: Author.

Educational Attainment	Number	Percentage
Not a High School Graduate	3,617,000	19.8%
High School Graduate	4,039,000	22.1%
Some College/No Degree	2,848,000	15.6%
Associate's Degree	782,000	4.3%
Bachelor's Degree	1,216,000	6.7%
Advanced Degree	692,000	3.8%

Communication

Although discrimination cannot be discounted, the reluctance of the Hispanic American culture to speak English has also contributed to their employment problems; in all likelihood, their ability and reluctance to speak English has also hindered their acculturation. Some Hispanics do not feel confident with their English-speaking skills and, therefore, seek employment only in Spanish-speaking neighborhoods. Others seek jobs that require only minimal speaking. Some feel frustration as employers refuse to employ Hispanics with limited English-speaking abilities. Those who are employed often feel that their limited ability to speak English reduces their chances of promotion and career advancement. Regardless of the reasons, lack of communication skills often results in Hispanics being unable to build the social and employment networks needed for economic and social success. Lack of English communication skills also affects many Hispanics' educational opportunities. Although they see the need for education and employment training, their communication skills prohibit them from filling out applications, seeking financial assistance, and actually attending classes.

The communication problem is not only a first-generation problem. Many second- and third-generation Hispanics continue to have difficulty with English. Even younger generation Hispanic Americans tend to speak Spanish or "Hispanicized English" in the home. Their limited English-language skills have been debilitating and have contributed to increased discrimination and lack of opportunity.

Families

Table 13.5 shows U.S. Census Bureau (2004) statistics for the number of children in Hispanic American families.

Table 13.5
Hispanic Families and Their
Children (Under Age 18)
Source: Statistical abstracts of the
United States 2004–2005
(124th ed.), by U.S. Census Bureau,
2004, Washington, D.C.: Author.

Family size	Number
No Children	3,385,000
1 Child	2,097,000
2 Children	2,032,000
3+ Children	1,575,000

To avoid generalizations about the entire Hispanic culture, our discussion here is organized around the three prominent Spanish-speaking groups currently residing in the United States: Puerto Ricans, Mexicans, and Cubans.

Puerto Ricans.   Although cultural differences exist between Puerto Ricans raised in Puerto Rico and those raised in the United States, both groups differ distinctly from the dominant European American culture, and both suffer disadvantages in that culture.

Puerto Rican families provide economic and emotional support. The family is viewed as the only area where people are free to be themselves and where people come for affection and love, but the family is also an institution that historically has oppressed women. Underlying this gender division of labor is a patriarchal ideology that emphasizes men's sexual freedom, virility, and aggressiveness, and women's sexual repression and submission (Toro-Morn, 1996).

Puerto Ricans place value on personalism, another cherished cultural characteristic. Puerto Ricans define their self-worth in terms of qualities that give them self-respect and earn them the respect of others. For example, a man can achieve respect by being able to protect and provide for his family and by being honorable and respectful in his behavior. Focusing on inner qualities allows people to experience self-worth, regardless of worldly success or failure. Respect plays a role in preserving the network of close personal relationships. Respect for authority is first learned in the home and then expands to the outside world. For example, many Puerto Ricans believe that children should call an adult by his or her first name only if they also use Don, Doña, Señor, or Señora. Also, making eye contact with strangers, especially women and children, is unacceptable (Garcia-Preto, 1996b).

A deep appreciation of family life characterizes Puerto Rican families, regardless of socioeconomic status. Because the family unit is fundamental, individuals tend to evaluate themselves in relation to other members of the family. Another important characteristic is the notion of male superiority, with the male considered to be the unquestioned head of the household. Although Hispanic women continue to redefine their roles, the women in Puerto Rican families still occupy clearly subordinate roles.

Mexicans.   As a group, Mexican Americans are typically proportionately more disadvantaged educationally and socioeconomically compared to their European counterparts; demographically speaking, these characteristics represent a real vulnerability for this group with regard to their mental health status and clearly suggest the need to ensure the presence of available, affordable, and effective health and mental health services for this population (Prieto, McNeill, Walls, & Gomez, 2001).

In a discussion of Mexican families, regional, generational, and socioeconomic variations make generalizations difficult. The following characteristics for the most part pertain to Mexican Americans of relatively poor and working-class backgrounds who migrated to the United States during the past three or four decades. First, the family includes grandparents, uncles, aunts, and cousins. Children who were orphaned or whose parents divorced may be cared for in the household of a relative. Second, a degree of interdependence characterizes this supportive network. Family functions such as caretaking, disciplining of the children, problem-solving, managing finances, and providing emotional support are shared. Third, the family protects the individual and demands loyalty. Family cohesiveness and respect for parental authority endure throughout an individual's lifetime. Autonomy and individual achievement are not particularly emphasized.

Cubans.   The Cuban American population shares many characteristics with Mexican Americans. The family is the most important social unit in Cuban life and is characterized by a bond of loyalty. This bond unites family members, as well as a network of friends, neighbors, and community members. As in other Hispanic cultures, the man is the leader and provider of the household. If the man is unable to find work, his self-esteem is damaged, and he may lose the respect of his wife and children. This loss of respect is likely to result in marital difficulties, especially if the wife assumes the role of economic provider.

Unique Challenges Confronting Hispanic American Adults

Regardless of the Hispanic group, professionals need to provide experiences that meet the needs of Hispanic immigrants. Holman (1997) maintains that two prescriptions for helping newly arrived immigrants are to (a) lessen the intimidation factors and (b) remove the communication barriers. More specifically, Holman suggests that professionals should (a) realize that some parents will lack formal education, (b) recognize that economic survival is a primary concern for many immigrant families, (c) validate parents' strengths and familial resources, (d) recognize that families bring a rich social context, and (e) familiarize families with the procedures and organization of their local schools.

Hispanic American adults, who are no longer children or adolescents in developmental transition, have major responsibilities, such as being financial providers. Poverty continues to be a problem among some Hispanic people. According to the U.S. Census Bureau (2004), 7,797,000 (22.6%) of Hispanics live below the poverty level.

Salgado and colleagues (2000) studied rural Mexican women to identify specific sexual practices, coping strategies in sex-related situations, and fears and concerns regarding sexual intercourse. The researchers sought to determine how these elements place Mexican women at risk for HIV/AIDS. The researchers concluded these rural Mexican women were at high risk for sexual-related transmission of HIV/AIDS; lacked the power to negotiate safe sex practices with their husbands due to the cultural norms that promote male dominance and female submissiveness; had information regarding HIV/AIDS transmission and ways of prevention (however, they did not evaluate their own risk); and considered sexual intercourse pleasing to their husbands and a part of the cultural obligations assigned to Mexican married women.

Salgado and colleagues (2000) suggested development of intervention programs that include the following:

1. Prevention strategies should not separate the risk for infection from the psychological, social, economic, and cultural contexts in which these women live.

2. Prevention strategies should emphasize the importance of women's roles in all societies, not only for their reproductive function but also as productive members of society.

3. Prevention strategies should acknowledge the fact that successful avoidance of HIV/AIDS will be possible only when women have the economic and social power to say "no" (p. 107) to their male partners without risking their lives or security for having made such a decision.

As A Focus on Research 13.4 explains, healthcare disparities exist for Hispanic Americans. Weinick, Jacobs, Stone, Ortega, and Burstin (2004) report that Hispanic Americans have poorer

A FOCUS ON RESEARCH 13.4

Hispanic Healthcare Disparities

Hispanic Americans are often treated as a monolithic ethnic group with a single pattern of healthcare utilization. However, there are considerable differences within this population. This healthcare disparity requires first understanding (and in fact, challenging) the myth that the Hispanic culture is a monolithic population. These authors examined the association between use of healthcare services and Hispanic Americans' country of ancestry or origin, language of interview, and length of time in the United States.

Weinick, Jacobs, Stone, Ortega, and Burstin (2004) report the following:

- Hispanics are less likely to be offered employer-sponsored health insurance and to be insured comparable to whites.

- Many Hispanics are recent immigrants to the U.S. and lack familiarity with healthcare systems.

- Some Hispanic fear being deemed a public charge.

- U.S. born Hispanic women are more likely to be insured, to receive certain healthcare services, and to have earlier detection of breast cancer than immigrant Hispanics.

- Some Hispanics face language barriers as a result of lack of providers who speak their native language.

Weinick, Jacobs, Stone, Ortega, and Burstin (2004) summarized that improvement efforts that rely on population data for Hispanics as a single group could miss important opportunities for more targeted initiatives that meet the needs of at-risk Hispanic subpopulations if improvements are planned for the entire Hispanic population without regard to factors such as language, duration of residence in the U.S., and country of origin.

Source: "Hispanic healthcare disparities: Challenging the myth of a monolithic Hispanic population," by R. M. Weinick, E. A. Jacobs, L. C. Stone, A. N. Ortega, and H. Burstin, 2004, *Medical Care, 42* (2), pp. 313–320.

health status and higher incidences of illnesses such as diabetes, human immunodeficiency infection, and cervical cancer compared with non-Hispanic whites. Despite this, Hispanics use fewer healthcare services and are less likely to have entered the health care system for any type of care than white non-Hispanic Americans.

Problems can result from discrimination, prejudice, and a lack of appropriate social skills for coping in a predominantly European American society. Counselors who understand the complexity of the Hispanic culture and the problems confronting Hispanic American adults will want to keep the following points in mind as they work with their clients:

• Recommending that the client speak only English may be too much to ask, especially of a first-generation Hispanic. Nonetheless, the client should be made aware that some proficiency in communicating in the language of the majority culture contributes to obtaining employment and to beginning the acculturation process.

• Hispanic Americans need help improving their educational attainment. They must be encouraged to finish high school and to seek entry into college. Only 6.7% had a bachelor's degree in 2000 (U.S. Census Bureau, 2004).

• Meeting the challenge with respect to education will allow Hispanic Americans to improve their employment possibilities. A move away from low-level jobs to positions of

UP CLOSE AND PERSONAL 13.3

Carla, a Hispanic American Adult

Carla, a Puerto Rican American, just turned 35, and her family life is causing her much concern. Her husband, Oscar, works intermittently as a laborer on various construction crews. Despite the fact that the family lives in a large and growing urban area, Oscar has been fairly lucky in getting jobs; however, he has been out of work for several weeks, and his chances of being called back to work in the near future appear to be slim. To make financial ends meet, Oscar and Carla have borrowed some money from their married son, who lives across the street in their predominantly Hispanic American neighborhood. But what will happen if Oscar is not called back to work soon? How will they make ends meet? Carla suggested that she apply for a job with a company that cleans offices at night, but Oscar was vehemently opposed. So Carla is stuck; she has no other choice but to do what Oscar says. And although the money is sorely needed, she realizes that

Oscar's pride is involved; after all, it is the man's responsibility to support the family.

Besides Oscar's layoff, there are other things to worry about: The neighborhood is becoming increasingly dangerous, her son Ramon is having school problems, her son Carlos's friends are a bad influence on him, and Carla cannot change Oscar's attitude about her taking a job. In the face of all this, Carla feels powerless. She wants to help her family financially and emotionally, but Oscar makes the decisions. He has the final word on everything, including money and child-rearing. Even though it is she who takes care of the children, Oscar tells her what behavior is appropriate for them. She sees that some younger women in the neighborhood are beginning to question their husbands. Many of them seem to be much more assertive than she. She sometimes wonders, "What would Oscar's reaction be if I just got a job and went to work?"

greater responsibility will require better education, the ability to speak English fluently, and the determination to fight discrimination by informing people about positive aspects of the Hispanic American culture and demanding guaranteed legal rights.

Counselors, especially those in college counseling centers, may be called upon to provide professional intervention for high-ability (or perhaps low-ability) students with learning disabilities.

Up Close and Personal 13.3 presents a portrait of Carla, a Hispanic American adult.

Hispanic American Elderly

Social and Cultural Description

Table 13.6 shows the numbers of Hispanic Americans aged 65 to 99 years living in the United States. Despite the growth of a large Hispanic American population, little systematic research has been conducted on elderly Hispanic Americans. Attempts to create generalizations about Cubans in Florida, Puerto Ricans in New York, and Mexicans in California are not likely to result in meaningful conclusions. Significant cultural differences, together with stereotypes about the elderly, frequently lead to misunderstandings; hence, counselors must identify specific subgroups and consider the individual client within this subgroup.

Table 13.6
Hispanic American Population
(Age 65 and Older)

Source: Statistical abstracts of the United States 2004–2005 (124th ed.), by U.S. Census Bureau, 2004, Washington, D.C.: Author.

Age	Number
65 to 69 years	683,000
70 to 74 years	539,000
75 to 79 years	397,000
80 to 84 years	244,000
85 to 89 years	119,000
90 to 94 years	54,000
95 to 99 years	16,000

Although the Hispanic American population is concentrated largely in the southwestern states, such as California and Texas, clusters reside in other geographic regions. The various subgroups tend to remain distinct with respect to location. For example, most Hispanic Americans in California and Texas are of Mexican descent, whereas a majority of those living in New York and New Jersey are of Puerto Rican descent.

Lack of education, unemployment, and low income pose problems for a significant segment of the Hispanic American community. Of all the minority elderly populations, Hispanic elderly are the least educated. The proportion without formal schooling is nine-fold greater than for elderly European Americans; most Hispanic Americans age 65 and older have little formal education. Not surprisingly, this lack of education has consequences that extend to employment and income. Income levels for elderly Hispanic Americans are dismal. Poverty rates are higher in nonmetropolitan areas than in metropolitan areas, and more Hispanic American women than men experience poverty. Table 13.7 shows the number of Hispanic American elders living in poverty.

Concern over potential health problems or declining health also characterizes Hispanic American elderly. They tend to have more activity limitations and spend more days per year in bed because of illness than other minority cultures. Common health problems include hypertension (high blood pressure), cancer, high cholesterol levels, diabetes, and arthritis (U.S. Census Bureau, 2004).

Zuniga (1997) cites four common myths about the Mexican American elderly that have the potential for affecting counseling intervention:

- *Myth 1: Mexican American elderly are surrounded by family systems that create a buffer for maladaptive behavior.* In reality, although more Mexican American elderly than European American elderly live with families, changes in family systems have occurred because of the stresses of modern living, increased acculturation rates, education and upward mobility, and the children relocating to various parts of the country. These factors often result in Mexican American elderly feeling alone and abandoned.

Table 13.7
Number/Percentage of Hispanic Americans Living in Poverty

Source: Statistical abstracts of the United States 2004–2005 (124th ed.), by U.S. Census Bureau, 2004, Washington, D.C.: Author.

Age	Number	Percentage
65 to 74 years	247,000	20.2%
75 years and older	192,000	23.1%

- *Myth 2: Mexican Americans encourage a reverence for elderly people, so in old age they take on crucial roles in their family and community systems.* Mexican American elderly sometimes serve as historians, counselors, or educators of the younger generations. Traditionally, the elderly have been given special status for their experience and wisdom. Yet, family structures have changed as generations have acculturated; support and respect for the elderly have declined. Younger generations sometimes do not want to listen to the stories of their elders; this reluctance contributes to the elderly feeling useless and unimportant in life.

- *Myth 3: Mexican Americans do not put their seniors into nursing homes; instead, they provide for their long-term care at home.* Although most Mexican Americans feel a sense of embarrassment when placing an elderly family member into a nursing home, the pressures of having multiple jobs, no caregiver in the home for the elder, and acculturation can result in family's placing the elder in a nursing home.

- *Myth 4: Mexican American families do not abuse their elderly family members.* Although research on this topic is somewhat sparse, evidence suggests that abuse does occur (e.g., economic exploitation, psychological and physical abuse). Abuse of the Mexican American elderly probably is rare, but counselors need to be aware that this problem does exist (Zuniga, 1997).

Communication

The low academic attainment and low socioeconomic conditions of elderly Hispanic Americans are caused, at least in part, by communication difficulties. The elderly often speak no English; specifically, one in four does not speak any English at all (Zuniga, 1997). Also, many older Hispanic Americans do not seek government benefits because of their inability to communicate in English. They feel frustrated and overwhelmed when they have to speak and write in English. Some take a bilingual person to help them with the application requirements.

To avoid communication problems, some elderly Hispanics tend to live in Spanish-speaking neighborhoods in which English is rarely spoken, which interferes with their acculturation. The convenience of being able to communicate in one's native language also undermines serious efforts toward learning to speak more fluent English. The growing number of newspapers and radio and television stations that are geared specifically toward Hispanic American audiences contribute to the problem.

Families

Hispanic American elderly are twice as likely to have difficulty with activities of daily living (e.g., preparing a meal, managing money) as non-Hispanic elderly. About one-third of elderly, almost twice as many as non-Latino elderly, live with children, relatives, or someone other than a relative (Zuniga, 1997).

The importance of family kinship networks among Puerto Rican Americans can be seen in their effort to provide for the elderly in their own homes. One study (Angel, Angel, McClellan, & Markides, 1996) examined preferred living arrangements of elderly Hispanics, specifically Mexican Americans. The study revealed that elderly people's behavior indicates a desire to live with the spouse while he or she is alive or with family members after the spouse's death. The researchers concluded that, for many older Mexican Americans, especially those who are more traditionally

UP CLOSE AND PERSONAL 13.4

Papa Rafael, a Hispanic American Elder

Papa Rafael, age 75, enjoys living close to his family. Having family members nearby means a great deal to him and provides many satisfying moments. His problems are not unlike those of many of his elderly friends in his predominantly Hispanic American community. Although the community includes diverse Hispanic cultures, most elderly worry about inadequate finances and failing health.

Right now, Papa Rafael's concerns are directed toward his family and their financial condition. His son has not worked in several weeks. He is aware that his daughter-in-law Carla wants to get a job, but in his view, "It just wouldn't be right." Papa Rafael wishes he could help his family financially, but he himself is fairly poor. He has a little money saved from when he was employed,

but this barely covers his own needs. Nothing is left over to share with his family. Besides, he thinks he needs to hold on to every penny now because the future is uncertain. Aside from his savings, his only other income is the meager government benefits he receives.

Papa Rafael is at a reflective age. He sees a changing Hispanic American culture and has been known to say, "Too many of our young people are like the Europeans." It shocks him to see how some children in the neighborhood treat their parents. Surely, respect for the elderly is not valued as it used to be, he thinks.

Papa Rafael's problems, like those of many elderly people, are associated with failing health and family issues. At times, these concerns seem almost too much for him to bear.

oriented (including the foreign-born), living with their children is a desirable alternative after the death of a spouse. Only a minority of elderly Mexican Americans in the study indicated a preference for a nursing home. Nevertheless, social change and cultural and structural assimilation take their toll on family life. For Mexican Americans, economic constraints limit options in living arrangements, and the necessity for women to work limits their availability as full-time caregivers for older parents (Angel et al., 1996).

In short, Hispanic American customs and practices include a respect for the elderly and a concern for their welfare. Keeping the elderly in the home, or at least in the immediate community so that younger generations can provide care, appears to be the current norm. It may be safely assumed, however, that younger generations will continue to lean toward stronger immediate families, which may leave the elderly in an increasingly precarious situation. Although this trend is not yet firmly established, it is quite possible that Hispanic American clients will increasingly bring such familial problems to counseling sessions.

Papa Rafael, an elderly Hispanic American, is featured in Up Close and Personal 13.4.

Unique Challenges Confronting Hispanic American Elderly

Although Hispanic American elderly have undoubtedly experienced economic, personal, and social progress, considerable hurdles remain: illiteracy, unemployment, malnutrition, language, poverty, and discrimination. The following five specific areas need immediate attention:

1. raising educational and income levels and decreasing the incidence of malnutrition,

2. increasing understanding of the role of the elderly in the family,

3. encouraging proficiency in English to allow the elderly to move out of Spanish-speaking enclaves,

4. directing attention to problems of the elderly and ridding the elderly of their stereotypical image, and

5. improving the general health status of the elderly, which will contribute to their overall well-being.

The extent to which Hispanic American elderly improve their lives will depend largely on the effort they put forth to raise their economic status and to improve their ability to speak English. Counselors working with elderly Hispanic Americans can contribute significantly to these efforts by understanding both the culture and the elderly period of the lifespan. Although challenges to both Hispanic Americans and counselors can be formidable, the future might reflect a genuine concern for the minority elderly and set the stage for long-overdue changes and accomplishments.

A Point of Departure: Challenges Confronting Counselors of Hispanic Americans

Mental health providers, regardless of their cultural background, will be challenged to understand some Hispanics' attitudes toward the healing professions. Three widespread ethnomedical systems are found among Hispanics in the United States—Espiritismo (spiritualism), Santeria, and Curanderismo—associated with the three major ethnic communities of Puerto Ricans, Cubans, and Mexicans. Each is a synthesis of beliefs and practices derived from separate neocolonial histories. Espiritismo is from a conjunction of European (French) and Afro-Caribbean traditions, and Santeria is from a conjunction of folk Catholicism and West African traditions (Koss-Chioino, 2000). Curandero literally means "healer" (Kossz-Chionio, 2000, p. 345). Stemming from the verb *curar* ("to heal"), *curanderos(as)* are recognized by Mexican Americans as having the special ability to heal. Curanderismo is a medical system, a view of healing with historical roots that combine Aztec, Spanish, spiritualistic, homeopathic, and scientific elements. Confusion often exists about the role of *curanderos(as)*, because these folk healers provide a wide range of services to their communities, and these services vary from region to region across the United States (Stauber, 1994).

Still other challenges confront counselors providing mental health intervention to Hispanic Americans. They will be called on to understand and respond appropriately to many Hispanic Americans' (a) reluctance to forsake Spanish and to commit to becoming proficient in English; (b) allegiance to cultural values and the stress often resulting from acculturation; (c) unemployment, poverty, and lack of education; and (d) stereotyping and discrimination. Non-Hispanic counselors might have a difficult time understanding this diverse culture of people. Also, counselors will be challenged to plan for Hispanic clients in the four lifespan stages. The problems of adolescents and the elderly will differ significantly, just as with other lifespan stages.

Summary

The rapidly increasing Hispanic American population and their many problems (e.g., lack of English-language skills, low educational attainment, unemployment, poverty, discrimination) suggest that counselors, especially those living in states with significant Hispanic populations, will be called on to provide culturally and lifespan-appropriate counseling intervention. Successful counseling, although not easy, is attainable. Counselors will need to prepare themselves professionally and personally to understand the diverse Hispanic cultures and heritages and to provide intervention that reflects these differences. The rewards of understanding Hispanic cultures and being able to provide effective intervention will be worth the time and effort expended.

Suggested Readings

Honda, K. (2005). Psychosocial correlates of smoking cessation among elderly ever-smokers in the United States. *Addictive Behaviors, 30*(2), 375–381. Honda found that strategies tailored to psychological distress and beliefs about smoking health would aid in successful cessation, especially for the Hispanic elderly.

Pole, N., Best, S.R., Metzler, T., & Marmar, C. R. (2005). Why are Hispanics at greater risk of PTSD? *Cultural Diversity and Ethnic Minority Psychology, 11*(2), 144–161. These authors studied posttraumatic stress disorders among Hispanic Americans and suggest that PTSD symptoms may be important for the prevention of mental illness.

Radina, M. E., & Barber, C. E. (2004). Utilization of formal support services among Hispanic Americans caring for aging parents. *Journal of Gerontological Social Work, 43* (2/3), 5–23. Maintaining that Hispanic caregivers are less likely to use formal support services than non-Hispanic white families, these researchers explore patterns of caregiving with respect to within-group differences.

Torres, L., & Rollock, D. (2004). Acculturative stress among Hispanics: The role of acculturation, coping, and intercultural competence. *Journal of Multicultural Counseling and Development, 32* (3), 155–167. These authors studied recently immigrated Hispanic adults and found a low sense of intercultural and intracultural proficiency may result in increased stress.

Counseling Hispanic American Clients

Questions to Be Explored

1. What unique challenges can counselors expect when intervening with Hispanic American children, adolescents, adults, and elders?

2. How can non-Hispanic counselors effectively plan counseling intervention for Hispanic American clients, considering their diverse cultural and individual differences?

3. How has a history of discrimination and injustice affected Hispanic Americans and their worldviews?

4. How can counselors address Hispanic Americans' tendency to underuse counseling services?

5. How can counselors conduct individual, group, and family therapy for Hispanic Americans?

6. What concerns and problems related to development might Hispanic American child, adolescent, adult, and elderly clients present to counselors?

7. How can counselors of differing cultural backgrounds and lifespan stages intervene with Hispanic Americans of other lifespan stages?

8. What additional sources provide information for professionals intervening with Hispanic American children, adolescents, adults, and elders?

Overview

The rapidly increasing Hispanic population (Contreras, Hendrick, & Hendrick, 1996; D'Andrea & Bradley, 1995; Santiago-Rivera, 1995; Smart & Smart, 1995) and Hispanics' economically disadvantaged status (Castaneda, 1994; D'Andrea & Bradley, 1995) suggest that counselors will be called on to provide professional intervention with this group of people. As emphasized in Chapter 13, counselors, social workers, and other professionals should use considerable caution when describing Hispanic Americans. This culture is composed of many diverse groups with historical, economic, social (D'Andrea & Bradley, 1995; Santiago-Rivera, 1995), individual, communication, generational status, rural/urban status, and social class level differences (Castaneda, 1994). The likelihood of counselors intervening with Hispanic American children, adolescents, adults, and elders is increasing. Effective counseling will require an understanding of Hispanic American clients, their respective developmental period, and how cherished cultural beliefs such as *machismo, respeto*, familism, *curerismo*, personalism, and *dignidad* will influence individual, group, and family therapy.

Counselors will need to understand cultural concepts such as *machismo, respeto*, and familism from a Hispanic perspective and how these cherished concepts affect these clients' daily lives and counseling outcomes. As with other cultures, counselors, regardless of their cultural background, have a responsibility to understand and counsel from the Hispanic client's worldview. The Hispanic American community is diverse with respect to almost every conceivable domain, including education level, income, family structure, length of residence in the United States, maintenance of traditional gender roles and cultural values, and occupation. The impact of stereotypes, however, may lead observers and in-group members to have one prototypic idea of what it means to be Hispanic in terms of behaviors, attitudes, and position in society (Niemann, 2001).

Another difference counselors will have to address is that many Hispanic Americans continue to show an allegiance to the Spanish language. Hispanic Americans may hold on to their native language for several reasons: (a) They expect to return to their native lands, (b) they live in Spanish-speaking enclaves, or (c) they lack the educational opportunities to learn English. Regardless of the reason, counselors likely will encounter clients with limited English-speaking abilities.

Hispanic American Children

Potential Problems Warranting Counseling Intervention

Problems that Hispanic American children may experience include

- failure to develop a strong cultural identity and a positive self-concept;
- adverse effects of stereotypes;
- distrust of and hostility toward European American professionals;
- Conflicts between use of "home language" and "school language"; as well as the child's belief that speaking English is disloyal to the "native tongue";
- inability to reconcile loyalties to conflicting values of Hispanic and European American cultures;
- different cultural expectations; for example, rigid gender roles—boys are "manly" and girls are "retiring and reserved";
- adverse effects of racism, injustices, and discrimination;
- physical, psychosocial, and intellectual differences;
- socialization to a peer-centered world;
- delayed psychosocial development if peers consider Hispanic American children inferior or troublemakers;

A FOCUS ON RESEARCH 14.1

Perceived School Environments, Perceived Discrimination, and School Performance Among Children of Mexican Immigrants

Using the Children of Immigrants Longitudinal Study, Stone and Han examined the influence of perceived discrimination. The overall purposes were to understand whether Mexican-origin youth perceived discrimination and also whether perceptions of discrimination in school environments affected school performance.

Their results were consistent with anthropological findings that suggest youth perceptions of their immediate environments and the larger social–cultural context are associated with their perceptions of discrimination and their performance in schools. Students who perceived poor-quality school environments had lower grades and were most likely to be generally off-track in schools. Stone and Han (2005) suggest it is important to note that the perceptions of poor school quality were positively related to perceptions of discrimination, suggesting that perceptions of discrimination may have effects on school performance.

Source: "Perceived school environments, perceived discrimination, and school performance among children of Mexican immigrants," by S. Stone, and M. Han, 2005, *Children and Youth Services Review, 27* (1), pp. 51–66.

- lack of personal resources caused by widespread low socioeconomic status; and
- reconciling family loyalties with individual desires during a time of transition from a parent-centered world to a peer-centered world.

Stone and Han (2005) maintain that the last two decades have witnessed enormous growth in the Latino student population. Recent estimates suggest the Latino drop-out rate is four times larger than that of White and twice as large as that of African American students. This is especially true of Mexican American students, who constitute the majority of the Latino student population. In A Focus on Research 14.1, Stone and Han examine how perceived discrimination affects school performance.

Counseling Considerations

Counseling Hispanic American children requires knowledge of individual Hispanic cultures whenever possible. Although Hispanic Americans are often considered a single cultural group because of their similarities in language, values, and traditions, the Hispanic American culture represents many heterogeneous subcultures, each possessing unique traits. Counselors of Hispanic American children should understand that these children have been taught to distrust European American professionals. This distrust can result in children being hesitant to disclose personal information.

When counseling Hispanic American children, counselors should understand

- their own cultural backgrounds, beliefs, values, and assumptions;
- Hispanic Americans' cultural backgrounds, as well as their historical and contemporary contributions;

- problems that Hispanic American children face and how individual children may be helped;
- difficulties Spanish-speaking children may encounter in bilingual settings, as well as their nonverbal mannerisms (e.g., preference for standing close);
- children's cognitive and psychosocial development;
- the importance of both immediate and extended families; and
- intricate relationships between culture and counseling and the role culture plays in counseling intervention.

Individual and Group Therapy.   What should counselors consider when planning intervention for Hispanic American children? Professionals will want to assist these children in coping with changing demands.

Counselors should consider four counseling priorities when intervening with Hispanic American children: (1) language, communication, and cognitive development; (2) expansion of career choice options; (3) personal respect and pride in the Hispanic culture; and (4) personal value exploration. Although all four factors are key to the effectiveness of the counseling process, counselors who respect and convey an appreciation for a child's cultural heritage can have a positive impact on children and their developing identities and self-concepts.

Counselors can also take other steps to improve their effectiveness in counseling Hispanic American children. Counselors will find it beneficial to be able to speak both English and Spanish fluently. They should also have firsthand experiences with, and an understanding of, the Spanish culture. Counselors will also find it beneficial to refine their helping characteristics, such as empathy, warmth, positive regard, congruence, and authenticity.

Group therapy has the potential for helping Hispanic American children work toward solving school and home problems. School counselors often perceive group counseling as particularly effective for furthering Hispanic American children's skills in expressing their feelings in English, stimulating self-respect and pride in Hispanic culture, and clarifying personal values.

Family Therapy.   The belief that a dysfunction within the family affects all family members in some manner especially holds true for Hispanic American families. Effective family counseling requires including all the children in family therapy, not just the child with the problem. The complex relationships surrounding the immediate and extended Hispanic American families contribute to the effectiveness of family counseling (Thompson & Rudolph, 1988).

The cultural concept of familism is so important that Hispanic parents and families teach their children early to sacrifice self-interest to help other family members and the family unit as a whole (Ho, 1987).

Up Close and Personal 14.1 looks at a counselor's efforts with Ramon, a Hispanic American child.

To enhance the effectiveness of family counseling with Hispanic Americans, the counselor should (a) respect the family's hierarchical structure by interviewing the parents first and then the children and by communicating in Spanish with the parents and in English with the children to delineate blurred generational boundaries (Falicov, 1996), and (b) recognize that Hispanic Americans learned early to be cooperative in interpersonal relationships (Ho, 1987).

UP CLOSE AND PERSONAL 14.1

Counseling Ramon, a Hispanic American Child

Eight-year-old Ramon was referred to the European American school counselor by his teacher, who was concerned about Ramon's academic achievement, communication problems, and self-concept. "I don't know what to do with Ramon," Mr. Perkins complained. "I encourage him, yet he just doesn't seem interested." After reading the referral sheet and speaking with Ramon, the counselor concluded that the child did have problems: low socioeconomic status, poor grades, weak self-concept, and communication difficulties. Plus, Ramon gave every indication of not trusting the counselor or the teacher.

The counselor, realizing he had to begin slowly, encouraged Ramon to speak with and trust him. In early sessions, the counselor chose to emphasize Ramon and his cultural background: his family, his language, and his life. Ramon hesitatingly began to trust and to speak—much to the counselor's surprise—in mixed English and Spanish. The counselor learned that

Ramon came from a traditional Puerto Rican family and Spanish was spoken in the home. The counselor also saw evidence of Ramon's reading difficulties and behavior problems.

The counselor decided that he had to work to improve Ramon's self-concept and arrange appropriate English instruction and remedial tutoring to help him catch up academically. The counselor recognized that he would have to proceed cautiously to convince Ramon he could still maintain his cultural identity and respect without getting into fights with other children. Finally, the counselor decided to arrange a conference with Ramon's parents, who might be able to help the boy if they knew exactly what to do. Although little could be done about Spanish being spoken in the home, the counselor would explain to the parents the conflict that Ramon experienced because of the dual language situation.

Hispanic American Adolescents

Potential Problems Warranting Counseling Intervention

Problems that Hispanic American adolescents may experience include

- failure to develop a positive Hispanic American identity and a healthy self-concept;
- commitment to such cultural values as *machismo, dignidad,* and *respeto,* which other cultures may misunderstand or reject;
- conflicts between other cultural expectations for "self-advancement" and the adolescent's commitment to family over self;
- failure to comply with traditional Hispanic family expectations: strict family roles, innate superiority of males, women assuming subordinate roles;
- academic problems;
- communication problems: reluctance to give up Spanish as the primary language, reluctance to move out of a Spanish-speaking enclave;
- developmental differences (e.g., height, weight);
- adverse effects of racism and discrimination; and
- media stereotypes, such as being gang members and participating in ganglike behavior.

Although HIV infections affect men of all cultures, Latino young men who have sex with men are contracting HIV at a disproportionately higher rate than young men of other cultures. In fact, among men between the ages of 15 and 22 years enrolled in the multisite Young Men's Survey, Latino's were twice as likely as their White counterparts to be HIV positive (Agronick, O'Donnell, Stueve, Doval, Duran, & Vargo, 2004). In Gender Perspectives 14.1, Agronick, O'Donnell, Stueve, Doval, Duran, & Vargo (2004) investigate this problem and report findings that suggest prevention programs to address these risky sexual behaviors.

According to Zayas, Kaplan, Turner, Romano, and Gonzalez-Ramos (2000), mental health clinicians in inner city mental health centers serving high concentrations of Hispanic American residents have observed that many of the adolescent Hispanic American females are referred after suicide attempts. The incidence of suicide attempts in adolescent Hispanic females is 21%, compared with 10.8% and 10.4% in African American and non-Hispanic adolescents, respectively. Also, adolescent Hispanic American girls are twice as likely as their African American and non-Hispanic American counterparts to have made suicide attempts requiring medical attention. On the bright side, the researchers report that the vast majority (80%) of adolescent Hispanic females do not attempt suicide. Zayas and colleagues propose an integrative counseling model that includes sociocultural, familial, psychological, and developmental domains. They discuss these domains in detail and explain how each appears to interact in the suicide attempts of Hispanic adolescent girls. One other point is worthy of mention. According to the authors, the

GENDER PERSPECTIVES 14.1

Sexual Behaviors and Risks Among Bisexual and Gay Latino Men

These authors bring attention to the challenge of young Latino men being HIV positive or having AIDS. One factor that plays a role in sexual behaviors is the prevalence of bisexuality. Although correct estimates are difficult to determine, Agronick, O'Donnell, Stueve, Doval, Duran, & Vargo, (2004) believe approximately 20% of men who have sex with men are bisexual. For bisexual and gay Latino men, the developmental passage may be complicated by strong sanctions against homosexuality that are supported by cultural norms stressing the importance of maintaining family and cultural connections. In fact, the strong value placed on family and religion might dictate a concealment of gay identity to protect the family from hurt or stigma.

Agronick, O'Donnell, Stueve, Doval, Duran, & Vargo, (2004) maintain that reaching bisexual men can be challenging. Some Latino men who have sex with men may not recognize themselves in HIV prevention programs primarily targeting gay-identified men and/or men of other cultural backgrounds. It will be important to develop media campaigns that specifically target the patterns of risky behaviors of bisexual men, and crucial to increase public service announcements featuring Latino men who engage in homosexual behavior. Prevention campaigns have the potential to reduce the rate of HIV infections and transmission among Latino men and their partners, members of communities that currently carry a disproportionately large burden of the AIDS epidemic.

This is a highly recommended article on a challenging problem facing young Latino men and their mental health professionals.

Source: "Sexual bahaviors and risks among bisexually and gay-identified young Latino men," by G. Agronick, L. O'Donnell, A. Stueve, A. S. Doval, R. Duran, and S. Vargo, 2004, *AIDS and Behavior, 8* (2), pp. 185–197.

research implies that adolescent Hispanic American girls who have attempted suicide may live in nuclear families that have less contact with extended families than do adolescents who do not attempt suicide. Having aunts, uncles, cousins, and others who can provide support, mentoring, and modeling to adolescent Hispanic girls may help prevent suicide attempts.

Counseling Considerations

Counselors need to understand the challenges facing adolescent Hispanic Americans. The Hispanic American male must eventually find gainful employment in a society where Hispanic American rates of unemployment and poverty run high and where limited education attainment prevents them from competing in the job market. The Hispanic American female probably will witness such social changes as greater equality among the sexes and more women in the workforce, perhaps at higher salaries than the often poorly educated Hispanic American men.

The diversity in Hispanic American cultural characteristics complicates a discussion of generic counseling strategies. Thus, counselors should seek knowledge of the specific population with whom they expect to interact.

When planning counseling intervention, counselors and psychotherapists need to remember that Hispanic American adolescents typically do not seek services themselves. Instead, they usually are referred by social service agencies. Also, parents who want counseling services for their adolescent might face a daunting task: Communication problems, cultural differences, and the lack of health insurance may make arranging for counseling even more difficult (Castaneda, 1994). When Hispanic Americans do seek counseling, they often give somatic attributes to depression, calling it a nervous condition (Santiago-Rivera, 1995). Gloria & Rodriguez (2000), writing specifically about counseling Latino students in university counseling centers (UCCs), maintain that UCC service providers should assess university environment, ethnic identity, acculturation, social support, and other psychosocial issues when providing counseling services and promoting academic persistence with Latino students. Scales and surveys should be identified to measure perceptions of the cultural environment, ethnic loyalty and cultural awareness, ethnic identity, acculturation, acculturative stress, and social support. Beginning the counseling relationship with a paper-and-pencil test might not be the most productive approach and, in fact, might lessen trust with some students. This is particularly true with Latinos, because many value personalism (Gloria & Rodriguez, 2000).

According to Gloria and Rodriguez (2000), asking clients questions such as the following might provide the necessary information when attending to psychosocial issues:

- How do you identify yourself (e.g., Latino, Chicano, Mexican American)?
- What does being Latino (or other self-identifier) mean to you?
- How difficult has it been for you to maintain your cultural values, beliefs, and behaviors on campus?
- What is your primary language?
- Who do you "hang-out" (p. 151) with on campus?
- What holidays and traditions do you and your family celebrate?
- As a Latino (or other identifier), what struggles and challenges have you encountered on campus?

- What expectations does your family have of you?
- Who have you sought help from on campus?
- Who do you seek help from in your home environment?
- If you were at home, how would you resolve these issues?

Researchers also report that less acculturated Mexican Americans are less likely than Whites and more acculturated Mexican Americans to receive mental health services. Less acculturated Mexican Americans tend to perceive psychiatric symptoms as physical problems rather than as emotional or mental problems (Santiago-Rivera, 1995).

When formulating counseling programs, effective counselors should understand several aspects of the Hispanic culture that influence counseling effectiveness. First, family structure and gender roles are important counseling considerations. For example, the extended family structure characteristically includes formalized kinship relations and loyalty to the family, which takes precedence over loyalty to others.

Abreu (2000) maintains that client expectations about counseling have long been considered important in the counseling process. Abreu concluded European American students expected counselors to be less directive and protective than did Chinese American, Iranian American, and African American students, who expected the counselor to be a more directive and nurturing authority figure. In addition, African Americans had lower expectations of personal commitment to the counseling process compared with their European American counterparts. Abreu also maintains that when given a choice, ethnic minority individuals in the United States prefer ethnically similar counselors over European American counselors.

For the most effective counseling intervention, professionals working with Hispanic American adolescents should listen carefully and offer feedback to the clients, identify and label potential problems, raise the clients' expectations for change, and describe the attitudes and feelings of clients according to their cultural perceptions.

Individual and Group Therapy.   The decision whether to use individual or group therapy must be reached with a solid understanding of the culture, the individual, and the advantages and disadvantages of each counseling modality. School counselors working with Hispanic American students sometimes find group counseling to be effective for developing students' skills in expressing their feelings in English, for stimulating self-respect and pride in the Hispanic culture, and for clarifying personal values.

The strengths and characteristics of the group therapist have a significant effect on the outcome and effectiveness of group counseling. Ideally, the group therapist should be young (under age 35) and trained at the master's level or higher. Preferably, all group therapists and the clinical supervisor should be of Hispanic or other ethnic backgrounds that can identify with the struggles adolescents experience. Of course, such a statement does not exclude therapists who have been trained to identify with the life experiences of ethnic minority youths (Baca & Koss-Chioino, 1997). Effective group therapists intervening with adolescents demonstrate

- culturally appropriate displays of firmness and well-defined boundaries;
- culturally appropriate expressions of validation, nurturing, warmth, caring, acceptance, sincerity, and openness;

- active ability to engage participants in either English or Spanish, including the use of culturally relevant humor;

- enthusiasm for cultural heritages expressed in language and communication, clothing, and knowledge of cultural events;

- sincere appreciation of youths; and

- capability to facilitate a sense of commonality. (Baca & Koss-Chioino)

Other effective group therapy techniques include teaching listening skills, focusing on feelings, and reinforcing group members' interactions. Some group counselors begin with individual adolescents and then progress to group therapy after establishing rapport and trust.

Family Therapy.   Family therapy offers particular promise with Hispanic Americans because of the high value placed on family kinship ties, unity, welfare, and honor. Many Hispanic Americans place major emphasis on the group rather than on the individual. This practice translates into a deep sense of family commitment, obligation, and responsibility. The family guarantees protection and caretaking for life as long as a person is a member of the family. A family expectation holds that when a person experiences problems, others will help (Garcia-Preto, 1996a).

Issues brought to family therapy sessions might include conflicts caused by adolescents feeling torn between two worlds. Some adolescents, especially girls, might be caught between the worlds of peers and families; they have spent their childhood in the United States and have learned some cultural rules of other societies, but at home they continue to be expected to behave according to cultural traditions of the family (Garcia-Preto, 1996a). For example, in some Cuban American families, the notion of female purity continues to be strong. In these families childrearing practices often emphasize protection of the girl's innocence even to the extent that chaperones in courtships still prevail (Bernal & Shapiro, 2005). Cuban American females could undoubtedly bring issues arising from such practices to family counseling sessions.

Counselors provide information on group dynamics, and family members actually try to help one another solve their problems. The counselor then meets separately with each family member in an attempt to improve communication skills for use in the group sessions and in private life. The family can be included in therapy in several ways. Counselors may choose to work with the whole family directly or request specific family members to attend counseling sessions. Or the counselor may work with one family member, who in turn works with the family as a group.

Christensen (1989) contends that the counselor should work with both the Hispanic American youth and the family in counseling. If such an arrangement is not possible, the counselor should at least meet with the family at some point. Because Hispanic Americans generally think the family can provide the greatest assistance, involving as many members as possible may result in a cooperative effort to help the client. By involving the family, the counselor also demonstrates awareness that the family can play a therapeutic role and that each person has something to offer.

When working with Puerto Rican adolescents, in particular, suggestions for counselors include

- using active, concrete, and specific counseling approaches;

- developing an awareness of the Puerto Rican culture and the adolescent developmental period;

UP CLOSE AND PERSONAL 14.2

Counseling Carlos, a Hispanic American Adolescent

Carlos, age 16, spoke in both English and Spanish as he told his 45-year-old European American counselor what had happened: He had been referred by the police to the counseling organization that worked with delinquent adolescents. Not having had any previous conflicts with the law, Carlos had been picked up with several other boys who had broken into a vacant store and had done several hundred dollars worth of damage. Carlos's parents had been notified, and his father and older married brother had come to the police station. Carlos further explained that he had been released because he had not actually taken part in the crime and because his father had agreed that Carlos would meet with the counselor.

During his first session, Carlos was cooperative. He discussed his academic problems, his poor self-concept, and his lack of European American friends. Although the counselor insisted that Carlos accept responsibility for his actions, he did believe that Carlos's friends were to blame for his encounter with the police.

In determining counseling priorities, the counselor decided to meet with Carlos on an individual basis for several sessions and then, if Carlos continued to disclose information, switch to group sessions with other Puerto Rican adolescents with similar problems. The counselor's first priorities were to help Carlos to better understand his culture, work to improve Carlos's self-concept, and help him understand his Hispanic identity. As secondary priorities, the counselor would attempt to convince Carlos to accept responsibility for his schoolwork and for selecting more appropriate friends.

- examining prejudices and attitudes toward Puerto Ricans;
- making home visits if possible and making reference to the family during sessions; and
- calling clients by their correct names.

Up Close and Personal 14.2 looks at a counselor's efforts with Carlos, a Hispanic American adolescent.

Hispanic American Adults

Potential Problems Warranting Counseling Intervention

Problems that Hispanic American adults may experience include

- conflicts caused by changing women's roles as women seek to change traditional roles to gain greater equality;
- negative effects of stereotypes that Hispanics are hotblooded, fighters, and drug dealers or gang members;
- the belief that all Hispanic adults, regardless of geographic origin, have the same cultural characteristics;
- commitment to long-held traditions of *respeto*, *machismo*, and *dignidad*, which may slow the acculturation process;

- language problems and communication barriers;

- differing cultural characteristics: allegiance to immediate and extended families, large families, patriarchal families, rigidly defined gender roles (in some cases), and belief of the inherent male superiority (in some cases);

- conflicts caused by the changing role of women (e.g., increasing numbers of Hispanic American women working outside the home);

- low socioeconomic status;

- difficulties encountered in achieving equal educational and employment opportunities in European American society;

- problems associated with midlife: meeting tasks and crises, marriage and family problems;

- lack of positive cultural and individual identity and difficulty in successfully meeting psychosocial crises and developmental tasks;

- frustrations caused by maintaining allegiance and commitment to Hispanic traditions while living in a predominantly European American society; and

- stress caused by the realities of the aging process (e.g., loss of stamina, impaired sexual functioning).

Counseling Considerations

It is essential for professionals planning counseling intervention to understand that Hispanic Americans underuse counseling services. An ethnomedical system, *curanderismo*, is associated with Puerto Rican Americans, Cuban Americans, and Mexican Americans (Koss-Chioini, 2000). Curanderos, often called folk healers, are consulted for many maladies and are trusted the most for folk illnesses with psychological components, such as *susto* ("fright"), *empacho* ("indigestion"), and *envidia* ("envy") (Falicov, 2005).

Similarly, Mexican Americans have a high rate of withdrawal from counseling. Reasons for withdrawal may include communication barriers, unfamiliarity with the mental health system, and counselor insensitivity. Several reasons might explain Hispanic Americans' underuse of counseling and their high withdrawal rates. First, there are too few counselors from Hispanic backgrounds. Second, values inherent in counseling and psychotherapy conflict with values inherent in the client's culture. Third, counselors fail to offer culturally responsive professional intervention (Atkinson, Casas, & Abreu, 1992). Fourth, communication barriers, another reason to underuse or withdraw from therapy, have been effectively addressed by letting the children interpret for the adults. However, counselors should recognize such an arrangement might put Puerto Rican parents in an inferior, powerless position.

Casas and Vasquez (1989) report that the behavioral approach is appropriate for many ethnic minority groups, including Mexican Americans. The behavioral approach has an environmental focus that usually empowers the client to effect change. Such intervention focuses on skill building and moves away from "blaming the victim," which is inherent in some insight-oriented therapies.

Ho (1987) suggests several counseling considerations that apply to most Hispanic American groups:

- Because of the counselor's position of authority, family members might consider it impolite or inappropriate to disagree with her or him during the counseling session.
- To maintain a good working relationship with the Hispanic family, especially with the father, the counselor's communicative style should be businesslike and nonconfrontational.
- Hispanics consider the exertion of personal power to be threatening, disrespectful, and Western; hence, it is likely to alienate them.

Gonzalez (1997) offers the following guidelines for mental health counselors with Mexican American clients:

- Engage in research and practices that focus on issues of immigration, acculturation, and bilingualism.
- Work within the profession to increase the availability and accessibility of bilingual and bicultural mental health services and staff.
- Direct mental health policies toward issues of Mexican American youths and their families.
- Work to build multicultural counseling competencies to provide the most effective professional intervention for all clients.

The counseling relationship will be affected by differing opinions of what constitutes appropriate behavior and differing expectations for the counseling intervention. It is important, therefore, to recognize individual differences and to acknowledge the diversity among Hispanic cultures. We now turn attention to several specific Hispanic American populations and offer counseling suggestions for each.

Latino Americans.   The counselor who understands the importance of *personalismo* to Latino American clients will want to greet them warmly, using the client's first name rather than a title. The counselor should employ small talk to build rapport and trust and should understand that because Latinos perceive psychological problems as physical problems, sessions should be scheduled promptly.

Brazilian Americans.   Most Brazilians come to treatment when an acute emotional crisis occurs and support is not available in their immediate network. Nonetheless, psychotherapy or counseling for emotional and family problems is not an alien concept for most middle-class Brazilians, especially younger generations. Compared with other ethnic groups, Brazilians in the United States seem more receptive to the idea of psychotherapy if a personal connection is made with a particular therapist, someone who can relate to them culturally and linguistically. Barriers do exist, however, such as communication barriers, time and financial constraints, and the scarcity of culturally sensitive counselors (Korin, 1996).

Mexican Americans.   Mexican Americans deserve individual consideration and counseling intervention based on their ethnohistory and culture. With respect to expectations for counseling, Mexican American clients expect more openness from counselors and prefer more formality from professionals. Also, Mexican Americans favor counseling that deals with present, rather than past, events and psychoanalytic techniques (Cherbosque, 1987).

For effective counseling, counselors who work with Mexican Americans should (a) assume the role of family intermediary who can translate cultural behaviors, justify conduct, encourage compromise and negotiation, and ameliorate imbalances in hierarchies; (b) be flexible with language, allowing the alternation of Spanish and English (if needed); (c) use an emotive tone, rather than a structured behavioral or contractual approach; (d) manifest genuine interest, rather than gaining data via referral sheets; and (e) encourage clients to express their reactions, both negative and positive (Falicov, 2005). The following counselor–client dialogue illustrates the client's frustrations in having to deal with several troublesome problems at once:

> COUNSELOR: Juan, workers' employment compensation will pay for your lost time, but the health insurance will pay only for the authorized medical treatment that you received for the accident you had at work.
>
> CLIENT: My eyes still don't work so I can see the assembly charts. I get so darn shaky whenever I think about all my money problems, bills, if I can't do the work, what's going to happen to my children . . .
>
> COUNSELOR: Yeah, I know, it seems like everything is hitting you all at once.
>
> CLIENT: Ha! You know, maybe it sounds crazy or something, but there's this woman in my neighborhood who has some things that she gives me and advises me how to feel better. It really helps.
>
> COUNSELOR: I can't really advise you on what type of treatment you should receive. If it helps and you feel better, why not use it? You're also getting the medical help for your visual problem. You're doing the most you can for yourself at this time.*

Another consideration for counselors is Mexican Americans' strong religious beliefs. The following case history attests to the powerful role of religious beliefs:

Jos, a young 35-year-old Spanish-speaking Mexican, came to the clinic complaining of trembling in his hands, sweating, and shortness of breath. He appeared to be a strong and straightforward individual. He stated that his work performance as an upholsterer had been deteriorating for several months. His major conflict focused on his wish to marry his girlfriend and the resulting need to decrease the amount of money he was sending to his parents and younger brothers and sisters in Mexico. He felt he would be committing a crime or a sin if he were to reduce his help to his family. He has sought advice in the mental health clinic because he thought he was going crazy. He had never experienced such sudden onsets of anxiety before. In addition to helping his patient express his feelings and his needs in short-term therapy, the therapist encouraged him to speak to a priest about his fears of committing a sin against his family.

---

*Dialogue from *Counseling and Development in a Multicultural Society* (pp. 433–434), by J. A. Axelson, 1999, Monterey, CA: Brooks/Cole. Reprinted with permission.

Jos did consult with a priest over several meetings and also completed eight sessions of short-term therapy. His anxiety diminished, his work improved, and he decided to propose marriage to his girlfriend when therapy ended.*

Sources of stress for Mexican American women include unfavorable conditions of poverty, such as substandard housing, depressed social status, limited education, and minimal political influence. Many women are struggling for increased equality and a greater range of personal and vocational options. In seeking such goals, Mexican American women find themselves in a double-bind: Not only are they treated as subordinate to men, but they are considered inferior as a result of their ethnic group membership. Mexican American women are caught between two worlds—one that tells them to preserve and to abide by traditional customs and another that tells them to conform to the teachings and beliefs of the dominant culture (Palacios & Franco, 1986, p. 127).

Casas and Vasquez (1989) point to potential problems the Mexican American woman confronts as she returns to school. Although most women may experience loss of income, change of status, or other adjustments, Mexican American woman may experience additional stress resulting from conflicts over commitment to children and her husband. The positive valuation of family and relationships can result in guilt and frustration when study schedules monopolize time. Other stresses may result from negative attitudes of peers and faculty members who doubt the woman's ability to succeed.

In A Focus on Research 14.2, Flores, Tschann, Marin, and Pantoja (2004) investigated the effects of acculturation on marital conflict among Mexican American husbands and wives.

Palacios and Franco (1986) offer several suggestions which, although directed toward counseling Mexican American women, are equally applicable in intervening with Mexican American men. Professionals should (a) identify mental health systems as appropriate sources of help by making personal appearances at meetings and by contacting doctors and clerics, (b) acquaint themselves with the most recent and effective innovations in counseling, and (c) ensure that bilingual informational materials explaining mental health services and how to use them are disseminated.

Puerto Rican Americans.

The counseling literature provides several suggestions for planning intervention with Puerto Rican Americans. First, the vast differences between first- and second-generation Puerto Ricans deserve recognition in counseling strategies. Second, Puerto Ricans often have problems with American school systems. Parents initially surrender responsibility for their children to the school system because they think it is a benevolent institution; later, they become suspicious of the schools and are unwilling to cooperate. Third, counselors working with Puerto Rican American clients should understand the Spanish-speaking culture and its attitudes toward the family. Counselors should also be aware that the high incidence of depression in low-income Puerto Rican women has been attributed to cultural factors, such as women's subordinate status.

---

*From *Effective Psychotherapy for Low–income and Minority Patients* (p. 47), by F. X. Acosta, J. Yamamoto, and L. A. Evans, 1982, New York: Plenum. Copyright 1982 by Plenum Publishing Company. Reprinted with permission.

A FOCUS ON RESEARCH 14.2

Marital Conflict Among Mexican American Husbands and Wives

Flores, Tschann, Marin, and Pantoja (2004) maintain that despite the growing literature on Mexican American families and increased research on family relationships, few studies have examined the marital functioning between Mexican American husbands and wives. These researchers investigated the effects of acculturation on marital conflicts among Mexican Americans.

They report that as individuals become more acculturated to European American cultural customs and take on more European American values, they may also develop less traditional gender role expectations within their marriages, which can be a source of marital conflict. Still, some Mexican American husbands and wives report that they have traditional gender role expectations of themselves and their spouses, even when the power balance is egalitarian.

They found that

- more acculturated husbands and wives engaged in less avoidance of conflict and were more expressive of their feelings in an argument;

- husbands and wives who were more acculturated reported more conflict concerning sex and consideration of the other; and

- bicultural and more acculturated husbands reported that their wives were more verbally and physically aggressive, compared with mono-Mexican husbands.

In summary, Flores, Tschann, Marin, and Pantoja (2004) suggest that mental health interventions with Mexican American husbands and wives need to consider the impact of acculturation differences on relationship dynamics in the marriage.

Source: "Marital conflict and acculturation among Mexican American husbands and wives," by R. Flores, J. M. Tschann, B. Marin, and P. Pantoja, 2004, *Cultural Diversity and Ethnic Minority Psychology, 10* (l), pp. 39–52.

Individual and Group Therapy.   The decision whether to use individual or group counseling may be difficult because of the tremendous diversity among Hispanic American groups. The choice of intervention approach should be based on which therapeutic mode is most beneficial for the individual client and culture. The selected approach should reflect the client's individual needs. socioeconomic status, place of birth, and language spoken.

Integrated groups composed of ethnic and non-ethnic members often reflect attitudes and behaviors of the external world and may provide more information and mutual understandings, as well as skills in interacting with each other. In contrast, homogenous groups of ethnic minorities provide the opportunity for more immediate trust and cultural understandings, which can enhance and foster group cohesion. Hispanic Americans may be more comfortable in a homogeneous, Spanish-speaking group if they can speak both Spanish and English without fear of offending non-Spanish speakers (Han & Vasquez, 2000).

Family Therapy.   Bean, Perry, and Bedell (2001) encourage therapists to understand the diversity among Hispanic Americans—for example, national origin, level of acculturation, length of U.S. residency, social class, and other demographic factors. A definitive set of therapeutic guidelines cannot be applied to every family. Even after accepting this diversity, it is important to initiate a standard for defining and evaluating culturally competent therapy with Hispanic American families.

These researchers offer the following guidelines for working with Hispanic American families:

- Use family therapy as the preferred treatment modality.
- Be prepared to collaborate with folk healers.
- Act as an advocate for the family with other helping agencies.
- Gather information on the immigration experience.
- Assess for level of acculturation.
- Be bilingual.
- Respect the father or father figure.
- Conduct separate interviews with family subsystems.
- Avoid forcing changes in family relationships.
- Provide the family with concrete suggestions that they can quickly implement.
- Engage the family during the first session with warmth and *personalismo*.

Counselors need to remember that because of the history of discrimination against Hispanic Americans, many clients distrust family therapists of the majority culture. Therapists should define their counseling roles carefully. They should show respect for the Hispanic culture by addressing the father first. Having an interpreter present might be necessary, because older family members may neither speak nor understand English. Counselors who are polite and willing to offer advice can develop rapport and trust and become a part of the family system.

It is important for family therapists to understand that the roles of family members in ethnic minority cultures may vary. For example, in African American families, the roles of husbands and wives tend to be relatively egalitarian, whereas in Hispanic American families, husbands often take a more dominant role. Counselors also need to be sensitive to family structure issues (Wilson, Kohn, & Lee, 2000).

The Hispanic American family can be included in counseling in several ways: (a) Ask specific family members to join in the counseling process, (b) work directly with the entire family, or (c) counsel one member of the family as a consultant who then works with the client or other family members.

Most Puerto Rican males do not like to ask for help, because asking for help might threaten their *machismo*. Often, wives ask the therapist to convince their husbands to come to therapy. The therapist should assess the situation carefully before interpreting the request as manipulative. Puerto Ricans who ask an outsider to intervene usually feel powerless and embarrassed, and they view authority figures as influential and this type of request as legitimate. Pushing a woman to do the convincing herself may alienate her and result in her withdrawal from therapy. Every effort should be made to include the husband by appealing to his sense of responsibility and to his traditional role as family head (Garcia-Preto, 1996b).

Studies of Cuban American family therapy suggests several guidelines for the engagement and treatment of Cubans. The counselor or psychotherapist should have family therapy skills, cultural competence, and sensitivity to cultural issues. More specifically, knowledge of the

UP CLOSE AND PERSONAL 14.3
Counseling Carla, a Hispanic American Adult

Carla, age 35, referred herself to a neighborhood mental health organization. Lately, she has been experiencing frustrations and stresses: her husband Oscar's job or the lack of one, the money the family has borrowed, Oscar's objection to her getting a job, problems with her son's progress in school, her inability to initiate change as other women can, her feelings of powerlessness, and her desire to put her husband's authority to the test. She has finally concluded that she should get a job and enroll in night school despite her husband's protests. "I want to improve my life," Carla says. "Oscar runs my life; I'm ready for a change."

The counselor, a 34-year-old European American woman, recognized that Carla needed immediate help and that she would be receptive to counseling. The counselor had some degree of multicultural expertise and understood some of the problems affecting contemporary Hispanic Americans. She told Carla that, although as a counselor she had a fairly good knowledge of the Hispanic culture, she still might make mistakes. She encouraged Carla to talk more about herself and what she wanted. She also advised Carla to consider the repercussions of her getting a job and attending school, as opposed to how she might feel if she failed to take action. The counselor decided that she would meet with Carla several times to counsel her as she moved against Oscar's authoritarian demands, and that individual therapy would be best for the first few sessions. Afterward group therapy might be appropriate, because the counselor knew other Hispanic American women in similar situations. Family therapy was not a possibility, because Oscar would stifle Carla's ambitions and monopolize the counseling session.

Spanish language is essential, because cultural issues are often best expressed in natural languages. Counselors also need to appreciate the phases of migration and the connectedness to the culture of origin and to evaluate the impact of the stress of migration, value conflicts, and developmental conflicts (Bernal & Shapiro, 2005).

Up Close and Personal 14.3 looks at a counselor's efforts with Carla, a Hispanic American adult.

Hispanic American Elderly

Potential Problems Warranting Counseling Intervention

Problems that Hispanic American elders may experience include

- inability to overcome stereotypes about the Hispanic culture and about being elderly;
- double jeopardy—being both Hispanic and elderly;
- vast intracultural differences that make generalizations difficult;
- problems associated with urban life: poverty, crime, low socioeconomic status, lack of education, unemployment, low standard of living, or unmet basic needs;
- illegal immigrant status;
- health-related problems: chronic ailments, frequent bouts with illnesses, lack of transportation to obtain medical services;

A FOCUS ON RESEARCH 14.3

Treating the Hispanic Elderly

In a succinct and interesting guest editorial, Buki (2005) offers several descriptive comments about geriatric psychiatric Hispanic patients, age 65 and older.

- Most know how to read and write in Spanish at a basic level.
- Most have low rates of both alcohol and substance abuse and many have stopped nicotine use.
- Most describe their early years as difficult, largely because they began working at a young age.
- Some report a history of verbal and physical abuse during years as political prisoners.
- Most common psychiatric diagnoses include anxiety disorders, social anxiety disorders, depression, and age-related cognitive decline and dementias.

- Many patients feel hopeless and have experienced suicial ideations.

Buki (2005) recommends psychological intervention that

- utilizes cognitive restructuring, medication, psychoeducation, support, and psychodynamic interventions;
- practices deep breathing and relaxation training; and
- takes about 25 minutes, because 45 minutes appear to be too long for patients' attention spans.

Source: "Treating the Hispanic elderly," by V. M. V. Buki, 2005, April, *Clinical Psychology News, 33* (4), pp. 8–9.

- developmental problems and psychosocial crises;
- allegiance to Spanish, hampering improvement in English;
- the patriarchal nature of the Hispanic American family and the inability to accommodate change; and
- lack of transportation, financial difficulties, and communication problems that hamper access to health services.

In A Focus on Research 14.3, Buki (2005), in a guest editorial for *Clinical Psychology News,* describes the condition of geriatric psychiatric Hispanic patients, aged 65 and older.

Counseling Considerations

Counselors confront several obstacles in planning professional intervention for elderly Hispanic American clients. First, the intracultural diversity among Hispanic Americans challenges counselors to understand the unique cultural characteristics of specific subgroups. Second, questions surrounding the problems and crises of the elderly years further complicate the counseling process. Third, the intensity of the elderly Hispanic's problems can be psychologically overwhelming to the counselor, as well as to the client. Aging, grief from loss, and relationship problems are common and may lead to crises if individuals do not have sufficient coping skills to deal with them (Casas & Vasquez, 1989).

Counselors should make every effort to understand what it is like to face the double jeopardy of being both Hispanic American and elderly. Retirement and reduced income are two issues faced by elderly Hispanic Americans, who (a) probably cannot afford to retire, or (b) do not have sufficient income to endure a reduction. Coping with these financial difficulties can result in a struggle to maintain one's integrity in times of despair, especially as one ages. Such problematic situations constitute an even greater challenge for the poor and uneducated Hispanic Americans confronted by racism and discrimination. The dismal picture of elderly Hispanic Americans also includes problems usually associated with the elderly lifespan period, such as loss of stamina, changes in physical appearance, and sometimes loss of sensory perceptions.

Professional intervention with Hispanic American elderly requires knowledge of elderly development, an ability to intervene with older clients, and culturally appropriate counseling skills to work with this cultural group. Two basic considerations crucial to the success of counseling elderly Hispanic Americans are (a) understanding what problems and issues might be raised during intervention, and (b) understanding what techniques and strategies may enhance the counseling relationship. The following discussion centers on specific steps the counselor can take to increase the likelihood of gaining the client's confidence, building rapport, and getting the client to disclose information freely.

The counselor working with elderly Hispanic Americans must first let the clients know that he or she understands and accepts the traditional Hispanic familial structure. A client must be confident that the counselor does not harbor negative feelings about the culture or subscribe to damaging stereotypes. Second, the counselor must be aware of the client's commitment to speaking Spanish and understand why it has persisted as such an important cultural characteristic. Third, the counselor should appreciate the possible reluctance of the client to take a young counselor seriously, especially a female counselor. Fourth, the counselor must work to build trust and encourage disclosure of relevant personal information.

Language can also be a barrier to effective communication, especially for older Hispanic Americans. Planning appropriately for communication barriers will be all-important. If elderly family members cannot speak English, then conducting the interview in Spanish is essential to engaging them. Older Puerto Rican Americans are often hesitant and afraid to learn English; they may feel humiliated when they try to speak English but are not understood and are asked to repeat themselves. Even when Puerto Rican Americans do speak English, lack of fluency may lead to distorted information and vagueness (Garcia-Preto, 1996b).

If a counselor needs an interpreter, it is best to use a co-counselor or paraprofessional, rather than a neighbor or friend. Finally, the Hispanic American client's need for respect, privacy, and dignity should not be overlooked.

As with other cultures and stages of the lifespan, counselors should consider the effects of being elderly, the effects of being a member of a particular culture, the complex relationship between age and culture, and the various intracultural and individual differences among elderly clients.

Individual and Group Therapy.   As always, the counselor's decision whether to use individual or group therapy should be based on the individual, the specific culture, and the reasons for counseling. Several generalizations, however, may be noted in dealing with

Hispanic Americans. Elderly Hispanic Americans, although generally not accustomed to disclosing significant information that may reflect poorly on the family, might be willing to discuss problems associated with aging in a group session. The elder's lack of experience with group counseling, however, would probably call for special effort on the part of the counselor to explain the group process, or the counselor may prefer to use individual therapy.

Family Therapy.   What do research and scholarly opinion offer for counselors working with elderly Hispanic Americans? With respect to family therapy with Puerto Rican Americans, Garcia-Preto (1996b) suggests that counselors should (a) speak Spanish (if possible) if communication in English presents a problem; (b) make the family comfortable by providing a warm and personal setting; (c) be active, personal, and respectful of the family's structure and boundaries; and (d) ask the family when the problems began, what types of solutions they have tried, and what their expectations are for change.

In all likelihood, the patriarchal nature of the Hispanic American family will dictate that only the father or husband will speak for the family. The possibility of the wife or children disagreeing with the head of the household is remote. Although some indications suggest that Hispanic American women are becoming more outspoken, they cannot be expected to disclose much personal information during the course of a family session.

Up Close and Personal 14.4 looks at a counselor's efforts with Papa Rafael, a Hispanic American elder.

UP CLOSE AND PERSONAL 14.4

Counseling Papa Rafael, a Hispanic American Elder

Papa Rafael, aged 75, referred himself to a community health organization for counseling. Although he was surprised that a 75-year-old man with difficulty speaking English had referred himself, the 48-year-old European American male counselor was eager to talk with Papa Rafael. Because he had come of his own volition, surely Rafael would be willing to discuss his problems and to disclose his feelings.

During the first session, the counselor explained the counseling process, assured confidentiality, and sought to establish trust and rapport. The client's problems became clear: his family's financial difficulties and his son's unemployment; his own meager government benefits; growing old poor; and concern that his family, like many others, might abandon traditional Hispanic beliefs. Rafael saw a solution to the family's financial woes, but it was not a satisfactory solution in his view: His daughter-in-law Carla could take a job to help make ends meet, but such a solution could also lead to "the downfall of the family." Women in his family had not worked outside the home; they had stayed home to care for the children. Who would cook, take care of the children, clean the house? The counselor understood how Rafael felt. Finances were a problem, and so was the threat of loss of traditional values. After assessing the situation, the counselor decided that he wanted to see Rafael again. Perhaps a group session would be appropriate because his other elderly clients were having similar difficulties. Because Rafael's problem involved the family, a family session might be in order. Meeting with Rafael, Oscar, and Carla to discuss their financial situation and possible solutions was an idea worth exploring.

A Point of Departure: Challenges Confronting Counselors of Hispanic Americans

Counselors who plan intervention based on the client's culture are perceived by clients as more competent than counselors who do not provide culturally appropriate strategies. Understanding the nature of the Hispanic American culture and knowing how to provide culturally appropriate counseling intervention for Hispanic Americans should be a goal of all counselors, especially considering the rapidly increasing population of this ethnic group.

Counselors of Hispanic Americans need to address numerous topics: cherished cultural concepts and beliefs, allegiance to Spanish and problems with limited English proficiency; problems associated with aging; low socioeconomic status; and racism and discrimination. The challenges will be to (a) understand clients, their individuality, and their respective Hispanic culture; (b) provide developmentally and culturally appropriate counseling intervention; and (c) understand Hispanics' reasons for underuse of, and early withdrawal from, counseling intervention. Professional training and firsthand contact with Hispanic American clients in the four lifespan stages are the most effective means of successfully meeting these challenges.

Summary

Counselors and psychotherapists undoubtedly will be called on to provide professional intervention with Hispanic Americans in the various lifespan stages. Rather than expect Hispanic Americans to acculturate toward the counselor's cultural perspective and worldview, the counselor has the professional responsibility to understand individual Hispanic American clients and their differences and problems and to provide appropriate counseling intervention. Counseling professionals will also need to know how individual Hispanic Americans, with their many cherished beliefs, traditions, and customs, will react to individual, group, and family therapies.

Suggested Readings

Ayalon, L., Arean, P. A., & Alvidrez, J. (2005). Adherence to antidepressant medications in Black and Latino elderly patients. *American Journal of Geriatric Psychiatry, 13* (7), 572–580. This study identified ethnic group differences in nonadherence and to determine predictors of nonadherence to antidepressant medications in older minority-group members.

Schwarzbaum, S. E. (2004). Low-income Latinos and dropout: Strategies to prevent dropout. *Journal of Multicultural Counseling and Development, 32,* 296–306. Schwarzbaum explores factors associated with dropout from counseling services and offers interventions and strategies that decrease counseling dropout rates.

Wilson, K. B., & Senices, J. (2005). Exploring the vocational rehabilitation acceptance rates for Hispanics versus non-Hispanics in the United States. *Journal of Counseling and Development, 83* (1), 86–97. These authors emphasize the need to research the Hispanic population, provide a review on vocational rehabilitation acceptance, and provide implications for counselors.

Understanding Lesbian, Gay, and Bisexual Clients

Questions to Be Explored

1. What terminology seems most appropriate when referring to lesbians, gay, and bisexual (LGB) clients and to related terms such as *homosexuality, sexual orientation*, and *queer*.

2. What demographics and historical and cultural contexts do counselors of LGB clients need to know?

3. What do the terms *coming out* and *identity development* mean? How do definitions vary? What does the literature say about coming out and identity development in several cultures?

4. What are the childhood, adolescent, adult, and elderly years like for LGB clients in terms of social and cultural descriptions, coming out and identity development, and challenges unique to the developmental period?

5. What challenges confront counselors of LGB clients?

6. What resources are available to counselors who want to improve their counseling effectiveness with LGB clients across the lifespan?

Overview

Previous chapters of this text have discussed clients of culturally different backgrounds and how counselors can address their various needs along the lifespan. Another premise of this book is that lesbians, gay men, and bisexual men and women have a culture of their own, in addition to their other cultures. Such individuals have their own worldviews, perspectives on same-sex and different-sex orientations, and experiences with injustices and discrimination. As more lesbians, gay men, and bisexual persons come out and let their sexual orientations be known, counselors increasingly will be called on to provide professional intervention throughout the lifespan. This chapter focuses on understanding LGB clients, their coming out and identity development, and the unique challenges they face in the lifespan continuum. As always, the emphasis will be on counselors understanding clients' cultures (mainly same-sex orientation in this chapter) and accepting the challenge to develop the attitudes, knowledge, and skills necessary to provide effective counseling intervention for LGB clients.

Lesbians, Gay Men, and Bisexuals

Terminology

Counselors working with LGB clients readily understand the need for constructive rather than destructive terminology. Therefore, there needs to be at least some discussion of words and labels such as *queer, gay, lesbian, bisexual, transgender, sexual orientation*, and *lifestyle* as well as abbreviated labels such as *LGB, LGBT*, and *LGBTQ*.

In this book, *gays* refer to males with a same-sex orientation, whereas *lesbians* refer to women with a same-sex orientation. *Bisexual* is defined as an individual who has "the capacity, regardless of the sexual identity label one chooses, to love and sexually desire both same- and other-gendered individuals" (Firestein, 1996). *LGB* is used as a convenient collective term to describe lesbians, gays, and bisexuals. The term, *LGBT* (lesbian, gay, bisexual, transgender) is not used because at this time, it is unclear whether the transgender rights movement will develop a significant and longlasting voice in gay/lesbian organizations. Another term, *GLBTQ*, stands for gay, lesbian, bisexual, transgender, and queer/questioning (MacGillivray & Kozik-Rosabal, 2000). In this volume, the term *LGB* will be used rather than *queer*, although "queer" is being reclaimed by the younger generation of LGBs and is considered more inclusive because it encompasses all nonheterosexual people (MacGillivray & Kozik-Rosabal). Here, *queer* will not be used as a noun, but only to show the cruelness of words. *Homosexual* is not a preferred term for LGBs because many people consider it to be exclusionary and too clinical (MacGillivray & Kozik-Rosabal). Also, Simon (1998) maintains that *homosexual* is often interpreted to mean "male homosexual" (p. 68). In this volume, *homosexual* is used as an adjective (e.g., the homosexual culture) and is rarely used as a noun. *Sexual orientation* is used to denote one's sexual orientation; *lifestyle* is rarely used because it suggests that sexual orientation is a choice. Again, whatever terminology counselors and other readers choose to use, terms should denote positive perspectives and respect for LGB clients, both as individuals and as a culture.

Demographics

Because LGB clients are in all four lifespan stages and live in all parts of the United States, it is difficult to provide specific demographics. One might expect LGB persons to live in larger urban areas, such as San Francisco, New York, and Chicago, but in reality, they also live in both suburban and rural areas. To avoid harassment, some LGB persons, especially those in rural areas and small towns, might be less likely to let their sexual orientation be known. They must deal daily with the problem of whether to hide their sexual orientation or risk the condemnation of the community. In such situations, teachers, ministers, and medical doctors might risk their professional status and financial livelihood if their sexual orientation becomes public. Such tendencies to hide one's sexual orientation make it difficult to determine accurate numbers and geographical locations for this group.

Some writers suggest that LGB persons comprise about 10% of the population (van Wormer, Wells, & Boes, 2000; Witt, Thomas, & Marcus, 1997). Still, some LGB persons might be reluctant to designate themselves as such. For example, some people have same-sex orientation yet never engage in same-sex relationships. Others might have had only one same-sex encounter and, therefore, do not classify themselves as lesbian or gay. Counselors need to determine when (and if) the client accepted his or her sexual orientation. In other words, some clients might actually be LGB and be unwilling to admit it to the counselor or to themselves.

Counselors might expect LGB clients to be primarily in the younger lifespan stages, but some writers (Berger, 1996) suggest that significant numbers of older people accept and deal with their same-sex orientations and the attendent prejudices, humiliation, and hurtful remarks. It is safe to assume that regardless of their geographic location, counselors will be called upon to intervene with LGB clients in all four lifespan stages. One key to effective professional intervention will be to consider homosexuality as a culture. LGB persons have a number of cultures, as do heterosexual people; however, one subculture of the former is their sexual orientation and the accompanying perspectives and views.

Historical and Cultural Contexts

In some cultures, homosexuality and bisexuality have been assumed to be mental illnesses. Hooker (1957) questioned this assumption because she found no difference between nonclinical samples of heterosexual men and homosexual men. Numerous subsequent studies have found no differences between heterosexual and homosexual groups on measures of cognitive abilities, self-esteem, and psychological well-being (American Psychological Association, 2000).

Counselors and their clients benefit when they understand both historical and contemporary perspectives of same-sex orientation. Most people currently know little about the everyday experiences of LGB persons in different historical periods. Also, much of what has been written focuses only on gay men. Attitudes appear to range from tolerance to oppression, with the norm in Western societies being hostility and condemnation. In fact, LGB persons have largely been invisible in history, and most existing knowledge is derived from religious and legal sanctions against same-sex relationships.

After World War II, the increasing visibility of lesbians and gay men was accompanied by increased public hostility, including police raids of lesbian and gay bars and efforts to remove homosexuals from government service. Many lesbians and gay men lived in fear that exposure could lead to loss of jobs, housing, or a place in the community. In 1955, the Daughters of Bilitis was founded in San Francisco as the first national lesbian organization. The last half of the 20th century witnessed the gradual flowering of lesbian publications, arts, organizations, and social services, ranging form softball teams to music festivals and lesbian health care clinics (Fingerhut, Peplau, & Ghavami, 2005).

In certain time periods and cultures, sexual orientation did not result in conflicts, whereas in others, considerable turmoil and violence surrounded the issue. For example, people with homosexual orientations have been honored among some American Indian tribes, tolerated in some countries such as Scandinavia, prescribed in ancient Greece among scholars, and condemned throughout much of the Anglo-Saxon world. Attitudes in the Far East have historically been benevolent. In Japan during the feudal period, male homosexual love was considered more manly than heterosexual love. In premodern China, where male brothels were common, parents often trained their sons to be prostitutes. Presently, among cultures in the United States, perhaps the greatest potential for cultural acceptance of diversity in sexual orientation lies in the traditional American Indian culture (Firestein, 1996). American Indians place value on "two-spirited people" (Reynolds & Hanjorgiris, 2000, p. 90), that is, people possessing masculine and feminine qualities. Many American Indian cultures recognize the existence of people whose spirits are both feminine and masculine, not only accepting them as part of nature but revering them as having particular spiritual qualities (Rust, 1996).

Whereas the contemporary European American model categorizes people as straight or gay, in countries such as Egypt, China, and Korea, men can have sex with other men as a sexual outlet devoid of connotations of identity and lifestyle. The Latino tradition assigns male homosexual identity only to the person assuming the receptive–passive role (Fukuyama & Ferguson, 2000).

Lesbian, gay, and bisexual people of color may experience multiple layers of oppression, as they often not only contend with the negative societal reactions to their sexual orientation but also may experience racial prejudice, limited economic resources, and limited acceptance within their own cultural community (Harper, Jernewall, & Zea, 2004). In A Focus on Research 15.1, Harper, Jernewall, and Zea provide a detailed look at LGB people of color.

Typically, people assume that someone who has sex with others of the same sex is homosexual (Herdt, 1997, p. 4). However, in some cultures throughout the world, and even in some communities of the United States, some people of both genders and of distinct ethnic groups

A FOCUS ON RESEARCH 15.1

Lesbian, Gay, and Bisexual People of Color

Major aspects of the Harper, Jernewall, and Zea (2004) article deal with heterosexism and oppression of LGB identity. The authors maintain that LBGs, or LBGTs if transgendered people are included, represent a collective group of individuals who experience varying degrees of heterosexism and oppression. Although the life experiences of these people vary tremendously, they are often marginalized and do not share the same basic rights as other citizens in society.

Heterosexism can be blatant and revengeful, or in other cases, more subtle—whether intentional or perpetuated without the oppressor's knowledge that she or he is being heterosexist. Many non-LGB people do not realize the heterosexist nature of most societies, because heterosexist language, icons, images, and messages are so pervasive within various realms of our society. Heterosexism also includes LBG youth being bullied, harassed, and physically abused in multiple settings, including school, home, and neighborhood. Violence is often perpetuated by peers, parents, and teachers. Heterosexist behavior can also include economic discrimination in which LGB people are discriminated against in the workplace, fired, or passed over for promotion because of their sexual orientation.

LGB people experience chronic and pervasive exposure to oppressive acts, which in turn affect their physical and mental health. Some LGB people may engage in behaviors that have been associated with internalized oppression, such as making self-deprecating remarks, failing to access needed mental health services, and placing themselves in situations that lead to harm or distress.

Source: "Giving voice to emerging science and theory for lesbian, gay, and bisexual people of color," by G. W. Harper, N. Jernewall, and M. C. Zea, 2004, *Cultural Diversity and Ethnic Minority Psychology, 10* (3), pp. 187–199.

engage in same-sex encounters, but they do not describe themselves as lesbian, gay, or bisexual. They may regard themselves as heterosexuals (Herdt, 1997, p. 4) who on occasion participate in homoerotic encounters for pleasure, money, or lack of other sexual opportunities. They may or may not actually be homosexual—both they and their counselors may have difficulty deciding whether these clients are truly lesbian or gay or whether they just occasionally participate in same-sex sexual activity.

Counselors who provide professional intervention for LGB clients should recognize contemporary contexts and attitudes toward homosexuality. Although acceptance of homosexuality has increased as more LGB persons have revealed their sexual orientations, many of these individuals continue to face discrimination and prejudice in schools, in the workplace, and in society. Many are afraid to let their sexual orientation be known; others have revealed their orientation and endured terrible consequences. Professionals working with LGB clients need to plan counseling intervention that recognizes the problems these clients face in a predominantly heterosexual society.

Coming Out and Identity Development

Any legitimate discussion of coming out should include a definition of the term. Counselors often find that the term has multiple meanings, depending on individual clients and the extent to which these clients have accepted their sexual orientation.

Multiple Definitions.   The coming out process can be defined in several ways. Smith (1997) defines *coming out* as the experience of acknowledging a lesbian, gay, or bisexual orientation to oneself and others. From this perspective, coming out is characterized by a person's development and acceptance of sexual orientation and identity. In some cases, coming out has been seen as an individual's sexual development related to self-acceptance and self-esteem (Smith). Other definitions include one's first sexual experience with another of the same sex, one being open with others about one's sexual orientation (even then the openness might be limited to family or close friends), and one's achieving self-recognition and self-acceptance. Sometimes, coming out or accepting one's sexual orientation comes long after a same-sex sexual experience. Regardless of the definition, most LGB persons consider coming out to be a significant life experience (Berger, 1996). Unfortunately, there is little of a substantive nature in the literature about cultural differences and coming out (Smith, 1997).

By acknowledging one's sexual orientation, an individual begins to reject the stigma and condemnation usually associated with being lesbian, gay, or bisexual. Counselors working with clients of various cultural backgrounds readily understand the importance of coming out, as well as how it relates to and affects self-acceptance, self-esteem, and self-validation. They also should recognize (and plan accordingly) that coming out depends on individual situations; that is, some LGB persons might first come out with family and close friends, yet be more reluctant with employers, teachers, or authority figures. Last, counselors should recognize that losses can accompany the coming out process. Example include the loss of a heterosexual lifestyle, loss of the rituals of marriage and divorce, loss of social acceptance of one's relationships, and loss of esteem of family and community (Smith, 1997).

Identity Models and Changes.   The acquisition of a gay or lesbian identity and its relevant developmental tasks, referred to as coming out, is generally considered to be a lengthy, often difficult process for LGB persons, with considerable variation depending on gender, race, ethnicity, social class, age, religion, and geographic location. The coming out process includes confronting negative social attitudes as well as one's own internalized oppression. This process occurs in the context of few role models, inadequate support systems, lack of legal protection and, for LGB persons in some cultural groups, added isolation and potential loss of primary cultural identification and community (Fassinger, 1991).

Van Wormer, Wells, and Boes (2000) maintain that, in the coming out process, the first stage is the initial or precoming out stage, during which an individual may not consciously recognize same-sex attraction but may experience uneasy feelings. During this stage, the person might defend himself or herself against any feelings associated with same-sex attractions and embrace heterosexuality. The second stage involves a beginning awareness of a same-sex romantic and sexual attraction. Individuals begin to examine heterosexist beliefs, that is, assuming everyone is heterosexual and that heterosexuality is preferred. During this stage, people choose to come out with someone about their feelings. In the third stage, people develop gay or lesbian friendships, perhaps a romantic/sexual partner relationship, and socialize with the gay and lesbian community. Through contacts in the LGB community, individuals develop a social support network within the context of their emerging identity. The fourth stage includes self-acceptance of a gay or lesbian identity, which is then incorporated into other aspects of one's life (i.e., social, political, personal). People describe their sexual orientation as who they are and integrate other developmental tasks into their LGB identity (van Wormer, Wells, & Boes, 2000).

Several other models of lesbian and gay identity development have been proposed. Although it is not feasible to explore in detail all the models of lesbian and gay identity development, several models are listed and briefly described. Two models, those of Falco (1991) and Troiden (1989), are examined in more detail. Last, McCarn and Fassinger's (1996) new model is discussed.

Cass Model.   Cass (1979) offers a six-stage model of lesbian and gay identity development that integrates the lesbian and gay identity with self-concept. Cass's model applies to both women and men and includes identity confusion, identity comparison, identity tolerance, identity acceptance, identity pride, and identity synthesis.

Coleman Model.   Coleman (1982) outlines a five-stage model that includes widespread identity disclosure as a developmental task of the final stage. Coleman discusses the force of social pressure at different stages of the coming out process. The Coleman model includes precoming out, coming out, exploration, first relationships, and integration.

Sophie Model.   Sophie (1985/1986) provides the first known model developed specifically for lesbians. This four-stage model includes first awareness, testing and exploration, identity acceptance, and identity integration.

Morales Model.   Morales (1989) proposes an identity model for visible racial/ethnic lesbian and gay individuals that attempts to incorporate their dual statuses. The five-stage model includes denial of conflicts, bisexuality versus homosexuality, conflicts in allegiances, establishing priorities in allegiances, and integrating various communities.

Falco Model.   In her book, *Psychotherapy with Lesbian Clients: Theory into Practice,* Falco (1991) proposes a generalized model for the sexual identity development of lesbians by combining and summarizing the models of other researchers. In the first stage, a person is aware of being different and begins to wonder why. In the second stage, she begins to acknowledge her lesbian feelings and may tell others. Sexual experimentation marks the third stage, as the person explores same-sex relationships while seeking a supportive community. She begins to learn to function in a same-sex relationship, establishing her place in the lesbian culture, while passing as heterosexual when necessary. In the final stage, she integrates her private and social identities (Wilson, 1996).

Troiden Model.   Troiden (1989) proposes a four-stage model of lesbian and gay identity formation that shows how lesbians and gay men see themselves as such and adopt corresponding lifestyles. The four stages are sensitization, identity confusion, identity assumption, and commitment. Each stage can be identified by its characteristics and personal behaviors.

Stage 1: Sensitization   During this stage, which occurs before puberty, most lesbians and gay men do not see homosexuality as personally relevant. They assume a sense of heterosexuality, if they think about their sexual status at all. Lesbians and gay men typically acquire social experiences during their childhood, however, that serve later as a basis for perceiving homosexuality in more relevant and personal terms. These experiences lend support to emerging perceptions of homosexuality.

Stage 2: Identity Confusion   Lesbians and gay men in this stage begin to perceive their sexual orientation during adolescence, when they reflect on the possibility that their feelings, behaviors, or both could be regarded as homosexual, which contradicts previously held self-images. The hallmark of this stage is identity confusion—inner turmoil and uncertainty surrounding ambiguous sexual status. Because their sexual identities are in limbo, these individuals can no longer accept their heterosexual identities as a given, yet they have not developed perceptions of themselves as homosexual.

During this stage, lesbians and gay men typically respond to identity confusion in several ways:

Denial: They deny the homosexual component of their feelings, fantasies, and activities.

Repair: They attempt to eradicate homosexual feelings and behaviors.

Avoidance: They recognize that their behaviors, thoughts, and fantasies are homosexual but see them as unacceptable and to be avoided.

Redefining: They reduce identity confusion by redefining behavior, feelings, and activities.

Acceptance: Women and men accept their behaviors; they accept that their feelings and fantasies may be homosexual and seek out additional sources of information to learn more about their sexual feelings.

Stage 3: Identity Assumption   Lesbians and gay men in this stage, during or after adolescence, develop a homosexual identity that becomes both a self-identity and a presented identity, at least to other lesbians and gay men. Defining oneself as lesbian or gay and presenting oneself as such to other lesbians or gay men are the first stages in a larger process of identity disclosure called "coming out" (Troiden, 1989, p. 59). The earmarks of this stage include self-definition as lesbian or gay, identity tolerance and acceptance, regular association with other lesbians or gay men, sexual experimentation, and exploration of the lesbian or gay subculture.

Stage 4: Commitment   Homosexuality is adopted as a way of life. The main characteristics of this stage include self-acceptance and comfort with the lesbian or gay identity and role. This commitment has both internal and external dimensions. It is indicated internally by (a) the fusion of sexuality and emotionality into a significant whole, (b) a shift in the meanings attached to homosexual identities, (c) a perception of the homosexual identity as a valid self-identity, (d) expressed satisfaction with the homosexual identity, and (e) increased happiness after self-defining as lesbian or gay. It is indicated externally by (a) same-sex love relationships, (b) disclosure of a homosexual identity to nonhomosexual audiences, and (c) a shift in the type of stigma management theories.

McCarn and Fassinger Model.   After examining the previously mentioned models, McCarn and Fassinger (1996) proposed a new model of lesbian identity:

Stage 1: Awareness

Individual Sexual Identity	of feeling or being different
Group Membership Identity	of existence of varying sexual orientations

Stage 2: Exploration

Individual Sexual Identity	of strong/erotic feelings for women
Group Membership Identity	of one's position regarding lesbians and gay men as a group

Stage 3: Deepening/Commitment

Individual Sexual Identity	to self-knowledge, self-fulfillment, and crystallization of choices about sexuality
Group Membership Identity	to commitment with reference group, with awareness of oppression and consequences of choices

Stage 4: Internalization/Synthesis

Individual Sexual Identity	of love for women and sexual choices into overall identity
Group Identity	of identity as a member of a minority group, across context

Bisexual Model.   Although many theories have attempted to explain the development of positive gay and lesbian identities, there has been little scholarly activity dedicated to bisexual identity development. According to Reynolds and Hanjorgiris (2000), "bisexuality is generally regarded as a behavior without an identity to back it up" (p. 44). Perhaps this is true, because bisexual sexual orientation can not be referred to with a singular noun. Unlike the lesbian and gay identity models, the development of bisexuality often presumes an absence of closure, partially owing to the fluidity of sexuality. Although the various bisexuality models have proposed diverse approaches to the coming out process, all have described the formation process as complex and multifaceted, complicated by a lack of social validation and lack of support from lesbians, gay men, and heterosexuals (Reynolds & Hanjorgiris).

Fox (1995) explained the following milestone events in bisexual identity development:

- *First Heterosexual Attractions, Behavior, and Relationships:* Bisexual men and women experience their first heterosexual attractions at about the same ages, in their early teens. This is somewhat earlier than for gay men and lesbians who have experienced heterosexual attractions. Bisexual women have their first heterosexual experience about 2 years earlier than bisexual men have their first heterosexual experience, in their middle to late teens. This is about the same as for gay men and lesbians who have sexual experiences with people of the opposite gender. Bisexual women have their first heterosexual relationships about 2 years earlier than bisexual men, in their late teens.

- *First Homosexual Attractions, Behavior, and Relationships:* Bisexual men experience their first sexual attraction toward other men in their early to middle teens, whereas bisexual women experience their first sexual attraction toward other women in their middle to late teens. This is later, by about 2 to 3 years, than for gay men and lesbians. Bisexual men have their first sexual experiences with other men in their middle to late teens, whereas bisexual women have their first sexual experience with other women in their early twenties. This is somewhat later than for gay men and lesbians. Bisexual men and women have their first same-sex relationships about the same ages, in their early twenties, which is about the same as for lesbians and gay men.

- *First Bisexual Attractions, Behavior, and Relationships:* Bisexual men and women first consider themselves bisexual at about the same ages, in their early to middle twenties. This is about 2 to 3 years later than the first homosexual self-identification for gay men and lesbians. For those bisexual men and women who have considered themselves gay or lesbian, the men self-identified as gay earlier than the women self-identified as lesbian, in their early twenties. This parallels the earlier homosexual self-identification of gay men compared with lesbians (Fox, 1995).

Culture and Gender.

It is interesting to see cultural and gender differences in the coming out process. Research does not provide a complete discussion of LGB persons in all cultural groups; however, the research that does exist shows the struggles LGB persons have as they come out.

African American gay men are similar to European American gay men on many dimensions; however, subtle differences can be found in the areas of vulnerability in occupations, family relationships (especially with extended family), religiosity, and attitudes toward sexual behavior. One study of both African American gay men and lesbians and the coming out process revealed concerns about finding validation in both gay and lesbian communities and the African American community and about integrating identities across these two dimensions (Fox, 1995). African American gay men placed less value on coming out than European American gay men because it could jeopardize the support they needed as members of a racial minority and because racial bias also exists in the gay and lesbian community (Adams & Kimmel, 1997).

Asian American lesbians and gay men often experience difficulty with the coming out process because open disclosure that one is lesbian or gay is seen as a threat to the continuation of the family line and a rejection of one's appropriate roles within the culture (Chan, 1989; Greene, 1997). The maintenance of family roles and conformity is an important and distinctive cultural expectation. Lesbian or gay offspring may be perceived as a source of shame, particularly to mothers, who feel responsible for preventing such occurrences (Chan; Greene).

Greek American lesbians experience unique struggles during the coming out process. Most Greek women have been taught for years that their role was to orient themselves toward a man. In fact, many Greek women learn early that they are only as good as the men they serve or will serve. A Greek woman's self-esteem is not based on individual merit but on her ability and willingness to serve a man. During the coming out process, this leaves the Greek American lesbian in the position to define herself and to find meaning in her life without a man (Fygetakis, 1997).

Hispanic American disapproval of homosexuality might be more intense than the homophobia found in the dominant European American community. A powerful form of heterosexist oppression occurs within Hispanic cultures, leaving many lesbian and gay members feeling reluctant to come out to avoid the ridicule and outcast status that would result from open acknowledgment of their sexual orientation. For the Hispanic American, coming out might be seen as an act of disloyalty against the culture and family. A lesbian or gay family member may maintain a place within the family and be quietly tolerated, but this does not constitute an acceptance of the individual or the individual's sexual orientation. Instead, the family adopts a perspective of denial and refuses to accept the sexual orientation of a LGB family member (Espin, 1984; Greene, 1997; Hidalgo, 1984; Morales, 1992).

Italian Americans also face unique struggles during the coming out process. Cerbone (1997) explained that Italian men are perceived as "earthy and lusty" (p. 121); Italian men are considered lovers, dark and suave romancers of women, or stallions in direct pursuit of women. Coming out means that the gay man does not meet the cultural expectation of what it means to be a virile Italian male. According to Cerbone, not only is coming out a difficult decision for the man, but he also faces the disapproval of the community and church, which expect men to act and behave in a particular manner.

Lesbian, Gay, and Bisexual Children

Unfortunately, little literature exists on LGB children, perhaps because it is not until the adolescence developmental period that most boys and girls begin to realize their sexuality, and in this case, their same-sex sexual orientation. However, some children as young as 5 or 6 years of age realize their attraction and interest in the same sex. Most research on LGB children focuses on topics such as living in a predominantly heterosexual society (and the accompanying harassment experienced by many LGB children), feeling different, and dealing with gender role conformity. What impact on children would result from parents keeping their sexual orientation a secret? How does the secret affect the family? Murray and McClintock (2005) examine these questions in A Focus on Research 15.2.

A FOCUS ON RESEARCH 15.2

Children of the Closet

Murray and McClintock examined whether a parent's nondisclosure of his or her homosexual or bisexual orientation within the family unit negatively affects self-esteem and anxiety in children. The authors hypothesized that the closeted parent would present issues that would affect children's psychological health. Potentially damaging dynamics, among others, include the lower self-esteem of the closeted parent and the effect of anxiety around secret-keeping.

Thirty-six subjects indicated that they had not known of their parent's sexual orientation until an average age of 16 for the children of lesbian and bisexual mothers and twenty-two for the children of gay or bisexual fathers.

Murray and McClintock looked specifically at (1) the social context–social stigma which includes the psychological fatigue of constant vigilance to keep a secret (the all-consuming task of passing oneself off as straight); (2) internalized homophobia, which includes the parent distancing herself or himself from the child, thus reducing intimacy to avoid disclosure; (3) self-esteem, which may be damaged as the parent's self-monitored

thoughts and behaviors leave little room for an expressed self with which the child can identify; and (4) anxiety, whereby keeping a family secret can result in lasting developmental and interpersonal consequences.

Murray and McClintock concluded that the children of lesbian mothers reported that their mother's secret sexual orientation affected them positively (6 responses); both positively and negatively (2 responses); not at all (2 responses); and negatively (2 responses). Children of lesbian mothers did not show a significant difference in trait anxiety, when compared to children of heterosexual mothers. Also, self-esteem was not affected. Children of gay fathers, however, often experienced a negative effect. This effect may have resulted from the length of the family secret or the fact that cultural attitudes toward gay men tend to be more negative than attitudes toward lesbians.

Source: "Children of the closet: A measurement of the anxiety and self-esteem of children raised by a non-disclosed homosexual or bisexual parent," by P. D. Murray, and K. McClintock, 2005, *Journal of Homosexuality, 49* (1), pp. 77–95.

Social and Cultural Description

It is nearly impossible to predict numbers of LGB children and the geographical location in which they reside. Researchers do not know how many LGB children exist and, in fact, many children might not realize their attraction toward the same sex. Still, some children have erotic or sexual fantasies that associate with sexual desire or lust. According to Friedman (1998), erotic fantasies are often experienced by many boys during the childhood years, well before puberty. In fact, the mean age of same-sex attraction has been reported to be 9.7 years for both boys and girls (Giorgis, Higgins, & McNab, 2000). Undoubtedly, LGB children do exist and might bring their unique problems to counseling sessions. Therefore, counselors need to recognize the challenges that these children face and be prepared to offer professional intervention that reflects children's sexual orientation and cultural backgrounds.

Some LGB children often know at a young age that something is different about them—the way they think, the way they feel, and what they like and do not like. Just because a child feels different does not mean that the child is necessarily lesbian, gay, or bisexual; however, emotional problems can result when children feel they are not like others. Some LGB persons report they realized their same-sex preference early in life. For example, van Wormer, Wells, and Boes (2000) tell of a 5 year-old boy who felt an attraction for other boys. Although LGB children might be too young to understand their feelings, they undoubtedly feel different and question themselves about why they are not like others. Then, they hear words such as *fag, homo,* or other derogatory terms. Although they might not understand the meaning of the words, they wonder if or know the words are directed at them. As they form a sexual identity, no child wants to be called derogatory names. They take on the cultural values of the majority, heterosexual society and deny their same-sex attractions.

Also, a child who is culturally different from the majority culture (regardless of the respective majority culture) might feel a double sense of oppression; that is, a child might also feel different because he or she is African American, Hispanic American, Arab American, or Asian American. The sad reality is that a child might feel different in more than one way. The child might be a cultural minority that is noticeably obvious and also harbor feelings of being attracted to the same sex.

Coming Out and Identity Development

Little research exists on children coming out or letting their sexual orientation be known. Although many young children might realize they differ in some way, they might not be old enough to realize their same-sex sexual orientation. Also, due to harassment and ridicule, most children will not engage in a coming out process. According to Herdt (1997), coming out and being out are so crucial to the creation of self-perceptions and stable, positive self-images that they would normally be considered as crucial to the sense of self in early childhood development.

Children growing up in more sexually tolerant environments may have experienced childhood sexual play with the same gender. Depending on the culture, such sexual play might have been encouraged; in other cultures the practice may be taboo. Years later, these children may wonder why the same-sex urges did not go away—their actions and desires had been repressed (Herdt, 1997). Still, as children, coming out (if they had even known the meaning of the term and process) would have been difficult or impossible due to parental punishments and peer harassment.

Identity formation refers to the development of a personal identity as core individual characteristics and social identity or as one's relation to others. The majority of the literature on childhood development is presumptively heterosexual, even though it is commonly known that children often have same-sex feelings and attractions. The omission of research on identity development in LGB children poses problems because it assumes these children either do not exist or they are so marginal that they are unworthy of study (van Wormer, Wells, & Boes, 2000, p. 65). In terms of identity formation, children face the developmental task of understanding and coming to terms with their sexual identity in an environment that denies and devalues their sexuality. Devaluing their sexual identity can negatively affect their social and psychological functioning (Schneider & Owens, 2000).

Many children feel challenged to demonstrate expected gender roles; that is, they are taught that boys and girls are expected to behave in specific ways. Still, all children who refuse to adhere to specific gender roles do not develop same-sex identities and orientations. Perceptive counselors realize they cannot determine who is lesbian, gay, or bisexual simply by appearance, personality, or behaviors (Bass & Kaufman, 1996).

When LGB children go through the process of understanding their sexual identity, they might experience considerable inner conflict. They do not understand their feelings and

UP CLOSE AND PERSONAL 15.1

Troy, African American and "Different"

Ten-year-old Troy was an African American boy in the fifth grade who seemed different from other boys his age. He liked to read and to be alone, and he did not participate in physical activities at recess.

Troy was required to take an active role in the physical education class. However, it was evident that he did not enjoy the physical activities; other boys did not want him on their teams, so he was always the last one chosen. One boy said, "We don't want the gay fag on our team." The coach heard the comment, but he chose not to take action. On several occasions, Troy made up excuses (e.g., having a hurt leg) so the coach would not make him play.

Troy was referred to the counselor, an Asian American man. During the third meeting with the counselor, Troy confided that he felt different. "I am not like them," he said, "I like to read; they don't. They like to play ball; I don't. I think I am more like the girls, but I don't think they like me either. It doesn't really matter—I am going to the middle school next year anyway." He never mentioned the possibility that he might have a different sexual orientation, and the counselor avoided seeking information in that area.

The teachers felt Troy was different and knew he was the recipient of considerable taunting and verbal abuse, but they did not take any deliberate action to help him. One teacher thought Troy might be gay and concluded that if he were, he should keep quiet about it. "He gets enough ridicule now," the teacher thought. Another teacher knew a problem existed but did not know what action to take. "Telling the others to stop picking on him might make the situation worse," the teacher said. In the meantime, Troy managed to make it through the day, although some days were far from pleasant. He stayed quiet most of the time, read more and more, and strove to avoid social contact.

their differences, especially when they perceive that society promotes opposite-sex attractions. As previously suggested, the problem of identity development grows more acute when the child comes from a culturally different background. Being a child in such an environment can result in problems such as confused sexual identity, guilt, and lower self-esteem, all of which counselors might be called on to address.

Up Close and Personal 15.1 looks at Troy, a 10-year-old African American boy who showed possible indicators of being gay.

Unique Challenges Confronting LGB Children

LGB children may face several challenges, all of which deserve counselors' attention. Even if children have not come out, other children might suspect their sexual orientation, thereby provoking displeasure and ridicule. Selected challenges facing LGB children and their counselors include the following:

1. School and societal messages emphasize (subtly or not so subtly) heterosexual attraction over homosexual attraction. Plus, peers might harass and call suspected LGB children names (e.g., "sissy," "fag," or "dyke"), provoking fear, humiliation, and self-hatred, which can have long-lasting negative effects on personal identity and self-esteem.

2. LGB children might assume that the majority of other children are heterosexual, recognize their own differences and, thus, assume they are wrong. Differences can take many forms;

sometimes differences indicate sexual orientation and at other times they do not. Schwartz and Blumstein (1998) maintain that some people erroneously suggest that effeminacy in boys and masculinity in girls are simply signs of the homosexuality that will manifest in late adolescence. Counselors need to avoid predicting future sexual orientations based on children's feminine or masculine behaviors. Similarly, Taylor, H.E. (2000) explains that boys are often uninterested in sports and like solitary rather than team interests; girls might like to be masculine and more interested in sports and generally lack heterosexual interests. Again, Taylor emphasizes the point that these types of differences do not *necessarily* (emphasis Taylor's) reflect sexual orientation.

3. LGB children may sometimes fear for their safety. Just because they are different, other children might pick fights or beat them up. In some particularly unfortunate situations, adults do not take appropriate action when they know a child is being harassed because of sexual differences.

4. In addition to their sexual orientation, children might also be of a culture different from the majority culture or perhaps disabled in some way. Forming a positive sexual and cultural identity can be even more difficult when children have to deal with several differences, especially in schools and communities that place major emphasis on heterosexualism and majority culture values.

Lesbian, Gay, and Bisexual Adolescents

Fortunately, more has been written on LGB adolescents than LGB children, probably because adolescents are developing sexually and also are developing sexual orientations. Selected authors such as Coleman and Remafedi (1989), Dubé and Savin-Williams (2000), Fygetakis (1997), Haeberle & Gindorf (1998), and van Wormer, Wells, and Boes (2000) have offered helpful information on understanding LGB adolescents.

Social and Cultural Description

Adolescence is the developmental period many boys and girls sense and act upon their LGB orientations. According to Giorgis, Higgins, and McNab (2000), the age of first homosexual activity is reported to be 13.1 years for boys and 15 years for girls. However, there have been some relatively small differences in these ages reported by other researchers. Dubé and Savin-Williams (2000) reported that youths, regardless of ethnicity, labeled their same-sex attractions at age 15 to 17 years. Referring only to bisexuals, Haeberle and Gindorf (1998) maintain that most bisexual people usually engage in such sexual activity in early to middle adolescence and young adulthood. It is possible for young people to develop passionate attachments to persons of the same gender during adolescence. In some cases, these emotional attachments may lead to physical sexual activity (Haeberle & Gindorf).

Minority culture adolescents often face double challenges owing to their same-sex orientations and their differing cultural backgrounds. They might face problems due to the majority culture's emphasis on personal independence compared to the minority culture's tendency toward group allegiance. Adherence to religious beliefs and family expectations for heterosexual unions and offspring affect African Americans, where close ties exist between church and community. Mexican Americans, Cuban Americans, and Puerto Rican Americans, as well as other cultures from primarily Catholic nations, would also be affected by adolescents' LGB orientations. Likewise, many Asian Americans (e.g., Chinese, Japanese, Koreans, Vietnamese, Thais, Cambodians, Philippinos) emphasize family tradition and adherence to community expectations. In addition, minority LGB persons are less likely than majority-culture Americans to have family support when they come out (van Wormer, Wells, & Boes, 2000). Also, Dubé and Savin-Williams (2000) suggested that perceptions of homophobia, fear of rejection, and avoidance of disclosure appear to be greater among ethnic sexual-minority youths.

Whereas European American cultures think adolescents should gain individuation from the family, Greeks think adolescence is a time when individuation occurs within the family. Adolescents learn to emulate their parents, take on more gender role-appropriate responsibilities, and develop their sense of increased maturity. Greek adolescents rarely discuss thoughts, feelings, or changing life values with their parents (Fygetakis, 1997). Fygetakis maintains that such family traditions would make it difficult for adolescent daughters to share their lesbianism. Although Fygetakis wrote primarily of Greek lesbians, adolescent males would also have difficulty sharing same-sex sexual orientations, especially considering the Greek culture's expectation for adolescents to accept gender role-appropriate responsibilities and behaviors.

Coming Out and Identity Development

Many LGB adolescents report feeling different since earliest childhood; however, contemporary studies (Hershberger & D'Augelli, 2000) have suggested that most adults who self-identify as lesbian or gay realize that their attractions to others of the same sex began during early adolescence. A developmental approach to sexual orientation must take into account the individual's developmental status. This means that same-sex eroticism will be experienced, thought about, and expressed not only in different ways at different ages but also in ways that reflect the individual's physical, cognitive, emotional, and social development at a particular point of personal development (Hershberger & D'Augelli).

Until quite recently, adolescent homosexuality was thought to be a passing phase on the road to heterosexuality; the possibility of a well-established homosexual identity was rejected (Coleman & Remafedi, 1989). Writers have devised various stage theories to depict the acquisition of a gay or lesbian orientation. They share the opinion that homosexual identification is not a sudden awakening during adulthood (Coleman & Remafedi; Troiden, 1989) but a gradual process that often begins with feeling different during childhood. These feelings take on sexual meanings during puberty as homosexual attractions occur. After a period of confusion, the individual typically adopts a gay or lesbian label but still may need years to reach a final stage of acceptance (Coleman, 1982; Coleman & Remafedi).

Sexual identification is not embraced immediately upon self-recognition; instead, it is a gradual coming out to oneself. Most individuals pass from awareness to positive self-identity between the ages of 13 and 20, with the process of establishing a positive lesbian, gay, or bisexual identity occurring earlier today than in the past. Few middle school students self-identify as lesbian, gay, or bisexual, compared with as high as 6% to 7% of high school students who describe themselves as primarily lesbian, gay, or bisexual. Still, even in middle school, evidence suggests lesbian, gay, and bisexual students feel different, even though they might not have the concepts to define the actual difference (Schneider & Owens, 2000).

Homophobia is a powerful force for not coming out during the adolescence developmental period. Herdt (1997) reports that being called "dyke" (p. 130) or "faggot" (p. 130) can be a detrimental blow to adolescents' self-esteem. Also, if they come out, many lesbian, gay, and bisexual adolescents do not believe that they can rely on traditional sources of support, such as their family, friends, peers, teachers, neighbors, clergy, and physicians. This perceived limitation on significant others' willingness to be supportive creates hurt, pain, and increased stress (Jones & Gabriel, 1998; van Wormer, Wells, & Boes, 2000). Adolescents who opt to come out also risk experiencing stigma and shame, and they fear the repercussions of coming out on their lives and safety, their overall well-being, and their social status and community prestige (Herdt).

Even under the threat of condemnation and harassment, some LGB persons come out during the adolescence stage. They have or are in the process of developing an LGB identity and are prepared to let their same-sex sexual orientation be known. Some have had heterosexual contacts, either experimentally or perhaps just to prove their heterosexuality to others; however, they become so certain of their same-sex sexual orientation that they decide to come out. The process may be more difficult for disabled adolescents or adolescents from culturally different backgrounds, who might already feel isolated and oppressed due to their culture and ethnicity and, therefore, may believe that coming out will only worsen their plight.

As a result of experiencing same-sex attractions or encounters in a predominantly heterosexual environment, adolescents' feelings of being different often result in identity confusion, the second stage of gay/lesbian identity development (Troiden, 1989). Characteristics of this stage include (1) feeling alone in every social situation, (2) feeling there is no one to talk to, (3) feeling the need to distance oneself emotionally from others, (4) fearing that same-sex friendships may be misinterpreted, and (5) feeling hopeless about the future (Martin & Hetrick, 1987; Ryan & Futterman, 1998; Taylor, H.E., 2000).

Giorgis, Higgins, and McNab (2000) maintain that lesbian and gay students face discrimination manifested in acts of isolation, physical abuse, and denial of basic rights of speech, assembly, and association. Counselors should

- keep in strict confidence when a student comes out,
- ask "Are you seeing anyone?" rather than "Do you have a boyfriend/girlfriend?"
- encourage library media specialists to purchase lesbian/gay friendly books,
- provide counseling services designed specifically for lesbian and gay students and their parents and families, and
- promote established policies to protect lesbian and gay students from harassment, violence, and discrimination.

Up Close and Personal 15.2 tells about Suzie, an Asian American adolescent who was not ready to come out and, in fact, tried to deny her same-sex sexual orientation even to herself.

UP CLOSE AND PERSONAL 15.2

Suzie, an Asian American Lesbian Adolescent

Suzie, a 16-year-old, third-generation, Asian American girl in the 10th grade refused to let her same-sex sexual orientation be known. In fact, she denied her feelings even to herself. Suzie came from a typical and "normal" middle-class home. The family attended church, they had big family gatherings, and they visited friends during vacation time each year. Both of Suzie's parents were heterosexual and, as far as she knew, no one in her family was homosexual. Suzie had several friends who were girls and, as far as she knew, none of them even suspected that she was feeling different. She had not even confided to her best friend that she might be a lesbian. She had dated several boys, tried to enjoy their company, and had even tried having sexual relations on two occasions. However, having sex with the boys was more for experimentation than for feelings of closeness with them. Her parents did not have any idea that she had had sexual relations with the boys, and it was clear that she did not want them to learn of her experiences. She had never had any physical contact with any of the girls she knew. She denied her feelings and thought (as she

said several years later), "I have too much to lose. My parents want me to go to college, and I know I need to—I will just have to face life somehow without people knowing I am a lesbian. Who knows? I might not be a lesbian anyway. As soon as I meet the right guy, I will be close to him, sex will be good, and I will forget these feelings. I have been feeling this way since I was 9 years old, and if I have been hiding my feelings all this time, I know I can keep hiding them."

Plus, as she confided several years later, another reason she would never let her feelings be known was because of the school. "I had heard all those names lesbians (although they might not actually have been lesbian, other students thought they were) were called. I would have been so embarrassed, especially if my parents had ever heard I was being called those names."

Suzie was in a bind. She had same-sex feelings that she continued to hide and deny to others and herself. She had no intention of ever letting anyone know. As she said later, "I was so embarrassed. No one could ever know about me."

Unique Challenges Confronting Lesbian, Gay, and Bisexual Adolescents

Although the challenges and stresses facing LGB adolescents are readily identifiable, such challenges and stresses can be so acute and so devastating to LGB adolescents that they need to be mentioned here. Selected challenges facing LGB adolescents include

- school and societal messages that heterosexuality is the norm and that homosexuality should be ignored;
- prejudice and discrimination in schools and society whereby LGB adolescents receive intentional or unintentional ill treatment;
- harassment, name-calling, and humiliation that some students (and teachers) inflict upon LGB students and heterosexual students who are perceived as lesbian, gay, or bisexual;
- safety and health risks such as suicide, drug and alcohol abuse, and risky sexual behaviors resulting in sexually transmitted diseases; and
- parents and family members who condemn LGB adolescents for their homosexuality.

Lesbian, Gay, and Bisexual Adults

These adults face a number of challenges, primarily due to society's rejection of homosexuality on moral and religious grounds, outright homophobia, or lack of knowledge of differing sexual orientations. Coming out also poses problems, either because LGB adults are reluctant to reveal their sexual orientations or because they fear loss of employment and social status as well as harassment and physical harm. Also, as previously suggested, counselors need to understand the unique situation facing minority LGB adults, because being a cultural minority plus being lesbian, gay, or bisexual can lead to multifaceted oppression and discrimination.

Social and Cultural Description

Although it is impossible to pinpoint specific numbers of minority LGB adults and their geographical location, they probably comprise about 10% of the population. LGB adults may be found in all cultures and all social classes.

The American Indian culture used the word *berdache* to describe a man or woman who departs from a socially constructed gender role and acquires traits and obligations of the opposite sex. Rather than crossing gender lines, the *berdache* actually blurs them, thus constituting a third sex. In traditional cultures, *berdaches* have married individuals of the same sex and these marriages were recognized by Indian law (Potgieter, 1997). Therefore, at least in the past, American Indian adults have tolerated same-sex sexual orientations; however, with the homophobia currently gripping American society, American Indian adults might be as reluctant as those of other cultures to reveal their homosexuality.

In the Asian American culture, open disclosure that one is lesbian or gay poses a threat to the continuation of the family line as well as a rejection of one's culturally accepted social roles. Lesbian or gay adults of other ethnic groups reported feeling discriminated against more because of race than sexual orientation, but Chan (1992) and Greene (1997) report that gay Asian men experience discrimination more because they were gay than because they were Asian. However, the persistent invisibility of Asian American lesbians and gay men within Asian communities is slowly changing with the development of lesbian and gay support groups within Asian communities (Greene).

Providing effective and culturally appropriate career counseling to gay and lesbian clients may seem similar to counseling heterosexual clients, yet Pope, Barret, Szymanski, Chung, Singaravelu, McLean, and Sanabria (2004) offer specific recommendations. Gender Perspectives 15.1 focuses on career counseling for gays and lesbians.

Western concepts of minority sexual orientations are influencing other countries. Discovering that one has an affectionate, erotic, or sexual attraction to others of their own sex has profoundly different meanings in China, Korea, and Japan. During the 19th and 20th centuries, this tolerant attitude was largely replaced by Western ideas that same-sex attraction was abnormal. A Focus on Research 15.3 looks at gay and lesbian Asians, Asian Americans, and immigrants from Asia and offers implications for counselors.

African Americans' cultural backgrounds include strong family ties that encompass nuclear and extended family members in complex networks of obligation and support. In African American families, gender roles for adults have been more flexible than in other cultures. The African American community is viewed by many of its lesbian and gay members as

GENDER PERSPECTIVES 15.1

Career Counseling for Gay and Lesbian Clients

After a discussion of the history and context of the emergence of an identifiable gay and lesbian culture, Pope, Barret, Szymanski, Chung, Singaravelu, McLean, and Sanabria (2004) recommend specific interventions directed at counselors, at individual counseling activities, at career counseling programs within institutions, and at advocacy and community action. They maintain that counseling interventions used with gay and lesbian people must either be learned during graduate school or through continuing education programs.

Program-focused interventions for career counseling include

- supporting gay and lesbian professionals as role models for students;

- providing information on national gay and lesbian networks of professionals and community

people such as the Association for Gay, Lesbian, and Bisexual Issues in Counseling;

- sharing information on existing local gay and lesbian resources;

- offering special programming, such as talks by lesbian and gay professionals;

- arranging career shadowing opportunities with other lesbian and gay professionals;

- facilitating internships or cooperative education placements in gay and lesbian owned or operated businesses; and

- establishing mentoring programs.

Source: "Culturally appropriate career counseling with gay and lesbian clients," by M. Pope, B. Barret, D. M. Szymanski, Y. B. Chung, H. Singaravelu, R. McLean, and S. Sanabria, 2004, *The Career Development Quarterly, 53* (2), pp. 158–177.

A FOCUS ON RESEARCH 15.3

Gay, Lesbian and Bisexual Asians

Kimmel and Yi (2004) reviewed past and contemporary thinking about gays, lesbians, and bisexual people, especially those of Asian descent. Some opinions were affected by Western thought, the work of Christian missionaries, and Asian allegiance to family expectations and honor.

Kimmel and Yi (2004) focus their attention on four aspects: differences between life in Asia and in the United States; differences between immigrants and nonimmigrants in the United States; differences of lifestyle variations; and age differences.

Kimmel and Yi offer four conclusions:

1. A gay, lesbian, and bisexual community is clearly emerging in Asia.

2. Gay men and lesbians in the United States are freer than in Asia to be open and to live their lives as sexual minorities.

3. Gender differences parallel those found in studies of lesbians and gay men in Western countries.

4. Nationality, culture, and ethnic background do make an important difference when studying Asian lesbians, bisexuals, and gay men.

Source: "Characteristics of gay, lesbian, Asians, Asian Americans, and immigrants from Asian to the USA." by D. C. Kimmel, and H. Yi, 2004, *Journal of Homosexuality, 47* (2), pp. 143–171.

extremely homophobic and rejecting of LGB persons. In fact, the strength of African American family ties often mitigate against outright rejection of lesbian and gay family members, despite clear rejection of lesbian and gay orientations (Greene, 1997).

As previously stated, Hispanic American cultures differ widely and represent a wide range of persons with different languages and different cultural norms. Consideration should be given to individual Hispanic cultures as well as to individuals within each culture. Generally speaking, in Hispanic cultures, women are expected to be submissive, virtuous, respectful of elders, and willing to defer to men; men are expected to provide for, protect, and defend the family. The Spanish language has few or no words for lesbians and gays that are not negative. There is a powerful sense of homophobia in the Hispanic community, which deters many lesbians and gay men from coming out (Espin, 1984; Greene, 1997).

Coming Out and Identity Development

Generally speaking, the largest number of lesbian and gay adults in the United States come out in their early 20s (Trujillo, 1997). However, one cannot assume all LGB adults have come out. Many adults have lived their entire lives without ever acknowledging their same-sex sexual orientation. These adults may consider coming out to be more risky and psychologically damaging than hiding their sexual orientation. In A Focus on Research 15.4, Parks, Hughes, and Matthews (2004) investigated the norms and expectations that women faced when they decided to identify as lesbian.

Simonsen, Blazina, and Watkins (2000) believe gay men experience gender role conflict that can affect attitudes about help seeking and psychological well-being. Gay men struggle with unique problems, such as being at odds with society's views, social condemnation, increased isolation, and decreased support and acceptance. Gay men who can share emotions and express affection experience less anger, anxiety, and depression and have a more favorable attitude toward seeking psychological help. The study results also suggested that gay men who have more conflicts about success, power, competition, and family issues also experience more anger, anxiety, and depression.

Simonsen, Blazina, and Watkins (2000) suggest that counselors should be sensitive to the importance of emotional and affection expression issues to the well-being of gay men and, where appropriate, incorporate those issues into counseling. They also note that gay men experience unique issues related to their sexual orientation; however, some concerns (e.g., emotionality, work and family conflicts) are similar to those experienced by heterosexual men. Therefore, although counselors should identify differences between gay men and heterosexual men, Simonsen, Blazina, and Watkins suggest that it is equally important to recognize the fundamental similarities between the two groups.

Particularly for cultural minority LGB adults such as Asian Americans, Hispanic Americans, and African Americans, coming out tests family acceptance and relationships. Some families, especially those that place emphasis on continuing the family line, may totally reject the coming out of a family member. Also, even if a family agrees to conceal a family member's same-sex sexual orientation, the family's allegiance to the church might still be reason to reject the LGB family member. Again, although coming out is difficult for LGB persons in all developmental stages, it can also be an emotional and traumatic event for adults, especially considering the potential loss of family, social status, and financial livelihood.

A FOCUS ON RESEARCH 15.4

Race/Ethnicity and Sexual Orientation: Intersecting Identities

Parks, Hughes, and Matthews (2004) report findings from a sample of African American, Hispanic American, and White American lesbians. The authors review sexual identity formation and describe sexual identity formation as a linear or sequential developmental process that begins with awareness of same-sex attraction, progresses through stages of testing and exploration, and culminates in personal acceptance and public acknowledgment of being gay or lesbian.

In their discussion, Parks, Hughes, and Matthews maintain that lesbians of color were less likely than their White counterparts to disclose their sexual identity to nonfamily groups, regardless of age. However, they found an interesting pattern of age-related differences in disclosure to family. Older women of color were more likely than younger women of color to be out to their families, whereas the opposite was true for White women: Older White women were substantially less likely than their younger counterparts to be out with their family members.

Parks, Hughes, and Matthews summarize that lesbians of color had to simultaneously confront and manage the triple oppressions of sexism, heterosexism, and racism that exist both within the dominant culture and within their own racial/ethnic groups. According to Parks, Hughes, and Matthews.

- challenges of these triple oppressions can be stressful and daunting tasks;

- stress and isolation place individuals at risk of negative health consequences, yet health-care providers cannot assume that lesbians will disclose information about their sexual orientation; and

- models of sexual identity development provide little guidance as to how individuals, particularly those of different races/ethnicities, will negotiate the identity development process.

Source: "Race/ethnicity and sexual orientation: Intersecting identities," by C. A. Parks, T. L. Hughes, and A. K. Matthews, 2004, *Cultural Diversity and Ethnic Minority Psychology, 10* (3), pp. 241–254.

An emotionally complex decision, the coming out process for LGB adults largely depends on expected consequences. For example, some LGB adults may confide in trusted friends in order to gain needed emotional support but choose not to tell coworkers in order to protect job security (Crosbie-Burnett, Foster, Murray, & Bowen, 1996).

Other considerations regarding the decision to come out may include a desire to protect other family members. LGB adults might want to avoid problems with the extended family, especially among the older generation, who might experience difficulty with a family member coming out. Also, LGB adults might choose not to tell elderly family members for fear of rejection, such as disinheritance (Crosbie-Burnett, Foster, Murray, & Bowen, 1996).

Oetjen and Rothblum (2000) maintain that depression is one of the most prevalent mental health problems in the United States today, affecting 2% to 19% of the country's population. Oetjen and Rothblum conclude that (1) lesbians, like heterosexual women, who feel unsupported are at risk for depression; (2) unlike women in general, relationship status does not predict depression in lesbians; however, relationship status satisfaction does; (3) their study disputed the popular belief that disclosure of sexual orientation is associated with depression in lesbians.

Up Close and Personal 15.3 looks at Carlos, a bisexual Hispanic American adult.

Carlos, a Bisexual Hispanic American Adult

Carlos, a 45-year-old professional, had been hiding his bisexuality for decades. He had been married for 23 years and had three grown children who, to the best of his knowledge, were heterosexual. He and his wife have had a good marriage, but she did not have any idea about his bisexuality (or at least she never gave any indication that she knew). They had enjoyed a good sex life and, generally speaking, were happily married. Carlos did not have any desire for a divorce; still, his feelings for men were equally as powerful as they were for women.

Because he worked in a professional position, he knew he could not come out. He was unwilling to risk his job, financial livelihood, and security. Also, his job offered another advantage. He had the opportunity to travel to distant cities where he met other men. He had enjoyed a number of encounters with men; in fact, these encounters were becoming increasingly frequent. In earlier years when he decided to move on his desires, he had had one encounter every 2 to 3 years. Now, the encounters were more frequent; he was taking more trips and having more sexual encounters with men. He was concerned that his increasing encounters with men might result in his being found out by his employer and by his wife. He was also concerned about the possibility of contracting AIDS from men he did not really know.

Unique Challenges Confronting Lesbian, Gay, and Bisexual Adults

Just as with LGB children and adolescents, being a LGB adult has several challenges. Although some of these challenges (e.g., prejudice, discrimination) apply to all LGB persons regardless of their developmental stage, others apply primarily to LGB adults. For example, LGB adults might experience

- problems with career needs and barriers due to their sexuality, especially those who come out in the workplace;
- prejudice, discrimination, and harassment in all aspects of society;
- problems that arise when lesbians, gay men, and bisexuals are in heterosexual marriages, as well as problems in adoption and parenting issues;
- challenges dealing with depression, especially in lesbians; and
- dangers resulting from risky behaviors: suicide, substance abuse, and HIV/AIDS.

Merrill and Wolfe (2000) maintain that battered gay and bisexual men suffer patterns, forms, and frequencies of physical, emotional, and sexual abuse similar to what has been documented by research on battered heterosexual and lesbian women. Domestic violence appears to be as common and as serious a problem in same-gender relationships as in heterosexual ones. Likewise, the most commonly reported reasons for staying—namely, hope for change and love for partner—appear to be universal to the experience of being battered, regardless of sexual orientation. Merrill and Wolfe offer several conclusions:

1. All people associated with and working with gay and bisexual battered men (and women) should avoid "recognition failure" (p. 24), whereby people fail to recognize behaviors that constitute domestic violence.

2. Most professionals should receive training in assessing and responding to same-gender battering; example, some helping professionals, when they arrive at a domestic violence scene, fail to realize that two women or two men can share a romantic relationship and that one can still be a victim of domestic violence.

3. Workers at battered women's shelters tend to admit women without completely assessing whether they are the victim or the batterer, who is seeking shelter as a ploy.

4. Workers tend to assume that "women are not as violent to one another" and "men can protect themselves" (p. 25) and, therefore, the man must be the perpetrator and the women must be the victim.

5. Mental health professionals should screen all clients for past and present history of relationship violence.

6. Mental health professionals should complete a full assessment and should develop an individualized treatment plan that respects the client's self-determination and the client's right to remain with a dangerous partner.

Lesbian, Gay, and Bisexual Elderly

Contrary to commonly accepted myths, elderly people remain sexually active and are generally satisfied with their sex lives (Jacobson & Grossman, 1996). Many people might think the elderly do not have same-sex urges. Not only might counselors neglect addressing their elderly clients' sexuality, they might also assume that all elderly people are heterosexual. Elderly LGB persons who have not come out might never let their sexual orientation be known.

Social and Cultural Description

Elderly LGBs face multiple challenges owing to their age, possible minority status, and same-sex sexual orientation. Older lesbians are thought to be nonexistent by both society and the lesbian community. Thus, elderly lesbians are in triple jeopardy because of age, gender, and sexual orientation. Gay men place more emphasis on youth, yet there is speculation that older gay men often learn to deal with their stigmatized status and, therefore, are better prepared to deal with aging than heterosexual men. Another commonly held belief is that young gay men find older gay men unattractive because of the reminder that they will also be old someday (van Wormer, Wells, & Boes, 2000).

The popular belief that older lesbians and gay men live their lives alone is a myth; living alone is not the norm for these individuals (Berger, 1996). The vast majority of older lesbians and gay men live with a partner, roommate, friends, or family members. Sharing an apartment or a home with another LGB person provides a haven from the outside hostile world. Some older LGB persons have meaningful relationships throughout their lives (van Wormer, Wells, & Boes, 2000). Perhaps the most important consideration for gay men is that their living situation can solve a range of political and social problems. Sharing a home with another person provides companionship and lightens the financial burden of housing. This companionship is important to gay men who might have few friends or to those who live in rural areas distant from an accessible gay community (Berger).

The plight facing minority LGB elderly can be multiply oppressive. The presence of any of these three conditions—minority status, elderly status, and same-sex sexual orientation—alone can create difficulties, but the presence of all three at once can make oppression more acute. Counselors need to understand the challenges associated with the elderly developmental period as well as those associated with being a minority and lesbian, gay, or bisexual.

Berger (1996) studied the social and socioeconomic status of older gay men and found that most were highly educated, held medium- to high-status occupations, had high incomes, and described themselves as in good or excellent health. In addition, more than half described themselves as somewhat or very liberal (Berger).

Coming Out and Identity Development

In Berger's (1996) study, older gay men were asked about their experiences coming out. As discussed previously, definitions of coming out vary. Some men in this study thought coming out meant their first sexual encounter with a man; others thought the term meant being honest with others about their sexual orientation; and others thought it meant self-recognition and self-acceptance. Regardless of their definition, they all considered coming out to be one of their most significant life experiences. It could also be a very difficult and frightening step that was taken only after years of soul-searching. With one exception, all the men had had their first same-sex sexual experience during early puberty or adolescence. Even though they recognized their same-sex sexual interests, some of the men had married and raised children before returning to same-sex interests in their 40s and 50s. Some of the men had their first experience with peers, usually friends

---

UP CLOSE AND PERSONAL 15.4

Calliope, an Elderly Greek American Lesbian

Calliope is 74 years old and is a lesbian. She has known for almost 60 years that sexually, she prefers women over men. It was difficult for Calliope when she was young, because her parents taught her a women's role was to serve a man. She was taught to do whatever was required to get a man and then do whatever was necessary to keep him. She listened attentively, because they were her parents, yet she knew from about age 12 or 13 that she had sexual feelings toward women. She did not tell her parents because, as she once said, "They would have thrown me out of the house." At age 19, Calliope moved out of the house and at age 24 moved in with another lesbian. True to her expectations, her father told her she could never come back to his house again (although Calliope never admitted to him that she was lesbian). In her lifetime, she had only had two

or three lovers, because her small community did not approved of lesbians. Now, she was 74, her lover had died from heart disease, and Calliope was living alone. She needed to live with someone to share housing costs, she continued to have sexual feelings for other women, and she was lonely. She was going to a lunch center for older people 3 times per week, but she wondered how much longer her health would allow her to attend. A counselor came several times a month to discuss concerns with the group, but she could not tell her about her "problems" in front of the entire group—not at her age. Although she had never married and had lived with women most of her adult life, she did not think that the people at the center knew she was lesbian. "If they knew, they probably wouldn't let me come," she once said.

from school or in the neighborhood. Only a small number had had sexual experiences with an older man (Berger).

In Berger's study, even same-sex experiences and self-recognition as a person who is sexually attracted to men did not guarantee a clear homosexual identity. It was necessary for the men to associate with other self-identified gay men. Just as there was a gap between same-sex sexual behavior and self-identification, there may also have been a time lag between self-identification and integration into the gay community (Berger, 1996).

Interestingly, the majority of gay men reported shame over their sexual feelings at some point in their lives, often during adolescence. Most gay men overcame their initial feelings of shame and guilt as they reached adulthood. In fact, older gay men are less anxious about their same-sex sexual relations than are their younger counterparts. As gay men age, they no longer have to conform to the mental image of the sexually active gay man in his 20s and 30s (van Wormer, Wells, & Boes, 2000).

Up Close and Personal 15.4 looks at Calliope, an elderly Greek American lesbian.

Unique Challenges Confronting Lesbian, Gay, and Bisexual Elderly

As for LGBs in the other developmental periods, it is important for counselors to consider challenges unique to LGB elderly, including

- deciding whether to come out during the elderly years (assuming the elderly person has not already come out);
- prejudice and discrimination in housing, retirement benefits, and medical attention;
- difficulties in obtaining assisted living facilities, nursing home care, and long-term health care stemming from their sexual orientation;
- psychosocial problems resulting from heterosexual family members, living arrangements, and society;
- problems associated with the elderly and risk factors such as suicide;
- challenges associated with increased health problems and the possibility of these problems being aggravated by HIV/AIDS and lack of proper medical attention; and
- problems stemming from being elderly in a society that ignores sexuality (especially LGB sexuality) of the elderly and, thus, does not work to address their needs.

A Point of Departure: Challenges Confronting Counselors of Lesbians, Gay Men, and Bisexuals

Counseling LGB clients in the various developmental stages will challenge counseling professionals, especially counselors who do not understand the effects of cultural diversity and same-sex sexual orientations. In order to provide effective counseling intervention, counselors must have the professional training, experience with minority LGB persons in the various lifespan stages, and a genuine professional motivation to effectively counsel LGB persons in the four lifespan periods. Specific challenges include

- understanding that LGB persons have a culture of their own, in addition to their own ethnicity;

- developing the counseling competencies (e.g., attitudes, knowledge, skills) necessary to counsel LGB persons in the various cultures and lifespan stages;

- understanding challenges faced by LGB persons in each lifespan period;

- providing counseling intervention (e.g., individual, group, and family) that reflects LGB persons' worldviews and same-sex sexual orientation;

- understanding discrimination, injustices, and harassment faced by LGB persons and making a commitment to address these issues whenever possible; and

- understanding and accepting one's own sexuality (homosexuality, bisexuality, or heterosexuality) and making a commitment to avoid letting one's sexuality interfere with counseling clients who have different sexual orientations.

Summary

As LGB persons come out in increasing numbers, counselors will be called on to provide counseling intervention to clients with same-sex sexual orientations in the various lifespan stages. Counselors will be unable to assume clients' heterosexuality; in fact, LGB clients will bring topics to counseling sessions unlike those of their heterosexual counterparts. Whereas minorities have long been plagued by discrimination, harassment, and prejudice, minority LGB clients will now bring issues related to sexual orientation in addition to the minority status issues. Counselors will be called on to understand different clients: LGB children and adolescents who are called hurtful names, LGB adults who are threatened with loss of employment and social status, and elderly LGB persons facing neglect and failure by others to understand their developmentally related problems. Understanding LGB persons will be the first step to effective counseling; knowing appropriate counseling strategies and techniques (discussed in Chapter 16) will be the second required step.

Suggested Readings

Beals, K. P., & Peplau, L. A. (2005). Identity support, identity devaluation, and well-being among lesbians. *Psychology of Women Quarterly, 29*, 140–148. Beals and Peplau investigate the association of identity support and identity devaluation with psychological well-being (e.g., self-esteem, life satisfaction, and depression).

Fingerhut, A. W., Peplau, L. A., & Ghavami, N. (2005). A dual framework for understanding lesbian experience. *Psychology of Women Quarterly, 29*, 129–139. These authors maintain that the diverse life experiences of contemporary lesbians are shaped by women's differing ties to two social worlds, the majority heterosexual society and the minority subculture of the lesbian or sexual-minority world.

Jensen, R. (2004). Homecoming: The relevance of radical feminism for gay men. *Journal of Homosexuality, 47* (3/4), 75–81. Jensen calls for a serious engagement with feminist politics—particularly critiques of pornography and the sex industry.

Lemelle, A. J., & Battle, J. (2004). Black masculinity matters in attitudes toward gay males. *Journal of Homosexuality, 47*(1), 39–51. These authors examine gender differences in attitudes toward homosexual men.

Todosijevic, J., Rothblum, E. D., & Solomon, S. E. (2005). Relationship satisfaction, affectivity, and gay-specific stressors in same-sex couples joined in civil unions. *Psychology of Women Quarterly, 29*, 158–166. After the legislation was enacted, Todosijevic, Rothblum, and Solomon examined a group of same-sex couples in Vermont to determine relationship satisfaction.

Vicario, B. A., Liddle, B. J., & Luzzo, D. A. (2005). The role of values in understanding attitudes toward lesbians and gay men. *Journal of Homosexuality, 49* (1), 145–159. These authors conclude that the values of *salvation, obedience, and national security* correlate with negative attitudes, and *broad-mindedness, a world of beauty, and imagination* correlate with positive attitudes.

Counseling Lesbian, Gay, and Bisexual Clients

Questions to Be Explored

1. How does counseling intervention differ for lesbian, gay, and bisexual (LGB) clients and heterosexual clients?

2. What are the American Psychological Association (APA) guidelines for counseling LGB clients?

3. What counseling concerns and issues are particularly relevant to LGB clients in each of the specific developmental stages?

4. How can counselors help LGB clients deal with harassment, prejudice, discrimination, and other types of physical and psychological abuse?

5. How can counselors provide effective individual, group, and family counseling for LGB clients in the four lifespan stages?

6. What factors should counselors consider when planning professional intervention for LGB clients who are also minority and/or disabled?

7. How can counselors provide professional intervention for LGB clients who have HIV/AIDS or who are experiencing bereavement because LGB friends and relatives have died?

8. How can counselors most effectively intervene with clients who are suicidal or engaged in substance abuse?

9. What special challenges might confront counselors of LGB clients that might not be experienced when working with heterosexual clients?

Overview

Currently, counselors may not have received professional training in techniques of counseling lesbian, gay, and bisexual (LGB) clients. Also, some counselors who are interested in culture and its effects on the counseling process may not have considered sexual orientation to be a

355

"culture." Most professionals agree that people have more than one culture and that lesbians, gay men, and bisexuals have a "same-sex sexual orientation" culture, just as heterosexual people share a culture of heterosexualism. However, counselors of LGB clients will want to improve their knowledge, attitudes, and skills because there are indications that lesbians, gay men, and bisexuals will increasingly make their sexual preferences known during counseling sessions. Until recently, and still the case for some clients, many LGB clients kept their sexual orientation to themselves, either due to embarrassment or fear of physical or psychological abuse, or harassment, prejudice, and discrimination. This chapter looks at the differences in counseling LGB clients, some special concerns and issues LGB clients might experience, and the use of individual, group, and family counseling for LGB clients in the four lifespan periods. Also, whenever possible, attention will be given to LGB clients who are minority and/or disabled.

Differences in Counseling Lesbian, Gay, and Bisexual Clients

Counselors who intervene with LGB clients encounter different challenges, concerns, and issues than those encountered while counseling heterosexual clients. One cannot assume that the only difference will be the client's sexual orientation. Table 16.1 shows difficult issues LGB clients might encounter.

Table 16.1 Differences in Counseling LGB Clients	LGB clients
	1. face challenges resulting from their different worldviews.
	    Example: Their sexual orientation will affect their individual experiences (and perceptions of those experiences) as well as their social, moral, religious, educational, economic, and political views.
	2. experience different types of discrimination and injustice.
	    Example: They experience discrimination because of their sexual orientation and their minority or disabled status, resulting in multiple types of jeopardy or discrimination.
	3. experience career problems caused by their coming out.
	    Example: They might feel their career will be jeopardized (or employment might actually be terminated) if they formally come out.
	4. experience family problems caused by coming out or perceived sexual orientation.
	    Example: Their family members object to their sexual orientation on moral, religious, or other grounds, resulting in loss of family support and family cohesiveness.

Other differences undoubtedly will surface as counselors intervene with LGB clients. The brief list in Table 16.1 provides only representative examples; counselors will need to consider individual LGB clients to determine the extent to which their sexual orientation affects counseling. The important point for counselors to remember is that a client's sexual orientation will affect the client's perceptions of problems, concerns, and issues. Just as Hispanic American counselors need to understand African American and other cultures' worldviews and culturally related issues, the heterosexual counselor needs to understand the differences in intervening with LGB clients and vice versa. In addition to understanding the differences in counseling LGB clients, it will be necessary to gain the knowledge, develop the attitudes, and refine the skills needed to intervene with these clients, just as this book has repeatedly recommended for counselors working with differing cultural groups.

What approach should the counselor take when the client does not know whether or not to come out? Should the counselor encourage the client to come out or to conceal his or her sexual orientation? These are difficult questions and the answer often depends on the individual client. The overriding counseling principle should be the welfare of the client. The counselor should try to establish a safe, comfortable climate so the client can come out if she or he wishes. The decision to come out should be strictly the client's decision. If the client is considering coming out, the counselor can help by discussing possible plans and their consequences; however, the final decision needs to be made by the client.

Guidelines for Psychotherapy With Lesbian, Gay, and Bisexual Clients

In 1975, the American Psychological Association (APA) adopted a resolution stating that homosexuality per se does not imply an impairment in judgment, stability, reliability, or general social and vocational capabilities. In 2000, the APA issued guidelines for psychotherapy with lesbian, gay, and bisexual clients. Specific purposes of the guidelines include providing practitioners with (a) a frame of reference for the therapy practices for lesbian, gay, and bisexual clients and (b) basic information and further references in the areas of assessment, intervention, identity, relationships, and the education and training of psychologists (APA, 2000). Table 16.2 provides an overview of the guidelines.

It is useful for counseling professionals to be aware of the nature and availability of community resources for LGB clients and their families. Particularly useful are those organizations that provide support to the parents, young and adult children, and friends of LGB clients; programs that provide assistance to victims of hate crimes; programs for LGB youth; and groups that focus on parenting issues, relationships, and coming out. There are also professional organizations for LGB persons of color groups for HIV/AIDS issues groups for socializing and networking in business and groups that provide spiritual assistance. Psychologists who are unfamiliar with available resources for LGB persons may obtain consultations or referrals from local agencies, state psychological associations, and the APA (APA, 2000).

Table 16.2
Guidelines for Psychotherapy with LGB Clients

Attitudes Toward Homosexuality and Bisexuality

Guideline 1: Psychologists understand that homosexuality and bisexuality are not indicative of mental illness.

Guideline 2: Psychologists are encouraged to recognize how their attitudes and knowledge about LGB issues may be relevant to assessment and treatment and seek consultation or make appropriate referrals when indicated.

Guideline 3: Psychologists strive to understand the ways in which social stigmatization (i.e., prejudice, discrimination) pose risk factors for the mental health and well-being of LGB clients.

Guideline 4: Psychologists strive to understand how inaccurate or prejudicial views of homosexuality or bisexuality may affect the client's presentation in treatment and the therapeutic process.

Relationships and Families

Guideline 5: Psychologists strive to be knowledgeable about and respect the importance of LGB relationships.

Guideline 6: Psychologists strive to understand the particular circumstances and challenges faced by parents who are lesbian, gay, or bisexual.

Guideline 7: Psychologists recognize that the families of LGB persons may include people who are not legally or biologically related.

Guideline 8: Psychologists strive to understand how a person's sexual orientation may have an impact on his or her family of origin and the relationship to that family.

Issues of Diversity

Guideline 9: Psychologists are encouraged to recognize the particular life issues or challenges that are related to multiple and often conflicting cultural norms, values, and beliefs that LGB persons of racial and ethnic minorities face.

Guideline 10: Psychologists are encouraged to recognize the particular challenges that bisexual individuals experience.

Guideline 11: Psychologists strive to understand the special problems that exist for LGB youth.

Guideline 12: Psychologists consider generational differences within LGB populations and the particular challenges that LGB older adults may experience.

Source: Developed from "Guidelines for psychotherapy with lesbian, gay, and bisexual clients," by American Psychological Association, 2000, *American Psychologist, 55* (2), pp. 1440–1451.

In the United States today, most lesbians have ties to two social worlds, the majority heterosexual world and the minority subculture of the lesbian or sexual-minority world. With differing degrees of comfort, lesbians navigate through these worlds as a regular part of life. Fingerhut, Peplau, and Ghavami (2005) in A Focus on Research 16.1 offer a framework for understanding identity in lesbian women, one that accounts for both minority and majority communities.

A FOCUS ON RESEARCH 16.1

A Dual-Identity Framework for Understanding Lesbian Experience

Fingerhut, Peplau, and Ghavami (2005) maintain the life experiences of contemporary lesbians are shaped by ties to two worlds. Their article presents a detailed conceptual analysis of a dual-identity framework that emphasizes lesbians' simultaneous affiliations with the lesbian world and the mainstream/heterosexual world. Their model captures the diversity among lesbians better than existing multidimensional identity models that consider connections only to lesbian and gay others. They conclude that factors that significantly affect identities include experiences of discrimination, feelings of homophobia, and life satisfaction.

These researchers also consider how best to conceptualize and assess key components of lesbian and mainstream identity. For example, how broadly or narrowly should the lesbian and gay male community be conceptualized? Breadth might range from a national lesbian and gay male community (e.g., a large organization that supports lesbians and gays); a local organization that serves both lesbians and gay males; sex-segregated lesbian groups (e.g., a lesbian support group or coffee shop); or more narrowly still to an individual's own social world.

***

Source: "A dual-identity framework for understanding lesbian experience," by A. W. Fingerhut, L. A. Peplau, and N. Ghavami, 2005, *Psychology of Women Quarterly, 29,* pp. 129–139.

Counseling Lesbian, Gay, and Bisexual Children

Counselors providing professional intervention with LGB children need to recognize the unique challenges of the childhood developmental period. For example, children may realize they are different in some way, but they may not understand how they differ or what the feelings of being different mean. Effective counselors of LGB or questioning children usually try to understand these children's worldviews and perceptions of their home, school, and community. Also, it will be imperative that counselors understand these children's perceptions of the problems that are bothering them. Being called "sissy" or "fag" on a daily basis can take a significant toll on a child. Telling a child to "just ignore those who call you names or laugh at you" will probably be ineffective. The counselor's challenge is to recognize that few children will have formally come out, so the counselor might not actually know whether the child has a same-sex sexual orientation.

Counseling Concerns and Issues

The LGB child (or a child whom others suspect is such) experiences concerns and issues that other children might not experience. Disabled children might be laughed at and taunted, but LGB children experience their own particular forms of fear, harassment, and prejudice.

LGB children often face a hostile school and societal environment. In many schools, the needs of LGB children largely go unnoticed and unmet. Their identity as a minority group is ignored, even though in many schools they are often the most hated group. As one of the few remaining minority groups that is victimized with few consequences for the perpetrators, LGB children are fair game for adults and other students to harass, demean, threaten, and even physically assault (Fontaine, 1998). Although parents and community members often consider schools to be safe places where teachers prohibit harassment, such is not always the case. Children are physically and psychologically abused on buses, playgrounds, hallways, and even in classrooms, while teachers either are unaware of it or choose to ignore it. LGB children are left to fend for themselves, although they often fear for their physical and psychological safety. They dread coming to school because they know they will be taunted by other students. They are called "gay," "fag," or "queer"; others are "beaten up" on the playground or on the way to school. Most school districts have policies against name-calling and harassment due to sexual orientation (or perceived sexual orientation), but all too often students who harass and cause physical or psychological damage go unpunished. Counselors can play significant roles in this area—they can encourage other students not to harass and taunt, and they can also encourage teachers and administrators to take strong and decisive action to stop harassment of LGB children.

LGB children often misunderstand the "differences" they feel. Although they might not realize that their feelings indicate a different sexual orientation, many feel a need to share their feelings with someone. However, whom do they tell? Do they share their feelings with a friend who might tell others? Do they tell a teacher or a counselor? Realistically speaking, telling any of these persons might be risky, especially for a child's fragile ego and self-esteem. LGB children may not understand their differences and thus may begin to develop a sense of self-hatred. The counselor has a difficult role in helping children who feel different. These children have not formally engaged in a coming out process, so the counselor should not automatically make assumptions about their sexual orientation. They may have same-sex orientation feelings, but the feelings might never be acted upon. However, the counselor can still attempt to help LGB children understand their perception of feeling different.

Another counseling concern or issue is when LGB children are from a culture different from the majority culture of the school (regardless of the school's majority culture). To be lesbian, gay, or bisexual or to be perceived as such and to be of a minority culture can result in multiple jeopardy for harassment. The presence of a disability is yet another reason for being harassed. Counselors who are effective with LGB children (or those children who are harassed because others suspect they are LGB) are sufficiently perceptive of other reasons for harassment. Counselors should make a commitment to take planned action to stop all harassment, whether owing to culture, disability, or perceived sexual orientation.

Counseling Considerations

Counselors of LGB children often must deal with several special considerations. Is the child's perceptions of feeling different a result of sexual orientation? Should sexual orientation even be mentioned during counseling sessions? Should all therapy be individual to avoid the possibility of harassment resulting from group therapy? How realistic is family therapy? These are difficult questions to answer, and a decision can be reached only through consideration of each individual case.

Individual and Group Therapy.   As discussed in Chapter 15, counselors and all professionals, as well as the general population, should refrain from assuming that a person is lesbian, gay, or bisexual based on that person's appearance or actions. Just because a boy is effeminate and prefers books over football does not mean he is gay or ever will be gay. The same is true with girls who prefer more rugged clothes to dresses, or soccer over cooking; she may or may not be lesbian, but counselors cannot make assumptions based solely upon preferences. Nor should counselors suggest to a client that he or she might be gay or lesbian. Same-sex sexual orientation is not a choice that a student makes in one day.

It is another matter if the child shares with the counselor that his or her "feelings of difference" include a same-sex sexual orientation. Some people have told us that they knew they had a same-sex sexual orientation as early as age 8 or 9. If, during individual therapy, the child openly confides to the counselor a same-sex sexual orientation, then the counselor has the professional responsibility to avoid judgmental statements, help the child to accept the feelings, help the child to understand the meaning of same-sex orientation, and agree to provide support and acceptance. The counselor should not engage in any attempts to change the child's sexual orientation. Likewise, the counselor should maintain strict confidentiality about the child's disclosure.

Schneider and Owens (2000) maintain that schools foster the attitude that heterosexism is the only natural and acceptable sexual orientation. Schneider and Owens think this heterosexual perspective is problematic for heterosexual children as well as for children who are questioning their sexual orientation. Children begin to feel sexual attractions, whether same-sexual, bisexual, or heterosexual. They are experiencing the developmental task of understanding and coming to terms with their sexual identity, and with hostile and abusive environments. Recommendations for schools fostering a supportive community can be accomplished at three levels:

1. *Institutional:* School leaders need to communicate to all educators and counselors that value is placed on safe, nurturing environments.

2. *Classroom:* Educators and counselors can discuss the fact that people differ and these differences have the potential to enhance our understanding of the world and one another.

3. *One-on-one:* Educators and counselors need to create a safe environment in which to learn and safe places where LGB students feel supported.

Unless the school has a sufficient number of LGB students who have formally come out, group therapy is probably not an effective means of intervention. Few, if any, elementary schools have group therapy solely for LGB students; the number of group therapy incidents might be higher in middle schools and high schools. Most children who think their perceptions of feeling different resulted from same-sex sexual orientations would be reluctant to share this information in a group therapy session owing to possible harassment and taunting.

Counselors can and should use group or class opportunities to discuss children's differences, the need to accept differences, and the need to avoid harassing others. In these group or class presentations, the counselor makes an individual decision about whether to refer to issues about people with same-sex sexual orientations—such a decision should be based on children's ages and developmental levels. For example, referring to same-sex sexual orientation might be risky for first graders but more realistic for sixth graders. The counselor might have to consider how broadly to consider the term "group therapy." If the term "group therapy" is sufficiently flexible to include class discussions, then diversity of all types should be discussed, with an emphasis on acceptance and positive treatment of others.

Family Therapy.   Some children may confide their perceptions of feeling different to their parents; however, in all likelihood, most children will not, especially if they know their feelings relate to (and if they understand the meaning of) their sexual orientation. Theoretically, children can disclose their same-sex sexual orientation during family therapy sessions, but from a practical perspective, this is unlikely. First, they may not know these feelings relate to sexual orientation. Second, they may be reluctant to share these feelings, especially if they come from a culture that believes children's behaviors reflect upon the mother's and father's parenting ability. In such cultures, the embarrassment they experience and the accompanying feelings of shame they bring to their families will be too great for most children to admit they feel different.

Assuming that a counselor does decide on family therapy and assuming the child does share feelings of same-sex sexual orientation, the counselor should strive to understand the parents' feelings (especially if they are both heterosexual) as well as their acceptance levels of the child's disclosure. The counselor should also help parents to understand the child's need for continued love and acceptance. The counselor should work to keep family therapy from becoming negative; for example, the counselor should prevent parents from assigning blame for their child's sexual orientation or prevent parents from reprimanding the child for being different. The session should not end with despair over the child's disclosure, disappointment with the child, or anger toward any person in the family therapy session. Up Close and Personal 16.1 focuses on a counselor's challenges with Troy, an African American boy who felt "different."

UP CLOSE AND PERSONAL 16.1

Counseling Troy, an African American Child

The counselor, an African American man, knew that Troy, a fifth grade African American boy, faced a number of problems: He avoided participation in physical activities, he felt he was "different" ("I am not like them," he once told the counselor), he avoided social contact, and he received considerable ridicule and verbal abuse from fellow students. The counselor concluded that Troy had sufficient problems to warrant special counseling. He decided against group therapy because Troy would be uncomfortable admitting his feelings and accompanying problems, and he decided against family therapy because Troy had indicated his parents did not know the problems he faced.

The counselor considered his intervention plan. He decided not to mention sexual orientation because Troy had never said his "different" feelings were sexually related. He would discuss Troy's feeling different and the origins of these feelings, his lack of participation in voluntary school activities, the ridicule and psychological abuse (and its negative effects), and his avoidance of social contact. He would also work on self-acceptance and self-esteem as well as his treatment of others, that is, giving others the impression that he was ignoring or avoiding them. He and Troy would also discuss Troy's apparent giving up on this year—as he said, "It (his different feelings and being called "gay fag") really doesn't matter—I am going to middle school next year anyway."

The counselor thought that Troy would receive as much or more psychological abuse at the middle school as he had received in the elementary school. Although he did not tell Troy that, he still wanted to work on Troy's self-esteem and the other negative effects of ridicule and taunting. Also, although he did not plan to ask Troy about his sexual orientation, he still planned his response should Troy disclose any same-sex feelings. "I don't want to look shocked, dismayed, or disappointed," the counselor thought. "It is imperative that Troy have someone to accept him, especially if he discloses information regarding his sexuality."

The counselor decided on two primary approaches. First, he planned to determine Troy's reasons for feeling different, and second, he planned to work on Troy's self-acceptance and self-esteem. He thought, "There might be a time when Troy will want to involve his parents, but this is probably not the time."

Counseling Lesbian, Gay, and Bisexual Adolescents

Counselors intervening with clients in the adolescent developmental stage need to remember that adolescents differ from both children and adults. All too often, people mistakenly view adolescents as older children or younger adults. However, adolescence is a distinct developmental period with its own unique challenges and developmental tasks. As previously mentioned, many children might not understand why they feel "different" and few will have engaged in a formal coming out process. Many adolescents have engaged in at least some form of sexual experimentation, either heterosexual, same-sex, or both. Most LGB adolescents fully understand their same-sex sexual orientation and many will have engaged in some type of same-sex sexual activity.

Counselors working with adolescents need to remember that this developmental period requires the achievement of specific developmental tasks, such as building wholesome attitudes toward self, sexual identity, and cultural identities; learning to get along with peers of all cultures and both sexes; developing positive attitudes and behaviors toward social groups; and achieving socially responsible and acceptable behavior. Perceptive counselors will bear in mind that because some developmental tasks vary with culture, such tasks may also vary with sexual orientation.

LGB adolescents face many of the same problems as their heterosexual counterparts, with the added burden of attempting to incorporate a stigmatized sexual identity. Schools often do little to provide support for LGB adolescents as they develop a sexual identity. Teachers usually avoid the subject of same-sex sexual orientations; when they do discuss the topic, it is often from a negative perspective. Nor do LGB adolescents view the counselor as a person with whom they

A FOCUS ON RESEARCH 16.2

Addictions Counselors' Attitudes and Behaviors Toward Gay, Lesbian, and Bisexual Clients

Matthews, Selvidge, and Fisher surveyed counselors to determine their attitudes and behaviors with all clients and with gay, lesbian, and bisexual clients. In their research review, Matthews, Selvidge, and Fisher report that whether or not gay men, lesbians, and bisexual individuals are at increased risk for substance abuse, they seem to have been at least using and abusing chemicals at rates comparable to those of heterosexual men and women.

General recommendations for counseling gay men, lesbians, and bisexuals include adapting paperwork to allow clients to indicate their sexual orientation (as well as the nature of the intimate relationships); offering educational activities, groups, and outreach programs; providing books and other literature specific for LGB individuals in waiting rooms; and

demonstrating tolerance and actual affirmation for LGB people. Addictions counselors should also be familiar with gay Alcoholics Anonymous and Narcotics Anonymous groups. Counselors should also understand and assist in striking the balance between an often very real need to secrecy regarding sexual orientation and the equally important need for honesty as part of a recovery program. Last, the presence of openly gay, lesbian, and bisexual people in the counseling centers can serve as positive role models for clients seeking help.

Source: "Addictions counselors' attitudes and behaviors toward gay, lesbian, and bisexual clients," by C. R. Matthews, M. M. D. Selvidge, and K. Fisher, 2005, *Journal of Counseling and Development, 83*, pp. 57–65.

can share problems (Fontaine, 1998). Studies have found that two-thirds of counselors surveyed expressed negative attitudes toward same-sex sexual orientations (Fontaine).

It is important that counselors understand the unique difficulties and risks that LGB adolescents face. Prominent concerns of LGB youth include social vulnerability and isolation and verbal and physical abuse, all of which have been associated with academic problems, running away, prostitution, substance abuse, and suicide (APA, 2000). LGB youth may experience estrangement from their parents when they reveal their sexual orientation. Parental rejection places LGB adolescents at increased risk for homelessness, prostitution, HIV/AIDS infection (caused by risky sexual behavior or other factors), and stress. Youth are also at increased risk for being victims of violence, even within their families, substance abuse, and attempting suicide (APA, 2000).

Matthews, Selvidge, and Fisher (2005) maintain it is difficult to determine the prevalence of addiction among the gay, lesbian, and bisexual population. In A Focus on Research 16.2, they look at addictions counselors' attitudes and behaviors toward gay, lesbian, and bisexual clients.

Counseling Concerns and Issues

As with other stages along the lifespan, LGB adolescents experience prejudice, discrimination, harassment, and name-calling in school and society. Some LGB adolescents actually fear for their physical and psychological safety. A survey of junior and senior high school students in New York reported more hostility toward gay adolescents than toward racial and ethnic minorities (Fontaine, 1998). The Institute for the Protection of Lesbian and Gay Youth in New York City reported that more than 40% of their clients had been victims of homophobic violence (Black & Underwood, 1998). When this violence occurs at school, dropping out seems to be the only solution to many victims (Black & Underwood). Speaking primarily of institutional homophobia and of lesbians, Black and Underwood maintain that educational institutions perpetuate homophobia by refusing to establish a homosexually affirmative environment and by refusing to deal with prejudice, discrimination, and abuse against lesbians in the same way they protect other oppressed groups. Schools can help lesbian adolescents neutralize the effects of homophobia by establishing homosexually affirmative school environments that provide external support for students with same-sex sexual orientation (Black & Underwood).

LGB adolescents also deal with the issue of coming out, another concern for which counselors need to provide professional intervention. Again, speaking only of lesbian adolescents, Black and Underwood (1998) defined coming out as "identifying and respecting one's homosexuality and disclosing this position to others" (p. 17). In doing so, the young woman moves from a socially approved existence to a socially condemned existence. Within the school environment, this move can result in the adolescent woman encountering everything from lack of support, isolation, rejection, and being ostracized to unfair discipline, taunting, harassment, verbal slurs, and persistent acts of violence. To make matters worse, adolescent lesbians are often reluctant to report these incidents because they fear they will be ignored, rejected, punished, or retaliated against by peers or school officials (Black & Underwood).

Upon disclosure of their lesbian orientation, these young women are often forced to drop out of school because they are unable to cope with the homophobia. Those who stay in school will often cope by varying the degree to which they are "out." For some adolescents, coming out is not a choice; they are forced out by peers who have discovered their same-sex sexual orientation.

Although coming out can produce psychological well-being, it can also be dangerous. Coming out prematurely presents the possibility of rejection as well as verbal and physical abuse. Coming out should be postponed until the adolescent gains a reasonable degree of self-worth and a support network. The lesbian adolescent needs to be secure in her identity before coming out because her self-doubt or hesitancy may heighten the confusion of others, thus making her acceptance more difficult. Counselors should advise adolescents to weigh the pros and cons of coming out while also examining their reasons for coming out. Anger, defiance, and acting out as one's reasons for coming out may need to be re-examined; self-actualization or a desire to no longer conceal one's sexual orientation requires support and encouragement (Black & Underwood, 1998).

Several developmental tasks occur during the coming out period. The first involves the development of interpersonal skills to meet and socialize with others with similar sexual orientations. Second, adolescents need to develop a sense of personal attractiveness and sexual competence. Third, it is helpful for the adolescent to realize that self-esteem is not based on sexual conquests, to help prevent seeing oneself in only a sexual manner (Black & Underwood, 1998).

Another concern or issue, dealing with suicide and substance abuse, affects significant numbers of LGB adolescents. Cooley (1998) report that suicide is the third leading cause of death of adolescents and maintain that researchers have not examined sexual orientation in their inquiries about adolescent suicide. In fact, the media often report adolescent suicides as accidents to avoid the issue of same-sex sexual orientation. Fikar (1992, cited in Cooley, 1998) reported that 1 in 10 heterosexual adolescents attempt suicide, compared with 3 in 10 homosexual adolescents. McFarland (1998) reported a survey of 131 gay and bisexual males, 14–21 years old; 30% reported at least one suicide attempt and nearly half of those who attempted suicide reported more than one attempt. Fikar's study revealed that the primary cause for suicide attempts is family problems (44%); however, 30% of those studied identified the cause as personal and interpersonal turmoil regarding their same-sex sexual orientation. Risk factors for lesbian and gay adolescent suicide include disclosure of sexual identity at an early age, low self-esteem, running away, substance abuse, and prostitution (Cooley, 1998).

Suicide and substance abuse are often related. McFarland (1998) reports that the age of initial substance use coincides with the age that many youths become aware of a lesbian or gay orientation. McFarland concludes that many LGB adolescents resort to alcohol and drug use to cope with their sexual orientation. The numbers are sufficiently high for counselors to plan appropriate intervention. For example, the substance abuse rate is two- to three-fold greater in LGB youths than for heterosexual youths. At least 30% of LGB adolescents have problems with alcoholism, a problem which is exacerbated by the fact that the only social outlets for many LGB youths are gay bars in the adult lesbian and gay community (Muller & Hartman, 1998).

Fourth, LGB adolescents often have difficulty dealing with parents and family members who condemn same-sex sexual orientations. LGB adolescents often experience alienation from family members; they face disownment, mistreatment, and disapproval or rejection from parents who react with shame, anger, and guilt (Muller & Hartman, 1998). Muller and Hartman found that nearly half of lesbian and gay adolescents were victims of violence inflicted by family members. Almost 30% of these clients were forced to leave their homes and, therefore, their schools because of conflicts and violence at home, solely because of their sexual orientation.

Fifth, LGB adolescents also deal with developmental and health concerns as well as HIV/AIDS. They deal with the typical developmental concerns (e.g., physical size, developmental tasks, socialization, cognitive abilities) that many heterosexual adolescents deal with daily, but LGB adolescents have another set of concerns related to their sexual orientation. Such concerns as whether to come out and its effects on sexual identities and self-esteem take a serious toll. Although the adolescent developmental period is a relatively healthy time of life, LGB adolescents know they are at increased risk for HIV/AIDS, especially when they have sexual relations with adolescents whom they do not know well. Counselors of LGB adolescents can play significant roles as they focus professional intervention toward health concerns, such as HIV/AIDS prevention, the need to have some information about partners' sexual history, and the need to choose an appropriate time (and appropriate reasons) for coming out.

Last, some LGB adolescents deal with being lesbian, gay, or bisexual, being from a different culture, and perhaps being disabled. As previously mentioned, being LGB and from a nonmajority culture can result in double jeopardy. Although there is not sufficient research on specific cultures to draw major conclusions, counselors know enough to conclude minority LGB adolescents can experience difficult situations.

In an excellent article on Asian American lesbian and gay adolescents, Chung and Katamaya (1998) explain how same-sex sexual orientation is at serious odds with the Asian American culture. There are neither organizations nor role models to help adolescents develop a lesbian or gay identity. Having a same-sex sexual orientation in Asian cultures conflicts with traditional gender roles for men (e.g., continuation of the family) and women (e.g., taking care of husband and children). Because traditional gender roles and the family system are central to most Asian cultures, violation of gender roles and threats to the family system are unacceptable. Therefore, same-sex sexual orientations are often condemned. Other reasons exist for same-sex sexual orientations being unaccepted in Asian cultures. Many modern Asian countries developed out of agricultural societies that relied primarily on human labor. Larger families meant more human power and economic potential. Therefore, men and women traditionally have been expected to get married and have many children so that they can secure greater economic status. Same-sex sexual orientations work against this economic tradition and, therefore, are condemned in most Asian cultures (Chung & Katamaya).

In conclusion, the American society deals with issues related to same-sex sexual orientations primarily at the adult level, and at the expense of adolescents. Even within the lesbian and gay communities, adolescents are not given adequate attention. Resources and services are almost exclusively for adults, possibly because the issue is too controversial and complex to deal with minors (Chung & Katayama, 1998; Savin-Williams, 1990). Counselors who understand the concerns of LGB adolescents realize that those who do not work out their concerns may direct their fears and hostility inward, resulting in low self-esteem and self-defeating behaviors (Omizo, Omizo, & Okamoto, 1998).

Counseling Considerations

LGB adolescents will be more likely than children to seek counseling intervention. Unlike children who often do not understand why they feel "different," LGB adolescents will likely understand their same-sex sexual orientations. Counselors might be called on to provide individual therapy for adolescents. Likewise, depending on the number of LGB adolescents and the level of school affirmation LGB students receive, counselors might be expected to have group therapy solely for LGB adolescents. Keeping in mind researchers who maintain that families often object vehemently to their adolescents' same-sex sexual orientation (Chung & Katamaya, 1998; & Muller & Hartman, 1998), counselors might need to plan family therapy to discuss adolescent and family concerns.

Individual and Group Therapy.   Counselors planning individual counseling therapy for LGB adolescents should base professional intervention on several beliefs. First, the adolescent who is disclosing a same-sex sexual orientation is overcoming considerable peer and cultural pressure to remain hidden. Therefore, a thorough history is needed to ascertain the adolescent's developmental level, values, and social mores. Questions about sexual activity should be asked in a nonjudgmental manner. The lack of same-sex activity or heterosexual activity may not indicate a lack of interest; instead, the lack might result from guilt, fear, insecurity, religious beliefs, parental injunctions, and lack of opportunity. Second, counselors should consider their attitudes, both cognitive and emotional, toward homosexuality. Counselors demonstrating positive attitudes can help alleviate the negative stigmatization felt by many LGB adolescents. Third, some counselors tend to minimize the adolescent's same-sex sexual orientations, which can be intimidating, overwhelming, and may actually increase anxiety. Counselors who genuinely want to help LGB adolescents show understanding and concern, so that these clients know their sexual orientation is neither being ignored nor condemned. Fourth, counselors should give clear and consistent messages that sexual orientation by itself does not determine a person's value, mental health status, and quality of life (Teague, 1992).

A group counseling experience for LGB adolescents can be a powerful and positive vehicle for acquiring the social identification and self-pride that enables successful life adjustment. Exposure to other LGB adolescents provides models for a variety of experiences, insights, and alternative behaviors in solving problems and developing healthy coping styles. This exposure will include information on how to resolve problems of identity disclosure, obtain support, manage a career, and build relationships.

Group counseling with LGB students has several advantages. First, a group allows a safe, secure atmosphere in which to establish trusting relationships that can encourage members to risk more authentic relationships outside the group. Second, the processes of reality testing, choosing goals and planning action, and modifying ideals and personal values tend to be accelerated in the group process. Third, the group experience tends to minimize the disadvantages of individual counseling for those LGB students who might be threatened by the intimacy inherent in client–counselor relationships (Teague, 1992).

A peer-oriented, self-help approach to group counseling defines LGB persons as members of an oppressed minority group as opposed to a group that is considered psychologically impaired. The group helps break the social isolation and can focus on personal adjustment rather than a shift in sexual orientation. Support groups seem to be the most valuable resources for lesbian and

Table 16.3
Group Counseling: Counseling Issues and Counselor's Roles

Counseling Issue: *Development of Social Identity*

Counselor's Roles

1. Avoid assuming all clients are heterosexual.
2. Understand the developmental stages and challenges of both heterosexual and homosexual youth.
3. Gain knowledge of same-sex sexual orientation in order to be able to dispel myths and negative stereotypes.
4. Provide intervention focused on developing positive self-esteem and self-acceptance.
5. Become aware of one's own homophobia.

Counseling Issue: *Isolation*

Counselor's Roles

1. Let LGB clients know they are not alone in the world—they have people who care about them.
2. Convince LGB clients that they have someone with whom they can confide their sexual orientation and their concerns and challenges.
3. Be informed and unbiased and begin eliminating internalized homophobia.
4. Be willing to engage in dialogue with clients and support clients in clarifying their feelings about sexual orientation.

Counseling Issue: *Educational Issues*

Counselor's Roles

1. Move toward destigmatizing homosexuality through professional development, support staff and services, addressing sexuality in the health curriculum, library services, and general curriculum changes (Anderson, 1994).
2. Commit to individuality of and fairness for all students, both heterosexual and homosexual.
3. Provide training for other educators in ways to promote individuality and equality.
4. Provide educative experiences in all discussions of sex education (both heterosexual and homosexual), including dating and relationships, parenting, sexually transmitted diseases, and available services.
5. Work to eliminate administrative discrimination in the hiring of lesbian and gay staff members.

Counseling Issue: *Family Issues*

Counselor's Roles

1. Help LGB adolescents and their family members in dealing with family issues.
2. Help adolescents and their families explore the possible consequences (both positive and negative) of coming out.
3. Seek help in dealing with anger, guilt, and concerns about religious issues, and the parents' own homophobia.
4. Help family members deal with the stigmatization of having a LGB family member.
5. Convince parents and family members that familial background appears to have nothing to do with the development of a same-sex sexual orientation.
6. Help parents and family members identify community resources.

Counseling Issue: *Health Risks*

Counselor's Roles

1. Address the health issues and possess the communication skills necessary to deal with sensitive health topics.
2. Ensure that LGB adolescents have sufficient information to protect themselves from HIV/AIDS.
3. Help LGB adolescents feel secure and comfortable discussing issues such as fear of HIV exposure, the need for HIV testing, test results, safe-sex practices, sexual orientation concerns, alcohol and drug use, and suicidal thoughts.
4. Increase LGB adolescents' awareness of evidence and indicators of victimization, suicidal tendencies, and substance abuse in clients, especially for LGB adolescents who are uncomfortable with their sexual orientation.

Source: Adapted from "Gay and lesbian adolescents: Presenting problems and the counselor's roles," by J. J. Cooley, 1998, *Professional School Counseling, 1*(3), pp. 30–34.

gay adolescents because they provide an opportunity for developing social skills, discussing the meaning of sexual identity and sexuality, finding support and understanding from peers, sharing information, and socializing (Teague, 1992).

Table 16.3 looks at counseling issues and the counselor's roles on group counseling for sexual minority youths.

Family Therapy.   Counselors who choose family therapy as a means of intervention are usually aware that problems often arise when LGB adolescents admit their sexual orientation to their family. Teague (1992) offers several suggestions for working with LGB adolescents and their families: (a) Be knowledgeable and comfortable with adolescents (and other family members) with same-sex sexual orientations, (b) resist the temptation to be overinquisitive and patronizing of the family, (c) be prepared to deal with fears of being stigmatized for working with LGB clients, (d) be able to communicate acceptance and understanding of the family, (e) gain exposure to functional families of LGB persons and a variety of LGB persons, (f) avoid "pseudo-insight" (p. 434) because problems may stem from factors unrelated to sexual orientation, (g) be guided by the family's sense of need, and (h) be familiar with and use LGB community organizations and resources to help the family.

Topics that counselors might choose to address during family therapy sessions include clarifying myths and stereotypes regarding what it is like to be lesbian, gay, or bisexual; encouraging LGB adolescents to socialize with people who can help them the most (e.g., other LGB persons and relevant support groups); and helping LGB adolescents and their family members realize that sexual orientation is only one facet of a person's life (Teague, 1992). Table 16.4 shows strategies for involving and educating parents and families of lesbian students. Up Close and Personal 16.2 describes a counselor's intervention with Suzie, a lesbian Asian American adolescent.

Table 16.4
Strategies for Helping Families
of Lesbian Students
Source: Adapted from "Young,
female, and gay: Lesbian students
and the school environment," by
J. Black and J. Underwood, 1998,
Professional School Counseling,
1(3), pp. 15–20.

1. Be sincere because these students might have been on guard most of their lives trying to determine who can and cannot be trusted.
2. Use the same-sex terminology the students use and remember that students might appear confused about their sexual orientation.
3. Respect confidentiality of students' sexual orientation and personal concerns.
4. Deal with feelings first—most young lesbians feel alone, guilty, ashamed, and angry.
5. Be supportive by explaining that many people have struggled with these same-sex sexual orientation issues and have lived healthy and happy lives.
6. Anticipate some confusion—understand that sexual orientation is a biological fact and counselors cannot talk students out of their sexual orientation.
7. Help but do not force—provide information on sexual orientation and identity development and allow students to work at their own individual pace.
8. Do not try to guess who is lesbian and who is straight and then lead clients into a preassumed direction.
9. Be aware of the potential for depression, especially as lesbians let go of their heterosexual identity.
10. Use role playing to prepare lesbian youth to handle a variety of situations.
11. Provide accurate information on how sexually transmitted diseases, including HIV/AIDS, can be passed among women.
12. Be informed when making referrals to community services and agencies.

UP CLOSE AND PERSONAL 16.2

Counseling Suzie, a Lesbian Asian American Adolescent

Suzie met with her counselor in the 12th grade. She had been recommended by one of her teachers, who thought she seemed unhappy and stressed. The counselor, a 45-year-old heterosexual man, agreed to meet with Suzie several times, mostly to satisfy the teacher.

After several meetings, the counselor saw no reason to continue. Suzie disclosed little about her personal life and nothing about her sexual orientation or her previous sexual relations with boys. Although the counselor made his confidentiality clear, Suzie was still unwilling to disclose personal information that the counselor might "tell" or that she would not want her

parents to know. The counselor learned that Suzie had a close family, and he perceived that something was bothering Suzie, but whatever the problem was, Suzie would not disclose it. Because there was no indication that Suzie was a lesbian or was disturbed by same-sex feelings, the counselor did not pursue the topic.

The closest any discussion came to sexual matters was when Suzie told him about the boys she had dated. However, she did not disclose that she had engaged in sexual relations. The counselor wondered why Suzie had not dated more boys, but assumed that Suzie's parents did not approve of her dating, especially non-Asian boys.

The counseling sessions were unproductive because Suzie refused to disclose information. Several years later, Suzie wished she had told the counselor about her feelings for other girls. She said, "I was embarrassed—I could not possibly let my counselor know I was one of those lesbians. What if my parents had found out? No, I just could not tell anyone."

Counseling Lesbian, Gay, and Bisexual Adults

Counseling LGB adults is both similar to and different from counseling children and adolescents. Some similar issues include homophobia, coming out, prejudice, and harassment, which affect LGB adults in much the same way as they affect LGB children and adolescents. Some differences during the adult development period include career barriers; issues surrounding adoption, parenting, and same-sex marriages; and bereavement issues. There may also be added health concerns that usually occur during the adult developmental period. Therefore, counselors of LGB adults need to plan for those challenges that cross developmental stages and also plan for challenges specific to the adult developmental period.

Counseling Concerns and Issues

MacGillivray and Kozik-Rosabal (2000) provide an excellent discussion of terminology in which they define GLBTQ as gay, lesbian, bisexual, transgendered, queer, and questioning. They describe the terms they prefer and provide rationales. In their article, they look at sexual orientation as "simply a state of being" (p. 289). Other topics explored include gender identity, the roles schools play in the creation and perpetuation of discrimination directed toward GLBTQ students, the difficulty of determining demographics of GLBTQ students, and the fact that being GLBTQ is not just an urban issue.

Interesting aspects offered by MacGillivray and Kozik-Rosabal include the following:

1. The term itself, GLBTQ, seems to support the inclusion the authors want: No adolescent is being excluded due to his or her sexual orientation.

2. The assertion is that GLBTQ is not just an urban issue—such students also attend schools in rural and suburban schools.

3. In addition to meeting the needs of GLBTQ students, schools need to prepare heterosexual students for democratic citizenship in communities with significant populations of politically active and out GLBTQ people.

MacGillivray and Kozik-Rosabal propose that educators have an enormous task before them as they make schools safe for GLBTQ students. Undoubtedly, counselors also will play significant roles, both helping GLBTQ students as well as helping heterosexual students accept diversity among all people.

Counselors of LGB adults will be called on to provide professional intervention for a number of concerns and challenges. One key to effective intervention for LGB adults is to remember that counseling efforts should reflect perspectives unique to the adult developmental period. First, many LGB clients face social stigmatization, violence, and discrimination. Living in a predominantly heterosexual society can cause considerable stress to nonheterosexuals. Also, belonging to a sexual minority can cause increased stress related to long-term daily hassles ranging from hearing antigay jokes to more serious problems, such as loss of employment, home, and custody of children or actual violence (APA, 2000). Also, many current laws and institutional regulations preclude LGB persons from full participation in society. For example, marriage, tax exemptions, and health benefits for domestic partners discriminate against LGB adults. Likewise, more subtle forms of culturally sanctioned discrimination are often officially condoned by governmental, religious, and other social institutions (Fontaine, 1998). Also, LGB adults sometimes fear for their physical and psychological safety, which results in their reluctance to come out and in their decision to limit their activities to predominantly homosexual communities.

Second, LGB adults face challenges associated with coming out. Will they be rejected by their social and business peers? Will their jobs be threatened? What is the right time (assuming there is a right time) for coming out? Will family members support the adult's same-sex sexual orientation and the decision to come out publicly? Because heterosexism and homophobia are so intense in Asian cultures, an openly homosexual lifestyle often is not an option; the consequences of disclosing one's sexual orientation is just too threatening. Most lesbians and gay men in Asian American societies suppress their sexual orientation and outwardly follow the expectations of a heterosexual lifestyle, although there might be some discreet homosexual activities. Most lesbian and gay Asian Americans eventually get married and have children. Consequently, in many Asian cultures, there might not be such a concept as a lesbian or gay identity (Chung & Katamaya, 1998).

Springer and Lease (2000) maintain that in the last two decades society has been faced with three related epidemics: HIV, AIDS, and the social, cultural, and political impacts of HIV/AIDS. One social impact of AIDS involves AIDS-related bereavement. Even with medical advancements, the disease and the bereavement continue. Gay men are among the most likely to be affected by multiple AIDS-related loss and bereavement because the gay community continues to be disproportionately affected by these diseases. Gay men perceive AIDS as being a threat to their own health as well as to that of their gay friends and partners. Also, the fear of being discriminated against decreases the likelihood that gay men will seek out medical and psychological services. Although gay men fear the discrimination they might face if they do reveal their gay status, they realize they will not receive relevant health care if they do not disclose their sexual orientation.

Counseling implications include the following:

1. Encourage clients to realize that it might be necessary to resolve additional losses of friends and partners.

2. Know and encourage clients to take advantage of the potential sources of support in the gay community.

3. Examine personal beliefs about gay men, HIV/AIDS, and AIDS-related deaths to determine homophobic attitudes and actual misinformation and stereotypes.

4. Help clients facilitate the acknowledgment of anger and feelings that their friends were not "careful enough" (p. 302).

5. Help HIV-positive gay men explore feelings of guilt or shame over the possibility that they have infected their lovers.

6. Plan for the fact that the loss of a partner is often not marked by the same societal rituals designed to aid the resolution of grief (e.g., memorial services, time off from work, support from family and friends).

7. Understand that families might not be a source of support during times of bereavement, particularly families who have rejected clients due to their sexual orientation.

8. Understand and plan appropriately for self-destructive behaviors, such as bitterness, alcohol and drug use, and aggressive behaviors that might result from multiple losses.

The reality of earning a living may be more apparent to lesbians than to heterosexual women. In fact, lesbians may realize that because they will not have a male wage earner, they need to earn more money because they may have to support themselves alone or with another woman (Hetherington & Orzek, 1989). Lesbian couples deal with many of the heterosexual stresses, plus a plethora of related complications and additional issues. In a survey by Winkelpleck and Westfield (1982), same-sex couples cited employment discrimination as one of the major issues they faced. Lesbian couples have numerous career-related issues to consider, including (a) how to present the relationship, (b) how to introduce one's partner, (c) how to openly acknowledge the relationship, if at all, and (d) how to deal with social events. Also, as expected, lesbians experience homophobia in the workplace. In their relationships, lesbian couples often must deal with fears about losing jobs or alienation from colleagues because of their sexual orientation (Hetherington & Orzek).

Career counselors working with LGB clients need to be sensitive to the fact that lesbian clients are a special group and need special assistance with self-exploration and job search strategies. Table 16.5 offers questions that counselors of LGB clients might need to explore.

Fourth, LGB adults deal with substance abuse, suicide, HIV/AIDS, and depression. Substance abuse in LGB populations has been adequately documented (Haeberle & Gindorf, 1998; Silverstein, 1991; van Wormer, Wells, & Boes, 2000); however, the seriousness of substance abuse needs to be brought to the attention of counselors working with LGB clients. Suicide also deserves counselors' consideration. Martin maintains that men with AIDS, ages 20 to 59, are

Table 16.5
Questions Counselors Might Need to Explore with LGB Clients

Source: Developed from "Career counseling and life planning with lesbian women," by C. L. Hetherington and A. Orzek, 1989, *Journal of Counseling and Development, 68,* pp. 52–57.

1. Is this career available to me as an "out" lesbian?
2. Had I determined how "out" I wanted to be before I chose this career?
3. Are there any work environments in this career that are more open to lesbians?
4. Is my sexual identity pertinent to this career?
5. How can I learn which companies have nondiscrimination policies?
6. How can I learn about the attitudes regarding homosexuality in the local communities where I want to live?
7. On my resumé, how should I communicate the lesbian and gay activities in which I have been involved?
8. How can I handle dual career issues?
9. How can I learn about companies that are sensitive to lesbian concerns?
10. How do I handle a situation when the presence of a spouse will be beneficial?

much more likely to commit suicide than comparably aged healthy men. This phenomenon underscores the need to assess suicide ideation and intent in individuals with HIV/AIDS. Several important factors in the assessment of suicide risk among persons with HIV/AIDS include multiple losses related to AIDS, intimate involvement with a person who died from AIDS, state of illness, recent disclosure of positive test results, discrimination and insults, personal history of homophobia-related losses, prevailing sense of danger in being gay, unsettled sexual identity, and lack of proper social and financial support (Martin, 1989).

The gay community has been disproportionately affected by HIV/AIDS. Counselors who plan professional intervention for infected LGB persons include topics such as risk-reduction education, knowledge of the diseases, safe-sex practices, and assistance with grieving the loss of loved ones. Counselors might also need to deal with clients who have learned of positive HIV test results. Because HIV is often understood as a "death sentence" (Martin, 1989, p. 68), depression and anxiety can result. Other topics include potential pain, disfigurement, possibility of death, feelings of being dirty and damaged, social rejection, and job loss. Anger might be targeted at former lovers or sexual partners, at oneself for being careless, and at the medical establishment for its apparent slowness in disseminating needed information. HIV/AIDS patients often undergo painful and frightening diagnostic and medical treatment procedures. In addition to providing emotional support during periods of anxiety, counselors can help patients with education, relaxation and guided imagery, and assistance in using existing coping methods that have been successfully used in the past. Counselors can also help patients who are near death to resolve unfinished business and personal issues. Making out wills and implementing a power of attorney for health care are among the last preparations for death. Decisions about where, how, and when to die must be confronted. When patients' decisions conflict with desires of families, friends, and health care providers, counselors may need to assist them in accepting patient decisions (Martin, 1989).

Many LGB persons, especially lesbians, often deal with depression. For example, lesbians might experience significant depression when they begin to accept their lesbian identity. Many little girls grow up dreaming of large weddings, lots of wedding presents, white dresses, and "Prince Charming" (Black & Underwood, 1998, p. 16). They often dream of being a perfect and devoted wife and mother; then, they are faced with accepting their lesbian identity, which can lead to depression in some cases (Black & Underwood).

LGB couples experience problems that are both similar and different from those of heterosexual couples. Problems can include communication difficulties, sexual problems, dual-career issues, and commitment issues. Problems that may be presented in therapy which are specific to LGB couples include the couple's disclosure of sexual orientation to their families, work colleagues, health professionals, and caregivers; differences between partners in the disclosure process; issues derived from the effects of gender socialization in same-sex couples; and HIV/AIDS status. External issues such as pressure from families of origin or current or former heterosexual partners may also arise (APA, 2000).

Fifth, LGB clients face issues associated with adoption, parenting, and same-sex marriages. As previously stated, Fontaine (1998) maintains that there are laws and institutional regulations that preclude full participation of LGB persons in society. An issue of growing concern is that LGB adults experience considerable frustrations with adoption, parenting, and same-sex marriages. LGB persons may not adopt children as do heterosexual couples, and often LGB adults lose their parenting rights when same-sex sexual orientations become known. Most states do not acknowledge same-sex marriages. These concerns will likely be increasingly debated as LGB persons continue to come out and as they demand equality.

There appears to be no significant differences in the capabilities of LGB parents compared with heterosexual parents. However, LGB parents face challenges not encountered by most heterosexual parents because of the stigma associated with homosexuality and bisexuality. Prejudice had led to institutional discrimination by the legal, educational, and social welfare systems. In a number of cases, LGB parents have lost custody of their children, have been restricted from visiting their children, have been prohibited from living with their domestic partners, or have been prevented from adopting or being foster parents based on their sexual orientation (APA, 2000).

LGB parents face the same problems and issues as those faced by heterosexual parents, such as how to maintain age-appropriate discipline or how to nurture children's self-esteem. However, LGB parents face additional complications, such as homophobia, secrecy, ambiguity of family roles and boundaries, and societal assumptions about their inadequacy to be effective parents. Also, the failure of the legal system to recognize the parental status and rights of many LGB persons contributes to increased parenting difficulties for LGB parents (Leslie, 1995).

Sixth, some LGB persons face additional problems when they are from a different culture and/or have a disability. Counselors have greater challenges when working with clients who have more than one difference. It will be necessary to understand the multifaceted discrimination these clients might face due to their same-sex sexual orientation, minority status, and disabling condition.

In offering professional intervention to racially and ethnically diverse LGB populations, it is not sufficient that psychologists simply recognize the racial and ethnic backgrounds of their clients. A multiple minority status may complicate and exacerbate the difficulties these clients experience. For example, clients may be affected by the ways in which their cultures view homosexuality and bisexuality (APA, 2000). LGB persons with disabilities may not have access to information, support, and services that are available to their nondisabled counterparts. Lack of social recognition for LGB persons in relationships affect those with ongoing medical concerns, such as medical coverage for domestic partners, family medical leave policies, hospital visitation, medical decision-making by partners, and survivorship issues (APA, 2000).

Seventh, many LGB adults face the challenge of dealing with grief and bereavement issues. Grief over the loss of friends and lovers has affected many members of the LGB community. Although LGB community members have provided mutual support in the grieving process, intervention is still necessary for some clients. Counselors working with LGB clients should explore the possibility of grief reactions when they perceive symptoms such as unusual fatigue and lethargy, unexplained anger, and depression and anxiety, especially when clients have had friends and lovers die from AIDS-related illnesses (Martin, 1989).

Counseling Considerations

The assessment and treatment of LGB clients can be adversely affected by therapists' explicit or implicit negative attitudes. For example, when heterosexual norms for identity, behavior, and relationships are applied to LGB clients, their thoughts, feelings, and behaviors may be misinterpreted as abnormal, deviant, and undesirable. Psychologists should strive to avoid making

GENDER PERSPECTIVES 16.1
Heterosexism, Sexism, and Lesbians

Szymanski (2005) maintains that LGB persons have experienced heterosexist events, including prejudice, harassment, discrimination, and violence, and that these experiences are related to adverse psychological, health, and job-related outcomes. Internalized heterosexism is correlated with a variety of negative health outcomes such as depression, little social support, and high levels of demoralization, and in some cases, increased psychological stress. Research has also shown that many women have experienced sexist events, including discrimination, harassment, rape, and sexual assault and that these experiences relate to psychological and health outcomes for these women.

Counselors need to assess both the heterosexist and sexist context in which their lesbian clients live and ask about their lesbian clients' experiences of prejudice, harassment, discrimination, and violence that are related both to their sexual orientation and their gender. Counselors can also help clients understand how living in both a heterosexist and sexist society might be influencing their mental health. Counselors might also become actively involved in social change efforts aimed at eradicating heterosexism and sexism in order to improve the lives of lesbians.

Source: "Heterosexism and sexism as correlates of psychological distress in lesbians," by D. M. Szymanski, 2005, *Journal of Counseling and Development, 83,* pp. 355–360.

assumptions that a client is heterosexual, even in the presence of apparent markers of heterosexuality (e.g., marital status), because LGB clients may be in a heterosexual marriage (APA, 2000).

Feminist therapy theorists have made significant contributions to enhancing counselors' understanding of how social, economic, political, and institutional factors affect women's lives and the particular problems that women bring to counseling. In Gender Perspectives 16.1, Szymanski (2005) examines the effects of external and internalized heterosexiam and internalized sexism on lesbians' mental health.

LGB adults need individual, group, and family therapy that reflects the needs of the adult developmental period. Although some issues (e.g., homophobia, prejudice, discrimination) affect LGB persons in all lifespan periods, counselors need to focus on specific issues faced by adults. Another challenge will be for the counselor to decide whether individual therapy, group therapy, or family therapy will be the most effective approach. Key issues for practice include an understanding of human sexuality; the coming out process, and how variables such as age, gender, ethnicity, race, disability, and religion may influence the process; same-sex relationship dynamics; family-of-origin relationships; struggles with spirituality and religious group membership; career issues and workplace discrimination; and coping strategies for successful functioning (APA, 2000).

Individual and Group Therapy.   LGB clients may be in individual counseling for any number of reasons, such as convenience, the counselor's decision, or because they have not formally come out and do not wish to share their sexual orientation with a group. One essential consideration in deciding whether to use individual or group therapy is whether the LGB client has come out and to whom. Although group therapy has a number of advantages, individual therapy is usually used until the client has formally engaged in a coming out process. Once the client has shared his or her sexual orientation and is comfortable with his or her sexuality, then often group counseling is recommended, so clients can know others' perspectives. Any of the previously discussed issues (e.g., prejudice and harassment, feeling unsafe, coming out, health concerns and disabilities) would be appropriate topics. These topics, however, might come from a heterosexual counselor unless the counselor is also LGB; therefore, it will be important to get the client to discuss concerns that he or she feels are worthy of discussion.

Again, if the client has come out and feels comfortable with his or her sexuality, group therapy can be useful because it provides a means for clients to learn others' perspectives. According to Han and Vasquez (2000), self-esteem and identity are central issues that could be discussed in group therapy. For many cultural groups, these issues are interwoven with being a minority in America, where stereotypes and prejudicial messages are pervasive. Low self-esteem can result from societal rejection of one's cultural group (or sexual orientation). Identity issues might result from self-estrangement and maladaptive psychological behavior, or confusion over one's identity (Am I Japanese? Or am I American?). These issues might grow even more acute for LGB clients as they deal with their sexual orientation and their minority status (and perhaps disabling conditions). According to Comaz-Diaz and Jacobsen (1987) and Han and Vasquez (2000), three therapeutic functions for group interventions include (1) reflection about the client's identity and societal/environmental sources that contribute to identity issues, (2) examination of the client's inconsistencies in self-identity, and (3) mediation between the client's ethnocultural identity and personal identity to achieve a more integrated and consolidated sense of self. These three therapeutic functions also need to be examined with regard to sexual orientation to determine how the client's sexual orientation affects his or her identity. In other words, counselors should explore how the relationship between culture and sexual orientation (and vice versa) affects identity formation.

Family Therapy.   Flores and Carey (2000), who specialize in family therapy for Hispanic Americans, presented several questions family therapists might ask:

1. Can therapists describe and define the intersection between being Hispanic and being a man without resorting to stereotypical and all encompassing descriptions?

2. How do we challenge internalized conceptions about the role, position, and power of family members?

3. Are we reconstructing a definition of men that reproduces heterosexist, patriarchal biases, addressing masculinity in universal terms while neglecting racial and cultural variations?

4. How do we integrate an affirmative practice in the treatment of Hispanic men?

Undoubtedly, counselors working with LGB Hispanic Americans and their families (as well as LGB persons and families from other cultures) can think of other questions that deserve to be answered in order to provide effective intervention for LGB family members.

Flores and Carey (2000) briefly explain how the Spanish language uses gender in oppositional terms for male and female: *el/ella, eso/esa, el/la*. By doing this, the nonheterosexual world is noticeably absent and neglects the realities of Hispanic LGB persons in families and couples

UP CLOSE AND PERSONAL 16.3

Counseling Carlos, a Bisexual Hispanic American Adult

Carlos finally had to admit to his bisexual life that he had long kept secret from his wife and employer. However, it was still not to them that he confided—he had to see a doctor. On one of his business trips to a large city, he had a sexual encounter with a man he met at a bar. Although this was not his first encounter, he said this was the first time he did not use protection. Afterward, his concerns about sexually transmitted diseases grew daily, and he made up excuses to avoid having sexual relations with his wife so he would not pass any possible infection to her. Finally, he went to a family practitioner (not his family doctor) to be tested for sexually transmitted diseases. The medical tests were negative, but the doctor strongly recommended counseling. Carlos agreed, mainly because if his bisexualism were discovered by his wife and employer, he could at least say he had entered counseling.

The counselor, a 40-year-old heterosexual Hispanic American man, met with Carlos and listened to his concerns: Carlos feared being found out by his wife and employer. As he said, "My wife and family would never understand this—I don't even understand it." The counselor knew group therapy was not practical in this case. He also concluded that family therapy was an impossibility because Carlos was so intent on concealing his bisexualism from his wife and employer. Therefore, the counselor chose individual therapy, but later admitted that he really did not know what Carlos hoped to accomplish. It was clear that Carlos had no intention of coming out; plus, he had no intention of trying to negate his bisexuality (even if that were possible).

The counselor planned several topics to discuss with Carlos: coming out (which already appeared to be impossible for Carlos), how to deal with the challenges brought on by his bisexuality, how his family and employer might react, how he could have safer sex in future bisexual encounters and, generally speaking, topics that Carlos considered important. Overall, the counselor felt that because Carlos never planned to come out, the goal should be to help Carlos accept his bisexuality and, as previously suggested, help him to use greater caution to engage in safe sex practices, which, after his recent scare, Carlos had probably already realized.

(p. 34). Being a male in the Hispanic world assumes that one is a heterosexual male; being manly is not associated with the "nonworld" of homosexuality (p. 34). Flores and Carey quote Stavans to summarize their position that "homosexuals have been a ubiquitous presence in the Hispanic world...they are the other side of Hispanic sexuality, a shadow one refuses to acknowledge" (Stavans, 1996, p. 155).

With sexual attitudes such as those described by Flores and Carey (2000), we question the effectiveness of family therapy for LGB Hispanic Americans. Likewise, considering Chung and Katamaya's (1998) position that same-sex sexual orientation is at serious odds with the Asian American culture, we also question the effectiveness of family therapy for LGB Asian Americans. In these cultures, men are expected to be "manly," providers, and patriarchal; women are expected to be nurturing and able to take care of their husband and family. Although times have changed owing to acculturation and changing mores, there are still gender and family role expectations that do not include being lesbian, gay, or bisexual.

However, counselors should consider family therapy if they think family members will be supportive of the LGB clients. Questions to be considered when deciding whether to use family therapy include

1. Will LGB clients openly disclose and discuss their sexual orientation and its effects on their lives (and their family members' lives)?

2. Will they risk losing family support?

3. Will family members be supportive or condemning?

4. Will the close ties of some families be more powerful than their condemnation of same-sex sexual orientations?

Other questions will undoubtedly be raised as counselors consider individual LGB clients and their families.

Up Close and Personal 16.3 describes a counselor's therapy approaches when working with Carlos, a bisexual Hispanic American adult.

Counseling Lesbian, Gay, and Bisexual Elderly

Two problems confront authors who write about the LGB elderly. First, there is a common misconception that the elderly do not have sex, are not interested in sex, or both. Second, there is a paucity of literature on counseling LGB elderly. There is a growing body of literature on the elderly and on LGB persons; however, literature on the two subjects combined—counseling the LGB elderly—is, unfortunately, somewhat more difficult to find. Also, as with previous discussions,

A FOCUS ON RESEARCH 16.3
Social Empowerment Strategies in Counseling Lesbian and Gay Male Clients

Savage, Harley, and Nowak (2005) explain that the social Empowerment Model (SEM) is based on a conflict theory that assumes society consists of separate groups that have advantages of power and control in relation to social, psychological, political, and economic systems. Lesbians and gay males constitute one group of people in the United States margininalized by the majority culture.

The concept of empowerment is frequently regarded as a desirable goal of self-advocacy. In addition, empowerment theory involves empowerment values, empowerment processes, and empowerment outcomes. Empowerment values consist of a belief system that governs how counselors and consumers work together. These values include a focus on health, adaptation, competence, and natural helping systems. Empowerment processes can be described as the mechanisms

through which people gain mastery and control over issues that concern them, develop a critical awareness of their environment, and participate in decisions that affect their lives. Empowerment outcomes refer to the consequences of individuals' attempts to gain control in their lives or the effects of intervention designed to empower these individuals.

In this highly recommended article, Savage, Harley, and Nowak explain how Social Empowerment Strategies can be applied and offer suggestions for future research.

_____

Source: "Applying social empowerment strategies as tools for self-advocacy in counseling lesbian and gay male clients," by T. A. Savage, D. A. Harley, and T. M. Nowak, 2005, *Journal of Counseling and Development, 83,* pp. 131–137.

it is imperative that this section focus as much as possible on LGB persons in the elderly developmental period. Although prejudice and discrimination challenges LGB persons in all developmental periods, it is necessary to look at the special challenges experienced by those in the elderly developmental period.

As marginalized populations, lesbians and gay males are frequently overwhelmed by a sense of powerlessness. For example, powerlessness manifests itself in various forms of oppression such as language, heterosexism, curtailment of civil rights, and criminalization of same-sex sexual contact. In A Focus on Research 16.3, Savage, Harley, and Nowak (2005) suggest social empowerment strategies in counseling lesbian and gay male clients.

Counseling Concerns and Issues

LGB persons in the elderly lifespan period experience the problems and challenges experienced by people in the other three lifespan periods, including dealing with a hostile social environment, fearing for physical and psychological safety, dealing with coming out issues, and dealing with suicide and substance abuse. Because all LGBs deal with these challenges, this section will focus on specific problems faced by the LGB elderly.

First, American society ignores elderly sexuality, especially in the LGB elderly population. Although stereotypes follow people in all developmental periods, two stereotypes about the elderly are that they either cannot function sexually or they have no interest in sex. Both stereotypes are wrong—many elderly people are interested in sex and continue to have the capacity to engage in sexual relations. The LGB elderly, like their heterosexual counterparts, continue their sexual interest. Another challenge for researchers and writers is that additional studies of the LGB elderly are needed so that recommendations can be made for mental health services and counseling professionals. A challenge for counselors is to recognize that sexual activity is not just for young and middle-aged people. Counselors who assume that the elderly have neither a sex life nor an interest in sexual activities make a serious mistake and should examine their personal stereotypes and assumptions.

Second, although all LGB persons experience prejudice and discrimination, the elderly also deal with problems in housing, assisted living facilities, nursing homes, retirement benefits, medical attention, and long-term health care. Some elderly LGB people experience discrimination as they attempt to find housing. Although they probably will not be told that their sexual orientation is the reason for being unable to find a place to live, realistically speaking, some landlords will not rent to LGB persons. Sometimes, LGB persons are told that the place has already been rented, or they will be quoted an exorbitant rental fee that far exceeds the value of the dwelling or comparable places in the neighborhood. Assisted living facilities and nursing homes often take deliberate action to deny access to elderly LGB people, perhaps because of outright prejudice or fear of HIV/AIDs and other diseases. Elderly LGB people face the typical problems that most elderly people experience, but they also experience problems associated with being lesbian, gay, or bisexual. Lack of legal rights and protection in medical emergencies and a lack of acknowledgment of couples' relationships, particularly following the loss of a partner, have been associated with feelings of helplessness, depression, and disruption of normative grief processes in LGB elderly (APA, 2000).

Third, some elderly LGB people deal with issues arising from their sexual orientation, minority status and, perhaps, having a disability. Although all elderly people probably experience discrimination at some time, the situation undoubtedly grows more acute when the elderly person has one or more of these risk factors for discrimination.

Fourth, some elderly deal with developmental and health concerns as well as HIV/AIDS. Most elderly people experience some health problems as they grow older. However, LGB elderly might also be concerned about their sexual orientation and related health problems such as HIV/AIDS. Unless they live with others (e.g., a roommate) of similar sexual orientation or in a LGB community, they might lack a support system to discuss developmental and health concerns. In order to receive the medical attention they need, elderly LGB people often feel required to share their sexual orientation, which may result in additional discrimination.

Counseling Considerations

Some counselors erroneously think sexual issues, particularly those surrounding same-sex sexual orientation, will not surface when counseling the elderly. Some counselors think the elderly will be more concerned with how long they will live, with whom they will live, and whether their health will decline. Although these are all legitimate concerns, LGB elderly may also be concerned with coming out issues, HIV/AIDS, and other sexual orientation issues. As with LGB clients in other lifespan periods, the counselor will be challenged to decide whether to intervene with individual, group, or family therapy.

Individual and Group Therapy.   Counselors working with elderly LGB people will want to consider their clients' personal circumstances in the decision to use individual or group therapy. Are there other elderly LGB people who are willing to meet as a group? Are they willing to disclose their sexual orientation and the related problems (if their problems relate to their sexual orientation)? Has the client in question engaged in a formal coming out process? Will individual or group therapy be most effective for the individual in question?

Fassinger (1997) outlined considerations in group interventions with older lesbians (aged 60 and older), a particularly invisible group. Fassinger contends that this group is triply oppressed owing to gender, age, and sexual orientation. Issues examined include life circumstances, physical health, mental health, family and friends, and retirement and leisure. The needs of older lesbians are similar to those of the general population, yet they also have unique needs. Fassinger offers the following recommendations for group work with this population:

1. Counselors need competence not only in group dynamics and processes, but also in addressing issues related to gender and sexual orientation.

2. Counselors need attitudes that include awareness of personal assumptions, values, biases, and culturally induced beliefs, as well as respect for differences and willingness to recognize personal limitations without feeling threatened.

3. Counselors need knowledge of the worldview of the client who is culturally different, including specific knowledge regarding the client's social, political, and cultural location.

4. Counselors need skills that allow them to develop appropriate strategies and techniques, including a varied repertoire and awareness of their therapeutic style.

Once the counselor makes the decision to use individual or group therapy, approaches might include topics such as coming out, health problems related to both sexual orientation and aging, discrimination and prejudice, problems with family (immediate and extended) acknowledging the elderly person's same-sex sexual orientation, financial concerns, housing problems, retirement benefits, medical attention and long-term health care, and any other problems that individual elderly LGB clients want to discuss. In addition, counselors will need to consider whether cultural diversity and disabling conditions result in multiple forms of jeopardy and contribute to the elderly LGB client's problems.

In both individual and group therapy, counselors should also consider the community in which the elderly LGB person resides. Is it accepting of diversity or is it homophobic? Does the elderly LGB client perceive the community as supportive or condemning? What community resources are available to assist the elderly LGB client? The acceptance of the community will be significant in elderly LGB clients' decisions to disclose their sexual orientation and the extent to which they feel the community will help them in their time of need.

Family Therapy.   As when counseling clients in the other lifespan periods, counselors need to consider whether family members will support or condemn elderly LGB clients. In some cases, family members think the elderly family member's sex life is nonexistent anyway, so trying

---

UP CLOSE AND PERSONAL 16.4

Counseling Calliope, an Elderly Greek American Lesbian

Calliope, a 74-year-old Greek American lesbian, had attended the senior lunch center for several years. Things in her life were about the same: She was lonely, she still had to share apartment costs, and she still had sexual feelings for women. The counselor, a 43-year-old heterosexual Greek American who worked at the lunch center, continued to discuss group concerns, but these sessions could not legitimately be called group counseling. The participants had general discussions concerning growing old, being somewhat poor, and having health problems. Because the lunch center group was relatively small, the counselor decided to have 20-minute individual "screening" sessions with participants. Then, she could decide which people needed individual counseling. She was not sure she could take on such a task, but she knew Calliope and several others seemed to want to discuss topics they were reluctant to disclose in the group.

During the first session, Calliope did not feel comfortable disclosing her lesbianism, yet the counselor felt she should see her another time or two. During the fourth session, Calliope disclosed that she had been a lesbian all her life. She had come out with a few close friends and had lived with two or three lesbian lovers, but she had never publicly come out, and she did not plan to do so, although the counselor assured her that she could still come to the lunch center. They discussed reasons for Calliope's not coming out earlier in life (e.g., her family expecting her to accept traditional Greek roles as wife and mother), why some LGB people tried to hide their same-sex sexual orientation all their life, and her fears of prejudice and discrimination, especially at her doctor's office. Plus, as Calliope said more than once, "If my landlord knew about the real me, I would probably have to move."

The counselor concluded that Calliope had no intention of ever coming out. She had concealed her sexual orientation all her life, and she would not come out now. Still, the counselor thought discussing Calliope's feelings about herself and her sexual orientation might prove helpful. The counselor thought, "Calliope disclosed her lesbianism to me, so I need to take her concerns seriously. I will talk with her several more times."

to address the client's sexual orientation is a moot point. As with other developmental periods, some family members will be supportive, others will not. The counselor should carefully consider whether including family members will contribute to or harm the elderly LGB client's situation. In some ways, if the family is supportive, family therapy can be helpful because the client then will see the support and assistance the family offers. Once the decision is reached to engage in family therapy, any of the above-mentioned topics will be appropriate. Again, the perceptive counselor will consider the individual LGB client to determine problems to be discussed and how family members can contribute to the counseling effort.

Up Close and Personal 16.4 looks at a counselor's efforts with Calliope, an elderly Greek American Lesbian.

A Point of Departure: Challenges Confronting Counselors of LGB Clients

Sometimes, counselors feel uncomfortable intervening with LGB clients, either due to homophobia or lack of professional training in working with this population. We recommend the following guidelines for counselors working with LGB clients:

1. Know the interrelatedness of client's developmental period, culture, sexual orientation, and disabling conditions—major premises of this book.

2. Consider sexual orientation to be a biological fact, rather than a matter of choice or preference.

3. Work toward eliminating any personal vestiges of homophobia and prejudicial feelings about LGB persons.

4. Know development in the four lifespan stages sufficiently well to know developmental issues and problems LGB clients in each lifespan period might experience.

5. Take deliberate and planned action to gain knowledge, refine attitudes, and develop the skills needed to provide effective professional intervention with LGB clients.

6. Refine individual, group, and family counseling skills; for example, know when to use each type of therapy and how to make a particular therapy work to achieve desired results in individual situations.

Summary

Counselors will increasingly encounter LGB clients in individual, group, and family counseling sessions. It will be important for counselors to feel competent and comfortable when planning professional intervention for LGB clients. Likewise, counselors need to recognize that

LGB persons have their own cultural mindsets and worldviews. In addition, more and more LGB persons are coming out, thereby disclosing their same-sex sexual orientations to either a few or all acquaintances. As LGB clients increasingly disclose their same-sex sexual orientation during counseling sessions, counselors need to feel comfortable discussing such orientations, knowing the unique challenges LGB clients face and the effects of culture and disabling conditions on those with same-sex sexual orientations. Counselors can also help LGB clients deal with society's continuing homophobia as well as prejudice and discrimination toward LGB clients' other differences, such as race/ethnicity or disability. Counselors who provide effective counseling for LGB clients will be making a significant contribution to this population, to the counseling profession, and to society.

Suggested Readings

Beals, K. P., & Peplau, L. A. (2005). Identity support, identity devaluation, and well-being among lesbians. *Psychology of Women Quarterly, 29*, 140–148. Beals and Peplau conclude that social support and social stressors specifically linked to sexual identity are associated with psychological well-being for lesbian women.

Fingerhut, A. W., Peplau, L. A., & Ghavami, N. (2005). A dual-identity framework for understanding lesbian experience. *Psychology of Women Quarterly, 29*, 129–139. This article presents a detailed conceptual analysis of a dual-identity framework that emphasizes lesbians' simultaneous affiliations with the lesbian world and the mainstream/heterosexual world.

Harkless, L. F., & Fowers, B. J. (2005). Similarities and differences in relational boundaries among heterosexuals, gay men, and lesbians. *Psychology of Women Quarterly, 29*, 167–176. These authors investigated the relative contributions of gender and sexual orientation as factors associated with both same- and opposite-sex couples.

Harper, G. W., Nadine, J., & Zea, M. C. (2004). Giving voice to emerging science and theory for lesbian, gay, and bisexual people of color. *Cultural Diversity and Ethnic Minority Psychology, 10*(3), 187–199. Lesbian, gay, and bisexual people of color often experience multiple layers of oppression in addition to racial prejudice, limited economic resources, and limited acceptance in their own cultural communities.

Lemelle, A. J., & Battle, J. (2004). Black masculinity matters in attitudes toward gay males. *Journal of Homosexuality, 47*(1), 39–51. Lemelle and Battle maintain that African American females may have more negative opinions toward homosexuals than their White counterparts.

Murray, P. D., & McClintock, K. M. (2005). Children of the closet: A measurement of the anxiety and self-esteem of children raised by a nondisclosed homosexual or bisexual parent. *Journal of Homosexuality, 49*(1), 77–95. These authors investigated whether a parent's nondisclosure of her or his homosexual or bisexual orientation within the family unit affects self-esteem and anxiety in children.

PART III

Professional Issues in Multicultural Counseling

Part III consists of Chapter 17 and the Epilogue. Chapter 17 explores a variety of issues of interest to scholars, practicing professionals, and students, including approaches to multicultural counseling, relevance of a lifespan perspective, research directions, ethics, stereotyping, and effects of diversity on professional intervention. The Epilogue provides readers with a look at potential future directions of multicultural counseling.

Issues in Multicultural Counseling

Questions to Be Explored

1. What issues will confront counselors as American society grows increasingly culturally pluralistic?

2. How inclusive should a definition of multicultural counseling be (e.g., should sexual orientation, gender, and disability be included in the definition)?

3. How can clients' diversity affect the effectiveness of counseling intervention?

4. What ethical and legal standards should be considered when counseling clients of differing cultural backgrounds?

5. How much cultural similarity can therapists assume in counseling clients of differing cultures?

6. How can counselors most effectively assess clients of differing cultural backgrounds, and how can spirituality be assessed?

7. What research issues remain to be resolved?

Overview

Counselors will increasingly intervene with clients of differing races, ethnic groups, cultural backgrounds, lifespan periods, gender, sexual orientation, and degree of disability. Some clients' problems will be specific to their particular culture, whereas other problems and frustrations will cross cultural lines. This chapter examines selected issues: (a) how inclusive a definition of multicultural counseling should be, (b) how clients' diversity can be addressed, (c) how ethical and legal standards affect intervention, (d) how assessment can be effective in multicultural settings, and (e) how counselors can address research concerns in the 21st century. This chapter also shows how these issues affect the counseling process and the counseling profession.

Issue 1: How Inclusive Should a Definition of Multicultural Counseling Be?

Defining the Issue

How inclusive should the multicultural counseling be? Some counselors think the definition should be restricted to interactions between counselors and clients of varying ethnic backgrounds, mainly because racism, injustices, and discrimination might be given short shrift if a more inclusive definition is adopted. Instead of broadening the definition, those who are opposed to an inclusive definition would prefer to use the phrase counseling multicultural populations when dealing with differences related to men and women, gay men and lesbians, elderly people, and people with disabilities. Other counselors maintain that unequal treatment and discrimination have widespread effects in the United States and are not limited to only racial and ethnic differences.

Individuals who differ from others have two important characteristics in common. First, clients usually cannot change their status, and they may experience discrimination because of differences. Second, equal respect for people from all cultures is a primary explicit value of multicultural counseling. At the same time, however, multiculturalism has been criticized as being too negative toward European cultures. Focusing multicultural counseling only on certain racial and ethnic minorities at the exclusion of others contradicts the concept of inclusiveness.

Our Position on Inclusiveness

We advocate an inclusive definition of multicultural counseling—one that includes lesbians, gay men, and bisexuals; people with disabilities; and European Americans. We think lesbians, gay men, bisexuals, and people with disabilities have a culture of their own, in addition to their actual culture. In this text, we have included chapters on lesbians, gay men, and bisexuals as well as European Americans. To the extent the research allowed, we included gender and disabilities perspectives. Our rationale for inclusiveness is as follows:

- LGB persons share specific cultural characteristics, experience injustices and discrimination similar to racial and ethnic minorities, and deserve counselors capable of providing effective professional intervention.

- The definition of multicultural counseling should include European Americans. European American clients, although extremely diverse, deserve to their have cultural worldviews recognized during counseling intervention. Just as we have advocated European American counselors understanding clients' differing cultural backgrounds, we advocate counselors of differing cultural backgrounds respecting and addressing European Americans' cultural backgrounds.

- People with disabilities have a culture of their own and often experience injustices. Because of their "culture of disability" and the threat of injustice, people with disabilities should be part of an inclusive definition of multicultural counseling. A Focus on Research 17.1 calls for counseling education students to have a specific counseling course that focuses on intervening with students with disabilities.

A FOCUS ON RESEARCH 17.1

Intervening With Students With Disabilities

Milsom and Akos (2003) think school counselors are not receiving sufficient training in working with students with disabilities, yet counselors are increasingly intervening with these students. Disability legislation has encouraged school counselor involvement with students with disabilities. This disability legislation along with position papers of professional counseling associations call for counselors to take active roles with students with disabilities. Roles can include individual and group counseling, serving on interdisciplinary teams, and assisting with behavior modification plans for students with disabilities. Even with legislation and professional association actions, research suggests that many school counselors have not been required to complete coursework that is related to students with disabilities.

In their investigative study, Milson and Akos found that 43% of counselor education programs required students to complete a disability course. Approximately two-fifths of the programs receive disability information. Because school counseling education program courses would be more likely to focus on counseling issues than would a disability course per se, Milsom and Akos think the counseling strategies course should be a part of the counseling education program. Milsom and Akos maintained that although many counseling students have informal opportunities to work with students with disabilities during their field experiences, it is troubling that only about 25% of the programs require (and provide supervision for) experiences with the disabled.

Source: "Preparing school counselors to work with students with disabilities," by A. Milsom, and P. Akos, 2003, *Counselor Education & Supervision, 43,* pp. 86–95.

Issue 2: How Can Counselors Perceive Clients' Diversity?

Counselor perceptions of clients' cultural backgrounds undoubtedly affect intervention strategies. As previously suggested, the events experienced during multicultural intervention may take a variety of forms, each having the potential for promoting or hindering the effectiveness of counseling. The stresses and strains of multicultural interaction may result in conflict that actually may increase or intensify clients' problems. Other counseling outcomes may result in improved relationships among people of varying cultural backgrounds. In any event, how the counselor and the client perceive their multicultural relationship and their perceptions of the actual outcome of the intervention warrants consideration. Considering our nation's growing diversity, counselors will continue to focus attention on several models of cultural deficiency/difference, conflicting opinions regarding counseling approaches, and the effects of verbal and nonverbal communication between counselor and clients.

Models of Cultural Deficiency and Difference

The study of differences in intelligence as a function of race has sometimes been flawed with inaccurate scientific data or faulty analysis. This situation has resulted in some researchers contributing, knowingly or unknowingly, to racism and stereotyping. The issue has far greater implications, however, than whether clients are categorized according to the genetic deficient model, the cultural deficit model, or the culturally different model. For example, counselors who believe that low intelligence and strong athletic ability characterize African Americans or that Asian Americans are by nature mathematically oriented will have a biased perception of the client.

The Genetic Deficient Model.   The genetic deficient model holds that culturally different people are genetically inferior. Scholarly opinion that was offered around the turn of the 20th century argued for the genetic intellectual superiority of Whites and the genetic inferiority of the "lower races." Some people considered minority cultures to be lacking desirable attributes and to be uneducable. Such mindsets undoubtedly resulted in discrimination and other forms of ill treatment. People forming friendships, college administrators making admissions decisions, and employers making employment decisions obviously considered some people to be genetically deficient and either consciously or unconsciously discriminated against them. Rather than considering a person's record of achievement or motivation for self-improvement, many people used the genetically deficient model as the basis for making such decisions. Although the genetic deficient model is not as powerful as it once was, some people continue to subscribe to the theory that genetic inheritance plays a significant role in the determination of intelligence, motivation, and ability to achieve academically and otherwise.

The Cultural Deficit Model.   In the cultural deficit model, social scientists described culturally different people as "deprived" or "disadvantaged" because they demonstrated behavior at variance with middle-class values, language systems, and customs. From a class perspective, middle-class people assumed that other cultures did not seek to advance themselves because of a cultural deficit. Thus, rather than attribute undesirable differences to genetics, social scientists shifted the blame to cultural lifestyles or values.

Both the genetic deficient and the cultural deficit models failed to address the implicit cultural biases that shaped these negative perceptions and inhibited the understanding of the role of sociopolitical forces. Both have been refuted and largely superseded by the culturally different model (Draguns, 1989).

The Culturally Different Model.   The culturally different model holds that people with culturally diverse backgrounds have unique strengths, values, customs, and traditions that can serve as a basis for enriching the overall counseling process. Researchers have begun to establish an information base documenting that cultural differences are not deficiencies and that the differences can be built upon as counseling progresses. In order for counselors to provide the most effective professional intervention, they must make deliberate attempts to capitalize on differences as resources, rather than disregard them or view them as deficits to be eliminated.

Proponents of the culturally different model believe that people of all backgrounds, regardless of lifespan period, still need to be aware of mainstream cultural values and knowledge. A degree of cultural compatibility is attained as counselors and clients increasingly develop an awareness of each other's cultural differences. In any event, people should not be condemned for their language, culture, age, sexual orientation, or other differences.

Etic–Emic Approaches.   Two basic approaches to multicultural study and related research are the etic and the emic. Kurasaki, Sue, Chan, and Gee (2000) define etic as culture-general concepts or theories and emic as culture-specific phenomena. They offer the example of the psychotherapist using catharsis, or the expression of pent-up emotions to relieve tension or depression directly. For a principle to be etic in nature, it should be applicable to different cultural groups. If it is not applicable to different cultural groups, the principle is emic, perhaps applicable only to a particular client or a particular cultural group.

Regardless of the etic or the emic approach, counselors should be cautious of theories and studies that fail to take into account individual differences among clients. The psychotherapist who assumes that nondirective techniques are effective with all clients may be confusing etics and emics to the extent that an individual client's needs are not met. In clinical practice, some researchers and clinicians believe that current psychotherapies based on Western modes of thought and treatment may be culturally inappropriate with certain members of ethnic minority groups; they advocate more culturally relevant forms of treatment. It is essential to have professional intervention consistent with clients' cultural lifestyles (Kurasaki, Sue, Chan, & Gee, 2000).

According to Draguns (1989), it is probably impossible to conduct counseling purely on the basis of etic or emic approaches. Counseling that ignores multicultural differences demonstrates cultural insensitivity; yet, counselors should not focus exclusively on such differences. Realistically speaking, neither the etic nor the emic approach can be used exclusively, because the emic approach accentuates the differences among groups and makes multicultural counseling a forbidding task, and the etic approach tends to overlook important cultural differences and may fail because of cultural insensitivity. The most effective counselors blend the two approaches (Das, 1995).

Autoplastic and Alloplastic Approaches.   People of all cultures adapt to their environmental situations by changing themselves, in an autoplastic approach; by changing the environment, in an alloplastic approach; or by combining the two approaches. The question has been raised concerning the extent to which multicultural psychotherapy and counseling lean toward changing the individual as opposed to helping the client change the environment. Traditionally, counseling has been directed at those who are socially and culturally deviant, with the goal of changing client behavior to be more conforming with the norms of the dominant majority group. The situation becomes more complex when the counselor considers multicultural situations. Does the counselor prepare the client to change external reality or help the client accommodate to that reality? Our increasingly pluralistic society expands the client's options as to the nature of personal relationships, reference groups, and ethnic and cultural identities. However, this issue continues to be crucial to counselors who must decide whether to foster assimilation or to encourage self-development.

The autoplastic–alloplastic distinction has the potential for creating controversy. How much should the client be helped to accept or change a situation? One must consider the role of culture in this regard. Whereas Hispanic Americans traditionally are socialized to accept and endure life gracefully, European Americans are taught to confront obstacles and, if possible, remove them. Traditionally, the European American counselor's mandate has been to reorganize and improve the client's personal resources, rather than to prepare the client to change the social structure (Draguns, 1989). What, then, should the counselor do when the client's attainment of goals is blocked by the obstacles of racism or discrimination?

Existentialist Approaches.   Although counseling usually draws on psychological theories, the existentialist approach to counseling emphasizes philosophical concepts. Developing an "I–thou" relationship allows for an exploration of questions that are crucial to the client's existence. In his explanation of existential counseling, Vontress (1996) explains that Western academicians classify philosophies into various categories such as rationalism, phenomenology, and pragmatism; however, he thinks these systems are variations on the same theme—the eternal quest to make sense out of our presence in the world.

Vontress (1996) recommends that counselors focus on four "worlds" or aspects of human existence to determine the nature of the client's adjustment to life: (a) *Eigenvelt* (the world of self); (b) *Mitwelt* (the world of relationships with others); (c) *Umvelt* (human beings' efforts to maintain harmonious relationships); and (d) *Uberwelt* (rapport with forces greater than oneself). These four worlds provide the basis for counseling and for knowing and determining clients' problems. However, Vontress does not use psychotherapeutic theory exclusively. Instead, he takes advantage of many ideas embedded in the writings of poets, novelists, and philosophers from around the world and places them into a framework that may give direction to clients from various cultural backgrounds. The counseling relationship should be imbued with a recognition of human mortality, a feeling of sympathy for the client, and the intimate I–thou rapport.

Existential philosophy and multicultural counseling both respect and recognize cultural differences as they organize human experiences in ways that reflect universal concerns of humankind. For counseling to be effective, counselors have a responsibility to explore their own and their clients' differences resulting from race, ethnicity, culture, gender, and sexual orientation.

Ivey et al. (1997) maintain that the existentialist point of view is an attitude toward the counseling interview and toward the meaning of life. These authors offer several main points concerning existentialist approaches to counseling:

- Our task is to understand what existence in the world means; these meanings vary from culture to culture.

- We know ourselves through our relationship with the world and, in particular, through our relationships with other people.

- Anxiety can result from a lack of relationship with ourselves, with others, or with the world at large or from a failure to act or choose.

- We are responsible for our own construction of the world. Even though we know the world only from a personal interaction, it is we who decide what the world means and who must provide organization for that world.

- The counselor's task is to understand the client's world as fully as possible and ultimately to encourage the client to be responsible for making decisions. However, existential counselors will also share themselves and their worldviews with clients when appropriate.

- Some people might not view the world as meaningful and, therefore, develop a negative and hopeless view of what they observe to be absurdity and cruelty of life.

- If a person sees the many possibilities in the world as difficulties, then that person has a problem. If a person sees problems as opportunities, then that person will choose to act.

Communication: Verbal and Nonverbal Language.   The outcome of any psychological intervention ultimately depends on the degree to which counselors and clients understand each other. Simply understanding a client's spoken language may not be enough, however. Other variables enter the picture. First, communication styles (both verbal and nonverbal) must be understood. We have already mentioned the Native American tendency to avoid eye contact, the tendency of some African Americans to "play it cool" and act "together," the Asian American confusion over whether to speak loudly or softly because of contrasting cultural expectations, and the Hispanic American tendency to maintain allegiance to the mother tongue. Second, the communication issue is further complicated when counselors consider the lifespan periods and generations of their clients. The language that children learn in American schools is quite different from the language used by a teenage drop-out dealing drugs on the street. Moreover, the language used by children and adolescents might differ from that of adult and elderly clients. Older clients are more likely to feel a sense of obligation to remain faithful to their native tongue.

Although all aspects of communication style are in play during a counseling session, some are likely to be more salient than others, depending on the individual and the culture. It may be very important with some clients to consider appropriateness of topics, tone of voice, or taking turns in conversation.

The complex issue of maintaining effective communication between counselor and client does not allow for broad generalizations. For example, the decision whether to seek an interpreter, to speak the client's native language (if the counselor is fluent in it), or to use a respected third party to assist with communication depends on the individual client, the nature of the client's problems, the extent of the language barrier, and how the client perceives the communication problem.

Lifespan Differences.   The fairly recent attention to lifespan development and the recognition of characteristics associated with each stage have resulted in more appropriate assessment and intervention. Counselors have long recognized that children differ from adults, but only recently have serious attempts been made to provide developmentally appropriate counseling and psychotherapy for adolescents and the elderly. The need for additional scholarly research on counseling and on the lifespan continuum becomes clear in the light of critical differences between lifespan stages and the myriad changes occurring during each stage. Complications arise from the fact that various cultures differ in their perception of lifespan stages.

Intracultural, Generational, Sexual Orientation, Disability, Geographical, and Socioeconomic Differences.   As mentioned in previous chapters, the tremendous diversity among clients makes generalizations difficult. Any number of examples can be offered as evidence that a "single" culture or ethnicity should not be the sole determining factor in reaching professional decisions. For example, considerable differences are found between relatively uneducated, lower-class African Americans living in the inner cities and highly educated, middle-class African Americans residing in the suburbs. Similarly, differences between first-generation Asian Americans and subsequent generations may be substantial. Differences may also occur as a function of geographic region of residency; for example, Hispanic Americans residing in Texas may exhibit characteristics different from those living in New York or Florida. Counseling professionals should have the knowledge and skill to intervene with individuals within a given culture, recognizing intracultural and individual differences as significant variables in planning appropriate intervention.

To understand gender issues for Asian American men means to understand traditional Asian masculinity development, acculturation and ethnic identity, immigration history, and Asian Americans men's experiences with racism in the United States. Nghe, Mahalik, and Lowe (2003) in Gender Perspectives 17.1 look at challenges facing Asian American men.

GENDER PERSPECTIVES 17.1

Vietnamese Men—Examining Traditional Gender Roles

Nghe, Mahalik, and Lowe (2003) sought to increase counselors' understanding of Vietnamese men in the United States by discussing masculine gender role of socialization influences from Vietnamese culture. Three areas are addressed: *Nhau* (or binge drinking), refugee experiences, and racism and stereotypes.

Nhau is a ritual of male bonding—it is a process in which males consume large quantities of alcohol in a relatively short period of time. Such male socialization takes place in a social environment that involves peers, family members, business acquaintances, and discussions of almost all topics. This ritual usually begins around the adolescent years—women are excluded from this male ritual.

The refugee experience often challenges males' perceptions of his ability to be the provider for the family. Being a refugee is a life-altering experience. Before coming to the United States, many Asian men suffered economic hardships that affected their abilities to provide for the family. They heard of the opportunities in the United States and were surprised to learn of the low wages, multiple jobs, 10 or more families in an efficiency unit, and problems with the English language.

Racism and stereotypes are also stressors for Vietnamese men. In the United States, masculinity is often seen as a reflection of the extent to which he has physical prominence. In traditional Vietnamese cultures, intellectual prowess is the most highly valued characteristic and at the top of the social scale. These forms of stereotyping are emasculating because intellectual prowess is not valued and the Asian male is seen as a caricature of a wimpy, feminine nerd.

The authors offer several implications for counselors. Counselors should understand that (1) psychological distress and help-seeking potentially undermine traditional masculine roles for Vietnamese men, (2) Vietnamese men will likely deal with stressors by using indigenous support systems and other coping mechanisms, (3) professional intervention should incorporate Asian customs, and (4) it is important to help Vietnamese American men identify U. S. masculinity messages that contribute to role strain for them.

Source: "Influences on Vietnamese men: Traditional gender roles, the refugee experience, acculturation, and racism in the United States," by L. T. Nghe, J. R. Mahalik, and S. M. Lowe, 2003, *Journal of Multicultural Counseling and Development, 31*(4), pp. 245–261.

Issue 3: What Ethical and Legal Standards Should Guide Counselors?

Counselors have an obligation to abide by the ethical standards subscribed to by the American Association for Counseling and Development (AACD) and the American Psychological Association (APA) and to respect other ethical standards. All ethical standards pertaining to the counseling profession and to research involving human subjects apply also to clients of differing cultural backgrounds.

Ethics Associated With Multicultural Counseling

How should counselors relate to clients with differing traditions, values, and customs? How can counselors really know their clients' values and mental health needs? According to Herlihy (1996), "Recognizing diversity in our society and developing intercultural competence are fundamental to ethical counseling practice" (p. 6).

The American Counseling Association's (ACA) Code of Ethics states that counselors should embrace a cross-cultural approach; specific standards related to nondiscrimination and multicultural competence permeate the code. Although the ACA Code of Ethics provides guidelines for sound multicultural practice in areas such as testing (Standard E.8), counselor training (Standards F.1.a and F.2.1), and access to technology (Standard A.12.c), counselor educators and practicing counselors need to work continuously toward culturally appropriate practice.

Sue (cited in Herlihy, 1996) suggests that ethical multicultural practice involves three primary goals:

1. self-awareness—becoming more aware of one's own values, biases, and assumptions regarding human behavior;

2. knowledge of cultural values, biases, and assumptions of diverse groups in our society; and

3. commitment to developing culturally appropriate intervention strategies at both the individual and system levels.

The counselor's ethical responsibility, however, is not only to understand the differing cultural orientations and values of clients, but also to examine cultural biases and stereotypes that affect clients. By gaining knowledge about clients' cultural differences and by assessing personal feelings, the counselor reaches a level of awareness that values are culture-specific, rather than right or wrong; that is, it is not for the counselor to judge the correctness of values esteemed by clients of other cultures.

Tjeltveit (2004) maintains that psychotherapy sessions and psychotherapy in general exist in the context of ethical questions and answers. Although psychotherapists often avoid them, ethical concerns and issues often arise. Tjeltvelt, in A Focus on Research 17.2, looks at ethical contexts of psychotherapy.

One example of an ethical dilemma is when school counselors decide whether to engage in multicultural counseling without having had sufficient multicultural training (Hobson & Kanitz, 1996). Some counselors have received little or no multicultural counseling training in their preparation training programs. Ethical standards of the ACA and the American School Counselor Association (ASCA) require members to treat each student as a unique individual and to provide services uniquely tailored to meet individual needs. Similarly, members are required to avoid practicing in areas where they are not professionally qualified. Hobson and Kanitz contend that the lack of multicultural training in master's degree programs means school counselors might not be aware of the importance of such training. Plus, the lack of adequate preparation increases the possibility that many school counselors unknowingly practice beyond their scope of competence. Thus, an ethical question exists: Should school counselors make their services available to all students at the risk of practicing beyond their scope of competence? Or should they limit their scope of practice to areas in which they feel confident, and therefore withhold services from clients of diverse backgrounds about whom they have not received training?

Ethics and ethical decision-making are critical elements of counseling practice, and a component of competent training in ethical decision-making should be a component of professional training programs. Cottone and Claus (2000) question whether ethical decision-making models really work. They maintain that there is much work to be done in ethics; surprisingly little research has been done on ethical decision-making or models of decision-making in counseling.

A FOCUS ON RESEARCH 17.2

The Ethical Contexts of Psychotherapy

Tjeltveit (2004) maintains that during counseling intervention, questions about what is good, what is bad, obligations, and virtues are an inescapable part of psychotherapy. Often left undiscussed, therapists and clients bring to the therapy a variety of ethical emotions, perceptions, behaviors, and convictions that profoundly shape counseling relationships. Ethics (and especially morality) is often seen as destructive and divisive. Rigid, moralistic, and misguided ethical rules can damage clients, at times producing conflicts. Therapists might feel if they discuss moral convictions, disagreement and divisiveness might occur.

Tjeltveit describes ethics in terms of the good (what is good), the bad (what is bad or not good), the obligatory (doing what one should do), and the virtuous (valued, stable qualities). He advocates a psychotherapeutic process that provides explicit or implicit answers to questions about what is good and bad, right and wrong, and virtuous. Such questions help create the ethical context of psychotherapy, a context that can prove disintegrative and destructive or integrative and constructive.

Source: "The good, the bad, the obligatory, and the virtuous: The ethical contexts of psychotherapy," by A. C. Tjeltvelt, 2004, *Journal of Psychotherapy Integration, 14*(2), pp. 149–167.

Although there are many models available, it is difficult to determine whether one model is better than another. In fact, the criteria for what makes a "better" (p. 281) model are not clearly defined. The authors conclude that additional dialogue on these matters is needed.

Lawrence and Kurpius (2000) maintain that many counselors in nonschool settings work with children during their practice. It is essential that counselors understand the legal and ethical issues relevant to working with minors. Attention should be given to four critical ethical issues: counselor competence, the client's right to confidentiality, the client's right to informed consent, and duties related to child abuse.

Lawrence and Kurpius (2000) maintain that working with minors can present a field of legal and "ethical landmines" (p. 135). Counselors need to protect themselves by being cautious and judicious. The authors suggest the following guidelines:

- Inform families of the limits of your abilities as defined by education, training, and supervised practice.
- Maintain familiarity with state statutes regarding privilege.
- Clarify policies concerning confidentiality with both the child and the parents at the first therapy session.
- If you choose to work with the minor without the parents' informed consent, ask the minor to provide informed consent in writing.
- Keep accurate and objective records of all interactions and counseling sessions.
- Maintain adequate professional liability coverage.
- When in need of help or advice, confer with colleagues and have professional legal help available.

Clearly, the many ethical and legal dilemmas surrounding the counseling profession are too complex to summarize here. It is apparent, however, that additional research is warranted to determine the effect of the differing perceptions of ethical matters when the cultural backgrounds of counselors and clients differ. Ethical decisions in counseling relationships become more complex when one works with clients who have differing worldviews and unique cultural perspectives of their lives.

Issue 4: How Can Counselors Most Effectively Assess Clients of Differing Cultural Backgrounds?

Assessment in counseling and psychotherapy includes interviewing, observing, testing, and analyzing data from cultural perspectives. Counselors should determine the extent to which diversity affects assessment as well as provide an adequate response to several questions. Numerous issues have arisen regarding cross-cultural testing and assessment. Concerns include (but are not limited to) assessment validity, the use of inappropriate norms, ethnocentrism and ethnorelativism, cultural stereotypes and prejudices, acculturation, and language barriers (Cofresi & Gorman, 2004).

The Extent to Which Cultural Diversity Affects Assessment

One basic issue concerns the extent to which cultural diversity affects assessment: Will a characteristic representative of a specific culture be mistakenly perceived and assessed by using European American middle-class standards? Will a counselor of an Hispanic or Asian cultural background mistakenly assess a European American or an African American client? Counselors need to make sure their cultural assumptions and worldviews have a minimum effect on clients of differing cultural backgrounds.

Five questions come to mind as counselors plan assessment in multicultural settings:

1. What needs to be assessed, and are those needs culturally based?
2. What types of assessment instruments reflect cultural perspectives and most effectively assess those needs?
3. What evidence do assessment instruments provide that indicates they are culturally responsive?
4. What precautions should counselors heed when interpreting assessment results?
5. What ethical and legal responsibilities are associated with multicultural assessment?

Several issues affect assessment with diverse populations. First is a "quest for the golden label" (Sedlacek, 1994, p. 549), or the idea that problems related to diversity can be solved if the right label can be determined. For example, what characteristics should be included in "diversity"? Can Black and African American be used interchangeably? Should gay men and lesbians be included in conceptualizations of diversity? Second is "the three musketeers" (p. 550), or the tendency to believe that one assessment measure can work equally well for all groups. Third is "horizontal research" (p. 551), or the tendency to do nondevelopmental research on nontraditional groups, that is, the tendency to include specific cultural groups in studies that were not designed with them in mind. Fourth is "bias is bias" (p. 551), or sampling bias in studies of diverse populations. Fifth is "I'm okay, you're not," (p. 552) the tendency to train few assessment specialists who are knowledgeable about diversity issues.

Also, counselors need to be fairly certain that assessment instruments are culturally appropriate. Without appropriate assessment strategies, counseling professionals are unable to diagnose problems, develop appropriate goals, and assess the outcomes of intervention. Initial client assessment, clinical judgments, selection of assessment instruments, and the outcomes of counseling evaluation are assessment factors that warrant attention.

Stanard, Sandhu, and Painter (2000) maintain that spirituality includes concepts such as transcendence, self-actualization, purpose and meaning, balance, sacredness, altruism, universality, and sense of a Higher Power. As an emerging fifth force in counseling and psychotherapy, spirituality is critical for sound mental health and effective growth and development.

Hinkle (1994) lists specific problems associated with cross-cultural assessment, including: (a) difficulty establishing equivalence across cultures, (b) lack of appropriate cultural norms, (c) composition of test items, and (d) differing attitudes across cultures toward testing. Population growth rates of culturally diverse groups are increasing; consequently, invalid clinical assessments associated with cultural bias are bound to occur. Cultural influences on testing can be minimized only through increased awareness, training, and instrument development, but they cannot be totally eliminated.

Hinkle (1994) suggests practical steps such as (a) increasing the awareness and knowledge of test items relevant to various cultures, (b) increasing the awareness and knowledge of tests developed for one culture and administered to persons with variable cultural backgrounds, and (c) increasing the awareness of the need for tests and testing procedures relevant to specific cultures and subsequent local test validation and advocacy of their use.

Until assessments and psychological evaluations are as fair as possible and common to all cultures, testing practitioners have a responsibility to continue to scrutinize the content of tests. Practitioners can contribute to test fairness by being aware of the difficulties involved in the comparison of test performance across cultures. Practitioners also need to share, in the literature and at professional meetings, their observations regarding cross-cultural testing (Hinkle, 1994).

Issue 5: What Research Concerns Will Be Relevant in the Future?

It goes without saying that counselors should stay abreast of research developments in the field; furthermore, they should conduct research of their own. In reality, however, the majority of counseling practitioners do not actively participate in research endeavors, nor do they always keep up with the latest developments reported in the literature. This section examines some research issues that are likely to confront counselors during the next decade.

The Multicultural Counseling Process

What research issues are particularly relevant to the multicultural counseling process? What areas must be considered to provide a more enlightened perspective on counseling clients in multicultural settings? Although research goals and methodologies in the various areas of counseling may be similar, a prerequisite to all research endeavors in a multicultural context is the understanding and acceptance that cultural differences significantly affect outcomes. Also, it must be understood that ethical standards and legal aspects relevant to the counseling profession also apply to research endeavors in multicultural situations.

Research Techniques and Outcomes

Whether counselors employ comparative group research designs, field studies, single-subject studies, or case studies, cultural differences should be taken into account. An important cultural consideration that may have a bearing on gathering research data is the possibility of a communication problem (verbal or nonverbal) between researcher and subject. For example, the researcher may construe the Native American tendency to gaze into space as indicative of boredom, or the researcher may not understand an Asian American's shyness or tendency not to disclose personal information, or the Hispanic American's valuing of family over self may be misinterpreted in a variety of ways. Although these represent only selected examples, the point is clear that researchers of one culture may make erroneous judgments with respect to the behavior of subjects of other cultures.

Multicultural Counseling and the Lifespan Continuum

Research undoubtedly needs to be directed toward the relationships between multicultural counseling interactions and the client's lifespan stage. These intricate relationships can be understood only by directing research toward (a) the multicultural aspects of the counseling relationship, (b) the actual counselor–client interactions, and (c) the counselor's perception of the client's lifespan stage. Specifically, attention needs to be focused on the actual effects of culture and the client's developmental period in the multicultural counseling endeavor.

Research Directions, Tasks, and Challenges

The ultimate determination of counseling effectiveness depends largely on a credible research base. In order for this base to accrue, studies must seek to synthesize knowledge of clients' cultures with that of lifespan differences. Selected research directions that will lead to greater multicultural awareness include the following:

- Evaluate the impact of multicultural counseling training.
- Determine which assessment instruments most effectively assess the needs of clients of differing cultural backgrounds.
- Determine client preference for counselor race or ethnicity (both intergroup and intragroup differences).
- Study identity development within the context of majority and minority status.
- Determine the effect of race and ethnicity on diagnosis, treatment, and counseling outcomes.

- Examine the relationship between therapist prejudice and differential diagnosis, process, treatment, and outcome.

- Examine multiple oppressions (e.g., the effects of being minority, gay or lesbian, and elderly; or being a Hispanic American with a disability).

- Ascertain approaches to culture and counseling beyond the current theoretical basis.

- Identify variables that explain past and present occurrences, as well as those that predict future events with respect to people, ideas, and cultures.

- Inform counselors of means of providing services based on new counseling theories and new training, so that counseling and psychotherapy services can be more equitably distributed among the multicultural society.

It is important to note that resolution of research issues will depend on collaborative efforts of researchers and counseling professionals. Practical solutions to counseling dilemmas can emerge only through such collaboration.

A Point of Departure

In the coming years, counselors will be faced with unresolved issues and unanswered questions. At least in some cases, this situation will affect the outcome of multicultural counseling and psychotherapy. Let us now look at some challenges confronting counselors in multicultural settings and consider the options open to counselors in meeting these challenges.

Challenges Confronting Counselors in a Culturally Pluralistic Society

How can counselors respond to the various unresolved issues in the field? What research priorities should counselors pursue? How can cultural approaches and lifespan approaches be integrated so as to enhance counseling interventions?

Counselors who wish to gain a better understanding of how culture, counseling and psychotherapy, and the lifespan approach are interrelated should consider the following recommendations:

- Actively seek to recognize basic issues pertaining to multicultural situations.

- Allow for multicultural encounters with clients of all cultures and at all stages of the lifespan.

- Keep abreast of research studies published in journals devoted to counseling and development in multicultural settings.

- Design and implement research studies with clients of differing cultural backgrounds.

- Understand one's own cultural background and commit to appreciating cultural differences, rather than making value judgments with respect to diversity.

If attention is focused in a methodical and deliberate manner on issues in need of resolution, then the effectiveness of the counseling process is likely to increase, even if the issues are not immediately resolved.

Summary

Counselors, now and in the future, will need to (a) determine the inclusiveness of the definition of multicultural counseling, (b) deal with the challenges of understanding clients' various diversities, (c) consider lifespan issues, (d) assess the effects of diversity on counseling intervention, (e) recognize the ethical and legal dimensions of counseling, and (f) conduct research on diversity and its effects on counseling intervention. The enthusiasm with which counselors and researchers tackle these tasks will greatly influence counseling efforts in multicultural situations.

Suggested Readings

Bodenhorn, N. (2005). American School Counselor Association Ethical Code changes relevant to family work. *Family Journal: Counseling & Therapy for Couples & Families, 13* (3), 316–320. Recent changes in the American School Counselor Association Ethical Code are outlined.

Frame, M. W., & Williams, C. B. (2005). Issues and insights: A model of ethical decision making from a multicultural perspective. *Counseling and Values, 49* (3), 165–179. These authors argue that the current Code of Ethics and Standards of Practice of the American Counseling Association does not adequately address the demands of working with non-White, non-Western clients.

Jennings, L., Sovereign, A., Bottorff, N., Mussell, M. P., Vye, C. (2005). Nine ethical principles of master therapists, *Journal of Mental Health Counseling, 27* (1), 32–47. These authors interviewed ten master therapists which resulted in the identification of nine ethical values.

Kitaoka, S. K. (2005). Multicultural counseling competencies: Lessons from assessment. *Journal of Multicultural Counseling and Development, 33* (1), 37–47. Kitaoka looks at multicultural counseling competencies from the perspective of quantitative assessment.

Lonborg, S. D., & Bowen, N. (2004). Counselors, communities, and spirituality: Ethical and multicultural concerns. *Professional School Counseling, 7* (5), 318–325. These authors explore the ethical implications of spiritual diversity in school counseling.

Tjeltveit, A. C. (2004). The good, the bad, the obligatory, and the virtuous: The ethical contexts of psychotherapy. *Journal of Psychotherapy Integration, 14* (2), 149–167. Tjeltveit calls for counselors to consider ethical questions such as what is good, what is bad, what are obligations, and what are virtues.

Epilogue

Increased knowledge of cultural diversity and lifespan development and improved understanding of how they are interrelated contribute to better relationships between clients and counselors and to more favorable outcomes. The goal of this epilogue is to tie together some recurrent themes of the preceding chapters. Considered here are the current status of multicultural counseling and the effects of cultural, intracultural, lifespan, sexual orientation, gender, and disability differences among clients; the continuing challenges associated with racism and discrimination; and the dangers of basing counseling decisions on erroneous generalizations.

Multicultural Counseling and Psychotherapy

Its Beginning

Multicultural counseling as a legitimate area of counseling specialization has evolved rather quickly during the past 30 years. This area began with a relatively small number of counselors and psychologists interested in cross-cultural differences (W. M. L. Lee, 1996). The growing interest in multicultural counseling is evidenced in the increasing numbers of multicultural studies and in the acceptance of this subspecialty in professional circles. As the United States continues to become increasingly more culturally diverse, counselors in public agencies, in schools, and in private practice will no doubt be challenged to provide effective counseling intervention for clients of many different cultures. Yet, many counselors may have been trained in traditional counselor education programs in which assessment and intervention techniques were based on middle-class European American standards and expectations.

A Rationale

The rationale for multicultural counseling is clear: Rather than expect clients of various cultural backgrounds to adapt to the counselor's cultural expectations and intervention strategies, multicultural counseling proposes that the counselor base intervention on each client's individual, intracultural, gender, socioeconomic, geographic, generational, sexual orientation, disability, and lifespan differences. Without doubt, this text has proposed and demonstrated that all clients, regardless of cultural background, need individual consideration that takes into account the client's cultural as well as many other differences.

Growing Acceptance: Present and Future

Considerable evidence suggests that multicultural counseling has gained professional respect and points toward an overall acceptance and a bright future: (a) the growth of the Association of Multicultural Counseling and Development (AMCD), (b) the *Journal of Multicultural Counseling and Development* and other prestigious journals listed in Appendix A,

(c) the growing number of multicultural counseling textbooks, (d) the various conferences and seminars addressing multicultural concerns and issues, and (e) the appearance of new college courses designed to enhance the counselor's knowledge and skills.

People and Their Diversity

To say that American society is growing more diverse is an understatement. Not only is the size of the minority population continuing to increase, but we are also seeing an increasing variety of cultures at all stages of the lifespan. From a historical viewpoint, culturally different people have been the recipients of cruel and inhumane treatment. Much has been written about the enormous problems that immigrants face on entering the United States. Consider, too, the unjust treatment directed toward American Indians; it is difficult to even guess at how many were enslaved or killed. Racism continues to exist, impeding the progress of all groups victimized by it.

Despite the grimness of the historical record, the 21st century can be a time for recognition and acceptance of others' diversity. Factors that may contribute to such recognition include (a) the efforts directed at children and adolescents (e.g., multicultural education courses in elementary and secondary schools), (b) the multicultural emphasis of the National Council for Accreditation of Teacher Education and the Council for Accreditation of Counseling and Related Educational Programs, (c) the increasing evidence that the nation actually benefits from cultural diversity, and (d) the growing number of organizations working to instill cultural pride.

Realities: Racism, Injustice, and Discrimination

As previously mentioned, racism, injustice, and discrimination continue to affect people in the United States. Although overt acts of violence and hatred, such as those of the skinheads and the Ku Klux Klan, may not be as overt as they have been in the past, the more covert forms of racism are widespread and continue to undermine people's progress and well-being.

Counselors of all cultures will have to deal with problems resulting from these realities; they will also have to sort through personal biases and long-held misconceptions with respect to race and ethnicity.

An Increasing Knowledge Base: Cultural Diversity and Lifespan Recognition of Cultural Diversity

The professional literature of the past several decades will increase counselors' knowledge of cultural diversity. More than ever before, counselors have access to objective information describing African American, American Indian, Asian American, European American, and Hispanic American cultural groups. No longer should counseling intervention be based on inaccurate generalizations about cultural differences. Through personal interaction with people of differing cultural backgrounds and through careful review of pertinent journals, books, and other resources, counselors can gain valuable insights into the unique problems of all clients. The American Indian concept of sharing, the African American unique dialect and concept of extended family, the Asian American concept of generational and family relationships, the European American respect for individualism, and the Hispanic American machismo and commitment to speaking Spanish can provide an accurate basis for counseling intervention. Equally important is the understanding that individuals may vary according to generation, socioeconomic status, gender, sexual orientation, disability, geographic location, and other variables.

Knowledge of Human Growth and Development

Counselors can benefit from the increasing knowledge of lifespan development. No longer should a counselor plan assessment and intervention without first considering the client's lifespan period and its unique characteristics, crises, and tasks; for example, the adolescent's view of the role of the family may be quite different from the elderly person's view or the child's view. The intricate relationship between culture and development can be seen in the generational differences between some younger and older Asian Americans. Although the work of some developmentalists (e.g., Erikson, Havighurst, Piaget) may be culturally specific and based on European American and middle-class norms, the growing body of developmental literature is providing a sound foundation for counseling across cultures and developmental periods.

Using the Knowledge Base to Enhance Counseling Effectiveness

There are numerous benefits of counseling intervention based on lifespan development. Counselors are better able to plan appropriate strategies if they understand, for example, (a) the child's problems growing up in a society that often discriminates against culture and age; (b) the adolescent's need to reconcile peer pressure and family expectations; (c) the adult's frustrations in coping with economic, educational, and employment discrimination; and (d) the daily reality of multiple jeopardy often faced by people who are elderly, LGB, disabled, or some combination thereof.

Responding to Individual and Cultural Diversity Differences

Classifying a client by culture or ethnicity may describe very little about the person. Each client should be considered on an individual basis, with the recognition that many differences affect the counseling process. It may be accurate to describe someone as an African American, but that description does not provide sufficient information with which to plan assessment and intervention. The problems of an unemployed African American man who never finished high school are very different from those of a college-educated African American man working in middle management. Along the same lines, the diverse Hispanic culture requires that counselors consider individual populations and individual clients. A Puerto Rican American living in New York is probably

quite different from a Mexican American residing in southern Texas.

Avoiding Stereotypes and Generalizations

Stereotypes and generalizations have the potential for severely damaging counseling relationships and intervention outcomes. It should be obvious that all minorities are not underachievers, that all adolescents are not sexually promiscuous, and that all elderly are not helpless. Stereotypical thinking continues to persist, however, even in people who are well-educated and who pride themselves on their sound logic and reason.

Stereotypes and generalizations not only apply to culture but also to the various lifespan periods. To characterize all children as carefree, all adolescents as troublemakers, all adults as prone to midlife crises, or all elderly as helpless and senile is an affront to individuals all along the lifespan continuum. The expectation that a client will demonstrate certain adverse behaviors because of age may even foster those behaviors.

What steps should be taken to reduce the presence of stereotyping and generalizations with respect to age groups? First, counselors should learn more about lifespan development and the unique problems of each stage. By so doing, the necessity of basing counseling decisions on accurate and objective information is likely to become clear. Second, counselors should seek firsthand experiences with people along the lifespan continuum. Third, counselors should strive to recognize the severe consequences of age-related stereotypical thinking for their clients.

Seeking Help in a Multicultural Society

Tendencies to Not Seek Professional Help

Counselors intervening in multicultural situations should recognize that, in some cultures, people tend to seek assistance from the immediate and extended family, rather than from professionals. Although logical reasons underlie this tendency, counselors are still faced with the need to explain the counseling process and its confidentiality to clients and to gear the first session to increase the likelihood of clients returning for additional sessions. Some cultural groups may avoid professional help because of a reliance on folk rituals. Others may be reluctant to disclose confidential matters to outsiders. Language and communication difficulties and transportation problems may also be factors. Although it is important for the counselor to be aware of a client's reluctance to seek counseling help, it is even more important to understand the cultural basis for the reluctance. With this understanding, the counselor is better able to foster receptivity to the counseling process and willingness to disclose significant personal information.

Sources of Mental Health Services

Counselors may encounter clients in various settings such as community mental health agencies, hospitals, schools, or private practice. Clients may seek counseling because of problems and frustrations associated with acculturation, racism and discrimination, or family relationships. Regardless of the problem or the counseling setting, counselors who understand multicultural groups will be more likely to address their clients' needs objectively and accurately.

The Future: A Time for Responsive Action

Multicultural counseling, lifespan development, and an understanding of the relationship between culture and development have progressed to a point where counseling professionals can take positive action to help clients from differing cultural backgrounds. To encourage such action, efforts should be directed toward training culturally effective counselors and promoting recognition of the relationship between cultural diversity and lifespan development.

Training Culturally Effective Counselors

The increasing likelihood that counselors will intervene in multicultural situations underscores the need for counselors to (a) understand their own cultural identities, (b) understand clients' cultural backgrounds, and (c) employ strategies that reflect cultural characteristics and expectations. Responsive counselor education programs will take into account the increasing cultural diversity in the United States by providing training and experiences designed to impart the knowledge and skills necessary for effective counseling in multicultural settings.

Recognizing the Relationship Between Cultural Diversity and Lifespan Development

Responsive action calls for counselor education programs that assist counselors in recognizing the relationship between cultural diversity and lifespan development. As previously stated, the Asian American elder has unique problems that the African American child or adolescent has not encountered or may never encounter. Intervention should be based on accurate knowledge of the client's culture and lifespan period and, of course, the client's many individual differences.

Summary

Multicultural counseling is beginning to come into its own. Increasing numbers of professionals are recognizing the need to consider a client's cultural background and valued cultural traditions and expectations. Continued advances in the area of lifespan growth and development are enhancing counselors' understanding of clients' developmental periods. In the 21st century, professionals will be better able to provide counseling services that are culturally and developmentally appropriate. It is hoped, in the years ahead, that the needs and problems that clients bring to counseling sessions will increasingly receive the kind of attention they deserve.

Selected Journals Recommended for Counselors in Multicultural Settings

American Psychologist

Published monthly by the American Psychological Association (1400 North Uhle St., Arlington, VA 22201), this journal focuses on all aspects of counseling and occasionally examines multicultural issues and concerns.

Child Development

Published six times per year by the Journals Division of the University of Chicago Press (5720 Woodlawn Ave., Chicago, IL 60637), this journal focuses on child development in all cultures. Periodically, the journal specifically addresses development in children of differing cultural backgrounds.

Counseling and Human Development

Published nine times per year, this journal examines counseling issues in the context of human development. Published by Love Publishing Company (1777 South Bellaire St., Denver, CO 80222), the journal usually includes a feature article that is more extensive than the rest.

Counseling and Values

Published in January, April, and October by the American Counseling Association (5999 Stevenson Ave., Alexandria, VA 22304-3300), this journal focuses on counseling and spiritual, religious, and ethical values.

Counseling Psychologist

Published quarterly by Sage Publications, this journal is the official publication of the Division of Counseling Psychology of the American Psychological Association. Each issue focuses on a specific theme of importance to the theory, research, and practice of counseling psychology. Special issues on aging (1984, Vol. 12, No. 2) and on cross-cultural counseling (1985, Vol. 13, No. 4) should be of interest to counselors in multicultural settings.

Counselor Education and Supervision

Published quarterly by the American Association for Counseling and Development, this journal is concerned with matters relevant to the preparation and supervision of counselors in agency or school settings. Multicultural counseling considerations are examined in occasional theme issues.

Cultural Diversity and Ethnic Minority Psychology

This journal quarterly (750 First St., NE, Washington, DC) publishes research and articles that promote the understanding and application of psychological principles and scholarly analysis of sociopolitical forces affecting minorities.

Gerontologist

Published bimonthly by the Gerontological Society of America (Department 5018, Washington, DC 20005-4018), this journal addresses concerns of the elderly of all cultures. Problems affecting minority cultures in particular are sometimes included.

Journal of Black Studies

Published four times annually by Sage Publications (2455 Teller Rd., Thousand Oaks, CA 91320), this journal discusses and analyzes issues related to people of African descent. Although counseling and development are not usually specifically addressed, this publication does provide a comprehensive examination of the Black culture.

Journal of Clinical Psychology

Published bimonthly by Clinical Psychology Publishing Company (4 Conant Square, Brandon, VT 05733), this journal directs attention to issues relevant to the clinician. Multicultural studies are occasionally included.

Journal of Counseling and Development

Published 10 times per year, by the American Association for Counseling and Development, this journal focuses on a broad range of topics for a readership composed of counselors, counseling psychologists, and student personnel specialists. Articles occasionally deal with multicultural issues and concerns.

Journal of Counseling Psychology

Published quarterly by the American Psychological Association, this journal contains articles reporting the results of empirical studies related to the various counseling areas.

Journal of Cross-Cultural Psychology

Published four times annually by Sage Publications, this journal contains cross-cultural research reports exclusively. The main emphasis is on individual differences and variation among cultures.

Journal of Gerontology

Published bimonthly by the Gerontological Society of America (Department 5018, Washington, DC 20005-4018), this journal publishes studies in which a variety of theoretical and methodological approaches are employed.

Journal of Mental Health Counseling

Published four times per year by the American Mental Health Counselors Association (801 N. Fairfax St., Suite 304, Alexandria, VA 22314), this journal contains a broad array of articles on most aspects of mental health counseling.

Journal of Multicultural Counseling and Development

Published four times per year by the American Association for Counseling and Development (5999 Stevenson Ave., Alexandria, VA 22304), each issue usually contains six or seven articles that focus on research, theory, or program application pertinent to multicultural and ethnic minority issues in all areas of counseling and human development.

Professional School Counselor

Published five times per year by the American School Counselor Association (801 N. Fairfax St., Suite 310, Alexandria, VA 22314), this journal contains articles on elementary, middle, and secondary school counseling.

Psychology of Women Quarterly

This quarterly journal (350 Main St., Malden, MA 02148) is a feminist scientific publication that contains articles on the psychology of women and gender.

Psychotherapy: Theory/Research/Practice/Training

Published quarterly, this journal (1390 S. Dixie Hwy, Suite 2222, Coral Gables, FL 33146-2946) contains a wide variety of research studies and theoretical articles relevant to the field of psychotherapy.

Suggested Multicultural Experiential Activities

The following activities can be used as a part of the multicultural counseling course. Feel free to modify them to reflect the needs and diversity of your class. If you use additional experiential activities, please send a description to either author for inclusion in future editions of this text.

1. Establish the tone for multiculturalism and its acceptance at the beginning of each class with an exercise in multiculturalism. Exercises may include a poem that relates to the topic, or a short story or music selection reflecting cultural diversity.

2. Use an ethnobiography to help the class get acquainted with the various backgrounds and differences of each class member. Such a biography will aid in building respect for differences in people and for clients in the future. Suggestions include students' names, why their parents gave them these names, what growing up was like, educational backgrounds, greatest successes, biggest failures, and ways in which students feel different.

3. Show *The Color of Fear*, an excellent video to facilitate discussion of topics of racial differences, social class, and gender issues. This powerful and thought-provoking video tells about a group of men from various backgrounds who discuss their feelings on these issues. Students can then react to the video and discuss their feelings about the issues.

4. Show *A Class Divided*, another excellent video, which tells about the "blue eye" experiment and brings attention to the unfair nature of discrimination. Then students can discuss their feelings and reactions to the video and to discrimination in general.

5. Replicate the "blue eye" experiment. Place all the students with blue eyes into one group and those with nonblue eyes into another group. Ask the blue-eyed students to wait in the hall. Explain to the nonblue-eyed students to treat the blue-eyed students in a discriminatory fashion. Invite the blue-eyed students back into the class with the "normal class." Toward the end of the class, each group can discuss how the discrimination felt.

6. Administer a cultural attitudes inventory to the class to determine attitudes demonstrated in books, television, and movies about cultures. Thinking about images portrayed in the media can help to explain some of the stereotypes that people have about cultures.

7. Arrange for a panel discussion of members of different cultures in an attempt to eliminate stereotypes by learning objective and factual information. Students in the class can ask questions about particular cultures to distinguish between fact and stereotype.

8. Ask students to do a cultural anthropology project by investigating people in their area and neighborhood. Selected and interesting topics might include what type of people live in the vicinity, how they arrived there, their reasons for selecting the area, and what they do there now. Such an exercise can be extended into the past several generations.

9. Arrange for a multicultural "adventure" by trying a culturally different type of food. Students in the class may cook the food, or they may go to an ethnic food restaurant they have never visited.

10. Have students think of at least one saying from five famous people from different cultural backgrounds.

Then analyze each saying in regard to cultural values.

11. Encourage class members to identify their family motto from their family of origin. What cultural values are implied by the motto?

12. Ask each class member to select an American Indian name and to explain its origin and significance.

13. Have students prepare a coat of arms in the shape of a shield that depicts various aspects of their cultural background and explain its meaning to the class.

14. Arrange for class members to visit with the elderly, because some people harbor stereotypes about older people and generally feel uncomfortable around them. Visiting a nursing home or senior center can be helpful in overcoming anxiety about counseling elderly clients. Students can tell or write about what they learned, such as stereotypes they had before visiting and how those stereotypes have changed.

15. Have the entire class set aside a time outside of or during class to visit a homeless shelter. The class can help clean and prepare meals for the people who live there. Students will benefit from helping the homeless and from learning about the reasons for homelessness and the problems faced by homeless people.

16. Arrange for class members to visit with people with disabilities, to help dispel stereotypes about such people. Students can share in class what they learned and how their newfound knowledge can be reflected during counseling intervention.

17. Ask class members to share experiences during which they felt discrimination. These experiences can be from racial and cultural discrimination or from any type of discrimination (e.g., disability, height, weight, religious affiliation, social class). How did they feel, and how might such discrimination be lessened?

18. Ask students to share experiences when they were the only one of their cultural group in a large group of people. Did they feel accepted by others or uncomfortable being the only one of their cultural group? What might they or others have done to lessen the feelings of anxiety (if anxiety existed) and promote mutual acceptance within the group?

19. Ask students to visit in the homes of people from another cultural background. How did the homes differ? What differences were seen in cultural backgrounds and expectations? Have students suggest how knowledge of home environments might contribute to the effectiveness of counseling, especially with children and adolescent clients.

20. Have individual students or small groups interview a gay man or lesbian or read about the problems (as well as the joys and satisfactions) faced by people with differing sexual orientations. What forms of discrimination or harassment do they experience? What do they think counselors need to know? How can the information the students gained contribute to their effectiveness when counseling gay and lesbian clients. The individual students or small groups can report to the class and create guidelines for improving the effectiveness of counseling intervention for gay and lesbian clients.

References

Abrams, R. D. (1993). Meeting the educational and cultural needs of Soviet newcomers. *Religious Education, 88* (2), 315–323.

Abrams, L., & Trusty, J. (2004). African Americans' racial identity and socially desirable responding: An empirical model. *Journal of Counseling and Development, 82* (3), 365–374.

Abreu, J. A. (2000). Counseling expectations among Mexican American college students: The role of counselor ethnicity. *Journal of Multicultural Counseling and Development, 28* (3), 130–143.

Adams, C. L., & Kimmel, D. C. (1997). Exploring the lives of older African American gay men. In B. Greene (Ed.), *Psychological perspectives on lesbian and gay issues: Vol 3. Ethnic and cultural diversity among lesbians and gay men* (pp. 132–151). Thousand Oaks, CA: Sage.

'African-American' becomes a term for debate. (2004, August 29). *The New York Times*. Retrieved April 2005, from http://www.nytimes.com/2004/08/29/national29african.html

Agronick, G., O'Donnell, L., Stueve, A., Doval, A. S. Duran, R., & Vargo, S. (2004). Sexual behaviors and risks among bisexually and gay-identified young Latino men. *AIDS and Behavior, 8* (2), 185–197.

Ahmed, N. R. (2003). Higher education, high incomes make Asian American market attractive. *National Underwriter Life & Health–Financial Services Edition, 107* (16), 8–10.

Akos, P., & Galassi, J. P. (2004). Training school counselors as developmental advocates. *Counselor Education & Supervision, 43*, 192–206.

Alba, R. D. (1985). *Italian Americans into the twilight of ethnicity.* Upper Saddle River, NJ: Prentice Hall.

Aldarondo, F. (2001). Racial and ethnic identity models and their applications: Counseling biracial individuals. *Journal of Mental Health Counseling, 23* (3), 238–252.

Alvarez, A. N., & Kimura, E. F. (2001). Asian Americans and racial identity: Dealing with racism and snowballs. *Journal of Mental Health Counseling, 23* (3), 192–204.

American Psychological Association. (2000). Guidelines for psychotherapy with lesbian, gay, and bisexual clients. *American Psychologist, 55* (2), 1440–1451.

Ananya, G., & Cole, D. G. (2001). Latina/o student achievement: Exploring the influence of student–faculty interactions on college grades. *Journal of College Student Development, 42* (1), 3–14.

Ancis, J. R., & Sanchez-Hucles, J. V. (2000). A preliminary analysis of counseling students' attitudes toward counseling women and women of color: Implications for cultural competency training. *Journal of Multicultural Counseling and Development, 28* (1), 16–31.

Ancis, J. R., & Szymanski, D. M. (2001). Awareness of White privilege among White counseling trainees. *The Counseling Psychologist, 29* (4), 548–569.

Anderson, J. (1994). School climate for gay and lesbian students and staff members. *Phi Delta Kappan, 75*, 151–154.

Angel, J. L., Angel, J., McClelland, J. L., & Markides, K. S. (1996). Nativity, declining health, and preference in living arrangements among elderly Mexican Americans: Implications for long-term care. *Gerontologist, 36* (4), 464–473.

Aponte, J. F., & Wohl, J. (2000). *Psychological intervention and cultural diversity* (2nd ed.). Boston: Allyn and Bacon.

Arbona, C., Flores, C. L., & Novy, D. M. (1995). Cultural awareness and ethnic loyalty: Dimensions of cultural variability among Mexican American college students. *Journal of Counseling and Development, 73*, 610–614.

Arnold, M. S. (1993). Ethnicity and training marital and family therapists. *Counselor Education and Supervision, 33*, 139–147.

Arredondo, P., & Glauner, T. (1992). *Personal dimensions of identity model.* Boston: Empowerment Workshops.

Arredondo, P., & Toporek, R. (2004). Multicultural counseling competence = Ethical practice. *Journal of Mental Health Counseling, 26*, 44–55.

Arredondo, P., Toporek, R., Brown, S. P., Jones, J., Locke, D. C., Sanchez, J., & Stadler, H. (1996). Operationalization of the multicultural counseling competencies. *Journal of Multicultural Counseling and Development, 24* (1), 42–78.

Arthur, N., & Achenbach, K. (2002). Developing multicultural counseling competencies through experiential learning. *Counselor Education and Supervision, 42* (1), 2–14.

Aspy, C. B., Oman, R. F., Vesely, S. K., McLeroy, K., Rodine, S., & Marshall, L. (2004). Adolescent violence: The protective effects of youth assets. *Journal of Counseling and Development, 82*, 268–276.

Atkinson, D. R. (2004). *Counseling American Minorities: A cross-cultural perspective* (6th ed.). New York: McGraw-Hill.

Atkinson, D. R., Casas, A., & Abreu, J. (1992). Mexican American acculturation, counselor ethnicity and cultural sensitivity, and perceived counselor competence. *Journal of Counseling Psychology, 39*, 515–520.

Atkinson, D. R., Furlong, M. J., & Poston, W. C. (1986). Afro-American preference for counselor characteristics. *Journal of Counseling Psychology, 33*, 326–330.

Atkinson, D. R., Morten, G., & Sue, D. W. (1998). *Counseling American minorities: A cross-cultural perspective* (5th ed.). Dubuque, IA: Brown.

Awe, T., Portman, A., & Garrett, M. T. (2005). Beloved women: Nurturing the sacred of leadership from an American Indian perspective. *Journal of Counseling and Development, 83* (3), 284–292.

Axelson, J. A. (1999). *Counseling and development in a multicultural society* (3rd ed.). Pacific Grove, CA: Brooks/Cole.

Ayalon, L., Arean, P. A., & Alvidrez, J. (2005). Adherence to antidepressant medications in Black and Latino elderly patients. *American Journal of Geriatric Psychiatry, 13* (7), 572–580.

Baca, L. M., & Koss-Chioino, J. D. (1997). Development of a culturally responsive group counseling model for Mexican American adolescents. *Journal of Multicultural Counseling and Development, 25* (2), 130–141.

Bailey, D. F., & Paisley, P. O. (2004). Developing and nurturing excellence in African American males. *Journal of Counseling and Development, 82*, 10–17.

Baker, F. M., Espino, D. V., Robinson, B. H., & Stewart, B. (1993). Assessing depressive symptoms in African American and Mexican American elders. *Clinical Gerontologist, 14*, 15–29.

Baptiste, D. A. (1987). Psychotherapy with gay/lesbian couples and their stepfamilies: A challenge for marriage and family therapists. *Journal of Homosexuality, 13*, 223–238.

Barker, N. C., & Hill, J. (1996). Restructuring African American families in the 1980s. *Journal of Black Studies, 27* (1), 77–93.

Barnes, P. W., & Lightsey, O. R. (2005). Perceived racist discrimination, coping, stress, and life satisfaction. *Journal of Multicultural Counseling and Development, 33*, 48–61.

Bass, E., & Kaufman, K. (1996). *Free your mind: The book for gay, lesbian, and questioning youth and their allies.* New York: Harper Perennial.

Bazargan, M., Bazargan, S., & King, L. (2001). Paranoid ideation among elderly African American persons. *The Gerontologist, 41* (3), 366–373.

Beals, K. P., & Peplau, L. A. (2005). Identity support, identity devaluation, and well-being among lesbians. *Psychology of Women Quarterly, 29*, 140–148.

Bean, R. A., Perry, B. J., & Bedell, T. M. (2001). Developing culturally competent marriage and family therapists: Guidelines for working with Hispanic families. *Journal of Marital and Family Therapy, 27* (1), 43–54.

Behrens, J. T. (1997). Does the White Racial Identity Attitude Scale measure racial identity? *Journal of Counseling Psychology, 44* (1), 3–12.

Belgrave, F. Z., Chase-Vaughn, G., Gray, F., Addison, J. D., & Cherry, V. R. (2000). The effectiveness of culture- and gender-specific intervention for increasing resiliency among African American preadolescent females. *Journal of Black Psychology, 26* (2), 133–147.

Belgrave, F. Z., Van Oss Marin, N., & Chambers, D. B. (2000). Cultural, contextual, and intrapersonal predictors of risky sexual attitudes among urban African American girls in early adolescence. *Cultural Diversity and Ethnic Minority Psychology, 6* (3), 309–322.

Bemak, F., & Greenberg, B. (1994). Southeast Asian refugee adolescents: Implications for counseling. *Journal of Multicultural Counseling and Development, 22*, 115–124.

Bepko, C., & Johnson, T. (2000). Gay and lesbian couples in therapy: Perspectives for the contemporary therapist. *Journal of Marital and Family Therapy, 26* (4), 409–419.

Berger, R. M. (1996). *Gay and gray: The older homosexual man* (2nd ed.). Binghamton, NY: Haworth.

Berk, L. E. (2004). *Development through the lifespan* (3rd ed.). Boston: Allyn and Bacon.

Bernal, G., & Shapiro, E. (2005). Cuban families. In M. McGoldrick, J. Giordano, & N. Garcia-Presto (Eds.), *Ethnicity and family therapy* (3rd ed., pp. 202–215). New York: Guilford.

Bernstein, A. C. (2000). Straight therapists working with lesbians and gays in family therapy. *Journal of Marital and Family Therapy, 26* (4), 443–454.

Bieschke, K. J., McClanahan, M., Tozer, E., Grzegorek, J. L., & Park, J. (2000). Programmatic research on the treatment of lesbian, gay, and bisexual clients: The past, the present, and the course for the future. In R. M. Perez, K. A. DeBord, & K. J. Bieschke (Eds.), *Handbook of counseling and psychotherapy with lesbian, gay, and bisexual clients* (pp. 309–335). Washington, DC: American Psychological Association.

Black, J., & Underwood, J. (1998). Young, female, and gay: Lesbian students and the school environment. *Professional School Counseling, 1* (3), 15–20.

Black male's life expectancy is declining. (1989, June 6). *Charlotte Observer,* p. 8A.

Block, C. J., & Carter, R. T. (1996). White racial identity attitude theories: A rose by any other name is still a rose. *Counseling Psychologist, 24* (2), 327.

Blustein, D. L., & Noumair, D. A. (1996). Self and identity in career development: Implications for theory and practice. *Journal of Counseling and Development, 74,* 433–441.

Bodenhorn, N. (2005). American School Counselor Association Ethical Code changes relevant to family work. *Family Journal: Counseling & Therapy for Couples & Families, 13* (3), 316–320.

Booker, M. (1999). Poetry, healing, and the Latin American battered woman. *Journal of Poetry Therapy, 13* (2), 73–79.

Bos, C. S., & Reyes, E. I. (1996). Conversations with a Latina teacher about education for language-minority students with special needs. *Elementary School Journal, 96,* 343–351.

Brayboy, B. M., & Deyhle, D. (2000). Insider–outsider: Researchers in American Indian communities. *Theory Into Practice, 39* (3), 163–169.

Broman, C. L. (2005). Marital quality in Black and White marriages. *Journal of Family Issues, 26* (4), 431–441.

Brook, J. S., Adams, R. E., Balka, E. B., Whiteman, M., Zhang, C., & Sugerman, R. (2004). Illicit drug use and risky behavior among African American and Puerto Rican urban adolescents: The longitudinal links. *Journal of Genetic Psychology, 165* (2), 203–221.

Brookins, C. C. (1996). Promoting ethnic identity development in African American youth: The role of rites of passage. *Journal of Black Psychology, 22,* 388–417.

Brown, L. B. (1997). *Two-spirit people: American Indian lesbian women and gay men.* New York: Haworth.

Brown, S. P., Lipford-Sanders, J., & Shaw, M. (1995). Kujichagulia—Uncovering the secrets of the heart: Group work with African American women on predominantly White campuses. *Journal for Specialists in Group Work, 20,* 151–158.

Brown, S. P., Parham, T. A., & Yonker, R. (1996). Influence of a cross-cultural training course on racial identity attitudes of White women and men: Preliminary perspectives. *Journal of Counseling and Development, 74,* 510–516.

Bruce, M. A. (1995). Brief counseling: An effective model for change. *School Counselor, 42,* 353–363.

Buki, V. M. V. (2005). Treating the Hispanic elderly. *Clinical Psychology News, 33* (4), 8–9.

Buriel, R. (1993). Acculturation, respect for cultural differences, and biculturalism among three generations of Mexican American and Euro-American school children. *Journal of Genetic Psychology, 154,* 531–543.

Burn, S. M. (2000). Heterosexuals' use of "fag" and "queer" to deride one another: A contributor to heterosexism and stigma. *Journal of Homosexuality, 40* (2), 1–12.

Bux, D. A. (1996). The epidemiology of problem drinking in gay men and lesbians: A critical review. *Clinical Psychology Review, 16* (4), 277–298.

Caldwell, L. D., & White, J. (2001). African-centered therapeutic and counseling interventions for African American males. In G. R. Brooks, & G. E. Glenn (Eds.), *The new handbook of psychotherapy and counseling with men: A comprehensive guide to setting, problems, and treatment approaches* (pp. 737–753). San Francisco: Jossey-Bass.

Casas, J. M. (2001). Directions and redirections in Chicano psychology. *The Counseling Psychologist, 29* (1), 128–138.

Casas, J. M., & Vasquez, M. J. T. (1989). Counseling the Hispanic client: A theoretical and applied perspective. In P. B. Pedersen, J. G. Draguns, J. Lonner, & J. E. Trimble (Eds.), *Counseling across cultures* (3rd ed., pp. 153–175). Honolulu: University of Hawaii Press.

Cass, V. C. (1979). Homosexual identity formation: Testing a theoretical model. *Journal of Homosexuality, 4,* 219–235.

Castaneda, D. M. (1994). A research agenda for Mexican American adolescent mental health. *Adolescence, 29,* 225–239.

Cataldo, J. K. (2001). The relationship of hardiness and depression to disability in institutionalized older adults. *Rehabilitation Nursing, 26* (1), 28–33.

Cerbone, A. R. (1997). Symbol of privilege, object of derision: Dissonance and contradictions. In B. Greene (Ed.), *Psychological perspectives on lesbian and gay issues: Vol 3. Ethnic and cultural diversity among lesbians and gay men* (pp. 117–131). Thousand Oaks, CA: Sage.

Cerwonka, E. R., Isbell, T. R., & Hansen, C. E. (2000). Psychosocial factors as predictors of unsafe sexual practices among young adults. *AIDS Education and Prevention, 12* (2), 141–153.

Chan, C. S. (1989). Issues of identity development among Asian-American lesbians and gay men. *Journal of Counseling and Development, 68* (1), 16–20.

Chan, C. S. (1992). Cultural considerations when counseling Asian American lesbians and gay men. In S. H. Dworkin & F. J. Gutierrez (Eds.), *Counseling gay men and lesbians: Journey to the center of the rainbow* (pp. 115–124). Alexandria, VA: American Association for Counseling and Development.

Chang, M. T. (2001). Is it more than about just getting along? The broader educational relevance of reducing students' racial biases. *Journal of College Student Development, 42* (2), 93–105.

Chapin, R., & Dobbs-Kepper, D. (2001). Aging in place in assisted living: Philosophy versus policy. *The Gerontologist, 41* (1), 43–50.

Cheatham, H., & Stewart, J. (Eds.). (1990). *Black families.* New Brunswick, NJ: Transaction.

Cherbosque, J. (1987). Differences between Mexican and American clients in expectations about psychological counseling. *Journal of Multicultural Counseling and Development, 15*, 110–114.

Cheston, S. E. (2000). A new paradigm for teaching counseling theory and practice. *Counselor Education and Supervision, 39*, 254–269.

Christensen, E. W. (1989). Counseling Puerto Ricans: Some cultural considerations. In D. R. Atkinson, G. Morten, & D. W. Sue (Eds.), *Counseling American minorities* (3rd ed., pp. 205–212). Dubuque, IA: Brown.

Chubbuck, S. (2004). Whiteness enacted, whiteness disrupted. The complexity of personal congruence. *American Educational Research Journal, 41* (2), 301–333.

Chung, R. C. (2001). Psychosocial adjustment of Cambodian refugee women: Implications for mental health counseling. *Journal of Mental Health Counseling, 23* (2), 115–126.

Chung, R. C. (2005). Woman, human rights, and counseling: Crossing international boundaries. *Journal of Counseling and Development, 83*, 262–268.

Chung, R. C., Bemak, F., & Wong, S. (2000). Vietnamese refugees' level of distress, social support, and acculturation: Implications for mental health counseling. *Journal of Mental Health Counseling, 22*, 150–161.

Chung, Y. B., & Katamaya, M. (1998). Ethnic and sexual identity development of Asian-American lesbian and gay adolescents. *Professional School Counseling, 1* (3), 21–25.

Cofresi, N. I., & Gorman, A. A. (2005). Testing and assessment issues with Spanish-English bilingual Latinos. *Journal of Counseling and Development, 82* (1), 99–107.

Coleman, E. (1982). Developmental stages of the coming out process. In J. Gonsiorek (Ed.), *Homosexuality and psychotherapy: A practitioner's handbook of affirmative models* (pp. 31–44). New York: Haworth.

Coleman, E., & Remafedi, G. (1989). Gay, lesbian, and bisexual adolescents: A critical challenge to counselors. *Journal of Counseling and Development, 68* (1), 36–40.

Collins, J. F. (2000). Biracial Japanese American identity: An evolving process. *Cultural Diversity and Ethnic Minority Psychology, 6* (2), 115–133.

Colmant, S. A., & Merta, R. J. (1999). Using the sweat lodge ceremony as group therapy for Navajo youth. *Journal for Specialists in Group Work, 24* (1), 55–73.

Comas-Diaz, L. (2001). Hispanics, Latinos, or Americanos: The evolution of identity. *Cultural Diversity and Ethnic Minority Psciyology, 7* (2), 115–120.

Comas-Diaz, L., & Jacobsen, F. M. (1987). Ethnocultural identification in psychotherapy. *Psychiatry, 50*, 232–241.

Conger, R. D., Wallace, L. E., Sun, Y., Simons, R. L., McLoyd, V. C., & Brody, G. H. (2002). Economic pressure in African American families: A replication and extension of the family stress model. *Developmental Psychology, 38* (2), 179–193.

Conley, D. (2000). 40 acres and a mule. *National Forum, 80* (2), 21–24.

Contreras, R., Hendrick, S. S., & Hendrick, C. (1996). Perspectives on marital love and satisfaction in Mexican and Anglo-American Rican couples. *Journal of Counseling and Development, 74*, 408–415.

Conyne, R. K. (2003). Group work issues: Past, present, and future. *Journal for Specialists in Group Work, 28* (4), 291–298.

Cook, D. A., & Helms, J. E. (1988). Visible racial/ethnic group supervisees' satisfaction with cross-cultural supervision as predicted by relationship characteristics. *Journal of Counseling Psychology, 35*, 268–274.

Cooley, J. J. (1998). Gay and lesbian adolescents: Presenting problems and the counselor's roles. *Professional School Counseling, 1* (3), 30–34.

Copeland, E. J. (1982). Minority populations and traditional counseling programs: Some alternatives. *Counselor Education and Supervision, 21*, 187–193.

Cortina, L. M., & Wasti, A. (2005). Profiles in coping: Responses to sexual harassment across persons, organizations, and cultures. *Journal of Applied Psychology, 90* (1), 182–192.

Cottone, R. R. (2001). A social constructivism model of ethical decision making in counseling. *Journal of Counseling and Development, 79*, 39–45.

Cottone, R. R., & Claus, R. E. (2000). Ethical decision-making models: A review of the literature. *Journal of Counseling and Development, 78*, 275–283.

Coy, D. R., & Kovacs-Long, J. (2005). Maslow and Miller: An exploration of gender and affiliation in the journey of competence. *Journal of Counseling and Development, 83*, 138–145.

Craig, H. K., & Washington, J. A. (1994). The complex syntax skills of poor, urban, African American preschoolers at school entry. *Language, Speech, and Hearing Services in Schools, 25*, 181–190.

Crawley, S. L. (2001). Are butch and fem working-class and antifeminist? *Gender and Society, 15* (2), 175–196.

Crosbie-Burnett, M., Foster, T. L., Murray, C., & Bowen, G. L. (1996). Gays' and lesbians' families-in-origin: A social–cognitive–behavioral model of adjustment. *Family Relations, 45* (4), 397–403.

Cross, T. A., Earle, K. A., & Simmons, D. (2000). Child abuse and neglect in Indian country: Policy issues. *Families in Society: The Journal of Contemporary Human Services, 81* (1), 49–58.

Cross, W. E. (1971). The Negro-to-Black conversion experience: Toward a psychology of Black liberation. *Black World, 20* (9), 13–27.

Curtis, R. C., Kimball, A., & Stroup, E. L. (2004). Understanding and treating social phobia. *Journal of Counseling and Development, 82*, 3–8.

Dade, L. R., & Sloan, L. R. (2000). An investigation of sex-role stereotypes in African Americans. *Journal of Black Studies, 30* (5), 676–690.

Dana, R. H. (2000). The cultural self as locus for assessment and intervention with American Indians/Alaska Natives. *Journal of Multicultural Counseling and Development, 28* (2), 66–82.

D'Andrea, M. D. (1995). Addressing the developmental needs of urban, African American youth: A preventive approach. *Journal of Multicultural Counseling and Development, 23*, 57–64.

D'Andrea, M. D., & Bradley, L. (1995). A comparative study of the worries of Mexican American and White students: Implications for school counselors. *Journal of Humanistic Education and Development, 33*, 183–192.

D'Andrea, M. D., & Daniels, J. (1996). What is multicultural group counseling? Identifying its potential benefits, barriers, and future challenges. *Counseling and Human Development, 28* (6), 1–16.

Das, K. D. (1995). Rethinking multicultural counseling: Implications for counselor education. *Journal of Counseling and Development, 74*, 45–52.

Davenport, D. S., & Yurich, J. M. (1991). Multicultural gender issues. *Journal of Counseling and Development, 70*, 64–71.

Day, S. M. (1995). American Indians: Reclaiming cultural and sexual identity. *SIECUS Report, 24* (1), 6–7.

DeBlassie, A. M., & DeBlassie, R. R. (1996). Education of Hispanic youth: A cultural lag. *Adolescence, 31*, 205–215.

De Korin, E. C., de Carvallho Petry, S. (2005). Brazilian families. In M. McGoldrick, J. Giordano, & N. Garcia-Preto (Eds.), *Ethnicity and family therapy* (3rd ed., pp. 166–178). New York: Guilford.

De Leon, B., & Mendez, S. (1996). Factorial structure of a measure of acculturation in a Puerto Rican population. *Education and Psychological Measurements, 56*, 155–165.

De Master, C., & Girodano, M. D. (2005). Dutch families. In M. McGoldrick, J. Giordano, & N. Garcia-Preto (Eds.), *Ethnicty and family therapy* (3rd ed., pp. 334–344). New York: Guilford.

Denevi, E. (2004). White on White: Exploring White racial identity, privilege, and racism. *Independent School 63* (4), 84–87.

Denis, A. B. (2001). Multiple identities . . . multiple marginalities: Franco-Ontarian feminism. *Gender and Society, 15* (3), 453–467.

DeRicco, J. N., & Sciarra, D. T. (2005). The immersion experience in multicultural counselor training: Confronting covert racism. *Journal of Multicultural Counseling and Development, 33*, 2–8.

Desselle, D. D., & Proctor, T. K. (2000). Advocating for the elderly hard-of-hearing population: The deaf people we ignore. *Social Work, 45* (3), 277–281.

DeVavas-Walt, C., Proctor, B. D., & Mills, R. J. (2004). *Income, poverty, and health coverage in the United States: 2003.* Washington, DC: US Census Bureau.

Deyle, D. (1995). Navajo youth and Anglo racism: Cultural integrity and resistance. *Harvard Educational Review, 65* (3), 403–444.

Diamond, L. M. (2000). Sexual identity, attractions, and behavior among young sexual minority women over a 2-year period. *Developmental Psychology 36* (2), 241–250.

Diaz, C. M., & Cohen, B. B. (2001). Cross-cultural contact in counseling training. *Journal of Multicultural Counseling and Development, 29* (1), 41–56.

Dinsmore, J. A., & England, J. T. (1996). A study of multicultural counseling training at CACREP-accredited counselor education programs. *Counselor Education and Supervision, 36*, 58–76.

Dodd, J. M., Garcia, F. M., Meccage, C., & Nelson, M. L. (1995). American Indian student retention. *NASPA Journal, 33*, 72–78.

Downing, N. E., & Roush, K. L. (1985). From passive acceptance to active commitment: A model of feminist identity for women. *Counseling Psychologist, 13* (4), 695–709.

Doyle, M. B. (2000). Transition plans for students with disabilities. *Educational Leadership, 58* (1), 46–48.

Draguns, J. G. (1989). Dilemmas and choices in cross-cultural counseling: The universal versus the culturally distinctive. In P. B. Pedersen, J. G. Draguns, J. Lonner, & J. E. Trimble (Eds.), *Counseling across cultures* (3rd ed., pp. 1–21). Honolulu: University of Hawaii Press.

Duan, C, & Vu, P. (2000). Acculturation of Vietnamese students living in or away from Vietnamese communities. *Journal of Multicultural Counseling and Development, 28* (4), 225–242.

Dubé, E. M., & Savin-Williams, R. C. (2000). Sexual identity development among ethnic sexual-minority male youths. *Developmental Psychology, 35* (6), 1389–1398.

Dudley-Grant, G. R. (2001). Eastern Caribbean family psychology with conduct-disordered adolescents from the Virgin Islands. *American Psychologist, 56* (1), 47–57.

Dufrene, P. M., & Coleman, V. D. (1992). Counseling Native Americans: Guidelines for group processes. *Journal for Specialists in Group Work, 17*, 229–234.

Dunne, G. A. (2000). Opting into motherhood: Lesbians blurring the boundaries and transforming the meaning of parenthood and kinship. *Gender & Society, 14* (1), 11–35.

Duys, D. K., & Hedstrom, S. M. (2000). Basic counselor skills training and counselor cognitive therapy. *Counselor Education and Supervision, 40*, 8–18.

Ebonics controversy focuses attention on minority achievement (1997). *American School Board Journal, 184* (3), 4–5.

Educating Hispanic students. (1995). *Education Digest, 61* (5), 15–19.

Edwards, D. E., & Edwards, M. E. (1989). American Indians: Working with individuals and groups. In D. R. Atkinson, G. Morten, & D. W. Sue (Eds.), *Counseling American minorities: A cross-cultural perspective* (3rd ed., pp. 72–84). Dubuque, IA: Brown.

Elden, R. N., Edwards, E. P., Leonard, K. E. (2004). Predictors of effortful control among alcoholic and non-alcoholic fathers. *Journal of Studies on Alcohols, 65* (3), 309–320.

Erickson, B. (2005). Scandinavian families: Plain and simple. In M. McGoldrick, J. Giordano, & N. Garcia-Preto (Eds.), *Ethnicity and family therapy* (3rd ed., pp. 641–653). New York: Guilford.

Erikson, E. (1950). *Childhood and society.* New York: Norton.

Erikson, E. (1963). *Childhood and society.* New York: Norton.

Erikson, E. (1968). *Identity: Youth and crisis.* New York: Norton.

Erikson, E. (1982). *The life cycle completed: A review.* New York: Norton.

Espin, O. (1984). Cultural and historical influences on sexuality in Hispanic/Latina women: Implications for psychotherapy. In C. Vance (Ed.), *Pleasure and danger: Exploring female sexuality* (pp. 149–163). London: Routledge & Kegan Paul.

Estrada, A. U., Durlak, J. A., & Juarez, S. C. (2002). Developing multicultural counseling competencies in undergraduate students, *Journal of Multicultural Counseling and Development, 30* (2), 110–123.

Evans, K. M., Kincade, E. A., Marbley, A. F., & Seem, S. R. (2005). Feminism and feminist therapy: Lessons from the past and for the future. *Journal of Counseling and Development, 83*, 269–277.

Everett, F., Proctor, N., & Cartmell, B. (1989). Providing psychological services to American Indian children and families. In D. R. Atkinson, G. Morten, & D. W. Sue (Eds.), *Counseling American minorities: A cross-cultural perspective* (3rd ed., pp. 53–71). Dubuque, IA: Brown.

Exum, H. A., & Lau, E. Y. (1988). Counseling style preference of Chinese college students. *Journal of Multicultural Counseling and Development, 16*, 84–92.

Falco, K. (1991). *Psychotherapy with lesbian clients: Theory into practice.* New York: Brunner/Mazel.

Falicov, C. J. (2005). Mexican families. In M. McGoldrick, J. Giordano, & N. Garcia-Preto (Eds.), *Ethnicity and family therapy* (3rd ed., pp. 229–241). New York: Guilford.

Farmer, T. W., Estell, D. B., Bishop, J. L., O'Neal, K. K., & Cairns, B. (2003). Rejected bullies or popular leaders? The social relations of aggressive subtypes of rural African American early adolescents. *Developmental Psychology, 39* (6), 992–1004.

Farmer, T. W., Price, L. N., O'Neal, K. K., Leung, M. C., Goforth, J. B., Cairns, B. D., & Reese, L. E. (2004). Exploring risk in early adolescent African American youth. *American Journal of Community Psychology, 33* (1), 51–60.

Fassinger, R. E. (1991). The hidden minority: Issues and challenges in working with lesbian women and gay men. *The Counseling Psychologist, 19* (2), 157–176.

Fassinger, R. E. (1997). Issues in group work with older lesbians. *Group, 21* (2), 191–209.

Faubert, M., Locke, D. C., & Lanier, S. P. (1996). Applying a cognitive–behavioral approach to the training of culturally competent mental health counselors. *Journal of Mental Health Counseling, 18* (3), 200–215.

Fejgin, N. (1995). Factors contributing to the academic excellence of American Jewish and Asian students. *Sociology of Education, 68*, 18–30.

Feng, J. (1994, June). Asian American children: What teachers should know. *ERIC Digest*, 1–2.

Ferch, S. R. (2001). Relational conversation: Meaningful communication as a therapeutic intervention. *Counseling and Values, 45*, 118–124.

Ferdman, B. M. (2000). 'Why am I who I am?' Constructing the cultural self in multicultural perspective. *Human Development, 43*, 19–23.

Ferdman, B. M. & Gallegos, P. I. (2001). Racial identity development and Latinos in the United States. In C. Wijeyesinghe & B. Jackson (Eds.), *New perspectives on racial identity development: A theoretical and practical anthology* (pp. 32–66). New York: New York University Press.

Fier, E. B., & Ramsey, M. (2005). Ethical challenges in the teaching of multicultural course work. *Journal of Multicultural Counseling and Development, 33*, 94–107.

Fikar, C. (1992). Gay teens and suicide. *Pediatrics, 89*, 519–520.

Finfgeld-Connett, D. L. (2005). Self management of alcohol problems among aging adults. *Journal of Gerontological Nursing, 31* (5), 51–58.

Fingerhut, A. W., Peplau, L. A., & Ghavami, N. (2005). A dual framework for understanding lesbian experience. *Psychology of Women Quarterly, 29*, 129–139.

Firestein, B. A. (1996). *Bisexuality: The psychology and politics of an invisible minority*. Thousand Oaks, CA: Sage.

Fish, L. S. (2000). Hierarchical relationship development: Parents and children. *Journal of Marital and Family Therapy, 26* (4), 501–510.

Fisher, T. A., & Padmawidjaja, I. (1999). Parental influences on career development perceived by African American and Mexican American college students. *Journal of Multicultural Counseling and Development, 27* (3), 136–152.

Fitzpatrick, J. P. (1987). *Puerto Rican Americans: The meaning of migration to the mainland* (2nd ed.). Upper Saddle River, NJ: Prentice Hall.

Flores, M. T., & Carey, G. (2000). *Family therapy with Hispanics: Toward appreciating diversity*. Boston: Allyn and Bacon.

Flores, R., Tschann, J. M., Marin, B., & Pantoja, P. (2004). Marital conflict and acculturation among Mexican American husbands and wives. *Cultural Diversity and Ethnic Minority Psychology, 10* (1), 39–52.

Folkenberg, J. (1986). Mental health of Southeast Asians. *ADAMHA News, 12* (1), 10–11.

Fontaine, J. H. (1998). Experiencing a need: School counselors' experiences with gay and lesbian students. *Professional School Counseling, 1* (3), 8–14.

Former students recall beatings, misery at institutions. (April 30, 1999). *The Virginian-Pilot*, pp. A21–A22.

Fox, R. C. (1995). Bisexual identities. In A. R. D'Augelli, & C. J. Patterson (Eds.), *Lesbian, gay, and bisexual identities over the lifespan: Psychological perspectives* (pp. 48–86). New York: Oxford.

Fraga, E. D., Atkinson, D. R., & Wampold, B. E. (2004). Ethnic group preferences for multicultural counseling competencies. *Cultural Diversity & Ethnic Minority Psychology, 10* (1), 53–65.

Frame, M. W., & Williams, C. B. (2005). Issues and insights: A model of ethical decision making from a multicultural perspective. *Counseling and Values, 49* (3), 165–179.

Friedman, R. C. (1998). Clinical aspects of bisexuality among men. In E. J. Haeberle, & R. Gindorf (Eds.), *Bisexualities: The ideology and practice of sexual contact with both men and women* (pp. 221–228). New York: Continuum.

Fuertes, J. N. (1999). Asian and African Americans' initial perceptions of Hispanic counselors. *Journal of Multicultural Counseling and Development, 27* (3), 122–135.

Fuertas, J. N. (2004). Supervision in bilingual counseling: Service delivery, training, and research considerations. *Journal of Multicultural Counseling and Development, 32* (2), 84–94.

Fuertes, J. N., Bartolomeo, M., Nichols, C. M. (2001). Future research directions in the study of counselor multicultural competency. *Journal of Multicultural Counseling and Development, 29* (1), 3–12.

Fukuyama, M. A., & Ferguson, A. D. (2000). Lesbian, gay, and bisexual people of color: Understanding cultural complexity and managing multiple oppressions. In R. M. Perez, K. A. DeBord, & K. J. Bieschke (Eds.), *Handbook of counseling and psychotherapy with lesbian, gay, and bisexual clients* (pp. 81–106). Washington, DC: American Psychological Association.

Furr, S. R., & Barret, B. (2000). Teaching group counseling skills: Problems and solutions. *Counselor Education and Supervision, 40*, 94–104.

Fygetakis, L. M. (1997). Greek American lesbians: Identity odysseys of honorable good girls. In B. Greene (Ed.), *Psychological perspectives on lesbian and gay issues: Vol 3. Ethnic and cultural diversity among lesbians and gay men* (pp. 152–190). Thousand Oaks, CA: Sage.

Gamst, G., Dana, R. H., Der-Karabetian, A., & Kramer, T. (2001). Asian American mental health clients: Effects of ethnic match and age on global assessment and visitation. *Journal of Mental Health Counseling, 23* (1), 57–71.

Garcia, J. G., Cartwright, B., & Winston, S. M. (2003). The Transcultural Integrative Model for ethical decision making in counseling. *Journal of Counseling and Development, 81* (3), 268–277.

Garcia-Preto, N. (1996a). Latino families: An overview. In M. McGoldrick, J. Giordano, & J. K. Pearce (Eds.), *Ethnicity and family therapy* (2nd ed., pp. 141–154). New York: Guilford.

Garcia-Preto, N. (1996b). Puerto Rican families. In McGoldrick, J. Giordano, & J. K. Pearce (Eds.), *Ethnicity and family therapy* (2nd ed., pp. 183–199). New York: Guilford.

Garcia-Preto, N. (2005). Latino families: An overview. In M. McGoldrick, J. Giordano, & N. Garcia-Preto (Eds.), *Ethnicity and family therapy* (3rd ed., pp. 153–165). New York: Guilford.

Garrett, J. T., & Garrett, M. W. (1994). The path of good medicine: Understanding and counseling Native American Indians. *Journal of Multicultural Counseling and Development, 22,* 134–144.

Garrett, M. T. (1999). Understanding the "medicine" of Native American traditional values: An integrative review. *Counseling and Values, 43* (2), 84–98.

Garrett, M. T., & Carroll, J. J. (2000). Mending the Broken Circle: Treatment of substance dependence among Native Americans. *Journal of Counseling and Development, 78* (4), 379–388.

Garrett, M. T., & Myers, J. (1996). The rule of opposites: A paradigm for counseling Native Americans. *Journal of Multicultural Counseling and Development, 24,* 89–104.

Garrett, M. T., & Pichette, E. F. (2000). Red as an apple: Native American acculturation and counseling with or without reservation. *Journal of Counseling and Development, 78* (1), 3–13.

Garrett, M. T., & Wilbur, M. P. (1999). Does the worm live in the ground? Reflections on Native American spirituality. *Journal of Multicultural Counseling and Development, 27* (4), 193–206.

Garrett, M. W. (1995). Between two worlds: Cultural discontinuity in the dropout of Native American youth. *School Counselor, 42,* 186–195.

Georgas, J. (1989). Changing family values in Greece: From collectivist to individualist. *Journal of Cross-cultural Psychology, 20,* 80–91.

Gil, A. G., Vega, W. A., & Dimas, J. M. (1994). Acculturative stress and personal adjustment among Hispanic adolescent boys. *Journal of Community Psychology, 22,* 43–54.

Giordano, J., McGoldrick, M., & Klages, J. G. (2005). Italian families. In M. McGoldrick, J. Giordano, & N. Garcia-Preto (Eds.), *Ethnicity and family therapy* (3rd ed., pp. 616–628). New York: Guilford.

Giorgis, C., Higgins, K., & McNab, W. L. (2000). Health issues of gay and lesbian youth: Implications for schools. *Journal of Health Education, 31* (1), 28–36.

Glauser, A. S., & Bozarth, J. D. (2001). Person-centered counseling: The culture within. *Journal of Counseling and Development, 79,* 142–147.

Gloria, A. M., & Rodriguez, E. R. (2000). Counseling Latino university students: Psychosocial issues for consideration. *Journal of Counseling and Development, 78,* 145–154.

Goh, M. (2005). Cultural competence and master therapists: An inextricable relationship. *Journal of Mental Health Counseling, 27,* 71–82.

Goldblum, P. (1987). Suicide: Clinical aspects. In Helquist, M. (Ed.). *Working with AIDS: A resource guide for mental health professionals.* San Francisco: University of California Regents.

Gollnick, D. M., & Chinn, P. C. (1990). *Multicultural education in a pluralistic society* (3rd ed.). Upper Saddle River, NJ: Merrill/Prentice Hall.

Gonzalez, G. M. (1997). The emergence of Chicanos in the 21st century: Implications for counseling, research, and policy. *Journal of Multicultural Counseling and Development, 25* (2), 94–106.

Grace, J. (1979). Coming Out Alive: A Positive Developmental Model of Homosexual Competence. Paper presented at the Sixth National Association of Social Workers Professional Symposium, Social Work Practice for the 1980s. San Antonio, TX.

Granello, D. H., Hothersall, D., & Osborne, A. L. (2000). The academic genogram: Teaching for the future by learning from the past. *Counselor Education and Supervision, 39,* 177–188.

Greene, B. (1997). Ethnic minority lesbians and gay men: Mental health and treatment issues. In B. Greene (Ed.).

Psychological perspectives on lesbian and gay issues: Vol 3. Ethnic and cultural diversity among lesbians and gay men (pp. 216–239). Thousand Oaks, CA: Sage.

Griffin, L. W., & Williams, O. J. (1993). Abuse in African American elderly. *Journal of Family Violence, 7,* 19–35.

Gunnings, T. S., & Lipscomb, W. D. (1986). Psychotherapy for Black men: A systematic approach. *Journal of Multicultural Counseling and Development, 14,* 17–24.

Gura, M. (1997). Fixated on Ebonics: Let's concentrate on the kids. *Educational Leadership, 54* (7), 87.

Gutierrez, J., & Sameroff, A. (1990). Determinants of complexity in Mexican American and Anglo-American mothers' conceptions of child development. *Child Development, 61,* 384–394.

Haddock, S. A., Zimmerman, T. S., & MacPhee, D. (2000). The power equity guide: Attending to gender in family therapy. *Journal of Marital and Family Therapy, 26* (2), 153–170.

Haeberle, E. J., & Gindorf, R. (1998). *Bisexualities: The ideology and practice of sexual contact with both men and women.* New York: Continuum.

Hale-Benson, J. E. (1986). *Black children: Their roots, culture, and learning styles.* Baltimore: Johns Hopkins University Press.

Han, A. Y., & Vasquez, M. J. T. (2000). Group intervention and treatment of ethnic minorities. In J. F. Aponte, & J. Wohl (Eds.), *Psychological intervention and cultural diversity* (2nd ed., pp. 110–130). Boston: Allyn and Bacon.

Hanna, F. J., & Green, A. (2004). Asian shades of spirituality: Implications for school counseling. *Professional School Counseling, 7* (5), 326–333.

Hardin, E. E., Leong, F. T. L., & Osipow, S. H. (2001). Cultural relativity in the conceptualization of career maturity. *Journal of Vocational Behavior, 58* (1), 36–52.

Harkless, L. F., & Fowers, B. J. (2005). Similarities and differences in relational boundaries among heterosexuals, gay men, and lesbians. *Psychology of Women Quarterly, 29,* 167–176.

Harper, G. W., Jernewall, N., & Zea, M. C. (2004). Giving voice to emerging science and theory for lesbian, gay, and bisexual people of color. *Cultural Diversity and Ethnic Minority Psychology, 10* (3), 187–199.

Harris, S. M. (1995). Psychosocial development and Black male masculinity: Implications for counseling economically disadvantaged African American male adolescents. *Journal of Counseling and Development, 73,* 279–287.

Hartman, J. S., & Askounis, A. C. (1989). Asian American students: Are they really a "model minority"? *School Counselor, 37,* 109–111.

Havighurst, R. J. (1972). *Developmental tasks and education* (3rd ed.). New York: McKay.

Hays, D. G., & Chang, C. Y. (2003). White privilege, oppression, and racial identity development: Implications for supervision. *Counselor Education & Supervision, 43,* 134–145.

Hays, D. G., Chang, C. Y., & Dean, J. K. (2004). White counselors' conceptualization of privilege and oppression: Implications for counselor training. *Counselor Education & Supervision, 43,* 242–257.

Hazler, R. J., & Mellin, E. A. (2004). The developmental origins and treatment needs of female adolescents with depression. *Journal of Counselor & Development, 82,* 18–24.

Heinrich, R. K., Corbine, J. L., & Thomas, K. R. (1990). Counseling Native Americans. *Journal of Counseling and Development, 69,* 128–133.

Heller, P. E., & Wood, B. (2000). The influence of religious and ethnic differences on marital intimacy: Intermarriage versus intramarriage. *Journal of Marital and Family Therapy, 26* (2), 241–252.

Helms, J. E. (1984). Toward a theoretical explanation of the effects of race on counseling: A Black and White model. *Counseling Psychologist, 12* (4), 163–165.

Helms, J. E. (1990). *Black and White racial identity: Theory, research, and practice.* Westport, CT: Greenwood.

Helms, J. E. (1994). Racial identity in the school environment. In P. Pedersen & J. C. Carey (Eds.), *Multicultural counseling in schools* (pp. 19–37). Boston: Allyn & Bacon.

Helms, J. E., & Carter, R. T. (1990). Development of the White Racial Identity Inventory. In J. E. Helms (Ed.), *Black and White racial identity: Theory and practice* (pp. 67–80). Westport, CT: Greenwood.

Henderson, G. (2000). Race in America. *National Forum, 80* (2), 12–15.

Henning-Stout, M. (1996). Que prodemos hacer? Roles for school psychologists with Mexican and Latino migrant children and families. *School Psychology Review, 25,* 152–164.

Henze, R., Lucas, T., & Scott, B. (1998). Dancing with the monster: Teachers discuss racism, power, and White privilege. *The Urban Review, 30* (3), 187–210.

Heppner, M. J., & O'Brien, K. M. (1994). Multicultural counselor training: Students' perceptions of helpful and hindering events. *Counselor Education and Supervision, 34,* 4–18.

Herdt, G. (1997). *Same sex, different cultures: Gays and lesbians across cultures.* Boulder, CO: Westview.

Herlihy, B. (1996). The 1995 ACA Code of Ethics: A user's guide. *Counseling and Human Development, 29* (1), 1–10.

Hernandez, H. (1989). *Multicultural education: A teacher's guide to content and practice.* Upper Saddle River, NJ: Merrill/Prentice Hall.

Herring, R. D. (1989a). The American Native family: Dissolution by coercion. *Journal of Multicultural Counseling and Development, 17,* 4–13.

Herring, R. D. (1989b). Counseling Native American children: Implications for elementary school counselors. *Elementary School Guidance and Counseling, 23,* 272–281.

Herring, R. D. (1990). Understanding Native American values: Process and content concerns for counselors. *Counseling and Values, 34,* 134–137.

Herring, R. D. (1992). Seeking a new paradigm: Counseling Native Americans. *Journal of Multicultural Counseling and Development 20,* 35–43.

Herring, R. D. (1996). Synergetic counseling and Native American Indian students. *Journal of Counseling and Development, 74,* 542–547.

Herring, R. D. (1997). *Multicultural counseling in schools: A synergetic approach.* Alexandria, VA: American Counseling Association.

Hershberger, S. L., & D'Augelli, A. R. (2000). Issues in counseling lesbian, gay, and bisexual adolescents. In R. M. Perez, K. A. DeBord, & K. J. Bieschke (Eds.), *Handbook of counseling and psychotherapy with lesbian, gay, and bisexual clients* (pp. 225–247). Washington, DC: American Psychological Association.

Hershenson, D. B. (2000). Toward a cultural anthropology of disability and rehabilitation. *Rehabilitation Counseling Bulletin, 43* (3), 150–157, 177.

Hetherington, C. L., & Orzek, A. (1989). Career counseling and life planning with lesbian women. *Journal of Counseling and Development, 68,* 52–57.

Hetrick, E. S., & Martin, A. D. (1987). Developmental issues and their resolution for gay and lesbian adolescents. *Journal of Homosexuality, 14,* 24–43.

Hidalgo, H. (1984). The Puerto Rico lesbian in the United States. In T. S. Darty & S Potter (Eds.). *Women identified women* (pp. 105–150). Palo Alto, CA: Mayfield.

Hill, M. R., & Thomas, V. (2000). Strategies for racial identity development: Narratives of Black and White women in interracial marriages. *Family Relations, 49,* 193–200.

Hines, P. M., & Boyd-Franklin, N. (2005). African American families. In M. McGoldrick, J. Giordano, & N. Garcia-Preto (Eds.), *Ethnicity and family therapy* (3rd ed., pp. 87–100). New York: Guilford.

Hinkle, J. S. (1994). Practitioners and cross-cultural assessment: A practical guide to information and training. *Measurement and Evaluation in Counseling and Development, 27,* 103–115.

Ho, M. K. (1987). *Family therapy with ethnic minorities.* Newbury Park, CA: Sage.

Hoare, C. H. (1991). Psychosocial identity development and cultural others. *Journal of Counseling and Development, 70* (1), 45–53.

Hobson, S. M., & Kanitz, H. M. (1996). Multicultural counseling: An ethical issue for school counselors. *School Counselor, 43,* 245–255.

Hoffman, R. M. (2004). Conceptualizing heterosexual identity development: Issues and challenges. *Journal and Counseling and Development, 82* (3), 375–380.

Holcomb-McCoy, C. C. (2000). Multicultural counseling competencies: An exploratory factor analysis. *Journal of Multicultural Counseling and Development, 28* (2), 83–97.

Holcomb-McCoy, C. C. (2001). Exploring the self-perceived multicultural counseling competencies of elementary school counselors. *Professional School Counseling, 4* (3), 195–201.

Holman, L. J. (1997). Meeting the needs of Hispanic immigrants. *Educational Leadership, 54* (7), 37–38.

Honda, K. (2005). Psychological correlates of smoking cessation among elderly ever-smokers in the United States. *Addictive Behaviors, 30* (2), 375–381.

Hooker, E. (1957). The adjustment of the male homosexual. *Journal of Projective Techniques, 21,* 18–31.

Hovey, J. D. (2000). Acculturative stress, depression, and suicidal ideation in Mexican immigrants. *Cultural Diversity and Ethnic Minority Psychology, 6* (2), 134–151.

Howard-Hamilton, M. F., & Behar-Horenstein, L. S. (1995). Counseling the African American male adolescent. *Elementary School Guidance and Counseling, 29,* 198–205.

Huang, S., & Waxman, H. C. (1995). Motivation and learning-environment differences between Asian American and White middle school students in mathematics. *Journal of Research and Development in Education, 28* (4), 208–219.

Huffman, S. B., Myers, J. E., Tingle, L. R., Bond, L. A. (2005). Menopause symptoms and attitudes of African American women: Closing the knowledge gap and expanding opportunities for counseling. *Journal of Counseling and Development, 83,* 48–56.

Hume, S. (2002). Demographics and diversity of Asian American college students. *New Directions for Student Services, 97*, 11–20.

Hwang, W. Chun, C., Takeuchi, D. T., Myers, H. F., & Siddarth, P. (2005). Age of first onset of major depression in Chinese Americans. *Cultural Diversity and Ethnic Minority Psychology 11* (1) 16–27.

Hyun, J. K., & Fowler, S. A. (1995). Respect, cultural sensitivity, and communication. *Teaching Exceptional Children, 28* (1), 25–28.

Ibrahim, F. A., & Arredondo, P. M. (1986). Ethical standards for cross-cultural counseling: Counseling or preparation, practice, and research. *Journal of Counseling and Development, 64*, 349–352.

Ibrahim, F. A., & Kahn, H. (1984). *Scale to Assess World Views (SAWV)*. Typescript. Storrs, CT: University of Connecticut.

Ibrahim, F. A., & Kahn, H. (1987). Assessment of worldviews. *Psychological Reports, 60*, 163–176.

Ibrahim, F. A., Ohnishi, H., & Sandhu, D. S. (1997). Asian American identity development: A culture-specific model for South Asian Americans. *Journal of Multicultural Counseling and Development, 25* (1), 34–50.

Ihle, G. M., Sodowsky, G. R., & Kwan, K. L. (1996). Worldviews of women: Comparison between White American clients, White American counselors, and Chinese international students. *Journal of Counseling and Development, 74*, 300–306.

Ingersoll, R. E., Bauer, A., & Burns, L. (2004). Children and psychotropic medication: What role should advocacy counseling play? *Journal of Counseling and Development, 82*, 337–343.

Israel, T., & Hackett, G. (2004). Counselor education on lesbian, gay and bisexual issues: Comparing information and attitude exploration. *Counselor Education and Supervision, 43*, 179–191.

Itai, G. I., & McRae, C. (1994). Counseling older Japanese American clients: An overview and observations. *Journal of Counseling and Development, 72*, 373–377.

Ivey, A. E., Ivey, M. B., & Simek-Morgan, L. (1997). *Counseling and psychotherapy: A multicultural perspective* (4th ed.). Boston: Allyn & Bacon.

Iyer, A., Leach, C. W., & Crosby, F. J. (2003). White guilt and racial compensation: The benefits and limits of self-focus. *Personality and Social Psychology Bulletin, 29* (1), 117–129.

Jackson, R. L. (1999). White space, White privilege: Mapping discursive inquiry into the self. *Quarterly Journal of Speech, 85*, 38–54.

Jacobson, S., & Grossman, A. H. (1996). Older lesbians and gay men: Old myths, new images, and future directions. In R. C. Savin-Williams & K. M. Cohen (Eds.), *The lives of lesbians, gays, and bisexuals: Children to adults* (pp. 345–373). Fort Worth, TX: Harcourt Brace.

Janevic, M. R., & Connell, C. M. (2001). Racial, ethnic, and cultural differences in the dementia caregiving experience: Recent findings. *The Gerontologist, 41* (3), 334–347.

Jennings, L., Sovereign, A., Bottorff, N., Mussell, M. P., Vye, C. (2005). Nine ethical principles of master therapists, *Journal of Mental Health Counseling, 27* (1), 32–47.

Jensen, R. (2004). Homecoming: The relevance of radical feminism for gay men. *Journal of Homosexuality, 47* (3/4), 75–81.

Johnson, I. H., Torres, J. S., Coleman, V. D., & Smith, M. C. (1995). Issues and strategies in leading culturally diverse counseling groups. *Journal for Specialists in Group Work, 20*, 143–150.

Johnson, P. (2001). Dimensions of functioning in alcoholic and nonalcoholic families. *Journal of Mental Health Counseling, 23* (2), 127–136.

Johnson, S. M., Makinen, J. A., & Millikin, J. W. (2001). Attachment injuries in couple relationships: A new perspective on impasses in couples therapy. *Journal of Marital and Family Therapy, 27* (2), 145–155.

Johnson-Garner, M. Y., & Meyers, S. A. (2003). What factors contribute to the resilience of African-American children under kinship care. *Child & Youth Care Forum, 32* (5), 225–269.

Jones, C. P. (2000). Levels of racism: The theoretical framework and a gardener's tale. *American Journal of Public Health, 90* (8), 1212–1215.

Jones, M. A., & Gabriel, M. A. (1998). *The Utilization of Psychotherapy by Lesbians and Gay Men: Findings from a Nationwide Study*. Unpublished Paper. New York: 1 Washington Square N. #2, 10003-6654.

Jones, S. R., & McEwen, M. K. (2000). A conceptual model of multiple dimensions of identity. *Journal of College Student Development, 41* (4), 405–413.

Kahn, J. H., Achter, J. A., & Shambaugh, E. J. (2001). Client distress disclosure, characteristics at intake, and outcome in brief counseling. *Journal of Counseling Psychology, 48* (2), 203–211.

Kao, G. (1995). Asian Americans as model minorities: A look at their academic performance. *American Journal of Education, 103*, 121–159.

Kaslow, N. J., Price, A. W., Wyckoff, S., Grall, M. B., Sherry, A., Young, S., Scholl, L., et al. (2004). Person factors associated with suicidal behavior among African American women and men. *Cultural Diversity and Ethnic Minority Psychology, 10* (1), 5–22.

Kasturirangan, A., & Williams, E. N. (2003). Counseling Latina battered women: A qualitative study of the Latina perspective. *Journal of Multicultural Counseling and Development, 31,* 162–178.

Keats, D. M. (2000). Cross-cultural studies in child development in Asian cultures. *Cross-Cultural Research, 34* (3), 339–350.

Kennedy, E., & Park, H. S. (1994). Home language as a predictor of academic achievement: A comparative study of Mexican American and Asian American youth. *Journal of Research and Development in Education, 29* (3), 188–194.

Killen, M., & Stangor, C. (2001). Children's social reasoning about inclusion and exclusion in gender and race peer group contexts. *Child Development, 72* (1), 174–186.

Killeya, L. A. (2001). Idiosyncratic role-elaboration, academic performance, and adjustment among African American and European American male college student athletes. *College Student Journal, 35* (1), 87–95.

Killian, K. G. (2001). Reconstituting racial histories and identities: The narratives of interracial couples. *Journal of Marital and Family Therapy, 27* (1), 27–42.

Killian, K. D., Agathangelou, A. M. (2005). Greek families. In M. McGoldrick, J. Giordano, & N. Garcia-Preto (Eds.), *Ethnicity and family therapy* (3rd ed., pp. 532–551). New York: Guilford.

Kim, B. L. (1996). Korean families. In M. McGoldrick, J. Giordano, & J. K. Pearce (Eds.), *Ethnicity and family therapy* (2nd ed., pp. 281–294). New York: Guilford.

Kim, B. L. C., & Ryu, E. (2005). Korean families. In M. McGoldrick, J. Giordano, & N. Garcia-Preto (Eds.), *Ethnicity and family therapy* (3rd ed., pp. 349–362). New York: Guilford.

Kim, B. S., & Lyons, H. Z. (2003). Experiential activities and multicultural counseling competence training. *Journal of Counseling and Development, 81* (4), 400–408.

Kim, B. S., Ng, G. F., & Ahn, A. J. (2005). Effects of client expectation for counseling success, client–counselor worldview match, and client adherence to Asian and European American cultural values on counseling process with Asian Americans. *Journal of Counseling Psychology, 52* (1), 67–76.

Kim, B. S., & Omizo, M. M. (2005). Asian and European American cultural values, collective self-esteem,

acculturative stress, cognitive flexibility, and general self-efficacy among Asian American college students. *Journal of Counseling Psychology, 52* (3), 412–419.

Kim, B. S., Omizo, M. M., & Salvador, D. S. (1996). Culturally relevant counseling services for Korean American children: A systematic approach. *Elementary School Guidance and Counseling, 31,* 64–73.

Kim, C. J. (2004). Imaging race and nation in multiculturalist America. *Ethnic and Racial Studies, 27* (6), 987–1005.

Kim, H., Rendon, L., & Valadez, J. (1998). Student characteristics, school characteristics, and educational aspirations of six Asian American ethnic groups. *Journal of Multicultural Counseling and Development, 26* (3), 166–176.

Kimmel, D. C., & Yi, H. (2004). Characteristics of gay, lesbian, Asian, Asian Americans, and immigrants from Asia to the USA. *Journal of Homosexuality, 47* (2), 143–171.

Kinnier, R. T., Tribbensee, N. E., Rose, C. A., & Vaughan, S. M. (2001). In the final analysis: More wisdom from people who have faced death. *Journal of Counseling and Development, 79,* 171–177.

Kitano, H. H. L. (1989). A model for counseling Asian Americans. In P. B. Pedersen, J. G. Draguns, J. Lonner, & J. E. Trimble (Eds.), *Counseling across cultures* (3rd ed., pp. 139–151). Honolulu: University of Hawaii Press.

Kitaoka, S. K. (2005). Multicultural counseling competencies: Lessons from assessment. *Journal of Multicultural Counseling and Development, 33,* 37–43.

Koch, L. M., Gross, A. M., & Kolts, R. (2001). Attitudes toward Black English and code switching. *Journal of Black Psychology, 27* (1), 29–42.

Korin, E. C. (1996). Brazilian families. In M. McGoldrick, J. Giordano, & J. K. Pearce (Eds.), *Ethnicity and family therapy* (2nd ed., pp. 200–213). New York: Guilford.

Koss-Chioino, J. D. (2000). Traditional and folk approaches among ethnic minorities. In J. F. Aponte, & J. Wohl (Eds.), *Psychological intervention and cultural diversity* (2nd ed., pp. 149–166). Boston: Allyn and Bacon.

Kostelnik, M. J., Stein, L. C., Whiren, A. P., & Soderman, A. K. (1988). *Guiding children's social development.* Monterey, CA: Brooks/Cole.

Krause, N. (2004). Lifetime trauma, emotional support, and life satisfaction among older adults. *The Gerontologist, 44* (5), 615–623

Kumashiro, K. K. (2000). Toward a theory of anti-oppressive education. *Review of Educational Research, 70* (1), 25–53.

Kung, W. W. (2001). Consideration of cultural factors in working with Chinese American families with a mentally ill patient. *Families in Society: The Journal of Contemporary Human Services, 82* (1), 97–107.

Kurasaki, K. S., Sue, S., Chun, C., & Gee, K (2000). Ethnic minority intervention and treatment research. In J. F. Aponte, & J. Wohl (Eds.), *Psychological intervention and cultural diversity* (2nd ed., pp. 234–249). Boston: Allyn and Bacon.

Lachman, M. E. (2004). Development in midlife. *Annual Review of Psychology, 55*, 302–332.

LaFountain, R. M., Garner, N. E., & Eliason, G. T. (1996). Solution-focused counseling groups: A key for school counselors. *School Counselor, 43*, 256–267.

LaFromboise, T. D., Foster, S. L., & James, A. (1996). Ethics in multicultural counseling. In P. B. Pedersen, J. G. Draguns, W. J. Lonner, & J. E. Trimble (Eds.), *Counseling across cultures* (4th ed., pp. 47–72). Thousand Oaks, CA: Sage.

LaFromboise, T. D., Trimble, J., & Mohatt, G. (1990). Counseling intervention and American Indian tradition: An integrative approach. *Counseling Psychologist, 18*, 628–654.

Laird, J. (2000). Gender in lesbian relationships: Cultural, feminist, and constructionists reflections. *Journal of Marital and Family Therapy, 26* (4), 455–467.

Langelier, R., & Langelier, P. (2005). French Canadian families. In M. McGoldrick, J. Giordano, & N. Garcia-Preto (Eds.), *Ethnicity and family therapy* (3rd ed., pp. 545–554). New York: Guilford.

Larrabee, M. J. (1986). Helping reluctant Black males: An affirmation approach. *Journal of Multicultural Counseling and Development, 14*, 25–38.

LaSala, M. C. (2000). Gay male couples: The importance of coming out and being out to parents. *Journal of Homosexuality, 39* (2), 47–71.

Laszloffy, T. A. (2005). Hungarian families. In M. McGoldrick, J. Giordano, & N. Garcia-Preto (Eds.), *Ethnicity and family therapy* (3rd ed., pp. 586–595). New York: Guilford.

Latino American. (1999, July 12). *Newsweek*, pp. 48–51.

Latino Americans: The face of the future. (1999, July 12). *Newsweek*, pp. 50–51.

Lawrence, G., & Kurpius, S. E. R. (2000). Legal and ethical issues involved with counseling minors in nonschool settings. *Journal of Counseling and Development, 78*, 130–136.

Lawson, D. M., & Brossart, D. F. (2004). The association between current intergenerational family relationships and sibling structures. *Journal of counseling and Development, 82*, 472–482.

Leck, G. (2000). Heterosexual or homosexual: Reconsidering binary narratives in sexual identities in urban schools. *Education and Urban Society, 32* (3), 324–348.

Lee, C. C. (Ed.). (1995a). *Counseling for diversity: A guide for school counselors and related professionals*. Boston: Allyn & Bacon.

Lee, C. C. (1995b). School counseling and cultural diversity: A framework for effective practice. In C. C. Lee (Ed.), *Counseling for diversity: A guide for school counselors and related professionals* (pp. 3–17). Boston: Allyn & Bacon.

Lee, E. (1996). In M. McGoldrick, J. Giordano, & J. K. Pearce (Eds.), *Ethnicity and family therapy* (2nd ed., pp. 249–268). New York: Guilford.

Lee, E., & Mock, M. R. (2005). Chinese families. In M. McGoldrick, J. Giordano, & N. Garcia-Preto (Eds.), *Ethnicity and family therapy* (3rd ed., pp. 302–318). New York: Guilford.

Lee, F. Y. (1995). Asian parents as partners. *Young Children, 50* (3), 4–8.

Lee, R. M. (2003). Do ethnic identity and other-group orientation protect against discrimination for Asian Americans? *Journal of Counseling Psychology, 50* (2), 133–141.

Lee, R. M. (2005). Resilience against discrimination: Ethnic identity and other-group orientation as protective factors for Korean Americans. *Journal of Counseling Psychology, 52* (1), 36–44.

Lee, R. M., & Dean, B. L. (2004). Middle-class mythology in an age of immigration and segmented assimilation: Implication for counseling psychology. *Journal of Counseling Psychology, 51* (1), 19–24.

Lee, R. M., Su, J., & Yoshida, E. (2005). Coping with intergenerational family conflict among Asian American college students. *Journal of Counseling Psychology, 52* (3), 389–399.

Lee, W. M. L. (1996). New directions in multicultural counseling. *Counseling and Human Development, 29* (2), 1–11.

LeMaster, P. L., & Connell, C. M. (1994). Health education interventions among Native Americans: A review and analysis. *Health Education Quarterly, 21* (4), 521–538.

Lemelle, A. J., & Battle, J. (2004). Black masculinity matters in attitudes toward gay males. *Journal of Homosexuality, 47* (1), 39–51.

Lemoine, Noma. A case for Ebonics: An interview. (1997). *Curriculum Review, 36* (7), 56.

Lemoire, S. J., & Chen, C. P. (2005). Applying person-centered counseling to sexual minority adolescents. *Journal of Counseling and Development, 83*, 148–154.

self-esteem. *Journal of Black Psychology, 30* (3), 307–328.

Peacock, J. R. (2000). Gay male adult development: Some stage issues. *Journal of Homosexuality, 40* (2), 13–30.

Pearson, J. L., Hunter, A. G., Ensminger, M. E., & Kellam, S. G. (1990). Black grandmothers in multigenerational households: Diversity in family structure and parenting involvement in the Woodlawn community. *Child Development, 62,* 434–442.

Pedersen, P. B. (1988). *A handbook for developing multicultural awareness.* Alexandria, VA: American Association of Counseling and Development.

Pedersen, P. B. (1996). The importance of both similarities and differences in multicultural counseling: Reaction to C. H. Patterson. *Journal of Counseling and Development, 74,* 236–237.

Pedersen, P. B., & Carey, J. C. (1994). *Multicultural counseling in schools: A practical handbook.* Boston: Allyn & Bacon.

Pedersen, P. B., Fukuyama, M., & Heath, A. (1996). Client, counselor, and contextual variables in multicultural counseling. In P. B. Pedersen, J. G. Draguns, J. Lonner, & J. E. Trimble (Eds.), *Counseling across cultures* (4th ed., pp. 230–248). Honolulu: University of Hawaii Press.

Pence, D. J., & Fields, J. A. (1999). Teaching about race and ethnicity: Trying to uncover White privilege for a White audience. *Teaching Sociology, 27,* 150–158.

Peng, S. S., & Wright, D. A. (1994). Explanation of academic achievement of Asian American students. *Journal of Educational Research, 87* (6), 346–352.

Pennachio, D. L. (2004). Caring for your Filipino, Southeastern Asian, and Indian patients: More than half of Asian Americans say their doctors don't understand their cultures: Sensitivity to diversity is essential for good patient care. *Medical Economies, 81* (2), 36–42.

Perez, B. (1995). Language and literacy issues related to Mexican American secondary students. *High School Journal, 78,* 236–243.

Perez, R. M., DeBord, K. A., & Bieschke, K. J. (2000). *Handbook of counseling and psychotherapy with lesbian, gay, and bisexual clients.* Washington, DC: American Psychological Association.

Peterson, J. V., & Nisenholz, B. (1987). *Orientation to counseling.* Boston: Allyn & Bacon.

Phan, L. T., Rivera, E. T., & Roberts-Wilbur, J. (2005). Understanding Vietnamese refugees women's identity development from a sociopolitical and historical perspective. *Journal of Counseling and Development, 83,* 305–312.

Phelps, E. P., Taylor, J. D., & Gerard, P. A. (2001). Cultural mistrust, ethnic identity, racial identity, and self-esteem among ethnically diverse Black university students. *Journal of Counseling and Development, 79* (2), 209–216.

Phinney, J. S. (2000). Identity formation across cultures: The interaction of personal, societal, and historical change. *Human Development, 43,* 27–31.

Phinney, J. S., & Rotherham, M. J. (1987). *Children's stage socialization: Pluralism and development.* Newbury Park, CA: Sage.

Pierce, L. L. (2001). Caring and expressions of stability by urban family caregivers of persons with stroke within African American family systems. *Rehabilitation Nursing, 26* (3), 100–107.

Pinsof, W. M., & Wynne, L. C. (2000). Toward progress research: Closing the gap between family therapy and research. *Journal of Marital and Family Therapy, 26* (1), 1–8.

Pitman, G. E. (2000). The influence of race, ethnicity, class, and sexual politics on lesbians' body image. *Journal of Homosexuality, 40* (2), 31–48.

Pizarro, M., & Vera, E. M. (2001). Chicana/o ethnic identity research: Lessons for researchers and counselors. *The Counseling Psychologist, 29* (1), 91–117.

Plantz, M. C., Hubbell, R., Barrett, B. J., & Dobrec, A. (1989). Indian child welfare: A status report. *Children Today, 18* (1), 24–29.

Pole, N., Best, S. R., Metzler, T., & Marmar, C. R. (2005). Why are Hispanics at greater risk of PTSD? *Cultural Diversity and Ethnic Minority Psychology, 11* (2), 144–161.

Ponterotto, J. G. (1987). Counseling Mexican Americans: A multimodal approach. *Journal of Multicultural Counseling and Development, 65,* 308–312.

Ponterotto, J. G. (1988). Racial consciousness development among White counselor trainee. *Journal of Multicultural Counseling and Development, 16,* 144–156.

Ponterotto, J. G. (1991). The nature of prejudice revisited: Implications for counseling intervention. *Journal of Counseling and Development, 70,* 216–224.

Ponterotto, J. G., Alexander, C. M., & Grieger, I. (1995). A multicultural competency checklist for counseling training checklist. *Journal of Multicultural Counseling and Development, 23* (1), 11–20.

Ponterotto, J. G., & Casas, J. M. (1987). In search of multicultural competence within counselor education programs. *Journal of Counseling and Development, 65,* 430–434.

Pope, A. (1999). Applications of group career counseling techniques in Asian cultures. *Journal of Multicultural Counseling and Development, 27* (1), 18–30.

Pope, M., Barret, B., Szymanski, D. M. Chung, Y. B., Singaravelu, H., McLean, R, & Sanabria, S. (2004). Culturally appropriate career counseling with gay and lesbian clients. *The Career Development Quarterly, 53* (2), 158–177.

Pope, R. L. (2000). The relationship between psychosocial development and racial identity of college students of color. *Journal of College Student Development, 41* (3), 302–311.

Population Reference Bureau (2000, June). Racial and ethnic diversity. *Population Bulletin, 55* (2), p. 16.

Porter, R. Y. (2000). Clinical issues and intervention with ethnic minority women. In J. F. Aponte, & J. Wohl (Eds.), *Psychological intervention and cultural diversity* (2nd ed., pp. 183–199). Boston: Allyn and Bacon.

Portman, T. A. A. (2001). Sex role attributions of American-Indian women. *Journal of Mental Health Counseling, 23* (1), 72–84.

Post, D. (2001). Region, poverty, sibship, and gender inequality in Mexican education: Will targeted welfare policy make a difference for girls? *Gender & Society, 15* (3), 468–489.

Poston, W. S. C. (1990). The biracial identity development model: A needed addition. *Journal of Counseling and Development, 69*, 152–155.

Potgieter, C. (1997). From Apartheid to Mandel's constitution: Black South African lesbians in the nineties. In B. Greene (Ed.), *Psychological perspectives on lesbian and gay issues: Vol 3. Ethnic and cultural diversity among lesbians and gay men* (pp. 88–116). Thousand Oaks, CA: Sage.

Potok, M. (2000). The year in hate. *National Forum, 80* (2), 32–36.

Powers, K. (2005). Promoting school achievement among American Indian students throughout the school years. *Childhood Education, 81* (6), 338–342.

Prey, L. L., & & Roysircar, G. (2005). Effects if acculturation and worldview for White American, South American, South Asian, and Southeast Asian students. *International Journal for the Advancement of Counseling, 26* (3), 229–248.

Prieto, L. R., McNeill, B. W., Walls, R. G., & Gomez, S. P. (2001). Chicanas/os and mental health services: An overview of utilization, counselor preference, and assessment issues. *The Counseling Psychologist, 29* (1), 18–54.

Quam, J. K., & Whitford, G. S. (1992). Adaptation and age-related expectations of older gay and lesbian adults. *The Gerontologist, 32*, 367–374.

Radina, M. E., & Barber, C. E. (2004). Utilization of formal support services among Hispanic Americans caring for aging parents. *Journal of Gerontological Social Work, 43* (2/3), 5–23.

Rahman, O., & Rollock, D. (2004). Acculturation, competence, and mental health among South Asian students in the United States. *Journal of Multicultural Counseling and Development, 32*, 130–142.

Ralston, P. A. (1993). Health promotion for rural Black elderly: A comprehensive review. *Journal of Gerontological Social Work, 20*, 53–76.

Ramasamy, R. (1996). Post-high school employment: A follow-up of Apache Native American youth. *Journal of Learning Disabilities, 29*, 174–179.

Ramirez, M. (1994). *Psychotherapy and counseling with minorities: A cognitive approach to individual and cultural differences.* Boston: Allyn & Bacon.

Ramirez, M. (1999). *Multicultural psychotherapy: An approach to individual and cultural differences* (2nd ed.). Boston: Allyn & Bacon.

Reeve, D. (2000). Oppression within the counseling room. *Disability & Society, 15* (4), 669–682.

Reeves, T., & Bennett, C. (2003). The Asian and Pacific Islander population in the United States: March 2002, *Current Population Reports*, P20–540, U.S. Census Bureau, Washington, DC.

Reid, R. (2001). Working with children with ADHD: Strategies for counselors and teachers. *Counseling and Human Development, 33* (6), 1–20.

Reis, S. M., McGuire, J. M., & Neu, T. W. (2000). Compensation strategies used by high-ability students with learning disabilities who succeed in college. *Gifted Child Quarterly, 44* (2), 123–134.

Reyes, L. R., Meininger, J. C., Liehr, P., Chan, W., & Mueller, W. H. (2003). *Nursing Research, 52* (1), 2–11.

Reynolds, A. L., & Constantine M. G. (2004). Feminism and multiculturalism: Parallels and intersections. *Journal of Multicultural Counseling and Development, 32*, 346–357.

Reynolds, A. L., & Hanjorgiris, W. F. (2000). Coming out: Lesbian, gay, and bisexual development. In R. M. Perez, K. A. DeBord, & K. J. Bieschke (Eds.), *Handbook of counseling and psychotherapy with lesbian, gay, and bisexual clients* (pp. 35–55). Washington, DC: American Psychological Association.

Reynolds, S. L., Saito, Y., & Crimmins, E. M. (2005). The impact of obesity on active life expectancy in older

American men and women. *The Gerontologist, 45* (4), 438–444.

Ricciuti, H. N. (2004). Single parenthood, achievement, and problem behavior in white, black, and Hispanic children. *Journal of Educational Research, 97* (4), 196–206.

Rice, F. P. (2001). Human development: A life-span approach. Upper Saddle River, NJ: Prentice Hall.

Rita, E. S, (1996). Filipino families. In M. McGoldrick, J. Giordano, & J. K. Pearce (Eds.), *Ethnicity and family therapy* (2nd ed., pp. 324–220). New York: Guilford.

Robinson, T. L. (2005). *The convergence of race, ethnicity, and gender: Multiple identities in counseling* (2nd ed). Columbus, OH: Merrill/Prentice-Hall.

Root, M. P. P. (2005). Filipino families. In M. McGoldrick, J. Giordano, & N. Garcia-Preto (Eds.), *Ethnicity and family therapy* (3rd ed., pp. 319–331). New York: Guilford.

Rosenthal, D. A. (2004). Effects of client race on clinical judgment of practicing European American vocational rehabilitation counselors. *Rehabilitation Counseling Bulletin, 47* (3), 131–141.

Rotheram-Borus, M. J., & Phinney, J. S. (1990). Patterns of social expectations among Black and Mexican American children. *Child Development, 6*, 542–556.

Rotter, J. (1975). Some problems and misconceptions related to the construct of internal versus external control of reinforcement. *Journal of Consulting and Clinical Psychology, 43*, 56–67.

Rowe, W., Bennett, S. K., & Atkinson, D. R. (1994). White racial identity models: A critique and alternative proposal. *Counseling Psychologist, 22* (1), 129–146.

Russell, G. (1998). *American Indian facts of life: A profile of today's tribes and reservations.* Phoenix, AZ: Russell.

Rust, P. C. (1996). Managing multiple identities: Diversity among bisexual men and women. In B. A. Firestein (Ed.), *Bisexuality: The psychology and politics of an invisible minority* (pp. 53–83). Thousand Oaks, CA: Sage.

Ryan, C., & Futterman, D. (1998). *Lesbian and gay youth: Care and counseling.* New York: Columbia University Press.

Ryan, D. J., & Harvey, S. J. (1999). Meeting the career development needs of students with disabilities. *Journal of Career Planning & Employment, 36*, 36–40.

Ryan, E. B., Jin Y., Anas, A. P., & Luh, J. J. (2004). Communication beliefs about youth and old age in Asia and Canada. *Journal of Cross-Cultural Gerontology, 19*, 343–360.

Sadeghi, M. Fischer, J. M., & House, S. G. (2003). Ethical dilemmas in multicultural counseling. *Journal of Multicultural Counseling and Development, 31* (3), 179–191.

Safran, S. P., Safran, J. S., & Pirozak, E. (1994). Native American youth: Meeting their needs in a multicultural society. *Journal of Humanistic Education and Development, 33*, 50–57.

Salgado de Snyder, V. N., Acevedo, A., de Jesu's Di'az-Pe'rez, M., Saldi'var-Guarduno, A. (2000). Understanding the sexuality of Mexican-born women and their risk for HIV/AIDS. *Psychology of Women Quarterly, 24*, 100–109.

Salzman, M. (2000). Promoting multicultural competence: A cross-cultural mentorship project. *Journal of Multicultural Counseling and Development, 28* (2), 119–124.

Sanchez, D. T., & Crocker, J. (2005). How investment in gender ideals affects well-being: The role of external contingencies of self-worth. *Psychology of Women Quarterly, 29*, 63–77.

Sanders, D. (1987). Cultural conflicts: An important factor in the academic failures of American Indian students. *Journal of Multicultural Counseling and Development, 15*, 81–90.

Sanders, G. L., & Kroll, I. T. (2000). Generating stories of resilience: Helping gay and lesbian youth and their families. *Journal of Marital and Family Therapy, 26* (4), 433–442.

Sanders, J. L., & Bradley, C. (2005). Multiple lens paradigm: Evaluating African American girls and their development. *Journal of Counseling and Development, 83*, 299–304.

Sandhu, D. S. (1995). Pioneers of multicultural counseling: An interview with Paul B. Pedersen. *Journal of Multicultural Counseling and Development, 23*, 198–211.

Sandhu, D. S. (1997). Psychocultural profiles of Asian and Pacific Islander Americans: Implications for counseling and psychotherapy. *Journal of Multicultural Counseling and Psychotherapy, 25* (1), 7–22.

Santiago-Rivera, A. L. (1995). Developing a culturally sensitive treatment modality for bilingual Spanish-speaking clients: Incorporating language and culture in counseling. *Journal of Counseling and Development, 74*, 12–17.

Satir, V. (1967). *Conjoint family therapy* (2nd ed.). Palo Alto, CA: Science & Behavior Books.

Saucier, M. G. (2004). Midlife and beyond: Issues for aging women. *Journal of Counseling and Development, 82*, 420–425.

Savage, T. A., Harley, D. A., & Nowak, T. M. (2005). Applying social empowerment strategies as tools for self-advocacy in counseling lesbian and gay male clients. *Journal of Counseling and Development, 83,* 131–137.

Savin-Williams, R. C. (1990). Gay and lesbian adolescents. *Marriage and Family Review, 14* (3/4), 197–216.

Schmitt, E. (2001, March 8). Census figures show Hispanics pulling even with Blacks. *The New York Times.* Retrieved April 2005, from http://www.nytimes.com/2001/03/08/national/08CENS.html.

Schneider, M. E., & Owens, R. E. (2000). Concern for lesbian, gay, and bisexual kids: The benefits for all children. *Education and Urban Society, 32* (3), 349–367.

Schwartz, P., & Blumstein, P. (1998). The acquisition of sexual identity: Bisexuality. In E.J. Haeberle, & R. Gindorf (Eds.), *Bisexualities: The ideology and practice of sexual contact with both men and women* (pp. 182–212). New York: Continuum.

Schwarzbaum, S. E. (2004). Low-income Latinos and dropout: Strategies to prevent dropout. *Journal of Multicultural Counseling and Development, 32,* 296–306.

Schwiebert, V. L., Myers, J. E., & Dice, C. (2000). Ethical guidelines for counselors working with older adults. *Journal of Counseling and Development, 78,* 123–129.

Scollon, C. N, Deiner, E., Oishi, S., Biswas-Diener, R. (2004). Emotions across cultures and methods. *Journal of Cross-Cultural Psychology, 35* (3), 304–326.

Scourby, A. (1984). *The Greek Americans.* Boston: Twayne.

Sears, J. T. (1992). Educators, homosexuality, and homosexual students: Are personal feelings related to professional beliefs? In K. M. Harbeck (Ed.), *Coming out of the classroom closet: Gay and lesbian students, teachers, and curricula* (pp. 29–79). Binghamton, NY: Harrington Park.

Sedlacek, W. E. (1994). Advancing diversity through assessment. *Journal of Counseling and Development, 72,* 549–553.

Semmier, P. L., & Williams, C. B. (2000). Narrative therapy: A storied context in multicultural counseling. *Journal of Multicultural Counseling and Development, 28* (1), 51–62.

Sharma, M. (2004). Substance abuse and Asian Americans: Need for more research. *Journal of Alcohol Drug Education, 47* (3), 1–3.

Shellman, J. (2004). "Nobody ever asked me before": Understanding life experiences of African American elders. *Journal of Transcultural Nursing, 15* (4), 308–316.

Shibusawa, T. (2005). Japanese families. In M. McGoldrick, J. Giordano, & N. Garcia-Preto (Eds.), *Ethnicity and family therapy* (3rd ed., pp. 339–348). New York: Guilford.

Shin, J. Y., Berkson, G., Crittenden, K. (2000). Informal and professional support for solving psychological problems among Korean-speaking immigrants. *Journal of Multicultural Counseling and Development, 28* (3), 144–159.

Silverstein, C. (Ed.). (1991). *Gay, lesbians, and their therapists: Studies in psychotherapy.* New York: Norton.

Simon, A. (1998). The relationship between stereotypes of and attitudes toward lesbians and gays. In G. M. Herek (Ed.). *Stigma and sexual orientation: Understanding prejudice against lesbians, gay men, and bisexuals* (pp. 62–81). Thousand Oaks, CA: Sage.

Simonsen, G., Blazina, C., & Watkins, C. E. (2000). Gender role conflict and psychological well-being among gay men. *Journal of Counseling Psychology, 47* (1), 85–89.

Skovholt, T. M. (2005). The cycle of caring: A model of expertise in the helping profession. *Journal of Mental Health Counseling, 27* (1), 82–93.

Smart, J. F., & Smart, D. W. (1995). Acculturative stress of Hispanics: Loss and challenge. *Journal of Counseling and Development, 73,* 390–396.

Smith, A. (1997). Cultural diversity and the coming out process: Implications for clinical practice. In B. Greene (Ed.). *Psychological perspectives on lesbian and gay issues: Vol 3. Ethnic and cultural diversity among lesbians and gay men* (pp. 279–300). Thousand Oaks, CA: Sage.

Smith, D. E., & Muenchen, R. A. (1995). Gender and age variations in the self-esteem of Jamaican adolescents. *Adolescence, 30,* 643–654.

Smith, R. L. (1993). Training in marriage and family counseling and therapy: Current status and challenges. *Counselor Education and Supervision, 33,* 89–100.

Smith-Adcock, S., Rogers-Huiman, B., Choate, L. H. (2004). Feminist teaching in counselor education: Promoting multicultural understanding. *Journal of Multicultural and Development, 32,* 402–413.

Sodowsky, G. R., & Johnson, P. (1994). Worldviews: Culturally learned assumptions and values. In P. Pedersen & J. C. Carey (Eds.), *Multicultural counseling in schools: A practical handbook* (pp. 59–79). Boston: Allyn & Bacon.

Solberg, V. S., Choi, K. H., Ritsma, S., & Jolly, A. (1994). Asian American college students: It is time to reach out. *Journal of College Student Development, 35,* 296–301.

Sophie, J. (1985/1986). A critical examination of stage theories of lesbian identity development. *Journal of Homosexuality, 12,* 39–51.

Speight, S. L., Myers, L. J., Cox, C. I., & Highlen, P. S. (1991). A redefinition of multicultural counseling. *Journal of Counseling and Development, 70* (1), 29–36.

Speight, S. L., Vera, E. M., & Derrickson, K. B. (1996). Racial designation, racial identity, and self-esteem revisited. *Journal of Black Psychology, 22*, 37–52.

Spencer-Rodgers, J. (2000). The vocational situation and country of orientation of international students. *Journal of Multicultural Counseling and Development, 28* (1), 32–49.

Spigner, C. (1994). Black participation in health research: A functionalist overview. *Journal of Health Education, 25* (4), 210–214.

Springer, C. A., & Lease, S. H. (2000). The impact of multiple AIDS-related bereavement in the gay male population. *Journal of Counseling and Development, 78*, 297–304.

Stanard, R. P., Sandhu, D.S., & Painter, L. C. (2000). Assessment of spirituality in counseling. *Journal of Counseling and Development, 78*, 204–210.

Stauber, D. (1994). Curanderismo in the Mexican American community. *Journal of Health Education, 25*, 345–349.

Stavans, I. (1996). The Latin phallus. In R. Gonzalez (Ed.), *Muy macho* (pp. 143–164). New York: Doubleday.

Steinman, K. J., & Zimmerman, M. A. (2004). Religious activity and risk behavior among African American adolescents: Concurrent and developmental effects. *American Journal of Community Psychology, 33* (3–4), 151–162.

Steward, R. J. (1993). Black women and White women in groups: Suggestions for minority-sensitive group services on university campuses. *Journal of Counseling and Development, 72*, 39–41.

Stone, S., & Han, M. (2005). Perceived school environments, perceived discrimination, and school performance among children of Mexican immigrants. *Children and Youth Services Review, 27* (1), 51–66.

Storm, C. L., Todd, T. C., Sprenkle, D. H., & Morgan, M. M. (2001). Gaps between MFT supervision assumptions and common practice: Suggested nest practices. *Journal of Marital and Family Therapy, 27* (2), 227–239.

Subia, B., Dauphinais, P., LaFromboise, T. D., Bennett, S. K., & Rowe, W. (1992). American Indian secondary school students' preferences for counselors. *Journal of Multicultural Counseling and Development, 20* (3), 113–122.

Sue, D. W. (1978). Worldviews and counseling. *Personnel and Guidance Journal, 56*, 458–462.

Sue, D. W. (1981). *Counseling the culturally different*. New York: Wiley.

Sue, D. W. (1996). Ethical issues in multicultural counseling. In B. Herlihy, & G. Corey (Eds.), *ACA ethical standards casebook* (5th ed., pp. 193–197). Alexandria, VA: American Counseling Association.

Sue, D. W., & Sue, D. (2003). *Counseling the culturally different* (4th ed.). New York: Wiley.

Sutton, C., & Broken Nose, M. A. (2005). American Indian families. In M. McGoldrick, J. Giordano, & N. Garcia-Preto (Eds.), *Ethnicity and family therapy* (3rd ed., pp. 43–54). New York: Guilford Press.

Suzuki, B. H. (1989). Asian American as the "model minority": Outdoing Whites? Or media hype? *Change, 21* (6), 13–19.

Swim, J. K., Miller, D. L. (1999). White guilt: Its antecedents and consequences for affirmative action. *Personality and Social Psychology Bulletin, 25*, 500–514.

Szymanski, D. M. (2005). Heterosexism and sexism as correlates of psychological distress in lesbians. *Journal of Counseling and Development, 83*, 355–360.

Taylor, H. E. (2000). Meeting the needs of lesbian and gay young adolescents. *The Clearing House, 73* (4), 221–224.

Taylor, M. J. (2000). The influence of self-efficacy on alcohol use among American Indians. *Cultural Diversity and Ethnic Minority Psychology, 6* (2), 152–167.

Teague, J. B. (1992). Issues relating to the treatment of adolescent lesbians and homosexuals. *Journal of Mental Health Counseling, 14* (4), 422–439.

Tharp, R. G. (1994). Intergroup differences among Native Americans in socialization and child cognition: An enthnogentic analysis. In P. M. Greenfield & R. R. Cocking (Eds.), *Cross-cultural roots of minority child development* (pp. 87–105). Hillsdale, NJ: Erlbaum.

Theodore, P. S., & Basrow, S. A. (2000). Heterosexual masculinity and homophobia: A reaction. *Journal of Homosexuality, 40* (2), 31–48.

Thomas, V. G. (2004). The psychology of Black women: Studying women's lives in context. *Journal of Black Psychology, 30* (3), 286–306.

Thomason, T. C. (1991). Counseling Native Americans: An introduction for non-Native American counselors. *Journal of Counseling and Development, 69*, 321–327.

Thomason, T. C. (2000). Issues in the treatment of Native Americans with alcohol problems. *Journal of Multicultural Counseling and Development, 28* (4), 243–252.

Thompson, C. L., & Rudolph, L. B. (1988). *Counseling children* (2nd ed.). Monterey, CA: Brooks/Cole.

Tjeltvelt, A. C. (2004). The good, the bad, the obligatory, and the virtuous: The ethical contexts of psychotherapy. *Journal of Psychotherapy Integration, 14* (2), 149–167.

Todosijevic, J., Rothblum, E. D., & Solomon, S. E. (2005). Relationship satisfaction, affectivity, and gay-specific stressors in same-sex couples joined in civil union. *Psychology of Women Quarterly, 29*, 158–166.

Tolliver, D. E. (2001). African American female caregivers of family members living with HIV/AIDS. *Families in Society: The Journal of Contemporary Human Services, 82* (2), 145–156.

Toperak, R. L., Ortaga-Villalobos, L., & Pope-Davis, D. B. (2004). Critical incidents in multicultural supervision: Exploring supervisees' and supervisors' experiences. *Journal of Multicultural Counseling and Development, 32* (2), 66–83.

Toro-Morn, M. I. (1996). Gender, class, family, and migration: Puerto Rican women in Chicago. *Gender and Society, 9*, 712–726.

Torres, L., & Rollock, D. (2004). Acculturative distress among Hispanics: The role of acculturation, coping, and intercultural competence. *Journal of Multicultural Counseling and Development, 32* (3), 155–167.

Townsend, K. C., & McWhirter, B. T. (2005). Connectedness: A review of the literature with implications for counseling, assessment, and research. *Journal of Counseling and Development, 83*, 191–201.

Trimble, J. E., & Fleming, C. M. (1989). Providing counseling services for Native American Indians: Client, counselor, and community characteristics. In P. B. Pedersen, J. G. Draguns, J. Lonner, & J. E. Trimble (Eds.), *Counseling across cultures* (3rd ed., pp. 177–204). Honolulu: University of Hawaii Press.

Troiden, R. R. (1989). The formation of homosexual identities. *Journal of Homosexuality, 17*, 43–73.

Trujillo, C. C. (1997). Sexual identity and the discontents of difference. In B. Greene (Ed.), *Ethnic and cultural diversity among lesbians and gay men* (pp. 266–278), Thousand Oaks, CA: Sage.

Tse, L. (1999). Finding a place to be: Ethnic identity exploration of Asian Americans. *Adolescence, 34* (133), 121–128.

Tseng, W. S., & Streltzer, J. (Eds.) (2001). *Culture and psychotherapy: A guide to practice.* Washington, DC: American Psychiatric Press.

Turner, W. L., Wieling, E., & Allen, W. D. (2004). Developing culturally based effective family-based research programs: Implications for family therapists. *Journal of Marital and Family Therapy. 30* (3), 257–270.

U.S. Census Bureau. (2000). *Statistical abstracts of the United States: 2000* (120th ed.). Washington, DC: Author.

U.S. Census Bureau. (2002). *Annual demographic supplement to the March 2002 Current Population Survey.* Washington, DC: Author.

U.S. Census Bureau. (2003). *Income, poverty, and health insurance coverage in the United States: 2003.* Washington, DC: Author.

U.S. Census Bureau. (2004). *Statistical abstracts of the United States: 2004–2005* (124th ed.). Washington, DC: Author.

U.S. Census Bureau. (2004–2005). *Statistical abstracts of the United States: 2004* (124th ed.). Washington, DC: Author.

Vander Zanden, J., Crandell, T., & Crandell, C. (2003). *Human development* (7th ed.). New York: McGraw-Hill.

Vander Zanden, J. W. (2000). *Human development* (7th ed.). New York: McGraw-Hill.

van Wormer, K., Wells, J., & Boes, M. (2000). *Social work with lesbians, gays, and bisexuals: A strengths perspective.* Boston: Allyn and Bacon.

Vasquez, M. J. T. (2001). Advancing the study of Chicana/o psychology. *The Counseling Psychologist, 29* (1), 118–127.

Vera, H., Feagin, J. R., & Gordon, A. (1995). Superior intellect?: Sincere fictions of the White self. *Journal of Negro Education, 64* (3), 295–306.

Vicario, B. A., Liddle, B. J., & Luzzo, D. A. (2005). The role of values in understanding attitudes toward lesbians and gay men. *Journal of Homosexuality, 49* (1), 145–159.

Vinson, T. S., & Neimeyer, G. J. (2000). The relationship between racial identity development and multicultural counseling competency. *Journal of Multicultural Counseling and Development, 28* (3), 177–192.

Vontress, C. E. (1988). An existential approach to cross-cultural counseling. *Journal of Multicultural Counseling and Development, 16*, 73–83.

Vontress, C. E. (1996). A personal retrospective on cross-cultural counseling. *Journal of Multicultural Counseling and Development, 24*, 156–166.

Wahoo, E., & Olson, L. (2004). Intimate partner violence and sexual assault in Native American communities. *Trauma, Violence, and Abuse: A Review Journal, 5* (4), 353–366.

Wainryb, C. (2004). The study of diversity in human development: Culture, urgencies, and perils. *Human Development, 47*, 131–137.

Want, V., Parham, T. A., & Baker, R. C. (2004). African Americans students' ratings of Caucasian and African

American counselors varying in racial consciousness. *Cultural Diversity and Ethnic Minority Psychology, 10*(2), 123–136.

Wastell, C. (1996). Feminist developmental theory: Implications for counseling. *Journal of Counseling and Development, 74*, 575–581.

Watari, K., Gatz, M. (2004). Pathways to caring for Alzheimer's disease among Korean Americans. *Cultural Diversity and Ethnic Minority Psychology, 10*(1), 23–28.

Watkins K. J., & Baldo, T. D. (2004). The infertility experience: Biophysical effects and suggestions for counselors. *Journal of Counseling & Development, 82*, 394–402.

Weeber, J. E. (2000). What could I know of racism? *Journal of Counseling and Development, 77*, 20–23.

Weinick, R. M., Jacobs, E. A., Stone, L. C., Ortega, A. N. & Burstin, H. (2004). *Medical Care, 42*(2), 313–320.

Werner, E. E. (1988). A cross-cultural perspective on infancy. *Journal of Cross-Cultural Psychology, 19*, 96–113.

Whang, P. A., & Hancock, G. R. (1994). Motivation and mathematics achievement: Comparisons between Asian American and non-Asian students. *Contemporary Educational Psychology, 19*, 302–322.

Wilbur, M. P. (1999). The Rivers of Wounded Heart. *Journal of Counseling and Development, 77*(1), 47–50.

Willis, A. I., & Lewis, K. C. (1999). Our known everydayness: Beyond a response to White privilege. *Urban Education, 43*(2), 245–262.

Wilmoth, J. M. (2001). Living arrangements among immigrants in the United States. *The Gerontologist, 41*(2), 228–238.

Wilson, A. (1996). How we find ourselves: Identity development and two-spirit people. *Harvard Educational Review, 66*, 303–317.

Wilson, K. B., & Senices, J. (2005). Exploring the vocational rehabilitation acceptance rates for Hispanics versus non-Hispanics in the United States. *Journal of Counseling and Development, 83*(1), 86–97.

Wilson, M. N., Kohn, L. P., & Lee, T. S. (2000). Cultural relativistic approach toward ethnic minorities in family therapy. In J. F. Aponte, & J. Wohl (eds.), *Psychological intervention and cultural diversity* (2nd ed., pp. 92–109). Boston: Allyn and Bacon.

Winawer, H., & Wetzel, N. A. (2005). German families. In M. McGoldrick, J. Giordano, & N. Garcia-Preto (Eds.), *Ethnicity and family therapy* (3rd ed., pp. 555–572). New York: Guilford.

Winkelpleck, J. M., & Westfield, J. S. (1982). Counseling considerations with gay couples. *The Personnel and Guidance Journal, 60*, 294–296.

Winker, A., & Daniluk, J. C. (2004). A gift from the heart: The experiences of women whose egg donations helped their sisters become mothers. *Journal of Counseling and Development, 82*, 483–495.

Witt, L., Thomas, S., & Marcus, E. (1997). Where do they get the numbers? In L. Witt, S. Thomas, & E. Marcus (Eds.), *Out in all directions: The almanac of gay and lesbian America* (pp. 363–366). New York: Warner.

Woodard, S. L. (1995). Counseling disruptive African American elementary school boys. *Journal of Multicultural Counseling and Development, 23*, 21–28.

Wrenn, G. C. (1962). The culturally encapsulated counselor. *Harvard Educational Review, 32*, 444–449.

Yager, T. J., & Rotheram-Borus, M. J. (2000). Social expectations among African American, Hispanic, and European American adolescents. *Cross-Cultural Research, 34*(3), 283–305.

Yagi, D. T., & Oh, M. Y. (1995). Counseling Asian American students. In C. C. Lee (Ed.), *Counseling for diversity: A guide for school counselors and related professionals* (pp. 61–83). Boston: Allyn & Bacon.

Yakushko, O., & Chronister, K. M. (2005). Immigrant women and counseling: The invisible others. *Journal of Counseling and Development, 83*, 292–298.

Yao, E. L. (1985). Adjustment needs of Asian American immigrant children. *Elementary School Guidance and Counseling, 19*, 223–227.

Yee, L. L. (1998). Asian children. *Teaching Exceptional Children, 20*, 49–50.

Yeh, C. (2001). An exploratory study of school counselors' experiences with and perceptions of Asian-American students. *Professional School Counseling, 4*(5), 349–356.

Yeh, C. (2003). Age, acculturation, cultural adjustment, and mental health symptoms of Chinese, Korean, and Japanese immigrant Youth. *Cultural Diversity and Ethnic Minority Psychology, 9*(1), 34–48.

Yeh, C., & Huang, K. (1996). The collectivistic nature of ethnic identity development among Asian American college students. *Adolescence, 31*, 645–661.

Yeh, C., & Wang, Y. (2000). Asian American coping attitudes, sources, and practices: Implications for indigenous counseling strategies. *Journal of College Student Development, 41*(1), 94–101.

Yoon, S. M. (2005). The characteristics and needs of Asian American grandparent caregivers: A study of Chinese American and Korean American grandparents in New York City. *Journal of Gerontological Social Work, 44*(3/4), 75–94.

Young-Kyong, E., Bean, R. A., & Harper, J. M. (2004). Do general treatment guidelines for Asian American families have applications to specific ethnic groups? The case of culturally competent therapy with Korean Americans. *The Journal of Marital and Family Therapy, 30* (3), 359–374.

Yu, A., & Gregg, C. H. (1993). Asians in groups: More than just a matter of cultural awareness. *Journal for Specialists in Group Work, 18,* 86–93.

Zane, N. W. S., Sue, S., Hu, L., & Kwon, J. H. (1991). Asian American assertion: A social learning analysis of cultural awareness. *Journal of Counseling Psychology, 38,* 63–70.

Zayas, L. H., Kaplan, C., Turner, S., Romano, K. Gonzalez-Ramos, G. (2000). Understanding suicide attempts by adolescent Hispanic females. *Social Work, 45* (1), 53–63.

Zila, L. M., & Kiselica, M. S. (2001). Understanding and counseling self-mutilation in female adolescents and young adults. *Journal of Counseling and Development, 79,* 46–52.

Zinnbauer, B. J., & Pargament, K. I. (2000). Working with the sacred: Four approaches to religious and spiritual issues in counseling. *Journal of Counseling and Development, 78,* 162–171.

Zsembik, B. A. (1993). Determinants of living alone. *Research on Aging, 15,* 449–464.

Zuniga, M. E. (1997). Counseling Mexican American seniors: An overview. *Journal of Multicultural Counseling and Development, 25* (2), 142–155.

Author Index

Subject Index